Rehabilitating Older and Historic Buildings

Rehabilitating Older and Historic Buildings

LAW
TAXATION
STRATEGIES

SECOND EDITION

STEPHEN L. KASS
JUDITH M. LaBELLE
DAVID A. HANSELL

JOHN WILEY & SONS, INC.

New York • Chichester • Brisbane • Toronto • Singapore

In recognition of the importance of preserving what has been
written, it is a policy of John Wiley & Sons, Inc., to have
books of enduring value published in the United States
printed on acid-free paper, and we exert our best efforts
to that end.

Copyright © 1993 by John Wiley & Sons, Inc.

All rights reserved. Published simultaneously in Canada.

Reproduction or translation of any part of this work
beyond that permitted by Section 107 or 108 of the
1976 United States Copyright Act without the permission
of the copyright owner is unlawful. Requests for
permission or further information should be addressed to
the Permissions Department, John Wiley & Sons, Inc.

This publication is designed to provide accurate and
authoritative information in regard to the subject
matter covered. It is sold with the understanding that
the publisher is not engaged in rendering legal, accounting,
or other professional services. If legal advice or other
expert assistance is required, the services of a competent
professional person should be sought. *From a Declaration
of Principles jointly adopted by a Committee of the
American Bar Association and a Committee of Publishers.*

Library of Congress Cataloging-in-Publication Data

Kass, Stephen L.
    Rehabilitating older and historic buildings : law, taxation,
strategies / Stephen L. Kass, Judith M. LaBelle, David A. Hansall. —
2nd ed.
      p.   cm. — (Real estate practice library)
    Includes bibliographical references and index.
    ISBN 0-471-57164-4 (cloth)
    1. Historic buildings—Law and legislation—United States.
 2. Real property and taxation—United States. 3. Tax incentives—
Law and legislation—United States. I. LaBelle, Judith M., 1948–
. II. Hansell, David A., 1953– . III. Title. IV. Series.
KF4310.K37   1993
344.73′094—dc20
[347.30494]   92-15741
                                                                           CIP

Printed in the United States of America

10 9 8 7 6 5 4 3 2 1

SUBSCRIPTION NOTICE

This Wiley product is updated on a periodic basis with supplements to reflect important changes in the subject matter. If you purchased this product directly from John Wiley & Sons, Inc., we have already recorded your subscription for this update service.

If, however, you purchased this product from a bookstore and wish to receive (1) the current update at no additional charge, and (2) future updates and revised or related volumes billed separately with a 30-day examination review, please send your name, company name (if applicable), address, and the title of the product to:

Supplement Department
John Wiley & Sons, Inc.
One Wiley Drive
Somerset, NJ 08875
1-(800)-225-5945

THE REAL ESTATE PRACTICE LIBRARY: REAL ESTATE DEVELOPMENT FROM WILEY LAW PUBLICATIONS

CONSTRUCTION OWNER'S HANDBOOK OF PROPERTY DEVELOPMENT
　　Robert F. Cushman and Peter J. King, Editors
DEVELOPING RETIREMENT FACILITIES (SECOND EDITION)
　　Paul A. Gordon
FOREIGN INVESTMENT IN UNITED STATES REAL ESTATE
　　Jeremy D. Smith
INSTITUTIONAL AND PENSION FUND REAL ESTATE INVESTMENT
　　Stephen P. Jarchow
MANAGING AND LEASING COMMERCIAL PROPERTIES
　　Alan A. Alexander and Richard F. Muhlebach
MANAGING AND LEASING COMMERCIAL PROPERTIES: FORMS AND PROCEDURES
　　Alan A. Alexander and Richard F. Muhlebach
MANAGING AND LEASING RESIDENTIAL PROPERTIES
　　Paul D. Lapides
PASSIVE ACTIVITY RULES: LAW AND TAX PLANNING STRATEGIES
　　Ronald D. Saake, Michael J. Novogradac, and Eric J. Fortenbach
REAL ESTATE DEVELOPMENT: STRATEGIES FOR CHANGING MARKETS
　　Stuart M. Saft
REAL ESTATE INVESTMENT TRUSTS: TAX, SECURITIES, AND BUSINESS ASPECTS
　　Stephen P. Jarchow
REAL ESTATE LIMITED PARTNERSHIPS (THIRD EDITION)
　　Theodore S. Lynn, Harry F. Goldberg, and Michael Hirschfeld
REAL ESTATE VALUATION: GUIDE TO INVESTMENT STRATEGIES
　　Terry Vaughn Grissom and Julian Diaz III
REHABILITATING OLDER AND HISTORIC BUILDINGS (SECOND EDITION)
　　Stephen L. Kass, Judith M. LaBelle, and David A. Hansell
RETIREMENT HOUSING CONSTRUCTION FINANCE DIRECTORY
　　David R. Evanson and Anthony J. Mullen
RETIREMENT HOUSING MARKETS: PROJECT PLANNING AND FEASIBILITY ANALYSIS
　　Susan B. Brecht
STRUCTURING REAL ESTATE JOINT VENTURES
　　Robert Bell
TAX GUIDE TO MANAGING AND LEASING COMMERCIAL PROPERTIES
　　Martin M. Shenkman

Preface

Few areas of law have grown as rapidly, or become as complex, in the past two decades as historic preservation. On the one hand, the widespread rediscovery of the built environment, by both the public and the development community, reflects increasing appreciation for the craftsmanship, design, and scale of thousands of older buildings in America's cities and towns, as well as for the economic, planning and tax benefits of rehabilitating historic structures for contemporary use. On the other hand, the allure of new construction, increased property taxes, and high returns on investment can lead property owners, municipalities, nonprofit organizations and even religious entities to seek to maximize development at the expense of historic structures and neighborhoods. While specific provisions of the Internal Revenue Code encourage historic preservation, others make all real estate investments, including rehabilitation projects, less attractive for investors.

These conflicting factors have shaped both the law and practice of historic preservation since the early 1970s. The legal issues relating to the rehabilitation process now include such diverse subjects as federal, state, and municipal taxation; securities and partnership requirements; federal and state constitutional law; zoning, environmental, and landmarks regulation; and the abatement of asbestos and hazardous substances. There are relatively few attorneys or accountants who feel confident advising a client on this array of issues in connection with a proposed rehabilitation project. Similarly, private developers seeking to undertake such projects, investment advisors counseling clients and prospective investors, and governmental officials responsible for approving and regulating rehabilitation projects often find it difficult to understand the legal, financial, and regulatory context within which they must function.

This book seeks to meet these needs by providing a guide to the process of rehabilitating historic and older buildings. It attempts to distill for lawyers, accountants, financial advisors, developers, government officials, and nonprofit organizations the principal components of the rehabilitation process and to set forth, as clearly as possible, the benefits and potential pitfalls of rehabilitation projects. This is neither a treatise nor an exhaustive exploration of the subject. Rather, this book is intended to provide an overview of an increasingly complex and important field and to provide a foundation from which lawyers, accountants, and others can explore specific problems in greater detail.

Since the publication of the first edition in 1985, there have been significant changes in the laws affecting historic preservation. These include the Tax Reform Act of 1986, revised Advisory Council procedures, the emergence of conservation easements and low-income housing credits as significant preservation tools, highly publicized conflicts between landmark commissions and religious property owners, and the devastating effect of "passive loss" rules on rehabilitation projects nationally. We have tried, through annual supplements, to help readers follow these and other developments; however, the sheer bulk of new laws, regulations, and judicial decisions now warrants more drastic relief. We have therefore sought, in this expanded edition, to incorporate all significant developments in the preservation field and to integrate them into a concise statement of current law and practice.

There are a number of new subjects that have received special attention. In January 1992, President Bush proposed, as part of his economic recovery program, revising the current "passive loss" rules for real estate investments. In response, Congress passed and sent to the President on March 20, 1992 its own tax reform program, which included significant changes in the passive loss rules. Although the President vetoed this legislation upon receipt, some revisions of the passive loss rules appear likely this year. Depending on the precise form of the new legislation, amendment of the passive loss rules could have a significant effect on historic preservation projects and could help to reverse what in recent years has been a disappointing decline in such projects. A discussion of the pending passive loss legislation appears in **Chapter Three**.

The National Affordable Housing Act of 1990 instituted new federal housing assistance programs, amended existing ones, and authorized significant appropriations to fund, among other things, residential rehabilitation projects. The 1990 Act, discussed in **Chapter Four**, thus reflects an increasing awareness of the severe housing crisis that affects millions of Americans, particularly those with low and moderate incomes. The Act does little, however, to redress the national shame of homelessness or to extend the reach of rehabilitation programs to the poorest families.

A recent federal case reveals a potentially important new relationship between historic preservation and federal laws relating to hazardous substances. As discussed in **Chapter Six**, environmental and preservation laws often work together to protect historic resources. However, in *Boarhead Corp. v. Erickson*, a federal appellate court held in January 1991 that CERCLA (the Comprehensive Environmental Response, Compensation and Liability Act of 1980) precludes judicial review of certain "superfund" clean-up activities, even if undertaken in violation of the National Historic Preservation Act. Other federal, state and local hazardous substance laws also bear on the rehabilitation process, particularly the treatment or removal of asbestos and toxic substances from historic buildings. Because of the growing importance of these issues to developers, lenders, community groups, and governmental regulators, a new **Chapter Eight** has been added that summarizes the applicable law in this area.

Another important development in preservation law has been the renewed surge of litigation over the constitutionality of landmark laws as applied to religious properties. In considering claims that landmarking of such properties violates the First Amendment's free exercise clause, courts have generally upheld landmark laws and procedures that limit, on a nondiscriminatory basis, the commercial use of landmarked religious property. However, courts have been somewhat more willing to protect clearly religious uses of property against the operation of local landmark laws. **Chapter Seven** contains a completely revised and up-dated discussion of these cases, including the U.S. Supreme Court actions in March 1991 in the cases of *St. Bartholomew's Church v. City of New York* and *First Covenant Church v. City of Seattle*.

A further area of concern to preservationists is the recent attack on the constitutionality of historic preservation ordinances under state constitutions. In its watershed *Penn Central* decision, the U.S. Supreme Court held that local landmark designations are a legitimate exercise of a state's police power and valid under the United States Constitution. However, as discussed in **Chapter Seven**, in 1991 the Pennsylvania Supreme Court held, in *United Artists Theater Circuit v. Philadelphia*, that Philadelphia's landmarks preservation ordinance was an unconstitutional "taking" of property in violation of the Pennsylvania constitution. This case was reargued before the Pennsylvania Court in October 1991; a final decision has not yet been released as this volume goes to press. Affirmance of the Court's earlier decision is likely to encourage similar challenges under other state constitutions and, possibly, an attempt to narrow or reverse the U.S. Supreme Court's *Penn Central* decision. This possibility is also raised, though less ominously, by another case recently decided by the U.S. Supreme Court, *Lucas v. South Carolina Coastal Council*, which is discussed in **Chapter Seven**.

Finally, **Chapter Nine** (which describes a number of sample rehabilitation projects) has been up-dated to reflect current developments in these projects and to add an account of a successful 10-year battle to preserve Alansten, the boyhood home of John Jay, our nation's first

Chief Justice. This account also describes the increasingly close relationship between preservation law and other forms of land use control, including zoning, subdivision approval, environmental review and public land acquisition.

As with the original edition of this work, we continue to appreciate reports from readers as to the progress of individual rehabilitation projects and suggestions of ways in which this revised edition can better contribute to an understanding of the ongoing task of preserving and rehabilitating America's built environment.

STEPHEN L. KASS
JUDITH M. LABELLE
DAVID A. HANSELL

New York, New York
May 1992

Acknowledgments

The authors wish to acknowledge and express their gratitude for the cooperation of the National Trust for Historic Preservation, Preservation Action, the Providence Preservation Society Revolving Fund, James Pickman & Associates, Inc., and the many other individuals and organizations who have provided us with material concerning rehabilitation projects or who have reviewed portions of the text. The authors also wish to thank their colleagues at Berle, Kass & Case in New York City for sharing their professional experience and for their patience during the preparation of both the original and revised editions of this work.

We also wish to thank those who assisted in the preparation of the original edition and periodic supplements over the last several years, including Stephen Warnath, Alan Epstein, Jeffrey Gracer, James Rubin, Florence Hutner, Deborah Goldberg, John Stephen, Martin Gitlin, David Jacobs, Elinor Colbourn, Helen Borrello, and Anna Barber. Debra-Ann Chait also deserves special recognition for her dedication in typing the original manuscript, and Peter Grandell for his skill and patience in typing both annual supplements and this revised edition. We also wish to thank Jeanne Littas, our original editor at John Wiley & Sons, Mark Dennison, her able successor, Ken Gesser, my present editor, and Nancy Marcus Land, our production manager, for their continuing interest and encouragement in connection with this second edition. Finally, we owe a special debt to James McClymonds, an exceptionally able student at New York Law School, for his skillful assistance in helping to bring this second edition to fruition.

Contents

1 Federal Income Tax Incentives for Rehabilitation   1

1.1   Evolution of Tax Treatment of Older Buildings   2
1.2   The Rehabilitation Tax Credit   4

     1.2.1   The Rehabilitation Percentage   5
     1.2.2   Qualified Rehabilitation Expenditure   5
     1.2.3   Qualified Rehabilitated Building   7
     1.2.4   Substantial Rehabilitation   8
     1.2.5   Retention of External Walls   10
     1.2.6   Recipients of the Rehabilitation Tax Credit   11
     1.2.7   Limit on Tax Offset   13
     1.2.8   Recapture of Tax Credits   14
     1.2.9   Effective Date and Transition Rules   15

1.3   Low-Income Housing Credit   16

     1.3.1   Amount of Credit   16
     1.3.2   Qualified Basis   18
     1.3.3   Qualified Low-Income Housing Project   20
     1.3.4   Interaction of Rehabilitation Credit and Low-Income Housing Credit   22

1.4   Depreciation   23

     1.4.1   Depreciation Systems   23
     1.4.2   Transition Rules   24

1.5   Preservation Easements   24

     1.5.1   Qualified Real Property Interest   25
     1.5.2   Qualified Organization   28
     1.5.3   Conservation Purposes   29

1.5.4　Valuation of Easement Donations　　30
　　　1.5.5　Interaction of Rehabilitation Tax Credit and
　　　　　　Preservation Easement Deduction　　33

1.6　Summary of Differences in Treatment of Historic and
　　　Nonhistoric Old Buildings　　33
1.7　Tax Treatment of Property Leased to Tax-Exempt
　　　Organizations　　34

　　　1.7.1　Tax-Exempt Use Property　　35
　　　1.7.2　Consequences of Tax-Exempt Participation　　36

1.8　Effectiveness of Rehabilitation Incentives　　37

2　Historic Preservation Certifications　　39

2.1　The National Register of Historic Places　　40

　　　2.1.1　Eligibility　　42
　　　2.1.2　The Standard of Evaluation　　43
　　　2.1.3　The Nomination Process　　44
　　　2.1.4　Owner Consent　　46
　　　2.1.5　Removal from the Register　　48

2.2　Certifications of Historic Significance　　49

　　　2.2.1　Standards for Evaluating Historic Significance　　50
　　　2.2.2　Certification Procedure　　51
　　　2.2.3　Application Requirements　　52
　　　2.2.4　Processing of Applications　　53

2.3　Certifications of Rehabilitation　　54

　　　2.3.1　Standards for Rehabilitation　　55
　　　2.3.2　Application of Standards　　58
　　　2.3.3　Certification Procedure　　60

3　Financing Rehabilitation: Private Syndication　　64

3.1　Limited Partnerships　　65

　　　3.1.1　Creation Governed by State Law　　66
　　　3.1.2　Role of General Partner　　67
　　　3.1.3　Role of Limited Partner　　68

3.2　Tax Treatment of Partnerships and Partners　　69

　　　3.2.1　Recognition as a Partnership by the IRS　　69
　　　3.2.2　Tax Benefits Available to Partners　　73
　　　3.2.3　Tax Shelter Registration　　76
　　　3.2.4　Passive Loss Rules; Alternative Minimum Tax　　77
　　　3.2.5　1992 Passive Loss Amendments (Proposed)　　79

3.3 Federal Securities Laws Affecting Limited Partnerships   81

    3.3.1 Regulation D   82
    3.3.2 General Provisions of Regulation D   83
    3.3.3 Exemptions under Regulation D   84
    3.3.4 Other Exemptions   85
    3.3.5 Fraud and Rule 10b-5   86

3.4 State Securities Regulation   89

    3.4.1 New York Securities Law Governing Real Estate Limited Partnerships   90
    3.4.2 California Securities Law Governing Real Estate Limited Partnerships   91

4 Financing Rehabilitation: Public and Nonconventional Sources   93

4.1 Public Sources: The Federal Government   95

    4.1.1 Historic Preservation Programs   95
    4.1.2 Community Revitalization and Development Programs   96
    4.1.3 Urban Development Action Grants   97
    4.1.4 Community Development Block Grants   98
    4.1.5 Federal Housing Administration Insurance Programs   101
    4.1.6 HUD Housing Programs as Rehabilitation Incentives   101
    4.1.7 Farmers Home Administration Programs   105
    4.1.8 Access to Credit   107
    4.1.9 Financing for Commercial Projects   108
    4.1.10 Special Purpose Funding   109

4.2 Public Financing: State and Local Aid   110

    4.2.1 Funding Sources   111
    4.2.2 Funding Entities   113

4.3 Nonconventional Sources for Financing Rehabilitation   113

    4.3.1 Revolving Funds   114
    4.3.2 Operation and Administration   114
    4.3.3 Funding   115
    4.3.4 Preservation Strategies   116
    4.3.5 Private Foundations   117
    4.3.6 Corporate Donations   119
    4.3.7 National Nonprofit Organizations   120
    4.3.8 Private Fundraising and Individual Donors   121

5 State and Local Incentives for Rehabilitation 122

5.1 Property Taxes 123

    5.1.1 Exemptions from Real Property Taxation 123
    5.1.2 Credit or Deduction Against Real Property Taxes 126
    5.1.3 Abatement Through a Lower Tax Rate 126
    5.1.4 Abatement for Rehabilitation or Renovation 128
    5.1.5 Assessment Based on Current Use of Property 128
    5.1.6 Assessment Based on Restricted Property Use 130
    5.1.7 Frozen Assessments 132

5.2 Local Building Codes 133

    5.2.1 Applicability to Existing Structures 134
    5.2.2 Historic Building Provisions 136

5.3 Transferable Development Rights 137

    5.3.1 Eligible Property 139
    5.3.2 Transfer Zone 140
    5.3.3 Rights That Can Be Transferred 141
    5.3.4 Conditions of Transfer 141

6 Federal and State Statutory Protection for Historic Buildings 144

6.1 The National Historic Preservation Act 145

    6.1.1 Section 106 Review 148
    6.1.2 Federal Agencies and Undertakings Affected 150
    6.1.3 Effects of a Federal Undertaking 151
    6.1.4 The Consultation Process 153
    6.1.5 Memorandum of Agreement 154
    6.1.6 Phased Development 155
    6.1.7 Enforcement of Section 106 Requirements 157
    6.1.8 Section 106 Litigants 158
    6.1.9 Procedural Issues in Section 106 Litigation 159
    6.1.10 Other Federal Agency Responsibilities Under the NHPA 161
    6.1.11 Section 110(f) (National Historic Landmarks) 162

6.2 Section 4(f) of the Department of Transportation Act 162

6.3 The National Environmental Policy Act 166

    6.3.1 Major Federal Action 167
    6.3.2 The EIS Process 170

Contents

  6.3.3 When Is an EIS Required? 171
  6.3.4 Participants 172
  6.3.5 Timing 173
  6.3.6 Contents of the EIS 173
  6.3.7 Judicial Review Under NEPA 175

6.4 Coordinating NEPA and the NHPA for Maximum Federal Statutory Protection 176
6.5 State Statutory Protection 177

  6.5.1 State Historic Preservation Statutes 177
  6.5.2 State Environmental Protection Statutes 178

7 Local Regulation of Historic Buildings 183

7.1 Structural Provisions of Local Preservation Ordinances 184

  7.1.1 Statement of Purpose 185
  7.1.2 Definitions 187
  7.1.3 Establishing the Administrative Body 187
  7.1.4 Creation and Makeup 188
  7.1.5 Scope of Authority 189
  7.1.6 Administrative Structure 191

7.2 The Historic Resources Inventory 191
7.3 The Designation Process 194

  7.3.1 Nomination 194
  7.3.2 Designation Standards 194
  7.3.3 General Criteria 195
  7.3.4 Historic Districts 196
  7.3.5 Procedural Standards 198
  7.3.6 Notice 199
  7.3.7 Prehearing 200
  7.3.8 Hearing 200
  7.3.9 Decision 201
  7.3.10 Appeal 202

7.4 Applications Relating to Alteration, New Construction, and Demolition 202

  7.4.1 Alteration and New Construction 202
  7.4.2 Standards 204
  7.4.3 Certificate of Appropriateness 206
  7.4.4 Demolition 207
  7.4.5 Economic Hardship Clause 210
  7.4.6 Maintenance 219
  7.4.7 Exclusion for Routine Maintenance 221
  7.4.8 Compliance Inspections 222

7.4.9 Publicly Owned Property 223
7.4.10 Religious Structures 224
7.4.11 Penalties 231

7.5 Certification of Local Statutes and Historic Districts 232

7.5.1 Certification of Statutes 233
7.5.2 Certification of Historic Districts 234

8 Asbestos and Other Hazardous Substances 235

8.1 Asbestos 235

8.1.1 National Emission Standards for Hazardous Air Pollution 236
8.1.2 Occupational Health and Safety Act 239
8.1.3 Asbestos Hazard Emergency Response Act 241
8.1.4 Comprehensive Environmental Response, Compensation, and Liability Act 242
8.1.5 Hazardous Materials Transportation Act 243
8.1.6 State Regulation of Asbestos 244

8.2 Other Hazardous Substances 245

8.2.1 PCB Regulation Under the Toxic Substance Control Act 245
8.2.2 Control of Hazardous Substances Under Federal and State Laws 247
8.2.3 Underground Storage Tanks 252

8.3 Asbestos and Other Hazardous Substances in Rehabilitation Projects: Avoiding Liability 253

8.3.1 Potential Liabilities 253
8.3.2 Avoiding Liability: Indemnification and Hold Harmless Provisions 255
8.3.3 Environmental Audits 256

9 A Rehabilitation Sampler 258

9.1 The Rehabilitation Program 259

9.1.1 Identifying the Property 259
9.1.2 Planning the Project 260
9.1.3 Structuring the Financing Package 261

9.2 Rehabilitation Projects 264

9.2.1 Small Residential Building (78 Hudson Street, Providence, Rhode Island) 265
9.2.2 Low-Income Housing (Kensington Square, New Haven, Connecticut) 269

- 9.2.3 Commercial Building (Hildreth Building, Lowell, Massachusetts)   272
- 9.2.4 Comprehensive Public Development Project (Forty-Second Street Development Project, New York, New York)   277
- 9.2.5 Combined Historic Rehabilitation and Low-Income Housing Credits (706-712 Huntington Avenue, Boston, Massachusetts)   282
- 9.2.6 Preserving the John Jay Estate (Rye, New York)   284
- 9.2.7 Initial Landmarking   286
- 9.2.8 Subdivision and SEQRA Review   289
- 9.2.9 Public Acquisition   290

APPENDICES

- A. National Historic Preservation Act, 16 U.S.C. §§ 470–470w-6   293
- B. National Park Service, "Historic Preservation Certification," Final Rule, 36 C.F.R. Part 67   326
- C. National Park Service, Historic Preservation Certification Application Form   349
- D. The Secretary's Guidelines for Rehabilitating Historic Buildings and Interpretations of the Secretary of the Interior's Standards for Rehabilitation   356
- E. Internal Revenue Service, Final Regulations Relating to Qualified Conservation Contributions, 26 C.F.R. Parts 1, 20, and 25   428
- F. Agreement of AAA Associates Limited Partnership Formed to Conduct Real Property Rehabilitation   450
- G. Rehab Associates Limited Partnership Pro Forma Accounting Projections with Accompanying Notes and Assumptions   469
- H. Securities and Exchange Commission, Regulation D-Rules Governing the Limited Offer and Sale of Securities Without Registration Under the Securities Act of 1933, 17 C.F.R. §§ 230.501-230.508   488
- I. National Park Service, "National Register of Historic Places"   501
- J. Advisory Council on Historic Preservation, Regulations Implementing Section 106 of the National Historic Preservation Act, 36 C.F.R. Part 800   521
- K. New York City Administrative Code, Chapter 8-A, "Preservation of Landmarks and Historical Districts"   538
- L. Current Text of S. 3196, a Bill to Amend the National Historic Preservation Act   561

INDEX   579

One

Federal Income Tax Incentives for Rehabilitation

Of the variety of social and economic factors that have contributed to the current interest in rehabilitation, the most important have probably been the federal income tax incentives for the rehabilitation of historic and certain other old buildings. While recent changes in the tax law make these incentives somewhat less powerful than they have been in the past, they will no doubt remain an important stimulus to rehabilitation efforts. Moreover, because recent tax law changes have removed tax benefits which once favored other types of investment, the incentives for rehabilitation have increased in relative importance. To understand the impact of these incentives, it is useful briefly to trace their history.

For many years, the federal tax structure reflected a policy bias favoring new construction over the rehabilitation of older buildings. The tax code was structured so that rehabilitation of an old building entailed the forfeiture of substantial tax benefits in relation to new construction. Because a new building could often be depreciated faster than a used one, preservation came to be viewed as less economically attractive than demolition and new construction. The ability to deduct demolition costs as an expense in the year in which the demolition occurred provided a further incentive to demolish rather than rehabilitate. These and other tax provisions compounded other economic incentives to replace rather than preserve older buildings, including the fact that rehabilitation of an older building often means forgoing an opportunity to construct a larger and more lucrative building on the same site. As a result of those considerations, the country lost innumerable structures that had contributed to its historic and architectural heritage.

Public awareness of the importance of preserving this heritage increased significantly as a result of activities relating to the Bicentennial and a renewed focus on the nation's cities. As the loss of buildings continued and preservation proponents gathered strength, the need to change the Internal Revenue Code as part of the preservation effort became increasingly clear.

1.1 EVOLUTION OF TAX TREATMENT OF OLDER BUILDINGS

Reform of the tax laws affecting existing structures began with the Tax Reform Act of 1976,[1] which provided two incentives intended to encourage rehabilitation of buildings on the National Register of Historic Places or in local historic districts. Owners of qualifying historic buildings were given a choice: They could amortize their rehabilitation expenditures over 60 months[2] (a significantly shorter period than those previously allowed, which were tied to the life of the improvements and generally averaged 25 to 30 years), or they could use the form of depreciation deduction available to owners of similar new construction.[3] Rather than being limited to the straight-line or 125 percent declining balance rates previously available, owners of substantially rehabilitated historic buildings could, depending on the type of project, use either the 150 or 200 percent declining balance rate for depreciation.

The 1976 Act also included two disincentives to demolition of certified historic structures or structures located in historic districts and certified as contributing to the significance of those districts.[4] The first disincentive required that such demolition costs be capitalized as part of nondepreciable land cost. Demolition costs relating to those structures could no longer be taken as current deductions.[5] (The Tax Reform Act of 1984 broadened this prohibition, and the Code now denies a deduction for costs of, or losses incurred in connection with, the demolition of any building, not only certified historic structures.[6]) The second disincentive required that depreciation of any structure which replaced a demolished historic structure be taken using the straight-line method.[7]

Two years later, in the Revenue Act of 1978, Congress provided a 10 percent investment tax credit as a further incentive for owners to

---

[1] Pub. L. No. 94-455, 90 Stat. 101 (1976).
[2] Former I.R.C. § 191 (repealed 1981).
[3] Former I.R.C. § 167(o) (repealed 1981).
[4] *See* § 2.2.
[5] Former I.R.C. § 280B.
[6] I.R.C. § 280B, *amended by* Pub. L. No. 98-369, § 1063, 98 Stat. 494, 1047 (1984).
[7] Former I.R.C. § 167(n).

rehabilitate commercial and industrial buildings that were more than 20 years old and had not been rehabilitated within the preceding 20 years.[8] The tax credit was intended to spur private investment in rehabilitation projects by providing an incentive of greater value than the depreciation deduction alone. Because a credit reduces tax liability dollar for dollar, it is worth more to the taxpayer than a deduction, which only reduces taxable income by a variable percentage reflecting the taxpayer's marginal bracket.[9] While making the investment tax credit available for qualified rehabilitation projects, however, the 1978 Act limited the manner in which the credit could be coupled with the incentives provided in 1976. An owner taking the investment tax credit for such a project could also use accelerated depreciation, but could not take advantage of the 60-month amortization period.[10]

The shift away from the bias favoring demolition and new construction over rehabilitation continued with the enactment of Section 212 of the Economic Recovery Tax Act of 1981 (ERTA).[11] This act replaced the amortization and depreciation incentives created by the 1976 Act and the 10 percent investment tax credit provided by the 1978 Act with a three-tier system of tax credits available for the substantial rehabilitation of qualified buildings, including qualified historic buildings. Among the changes to the Code made by ERTA, one of the most significant with regard to rehabilitation of most older buildings was the replacement of the previous depreciation system with the accelerated cost recovery system (ACRS).

Of even greater significance was the adoption of a new set of tax credits for rehabilitation of certain older structures. ERTA created three categories of favored buildings and provided for specified investment tax credits (equal to a percentage of the qualified rehabilitation expenditures) in connection with the rehabilitation of each category of building. To qualify for the investment tax credit, the rehabilitation would have to meet minimum standards intended to encourage significant rehabilitation projects that retained the integrity of the building. As discussed in § **1.8**, projects representing an investment of billions of dollars in the rehabilitation of certified historic structures alone have been undertaken using the ERTA tax credits.

---

[8] Former I.R.C. § 48(g).

[9] For example, a taxpayer in the 15-percent bracket with $50,000 taxable income has a federal tax liability of $7,500. If the taxpayer earned a $5,000 deduction, this would reduce taxable income to $45,000, resulting in a tax liability after the deduction of $6,750 (assuming no change in bracket). In contrast, the dollar-for-dollar offset that a taxpayer receives for a $5,000 tax credit allows the taxpayer to subtract the full $5,000, resulting in a total tax liability of $2,500.

[10] Former I.R.C. § 48(g)(2)(B)(iv).

[11] Pub. L. No. 97-34, 95 Stat. 172 (1981). Citations to the regulations promulgated in connection with these provisions were also changed by ERTA. Earlier references to 36 C.F.R. Part 1208 became 36 C.F.R. Part 67. Standards for evaluating National Register eligibility were changed from 36 C.F.R. Part 1202 to 36 C.F.R. Part 60.

The scheme created by ERTA remained virtually unchanged until the passage of the Tax Reform Act of 1986 (1986 Act).[12] The 1986 Act reduced the amount of the credit and altered the rules governing its availability. When viewed in relation to the dramatic changes made by the 1986 Act in other areas, however, the rehabilitation credit survived relatively unscathed. The 1986 changes in the rehabilitation credit have had less impact on subsequent use of the credit than have other changes in the tax treatment of real estate and investment income generally. These latter changes are described primarily in **Chapter Three**, and the prospective investor in a rehabilitation project should be thoroughly acquainted not only with the details of the credit itself, but also with the other tax provisions that may govern the degree to which an investor can benefit from the credit.

The 1986 Act also created a new low-income housing credit. While not primarily targeted at rehabilitation of older buildings, this credit can be used to support such activity, alone or in tandem with the rehabilitation credit.

1.2 THE REHABILITATION TAX CREDIT

Section 38 of the Code allows credits against income for investment in certain depreciable property known as "Section 38 property." One category of investments eligible for a tax credit is the expense of rehabilitating certain older buildings. The credit allowed for these expenses, known as "qualified rehabilitation expenditures," is determined by multiplying the portion of the basis of the property which is attributable to such expenditures by a specified percentage, referred to below as the "rehabilitation percentage."[13]

To determine whether a rehabilitation tax credit will be available in connection with any particular rehabilitation project, several factors must be analyzed, including (1) the age of the building and the use to which it will be put after rehabilitation, (2) the taxpayer's adjusted basis in the building and the total rehabilitation costs to be incurred, (3) the timing of the rehabilitation process, and (4) the physical changes to be made to the building. In addition, as explained in detail in **Chapter Two**, if the building is a "certified historic structure," additional requirements must be met, particularly with regard to the type of physical alterations made.[14]

---

[12] Pub. L. No. 99-514, 100 Stat. 2085 (1986).

[13] I.R.C. § 47(a) (West Supp. 1991).

[14] It is critical that a determination be made at the beginning of the planning process whether the building under consideration is a certified historic structure. If it is, a qualifying rehabilitation will result in a 20-percent tax credit. *See* § **1.2.1**. However, if such a structure is rehabilitated in a manner which does not qualify under the applicable standards, no tax credit will be available. *See* § **1.6**. If a building has not been certified, the

1.2.1 The Rehabilitation Percentage

The rehabilitation percentage varies with the class of building, as follows:

Class of Building	Rehabilitation Percentage[15]
First placed in service before 1963	10
Certified historic structure	20

A certified historic structure is one that is either (1) listed on the National Register of Historic Places or (2) located in a registered historic district (a district (A) itself listed on the National Register or (B) designated under any appropriate state or local statute and certified by the Secretary of the Interior as meeting substantially all the requirements for listing in the National Register) and certified by the Secretary of the Interior as being of historic significance to that district.[16] Except under the transition rules discussed in § 1.2.9, the credit is no longer available for buildings that were first placed in service after 1936, regardless of how old they may be, unless they meet the requirements for certified historic structures which are discussed in further detail in **Chapter Two**. The transition rules will also allow some rehabilitation projects to continue to qualify for the 25-percent credit for certified structures, as well as 10- and 13-percent credits for 30- and 40-year-old buildings, respectively.

1.2.2 Qualified Rehabilitation Expenditures

"Qualified rehabilitation expenditures," the amount to which the rehabilitation percentage is applied to determine the amount of the rehabilitation tax credit which is available, means any amount (1) properly chargeable to capital account, (2) incurred in connection with the rehabilitation of a qualified rehabilitated building, and (3) incurred for property (or an addition or improvements to property) which is either nonresidential real property, residential rental property, or property with a class life of more than 12.5 years under the new depreciation guidelines.[17] (As discussed in

---

decision whether to seek certification may depend on a comparison at the outset of the marginal benefit of the 20-percent (vs. 10-percent) credit with the incremental cost of a certified rehabilitation. If the building is in a registered historic district, however, it must be certified either as significant or nonsignificant to benefit from any credit, as explained in **Ch. Two**.

[15] I.R.C. § 47(a).
[16] I.R.C. § 47(c)(3).
[17] I.R.C. § 47(c)(2).

§ 1.2.3, however, residential property is eligible for the rehabilitation credit only if it qualifies as a certified historic structure and is used in a trade or business.)

In general, the 1986 Act did not change the rules governing the capitalization of expenses for purposes of calculating qualified rehabilitation expenditures. As before, such expenditures include most hard construction costs, such as removal, installation, or reconstruction of walls; plumbing; wiring; flooring; installation of heating or air conditioning systems; and so on. Also included are many "soft costs" incident to rehabilitation. To the extent that these represent fees for services (legal, architectural, etc.) in connection with the acquisition or development of real property, they are properly allocable to basis, and hence qualify for the rehabilitation credit.[18] The expenses of organizing a partnership or other entity to conduct a rehabilitation must be amortized over a period of not less than 60 months.[19] Moreover, expenses relating to a loan obtained to purchase or develop property (appraisal fees, title costs, commitment fees) should be amortized over the term of the loan.[20]

The 1986 Act repealed the provision that formerly permitted amortization of construction period interest and taxes over 10 years.[21] Instead, the new law generally requires that interest on debt incurred to "construct, build, install, manufacture, develop, [or] improve" real property be capitalized and deducted over the life of the property rather than deducted as incurred or amortized on a more accelerated basis.[22] Furthermore, if construction costs with respect to a property exceed the amount of debt incurred directly to finance the construction, interest on other loans which might have been avoided had construction expenditures not been incurred may also have to be capitalized, up to the full amount of construction expenses.[23] This provision is intended to prevent circumvention of the capitalization rules by the incurring of debt that is not directly linked to construction activities. Construction period taxes must also be capitalized.

The rules excluding from qualified rehabilitation expenditures the cost of acquiring a building, as well as costs attributable to enlargement of an

---

[18] Treas. Reg. § 1.48-11(c) (1985); see, e.g., Surloff v. Commissioner, 81 T.C. 210 (1983); Cagle v. Commissioner, 63 T.C. 86 (1974), aff'd, 539 F.2d 409 (5th Cir. 1976).

The IRS has adopted regulations relating to the investment tax credit for rehabilitated buildings, which do not incorporate changes made by ERTA or the 1986 Act and which generally apply only to expenditures incurred by December 31, 1981. Regulations governing subsequent expenditures were adopted in 1988. See Treas. Reg. § 1.48-12 (1988).

[19] I.R.C. § 709 (West 1988).

[20] See, e.g., Rev. Rul. 81-160, 1981-1 C.B. 312; Rev. Rul. 70-360, 1970-2 C.B. 103; Enoch v. Commissioner, 57 T.C. 781 (1972).

[21] Former I.R.C. § 189 (repealed 1986).

[22] Temp. Treas. Reg. § 1.263A-1T(a)(5)(ii) (as amended 1987).

[23] I.R.C. § 263A(f) (West Supp. 1991).

existing building, have not been changed.[24] Thus, as before, increases in building volume will not generate expenses eligible for the credit, but increases in usable floor area due to internal remodeling may qualify.[25] Exterior elevators or stairwells may not be treated as ineligible expansions in the case of certified rehabilitations, if the Secretary of the Interior rules that the interior placement of these facilities would destroy significant architectural or historic features.[26] Also continued is the prohibition on the use of the rehabilitation credit with respect to any rehabilitation expenses that are not depreciated using the straight-line method (although the new depreciation guidelines would bar this in any event). Qualifying expenses must be incurred in connection with rehabilitation, not new construction.

Lessees may take their expenditures into account for purposes of the rehabilitation credit only if the remaining term of the lease, on the date that rehabilitation is completed, exceeds 27.5 years in the case of residential property or 31.5 years in the case of commercial property.[27]

The rules governing certification of property and of rehabilitation work, discussed in **Chapter Two**, have not been changed. Thus expenses incurred in the rehabilitation of a certified historic structure, or a structure located in a registered historic district, qualify for the credit only if the rehabilitation has been certified by the Secretary of the Interior (in which case the building is eligible for the 20-percent credit). This requirement may be avoided with respect to a building located in a registered district but not individually certified, if the Secretary of the Interior certifies that the building is not of historic significance to the district (in which case the building is eligible for the 10-percent credit). This "decertification" of the building must occur prior to the commencement of the rehabilitation of the building unless the taxpayer can certify to the Secretary of the Treasury that, at the time rehabilitation began, the taxpayer in good faith was not aware of the requirement to obtain such certification.[28] Otherwise, no credit can be taken.

1.2.3 Qualified Rehabilitated Building

Investment tax credits are available only with regard to the rehabilitation of qualified rehabilitated buildings. As discussed in **§ 1.2.1**, the eligibility for the rehabilitation credit of a building that is not a certified historic structure is no longer determined by the age of the building, but rather by the year in which it was placed in service. Such a building

---

[24] I.R.C. § 47(c)(2)(B)(ii)-(iii).
[25] Treas. Reg. § 1.48-11(c)(7).
[26] *See* Priv. Ltr. Rul. 83-04-001 (May 29, 1981).
[27] I.R.C. § 47(c)(2)(B)(vi).
[28] I.R.C. § 47(c)(2)(B)(iv).

cannot qualify for the credit unless it was placed in service prior to 1936.[29] In addition, the credit cannot be taken if a building (other than a certified historic structure) is used for residential purposes. A certified historic structure, as under prior law, may be used for either residential or nonresidential purposes. The use must, however, be one that is depreciable to the taxpayer (e.g., the taxpayer's personal residential use would not qualify). As under prior law, use for transient lodging (e.g., inns or hotels) is not deemed residential and hence can qualify for either credit.[30]

In addition to satisfying these age and use tests, the building (and its structural components) must have been "substantially rehabilitated," must have been placed in service before the beginning of the rehabilitation, and must meet certain requirements as to the retention of external walls and internal structural framework in the rehabilitation process.

1.2.4 Substantial Rehabilitation

A building will be treated as having been substantially rehabilitated only if the qualified rehabilitation expenditures during the 24-month period selected by the taxpayer (and ending with or within the taxable year for which the credit is sought) exceed the greater of:

1. The prerehabilitation adjusted basis of the building (and its structural components); or
2. $5,000.[31]

The adjusted basis of the building (and its structural components) is determined as of the later of the first day of the 24-month period selected by the taxpayer or the holding period of the building as defined in Section 1250(e) of the Internal Revenue Code.[32] For this purpose, land costs are excluded from prerehabilitation basis.[33]

When a major portion of a building is rehabilitated independently, it is likely that it will be treatable as a separate building in determining whether it is a qualified rehabilitated building, and basis may be allocated to the rehabilitated portion. Expenditures for work that affects more than

---

[29] I.R.C. § 47(c)(1)(B). The term "placed in service" refers to the earlier of the taxable years in which either (1) depreciation on the building began or (2) the property was available for its intended use. Treas. Reg. § 1.46-3(d)(1) (as amended 1988). *Cf.* Prop. Treas. Reg. § 1.168-2(l)(2), 49 Fed. Reg. 5940 (1984) (providing a consistent definition for ACRS purposes).

[30] I.R.C. § 50(b)(2) (West Supp. 1991).

[31] I.R.C. § 47(c)(1)(C)(i).

[32] For these purposes, the determination of the beginning of the holding period is made without regard to any reconstruction by the taxpayer in connection with the rehabilitation.

[33] S. Rep. No. 97-144, 97th Cong., 1st Sess. 177–78 (1981).

that portion of the building, however, must also be allocated.[34] Under the regulations, for a part of a building to be considered a major portion of the building, it must generally consist of clearly identifiable parts of the building (e.g., the first five stories of a seven-story building or a wing of a building). The determination is to be made "on the basis of all the facts and circumstances."[35]

The treatment of expenditures incurred within the 24-month period but paid for after that time is not settled. The regulation governing pre-ERTA expenses provides that all taxpayers, regardless of their accounting method, will be treated as being on the accrual basis.[36] With this approach, all expenses incurred as well as paid during the 24-month period would be aggregated in determining whether the building was substantially rehabilitated.

The statute provides an alternative to the 24-month period for phased rehabilitation projects, which allows rehabilitation expenditures to be aggregated over a 60-month period. This option is not intended to be available for projects that unintentionally extend past their original completion date and incur costs after the conclusion of the 24-month period. To qualify under this provision, the architectural plans and specifications for the project must be completed before the rehabilitation begins and must set forth the phases in which the project will be completed.[37] The rehabilitation tax credit may be taken when a certified historic building is first placed in service in a phased rehabilitation project even though the "substantial rehabilitation" test has not been satisfied, as long as the project is intended to be completed within the 60-month measuring period.[38]

Although these objective criteria for satisfying the substantial rehabilitation test may aid in the administration of the tax law, the test has been criticized for several reasons. First, the criteria may encourage developers to make expenditures solely to meet the substantial rehabilitation test even though the expenditures are not otherwise necessary. Second, the substantial rehabilitation standards make rehabilitation projects more difficult in areas where building values are high. In cities such as New York, the purchase price of an old building often exceeds the amount which would ordinarily be spent to rehabilitate it, thus making it impossible to meet the substantial rehabilitation test and qualify for the tax credit unless the transaction is restructured for this purpose. In some

---

[34] Treas. Reg. § 1.48-11(b)(5). *See, e.g.*, Priv. Ltr. Rul. 82-26-125 (March 31, 1982) (ruling that the first floor of a nonhistoric building was a "separate building" for this purpose). *But see*, Alexander v. Commissioner, 97 T.C. 15 (1991) (holding that tax credit could not be taken for the rehabilitation of a rental unit that occupied the entire first floor of a building when the taxpayer owned the entire building).

[35] Treas. Reg. § 1.48-11(b)(5)(ii).

[36] Treas. Reg. § 1.48-11(c)(3).

[37] I.R.C. § 47(c)(1)(C)(ii). For an example of a phased rehabilitation approved by the IRS, *see* Priv. Ltr. Rul. 83-38-048 (June 20, 1983).

[38] Ford v. United States, No. 1:89-cv-1850-HTW, 1990 U.S. Dist. LEXIS 16337 (N.D. Ga. Nov. 15, 1990).

cases, developers have attempted to avoid this problem by creating a partnership to undertake the rehabilitation of the building and having the current owner transfer the building to the partnership as its contribution to capital. The partnership can then use the owner's existing adjusted basis, which, especially if the building has been depreciated, may be low enough to allow the rehabilitation to qualify under the substantial rehabilitation test.

This technique may, however, have drawbacks as well. If the property is transferred to the partnership at less than its current market value, the partnership will forgo the opportunity to depreciate the increment between the transferring partner's basis in the property and its fair market value.

Owners may wish to consider other ways to reduce the adjusted basis of a building so as to decrease the amount which must be spent to qualify as a substantial rehabilitation.[39] The purchaser of a property for rehabilitation may wish to allocate the purchase price as heavily as possible to the cost of land, which is not included in the substantial rehabilitation test, rather than to the cost of the building (although this will reduce the purchaser's basis for later depreciation of the building). The purchaser must be able to substantiate any allocation which is made. It may be desirable for the seller, or the purchaser prior to beginning rehabilitation, to make a charitable contribution of a facade easement (as discussed in § 1.5) on the building, thereby reducing basis.[40] In some circumstances, it may be necessary to delay rehabilitation of a building until its basis is reduced, through accelerated cost recovery depreciation deductions,[41] to the point at which rehabilitation becomes financially viable.

Alternatively, there may be ways to increase qualified rehabilitation expenditures to satisfy the substantial rehabilitation test. An owner may, for example, be able to capitalize as rehabilitation costs certain expenditures that might otherwise be immediately deductible as current expenditures. Each of these approaches, however, may involve other adverse tax consequences or may simply not be appropriate or possible in the circumstances of a given project. It is essential, therefore, that each of these approaches be thoroughly explored with the owner's tax advisor before they are employed.

1.2.5 Retention of External Walls

The 1986 Act adopted a two-part test governing the requirements for retention of the external walls of a building as part of a rehabilitation.[42] The

---

[39] For a more detailed discussion of these and other approaches, see Luxemberger, "Getting to 'Substantially Rehabilitated' in the Most Economical Way: One Aspect of the Rehabilitation Tax Credit," 1 *Preservation L. Rep.* 2036 (1982).

[40] *See* § 1.5.

[41] *See* § 1.4.

[42] I.R.C. § 47(c)(1)(A)(iii).

rehabilitation of a certified historic structure need no longer comply with the retention-of-walls requirements. Satisfying the Department of the Interior's certification standards would be sufficient with respect to any structural work done as part of a project. According to the Senate Committee Report, this change was intended to give the Secretary of the Interior "appropriate flexibility" in evaluating certification applications.[43] The Report also states, however, that rehabilitations eligible for the 20-percent credit should continue to be "true rehabilitations," and indicates the Committee's expectation that the "Secretary of the Interior will continue generally to deny certification to rehabilitation during which less than 75 percent of the external walls are not [sic] retained in place."

With respect to rehabilitations of buildings other than certified historic structures, three conditions must be met:

1. At least 50 percent of the existing external walls must be retained in place as external walls.
2. At least 75 percent of the existing external walls must be retained in place as either internal or external walls.
3. At least 75 percent of the existing internal structural framework must be retained in place.[44]

The purpose of these requirements, according to the Senate Committee Report, is to prohibit the credit in connection with "gut" rehabilitations, in which only the external shell of a building is left in place. The Report defines a building's internal structural framework to include "all load-bearing internal walls and any other internal structural supports, including the columns, girders, beams, trusses, spandrels, and all other members that are essential to the stability of the building."[45]

1.2.6 Recipients of the Rehabilitation Tax Credit

Generally, the taxpayer who owns the qualified rehabilitated building is eligible to take advantage of any available investment tax credit. The determination of ownership is made when the property is placed in service.[46] Consequently, the taxpayer taking the credit is not necessarily the taxpayer who owned the property during the rehabilitation. This provision is particularly significant in facilitating syndication of rehabilitation projects, as discussed in **Chapter Three**, because it permits the credit to be passed through to limited partners who may not have been investors in the original purchase of the property. In addition, there are some circumstances in which the tax credits may be passed through to the lessee of a rehabilitated building.

---

[43] S. Rep. No. 99-313, 99th Cong., 2d Sess. 754 (1986).
[44] I.R.C. § 47(c)(1)(A)(iii).
[45] S. Rep. No. 99-313, 99th Cong., 2d Sess. 754 (1986).
[46] Treas. Reg. § 1.48-11(c)(3).

The regulations governing the investment tax credit establish a formula for determining a transferee's basis in qualified rehabilitation expenditures in cases in which a transfer is made after rehabilitation has occurred but before a building has been placed in service. A transferee who wishes to take advantage of the credit may treat as paid or incurred by the transferee qualified rehabilitation expenditures equal to the lesser of (1) the amount of such expenditures incurred before the date of acquisition by the transferee or (2) that portion of the transferee's costs of acquisition that was attributable to such expenditures.[47]

There are several situations in which the ability to pass along rehabilitation expenditures to a transferee may be especially helpful. One is the case of a condominium conversion. Purchasers of condominium units for depreciable purposes are eligible for the rehabilitation credit for those expenditures that relate to their individual units and their proportionate shares of common areas.[48] Qualified rehabilitation expenditures incurred by a condominium developer may be taken into account by purchasers for purposes of calculating the amount of the credit for which they are eligible, so long as the units are acquired prior to their being placed in service (i.e., made available for rent as commercial units or for use in a trade or business, whichever is earlier).[49]

A lessor of property eligible for the rehabilitation tax credit may elect to treat its lessee as a purchaser of the property.[50] If the lessor does so, the lessee is treated as the actual owner and may take the tax credit. A number of conditions apply to such elections,[51] including that the lessee be the original user of the property. If the lease term is less than the class life of the property (as discussed in § 1.4), the lessor may only pass through a fraction of the credit, determined by the ratio between the lease term and the class life of the property.

Passing the tax credit through to a transferee may also be important when rehabilitated property is transferred to a partnership. This must be done before the property is placed in service if the partnership is to be eligible for the credit, and all partners who wish to share the benefits of the credit must also have joined prior to that time. Similarly, if property is to be transferred from a partnership to other entities or individuals, this must occur before it is placed in service if the transferees are to be eligible for the credit.[52] Moreover, the allocation of profits among the partners

---

[47] Treas. Reg. § 1.48-11(c)(3)(ii)(B).

[48] *See, e.g.,* Priv. Ltr. Rul. 83-47-047 (Aug. 22, 1983); Priv. Ltr. Rul. 83-40-021 (June 28, 1983); Priv. Ltr. Rul. 83-05-104 (Nov. 3, 1982).

[49] A purchaser may, apparently, take the credit in the year his or her unit is placed in service even if other units are not purchased or placed in service in that year. *See* Priv. Ltr. Rul. 87-31-005 (March 27, 1987).

[50] I.R.C. § 50(d)(5); Treas. Reg. § 1.48-11(d)(1).

[51] Treas. Reg. § 1.48-4 (as amended 1972).

[52] *See* Priv. Ltr. Rul. 85-06-036 (Nov. 9, 1984).

may not be altered for five years after the property is placed in service, or a disposition of Section 38 property will be deemed to have occurred and some or all of the credit taken will be recaptured.[53]

As noted previously, the rehabilitation tax credit is available in the year the rehabilitated building is placed in service.[54] As a general matter, property is deemed to have been placed in service when it is "placed in a condition or state of readiness and availability for a specifically assigned function, whether in a trade or business, in the production of income, in a tax-exempt activity, or in a personal activity."[55] This is often demonstrated by an objective event such as the receipt of a certificate of occupancy from the appropriate governmental authority. However, the IRS will not necessarily accept such an event as determinative of when a building is placed in service.[56]

1.2.7 Limit on Tax Offset

One of the major impacts of the 1986 Act has been to limit the usefulness of many tax benefits, including the rehabilitation credit, for most taxpayers who would previously have utilized them. While the rehabilitation credit can, as before, be carried backward or forward, the new passive loss rules tightly restrict the value of the credit to most investors. The Technical Corrections and Miscellaneous Revenue Act of 1988 (TAMRA)[57] sets forth in I.R.C. Section 42(h)(1)(E) the conditions that must be satisfied for taxpayers to carry over credits.

The amount of the rehabilitation tax credit which a taxpayer may claim in any taxable year (other limitations not withstanding) may not exceed $25,000 plus 75 percent of the taxpayer's liability for tax in excess of $25,000.[58] If the taxes for which the taxpayer would otherwise be liable in the year the property is put in service are less than the amount of the credit for which he or she is eligible, the excess credit may be carried back to the three taxable years preceding the year in which the unused credit accrued and applied to the taxes paid on those years (starting with

---

[53] Treas. Reg. § 1.47-6 (1967).

[54] Treas. Reg. § 1.46-3(d)(4)(i).

[55] Treas. Reg. § 1.46-3(d)(1), § 1.48-11(d)(2).

[56] *See, e.g.*, Priv. Ltr. Rul. 84-15-003 (Dec. 15, 1983) (ruling that the installation of drywall and water and electrical meters, not the issuance of a temporary certificate of occupancy, determined when an apartment was "in a condition or state of readiness and availability for occupancy," and finding that the taxpayer had failed to demonstrate a sufficient connection between the issuance of a certificate and the time an apartment was ready for occupancy).

[57] Pub. L. No. 100-647, 102 Stat. 3342 (1988) (codified, as amended, in scattered section of 26 U.S.C.).

[58] I.R.C. § 38(c) (West Supp. 1991). This limit is decreased in the case of certain persons and entities. I.R.C. § 38(c)(2).

the most recent).[59] If the tax paid during the three prior years does not fully offset the unused credit, the remainder may be carried forward and offset against taxes that would otherwise be due during the 15 years following the year in which the credit became available.[60] The ability to maximize the tax offset power of the credit in this manner was, prior to the 1986 Act, an important incentive in attracting syndication investors to a rehabilitation project.

Few taxpayers, however, are now likely to be able to benefit from the full value of even these credits because the ability to utilize credits (including both the rehabilitation credit and the low-income housing credit discussed in § 1.3) is further restricted by the 1986 Act. Even if a taxpayer were able to carry credits forward as just discussed, the ability to take those credits in future years is limited by the new passive loss rules. Under these rules, taxpayers may only use credits and losses from so-called "passive" activities (including most real estate investment) to offset income from other passive activities. These rules are discussed in greater detail in § 3.2.4. Investors should also be aware of the possible impact of the alternative minimum tax, expanded in scope and amount by the 1986 Act, on the tax offset effect of the rehabilitation credit. This is also discussed in § 3.2.4.

1.2.8 Recapture of Tax Credits

After claiming an investment tax credit, the taxpayer must hold the rehabilitated building for five full years after the property is placed in service to avoid being subject to a recapture of the credit.[61] This includes a requirement to hold any interest in the property, including a limited partnership interest. The percentage of the credit that is recaptured is determined by the amount of time that has elapsed since the property was placed in service and is calculated according to the following schedule:

If Disposition of Property Occurs Within	The Percentage of the Credit Recaptured Is:[62]
One full year after placed in service	100
One to two full years after placed in service	80
Two to three full years after placed in service	60
Three to four full years after placed in service	40
Four to five full years after placed in service	20

---

[59] I.R.C. § 39 (West Supp. 1991).
[60] Note that any recapture of the tax credit will result in an adjustment to the carryback or carryover. *See* I.R.C. § 50(d)(3).
[61] I.R.C. § 50(a)(5).
[62] I.R.C. § 50(a)(1)(B).

To determine the taxpayer's tax liability for the taxable year in which the disposition is made, one must first determine the amount of credit that has been taken in all prior taxable years as a result of qualified investment in the property. The amount of the credit that will be recaptured is determined by multiplying the applicable recapture percentage by the total prior credit taken. This recapture amount is added to the taxpayer's current tax liability.

However, current tax liability is adjusted only with regard to credits actually taken. If the taxpayer had excess credits which could not be fully used in the year they became available and which have been carried back or carried over, such carrybacks and carryforwards are adjusted.[63] Any portion of the credit which has not yet been taken will not affect current tax liability on disposition of the property.

Most dispositions and changes in the nature of the use of the building result in recapture of the tax credit previously taken for rehabilitation. This includes sale, like-kind exchanges, and conversion of commercial property to rental or personal use.[64] It also includes gifts of rehabilitated property. Transactions that do not trigger recapture include transfer by reason of death, transfer between spouses incident to divorce, and certain sale-and-leaseback arrangements.[65]

While recapture generally applies to casualty losses, replacement property will usually be treated as eligible for the credit. Casualty damage, such as that due to fire, will probably not trigger recapture so long as it does not cause structural damage amounting to a disposition of the property, or cause a change in use so substantial as to constitute a cessation of use as qualifying property. However, any insurance proceeds exceeding the cost of repair and restoration would be subject to recapture.[66]

1.2.9 Effective Date and Transition Rules

The changes in the rehabilitation tax credit made by the 1986 Act apply generally to rehabilitated property placed in service after December 31, 1986. Certain transition provisions do, however, continue the old rules in some instances, so long as a building is placed in service by January 1, 1994. Such a building will not be subject to these changes if the property (including any leasehold interest) was acquired before March 2, 1986, or acquired later pursuant to a contract binding on March 1, 1986, and either:

---

[63] I.R.C. § 50(a)(3).
[64] Treas. Reg. § 1.47-2 (as amended 1972).
[65] Treas. Reg. § 1.47-3 (as amended 1988).
[66] Priv. Ltr. Rul. 85-21-010 (Feb. 14, 1985).

1. Parts 1 and 2 of the Historic Preservation Certification Application (see **Chapter Two**) were filed with the Department of the Interior before March 2, 1986, or
2. The lesser of $1 million or 5 percent of the cost of the rehabilitation was incurred before March 2, 1986, or was required to be incurred pursuant to a written contract which was binding on March 2, 1986.[67]

In addition, for properties placed in service after December 31, 1986 and subject to these transition rules, the 15- and 20-percent credits are reduced to 10 and 13 percent, respectively.[68] The 25-percent credit is unchanged for transition projects.

1.3 LOW-INCOME HOUSING CREDIT

The structure of real estate tax incentives left in the wake of the 1986 Act, TAMRA, and the 1989[69] and 1990 Omnibus Budget Reconciliation Acts[70] (collectively, OBRA) makes low-income housing a potentially advantageous component of a rehabilitation project. The 1986 Act substitutes for the 60-month amortization for low-income housing rehabilitation[71] a new low-income housing tax credit.[72] The new credit provides a generous tax incentive for the development of low-income housing, through both new construction and rehabilitation. It also contains stringent requirements as to the income limitations that must be used in selecting tenants for housing financed with the credit, maximum rents that may be charged, and time periods over which units must remain in low-income tenancy. If a project can meet these requirements, the credit can be an important part of the financing package for a rehabilitation project. Particularly in light of the reduction in the rehabilitation credit and the other tax changes making real estate a less beneficial investment, it is in the interest of project sponsors to investigate all available incentives for which a project, depending on its nature, may qualify.

1.3.1 Amount of Credit

As created by the 1986 Act and modified by OBRA, the low-income housing credit is available for projects placed in service between January 1,

---

[67] Tax Reform Act of 1986 § 251(d)(2), *amended by* TAMRA § 1002(k).
[68] *Id.* § 251(d)(5).
[69] Pub. L. No. 101-239, 103 Stat. 2106 (1989).
[70] Pub. L. No. 101-508, 104 Stat. 1388 (1990).
[71] I.R.C. § 167(k) (repealed 1986).
[72] I.R.C. § 42 (West Supp. 1991).

1987 and June 30, 1992.[73] (Under certain circumstances, a credit may also be claimed for eligible property financed with tax-exempt bonds if the building is placed in service before July 1, 1994)[74] The amount of the credit, which applies at two different rates to different types of expenditures, may vary on a month-to-month basis for buildings placed in service after 1987. For buildings placed in service during 1987, the applicable credit amounts were 9 and 4 percent.[75] These percentages could be taken as a credit annually over a 10-year period for an aggregated credit of either 90 or 40 percent. Each state, however, has the discretion to reduce the credit percentage where a smaller credit percentage, coupled with other financing and rental assistance, would be sufficient to operate a project.[76]

The 9-percent credit is available for new construction costs and for rehabilitation costs if, during any 24-month period, they equal or exceed the greater of 10 percent of the adjusted basis of the building (as determined in a specified manner as of the first day of the period) or $3,000 per low-income unit.[77] These costs do not qualify for the 9-percent credit, however, if they are "federally subsidized"—financed by means of either tax-exempt obligations or below market federal loans.[78] If these expenses are federally subsidized, the taxpayer has the option of reducing the basis of the project eligible for the credit by the amount subsidized, or including the subsidized costs in the amount eligible for the 4-percent credit.

The 4-percent credit, in addition to federally subsidized construction or rehabilitation costs as described previously, is available for building acquisition costs and rehabilitation costs associated with the acquisition of a building. The latter costs may not exceed the amounts specified in the preceding paragraph per unit; if they do, they will be treated as attributable to a separate new building, and hence will be eligible for the 9-percent credit.[79] No credit is available for land, as opposed to building, costs.

For buildings placed in service after 1987, the credits are to be adjusted so that their present value, over the 10-year period, will equal 70

---

[73] Section 107 of the Tax Extension Act of 1991, Pub. L. No. 102-227 (1991), extended the low-income housing tax credit program for six months past the December 31, 1991 expiration date in the statute. Hearings on whether to extend or terminate the tax credit were held on January 28–29, and February 29, 1992, in the House Ways and Means Committee. H.R. 4210, 102d Cong., 2d Sess. (1992), which passed the House on February 27, 1992, contains a permanent extention for the low-income housing tax credit effective after June 30, 1992. As of March 2, 1992, the Senate Finance Committee is considering similar legislation.

[74] I.R.C. § 42(o)(2).
[75] I.R.C. § 42(b)(1).
[76] I.R.C. § 42(m)(2).
[77] I.R.C. § 42(e).
[78] I.R.C. § 42(i)(2).
[79] I.R.C. § 42(e).

and 30 percent of costs, respectively.[80] The credits are to be calculated monthly based on fluctuations in interest rates as determined by the Treasury Department and are intended to ensure that the true economic recovery of project costs remains relatively constant, despite interest rate changes. The taxpayer may elect to fix the credit percentage for the full 10-year credit period at the earlier of (1) the date the project is placed in service or (2) the date the taxpayer enters into a binding agreement with the state agency with respect to the project. In this way, the taxpayer need not remain at risk for increases in the interest rate until the building is placed in service.[81]

For buildings placed in service after 1989, the 70-percent credit is available for new construction costs and for rehabilitation costs if, during any 24-month period, they equal or exceed the greater of $3,000 per low-income unit, or 10 percent of the unadjusted basis. If this new substantial rehabilitation standard is met, the existing portion of the building is eligible for the 30 percent credit. Exceptions to the new substantial rehabilitation standard are available for buildings acquired by a taxpayer from a governmental unit, and for federally assisted buildings under certain conditions.[82] Individuals who invested in eligible property prior to October 26, 1990 may elect to claim a credit equal to 150% of the otherwise allowable credit for the next tax year. This election is binding on successors, and the increased credit is recaptured in future years. For partnership property, the election is made by the partnership.[83]

The amount of this credit that will be available overall is not unlimited. An annual allocation of credits is made to each state, on the basis of $1.25 per state resident per year.[84] A project sponsor must apply to the state's designated housing credit agency (in most states, the housing finance agency) for a credit allocation to be assured of receiving a credit at the time that a project is placed in service. Most projects financed with tax-exempt bonds, however, will be eligible for the credit independent of the state cap, and without the need for an express allocation.

1.3.2 Qualified Basis

The amount of project costs on which the credit is calculated is known as "qualified basis." Qualified basis is equal to the product of "eligible basis" multiplied by the "applicable fraction" of low-income units to all units in the project.[85] Each of these items is determined as follows:

---

[80] I.R.C. § 42(b)(2).

[81] I.R.C. § 42(b)(2)(A).

[82] I.R.C. § 42(e)(3).

[83] 1990 OBRA § 11407(c). *See also* Rev. Proc. 91-7.

[84] I.R.C. § 42(h)(3)(C). For calendar year 1990, the annual allocation of credits was originally made on the basis of $0.9375 per state resident per year. This was restored to $1.25 by 1990 OBRA § 11407(a)(2).

[85] I.R.C. § 42(c)(1).

1. Eligible basis generally includes acquisition, construction, and rehabilitation costs for an entire building, not only for the low-income portion. These costs may be included, however, only if the average quality of the non low-income units in the building is not higher than that of the low-income units[86] unless (1) the cost of those units does not exceed the average cost of low-income units by more than 15 percent and (2) the differential is excluded from eligible basis.[87] The Conference Committee Report states that units are of comparable quality if construction or acquisition costs (including, presumably, rehabilitation costs) are comparable, and if the units are provided in similar proportion to low-income and other tenants. In addition, the costs of amenities may be included only if they are provided at comparable cost for low-income and other tenants, or are available to all tenants on a comparable basis.[88] Amenities may include items of personal property.

Under the 1989 OBRA, an increase in eligible basis is available for certain buildings in high cost areas. The eligible basis of a building that is located in a census tract (or, in certain cases, a census enumeration district) in which 50 percent or more of the households have an income that is less than 60 percent of the area median gross income, or in an area designated by the Secretary of HUD as one that has high construction, land, or utility costs, is deemed to be 130 percent of eligible basis claimed for depreciation.[89]

Eligible basis must be reduced by the amount of any federal grants that are made to support a project at any time during the 15-year period during which the project must comply with the low-income unit requirements and it may not include expenditures for which the taxpayer elects to take a depreciation deduction under Section 167(k) (as in effect the day before the enactment of 1990 OBRA).[90] Moreover, as previously discussed, the taxpayer may elect to reduce eligible basis by the amount of other federal subsidies.

2. The applicable fraction equals the lesser of (1) the ratio of low-income units in a building to all units, or (2) the ratio of the floor area of low-income units to the floor area of all units.[91] In making this calculation, only units actually occupied by low-income tenants may generally be included, whereas the determination of the total number of units includes all units, whether presently occupied or not.[92]

---

[86] I.R.C. § 42(d)(3)(A).

[87] I.R.C. § 42(d)(3)(B).

[88] Conf. Rep. No. 99-841, 99th Cong., 2d Sess. II-89 and II-90 (1986).

[89] I.R.C. § 42(d)(5)(C). Federally subsidized buildings are also eligible for the 30 percent increase. See I.R.S. Announcement IR-91-112 (July 17, 1991).

[90] I.R.C. § 42(d)(5)(B), (C).

[91] I.R.C. § 42(c)(1)(B).

[92] Conf. Rep. No. 99-841, 99th Cong., 2d Sess. II-89 (1986).

An additional requirement applies to the eligibility of any building for the low-income housing credit. At least 10 years must have elapsed between the date of acquisition by the taxpayer claiming the credit and the later of (1) the last date that the building was placed in service or (2) the date of the most recent nonqualified substantial improvement of the building.[93] (Placement in service includes acquisition of the building by a new owner.) The 10-year requirement applies whether the building was previously placed in service by the taxpayer or by another owner. However, a number of exceptions apply to the 10-year rule, including a rule (contained in the *Blue Book*) that under certain circumstances, the acquisition of a building by a not-for-profit organization may not be deemed a placement in service.[94] This might, for example, permit a not-for-profit owner to transfer the building to another entity that will undertake the rehabilitation, without running afoul of the 10-year requirement. The Treasury Department may also waive the 10-year rule if (1) the building is federally assisted, (2) federal mortgage funds are at risk, and (3) certain defined federal actions have been taken with respect to the building.[95]

The 1989 Act contains two additional exceptions to the 10-year rule. The Secretary may waive the rule with respect to certain federally assisted low-income buildings on which the mortgage is subject to prepayment if the exception is necessary to avert conversion of the property to market rate use and with respect to certain buildings acquired from failed financial institutions.[96]

1.3.3 Qualified Low-Income Housing Project

A project qualifies for the low-income housing credit only if several conditions are met. The first relates to income requirements for tenancy. To qualify for the credit, either (1) 20 percent or more of the residential units in a project must be occupied by tenants whose income is 50 percent or less of the area's gross median income, or (2) 40 percent or more of the units must be occupied by tenants whose income is 60 percent or less of the area's gross median.[97] These numbers represent merely threshold requirements; if a larger number of units contain low-income tenants, the proportion of eligible basis that may be included in qualified basis will be

---

[93] I.R.C. § 42(d)(2)(B).

[94] Staff of the Joint Committee on Taxation, *General Explanation of the Tax Reform Act of 1986* 159 (1986) [hereinafter *Blue Book*].

[95] Treas. Reg. § 1.42-2(b) (1990).

[96] I.R.C § 42(d)(6).

[97] I.R.C. § 42(g)(1). A special rule for New York City allows a project to qualify if 25 percent of the units are occupied by tenants with incomes under 60 percent of the median. I.R.C. §§ 42(g)(4), 142(d)(6).

higher, resulting in a larger credit. Qualifying income standards may be adjusted for household size.

The choice of a qualifying standard, and the number of units to be included in qualified basis, must be made when the project is placed in service. If additional units are subsequently rented to low-income tenants, an additional credit equal to ⅔ of the applicable percentage may be taken on the qualified basis attributable to the additional units.[98]

Second, tenants occupying low-income units may not be required to pay more than 30 percent of their income in rent.[99] For purposes of the 30-percent requirement, rent does include a utility allowance, but does not include federal rent subsidies, or, apparently, any other rental assistance payment not made by the tenant.[100]

Finally, a project must continuously meet the low-income occupancy requirements for a period of 30 years pursuant to an extended low-income housing commitment. Such a commitment must be made with the housing credit agency and it must be binding on all successors of the project owners and recorded pursuant to state law as a restrictive covenant. If, at the end of the initial (15-year) compliance period, the project owner(s) is unable to transfer the property for continued low-income use, the allocating agency has one year to find an eligible buyer at a specified price based on outstanding indebtedness and investor equity contributions. The project owner(s) may trigger this one-year period by providing written notice to the agency at any time after the fourteenth year of the compliance period. If no such buyer is located, the property may be converted to market rate use, with the qualification that existing low-income tenants may not be evicted within three years after the termination of the extended compliance commitment.[101]

A tenant may continue to be considered low-income as long as the tenant's income does not rise more than 40 percent above the qualifying income standard (or 70 percent in the case of a "deep rent skewed" project in which the occupants earn and pay rent at specified levels that are even lower than those necessary to establish the project as a qualified low-income housing project). If it does, the tenant may remain in the unit, but the next vacant unit of comparable or smaller size must be rented to a low-income tenant (or a tenant whose income does not exceed 40 percent of area median gross income in the case of a deep rent skewed project), so that the overall proportion continues to meet the requirements.[102] Moreover, the tenant may not be charged more than 30 percent of the qualifying income standard as rent, regardless of increases in the tenant's actual

---

[98] I.R.C. § 42(f)(3)(A).
[99] I.R.C. § 42(g)(2).
[100] Conf. Rep. No. 99-841, 99th Cong., 2d Sess. II-94 (1986).
[101] I.R.C. § 42(h)(6).
[102] I.R.C. § 42(g)(2)(D).

income. If the project does not continue to comply with the low-income proportionality requirements, recapture penalties are imposed.[103]

The recapture risk may be of particularly serious concern to potential investors, given the lengthy compliance period. If an individual unit ceases to be occupied by a low-income tenant, the project loses only the accelerated portion of the credit (reflecting the fact that the entire credit is taken over 10 years while the project must remain in compliance for a longer period). If the project falls below the qualifying standard, however, a portion of the entire credit is recaptured. According to the Blue Book, there will be no recapture as long as any noncompliance is corrected within a reasonable period from the time at which it was discovered or should have been discovered, and project owners are not required to evict tenants in order to restore compliance.[104] If a project is sold or ownership otherwise transferred, recapture may be avoided if an adequate compliance bond is posted with the Treasury Department.[105]

1.3.4 Interaction of Rehabilitation Credit and Low-Income Housing Credit

Assuming that all of the requirements for both credits are met, nothing in the 1986 Act prevents the rehabilitation tax credit and the low-income housing tax credit from being taken together with respect to a project.[106] In general, substantial rehabilitation expenditures that would qualify for the rehabilitation credit could also qualify for the 9-percent low-income housing credit. Residential rental projects that would qualify for the low-income housing credit are, however, only eligible for the rehabilitation credit if they involve certified historic structures.

If both credits were to be utilized, the 20-percent rehabilitation credit would be figured first. The basis of the building on which the amount of the low-income housing credit would be calculated would have to be reduced by the full amount of the rehabilitation credit taken. Thus, while the amount of costs recovered using both credits would not be completely additive, the total benefit obtained from the credits taken together could potentially be substantially greater than either alone. This could be particularly valuable in the case of mixed-use projects, only a portion of which would qualify for the low-income housing credit alone.

---

[103] I.R.C. § 42(j).

[104] *Blue Book, supra* note 94, at 166.

[105] I.R.C. § 42(j)(6). Under the 1989 OBRA, the Treasury Department is directed to issue guidance on recapture within six months of the OBRA's passage.

[106] Conf. Rep. No. 99-841, 99th Cong., 2d Sess. II-89 (1986).

1.4 DEPRECIATION

The 1986 Act reduced real estate depreciation benefits in two primary ways. First, it generally discontinued the use of accelerated depreciation schedules and mandated use of the straight-line method with respect to real property.[107] Second, it substantially lengthened the recovery period from the 19-year period generally applicable under prior law.

Because the new law requires that straight-line depreciation be used with respect to the types of property eligible for the rehabilitation tax credit, taxpayers may no longer choose whether to use accelerated depreciation (and forego the credit) or use straight-line depreciation (and qualify for the credit). Similarly, accelerated depreciation is no longer recaptured upon disposition of a property.

1.4.1 Depreciation Systems

Under the revised accelerated cost recovery system (ACRS) created by the 1986 Act, all residential rental property will be depreciated over a 27.5-year recovery period on a straight-line schedule.[108] Nonresidential real property must be depreciated over a 31.5-year period, also on a straight-line basis.

The 1986 Act also established an alternative depreciation system, which further extended the depreciation period and reduced annual deductions. Under this alternative, both nonresidential real property and residential rental property are depreciated on a straight-line basis over 40 years.[109] As discussed in § 1.7.2, tax-exempt use property must be depreciated on this 40-year schedule. In addition, the difference between the depreciation deductions allowable under the revised ACRS and those allowed by the alternative depreciation system may in some instances be treated as an item of tax preference subject to the alternative minimum tax. An election to use the alternative depreciation system may be made on an asset-by-asset basis.

Under all depreciation formulas, the midmonth convention applies to real property.[110] This convention provides that a building placed in service or disposed of at any time during a month is treated as if it were placed in service or disposed of in the middle of that month.

The basis of property on which depreciation deductions are figured must be reduced by the full amount of any rehabilitation credit that is taken with respect to that property.[111] This differs from prior law,

---

[107] I.R.C. § 168(b)(3) (West Supp. 1991).
[108] I.R.C. § 168(c).
[109] I.R.C. § 168(g).
[110] I.R.C. § 168(d).
[111] I.R.C. § 50(c)(1).

which required only a 50-percent basis adjustment if the rehabilitated property was a certified historic structure.

1.4.2 Transition Rules

In general, the new depreciation rules apply to property placed in service after December 31, 1986. However, the old rules continued to apply to real property that was constructed, reconstructed, or acquired pursuant to a written contract that was binding as of March 1, 1986, so long as the property is placed in service before January 1, 1991.[112] A contract is considered binding if it is enforceable under state law against the taxpayer, and may be considered binding even if subject to a condition, so long as the condition is not within the control of either party or a predecessor in interest.[113]

A taxpayer would also be able to take advantage of the old depreciation schedules with respect to constructed or reconstructed property if (1) the lesser of $1 million or 5 percent of the cost of the property was incurred or committed as of March 1, 1986, (2) construction or reconstruction began by that date, and (3) the property was placed in service before January 1, 1991.[114] For purposes of this rule, construction is defined as "physical work of a significant nature," and is not deemed to include "preliminary activities such as planning or designing, securing financing, exploring, researching, or developing."[115]

1.5 PRESERVATION EASEMENTS

Under the terms of the Tax Treatment Extension Act of 1980, certain donations of easements affecting historic buildings or districts are eligible for charitable contribution deductions under Section 170 of the Code. The most common application of this provision involves gifts of facade easements, which restrict future alteration or demolition of building facades and thereby preserve an important part of the character of a historic structure. Alone or in tandem with the rehabilitation tax credit, the donation of a facade easement can contribute significantly to making restoration of historic buildings financially attractive. Investors should be aware, however, that the IRS may challenge deductions relating to these donations, and that strict compliance with the substantiation requirements discussed in § **1.5.4** may be essential to a determination of validity. In addition, all of the requirements of the IRS

---

[112] Tax Reform Act of 1986 § 203(b), *amended by* TAMRA § 1002(c)(4), (6), (7).
[113] Conf. Rep. No. 99-841, 99th Cong., 2d Sess. II-55 (1986).
[114] Tax Reform Act of 1986 § 203(b), *amended by* TAMRA § 1002(b)(4).
[115] Conf. Rep. No. 99-841, 99th Cong., 2d Sess. II-56 (1986).

regulations relating to donations of partial interests in real property must be met and, where possible, the precise language of the regulations should be incorporated in the easements.

The IRS first ruled on the deductibility of open space easements in gross in 1964;[116] subsequent regulations provided that easement gifts were not subject to limitations otherwise applicable to donations of partial interests in property.[117] The Tax Reform Act of 1976 codified a deduction for gifts of a "lease on, option to purchase or easement with respect to real property of not less than 30 years' duration" given to a conservation organization.[118] All of these earlier attempts to recognize, for tax purposes, the legitimate interests motivating preservation easements were superseded in the 1980 legislation.

The 1980 Act created a federal income, gift, and estate tax deduction for a "Qualified Conservation Contribution."[119] As defined in Section 170(h) of the Code, the term "Qualified Conservation Contribution" means a gift (1) of a "qualified real property interest," (2) to a "qualified organization," and (3) to be used exclusively for conservation purposes. Each of these conditions, discussed in greater detail in the following sections, must be met to qualify for the deduction, and the Treasury has adopted regulations providing additional elaboration on the statutory requirements.[120] In principle, however, it is clear that appropriate facade easements do fall within the terms of the statute's definition, and hence qualify for a charitable deduction.

A useful source of information on conservation easements are the publications of the Conservation Tax Program, a service of the Land Trust Alliance, 900 17th Street, NW, Washington, DC, 20006. These cover tax developments affecting land conservation in general, including issues relating to easement donations.[121]

1.5.1 Qualified Real Property Interest

To receive a tax deduction, the easement that is donated must be "a restriction (granted in perpetuity) on the use which may be made of the real property."[122] Moreover, the regulations make clear that the easement must be enforceable.[123] This entails the rights of a donee to inspect the property to determine whether the terms of conveyance have been

---

[116] See Rev. Rul. 64-205, 1964-2 C.B. 62.
[117] Treas. Reg. § 1.170A-7(b)(1)(ii) (as amended 1986).
[118] Pub. L. No. 94-455, § 2124(e), 90 Stat. 1525, 1919 (1976).
[119] I.R.C. § 170(f)(3)(B)(iii) (West Supp. 1991).
[120] See Treas. Reg. § 1.170A-14 (as amended 1988).
[121] For a detailed discussion of the federal laws affecting conservation easements, see generally S. Small, *The Federal Tax Law of Conservation Easements* (Land Trust Exchange 1989).
[122] I.R.C. § 170(h)(2)(C).
[123] Treas. Reg. § 1.170A-14(g)(1).

complied with, to enforce the easement restrictions by resort to appropriate legal proceedings, and to compel restoration of the property to its condition prior to the donation.[124] The regulations also require that any mortgage on the property be subordinated to the rights of the donor organization to enforce the conservation purposes of the easement in perpetuity. All of these powers should be affirmatively stated in the document creating the easement. In addition, it may be advisable for the donor to get a legal opinion that the easement will be enforceable in perpetuity under state law.

Compliance with the perpetuity requirement may be somewhat problematic. State law often provides procedures for relaxing or terminating property restrictions that impair the conveyance of marketable title or are otherwise determined by courts to constrain unduly the use of property.[125] Many states bar the original grantee from assigning an easement.[126] Some states have recording statutes requiring that restrictions on the use of property be rerecorded at periodic intervals.[127] As a legal matter, any of these restrictions makes it impossible to guarantee that the easement will be perpetual. Some, but not all, of these assignment restricting and recording statutes contain exceptions for easements granted for conservation purposes.[128] Absent such exception, however, there is an unresolved conflict between the property right that can be created under state law and the requirements of the federal tax laws.

That conflict is averted under the Uniform Conservation Easement Act (Uniform Act), adopted by the National Conference of Commissioners on

---

[124] A U.S. Claims Court recently upheld a scenic easement in which the donor retained the right to subdivide the land, build houses, cut timber and farm, and a reversion of the easement upon condemnation of the underlying property. Since the terms of the easement restricted industrial or commercial activities, placement of mobile homes, camping accommodations, signs or advertising materials on the land, construction of roads or utilities lines other than for residential purposes, or mining or mineral extraction, the court concluded that "material limitations" were placed on the property that "enabled the Conservancy to adequately preserve the scenic quality of the easement property." The reversion did not make the donation valueless since the easement agreement conveyed to the Conservancy "forever an easement in perpetuity," making the Conservancy a public fiduciary. "In the event of a taking action by the government, the easement and the underlying land remains entrusted to the public. In other words, the easement cannot revert back to the [donor]." McLennan v. United States, No. 129-87T (Cl. Ct. May 5, 1991).

[125] For example, New York's "cy pres" statute permits a court to remove restrictions from dispositions for "religious, charitable, educational or benevolent purposes" if a determination is made that "circumstances have so changed . . . as to render impracticable or impossible a literal compliance" with the terms of those restrictions. N.Y. Est. Powers & Trusts Law § 8-1.1(c) (McKinney 1992).

[126] See Netherton, "Restrictive Agreements for Historic Preservation," 12 *Urb. Law.* 54 (1980).

[127] See Madden, "Tax Incentives for Land Conservation: The Charitable Contribution Deduction for Gifts of Conservation Easements," 2 *B.C. Envtl. Aff. L. Rev.* 105, 107 (1983).

[128] See, e.g., Mass. Gen. Laws Ann. ch. 184, § 26(c) (West 1991).

Uniform State Laws in 1981.[129] The Uniform Act, which has been adopted in New York and many other states, removes obstacles to the creation of perpetually enforceable easements in gross for conservation and historic preservation purposes. However, it limits the categories of easement holders possessing the right to permanent protection to governmental bodies and charitable organizations devoted, *inter alia*, to conservation purposes.

Conflict between state law and the perpetuity provision could, at least theoretically, arise in a different context. A recent IRS challenge to an easement donation questioned the easement's compliance with the perpetuity requirement in light of a California statute permitting landowners to petition the governing body of a city or county for abandonment of an open space easement. The Tax Court noted that, under the California statute, abandonment is permissible only upon a finding that no public purpose would be served by preserving the land as open space. The court found that the likelihood of such a finding being made was so remote as to be negligible, and upheld the taxpayer's right to claim a deduction.[130]

If the terms of the easement permit future development of land or alteration to buildings within a registered historic district, the regulations require that the development or alteration conform to local, state, or federal standards applicable to construction or rehabilitation.[131] This would presumably include the Secretary of the Interior's Standards for Rehabilitation, discussed in **Chapter Two**. Although this requirement does not expressly apply to properties individually listed in the National Register, it would be prudent to include the requirement in drafting any easement to comply with these provisions.

Another requirement of the regulations is that the easement prohibit subsequent transfer from the "qualified organization" to which it is originally granted unless two conditions are met. The subsequent transferee must also be a "qualified organization," under the rule explained in **§ 1.5.2**, and future transfers must be contingent on assurances that the conservation purposes for which the gift was made will continue to be carried out.[132] If the property as to which the easement is granted is subject to a mortgage, the mortgagee must subordinate its rights to the right of the grantee organization to enforce the conservation restrictions in perpetuity.[133]

The easement must also give the donee the right to receive a fair market value for the property interest, equal to a minimum ascertainable share of the fair market value of the entire property.[134] This represents a

---

[129] *See* 12 U.L.A. 63 (Supp. 1991).
[130] Stotler v. Commissioner, 1987 T.C. Memo 275.
[131] Treas. Reg. § 1.170A-14(d)(5)(i).
[132] Treas. Reg. § 1.170A-14(c)(2).
[133] Treas. Reg. § 1.170A-14(g)(2).
[134] Treas. Reg. § 1.170A-14(g)(6)(ii).

significant limitation on the donor's remaining rights in the property, including the right to dispose of it. If the restriction is extinguished for any reason, on subsequent sale or exchange of the property the donee would be entitled to a share of the proceeds equal to the proportionate value of the original restriction. This would be true even if the easement is extinguished against the donor's wishes for example, by order of a court on application of another party (as in a condemnation proceeding). Moreover, any proceeds received by the donee must be used in a manner consistent with the purposes of the original grant.[135]

The regulations require some visual public access to the donated property.[136] In the case of a historically important land area, this does not necessarily entail access to the entire property, but the public access provisions must insure sufficient public benefit to justify a tax benefit from the donation. If the land area or structure is not visible from a public way, the easement must give the public the opportunity on a regular basis to view the historic characteristics and features of the property.

The regulations list factors to be considered in evaluating the degree of public access, which essentially balance the historic significance and features of the property against the hazards or intrusions which public access might create.[137] Access is to be determined with reference to the terms of the easement rather than the amount actually provided by the donee organization, unless the donor was aware of facts indicating that the donee would provide significantly less access than the terms of the easement would allow.

1.5.2 Qualified Organization

For the donation of an easement to be deductible, the donee must be a qualified organization, of which there are several types. The organization may be a governmental unit, a publicly supported charity as defined in Section 509(a)(2) of the Code, or a charitable organization as defined in Section 509(a)(3) of the Code and controlled by a governmental unit or a publicly supported charity. It is beyond the scope of this book to describe the IRS's public support requirements in detail, but it should be noted that, in general, entities such as schools and churches will probably not qualify as recipient organizations. Easements are typically donated to charitable organizations that have preservation of historic and architectural resources among their purposes.[138] Although many easements are valued at zero on the books of nonprofit donees, donors and donees should consider securing professional advice on

---

[135] Treas. Reg. § 1.170A-14(c)(2).
[136] Treas. Reg. § 1.170A-14(d)(5)(iv)(A).
[137] Treas. Reg. § 1.170A-14(d)(5)(iv)(B).
[138] See, e.g., B. Hopkins, *The Law of Tax-Exempt Organizations* (New York: John Wiley, 1987).

whether, in an unusual case, the receipt of an extremely valuable easement could jeopardize the donee's "publicly supported" status.

The regulations require that a donee organization "have the resources to enforce the restrictions" and "have a commitment to protect the conservation purposes of the donation."[139] The regulations suggest that an established group dedicated primarily or substantially to conservation purposes would automatically meet both prongs of this test. Presumably, a governmental unit with revenue-raising powers would as well. The regulations do not require that funds actually be set aside to enforce the easement restrictions. As a practical matter, however, it may be useful to establish an endowment for meeting future costs of maintaining and enforcing the easement. Methods for doing so include requiring the donor to contribute a percentage of the value of the easement, or of the unrestricted value of the property; requiring a contribution based on the salable or rentable floor area of the building; or capitalizing, on an organization-wide basis, the costs of administering an entire easement program and assessing all donors proportionately.[140]

1.5.3 Conservation Purposes

Among the allowable conservation purposes for which an easement may be granted under the statute is "the preservation of a historically important land area or a Certified Historic Structure."[141] The definition of "certified historic structure" for this purpose is substantially similar to that applicable to the rehabilitation tax credit, but with two significant differences. First, the building must actually be listed on the National Register or certified as being significant to a National Register district by the due date (including extensions) of the taxpayer's return for the year of transfer.[142] Second, both depreciable and nondepreciable structures qualify, thus making private residences eligible for easement donations.[143]

Lack of certification, however, does not necessarily exclude a building within a historic district from eligibility for protection through an easement donation. Under the regulation, the term "historically important land area" includes:

1. An independently significant land area including any related historic resources that meets the National Register criteria (such as an archaeological site or a Civil War battlefield)

---

[139] Treas. Reg. § 1.170-14(c)(1).

[140] Coughlin, "Historic Preservation Easements," in *Historic Preservation Law: Tax Planning for Old and Historic Buildings* (American Law Institute, 1984) pp. 344–45.

[141] I.R.C. § 170(h)(4)(A)(iv).

[142] I.R.C. § 170(h)(4)(B).

[143] Treas. Reg. § 1.170A-14(d)(5)(iii).

2. Any land area within a registered historic district including any buildings on the land area that can reasonably be considered as contributing to the significance of the district
3. Any land area adjacent to a National Register property "where the physical or environmental features of the land area contribute to the historic or cultural integrity of the property."[144]

Thus, under item 2, the protection of an uncertified but significant building within a registered district may be an acceptable "conservation purpose."[145] It is not entirely clear how the "significance" requirement for this purpose relates to the certification of significance for purposes of the rehabilitation tax credit, but it would certainly be advisable to obtain such a certification where possible, even if the regulations appear not to require it.

A gift to achieve a statutorily enumerated conservation purpose will not be permitted if it would also result in or allow the destruction of other significant conservation purposes.[146] The regulations illustrate this provision with the example of preservation of farmland for purposes of flood prevention and control, which would not be eligible for a deduction if the use of pesticides in the operation of the farm could damage a significant natural ecosystem. Uses that are destructive of conservation interests are permissible only if necessary for the protection of the conservation interests which the contribution is intended to further.[147] Thus the regulations indicate that a deduction for an easement to preserve an archaeological site would not be disallowed because site excavation might impair a scenic view. How the IRS will balance competing considerations of this sort in practice remains to be determined.

1.5.4 Valuation of Easement Donations

Except in the rare instance in which a marketplace value for the easement can be established, its value is to be determined by taking the difference between the fair market value of the land before the donation and its fair market value afterward.[148] This is consistent with prior

---

[144] Treas. Reg. § 1.170A-14(d)(5)(ii).

[145] See 3 Preservation L. Rep. 1025 (1984), with respect to Priv. Ltr. Rul. 84-10-034 (Dec. 2, 1983), upholding the deductibility of an easement to protect a noncertified structure.

[146] Treas. Reg. § 1.170A-14(e)(2).

[147] Treas. Reg. § 1.170A-14(e)(3).

[148] Treas. Reg. § 1.170A-14(h)(3)(i). The Tax Court recently found that the value of an open space easement was equal to 43.8 percent of the value of the property on which it was located. Higgins v. Commissioner, 1990 T.C. Memo 103. For a discussion of the case, see 9 Preservation L. Rep. 1034 (1990). In a subsequent decision, the Tax Court declined to assess attorney's fees against the Service despite the taxpayer's success on the merits. See Higgins v. Commissioner, 1990 T.C. Memo 602.

revenue rulings by the IRS,[149] and with judicial decisions on the issue of valuation of easements.[150] In making this determination, the taxpayer must consider not only current uses of the property but also future uses permitted by the conservation restriction, adjusted for the likelihood that those future uses will actually be undertaken. To serve as the basis for valuation, a future use must be not merely possible, but at least reasonably probable.[151] Costs imposed upon the owner of property by the easement agreement (insurance and maintenance, for example) may also be included in the valuation process.

Land use or other restrictions applicable to property and limiting its use must be considered in assessing the degree to which an easement diminishes the property's value.[152] A building's presence within a historic district may, for example, already restrict the owner's ability to alter or demolish it, depending upon the stringency of the municipality's preservation ordinance. If an owner's hands are already substantially tied, the easement restriction might not cause much additional diminution in value (although it may, on the other hand, provide greater assurance that the restriction will apply in perpetuity, since ordinances can always be amended or repealed). Where land values are high (particularly in urban centers) and land use restrictions less strict, an easement preserving an underbuilt structure may substantially reduce the market value of the property by foreclosing the realization of its development potential. If an easement is donated on a historic property as to which a rehabilitation credit has been taken, the value of the easement may be somewhat reduced by the fact that an owner is unlikely to make substantial alterations during the five-year period that the credit is subject to recapture. For these and other reasons, easement valuation in an urban setting may be particularly complex.

When an easement has the effect of raising the value of any other property owned by the donor or a related person (whether or not that property is contiguous to the donated property), the amount of the deduction must be decreased by the increase in value of the other

---

[149] *See, e.g.*, Rev. Rul. 73-339, 1973-2 C.B. 68; Rev. Rul. 76-376, 1976-2 C.B. 53.

[150] *See, e.g.*, Thayer & Thayer v. Commissioner, 1977 T.C. Memo 370.

[151] *See, e.g.*, Stanley Works & Subsidiaries, 87 T.C. 389 (1986); Todd v. United States, 617 F. Supp. 253 (W.D. Pa. 1985). For a recent case in which the Tax Court considered the loss of development rights as substantially contributing to the value of the easement, *see* Dorsey v. Commissioner, 1990 T.C. Memo 242 (1990). For a discussion of this and other recent cases regarding the valuation of easement donations, *see* 9 *Preservation L. Rep.* 1099 (1990). For information regarding easement valuation, see the revised edition of *Appraising Easements*, recently published by the National Trust for Historic Preservation and The Land Trust Alliance.

[152] *See, e.g.*, Schapiro v. Commissioner, 1991 T.C. Memo 128 (potential for subdivision of property in appraisal of easement value proper); Hilborn v. Commissioner, 85 T.C. 677 (1985).

property.[153] The amount of the deduction is the net benefit to the donor or related person. If the net result is a financial benefit to the landowner, no deduction is allowed.

Both donors and donees of easements must comply with the procedural requirements governing charitable contributions of appreciated property.[154] If the claimed value of the easement exceeds $5,000, the taxpayer must have an appraisal done by a "qualified appraiser" who is not the donor taxpayer, the donee, a party to the transaction in which the taxpayer acquired the property, or a person related to any of these. The appraisal, which must be done no more than 60 days prior to the date of the contribution, must include information specified in the regulations, including a description of the property, any restrictions on the recipient's use or disposition of the property, and the appraised value of the property, including the method of valuation. The taxpayer must attach an appraisal summary on the appropriate IRS form to his or her tax return, providing information required by the regulations, and signed by both the appraiser and a representative of the donee organization. The signature of the donee does not indicate that it concurs in the appraisal, but rather signals its recognition that, if it sells, exchanges, or disposes of the easement within two years of receipt, it must file an information report with the IRS, identifying the donor, describing the property, and giving the date of contribution, date of disposition, and the amount received on disposition.

The IRS has in past years aggressively audited returns claiming deductions for easement donations, and challenged allegedly inflated appraisals.[155] To minimize conflict, it is important that easement values be accurately appraised. To assist taxpayers in this respect, the National Trust for Historic Preservation has published the second edition of a pamphlet entitled *Appraising Easements: Guidelines for Valuation of Historic Preservation and Land Conservation Easements*, which prospective donors may wish to consult.[156]

---

[153] Treas. Reg. § 1.170A-14(h)(3)(i).

[154] Treas. Reg. § 1.170A-13 (as amended 1988).

[155] *See, e.g.*, Akers v. Commissioner, 1984 T.C. Memo 490, *aff'd*, 799 F.2d 243 (6th Cir. 1986), *cert. denied*, 479 U.S. 1086 (1987) (IRS disallowing an easement deduction entirely, and the Tax Court reducing the value of the donated easement to $114,000 from the claimed value of $789,000). *See also* Penico, "Valuation of Preservation Easements," 3 *Preservation L. Rep.* 2069 (1984). In public information release I.R. 84-125 (December 10, 1984), however, the Commissioner of Internal Revenue stated that the IRS would review donated easements on a case-by-case basis, and that deductions would be allowed if a taxpayer's appraiser used the before-and-after method and applied sound appraisal practices in calculating the value of a donation. When the IRS challenges an appraisal and the claimed value of a taxpayer's gift is sufficiently greater than the value found to be correct by the Tax Court, the Court may apply a penalty of an increased interest rate to the underpayment of tax. See Losch v. Commissioner, 1988 T.C. Memo 230 (applying the penalty when the claimed value exceeded the correct value by more than 150 percent).

[156] *See also*, Diehl and Barrett, *The Conservation Easement Handbook* (1988). These and other publications are available from The National Trust for Historic Preservation, 1785 Massachusetts Ave., NW, Washington, DC 20036.

1.5.5 Interaction of Rehabilitation Tax Credit and Preservation Easement Deduction

To maximize tax benefits for rehabilitation of old buildings, owners may wish to take advantage of both rehabilitation tax credits and deductions for donation of facade easements. Timing may, however, be of central importance. The regulations require that the basis of property be reduced in the case of an easement donation, and in an amount proportionate to the amount of predonation basis allocable to the easement.[157] If an easement is granted after a rehabilitated building has been placed in service, the reduction in basis attributable to the easement might be treated as a disposition of Section 38 property, and will trigger recapture of a portion of the rehabilitation tax credit.[158]

Timing of the gift may have other implications as well. If the donation is made while the property remains unrehabilitated, it may reduce adjusted basis for purposes of meeting the "substantial rehabilitation" test of eligibility for the investment credit.[159] Moreover, the timing of the gift may determine the allocation of basis reduction between the land and building basis account and the rehabilitation basis account, which in turn may affect the amount of the rehabilitation credit for which the taxpayer is eligible.[160] These are only a few of the many complex issues that may arise in attempting to coordinate use of these two provisions.

1.6 SUMMARY OF DIFFERENCES IN TREATMENT OF HISTORIC AND NONHISTORIC OLD BUILDINGS

To summarize, it may be useful to note the major differences in tax treatment between rehabilitations of historic and nonhistoric structures, after the 1986 Act.

1. The rehabilitation of a certified historic structure (including a structure located in a historic district which is certified as contributing to the significance of that district) is, if the rehabilitation itself is certified, eligible for a 20-percent rehabilitation tax credit. On the other hand, rehabilitation of a building which was placed in service before 1936 (which has received a certification of nonsignificance if it

---

[157] Treas. Reg. § 1.170A-14(h)(3)(iii).

[158] *See* Rev. Rul. 89-90, 1989-2 C.B. 3. *See also*, Rome I, Ltd. v. Commissioner, 96 T.C. 2 (1991) (ruling that grant of historical facade easement constitutes a disposition of the underlying real property, thereby triggering the recapture of a portion of the rehabilitation tax credit and a reduction in the basis of the underlying property).

[159] *See* § **1.2.4**.

[160] For a general discussion of these issues, *see* Luxemburger, "Preservation Easements and Rehabilitated Buildings: Preservation Easements and Mortgaged Property," 10 *J. Real Est. Tax* 273 (1983).

is located within a registered historic district) is eligible for a 10-percent tax credit. No other rehabilitation credit will be available after the transition period established by the 1986 Act.

2. To qualify for a tax credit, a rehabilitation of a certified historic structure must in turn be certified as meeting the Secretary of the Interior's Standards for Rehabilitation (see **Chapter Two**). On the other hand, rehabilitation of a noncertified structure, or of a structure within a historic district that has been certified as not contributing to the significance of that district, need not be a certified rehabilitation to qualify for the credit, but must meet the other requirements. Thus although the potential tax benefit for a certified rehabilitation is greater, such a rehabilitation must overcome an additional, and in some instances costly, statutory hurdle. The incremental benefit will often be greater than under prior law; it is now 10 percent in all cases, whereas previously it was only 5 percent for buildings that were 40 or more years old.

3. The rehabilitation tax credit applies to a certified rehabilitation of an appropriately certified historic structure regardless of age, while a noncertified structure must have been placed in service prior to 1936 to qualify.

4. Residential rental property is eligible for the credit only if it is a certified historic structure and is used in a trade or business.

5. To qualify for a charitable contribution deduction under the regulations, an easement generally must be donated to protect a certified historic structure or a building within a historic district, so long as the building can reasonably be considered as contributing to the significance of the district.

1.7 TAX TREATMENT OF PROPERTY LEASED TO TAX-EXEMPT ORGANIZATIONS

Prior to the Tax Reform Act of 1984, historic property used but not owned by a tax-exempt organization was generally eligible for the rehabilitation tax credit on the same basis as other property.[161] In addition, taxpayers could use ACRS to depreciate property used but not owned by tax-exempt organizations. The combined effect of these two provisions was to encourage a large volume of transactions in which tax-exempts would sell property to taxable entities and then lease it back, thereby reaping the benefits of investment credits and depreciation deductions which would otherwise have been unavailable.

The significant revenue losses occasioned by these transactions led Congress to tighten the tax treatment of property used by tax-exempt organizations. A new set of rules, described by one commentator as

---

[161] *Cf.* I.R.C. § 50(b)(3).

"grotesquely intricate,"[162] was adopted in the 1984 Act.[163] Under the new provisions, the involvement of a tax-exempt organization in a historic rehabilitation may bar or at least limit the eligibility of the project for federal tax incentives. There may still be substantial advantages from the involvement of tax-exempt entities in historic preservation work (such as the availability of tax-exempt financing[164] or charitable contributions[165] to support the work), but both the benefits and detriments of tax-exempt participation should be considered carefully in deciding how best to structure a preservation or rehabilitation project.

1.7.1 Tax-Exempt Use Property

These provisions apply to a category of property known as "tax-exempt use property." Real property becomes tax-exempt use property to the extent that it is leased to a tax-exempt entity under a "disqualified" lease. A lease of property to a tax-exempt entity is a disqualified lease if:

1. The tax-exempt entity participates in financing the property through tax-exempt obligations, whether before or after financing is committed,
2. The lease governing the tax-exempt entity's use contains a purchase or sale option, or the equivalent,
3. The lease has a term exceeding 20 years, or
4. The lease is entered into after a sale, lease, or other, transfer of the property from the tax-exempt entity, and the property has been used by the entity prior to the transfer.[166]

A service contract arrangement governing use of a particular property may be treated as a "disqualified lease" for this purpose, depending on the degree to which it possesses the characteristics of a lease. The determination will be made by evaluating a number of factors, including whether the tax-exempt entity has physical possession, control, or a significant possessory or economic interest in the property; whether the service provider bears any economic risk in the event of nonperformance; whether the service provider concurrently uses the property for the benefit of parties unrelated to the tax-exempt entity; and whether the total contract price substantially exceeds the rental value of the property.[167]

---

[162] J. Eustice, *The Tax Reform Act of 1984: A Selective Analysis* 5-40 (1984).
[163] Pub. L. No. 98-369, § 31, 98 Stat. 494, 509 (1984).
[164] *See* § **4.2.1**.
[165] *See* § **4.3.8**.
[166] I.R.C. § 168(h)(1)(B)(ii).
[167] I.R.C. § 7701(e)(1) (West Supp. 1991).

Notwithstanding these provisions, depreciable real property will not generally be treated as tax-exempt use property unless the tax-exempt entity uses more than 35 percent of the property in a disqualified manner.[168] Moreover, property will not be deemed tax-exempt use property if it is predominantly used by a tax-exempt entity in an unrelated trade or business that produces income taxable as unrelated business income.[169] Nor will it be treated as tax-exempt use property if the use is subject to a short-term lease, generally 3 years or less.[170]

The definition of "tax-exempt entity" is broader than might be expected in one potentially significant respect. For purposes of the limitations on depreciation and investment credits, tax-exempt entities are deemed to include: federal, state, and local government bodies; organizations that are exempt from normal federal income taxes; and "any foreign person or entity."[171] However, foreign investors are not treated as tax-exempt entities with respect to a property if 50 percent or more of the income derived by the foreign investor from the use of the property is subject to U.S. income tax.

The Code also treats as tax-exempt entities those taxable entities that are controlled by tax-exempt entities.[172] "Control" means ownership of 50 percent or more of the stock.[173] This provision may be avoided if the tax-exempt controlled entity so elects, but in that case, any gain recognized by the controlling entity from disposition of an interest in the controlled entity will be taxable as unrelated business income, as will dividends or interest received or accrued.[174]

1.7.2 Consequences of Tax-Exempt Participation

Several significant results flow from a determination that any portion of a rehabilitated or to-be-rehabilitated building represents tax-exempt use property. First, the rehabilitation credit will not apply to expenditures attributable to the rehabilitation of any part of a building which is tax-exempt use property. This restriction is, however, subject to the 35-percent threshold. If a rehabilitated building becomes tax-exempt use property within 5 years after the rehabilitation occurs, this will be treated as a disposition and the credit will be recaptured.

Second, under the 1986 Act, the alternative depreciation system must be used to calculate deductions for tax-exempt use property.[175] This

---

[168] I.R.C. § 168(h)(1)(B)(iii).
[169] I.R.C. § 168(h)(1)(D).
[170] I.R.C. § 168(h)(1)(C).
[171] I.R.C. § 168(h)(2)(A).
[172] I.R.C. § 168(h)(6)(F)(i).
[173] I.R.C. § 168(h)(6)(F)(iii)(I).
[174] I.R.C. § 168(h)(6)(F)(ii).
[175] I.R.C. § 168(g)(1)(B).

requires that such property be depreciated over a 40-year period.[176] In any event, the recovery period cannot be less than 125 percent of the term of the lease,[177] a limitation which will be significant only in the case of long-term leases. First-year deductions are computed based on the number of months of the taxable year in which the property is placed in service.

Finally, the rules contain restrictions to prevent the use of partnerships or other pass-through entities to circumvent their application.[178] If property that is otherwise not tax-exempt use property is owned by a partnership in which a tax-exempt entity is a member, the tax-exempt's proportionate share of the property will be treated as tax-exempt use property, unless the allocation of partnership items (income, deduction, gain, loss, credit, and basis) is a "qualified allocation."[179] An allocation is qualified if (1) the tax-exempt entity receives the same distributive share of all partnership items, (2) the share remains the same throughout the tax-exempt entity's participation in the partnership, and (3) the allocation has a substantial economic effect.[180]

1.8 EFFECTIVENESS OF REHABILITATION INCENTIVES

Until the passage of the 1986 Act, it was clear that the federal tax incentives for rehabilitation had successfully increased private investment in historic preservation and in the efforts to rehabilitate the nation's stock of older buildings. The pace of rehabilitation activity has slowed substantially since the Act went into effect. In fiscal year 1986, 2,964 rehabilitation jobs were completed nationwide; in fiscal year 1989, 994 projects were carried out; this dropped to 814 projects in 1990, and to 678 projects in 1991. Investment also dropped from a peak of $2.4 billion in fiscal year 1985 to $927 million in fiscal year 1989, $750 million in 1990, and $608 million in 1991. The number of applications for new rehabilitation projects decreased 25 percent between fiscal years 1989 and 1990, and decreased another 18 percent between fiscal years 1990 and 1991.[181]

Nevertheless, the magnitude of the program should not be underestimated. Since the inception of the tax incentives program in 1976, a total of nearly 23,265 projects have been approved. An NPS sample of

---

[176] I.R.C. § 168(g)(2)(C).
[177] I.R.C. § 168(g)(3)(A).
[178] I.R.C. § 168(h)(5), (6).
[179] I.R.C. § 168(h)(6)(A).
[180] I.R.C. § 168(h)(6)(B); see § **3.2.2**.
[181] Information in this section is from National Parks Service, *Tax Incentives for Rehabilitating Historic Buildings, Fiscal Year 1989 Analysis* (March 1990) and updated with information from the same reports issued for fiscal years 1990 and 1991.

projects approved in fiscal year 1990 indicates that 74 percent of those projects would not have been undertaken without the preservation tax incentives. Thus, the program continues to function, albeit at a reduced level compared to earlier years.

Approximately 40 percent of the projects approved in fiscal year 1990 were used for housing. Of the 1,730 housing units created in 1990, approximately 1,288 of the units were for low- and moderate-income housing. Since the program began in 1976, approximately 120,000 housing units have been rehabilitated (or converted from other uses), including approximately 21,600 low- and moderate-income units.

Two

Historic Preservation Certifications

Eligibility for the federal tax incentives discussed in **Chapter One** requires compliance with the certification procedures established by the National Park Service (NPS). While the Internal Revenue Code vests the Secretary of the Interior with responsibility for the certification program, the Secretary has delegated virtually all operating authority to the director of the NPS. Within the NPS, the associate director for cultural resources has responsibility for administration of the tax incentive program, but the Technical Preservation Services Division has day-to-day responsibility for the program. In addition, state historic preservation officers (SHPOs) play an important role in reviewing certification applications and in making recommendations to the NPS.

The certification process, which remained largely unchanged by the 1986 Act, involves two steps. First, to be eligible for the 20-percent rehabilitation tax credit, a building must qualify as a "certified historic structure." Any building individually listed on the National Register of Historic Places comes within this definition, as does any building that is certified as contributing to the historical significance of a registered historic district.[1] To be eligible for the 10-percent credit, a building other than a certified historic structure must have been placed in service before 1936. Second, the rehabilitation project undertaken on the certified historic structure must itself be certified as meeting NPS

---

[1] 36 C.F.R. § 67.2 (1991).

requirements.[2] This chapter will first describe the process of listing on the National Register and then discuss the requirements for certification of both historic structures and rehabilitation activities.

2.1 THE NATIONAL REGISTER OF HISTORIC PLACES

The National Register of Historic Places is the official list of this nation's historic and cultural resources. The National Historic Preservation Act (NHPA),[3] discussed in greater detail in **Chapter Six**, authorizes the Secretary of the Interior to expand and maintain the National Register of buildings, districts, sites, structures, and objects which because of their significance in history, architecture, archaeology, engineering, and culture are worthy of preservation.[4] The property may be significant on a national, state, or local level.[5]

Administered by the Keeper of the National Register within the NPS, the Register is intended to be a comprehensive national inventory of historic properties. A cumulative list of the more than 55,000 properties listed in the National Register is available through the American Association of State and Local History, 172 Second Avenue North, Suite 202, Nashville, TN 37201. Notices of the most recent properties removed from or determined eligible for the National Register appear periodically in the Federal Register.[6]

A national inventory serves several purposes. The most important result of listing is that any action by a federal agency that affects listed

---

[2] *See* § **1.2.1**.

[3] 16 U.S.C.A. §§ 470–470w-6 (West 1985 & Supp. 1991).

[4] 16 U.S.C.A. § 470a(a)(1)(A). Original authorization to survey "historic and archaeological sites, buildings, and objects for the purpose of determining which possess exceptional value as commemorating or illustrating the history of the United States" was granted under the Historic Sites Act of 1935, ch. 593, § 2, 49 Stat. 666 (1935) (codified at 16 U.S.C.A. § 462(b) (West 1985)).

[5] 36 C.F.R. § 800.2(d) (1991). An example of a site that the Secretary of the Interior found to be eligible for the National Register without being of national significance is Hawaii's Moanatua Valley. The Advisory Council on Historic Preservation found that:

> the historical and cultural significance of the [Moanatua] [V]alley stems from Hawaiian folklore and tradition and continues into the 20th century. The valley contains Kamanui, the valley of the great power, and Waolani, the valley of the spirits which was, in tradition, "the dwelling place of the gods." The forest of the valley remains a traditional natural state associated with the legend and history of the area.

> The valley was the property of the royal house of Oahu, the scene of battles and other exploits which are extolled in the ancient Hawaiian chants, the Kahikilaulani. . . .

Stop H-3 Ass'n v. Coleman, 533 F.2d 434, 436 n.1 (9th Cir.), *cert. denied*, 429 U.S. 999 (1976). Other examples from throughout the country can be located by consulting the Federal Register.

[6] 54 Fed. Reg. 35,854 (1989).

or eligible property is subject to the review and comment procedures of Section 106 of NHPA, discussed more fully in **Chapter Six**. The Register also functions as a central reference tool for anyone contemplating action that may affect a building suspected of having significance. It can be consulted in designation proceedings to suggest, by comparison, whether other properties should be considered for protection. Finally, inclusion in the Register makes a property eligible for financial assistance in the form of tax benefits, grants, and loans.

The NPS has issued proposed amendments to the regulations that implement the National Register provisions of the NHPA. These proposed changes[7] were expected to be implemented some time during fiscal year 1988, but have not been published as of January, 1992. For the most part, they do not change the criteria or qualifications for eligibility or listing. They are intended rather "to consolidate and update the procedures" governing the listing in the National Register of Historic Places and determinations of eligibility for inclusion in the National Register, which can now be found at 36 C.F.R. Parts 60 and 63.[8] Because both listing properties in the National Register and determining their eligibility for inclusion in the Register are based on generally similar criteria, combining the procedures for both into one rule is expected to be more efficient than the current system: "The intended effect of this action is to clarify, streamline, and bring up-to-date the various administrative procedures for identification of historic and archaeological properties."[9]

Many of the changes in the proposed regulations are organizational and nonsubstantive. For example, the definitions would no longer all be contained in the same section, and analogous provisions relating to listing and eligibility would be reorganized to render the procedures uniform where appropriate. In addition, appeals procedures for resolving questions of the historic significance of properties for federal tax benefit certification purposes (although they would appear in different sections of the regulations) would still be subject to the same standards, guidelines, and criteria.

Other elements of the proposal, however, would effect changes that warrant specific mention. Under the proposed procedures, federal agencies would have the option to notify private owners and appropriate local officials when privately owned inholdings surrounded by federal lands are included in a nomination of federal property. Otherwise, the appropriate State Historic Preservation Officer (SHPO) would notify the private owner when the nomination is forwarded to the state for review.[10]

---

[7] 51 Fed. Reg. 28,204–16 (1986).

[8] *Id.* at 28,204.

[9] *Id.*

[10] *Id.* at 28,205.

The proposed rule would also change the procedure to be followed when a SHPO disagrees with the recommendation of the State Review Board. Under the proposed regulation, the SHPO would be required to notify the Board of its disagreement within 10 days. A decision by the SHPO not to nominate a property recommended by the Board could be appealed by the Board or any individual under Section 60.11, which governs appeals to the Keeper of the Register.

The grounds for removal of properties from the National Register would be both broadened and reduced from four to two. Under the proposal, the two new grounds would be "(1) the property does not now meet the National Register criteria; or (2) there has been prejudicial procedural error in the nomination or listing process."[11] This change, however, should not lead to substantially different results than under the current regulation; the limiting clauses in the current language have been eliminated while the general principles have been retained.

In addition, a new protective provision has been inserted for the benefit of owners of listed property who have, in good faith, qualified for a federal income tax credit for the certified rehabilitation of that property, when the property is later removed from the National Register under proposed new Section 60.9(a). In combination with Section 60.9(e), which would enable the Keeper to determine the effective date of removal from the National Register, the new provision would permit the Keeper to take into account the effect of the delisting on an owner's tax circumstances.

2.1.1 Eligibility

Several broad categories of property are eligible for inclusion in the Register: "Districts, sites, buildings, structures, and objects significant in American history, architecture, archaeology, engineering, and culture"[12] may be considered. These terms are fully defined and examples of each are provided in the regulations:[13]

> (a) *Building.* A building is a structure created to shelter any form of human activity, such as a house, barn, church, hotel, or similar structure. Building may refer to a historically related complex such as a courthouse and jail or a house and barn.
>
> * * *
>
> (d) *District.* A district is a geographically definable area, urban or rural, possessing a significant concentration, linkage, or continuity of sites, buildings, structures, or objects united by past events or aesthetically by

---

[11] *Id.* at 28,214.
[12] 16 U.S.C.A. § 470a(a)(1)(A).
[13] 36 C.F.R. § 60.3 (1991).

plan or physical development. A district may also comprise individual elements separated geographically but linked by association or history.[14]

* * *

(j) *Object.* An object is a material thing of functional, aesthetic, cultural, historic, or scientific value that may be, by nature or design, movable yet related to a specific setting or environment.

* * *

(l) *Site.* A site is the location of a significant event, a prehistoric or historic occupation or activity, or a building or structure, whether standing, ruined, or vanished, where the location itself maintains historical or archaeological value regardless of the value of any existing structure.

* * *

(p) *Structure.* A structure is a work made up of interdependent and interrelated parts in a definite pattern of organization. Constructed by man, it is often an engineering project large in scale.[15]

Although one tends to think of landmarks in terms of old buildings and battlefields, for National Register purposes this is too limited a view. Almost any type of physical property is potentially eligible for inclusion in the National Register.

The regulations, however, do identify several types of property that are to be less favored when nominated for inclusion in the National Register. Cemeteries and individual graves, or birthplaces of historical figures; religious, commemorative, relocated, or reconstructed properties; and properties whose significance can be traced to the past 50 years are not, as a general rule, eligible for listing.[16]

2.1.2 The Standard of Evaluation

In evaluating the "significance" of nominated property, several criteria are applied. The quality of significance in American history, architecture, archaeology, engineering, and culture is present in districts, sites, buildings, structures, and objects that possess integrity of location, design, setting, materials, workmanship, feeling, and association, and

---

[14] Districts composed of geographically separated elements are known as thematic districts.

[15] It should be noted that a "structure," for National Register purposes, is not synonymous with a "structure" for rehabilitation tax credit purposes and that a given structure could qualify for the former but not the latter. A historic ship would be an example of such a structure.

[16] 36 C.F.R. § 60.4. However, broad categories of exceptions provide numerous havens within the general rule to protect specific properties. Sherfy & Luce, *How to Evaluate and Nominate Potential National Register Properties that Have Achieved Significance within the Last 50 Years* (Washington, DC: Heritage Conservation and Recreation Service, U.S. Department of Interior, 1979).

1. That are associated with events that have made a significant contribution to the broad patterns of our history; or
2. That are associated with the lives of persons significant in our past; or
3. That embody the distinctive characteristics of type, period, or method of construction, or that represent the work of a master, or that possess high artistic values, or that represent a significant and distinguishable entity whose components may lack individual distinction; or
4. That have yielded, or may be likely to yield, information important to prehistory or history.[17]

Given the number and type of criteria to be applied, the determination of a property's significance necessarily contains an element of subjectivity. For purposes of the Register, properties of national, state, and local significance are treated equally.

2.1.3 The Nomination Process

The nomination process begins by submitting a standard nomination form[18] to the SHPO.[19] The nomination form may be completed by one of a number of interested parties including the property owner, the municipality within which the property is located,[20] or a preservation group. Although most nominations originate at the local level, the SHPO may also initiate the process.[21]

The SHPO must respond to the applicant submitting the nomination form within 60 days, providing a technical opinion indicating whether the form adequately documents the property and whether the property appears to meet the National Register criteria.[22] It is the applicant's responsibility to provide additional documentation, if necessary. If documentation is adequate, the SHPO must schedule the property for consideration

---

[17] 36 C.F.R. § 60.4.

[18] The nomination form is available from the Department of Interior, participating federal agencies, and state historic preservation offices. *Id.* § 60.5. Completed nomination forms must be "adequately documented" and "technically and professionally correct and sufficient." To meet these requirements the forms and accompanying maps and photographs must be completed in accord with requirements and guidance in the NPS publication, *How to Complete National Register Forms* and other NPS technical publications on this subject. 36 C.F.R. § 60.3(i).

[19] The State Historic Preservation Officer is the person in each state selected to administer the state's historic preservation program including identifying and nominating eligible properties, and administering applications for listing historic properties in the National Register. 36 C.F.R. § 60.3(m); *see generally* 36 C.F.R. Part 61.

[20] To nominate property the local government must be certified by the Secretary of Interior and by the SHPO. 16 U.S.C.A. § 470a(c); 36 C.F.R. § 61.5(d)(1) (1991).

[21] 36 C.F.R. § 60.6(a).

[22] *Id.* § 60.11(a).

at the earliest possible meeting of the State Review Board, and must give the applicant at least 75 days' notice of that meeting.

The state review board conducts the initial review of a nomination.[23] State review boards meet at least three times a year to evaluate nominations. The property owner, community officials, and the general public are notified[24] of the review process and their input regarding the nomination is solicited as part of this evaluation.

The review board will determine whether the property meets National Register criteria based on its consideration of the nomination form and supporting documents, comments presented to it, and possibly an on-site investigation by the review board or its staff. If the review board determines that the property meets the designation criteria, that recommendation is forwarded to the SHPO for review. If the board does not so find, then the nomination is disapproved and is not sent to the SHPO for any further deliberation.

The review board's favorable decision to list the property on the Register, if concurred in by the SHPO, is forwarded to the Keeper of the National Register. Even if the SHPO does not agree, the nomination may reach the federal level by several avenues. The SHPO may still submit the nomination with relevant material, the opinion of the state review board, and his dissenting opinion. If he chooses not to do so, he must advise the applicant of that fact within 45 days. Nominations disputed by the SHPO and the state review board are substantively reviewed by the Keeper of the Register. Alternatively, the property owner or the local government may appeal the SHPO's action to the Secretary of the Interior.[25]

A federal agency may nominate a property to the National Register without going through the state nominating process. By law, each federal agency must establish a method to identify, inventory, and nominate property which it owns or controls that appears to be eligible for National Register listing.[26] These nominations are made to the Secretary of the Interior rather than to the SHPO, but the SHPO and the affected community must be allowed to comment. Each federal agency must also appoint a "preservation officer" to implement the agency's program.

Applications that have made their way through the state or federal agency nominating process and have thus far been approved are forwarded to the Keeper of the National Register, where the nominated property is once again reviewed for compliance with the National Register

---

[23] A review board must consist of no fewer than five members, a majority of whom must generally be recognized professionals in the fields of history, prehistoric and historic archaeology, architectural history, architecture, and historic architecture. Members are designated by the SHPO unless state law provides for membership by other means. *Id.* § 60.4(e).

[24] The review process is outlined in 36 C.F.R. § 60.6(b),(c),(d).

[25] 16 U.S.C. § 470a(a)(5).

[26] *Id.* § 470h-2(a)(2). *See* Wilson v. Block, 708 F.2d 735, 754 (D.C. Cir. 1983), *cert. denied,* 464 U.S. 956 (1983).

criteria. Notice that property has been nominated for National Register listing is provided in the Federal Register.[27] Any person or organization that supports or opposes a nomination may petition the Keeper to accept or reject the nomination.[28] If conformance is found, the nomination is approved and the property designated. If there is insufficient information upon which to base a decision, the application is sent back to the state level for supplementation.

Unless there is a dispute between the SHPO and the state review board, or unless the Keeper of the Register receives a petition from a person or organization objecting to the state's approval of the nomination and requesting the Keeper to substantially review the nomination, review by the Keeper will not typically amount to a *de novo* fact finding. More frequently the Keeper only considers the information in the application.

Moderate procedural safeguards are provided for this process. A 15-day comment period is required, and notice for the comment period is published in the National Register.[29] This period may be waived if necessary, usually at the property owner's request. However, the form of the review is not specified in the regulations, nor do they require written findings evaluating the property's characteristics vis-à-vis the criteria.

The property is officially designated for listing upon the signature of the Secretary of Interior. Notice of the listing is provided to the owner, the SHPO, and the members of Congress representing the district where the property is located. The SHPO, in turn, is required to inform the owners and the chief elected official of the relevant municipality of the listing.[30]

The failure to nominate property may be appealed to the Keeper of the Register by any individual or by the local government with an interest in the property.[31] However, the preamble to the regulations implementing the 1980 amendments states that appeal is discouraged "in cases where there is a general consensus of opinion among involved State and/or Federal officials that a property is not eligible."[32]

2.1.4 Owner Consent

A property may not be listed on the National Register if its owner objects.[33] This owner consent provision was enacted when the tax laws provided significant disincentives for some private actions affecting Register

---

[27] 36 C.F.R. § 60.6(q).
[28] *Id.* § 60.6(t).
[29] *Id.* § 60.13(a).
[30] *Id.* § 60.6(u).
[31] *Id.* § 60.12.
[32] 48 Fed. Reg. 46,306 (1983).
[33] 16 U.S.C. § 470a(a)(6).

buildings. Its enactment also reflected the resistance to Register listing caused by the fact that such listing may trigger the application of state regulation of actions affecting the property.

An owner is defined as "those individuals, partnerships, corporations or public agencies holding fee simple title to property."[34] Ownership does not include holding easements or less than fee interests, including leaseholds of any nature. After receiving notification that the state has initiated nomination procedures, the owner who wishes to object must submit to the SHPO a notarized statement certifying ownership of the property, in whole or in part, and the fact of his objection.[35] In the case of properties within a historic district, a majority vote of the owners within the proposed district can block the designation.[36] When the owner or majority of owners objects to the nomination, it is still submitted to the Keeper of the Register, but only for a determination of eligibility.[37] If the Keeper determines that this property is eligible, the SHPO notifies the appropriate elected local official.

A property that is eligible for listing, but is not listed because its owner objects, is nevertheless afforded the procedural protection of Section 106 of the Act, discussed in **Chapter Six**.[38] Many state environmental and preservation statutes also apply to Register-eligible property as well as to property that is actually listed. However, the owner of eligible but nonlisted property will not be eligible for the tax benefits or grants made available to registered property.

It is not clear whether the owner-consent provisions of the 1980 amendments apply to lands owned or controlled by the federal government. This question has particular significance to western states with enormous expanses of federal land, where frequent differences of opinion occur between the SHPO and federal agencies over the historic significance of sites on federal lands. The Reagan administration took the position that it had the right to withhold consent. A 1982 letter to all SHPOs from the Keeper of the Register directed that nominations for listing of property under federal ownership or control include a letter from the relevant federal agency preservation officer approving of the listing.[39] The Bush administration still maintains this position.

---

[34] 36 C.F.R. § 60.3(k).

[35] *Id.* § 60.6(g).

[36] *Id.* An owner cannot accumulate voting power based on property units owned or shares of a property. Each owner gets one vote. It is also irrelevant that the particular property in a historic district does not contribute to the significance of the district.

[37] 36 C.F.R. § 60.6(n), (s).

[38] *See* § **6.1.1**.

[39] *See* 3 *Preservation L. Rep.* 1006 (1984). For a discussion of the constitutionality of owner consent provisions, see Miller, "Owner Consent Provisions in Historic Preservation Ordinances: Are They Legal?" 10 *Preservation L. Rep.* 1020 (1991).

2.1.5 Removal from the Register

The grounds for removal of property from the National Register are articulated in the regulations.[40] Generally, it is not a simple matter to change the status of property that has been determined to have met the criteria for listing—it must be shown that it presently does not, or that it never did, meet the criteria for eligibility. Among the grounds for removal are errors in the original determination due to substantive, technical, or procedural flaws, or the availability of new information pertaining to eligibility. Alterations made after December 12, 1980, that changed the character of the property to the extent that it no longer meets the criteria are also a basis for removal.

There may be instances in which delisting from the Register is necessary to allow an owner to benefit from any of the rehabilitation tax credits discussed in **Chapter One**. When preparations were being made for recent full-scale renovation of the National Press Building in Washington, DC, for example, it was discovered that the facade of the building had been so badly stripped that a certified rehabilitation was impossible. Only by removing the building from the Register was the owner able to take advantage of the 20-percent tax credit,[41] for which certification of restoration work is not required. Owners should, in this and other situations, weigh the benefits of the enhanced credit for a certified rehabilitation against the possibly increased cost or difficulty of undertaking such a rehabilitation in deciding whether to seek listing or delisting of a building.

The case of *Amoco Production Co. v. United States Department of Interior*,[42] illustrates the possible consequences of failing to adequately consider such possibilities. Amoco sought and obtained listing of its Philcade Building, located in downtown Tulsa, Oklahoma, in order to take advantage of the 25-percent tax credit then available for the rehabilitation of certified historic structures. Relying on the state preservation officer's advisory approval of its plans, Amoco began construction work on the building before obtaining final Park Service certification for the rehabilitation. When the National Park Service later denied the application for rehabilitation on the grounds that the work was not consistent with the historic character of the property and did not meet the Secretary of the Interior's "Standards for Rehabilitation," Amoco sought delisting in order to take advantage of the 20-percent tax credit then available for the restoration of buildings over 40 years old.

The Keeper of the Register denied delisting, and Amoco appealed on equitable grounds. The district court, in affirming the Keeper's decision, held that equitable considerations did not favor delisting. The court pointed out that Amoco was aware of the tax credit requirements prior to

---

[40] 36 C.F.R. § 60.15.

[41] Today this tax credit would be only a 10-percent tax credit pursuant to the 1986 Act.

[42] 763 F. Supp. 514 (N.D. Okl. 1990).

its attempt to have the building listed and was equally aware of the risk involved in beginning construction before Park Service certification. Moreover, allowing the retroactive delisting of a property that was improperly rehabilitated in order to allow the owner to take advantage of the lower tax credit would undermine Congress' intent with regard to the rehabilitation of historic structures. Since Amoco had placed itself in its unfavorable position, the court held that the National Park Service had acted properly in this situation.

2.2 CERTIFICATIONS OF HISTORIC SIGNIFICANCE

In addition to buildings individually listed on the National Register, any building that is certified as contributing to the historic significance of a registered historic district is eligible for the 20-percent rehabilitation tax credit.

There are two ways to establish that a particular district qualifies as a Registered Historic District, within which non-National Register properties may be certified for tax benefits. First, the district itself may be listed on the National Register. Second, the district may have been designated as historic under a certified state or local preservation statute. The process for certification of such local statutes is described in **Chapter Seven**.[43] In the latter case, the district must, in addition to local designation, be certified by the NPS as "meeting substantially all of the requirements for listing of districts in the National Register."[44]

An owner contemplating rehabilitation may also request preliminary certification that a building not yet on the National Register appears to meet National Register criteria, or that a building located within a potential historic district appears to contribute to the significance of that district. Preliminary certification is not binding, and does not guarantee that the NPS will ultimately issue a final certification for the building in question. Thus, owners who proceed with rehabilitation on the strength of a preliminary certification do so at their own risk.[45] Nevertheless, preliminary certification often provides useful guidance, particularly when a rehabilitation project is to be syndicated.

Requests for preliminary determinations of significance, moreover, must be accompanied by assurances of future state action consistent with the purported historic significance of the building in question. Thus, for instance, if the building does not fall within the existing boundaries of a historic district, written assurances must be provided

---

[43] *See* § **7.5.1**.

[44] 36 C.F.R. § 67.2 (1991).

[45] *Id.* § 67.4(f). The taxpayer may assume that the listing will occur and take the tax benefits pending the listing without penalty if the listing occurs within 30 months of the first deduction. *See A Handbook on Historic Preservation Law* 155 (C. Duerksen ed., 1983).

from the appropriate local official that the district is to be expanded. Likewise, if a certification request is made for a building situated within a geographic district but outside that district's established period of significance, a preliminary determination will be issued only if a local official provides written assurance that the district documentation is being revised to expand the historical timeframe upon which its significance is based. Alternatively, owners requesting preliminary determinations of significance may submit written assurances from the SHPO that the SHPO plans to nominate the property or the district in which the property is located.[46] If the district in question has been nominated but not yet registered as historic, the SHPO must verify in writing that the nomination is being revised so that the building will fall within the district's area and period of significance.

The owner of a building within a registered district does not have the option either to seek certification and the 20-percent tax credit or to forego certification and undertake a rehabilitation which is eligible for only the 10-percent tax credit. In order to be able to obtain the lesser tax credits he must obtain a certification that the building is not of significance to the district within which it is located. Otherwise, to obtain any tax credit he must, as described next, undertake a fully certified and approved rehabilitation.[47]

2.2.1 Standards for Evaluating Historic Significance

In reviewing buildings located within registered historic districts to determine if they contribute to the significance of their districts, the NPS applies its "Standards for Evaluating Significance within Registered Historic Districts."[48] A building will be deemed as contributing, and hence as likely to be certified, if by location, design, setting, materials, workmanship, feeling, and association it adds to the district's sense of time, place, and historical development. A building will not be found to contribute, and therefore will be certified as nonsignificant, if it fails to add to the district's sense of time, place, and historical development. This also applies when a building has been so altered or has so deteriorated that its overall integrity and the characteristics just listed have been irretrievably lost.

Buildings constructed within the past 50 years generally will not be considered to contribute to the significance of a historic district unless strong justification of their historical or architectural merit is provided, or unless the historical attributes of the district itself are considered to be less than 50 years old. An owner seeking a certification of

---

[46] 36 C.F.R. §§ 67.4(f), 67.5(c).

[47] I.R.C. § 47(c)(2)(B)(iv) (West Supp. 1991).

[48] 36 C.F.R. § 67.5.

nonsignificance may submit a condemnation order as evidence of physical deterioration, but that alone will not be considered sufficient evidence of loss of integrity. It may also be necessary to submit a structural engineer's report to help substantiate physical deterioration or structural damage.[49]

The owner of a deteriorated or partially demolished historic building who wishes to undertake a certified rehabilitation may have trouble obtaining a certification of significance. Even if the rehabilitation plans call for the most accurate possible reconstruction of the building, the NPS may find that prior to the reconstruction, the time at which its determination must be made, the building does not retain sufficient structural integrity or historical significance.

2.2.2 Certification Procedure

A request for a certification of historic significance, or for certification of rehabilitation, must be made by means of a Historic Preservation Certification Application (NPS Form No. 10-168), which can be obtained from NPS regional offices or from appropriate state officials and which is reproduced in **Appendix C** of this book. Part 1 of the application pertains to certification of historic significance or nonsignificance, while Part 2 is used to request certification of rehabilitation projects. Although Parts 1 and 2 need not be submitted together, Part 2 of the application will not be processed until an adequately documented Part 1 has been received and acted upon, unless the building in question is already a certified historic structure.

Generally, only the fee simple owner of a building may submit an application for certification.[50] If, in appropriate circumstances, the application is made by another individual or entity, the application must be accompanied by a written statement from the owner indicating that he is aware of the application and has no objection to the request for certification. In certain situations, the NPS may undertake a certification determination at the request of a state official or on its own initiative, but only if notice is provided to the owner.

For purposes of the 10-percent rehabilitation tax credits (for nonhistoric buildings), buildings situated within registered historic districts are presumed to contribute to the significance of those districts unless certified as nonsignificant before the project is initiated. If an owner begins or completes demolition or substantial alteration without knowledge that certification is required, he may still request certification that the building was not of historic significance before the work was undertaken. If he does so, however, the owner must certify to the

---

[49] *Id.* § 67.5(b).
[50] *Id.* § 67.3(a)(1).

Secretary of the Treasury that at the time demolition or alteration was initiated, he was in good faith unaware of the certification requirement.[51]

The last point may be of critical importance for any purchaser of a building within a National Register district. It is entirely possible that a purchaser may buy property within a registered or nominated district without knowledge that the property has been or will be deemed "contributing," or, for that matter, without knowledge that the property falls within the boundaries of such a district at all. Accordingly, any buyer of urban property who intends to take advantage of the investment tax credit for rehabilitation (even at 10 percent) should, as a routine precaution, investigate the status of the property he intends to purchase, as well as the possibility that it is located within a historic district, to determine whether these restrictions will apply.

2.2.3 Application Requirements

An application for certification of significance or nonsignificance must, at a minimum, provide the following documentation:[52]

1. The address of the property, and the name if one exists.
2. The nature of the certification request.
3. The name, address, and telephone number of the authorized project contact to whom all inquiries should be addressed.
4. The name, address, and telephone number of the building owner.
5. The name of the historic district in which the building is located.
6. A brief description of the physical appearance of the building, both exterior and interior, including architectural details, alterations, and date of construction.
7. A brief statement of the significance of the building, summarizing its significance to the distinctive historical and visual character of the district.
8. Current photographs of the building, as well as photographs prior to alteration if rehabilitation has been completed.
9. Sketch maps indicating the building's location within the district.
10. The signature of the owner requesting or concurring in the request for an evaluation.

If a building has been or is to be moved into a historic district, additional documentation must be provided in the application. Information must be submitted discussing the effect of the move on the building's

---

[51] I.R.C. § 47(c)(2)(B)(iv)(III).
[52] 36 C.F.R. § 67.4(c).

appearance and on the distinctive historical and visual character of the district, describing the new setting and general environment of the proposed site, and identifying the method of moving to be used. The moving of historic buildings from their original sites is discouraged. If a building is to be moved as part of a rehabilitation for which certification is sought, the nature of the procedure to be followed by the owner depends on whether the building is individually listed on the National Register or is within a registered historic district.[53]

A single application may generally be submitted to request certification of the historic significance of groups of related buildings within a historic district. However, documentation must be offered for every building proposed for certification. In addition, buildings whose functional relationship contributes to their historical significance (for instance, a mill complex or a residence and carriage house) may be treated as a single unit for purposes of certification as contributing or noncontributing to the historic district.

2.2.4 Processing of Applications

The manner in which certification applications are processed depends on whether the state in which the property is located has elected to participate in the review of certification requests. In participating states, completed applications are sent to the appropriate state official, generally the SHPO. Thirty-day review periods are permitted at the state and federal levels, respectively. In nonparticipating states, certification requests should be sent directly to the appropriate NPS regional office. Review of completed requests should generally be completed within 60 days (30 days at the state level and 30 days at the federal level).

Failure to process certification applications in a timely manner appears to have been the primary complaint voiced in regard to the entire certification program.[54] Increased processing time can increase the cost of rehabilitation projects, and may deter property owners from participating in the program at all. At least one NPS regional office was unable to comply with the time limits that were subsequently shortened by the 1984 amendment of the certification regulations.[55] Whether the new time limits, which are not mandatory, can be enforced remains to be seen.

The owner or his duly authorized representative may appeal from any grant or denial of certification. Appeals must be made in writing and sent to the Chief Appeals Officer, Cultural Resources, National Park Service,

---

[53] *Id.* § 67.4(h).

[54] "Federal Taxation and the Preservation of America's Heritage: A Report Prepared for the Advisory Council on Historic Preservation by the National Trust for Historic Preservation" at IV-6 (1983).

[55] "Historic Tax Certification Backlogs Not a Problem, Says Interior Department," [11 Current Developments] *Hous. & Dev. Rep.* (BNA) 182 (1983).

U.S. Department of the Interior, P.O. Box 37127, Washington, DC 20013-7127. The chief appeals officer must receive the appeal within 30 days of receipt of the contested decision by the complaining party. The appellant may request a meeting to discuss the appeal, and the appropriate state official will be notified that the appeal is pending. The chief appeals officer will review the appeal and the written record of the decision in question as promptly as circumstances permit.[56]

The denial of a preliminary determination of significance is not automatically appealable, although an appeal may be granted on a case-by-case basis at the discretion of the chief appeals officer. If an appeal is not permitted, the owner must seek recourse to the usual process of nomination for inclusion in the National Register.

2.3 CERTIFICATIONS OF REHABILITATION

Before an owner may take advantage of the tax benefits for rehabilitation of a historic building, he must also obtain a determination that the project undertaken qualifies as a "certified rehabilitation." This is true whether the property is listed on the National Register or has been certified by the NPS as contributing to the historic significance of the registered district in which it is located. The purpose of this second-stage certification is to insure that the historic character of a building is preserved in the process of rehabilitation.

Owners contemplating rehabilitation projects should bear in mind two general factors which are of primary concern to the NPS. First, it is essential to identify the historic materials and features, and the unique craftsmanship they represent, which make their buildings worth preserving. Second, owners must insure that, to the greatest extent possible, these attributes will be retained, protected, and repaired in the process of rehabilitation. Removal or replacement, even with materials and features which appear to be historic, may jeopardize certification. Integrating efficient contemporary uses with preservation of historic features will often be a challenging task.

The definition of "rehabilitation project," for certification purposes, is extremely broad. It includes "all work on the interior and exterior of the certified historic structure(s) and its site and environment," as well as "related demolition, new construction, or rehabilitation work which may affect the historic qualities, integrity, or site, landscape features, and environment of the certified historic structure(s)."[57] All elements of the rehabilitation must meet the Standards for Rehabilitation, discussed in this chapter, and no portion of a project may be exempted. Thus an owner

---

[56] 36 C.F.R. § 67.10(a).

[57] *Id.* § 67.6(b).

may not choose to undertake one portion of a project in accordance with the Standards for Rehabilitation to obtain the 20-percent tax credit, and forego any tax credit on the remainder of the project in order to avoid the application of the standards to that part of the project. If the NPS believes that a project submitted for certification does not in fact include the entire rehabilitation undertaken, it may choose to deny a rehabilitation certification, or alternatively, to withhold its decision until the Internal Revenue Service, by means of a private letter ruling, determines the proper scope of the rehabilitation project to be reviewed. In making their determinations, the NPS and the IRS will consider all the facts and circumstances surrounding a particular application, but will give particular attention to these issues: (1) whether previous demolition, construction, or rehabilitation work, irrespective of ownership or control at the time, was in fact undertaken as part of the rehabilitation project for which certification is sought; and (2) whether property conveyances, reconfigurations, ostensible ownership transfers, or other transactions were intended to limit the scope of a rehabilitation project for review purposes without substantially altering the beneficial ownership or control of the property.

In deciding whether to certify a rehabilitation project, the NPS will evaluate the condition of a structure after rehabilitation in relation to its condition prior to the commencement of rehabilitation. In addition, the project will be evaluated in the broadest possible context. Thus, for instance, if rehabilitation involves a number of structures which have been judged to have been functionally related to serve an overall purpose (again, a mill complex or a residence and carriage house are the typical illustrations), the NPS will consider certification based upon the merits of the overall project rather than on its individual components. Where there is no historical relationship among structures that are part of a rehabilitation project, a certification decision will be made for each certified historic structure. Demolition of a structure as part of a project involving multiple components will generally result in denial of certification of a project. Similarly, if a building in a historic district is to be rehabilitated, review will encompass the effects of the alteration on both the historic structure itself and on the district in which it is situated.

2.3.1 Standards for Rehabilitation

As guidelines in evaluating rehabilitation projects, the NPS applies its Standards for Rehabilitation.[58] The regulations call for the standards to be applied "to specific rehabilitation projects in a reasonable manner, taking into consideration economic and technical feasibility."[59] Nevertheless, a project must comply with each of the 10 standards, or it will not

---

[58] *Id.* § 67.7(a).
[59] *Id.* § 67.7(b).

be approved. The text of the standards was revised in the 1990 amendment of Part 67, but the application of either the previous or revised version of the standards to a project should have the same effect.[60] The revised standards are:

1. A property shall be used for its historic purpose or be placed in a new use that requires minimal change to the defining characteristics of the building and its site and environment.
2. The historic character of a property shall be retained and preserved. The removal of historic materials or alteration of features and spaces that characterize a property shall be avoided.
3. Each property shall be recognized as a physical record of its time, place, and use. Changes that create a false sense of historical development, such as adding conjectural features or architectural elements from other buildings, shall not be undertaken.
4. Most properties change over time; those changes that have acquired historic significance in their own right shall be retained and preserved.
5. Distinctive features, finishes, and construction techniques or examples of craftsmanship that characterize a historic property shall be preserved.
6. Deteriorated historic features shall be repaired rather than replaced. Where the severity of deterioration requires replacement of a distinctive feature, the new feature shall match the old in design, color, texture, and other visual qualities and, where possible, materials. Replacement of missing features shall be substantiated by documentary, physical, or pictorial evidence.
7. Chemical or physical treatments, such as sandblasting, that cause damage to historic materials shall not be used. The surface cleaning of structures, if appropriate, shall be undertaken using the gentlest means possible.
8. Significant archaeological resources affected by a project shall be protected and preserved. If such resources must be disturbed, mitigation measures shall be undertaken.
9. New additions, exterior alterations, or related new construction shall not destroy historic materials that characterize the property. The new work shall be differentiated from the old and shall be compatible with the massing, size, scale, and architectural features to protect the historic integrity of the property and its environment.
10. New additions and adjacent or related new construction shall be undertaken in such a manner that if removed in the future, the

---

[60] *Id.*

essential form and integrity of the historic property and its environment would be unimpaired.[61]

To assist in applying and implementing the Standards, the NPS has adopted "Guidelines for Rehabilitating Historic Buildings."[62] These reflect a general hierarchy from least to most intrusive means of rehabilitating structures in order to accommodate efficient contemporary uses. Not surprisingly, they represent a strong preference for the most minimal rehabilitative activity which can possibly be undertaken. Building owners are instructed initially to identify, retain, and preserve those architectural materials and features which are important in defining the historic character of a structure. Once this is done, work should be done as necessary to protect and maintain the materials and features which have been identified, but with the least degree of intervention possible. Protective work to be undertaken includes such things as rust removal, caulking, limited paint removal, reapplication of protective coatings, or installation of fencing or alarm systems.

If protective maintenance is not adequate to preserve historic features, then repair work should be undertaken. Again, the guidelines call for the least intrusion possible. Patching, splicing, reinforcing, and the like are preferable to more substantial alteration. Also, use of the original material is always desirable, although substitutes are acceptable if the form and design of the substitute convey the same visual appearance as the remaining parts of the original material or feature.

If repair is impossible, the next-best option is replacement of an entire character-defining feature. The guidelines emphasize, however, that removal and replacement are never recommended when a feature, however damaged or deteriorated, can be repaired and preserved. If replacement is essential, use of the original material is, again, preferable but not essential. If an entire interior or exterior feature is missing and irretrievable (for instance, a cast iron facade, or a principal staircase) and adequate historical, pictorial, and/or physical documentation exists so that the original feature can be accurately reproduced, design and construction of a new feature based upon that information may be appropriate. A new design, which is compatible with the remaining features of the building, may also be acceptable.

Finally, though least desirable, physical alterations or additions to historic buildings may be necessary to allow continued use, to meet health and safety code requirements, or to meet energy conservation objectives.

---

[61] 9 *Preservation L. Rep.* 1030 (1990) contains a useful discussion of changes effected by the revision of these standards.

[62] National Park Service, U.S. Dep't of Interior, *The Secretary of the Interior's Standards for Rehabilitation and Guidelines for Rehabilitating Historic Buildings* (revised 1983). The NPS Guidelines are included in **App. D.**

These must not radically change, obscure, or destroy character-defining spaces, materials, features, or finishes of the structure. Interior alterations are generally preferable to exterior, and interior solutions are certainly preferable to exterior additions. The regulations warn of particular rehabilitative techniques which are generally not appropriate for historic buildings and which are likely to lead to denial of certification.[63] Physical treatments which may cause or accelerate deterioration of buildings are to be avoided; these include improper repointing techniques, improper exterior masonry cleaning methods, and the introduction of insulation into cavity walls of historic wood frame buildings where damage to historic fabric would result. Certification denial will also result from exterior additions that duplicate the form, material, style, and detailing of a structure to the extent that they compromise its original historic character.

2.3.2 Application of Standards

Based upon its experience in reviewing and evaluating rehabilitation projects, the NPS has identified a number of special problem areas which are most likely to result in certification denial if not properly handled.[64]

1. New heating, ventilating, and air-conditioning (HVAC) systems. Justification must be provided before installing window-mounted or through-the-wall HVAC units. This should include the effect of the new equipment and ductwork on the building fabric, a description of alternative systems considered and why the system in question was chosen, and a life cost analysis comparing the system proposed for use with two or more alternative systems. In general, owners are strongly encouraged to utilize systems which cause least damage to the historic fabric of the building.

2. Window replacement. Owners must justify the replacement of existing window sash with evidence, including photographs, of severe deterioration, and must provide data on the cost of repairing existing sash versus installing new sash. Where replacement is warranted and where windows are an integral part of the building's design and character, new sash should match the original in material, size, general pane configuration, and reflective qualities. Owners are encouraged to repair and retain existing sash where such sash add to the historic and architectural character of the building.

---

[63] 36 C.F.R. § 67.7(c).

[64] *See* Rogers, "Reasons for the Denial of Certification for the 25 Percent Investment Tax Credit," 3 *Preservation L. Rep.* 2001 (1984); National Park Service, "Preservation Briefs" (series designed to assist in handling problems common in preservation prior to commencement of work).

3. Removing interior plaster work and exposing masonry surfaces. Documentation of the existing condition of the interior walls, and the effect on existing woodwork, should be provided before undertaking work of this type. In general, owners are discouraged from exposing bare masonry surfaces unless this condition is supported by historical evidence.

4. Exterior masonry cleaning. Cleaning should be accomplished by the gentlest means possible, and an indication should be provided that other cleaning methods were considered but found less appropriate for the condition of the material to be cleaned. Owners are strongly encouraged to clean masonry only when necessary to halt deterioration or to remove graffiti and stains.

5. Exterior masonry repair. Documentation should indicate which areas require repair, and should provide evidence that repointing mortar will match the original in composition, proportions, color, and texture. Owners are encouraged to repoint only those portions of a building that require repair.

6. Storefront alterations. Before altering an existing storefront, information should be provided on when the existing storefront was constructed; what physical conditions are present; and if a historical treatment is planned, on what research or physical evidence the proposed new storefront designs are based. Owners are strongly discouraged from introducing a storefront or new design element on the ground floor which alters the character of the building and its relationship with the street, or which causes destruction of significant historic fabric.

7. Incompatible new use or addition. Even when the economic viability of a historic building requires alteration to accommodate a new use or expansion to accommodate existing uses, any changes made must comply with the Standards for Rehabilitation. Economic hardship may be grounds for alteration under local law, but it is not a sufficient condition for certification. The standards do not necessarily discourage additions, but they must be compatible with the building and the neighborhood. At the same time, however, additions should be clearly distinguishable from the original building and should not attempt to give the property an earlier appearance.

8. Incompatible treatments to building interior or rear or secondary elevations. As with alterations or additions, evaluation of interior, rear or secondary elevation treatments for certification purposes may differ from the scrutiny required under local law. Many local ordinances, for example, permit a commission to analyze only proposed treatments of building exteriors. Certification decisions, however, are based upon an entire project, and involve review of all impacts upon a building. It is important to emphasize that issuance by a local commission of a certificate of appropriateness for an alteration by no means guarantees NPS certification.

The regulations acknowledge that, in limited cases, "it may be necessary to dismantle and rebuild portions of a certified historic structure to stabilize and repair weakened structural members and systems."[65] Extreme intervention of this type will be considered as part of a certified rehabilitation if three conditions are met:

1. The necessity for dismantling is justified in supporting documentation.
2. Significant architectural features and overall design are retained.
3. Adequate historic materials are retained to maintain the architectural and historic integrity of the overall structure.

As further guidance in applying the Standards for Rehabilitation, the NPS, through the Technical Preservation Services Division, periodically published a now discontinued bulletin entitled *Interpreting the Secretary of the Interior's Standards for Historic Preservation Projects*. These publications briefly describe a particular application for certification of a rehabilitation project, state whether the request was approved or denied, and explain the rationale for the positive or negative determination. While the decisions discussed relate to the particular facts and circumstances of a given application, they do highlight the sorts of rehabilitative techniques which are likely to encounter disapproval from the NPS. A number of the major bulletins will be found in **Appendix D**.

2.3.3 Certification Procedure

The NPS will review any proposed, ongoing, or completed rehabilitation project for compliance with the Standards for Rehabilitation. Owners are encouraged to obtain a determination of compliance before undertaking work. Prior approval enables owners to proceed knowing that the work meets necessary requirements, and will also expedite certification of the completed project. Owners who undertake rehabilitation projects without securing approval in advance do so at their own risk. Not surprisingly, most certification denials have arisen in situations in which the SHPO or NPS has not been consulted until after work has been substantially completed.

Projects involving the use of federal funds such as grants from the Department of Housing and Urban Development or Urban Development Action Grants generally require certification prior to the final commitment of the federal funds.

If a proposed or ongoing project has been approved, the owner must promptly report to the NPS substantive changes in the work as described in the application.[66] This must be accomplished by written statement, through the SHPO. The NPS will notify the owner if the revised project continues to meet the standards, and the owner can thereby assure continued conformance.

---

[65] 36 C.F.R. § 67.7(d).
[66] *Id.* § 67.6(d).

Whether or not prior approval is obtained, final certification of the rehabilitation will be issued only after the project has been completed. Requests for certification are made by means of Part 3 of the Historic Preservation Certification Application, discussed in § 2.2.2, which is entitled, "Request for Certification of Completed Work." Requests must include the project completion date; a signed statement indicating that, in the owner's opinion, the completed project meets the Standards for Rehabilitation and is consistent with the work described in Part 2 of the application; a statement of costs attributed to the rehabilitation; and photographs adequate to document the completed work.

The NPS charges fees for processing rehabilitation certification requests.[67] For reviewing proposed or ongoing rehabilitation projects estimated to cost over $20,000, the fee is $250; no fee is charged for projects under that amount. Fees for reviewing completed projects depend upon the dollar amount of costs attributed solely to the rehabilitation in the Historic Preservation Certification Application, in accordance with the following table:

Size of Rehabilitation	Fee
$20,000 to 99,000	$ 500
100,000 to 499,000	800
500,000 to 999,000	1,500
1,000,000 or more	2,500

If review had already been undertaken before a project was completed, the initial fee of $250 will be deducted from these fees.

Generally, each rehabilitation of a separate certified historic structure is considered a separate project for purposes of computing fees. If, however, the project involves structures judged to have been functionally related to serve an overall purpose, the fee for preliminary review will be $250 and the fee for final review will depend upon total project costs. If multiple projects under the same ownership (for example, row houses or loft buildings) are submitted for review at the same time, the maximum total fee is $2,500. The fee for preliminary review will be $250 per building, and the fee for final review will be based upon total rehabilitation costs, up to a maximum of $2,500. If $2,500 has already been expended in preliminary fees, no further fee will be charged.

Upon receipt of a completed application, the NPS will determine if the project is consistent with the Standards for Rehabilitation, in accordance with the timetable described in § 2.2.4. If a project does not meet the standards, a letter will be sent to the owner explaining the reasons for that determination, and where possible, advising him of the revisions necessary to meet the standards.[68] It should be noted again

---

[67] *Id.* § 67.11.

[68] *Id.* § 67.6(c), (f).

that prior approval of a project by federal, state, or local agencies does not ensure certification by NPS. The Standards for Rehabilitation take precedence over other regulations and codes in determining whether a rehabilitation project is consistent with the historic character of a building and/or the district in which it is located.[69] If certification is denied, that determination may be appealed as discussed in § 2.2.4.

The large majority of projects presented to the NPS are certified.[70] Of a total of 7,009 certification decisions made between fiscal years (FY) 1977 and 1983, 683 initial denials were issued, amounting to 9.7-percent initial denial rate. In FY 1983 alone, 245 requests for certification were denied, representing 10 percent of the decisions rendered. The initial denial rates for the project certifications in fiscal years 1988, 1989, 1990, and 1991 were 12.2 percent, 11.5 percent, 5.8 percent, and 5.5 percent, respectively. The rate of appeals of initial denials has risen in recent years. From FY 1977 through FY 1980, an average of 26 percent of initial denials were appealed. In FY 1983, 27 initial denials, or 52 percent, were appealed. More recently, the rate of appeals of denials of certifications of rehabilitations rose from 66 percent in FY 1987 to 94 percent in FY 1988. In FY 1991, however, the rate of appeals declined to 73 percent.

The number of denials overturned on appeal has declined somewhat. From FY 1977 through FY 1980, 56 percent of initial denials were overturned; in FY 1983, 44 percent of appeals resulted in reversal. In FY 1988, 1989, and 1990, 43 percent, 40 percent, and 39 percent respectively, of appeals resulted in reversal. However in FY 1991, the percent of reversals on appeal increased to 61 percent.

According to the NPS, submission of information on appeal and professional error account for essentially all reversals on appeal; reversals rarely result from procedural error. This statistic highlights the importance of providing complete information in the certification application, to minimize the danger of initial denial and reduce ultimate processing time.

A recent federal district court decision emphasizes the discretionary nature of NPS authority in reviewing certification applications for rehabilitation. In *Amoco Production Company v. Department of Interior*,[71] Amoco contended that the NPS' denial of certification of the rehabilitation of Amoco's Philcade Building in Tulsa, Oklahoma, was unreasoned and conclusory. The NPS issued an original denial and two subsequent denials in response to Amoco's petition for reconsideration of the original

---

[69] *Id.* § 67.7(e).

[70] All statistics are taken from "Tax Incentives for Rehabilitating Historic Structures: Facts and Figures 1977–1983" (National Park Service 1984), available from the National Trust for Historic Preservation; National Park Service, "Tax Incentives for Rehabilitating Historic Buildings; Fiscal Year 1989 Analysis" (March 1990); and National Park Service, "Tax Incentives for Rehabilitating Historic Buildings; Fiscal Year 1991 Analysis" (Dec. 1991).

[71] 763 F. Supp. 514 (N.D. Okla. 1990).

denial. In rejecting Amoco's claim, the Court stated that the NPS analysis of the chief historic features of the building, although different from Amoco's, was not unreasonable. The Court also rejected Amoco's attempt "to bind National Park Service's discretionary authority to precedent." Moreover, the Court denied Amoco's request for equitable relief in the form of delisting the property from the National Register in order to enable Amoco to claim the former 20-percent tax credit with respect to its rehabilitation expenditures. The Court stated that, in establishing the procedures relating to the tax credit, Congress sought, not only to provide incentive for rehabilitation, but also to provide a strong disincentive for failure to rehabilitate historic structures properly. Accordingly, the Court found that to grant Amoco relief would not further Congressional intent with respect to rehabilitation.[72]

Receiving certification from the NPS does not entirely discharge a building owner's obligations. The NPS reserves the right to make inspections at any time up to five years after completion of the rehabilitation. Certification may be revoked, after 30 days' notice to the owner, if it is determined that the rehabilitation was not undertaken as presented in the application and supporting documentation, or that the owner, upon obtaining certification, undertook further unapproved alterations as part of the rehabilitation project which were inconsistent with the standards.

---

[72] For two other examples of the federal courts' deference to NPS, both in promulgating and applying its certification regulations, *see* Schneider Partnership v. United States Department of Interior, 693 F. Supp. 223 (D.N.J. 1988), and St. Charles Associates v. United States, 671 F. Supp. 1074 (D. Md. 1987), *aff'd*, 907 F.2d 1139 (4th Cir.), *cert. denied*, 111 S. Ct. 258 (1990).

Three

Financing Rehabilitation: Private Syndication

An initial and important step in historic rehabilitation, as in any real estate venture, is the choice of ownership entity or syndicate.[1] The decision is guided by an evaluation of which vehicle will best achieve the purposes of raising the equity capital and securing the financing needed to acquire and rehabilitate the building and, thereafter, assuring its ongoing operation. For several reasons, which will be discussed in this chapter, the limited partnership has been the preferred form of association.

In addition to organizational advantages, a real estate limited partnership can offer numerous tax benefits. While the Tax Reform Act of 1986 extends the coverage of the at-risk rules to include real estate investment, a limited partner can still include in basis a proportional share of "qualified nonrecourse financing," as discussed next. Under present law, properly managed real estate investments may produce

---

[1] For a thorough discussion of this subject, see T. Lynn & H. Goldberg, *Real Estate Limited Partnerships* (2d ed. 1983). *See generally* Madison & Dwyer, *The Law of Real Estate Financing* (1981 & Supp. 1984). Entity choices include tenancy in common, joint venture, general partnership, limited partnership, corporation, land trust, or real estate investment trust.

deductions larger than the amount invested. One who invests as a limited partner can normally claim a share of both depreciation of the building and deductions for other business expenses of the partnership, such as interest on borrowed funds. The advantages of undertaking the rehabilitation of a historic or other old building through a partnership may be further enhanced by the availability of investment tax credits that may be shared among the individual investors. However, an investor's ability to utilize fully the share of credits and losses attributable to a limited partnership interest is restricted by the new passive loss rules discussed in § 3.2.4. These rules severely limit the amount of nonpassive source income which individual (but not certain corporate) taxpayers may offset with losses and credits from most real estate investments. As a result, the limited partnership may no longer retain all of its attraction as a form of investment entity, and investors may look to other vehicles. These could include, for example, corporate entity investment, either directly or through corporate participation in partnerships. In any event, investment partnerships emphasizing true economic return, rather than tax benefits, would not be hampered by the passive loss limits.

Projects undertaken through limited partnerships will often go through the syndication process, discussed more fully in this chapter and in **Chapter Eight**. This involves the preparation of a memorandum or prospectus for potential investors, which discloses all material information relating to the project, as required by federal and state laws governing securities offerings. The memorandum or prospectus typically contains pro forma financial projections of income (and losses) over an extended period, both for the project as a whole and for each prospective limited partner. Portions of a typical pro forma projection, showing expected cash-flow and after-tax consequences of a project over a 17-year period, for both general and limited partners, are found in **Appendix G**.

3.1 LIMITED PARTNERSHIPS

Limited partnerships are a valuable financing tool in the rehabilitation process. Most simply, a limited partnership allows an investor to pool resources with other investors to rehabilitate a building in a manner that the individual investor may not have the resources to accomplish alone. In addition to providing a vehicle by which individual investors can extend their financial reach by pooling resources, the law provides incentives which may make this form of association more advantageous to the investors than others.

A limited partnership is a partnership created under state statute that allows an investor to contribute or lend money or property to a business or venture managed by at least one general partner, without subjecting the investor-limited partner's personal assets to the full risk of the enterprise. The Uniform Limited Partnership Act (ULPA)[2] defines a limited partnership as "a partnership formed by two or more persons . . . having as members one or more general partners and one or more limited partners. The limited partners as such shall not be bound by the obligations of the partnership." In addition to limiting an investor's liability, the limited partnership form provides an investor with tax benefits that other organizational forms do not.[3]

To receive this favorable treatment, a limited partner must remain passive in the management of the partnership's affairs. All management and control of the partnership's business and property must be left to the general partner(s). The investor who does not heed this requirement and seeks to participate in business decisions risks a finding that he is a general partner, not a limited partner, thereby exposing himself to full personal liability.[4] However, if this restriction is heeded, the limited partnership can combine the legal and business benefits available from the corporate form of organization with the tax advantages otherwise available only to individuals. While a corporation can offer similar limitations on liability, corporate shareholders do not enjoy the tax benefits that limited partners do: Profits are taxed at both the corporate and the individual level, and tax deductions and credits for which the corporation is eligible cannot be passed through to the investor.[5] A general partnership or individual ownership, on the other hand, may provide the same tax benefits as a limited partnership, but general partners and individual investors bear full personal liability for the obligations and liabilities incurred in real estate ventures. For these reasons, limited partnerships have been a popular vehicle for investors wishing to contribute capital for the purpose of rehabilitating old buildings.

3.1.1 Creation Governed by State Law

A limited partnership is created under state statute.[6] Every state (except Louisiana) and the District of Columbia has enacted a statute that governs the formation and conduct of a limited partnership. These statutes are based on either the original 1916 ULPA[7] or a version of the 1976

---

[2] 6 U.L.A. 559–631 (1969 & Supp. 1991).

[3] *See* § 3.2.3.

[4] *See* U.L.P.A. § 7.

[5] Some of the advantages of limited partnerships can be achieved, in appropriate circumstances, by adopting the corporate form and electing to be treated as a Subchapter S corporation. This form will, for example, permit direct pass-through of profits and losses to shareholders. However, there may also be disadvantages to Subchapter S election. It may, for instance, subject an entity to statutory provisions which reduce the total amount of losses which can be passed through to investors when compared to limited partnerships. Fuller consideration of the Subchapter S provisions is beyond the scope of this book.

[6] There were no limited partnerships under common law.

[7] The original ULPA is located at 6 U.L.A. 559 (1969).

revised ULPA, adopted by the National Conference of Commissioners on Uniform State Laws in 1976 and amended in 1985. Although specific state statutes may parallel the language of these model acts, the precise wording and scope of each state's statute may differ from the model acts, and the specific statute of the appropriate jurisdiction should always be consulted.

Generally, a limited partnership must file a certificate in a central recording office of a designated public official in the jurisdiction. The certificate must specify such things as a description of the partnership and its business, the names of the general and limited partners, the amount of cash or other property contributed by the limited partners, provisions governing dissolution of the partnership, requirements for assignment of partnership interests, and provisions governing distributions of partnership property. In some cases, the partnership agreement is filed in lieu of, or in combination with, the certificate. The agreement is often filed as a subsequent amendment to a short-form certificate once it has been prepared.

Completion of the certificate is crucial. Failure to conform to the requirements of the state's law subjects the limited partners to the risk of the loss of limited liability. However, substantial compliance in good faith with the certificate filing requirements is sufficient to form a limited partnership.[8]

3.1.2 Role of General Partner

A general partner in a limited partnership is subject to all of the liabilities of a partner in a general partnership.[9] This includes full liability for all debts and obligations incurred by the partnership, as well as for wrongful acts performed by other partners.[10] A general partner in a limited partnership also possesses most of the rights and powers a partner would exercise in a general partnership. Certain of these powers, however, must be specifically provided for in the partnership agreement or by the unanimous written consent or ratification of all the general partners.[11] Without such agreement, for example, a general partner may not confess judgment against the partnership; admit a person as a general or limited partner; or continue the business with partnership property on the death, retirement, or insanity of a general partner.

General partners owe a fiduciary duty to the partnership and to the limited partners.[12] They may be liable to the limited partners if they breach the duty of fair dealing in their conduct of the partnership

---

[8] U.L.P.A. § 2(2).
[9] *Id.* § 9.
[10] Unif. Partnership Act §§ 24–26, 6 U.L.A. 324–53 (1969).
[11] U.L.P.A. § 9.
[12] *See, e.g.,* Korn v. Franchard Corp., 388 F. Supp. 1326 (S.D.N.Y. 1975).

business. Moreover, general partners act as agents of the partnership, and commitments within their actual or apparent authority are binding on the entity as a whole.[13]

A limited partnership automatically dissolves upon death, retirement, or insanity of a general partner, unless the certificate authorizes the remaining general partners to continue the business, or all of the members consent to their doing so, and the business is in fact continued.[14] In order to avoid adverse tax consequences[15] and repetition of the administrative formalities of formation, it is often advisable to provide for these contingencies in the partnership agreement.

3.1.3 Role of Limited Partner

Generally speaking, the limited partner has fewer rights and powers, because he has entrusted management of the enterprise to the general partners. The limited partner may, however, take steps to insure that his investment is being protected. He has a right to inspect the partnership books, to demand full information about the partnership activities, to receive a share of partnership profits or compensation as provided in the certificate, and to compel a dissolution in certain circumstances.[16] He may also be able to bring an action against the general partners for breach of their fiduciary duty.[17] Moreover, upon the occurrence of certain conditions precedent or after giving specified notice, a limited partner may demand the return of his original contribution.[18]

A limited partner may assign his partnership interest, but, absent amendment of the certificate, the assignee succeeds only to the economic rights in that interest.[19] The assignee is entitled to receive a share of the profits and other compensation, or to a return of the original contribution, but can exercise none of the other rights possessed by the limited partner. However, if the certificate is properly amended, the substitute limited partner acquires all rights and powers associated with the interest, as well as all restrictions and liabilities, except for those liabilities of which he was not aware or on notice when he became a limited partner. Assignment of a limited partnership interest and admission of the assignee as a limited partner often requires consent of some or all of the other partners, pursuant to the partnership agreement.

---

[13] U.L.P.A. § 9.

[14] *Id.* § 10.

[15] *See* Lynn & Goldberg, *supra* note 1, ch. 8.

[16] U.L.P.A. § 10.

[17] *See* Lerman v. Tenney, 425 F.2d 236 (2d Cir. 1970); Riviera Congress Assocs. v. Yassky, 268 N.Y.S.2d 854 (App. Div.), *aff'd*, 223 N.E.2d 876 (1966).

[18] U.L.P.A. § 16.

[19] *Id.* § 19.

So long as a limited partner does not take part in the control of the business, he does not assume the liability of a general partner.[20] His financial liability to the partnership is limited to making up the difference between the amount of his capital stated in the certificate and the amount actually contributed.[21] (If he does not make up this difference, cash distributed to him may have to be repaid unless the certificate is amended.) The case law is unclear in identifying those powers whose exercise will abrogate limited liability.[22] Some state versions of the ULPA do specify particular powers which may be granted to limited partners without burdening them with general liability.[23] The applicable statutory and decisional law should be carefully consulted by the drafter of a limited partnership agreement to avoid potentially troublesome involvement of limited partners in the business affairs of the partnership.

3.2 TAX TREATMENT OF PARTNERSHIPS AND PARTNERS

A partnership is not a taxable entity under the Internal Revenue Code.[24] Instead, the tax consequences of the actions of the partnership flow through to the individual partners. The income, gain, loss, deductions, and credits of the partnership become the income, gain, loss, deductions, and credits of the individual partners. The ability to escape taxation at the entity level is often a primary reason for using the partnership form.

3.2.1 Recognition as a Partnership by the IRS

A limited partnership recognized under a state statute will not necessarily be recognized as such for federal income tax purposes.[25] This is because the IRS's definition of a limited partnership varies from that of the states. Since one of the primary reasons why individuals choose to organize as a limited partnership is to take advantage of tax benefits, attention must be paid to the independent criteria of the federal tax laws.[26]

For tax purposes, the question is whether the business entity will be classified as one with the characteristics of a partnership or with the features of a taxable association or corporation.[27] This question often

---

[20] *Id.* § 7.

[21] *Id.* § 17.

[22] *See, e.g.,* Weil v. Diversified Properties, 319 F. Supp. 778 (D.D.C. 1970) and cases cited therein.

[23] *See* U.L.P.A. § 7.

[24] I.R.C. § 701 (West 1988). However, the partnership is required to file an information income tax return form. I.R.C. § 6031 (West 1989).

[25] Treas. Reg. § 301.7701-1(c) (as amended 1977).

[26] *See generally* Lynn & Goldberg, *supra* note 1, ch. 2.

[27] A partnership, for federal tax purposes, "includes a syndicate, group, pool, joint venture, or other unincorporated organization through or by means of which any business, financial

arises in the context of a request by the partnership for an advance ruling by the IRS on its tax status.[28] The answer is based on the result of a balancing test. The factors to be weighed are the presence or absence of characteristics that have been identified as typifying the corporate form. For purposes of this test, the six characteristics of a corporation that the Treasury regulations identify are as follows:

1. Associates
2. An objective to carry on business and divide gains therefrom
3. Continuity of life
4. Centralization of management
5. Liability for corporate debts limited to corporate property
6. Free transferability of interests.[29]

Since the first two characteristics associates and business undertaken for common purposes are shared by both corporate entities and partnerships, the inquiry focuses on the latter four characteristics. To obtain recognition as a partnership for federal tax benefits, it is necessary to show that two of these four remaining corporate characteristics are not present and that the entity "has no other characteristics which are significant in determining its classification."[30]

The IRS is most likely to find that the two characteristics of corporate association not present are continuity of life and free transferability of interests, with the possible addition of limited liability. The case law[31] leads to the conclusion that when investors are organized under the terms of the ULPA, the resulting entity will be treated as a limited partnership for federal tax purposes.

A limited partnership agreement drafted according to a state statute which corresponds to the ULPA lacks continuity of life, because a general partner has the power to dissolve the partnership.[32] The agreement and certificate should additionally state that the entity's life dissolves upon the occurrence of a certain event, which may be the termination of the partners' relationship based on the death, insanity, retirement, resignation, bankruptcy, or expulsion of a general partner. The partnership may in fact continue based on the consent of the remaining general

---

operation, or venture is carried on, and which is not . . . a corporation or a trust or estate." I.R.C. § 761(a).

[28] See Rev. Proc. 89–12, 1989–1 C.B. 798, *amplified*, Rev. Proc. 91–13, 1991–6 I.R.B. 16.

[29] Treas. Reg. § 301.7701-2(a)(1) (as amended 1983). See Morrissey v. Commissioner, 296 U.S. 344 (1935).

[30] Treas. Reg. § 301.7701-2(a)(3).

[31] See, e.g., Larson v. Commissioner, 66 T.C. 159 (1976); Zuckman v. United States, 524 F.2d 729 (Cl. Ct. 1975). These cases rejected IRS attempts to interpret the regulations restrictively to find limited partnerships organized under the U.L.P.A. to be taxable associations.

[32] Treas. Reg. § 301.7701-2(b)(3).

partners or members, provided the consent is given after the event which triggers dissolution.[33] Prior consent by a provision for automatic continuation or even a fixed date when the partnership will dissolve may not be sufficient to avoid the continuity of life characteristic and may be seen by the IRS as an indication that the entity is not to be treated as a partnership for tax purposes. In the case of a limited partnership formed in a state with a statute corresponding to ULPA or the revised ULPA, in the event of the removal of the general partner, at least a majority in interest of limited partners must be required to elect a new general partner to continue the partnership in order for the IRS to rule that continuity of life is lacking.[34]

Limited partnership agreements drafted in accordance with the ULPA also will lack the corporate characteristic of free transferability of interests, which refers to the ability of members to substitute fully a person outside the organization for themselves.[35] If consent of the other members of the organization is required prior to this substitution or if something less than all of the powers of the interest can be conferred, then this does not constitute free transferability.

The corporate characteristics of limited liability are not present when some member of the entity is personally liable for the debts and obligations of the organization.[36] In a limited partnership, the general partner has personal liability. There are, however, circumstances in which the general partner is not deemed to be personally liable, and such circumstances could lead the IRS to challenge the characterization of the entity as a partnership. A general partner may not be considered personally liable if he does not hold substantial assets, exclusive of his interest in the partnership, which could be reached by a creditor, and if he is mere "dummy" acting as an agent of the limited partners.[37] For individuals acting as general partners, the definition of "substantial assets" is not well-defined in either the regulations or case law.

In considering whether to issue an advance ruling classifying an entity with corporate general partners as a limited partnership, the IRS will generally deem an entity to lack limited liability if the net worth of corporate general partners equals and is expected to continue to equal at least 10 percent of the total contributions to the limited partnership. In the case of an entity in which the only general partners are corporations that do not satisfy this condition, the IRS will apply close scrutiny to determine whether the partnership lacks limited liability; the entity must demonstrate that the general partners have substantial assets that could

---

[33] *See* Rev. Rul. 74–320, 1974-2 C.B. 484, *modified,* Announc. 75–23, 1975-11 I.R.B. 87.
[34] Rev. Proc. 89–12.
[35] Treas. Reg. § 301.7701-2(e)(1).
[36] *Id.* § 301.7701-2(d)(1).
[37] *Id.* § 301.7701-2(d)(2).

be reached by a creditor of the entity or that the general partners individually and collectively will act independently of the limited partners.[38]

Centralization of management is another characteristic of corporate organization. According to the regulations, centralization of management exists when the limited partners own "substantially all the interests" in the limited partnership.[39] Avoiding centralization of management in drafting a limited partnership agreement is difficult for two reasons. First, the concept of substantially all the interests is not clearly defined in the regulation or case law. And second, many limited partnerships are formed to obtain investment capital for which an ownership interest in most of the entity's profit is exchanged. It would seem that this might well be characterized as substantially all the interests. Avoiding centralization of management is perhaps most easily accomplished by giving the limited partners a right to take part in the conduct of the business in certain respects. That, however, runs the risk of jeopardizing their limited liability.

There is a rule of thumb used by the IRS to trigger its assertion of centralization of management. Centralization of management may be deemed to exist if the general partners own less than twenty percent of the partnership's capital and profits.[40] Since over eighty percent is often owned by limited partners, especially in the early years, most limited partnerships investing in real estate will be found to possess the corporate characteristic of centralized management. The IRS will not rule that a partnership lacks centralized management unless limited partnership interests, excluding those held by general partners, do not exceed 80 percent of the total partnership interests; in addition, in connection with an advance ruling, the IRS will consider all the facts relating to centralized management, including whether limited partners directly or indirectly control the general partners.[41]

Structuring a limited partnership to undertake a rehabilitation project requires a balancing of the business needs of the parties, the requirements of state partnership law, and the characteristics evaluated by the IRS. Beyond the substantive requirements and the special conditions discussed previously relating to partnerships with corporate general partners, a limited partnership wishing to obtain an advance ruling on its tax classification must satisfy additional conditions. Under Revenue Procedure 89-12,[42] the general partner or partners must, except as described in the next sentence, have at least a 1-percent interest in each material item of partnership income, gain, loss, deduction, or credit. If the partnership has

---

[38] Rev. Proc. 89–12.

[39] Treas. Reg. § 301.7701-2(c)(4).

[40] Staff of Joint Committee on Internal Revenue Taxation, 94th Cong., 1st Sess., *Tax Shelters: Use of Limited Partnerships, Etc.* 4 (Comm. Print 1975).

[41] Rev. Proc. 89–12.

[42] *Id.*

total contributions exceeding $50 million dollars, the general partner's or partners' aggregate interest in each item must be one percent divided by the ratio of total contributions to $50 million, but in no event can it be less than 0.2 percent. Second, the general partner or partners must maintain an aggregate capital balance equal to the lesser of the total positive capital account balances for the partnership or $500,000. However, if at least one partner contributes substantial services to the partnership, this rule does not apply provided the partnership provides that, upon dissolution and termination of the partnership, the general partners will contribute an amount equal to (a) any deficit balances in their capital accounts, (b) the excess of 1.10 percent of the total capital contributions of the limited partners over the capital previously contributed by the general partners, or (c) the lesser of (a) and (b). These rules apply to requests for advance rulings and are not intended to be substantive rules for the determination of partner and partnership status.

3.2.2 Tax Benefits Available to Partners

A limited partnership is an attractive method of organization because of the tax benefits available to each partner. The tax benefits accrue because the partnership is not itself a taxable entity. All tax benefits pass through the partnership to the individual partners. The partners are then taxed on their distributive shares of these gains, losses, income, and credits.

Limited partners thus enjoy the tax benefits available for old building rehabilitation described earlier in this book. This includes the investment tax credit of up to 20 percent on rehabilitation expenses.[43] To the extent permitted by the at risk rules, this can be based on the fully leveraged cost of the rehabilitation of the property, rather than the basis of the partners' direct investment.[44] In addition, the partnership can depreciate the cost of the building plus the expenses of rehabilitation, for another potentially sizable deduction. The depreciation deduction may be taken only when the building is first placed in service.[45]

The Tax Reform Act of 1986 extends the at risk rules to include real estate investment. In principle, this means that real property investors, like investors in other types of property, may not claim losses in excess of the amount they actually have placed at risk in an investment. Normally, this would include cash or property actually contributed to the partnership as well as borrowed funds as to which a partner is personally liable. The new law, however, provides relief from the otherwise harsh application of this rule in one major respect. An investor (including the holder of

---

[43] *See* § 1.2.1.

[44] *See* § 1.4. Under the 1986 Act, basis must be reduced by the full amount of any rehabilitation credit taken with respect to a property. I.R.C. § 50(c)(1) (West Supp. 1991).

[45] Treas. Reg. § 1.167(a)-10(b) (1960).

a limited partnership interest) may treat as being at risk an appropriate share of "qualified nonrecourse financing."[46] This generally includes financing from a commercial or institutional lender or financing which is extended or guaranteed by a government agency, if the financing is secured by the real property. Qualified nonrecourse financing would generally not include seller financing. If the lender and borrower are related individuals or entities in certain defined ways, the terms of the financing must be commercially reasonable to be deemed qualified.

In general, even qualified nonrecourse financing may only be used to the extent of 80 percent of the credit base of property qualifying for an investment tax credit (including the rehabilitation tax credit). An exception from this and other limitations is, however, provided with respect to the low-income housing credit. Financing may qualify even if its source is a party that would otherwise be deemed "related" under the general rules. Moreover, seller financing from a tax-exempt entity whose exempt purposes include fostering low-income housing qualifies up to 60 percent of the basis of low-income housing property.[47]

A partner can also claim a deduction based on partnership losses. The amount of the deduction is limited by the basis of the partner's interest in the partnership,[48] which is equal to the cost of the partner's share in that entity. This cost is the amount of cash and the value of property contributed to the partnership, as well as any obligations or liabilities of the partnership assumed by the partner, reduced by any return of capital or property.[49] Because basis may include a proportionate share of qualified nonrecourse liabilities, it may exceed the amount for which a partner is personally liable.

During the construction period, costs will be incurred that are not associated directly with actual construction. Among these are interest on construction loans, taxes, various financing, service and management fees, and other "soft" costs.[50] Some of these expenses are deductible by the partner in the taxable year in which they are incurred. The general rules are that the expense must be ordinarily and necessarily incurred in the course of profit-seeking activities, that the useful life of the asset acquired not extend beyond the taxable year, and that the expense be in a reasonable amount and for a stated purpose.[51]

Some costs may not be immediately deducted, but must be added to the basis of the partnership's property and depreciated or amortized over the

---

[46] I.R.C. § 465(b)(6) (West Supp. 1991).

[47] Staff of the Joint Committee on Taxation, *General Explanation of the Tax Reform Act of 1986* 172 (1986) [hereinafter *Blue Book*].

[48] I.R.C. § 704(d) (West 1986).

[49] I.R.C. §§ 705(a), 722, 742 (West 1988); Treas. Reg. §§ 1.722-1, 1.742-1 (1960).

[50] For a detailed discussion of the tax implications of these costs, see Lynn & Goldberg, *supra* note 1, at 117.

[51] Treas. Reg. § 1.162-3, -7 (1960).

property's useful life.[52] These include costs of construction (which include builder's fees and profits, raw materials, and labor utilized in construction); furniture; fixtures; equipment; and architectural, landscape, design, and legal fees associated with the project. Under the 1986 Act, construction period interest and taxes must be capitalized rather than immediately deducted.[53]

Often, most or all of the partnership tax benefits are allocated to the limited partners to attract potential investors. A limited partner's tax benefits from the partnership's activity are allocated according to the partner's distributive share. This share is generally set out in the partnership agreement,[54] which should specify the partners' respective shares of income, gain, credit, deduction, and loss. If the partnership agreement does not address any of these items, the partner's distributive share is determined by his or her interest in the partnership.

Under some circumstances, it is also possible to make "special allocations" of specific partnership items. This may be intended to make investment in the partnership especially advantageous for particular individuals, or to allocate tax benefit items to those partners for whom they will do the most good. Special allocations must be defensible, however, and can be subject to challenge and disallowance if they cannot be justified. Under the Tax Reform Act of 1976, special allocations are permissible only if they can be shown to have "substantial economic effect."[55] If the special allocation is disallowed, any affected items are reallocated in accordance with the partner's interest in the partnership, which is determined by taking into account all the facts and circumstances of a given situation. The IRS has adopted regulations establishing a two-part test for determining whether a special allocation has substantial economic effect. An allocation will be deemed to have economic effect if the economic benefit or burden of the allocation accrues to or is borne by the partner to whom the allocation is made. This in turn generally requires that

1. The partner's capital accounts are maintained in accordance with the allocation.
2. Liquidation proceeds are distributed in accordance with capital account balances, and
3. Following distribution of such proceeds, any deficits in the partner's capital accounts must be restored.[56]

---

[52] *Id.* § 1.263(a)-1 (as amended 1972).
[53] I.R.C. § 263A (West Supp. 1991).
[54] *Id.* § 704(a).
[55] *Id.* § 704(b)(2).
[56] Treas. Reg. § 1.704-1(b)(2)(ii) (as amended 1991).

An economic effect is substantial under the regulations if there is a reasonable possibility that the allocation will substantially affect the dollar amounts received by the partners, independent of tax consequences. An allocation is not substantial if

1. The after-tax economic consequence to at least one partner may, as a result of the allocation, be enhanced in present value terms, and
2. The after-tax economic consequence to no other partner will be diminished, in present-value terms.[57]

Special allocations of tax credits are deemed not to have economic effect, and are therefore generally not permitted. However, an exception to this rule is provided for certain allocations of investment tax credits, including the rehabilitation and low-income housing credits.[58]

The ability of individual partners to utilize the tax benefits which accrue to them may be limited by the new passive loss limitations discussed in § **3.2.4.** Thus, before investing in a real estate limited partnership, an investor must ascertain whether the tax benefits accruing to the partnership interest will have personal tax sheltering advantages, and to what extent. Under the strict new loss rules, these advantages may be limited.

3.2.3 Tax Shelter Registration

In an effort to crack down on tax shelter abuses, the Tax Reform Act of 1984 adopted new provisions mandating registration of certain tax shelters and listing of tax shelter investors. These requirements will be applicable to many real estate limited partnerships, and promoters must be careful to comply with them before any limited partnership interests are offered for sale.

Section 6111 of the Internal Revenue Code[59] requires registration of tax shelters if two conditions are met. First, the investment must have been represented as offering a "tax shelter ratio" of better than two to one. The tax shelter ratio is the ratio, in a given year, which the aggregate deduction plus 350 percent of the credits potentially allowable to an investor bears to the total amount invested by the investor. Second, the investment must either be (1) required to be registered under federal or state securities law; (2) exempt from registration under a provision requiring the filing of a notice with a federal or state agency regulating securities; or (3) substantial, that is, involving five or more anticipated investors and an aggregate amount exceeding $250,000. Pursuant to temporary

---

[57] *Id.* § 1.704-1(b)(2)(iii).
[58] *Id.* § 1.704-1(b)(4)(ii).
[59] I.R.C. § 6111 (West 1989).

regulations issued by the IRS,[60] registration is accomplished by filing Form 8264, "Application for Registration of a Tax Shelter."

The new law also requires that any organizer or seller of a "potentially abusive tax shelter" must maintain a list of investors available to the IRS upon request.[61] A potentially abusive tax shelter is one required to register under Section 6111, or one which the Secretary of the Treasury determines by regulation to have the potential for tax avoidance or evasion. The information provided by these registration and filing requirements is intended to enable the IRS to monitor tax shelters more efficiently, and increased auditing of such shelters can be anticipated. The IRS has announced that it will issue prefiling notification letters to investors in certain potentially abusive tax shelters, thereby warning such investors that their returns will be audited if they claim tax benefits from the shelter.[62]

3.2.4 Passive Loss Rules; Alternative Minimum Tax

Real estate limited partnerships have traditionally appealed to high-income investors seeking to shelter their otherwise taxable income with the losses and credits that real estate projects can generate. Under the passive loss rules now in place, however, investors generally may no longer use credits and losses generated by real estate syndication projects to shelter "active" income (income from wages, salaries, or business ventures in which the individual materially participates) or portfolio income (income from interest, dividends, and other sources not derived in the ordinary course of a trade or business).[63] This rule applies to individual taxpayers, estates, trusts, personal service corporations, and closely held C corporations. It does not apply to publicly held corporations.

If a taxpayer does not have sufficient passive income in a given year against which to offset passive credits and losses, those credits and losses are suspended and may be carried forward indefinitely until they can be utilized. Upon the disposition of a taxpayer's entire interest in a property, all suspended deductions may then be taken against income from any source.[64] Credits, however, continue to be subject to the rules and are allowable only against passive income.[65]

While the determination of the nature of an activity is generally a factual one, the treatment of certain activities and interests is specifically

---

[60] Temp. Treas. Reg. § 301.6111-1T (as amended 1986).

[61] I.R.C. § 6112 (West 1989).

[62] Rev. Proc. 83–78, 1983–2 C.B. 595.

[63] I.R.C. § 469(a) (West Supp. 1991). Temporary regulations interpreting the passive loss provisions of I.R.C. § 469 may be found at Treas. Reg. § 1.469-1T (as amended 1991). Interest expense allocable to passive activities is also treated as a passive activity expense, and the Service has adopted allocation rules. Temp. Treas. Reg. § 1.163-8T (1987).

[64] I.R.C. § 469(g) (West Supp. 1991).

[65] *Blue Book, supra* note 47, at 225.

defined and these definitions apply to the treatment of credits and losses as well as income. Rental activities are automatically treated as passive,[66] and limited partnership interests will be treated in this manner as well.[67] However, two exceptions to these rules provide some relief for participants in real estate projects.

First, an individual who actively participates in rental real estate activity may use losses or credits attributable to that activity to offset up to $25,000 of active income annually.[68] This provision phases out above an income level of $100,000 at the rate of $1 for each $2 of income, with a complete phaseout at $150,000. In addition, a taxpayer may use the rehabilitation credit and the low-income credit to offset up to $25,000 in active income annually, regardless of whether the taxpayer actively participates in the venture generating the credits. This provision phases out at the same rate as that just discussed, but between the income levels of $200,000 and $250,000. Thus those high-income taxpayers who previously represented a large proportion of investors in syndicated rehabilitation projects may no longer be able to use the rehabilitation credit to shelter any active income.

However, under the Omnibus Budget Reconciliation Act of 1989, the phaseout provisions are eliminated for low-income housing tax credits. This exception is available only for properties placed in service after 1989. If the property is held through a partnership or other "pass-thru" entity, the taxpayer's interest in the partnership or entity must be acquired after 1989.[69]

Prospective investors should also be aware of the possible impact of the expanded alternative minimum tax on the benefits they may be able to receive from losses and credits attributable to real estate activities.[70] Certain tax preference items that may be deducted in calculating regular tax liability may not be deducted for purposes of the alternative minimum tax. Passive losses, for example, even to the extent that they can offset regular tax, may not be taken as deductions against the minimum tax. Moreover, tax credits (except for the low-income housing credit) cannot be used to reduce minimum tax liability. And the appreciated value of property given as a charitable deduction (including facade easements) is subject to minimum tax. Because the alternative minimum tax is likely to affect more taxpayers than it did prior to the 1986 Act (as well as more of the tax benefits generated by real estate investment), it is a more important factor in all areas of tax planning.

---

[66] I.R.C. § 469(c)(2).

[67] *Id.* § 469(h)(2). The 1986 Act provides that a limited partnership interest may not be treated as an interest with respect to which a taxpayer materially participates, and hence not as a source of losses or credits from active, rather than passive, sources.

[68] *Id.* § 469(i).

[69] *Id.* § 469(i)(3)(C).

[70] *Id.* §§ 55–59.

The combined effect of these provisions has been substantially, although not entirely, to restrict the degree to which individuals investing in real estate projects for the purpose of generating tax losses can continue to utilize the rehabilitation tax credit. To maximize tax benefits, investment in rehabilitation projects will, in all likelihood, have to be made to a greater degree for the purpose of generating a true economic return rather than garnering tax benefits.

3.2.5 1992 Passive Loss Amendments (Proposed)

In June, 1992, as this edition was going to press, new rules concerning passive losses and depreciation were being considered by Congress and the President. If enacted, these proposals have the potential to mitigate the adverse effect that current passive loss rules have had on historic preservation projects.

In his 1992 State of the Union address, President Bush proposed revisions to the passive loss rules to encourage investment in real estate development. Subsequently, both Republican and Democratic representatives introduced bills in the House of Representatives to affect such changes. The Democratic version (H.R. 4210, introduced by Representative Rostenkowski)[71] passed the House on February 27, 1992. Under the House bill, real property operations, undertakings, and activities of a taxpayer engaged in the real property business were treated as nonrental trade or business activity.[72] However, this treatment would not extend to limited partner interests or to any activity relating to property placed into service after the date of enactment of the bill. Moreover, 20 percent of the items of income, gain, loss, deduction, or credit allocable to any real property rental activity would continue to be treated as items allocable to a passive activity.

The requirements for qualifying for the real property business exemption were narrowly tailored under the House bill. An individual engaged in the real property business was defined as someone who spends at least 50 percent of his or her working time and more than 500 hours during a year in real property operations, including construction, reconstruction, rental, management and finance operations.[73] Working time includes time spent as an employee, sole proprietor, S corporation shareholder, partner in a partnership, or beneficiary of a trust or estate. Closely held C corporations would qualify for the exemption if one or more shareholders owning stock representing more than 50 percent of the outstanding stock of the corporation materially participate in the aggregate real property activities of the corporation, or conform to other specific requirements.

---

[71] H.R. 4210, 102d Cong., 2d Sess. (1992).
[72] *Id.* § 2201(a).
[73] *Id.*

On March 12 and 13, 1992, the Senate passed amendments to the House bill that narrowed the application of the new passive loss rules. Under the Senate version, the passive loss rules apply to activities in the performance of "qualified real estate services," including the construction, substantial renovation, and management of real property or the lease-up and sale of qualified real property. The rules applied to rental activities with respect to "qualified real property," which was defined as rental property in which a taxpayer owns more than a *de minimis* interest.

In order to qualify for the passive loss credit under the Senate version, the taxpayer must materially participate in the performance of real estate services or rental activities. The rules would not apply to non-owner employees of a qualified real estate service unless the employee owns more than a *de minimis* interest in the employer, nor would they apply to closely held C corporations. Furthermore, the rules would not apply to properties placed in service or substantially renovated after March 3, 1992.

Under the Senate version, aggregate losses from applicable rental activities could not exceed the sum of the aggregate income from such activities, the net income from passive activities to which the rules do not apply, and an amount equal to 80 percent of the lesser of the net income from the performance of qualified real estate activities or the taxable income from rental activities. Unused deductions or credits from rental activities could not be applied against the following taxable year, but could be carried over to calculate aggregate losses.

A Conference Report adopted by the Joint Congressional Committee on Taxation on March 20 contained provisions that, in general, allowed real estate developers to deduct losses from rental real estate against other real estate activities, largely along the lines contained in the Senate bill.[74] Under the Conference Report, the definition of qualified real estate services was changed to include services in the construction, substantial renovation, leasing, or brokerage of real property, provided that, in the case of leasing or brokerage, the taxpayer spends more than 500 hours during the taxable year performing such services. The Conference Report was approved by both the House and Senate on March 20 but was vetoed by the President upon its receipt at the White House later that day. Although the veto apparently will not be overridden, it is possible that, in view of the strong support for revisions in the passive loss rules, a revised version of the Conference bill will be enacted sometime in 1992.

Whatever their final form, the enactment of new passive loss rules should encourage greater investment in real property development, as investors seek to shelter their otherwise taxable income with losses and credits generated by other real estate projects in which they are involved. This may be expected to be generally helpful for persons seeking private

---

[74] H.R. Rep. No. 102–461, 102d Cong., 2d Sess. (1992).

sources of financing for historic rehabilitation projects, though neither the House, Senate, nor Conference bills sought to relieve limited (as opposed to general) partners of the current passive loss requirements.

3.3 FEDERAL SECURITIES LAWS AFFECTING LIMITED PARTNERSHIPS

Although neither the Securities Act of 1933 nor the Securities Exchange Act of 1934 mentions limited partnership interests by name,[75] it is well-established that such interests constitute "securities" whose issuance, sale, and transfer is subject to federal and state regulation. The Supreme Court has defined "security" as "an investment in a common venture premised on a reasonable expectation of profits to be derived from the entrepreneurial or managerial efforts of others."[76] The typical limited partnership interest involves a sharing of risks and benefits of a profit-seeking enterprise without direct involvement in the control of the business, and thus clearly falls within this definition.[77]

In general, federal law requires registration of securities offerings, registration of broker-dealers, and compliance with disclosure and anti-fraud provisions. Section 5 of the Securities Act of 1933 requires registration prior to the sale of securities, unless the issuance in question falls within one of the several strictly defined categories of exemption. Registration is a time-consuming and expensive process. Thus, qualifying for an exemption is quite advantageous. Offerings of interests in real estate limited partnerships undertaking preservation or rehabilitation work will often fall within one of the available exemptions, which are therefore discussed at some length in this chapter. It should be noted, however, that full disclosure of all material information relating to an offering is required whether a security must be registered or not, and that the anti-fraud provisions, discussed next, apply regardless of any registration requirement.[78]

---

[75] The Securities Act of 1933 is codified at 15 U.S.C. §§ 77a–77aa, and the Securities Exchange Act of 1934 at 15 U.S.C. §§ 78a–78jj. Citation will be made to the sections of the acts rather than to the U.S. Code. The securities acts variously define "security" as "certificate of interest or participation in any profit-sharing agreement," "investment contract," and "instrument commonly known as a 'security.'" Securities Act of 1933 § 2(1); Securities Exchange Act of 1934 § 3(a)(10).

[76] United Housing Foundation v. Forman, 421 U.S. 837, 852 (1975); *see also* SEC v. W.J. Howey Co., 328 U.S. 293, 301 (1946).

[77] *See* Goodman v. Epstein, 582 F.2d 388 (7th Cir. 1978), *cert. denied*, 440 U.S. 939 (1979). There may, however, be special situations in which a limited partnership interest does not qualify as a security, as, for example, if the limited partner contributes some managerial skills to the enterprise. *See* Frazier v. Manson, 651 F.2d 1078 (5th Cir. 1981).

[78] *See* Securities Act of 1933 §§ 12(2), 17; Securities Exchange Act of 1934 § 10(b); SEC Rule 10b-5, 17 C.F.R. § 240.10b-5 (1991).

The new passive loss rules discussed in § **3.2.4** may alter the structuring of limited partnerships in ways that will affect their treatment under the federal securities laws. In the past, limited partnership offerings were often made to a relatively small number of wealthy, sophisticated investors, and therefore could frequently qualify, as private placements, for exemption from registration requirements. Because the degree to which these investors can individually benefit from rehabilitation-generated tax credits and losses is now severely limited, some syndicators have begun structuring partnerships which seek a smaller investment of funds from a larger number of individuals.

This may mean that many rehabilitation syndications will no longer be exempt from registration, which has important implications. First, the registration process significantly increases the time and cost associated with putting together a partnership offering. Second, registered public offerings may be targeted toward investors who are, on the whole, less sophisticated than those who participate in private placements, and who may also be less likely to have a prior relationship with the offeror. While registration statements and private placement memoranda are held to the same disclosure standards under the antifraud regulations of the Securities Exchange Commission, as a practical matter a public offering of limited partnership interests in rehabilitation projects may expose the issue to a higher risk of claims under Rule 10b-5 than is the case in the private placements that have characterized such projects in the past. A thorough understanding and disclosure of the tax issues and risks summarized in this volume is therefore important in the preparation of registration statements offering interests in such projects to the public at large.

3.3.1 Regulation D

In 1982, the Securities and Exchange Commission (SEC) adopted Regulation D,[79] which set out the criteria for several categories of exemption from the registration requirement of Section 5. Regulation D, which comprises SEC Rules 501–508, superseded pre-existing exemption standards in several respects and introduced some new concepts and definitions that are critical in determining whether an issuance of securities qualifies for exemption. Regulation D is not exclusive and attempted compliance with its provisions does not prohibit an issuer from claiming any other exemption that may be available. Nevertheless, complying with the relatively clear and straightforward terms of Regulation D will generally be easier than attempting to justify exemption on some other ground, and anyone planning or assisting with an offering should be thoroughly familiar with its provisions. The text of Regulation D is found in **Appendix H**.

---

[79] 17 C.F.R. §§ 230.501–.508 (1991).

3.3.2 General Provisions of Regulation D

A central concept in Regulation D is that of the "accredited investor." Exemption requirements, as explained in this chapter, are somewhat more liberal when accredited investors constitute some or all of the purchasers in a given offering. Under Rule 501(a), accredited investors include banks, insurance companies, investment companies, and private business development companies. Charitable organizations with assets exceeding $5 million also qualify. Individuals must meet one of several financial requirements to qualify as accredited investors. These requirements are satisfied by anyone whose net worth exceeds $1 million, or whose annual income exceeds $200,000.

Under the doctrine of integration, the SEC may treat several ostensibly distinct offerings as one combined offering for purposes of determining eligibility for exemption from registration. If this were not so, issuers might be tempted to subdivide offerings into enough units to qualify for the small offering exemption, and the intent of the registration requirement would be thwarted. Conversely, if no limitations on integration existed, an offering solely to intrastate residents might be integrated by the SEC with one of broader scope, thus making the former ineligible for the intrastate offering exemption.

Rule 502(a) adopts a "safe harbor" rule, compliance with which will insure that integration does not occur. If there are no offers or sales of securities by or for the issuer of the same or a similar class of securities during the six-month periods before and after a Regulation D offering, there will be no integration of that offering with offers or sales outside that time period. If the safe harbor requirements are not met, integration will depend upon the facts and circumstances of the particular issuance. In making a determination, the SEC will consider a number of factors,[80] including whether the offerings are part of a single plan of financing, whether they are made at or about the same time, and whether they are made for the same general purpose.

Rule 502(b) specifies the type of information which must be furnished to potential investors under Regulation D. The specific disclosure requirements applicable to an offering depend upon its nature and the exemption for which it qualifies. No specific disclosure conditions are imposed upon small offerings under Rule 504, or to offerings solely to accredited investors under Rules 505 and 506. Real estate limited partnerships are not typically subject to the periodic reporting requirements of the Securities Exchange Act, and so will be required to comply with the set of Rule 502(b) information requirements applicable to nonreporting, rather than reporting, entities.

In general, the rule requires nonreporting issuers to furnish information "to the extent material to an understanding of the issuer, its

---

[80] Securities Act Release No. 4434, 26 Fed. Reg. 11,896 (1961); Securities Act Release No. 1459, 27 Fed. Reg. 11,316 (1962).

business, and the securities being offered." More specifically, for offerings up to $2 million, the issuer must provide information of the kind required in Part II of SEC Form 1-A, an offering statement for securities exempt from registration. For offerings up to $7.5 million, the issuer must provide the same kind of information as required in Part I of Form S-18, a prospectus for offerings not to exceed $7.5 million. For larger offerings, the issuer must provide the same kind of information as would be required in Part I of a registration statement filed under the Act on the form that the issuer would be entitled to use. It is not official or binding, however, and not all of the information detailed in the guide need necessarily be included in the statement.

Rule 502(b) also requires an issuer to give each purchaser an opportunity to ask questions about the terms and conditions of the offering, and to supply additional information which can be acquired without unreasonable effort and which is necessary to verify the accuracy of information already disclosed.

3.3.3 Exemptions under Regulation D

When all of its general requirements are met, Regulation D provides three exemptions from registration for offerings by real estate limited partnerships. Under Rule 504, an issuance is exempt if the aggregate offering price does not exceed $1 million.[81] If the offering complies with this dollar limitation, there are no restrictions as to number or type of offerees or investors. Nor is there any specific information disclosure requirement under Rule 502(b). There may, however, be state disclosure standards, and federal antifraud rules discussed herein, that will apply in any event.

To obtain exemption under Rule 505, the offeror must comply with two sets of restrictions. First, the total amount of the offering cannot exceed $5 million,[82] and as with the other Regulation D exemptions, the integration standards of Rule 502(a) apply. Second, the entity issuing the securities (here, limited partnership interests) must reasonably believe that there are not more than 35 purchasers in the given offering. In calculating the number of purchasers, however, accredited investors may be excluded.

---

[81] This amount must be reduced by the
   aggregate offering price for all securities sold within the twelve months before the start of and during the offering of securities under this [Rule 504] in reliance on any exemption under section 3(b) of the Act or in violation of section 5(a) of the Act, provided that no more than $500,000 of such aggregate offering price is attributable to offers and sales of securities without registration under a state's securities laws.

17 C.F.R. § 230.540(b)(2).

[82] This amount must again be reduced by the "aggregate offering price for all securities sold within the twelve months before the start of and during the offering of securities under this [Rule 504] in reliance on any exemption under section 3(b) of the Act or in violation of section 5(a) of the Act." *Id.* § 230.505(b)(2).

The first criterion for exemption under Rule 506, like Rule 505, is that the issuer reasonably believe there are no more than 35 purchasers in the offering, excluding accredited investors. The second criterion is somewhat more complex. The issuer must reasonably believe that each purchaser who is not an accredited investor "either alone or with his purchaser representative(s) has such knowledge and experience in financial and business matters that he is capable of evaluating the merits and risks of the prospective investment." The specific content of this "sophistication" requirement is not spelled out in the rule, and will probably involve a number of factors, including the complexity of the offering, the amount of information disclosed, and the level of knowledge of the purchaser. If the purchaser himself does not possess adequate sophistication, the rule will be satisfied if his representative, who assists him in evaluating the prospective investment, is sufficiently knowledgeable. The status of the representative must, however, be acknowledged by the purchaser in writing, and certain conflicts of interest between the issuer and representative must be either disclosed or avoided altogether.[83]

3.3.4 Other Exemptions

Regulation D was intended to simplify the conditions of eligibility for several of the statutory exemptions from registration under the Securities Act of 1933. Its procedures do not, however, represent the exclusive means of complying with the statute. An issuer who does not wish to satisfy all of the requirements of Regulation D, cannot do so, or attempts to do so and fails, may attempt to avail himself of other avenues to the statutory exemptions discussed next.[84] In seeking such exemption, however, the burden of proof as to each requisite element is on the issuer.[85] Thus, compliance with Regulation D wherever possible is likely to be the preferable course.

Section 4(2) of the Securities Act exempts from registration "transactions by an issuer not involving any public offering." The Supreme Court has held that the construction of this exemption "should turn on whether the particular class of persons affected need the protection of the Act."[86] The SEC adopted Rule 506, which replaced Rule 146, as one means of compliance with the statutory "private placement" exemption. An issuer can, however, claim to fall within Section 4(2) even without complying with Rule 506.

---

[83] "Purchaser representative" is defined in Rule 501(h).

[84] Rule 508 of Regulation D provides that a person who fails to comply strictly with Rules 504, 505, and 506 will not lose his exemption from the registration requirements of Section 5 of the Securities Act, provided that he shows that his failure was insignificant and did not pertain to a term intended to protect him and that he made a good faith and reasonable effort to comply with applicable conditions. The failure, however, is actionable by the SEC under Section 20 of the Securities Act.

[85] *See* Lively v. Hirschfeld, 440 F.2d 631, 632 (10th Cir. 1971).

[86] SEC v. Ralston Purina Co., 346 U.S. 119, 125 (1953).

Both Regulation D and the older Regulation A, which provides a somewhat more complicated exemption procedure, were adopted under the authority of Section 3(b) of the Securities Act of 1933, which authorized the SEC to create exemptions for small offerings. As just discussed, however, the SEC regulations are not all-encompassing, and failure to comply with their requirements does not automatically make the statutory exemption of Section 3(b) unavailable. An offeror may be able to demonstrate eligibility for exemption directly under the terms of the statutory provision. In addition, Section 4(6) of the Securities Act, enacted in 1980, offers an exemption related, although not identical, to that of Section 3(b). Basically, Section 4(6) exempts transactions in which the total offering price is less than $5 million, and in which there is no advertising or public solicitation. Each section may, in certain circumstances, offer an exemption where the specific requirements of the other, or of the subsidiary regulations, would not.

Section 3(a)(11) of the Securities Act exempts from registration offerings extended only to residents of the state in which the issuer does business. This exemption is somewhat less useful than it appears. An offer to even a single nonresident makes the exemption inapplicable, so an issuer should be certain that he will qualify for the exemption before placing reliance upon it. Rule 147[87] defines the significant terms in Section 3(a)(11) in a rather technical manner. Exemption under either the statute or the rule does not provide exemption from registration requirements under the state securities laws.

3.3.5 Fraud and Rule 10b-5

Even when an offering qualifies for one of the exemptions just discussed, the issuer must be careful not to run afoul of the anti-fraud provisions of the securities laws. In general, the issuer's duty is twofold: He must not misrepresent any material fact in the disclosure provided to potential purchasers of the security, nor may he withhold any material information. If he does either of these, he risks a claim for rescission of the purchase agreement or for damages under, *inter alia,* Rule 10b-5 of the SEC.[88]

Rule 10b-5 was issued to enforce Section 10(b) of the Securities and Exchange Act, which contains a general prohibition on the use of manipulative or deceptive devices in connection with the purchase or sale of any security. This broad antifraud provision is fleshed out by Rule 10b-5, which makes it unlawful, in connection with the purchase or sale of any security

---

[87] 17 C.F.R. § 230.147 (1991).
[88] *Id.* § 240.10b-5.

(a) to employ any device, scheme or artifice to defraud;

(b) to make any untrue statement of a material fact or to omit to state a material fact necessary in order to make the statements made, in the light of the circumstances under which they were made, not misleading; or

(c) to engage in any act, practice, or course of business which operates or would operate as a fraud or deceit upon any person.

Because limited partnership interests generally qualify as securities, a general partner selling such interests is likely to be subject to this proscription.[89]

The breadth of Rule 10b-5's coverage can perhaps best be illustrated by listing the elements of a fraud claim under that rule:

1. Purchase or sale. Under the so-called *Birnbaum* doctrine,[90] adopted by the Supreme Court in *Blue Chip Stamps v. Manor Drug Stores*,[91] only a purchaser or seller of securities can maintain an action under Rule 10b-5. An individual who asserts that he or she decided not to buy or sell as a result of the misrepresentation or omission of material information is barred from bringing a fraud claim under the rule.

2. Manipulation or deception. The rule reaches a broad range of untrue statements, misleading statements, or omissions. The fraudulent statements can be made in any manner: in filings with the SEC, in disclosure statements to offerees, or in oral communications. In the partnership context, allegations of misrepresentation by general partners of the value and permanence of their contributions to the partnership, and of the transfer of other businesses to the partnership, have been held to support a 10b-5 claim by the limited partners.[92] The withholding of information about obstacles to accomplishing the object of the partnership, prior to the final payment of the limited partners' contributions, has also been held to be fraudulent under 10b-5.[93]

3. Materiality. For purposes of Rule 10b-5, information misrepresented or omitted is considered material if a reasonable man, in determining his or her choice of action as to the transaction in question, would attach importance to the information.[94] If the offeree's decision whether to buy, or the investor's decision whether to sell, would reasonably be affected by the information, it is material.

---

[89] *See, e.g., Goodman*, 582 F.2d at 406.

[90] Birnbaum v. Newport Steel Corp., 193 F.2d 461 (2d Cir. 1952), *cert. denied*, 343 U.S. 956 (1952).

[91] 421 U.S. 723 (1975).

[92] McGreghar Land Co. v. Meguiar, 521 F.2d 822 (9th Cir. 1975).

[93] *Goodman*, 582 F.2d at 414.

[94] SEC v. Texas Gulf Sulphur Co., 401 F.2d 833, 849 (2d Cir. 1968), *cert. denied*, 394 U.S. 976 (1969).

4. Scienter. Although the terms of neither the statute nor the rule seem to require it, the Supreme Court has imputed a requirement that the putative offender must have acted with scienter, or intent to deceive, manipulate, or defraud in order to be liable under 10b-5.[95] Under this view, mere negligent conduct does not rise to the level of fraud and hence is not actionable under this provision.

5. Reliance or causation. There must be a causal relationship between the fraudulent act and the sale or purchase in order to state a 10b-5 claim. Where the alleged act involves misrepresentation, the plaintiff must demonstrate that he relied on the misrepresentation.[96] Where the fraud involves omission, however "positive proof of reliance is not a prerequisite to recovery. All that is necessary is that the facts withheld be material in the sense that a reasonable investor might have considered them important in the making of this decision."[97]

The Securities Act contains a broad antifraud provision that forbids substantially the same conduct as Section 10(b) of the Securities Exchange Act. Section 17(a) of the Securities Act[98] makes it unlawful to use fraudulent devices in the offer or sale of any securities in interstate commerce. Section 17(a) applies solely to the sale of securities, rather than purchase or sale, but it is typically in relation to sale that fraudulent activities are alleged. The major difference between the two relates to the availability of private enforcement. It is well-established that private suits may be brought by aggrieved parties under Section 10(b).[99] The federal circuits are split, however, as to the availability of a private remedy under Section 17(a),[100] and the Supreme Court has repeatedly declined to resolve the question.[101]

---

[95] *See* Ernst & Ernst v. Hochfelder, 425 U.S. 185 (1976).

[96] *See, e.g.,* Safecard Serv. v. Dow Jones & Co., 537 F. Supp. 1137 (E.D. Va. 1982); *aff'd without opinion,* 705 F.2d 445 (4th Cir.), *cert. denied,* 464 U.S. 831 (1983).

[97] Affiliated Ute Citizens v. United States, 406 U.S. 128, 153–54 (1972). In *Basic, Incorporated v. Levinson,* the Supreme Court held that an investor's reliance on public material in representations may be presumed, subject to rebuttal, for purposes of a 10b-5 action. 485 U.S. 224, 248–49 (1988). For a discussion of the decision and 10b-5 claims in general, see H. Bloomenthal, *Securities Law Handbook* (1990–91 ed.).

[98] 15 U.S.C.A. § 77q(a) (West 1981).

[99] *Ernst & Ernst,* 425 U.S. at 196.

[100] The Fourth, Fifth, Eighth, and Ninth Circuits are among those that have rejected a private right of action. *See* Newcome v. Esrey, 862 F.2d 1099 (4th Cir. 1988); *In re* Washington Pub. Power Supply Sys. Sec. Litig., 823 F.2d 1349 (9th Cir. 1987); Deviries v. Prudential-Bache Sec., 805 F.2d 326, 328 (8th Cir. 1986); Landry v. All Am. Assurance Co., 688 F.2d 381, 387–91 (5th Cir. 1982). The Second Circuit, which has implied such a right, *see* Kirshner v. United States, 603 F.2d 234 (2d Cir. 1978), *cert. denied* 442 U.S. 909 (1979), has since expressed doubt as to the correctness of its decisions. *See* Yoder v. Orthomolecular Nutrition Inst., 751 F.2d 555 (2d Cir. 1985).

[101] *See* Bateman Eichler, Hill Richards, Inc. v. Berner, 472 U.S. 299, 303 n.9 (1985); Herman & MacLean v. Huddleston, 459 U.S. 375, 378 n.2 (1983).

3.4 STATE SECURITIES REGULATION

The power of the states to regulate securities activities is specifically reserved by the federal securities laws.[102] The legal requirements imposed by a state are independent of the requirements under federal law. Thus, in addition to any federal requirements, a securities transaction in the form of a transaction involving limited partnership shares may be subject to the further requirements of those states where the interests are being offered or sold.[103]

Every state has enacted laws regulating securities. These "blue sky" laws[104] typically contain any or all of three central components: (1) registration requirements for securities to be sold in the state, (2) antifraud and disclosure requirements, and (3) registration requirements for brokers and dealers. Some states also have suitability requirements governing both investors and the merits of the offering. Although the types of restrictions are generally similar, the specific provisions of various blue sky laws vary significantly.

Many states require that securities be registered with a state's securities officer or commission prior to sale within the state. This frequently involves filing an application form with a filing fee, providing disclosure information through a prospectus or memorandum, and furnishing other material exhibits and additional information. This process is simplified in some states that utilize a method called coordination, by which a copy of the prospectus and information filed under the Securities Act of 1933 is submitted in full or partial satisfaction of the state requirement. If the offering is not registered with the SEC, then the issuance must meet the state's "qualification" requirements before any sales can be made. In this regard, the powers of some state securities commissions are broader than those of the SEC. While the SEC can only require full disclosure prior to an offering, some state securities administrators can actually refuse registration of offerings if they find them unfair to investors.

Sales of limited partnership interests may benefit from exemptions from registration that exist in many states. Generally, these involve offerings to a limited number of investors, but their precise terms vary significantly. Some count offerees, others purchasers, and the maximum number allowed varies from 3 to 50. Moreover, New York and New Jersey require compliance with laws relating specifically to real estate syndications, in addition to their general securities laws.

In some states, exemptions are self-activating: Qualifying issuances do not have to comply with any procedural requirements. Other states

---

[102] Securities Act of 1933 § 18; Securities Exchange Act of 1934 § 28(a).

[103] *See generally* Lynn & Goldberg, *supra* note 1, ch. 10.

[104] The term *blue sky* comes from a U.S. Supreme Court case, Hall v. Geiger-Jones Co., 242 U.S. 539 (1917), which described the aim of these laws as the prevention of "speculative schemes which have no more basis than so many feet of blue sky."

require the filing of a notice or other information with the state securities commission. In some states, the rules of eligibility for exemption are clearcut; in others, availability of the exemption rests within the broad discretion of the commission. The securities laws of New York and California are representative of approaches taken by different states, and are discussed in some detail in the following sections.

3.4.1 New York Securities Law Governing Real Estate Limited Partnerships

Sales of limited partnership interests in real estate which are offered in New York must comply with the Real Estate Syndicate Act.[105] Any public offering of securities which "consist primarily of participation interests or investments in one or more real estate ventures" is subject to the act's requirements.[106]

No public offering of these interests may be made in or from New York until an offering statement or prospectus has been submitted to the Department of Law. The information that must be included in the submission is described in detail in Section 352- e(1)(b) of the General Business Law, and includes a description of the property, the nature of the interests being offered, and information on the principals involved in the offering. Whether New York filing requirements apply depends upon whether the offering is made in New York, not whether the property is located there.[107]

The statute does not define the parameters of a "public" offering. In certain circumstances, however, the attorney general in his discretion will furnish a "no action" letter confirming that registration is not required. This is generally possible when an offering is made to no more than nine offerees who are wealthy and sophisticated and who have a preexisting relationship with one or more principals of the issuer or promoter.

In addition, an issuer may apply for an exemption from Section 352-e filing requirements under Section 352-g. That section permits an exemption, at the attorney general's discretion, for an offering to up to 40 individuals, or for an offering which has been either registered under, or exempted from, the federal securities laws. The first basis of exemption requires that the entire offering throughout the world be made to no more than 40 people. If the number of offerees cannot be controlled (and the application should indicate how the number will be restricted), this exemption will not be available. The attorney general may, in addition, require some representation as to the net worth of the investors to establish exemption on this ground.

---

[105] N.Y. Gen. Bus. Law § 352-e to 352-j (McKinney 1984 & Supp. 1992).
[106] Id. § 352-e.
[107] *See* Ledgebrook Corp. v. Lefkowitz, 354 N.Y.S.2d 318 (Sup. Ct. 1974).

Alternatively, an issuer may seek exemption on the basis that the offering has been exempted from federal securities law registration. The exemptions may not be precisely coextensive, however. For example, New York does not accept the Regulation D provisions for distinguishing accredited from nonaccredited investors. While the attorney general does not impose a uniform standard in determining whether an offering is suitable for all potential investors without registration, he may require that some showing be made that all purchasers, not just accredited investors, meet an adequate suitability standard. Section 352-g will also provide exemption from offerings exempted under Section 4(2) of the Securities Act of 1933,[108] where Regulation D exemption cannot be obtained. Intrastate offerings exempted under Section 3(a)(11) of the Securities Act,[109] however, are not eligible for a New York exemption under Section 352-g.

If an issuer falls within the scope of Section 352-e, he will also be required to register as a securities "dealer" under Section 359-e. Exemption from the dealer registration requirements is available, however, if the issuer is involved only in a limited offering of real estate limited partnerships to no more than 40 individuals.[110] Application for both exemptions (from the public offering and securities dealer registration requirements) can be filed together with the Department of Law. It should be noted that, as a general matter, using a broker or dealer as an agent in selling partnership interests will not exclude an issuer from the definition of a dealer.[111]

3.4.2 California Securities Law Governing Real Estate Limited Partnerships

Securities transactions in California are governed by the Corporations Code.[112] The statute requires the issuers of securities in California to comply with qualification requirements, analogous to registration procedures under federal law and filing procedures under New York law.

There are two means of avoiding the burden of the California qualification requirements that may be available to offerors of limited partnership interests. The first is the limited offering exemption.[113] The criteria for this exemption largely follows those of federal Regulation D, but with some variations. The statute requires a maximum of 35 purchasers, with some of the same exclusions from the count as are permitted under SEC Rule 501: purchasers of at least $150,000 of securities in the offering,

---

[108] *See* § 3.3.4.

[109] *Ibid.*

[110] N.Y. Gen. Bus. Law § 359-f(2)(d) (McKinney 1984).

[111] *Id.* § 359-e(1)(a).

[112] Cal. Corp. Code §§ 25000–25706 (West 1977 & Supp. 1992).

[113] *Id.* § 25102(f) (West Supp. 1992); Cal. Code Regs. tit. 10, § 260.102.13 (1991).

purchasers with net worth exceeding $1 million or annual income exceeding $200,000, and certain persons affiliated with the offeror. Every purchaser must have either a pre-existing personal or business relationship with the offeror or an individual associated with it, or personally or together with his professional advisers be capable of protecting his own interests in connection with the transaction. There is no limit on the number of offerees under this exemption, nor is any particular disclosure required.

The commissioner of corporations may also, in certain circumstances, permit an offering to be qualified by means of a limited offering qualification, which relieves the offeror of the duty of compliance with some or all of the requirements.[114] Eligibility for this treatment depends upon meeting suitability requirements for California investors (generally, net worth of $250,000 to $500,000 or more and substantial income) and providing investors with written disclosure of areas in which the offering does not meet the commissioner's usual standards. There will also be restrictions on transfer of partnership interests.

---

[114] Cal. Code Regs. tit. 10, §§ 260.140–260.140.139 (1990).

Four

Financing Rehabilitation: Public and Nonconventional Sources

Having put together the appropriate organizational structure for undertaking a rehabilitation project, the next step is to obtain the necessary funding. In most cases, syndicates will first approach banks or other private lenders for construction period or longer term mortgage financing. In addition, however, there are public and private sources of preservation and rehabilitation funding that should be explored in putting together the most advantageous funding package.

In recent years, public funds earmarked exclusively for rehabilitation have become quite scarce. However, a number of governmental funding sources exist which, while not primarily designed to support rehabilitation, can be used for that purpose. One example of such a program source is the federal Urban Development Action Grant (UDAG) program, discussed in greater detail in this chapter. While development often means new construction, it is also true that rehabilitation can be an important tool in community development and revitalization. Other housing and urban development programs similarly make funds available for rehabilitation programs, the preservationist will encounter an application process that placed no special emphasis upon the goal of preservation. Under the UDAG program, for instance, urban development is the objective, and that end will be sought without a programmatic preference for either rehabilitation or new construction. Consequently, it will be necessary to develop more aggressive strategies to "sell" rehabilitation proposals to these funding sources.

Similarly, foundation and corporate donors may not give special priority to preservation projects, but may be willing to provide support for them. The primary objective of such funding sources may be civic improvement or cultural development, goals to which historic preservation can make a significant contribution. The challenge, again, is to demonstrate that rehabilitation can compete for funding in these categories.

Not only should more varied sources for funding be explored, but financing should be sought for limited portions of a project. For example, certain energy programs may provide assistance for insulating old houses. With less money available, no single source is likely to cover all financing needs, and owners should be familiar with the full breadth of available programs in order to assemble a financing package.

There are a number of factors that a developer should consider in attempting to build a broader financial base.

1. Eligibility. Each funding source has its own eligibility criteria. An applicant must determine whether the funding source considers the project eligible for financial support.

2. Use of structure. Some funding sources are available only if the building is put to a particular use. Thus, an applicant who intends to rehabilitate a building as, for example, a senior citizen community center, may find that the project qualifies for funding not because it is a rehabilitation project, but because it will benefit senior citizens.

3. Project location. Some funding programs seek to provide incentives aimed at improving the condition of particular areas. Thus, a program may make funds available only for use in urban neighborhoods, rural areas, or commercial districts.

4. Size of undertaking. The size of the undertaking is a significant consideration, since it affects both the type and amount of financial assistance that must be injected to get the project off the ground. In some cases, private financing will suffice to initiate a venture; in other circumstances, a large grant or loan guarantee will be required before other financing is forthcoming.

5. Project time constraints and the funding bureaucracy. The time that elapses between submitting an application and receiving funding approval varies among programs. The applicant attempting to assemble a funding package must coordinate agency schedules with his own funding requirements.

Since both sources and amounts of funding available change over time, current information on public and private funding sources is essential. Up-to-date information can be acquired from reference sources at many community and university libraries. Libraries of nonprofit organizations can be extremely helpful and many of these are accessible to the general public.[1]

4.1 PUBLIC SOURCES: THE FEDERAL GOVERNMENT

A wide array of financing assistance is potentially available at the federal level. It ranges from direct grants and loans to indirect forms of assistance such as tax incentives and loan guarantees. In addition to absorbing part of project costs, government financing assistance can lower interest rates or extend a loan's term, or share some of the project's risk by providing protection for private lenders. The types of assistance include the following:

1. Formula grant. Allocation of money to states or their subdivisions according to a distribution formula prescribed by law or administrative regulation, with or without restrictions on the purposes for which funds may be used.

2. Project grant. The funding of specific projects for a fixed period.

3. Direct payments for specified use. Financial aid provided directly to eligible beneficiaries by the federal government with restrictions on how the money is spent.

4. Guaranteed/insured loans. Loan guarantee or insurance programs to protect a lender and thereby encourage it to extend financing it might not otherwise provide. These programs insure the lender against default in whole or in part by the borrower. Many lending institutions which have not previously loaned money for rehabilitation projects view them as a larger risk than conventional construction programs, and indemnification may be essential to their participation.

5. Direct loan. Direct lending of federal moneys for a specific period of time, without interest or at below-market rates.

4.1.1 Historic Preservation Programs

Federal assistance targeted for historic rehabilitation has been dramatically reduced in recent years. While many of the programs remain authorized and intact in name, appropriations have been slashed. Programs that once provided grants and loans to eligible projects now may insure

---

[1] For the most current information regarding the funding status and application procedures of all of the following federal funding programs, see U.S. Office of Management and Budget, *Catalogue of Federal Domestic Assistance*, supplemented periodically.

loans only if the applicant can find financial backing privately. Other programs no longer participate in rehabilitation at all and are limited to property surveying and information dissemination.

The National Historic Preservation Fund grants program, authorized by the National Historic Preservation Act (NHPA),[2] continues to be funded in FY 1992. Once a source of funds for acquisition or development of historic properties, however, historic preservation grants-in-aid are no longer available for that purpose. Since FY 1983, grant uses have been restricted to financing state staff salaries, equipment, materials, and travel necessary to expand and maintain the National Register. In FY 1983, $51 million was appropriated; that was reduced to $25.48 million for FY 1985,[3] and $23.73 million for FY 1986. In fiscal year 1987, the appropriation for Historic Preservation Fund programs was $24.25 million of which $4.25 million was allocated to the National Trust. Since the 1980s, appropriations have gradually increased. In FY 1990, $32.75 million was allocated to the Historic Preservation Fund; for FY 1991, $34.665 million was appropriated to the Fund, of which $5.77 million was allocated to the National Trust. For FY 1992, Congress appropriated $35.931 million to carry out the provisions of the NHPA.

The historic preservation grant program is administered by the National Park Service (NPS). States, territories, and the National Trust may apply to the Secretary of Interior for annual grants for anticipated projects. These entities may subgrant to public and private parties to accomplish program objectives. States must subgrant 10 percent of the funds to local governments that have met certain requirements.

Assistance is provided on a formula and matching grant basis. Federal grants can fund up to 50 percent of project costs, while the remaining 50 percent must come from state and/or private funds and/or allowable in-kind donations. However, if the funds are for state and local historic resource surveys, the federal share is increased 70 percent.[4]

To become eligible for these funds, a state must appoint a state historic preservation officer (SHPO) to oversee a program of federally specified preservation activities, including participation in the National Register nomination process. Within the federally mandated framework, however, each state makes its own decisions regarding which projects to fund.

4.1.2 Community Revitalization and Development Programs

The U. S. Department of Housing and Urban Development (HUD) administers a number of community development programs which may be

---

[2] 16 U.S.C.A. § 470a(d) (West 1985).
[3] 3 *Preservation L. Rep.* 1059 (1984).
[4] 16 U.S.C.A. § 470b(a)(3).

used to assist rehabilitation activities. Although not intended exclusively for preservation funding, HUD's block grant programs have provided more funding for these activities than have programs tailored specifically for preservation. These programs provide a variety of financing, including direct grants, loans, guaranteed loans, and mortgage insurance. Many communities have developed memoranda of agreement to facilitate the historic preservation process once such block grants are distributed.

A group of the more significant programs are under the general supervision of HUD's Office of Community Planning and Development. However, it is important to note that these programs often have their own offices with separate administering officials.

4.1.3 Urban Development Action Grants

States, local governments, and urban counties may, at least in theory, obtain an Urban Development Action Grant (UDAG) to help alleviate severe economic distress or physical and economic deterioration in particular areas.[5] A UDAG is awarded on a competitive basis as a categorical grant—that is, a grant to support projects of a statutorily defined nature. These units of nonfederal government then use the federal funds for loans to developers of eligible projects that will spur economic development in distressed areas. Among the project uses to which these grants can be applied is preservation and restoration of historic properties.

No UDAG appropriations were made after FY 1989. Consequently, although the program remains on the books, for all practical purposes, it is no longer in effect. (The funding recaptured under the UDAG program in 1990 (approximately $50 million) was transferred to the Community Development Block Grant program.) The program is nevertheless described in general outline because some on-going projects are still using UDAG funds.

While regulatory authority for implementing the UDAG program was vested in HUD's Office of Community Planning and Development, many crucial decisions were made at the local level, including how aggressively the local government will compete to obtain UDAG funds from the federal government. The UDAG program was a large federal development assistance undertaking, both in dollars expended and the number of projects funded, but funding became increasingly competitive as appropriations were reduced and more communities became aware of the prospective benefits of UDAG support. The purpose of the UDAG program was to provide sufficient public financial support for individual qualifying projects so as to spur private investment. In this sense, UDAGs were a catalyst. They could not be the sole source of a project's support, but did leverage their financing with other private or public funds committed to

---

[5] 42 U.S.C.A. § 5318 (West 1983 & Supp. 1991).

a project. UDAGs were designed to bridge the gap between the return on investment a private investor could expect in a profitable location and that anticipated in a deteriorated area.[6] Support from UDAG funds were therefore available only when necessary to bring a project to fruition.

New York City, for example, has loaned UDAG funds to project developers at rates that are generally below the market rate, under the auspices of the New York City Economic Development Corporation. UDAG funds have been used in New York City for acquisition of land and acquisition, construction, and replacement of buildings. The loans have been sizable; their average amount is $300,000.

Under the provisions of the Housing and Community Development Act of 1987, 65 percent of funds would be awarded on the basis of area economic distress and project merit and 35 percent would be awarded on the basis of merit alone.[7] Although specific criteria varied somewhat depending upon the size of the recipient community, these general categories were employed to evaluate economic distress: (1) the percentage of housing constructed before 1940, (2) per capita income change, (3) the percentage of poverty, (4) population growth lag or decline, (5) job lag or decline, (6) unemployment, and (7) unemployment criteria used to establish the Labor Surplus Area designation.[8] Standards for project merit included: the ratio of private funds committed to grant monies; number of permanent jobs created, especially for low-income persons and minorities; and job training provided.[9] In addition, to achieve eligibility, a locality must have "demonstrated results in providing housing for low- and moderate-income persons and in providing equal opportunity in housing and employment for low- and moderate-income persons and members of minority groups."[10]

4.1.4 Community Development Block Grants

Community Development Block Grants (CDBGs)[11] are also administered by HUD's Office of Community Planning and Development. These grants are designed to assist communities in meeting development needs, particularly by providing housing to their citizens, enhancing both their neighborhood and business environments, and broadening economic opportunities for low- and middle-income individuals. One of the objectives of the program is the restoration and preservation of buildings of special

---

[6] *A Handbook on Historic Preservation Law* 324 (C. Duerksen ed., 1983) [hereinafter *Handbook*].
[7] 42 U.S.C.A. § 5318(d)(4).
[8] 24 C.F.R. § 570.452 (1991).
[9] 42 U.S.C.A. § 5318(d)(1)(C).
[10] *Id.* § 5318(b)(1).
[11] Statutory authorization for CDBGs is found in 42 U.S.C.A. §§ 5301–17 (West 1983 & Supp. 1991).

value for historic, architectural, or aesthetic reasons.[12] In recent years, about one-third of all CDBG funds have been spent on projects with some rehabilitation component. In FY 1987, the CDBG program was funded at a total of $3.8 billion, of which $3 billion represented new appropriations and $804 million constituted carryover and recapture funding. New appropriations of approximately $3 billion were approved for each of fiscal years 1988, 1989, and 1990, new appropriations of $3.2 billion were approved for FY 1991, and new appropriations of $3.4 billion were approved for FY 1992.

Metropolitan cities, urban counties, certain units of local government, and suburban areas are eligible for these funds, although the requirements for cities of differing populations vary. Communities with a population exceeding 50,000 receive the grant as an entitlement; the amount of grant assistance is determined by a statutory formula. Other entitlement recipients are central cities of federally designated standard metropolitan statistical areas (SMSAs) and urban counties with a population of more than 200,000 excluding entitlement cities. Communities with a population of less than 50,000 are eligible on a competitive basis. Although the actual applicants are units of state, county, and local government, the benefits are intended to pass through to low- and moderate-income residents (generally defined as families with less than 80 percent of the median family income for the area). Grantees must spend at least 70 percent of the funds they receive on activities to benefit these residents.

There are many possible uses of CDBGs for rehabilitation projects. Communities develop their own programs and funding priorities consistent with federal standards and the program's primary aims of benefiting low- and moderate-income persons, eliminating blight or slums (or preventing their formation), and meeting urgent community development needs. Localities exercise significant discretion. Some of the activities that communities may fund for rehabilitation purposes include acquisition of property, relocation, code enforcement, energy efficiency maintenance, rehabilitation counseling, direct expenditures for rehabilitation of residential and nonresidential structures, and the establishment of revolving funds for these purposes. Moreover, the regulations specifically provide that "CDBG funds may be used for the rehabilitation, preservation, and restoration of historic properties, whether publicly or privately owned." Not all publicly owned buildings, however, are eligible for CDBG funds. Such funds cannot be used for the preservation of "buildings for the general conduct of government." Accordingly, city halls, state houses, and municipal buildings are ineligible.[13] Historic properties are defined to include those listed or eligible for listing on the National Register,

---

[12] *Id.* § 5301(c)(7).
[13] *Id.* § 5305(a)(2).

those listed on a state or local inventory of historic properties, or those designated as state or local landmarks or historic districts.[14]

Communities may use the funds to support their own rehabilitation projects, or they may contract with other local agencies or nonprofit organizations to carry out all or part of their neighborhood revitalization programs. Communities may also designate subgrantees, such as neighborhood-based nonprofit organizations, Section 301(d) Small Business Investment companies, or local development corporations, to engage in projects designed to revitalize a neighborhood or enhance community economic development. CDBG funds may also be used by cities to provide financial assistance to profit-making businesses to engage in these activities, so long as they meet program objectives.

Citizen participation regarding the use of CDBG funds is required. Grantees must submit and certify compliance with a citizen participation plan that meets each of six goals.[15] The plan must encourage participation by low- and moderate-income citizens; provide for reasonable and timely access to local meetings, information, and relevant records; allow for technical assistance to representatives of low- and moderate-income citizens who wish to submit proposals for CDBG projects; provide for adequate notice of hearings to be held at various stages of the program; accommodate non-English-speakers if a substantial number are expected to attend the hearings; and require timely written response to written complaints from citizens.

CDBGs offer greater flexibility than any other community development program. Financial assistance may take the form of grants, loans, loan guarantees, interest subsidies on private loans, or principal-subsidized loans.

In New York City, one use of federal community development funds has been to provide low-interest home improvement loans. Low- and moderate-income families who are owner-occupants of one to four-unit homes are eligible to borrow up to $10,000 for such purposes as rehabilitation. If the home is in a historic district, the city's Department of Housing Preservation and Development will provide assistance in meeting the Landmarks Preservation Commission's standards for approval of the work. Application for the loans is made at participating lending institutions which provide Federal Housing Administration Title I loans, discussed in § 4.1.5. Supplementing commercially available moneys with public funds allows a reduction of interest rates to well below the market rate. Beaumont, Texas, has used a CDBG to create a Historic Preservation Loan Program.[16]

---

[14] *See* 24 C.F.R. § 570.202(d) (1991).

[15] 42 U.S.C.A. § 5304(a)(3); 24 C.F.R. § 570.301(b) (1991).

[16] For a description of the project, see "Loan Program and Tax Abatements in Beaumont, Texas," *Preservation L. Update* (Nat'l Ctr. Preservation L., Washington, DC), Dec. 28, 1990.

4.1.5 Federal Housing Administration Insurance Programs

The Federal Housing Administration (FHA) administers a large number of guaranteed and insured loan programs. By sharing the risks involved in extending credit with private lenders, the government hopes to encourage a better flow of financing for targeted activities. FHA loan insurance programs require the benefited projects to meet HUD standards for rehabilitation. These standards are expressed either as minimum design criteria (including construction standards) or as minimum property standards.

Under the Title I Home Improvement Loan Insurance program,[17] HUD insures loans that applicants obtain through private lending institutions for improvements, repairs, and alterations of both residential and commercial buildings. Participating private lenders process applications and determine eligibility criteria. Loans may be extended up to $8,750 per unit, to a maximum of $43,750 in a multiple-unit building. Single-unit structures can receive a maximum of $17,500 ($20,000 where financing the installation of a solar energy system is involved). To finance the preservation of a historic structure, a loan not to exceed $15,000 per family unit may be insured. The maximum term of the loan is 15 years.

The Historic Preservation Loan Program[18] insures loans for rehabilitation of properties either listed on the National Register or certified by the Secretary of the Interior as meeting National Register criteria. Administered by HUD, this program is a variant of Title I property insurance designed to stimulate lending in depressed areas.[19]

Rehabilitation Mortgage Insurance, also known as 203K loans,[20] represent another program that may be available as a source of rehabilitation funds. Through the FHA, HUD provides loan guarantees and insurance to protect lenders against loss on residential financing. These loans may be provided to individuals to finance both the acquisition and rehabilitation of one to four-family dwellings. In addition, the loans may be used to refinance outstanding debts from rehabilitation activities.

4.1.6 HUD Housing Programs as Rehabilitation Incentives

Housing assistance programs provide an incentive to rehabilitate building sites either through direct loans, loan guarantees, or rent subsidies. In theory, the latter provide an indirect incentive to rehabilitate because an owner, after rehabilitating, can (subject to local rent control or stabilization laws) charge low- and middle-income tenants the market rate for these units and the federal government will cover the difference between

---

[17] 12 U.S.C.A. § 1703 (West 1989 & Supp. 1991).

[18] *Id.*

[19] *See Handbook, supra* note 6, at 313–14.

[20] 12 U.S.C.A. § 1709(k) (West 1989).

this market rate and a fixed percentage of the tenant's income. However, the bulk of federal rental subsidies were provided through HUD's Section 8 housing assistance payments program.[21] In 1983, that program was amended to deny further funding for new construction or for substantially rehabilitated housing. The moderate rehabilitation program remained in effect, but the Section 8 program overall no longer provided much assistance for preservation and restoration of old and historic buildings. Two new programs were enacted in 1983, however, as part of the Housing and Urban/Rural Recovery Act,[22] and were designed to fill part of the void left by the restriction of Section 8 assistance.

In late 1990, Congress enacted the Cranston-Gonzalez National Affordable Housing Act[23] (1990 Housing Act), a comprehensive act that both instituted major new programs and revised existing national housing programs. The 1990 Housing Act repealed the 1983 programs, as well as the Urban Homestead program.[24] In addition, the Section 8 Moderate Rehabilitation grant program was terminated except for grants for single room occupancy dwellings under the Stewart B. McKinney Homeless Assistance Act. However, because binding commitments entered into prior to October 1, 1991, will be honored, the programs are discussed next.

Three major programs available for historic preservation repealed by the 1990 Housing Act were the Housing Development Grants program, the Rental Rehabilitation program, and the Urban Homestead program. Patterned after the UDAG program, Housing Development Grants (HODAGs)[25] were awarded by HUD to localities which, in turn, provide funds as grants or loans to sponsors of new construction or substantial rehabilitation projects, including historic preservation. Subsidies were used for rental, cooperative, or mutual housing projects and could fund up to 50 percent of construction or rehabilitation costs. Funding was available to 1,470 cities nationwide, based upon the extent of housing built before 1940 occupied by low-income households, overcrowding among those households, the level and duration of rental housing vacancies, and the need for new housing. Projects receiving assistance had to remain as rental housing for at least 20 years.

Appropriations for this program were modest in comparison to those which had been available under Section 8. Two hundred million dollars was available in FY 1984, and $115 million in FY 1985. As of the first application deadline, August 14, 1984, $510 million in grant funds had been requested. In fiscal year 1987, HODAG funding consisted of $99.5 million of new appropriations and $10 million of recaptures. Appropriations for the program were decreased to $75 million for each of fiscal

---

[21] 42 U.S.C.A. § 1437f, *repealed by* Pub. L. No. 98–181, 97 Stat. 1153 (1983).

[22] Pub. L. No. 98-181, 97 Stat. 1153 (1983).

[23] Pub. L. No. 101-625, 104 Stat. 4079 (1990).

[24] *Id.* § 289, 104 Stat. 4128.

[25] 42 U.S.C.A. § 1437*o* (repealed 1990).

years 1988 and 1989 in the Housing and Community Development Act of 1987.[26] The Act terminated the HODAG program altogether as of October 1, 1989.[27]

The Rental Rehabilitation Program was also enacted in 1983.[28] As amended by the Housing and Community Development Act of 1987, the program provided funds for rehabilitation of privately owned property or property that would be privately owned after rehabilitation.[29] Funds were awarded by formula, not competitively, to states and eligible localities. The appropriation for each of fiscal years 1988 and 1989 was approximately $125 million, and the appropriation for fiscal year 1991 was approximately $70 million.[30]

Rehabilitation projects undertaken pursuant to this program must have been located in low-income neighborhoods.[31] In addition, the rehabilitation could not cause the involuntary displacement of low-income families by families that are not low-income.[32]

The Housing and Community Development Act of 1987 amended the Rental Rehabilitation Program in a number of additional ways benefiting grant recipients. Most important was an amendment permitting grant recipients to use up to 10 percent of their grants for administrative costs.[33] The prior ban on use of grant monies for administration of the program often foreclosed participation by eligible localities that could not afford to run the program.

The new amendments also increased the per-unit average limit on grants. The higher limits provided a greater incentive to rehabilitate larger units and made it easier to market the program to developers. Grants for moderate rehabilitation could cover as much as 50 percent of rehabilitation expenses, up to a maximum of $5,000 per unit for a unit with no bedrooms, $6,500 per one-bedroom unit, $7,500 per two-bedroom unit, and $8,500 per unit for a unit with three or more bedrooms. In areas of high costs, the Secretary could adjust these limits upwards.[34] Moderate rehabilitation funds could be used only to correct substandard conditions, make essential improvements, or repair major systems in danger of failure.[35]

---

[26] *Id.* § 1437*o*(a)(3).
[27] Housing and Community Development Act of 1987, Pub. L. No. 100-242, § 152, 101 Stat. 1815, 1855 (1988).
[28] 42 U.S.C.A. § 1437*o*.
[29] *Id.* § 1437*o*(a)(1)(A).
[30] *Id.* § 1437*o*(a)(3).
[31] *Id.* § 1437*o*(c)(2)(B).
[32] *Id.* § 1437*o*(c)(2)(F).
[33] *Id.* § 1437*o*(h)(2).
[34] *Id.* § 1437*o*(c)(2)(E).
[35] *Id.* § 1437*o*(c)(2)(D).

A third amendment established a two-year rural rehabilitation demonstration program. States participating in the demonstration were authorized to reallocate unused program funds from prior fiscal years to areas receiving Farmers Home Administration housing assistance. The demonstration, originally planned to run only until September 30, 1989, was extended until September 30, 1991.[36]

Under the Urban Homesteading program,[37] individuals could obtain properties at low cost from local governments by agreeing to rehabilitate them to code standards within 3 years. They also had to agree to live in the rehabilitated building for a minimum of 5 years. Title was conveyed after the 5-year period expired. Properties that were used for the homesteading program generally were transferred to the local government from the federal government through HUD, the Veterans Administration, the Federal Housing Administration, or the Farmers Home Administration, which acquired the properties through foreclosure in their mortgage programs. HUD issued new Urban Homesteading regulations which gave priority to prospective homesteaders whose current housing failed to meet applicable local health and safety standards, who currently paid more than 30 percent of their adjusted gross income for rent, and who had little prospect of obtaining improved housing within the foreseeable future.[38]

The 1990 Housing Act, while terminating each of the three programs just discussed, creates several new important programs. The central feature of the new legislation is the HOME program, for which Congress authorized appropriations of $1 billion for FY 1991 and $1.5 billion for FY 1992. The HOME program is designed to assist participating state and local governments carry out comprehensive housing strategies. In order to participate and receive funding under the HOME program, a state or local jurisdiction will have to comply with procedures established by the Secretary of HUD.[39] The National Homeownership Trust and the HOPE grant program are among the other programs established under the 1990 Housing Act; these programs are designed to help low and moderate income families purchase their first homes by providing them with grants and other financing assistance. Programs for persons with special needs (including the elderly, persons with disabilities, and persons with AIDS) are among other programs established under the 1990 Housing Act.

Several features of the HOME program should effectively encourage rehabilitation. Pursuant to Section 212 of the 1990 Housing Act, HOME funds are available for, among other things, "moderate or substantial rehabilitation."[40] Participating jurisdictions will generally be required to give a preference to rehabilitation of substandard housing; however,

---

[36] Housing and Community Development Act of 1987 § 311.

[37] 12 U.S.C.A. § 1706e (repealed 1990).

[38] *See* 24 C.F.R. §§ 590.1–590.31 (1991).

[39] *See* 24 C.F.R. §§ 91.1–91.99 (1991); 56 Fed. Reg. 34,094 (1991).

[40] 42 U.S.C.A. § 12742(a) (West Supp. 1991).

they may avoid the preference by establishing that rehabilitation is not the most cost effective way to meet their housing supply needs or that their needs cannot be met through the rehabilitation of existing housing stock.[41]

The 1990 Housing Act also directs the HUD Secretary to develop model programs that participating jurisdictions may adopt, including a rental rehabilitation and rehabilitation loan program.[42] The model rental rehabilitation program will be designed to benefit neighborhoods in which the median income does not exceed 80 percent of the area median income and in which rents are not expected to change materially over time.[43] The amount of a subsidy under the program shall generally not exceed 50 percent of the total rehabilitation cost of the subsidized project, and the program shall generally comport with guidelines specified under the repealed Rental Rehabilitation program discussed above. The model rehabilitation loan program will be designed to make direct loans to finance the rehabilitation of low- and moderate-income single family groups and multifamily residential properties.[44] The Act sets forth additional guidelines for the program and permits the Secretary of HUD to specify, among other things, that the financed property is residential, owner occupied and located in an area that contains a substantial number of dwellings in need of rehabilitation.

Finally, HUD is considering administrative guidelines to determine, on a case-by-case basis, when housing assistance would constitute an appropriate level of assistance when combined with the Low Income Housing Credit discussed in § 1.3, or with assistance from other federal, state, or local government agencies.[45] The guidelines, which are already being applied to some tax credit cases, are to assure that participants in multifamily projects do not receive excessive compensation by combining HUD programs with low-income housing credits, and to assure that new or additional HUD assistance is "not more than is necessary to provide affordable housing after taking account of" any other government assistance.

4.1.7 Farmers Home Administration Programs

Low- and moderate-income households in rural areas are eligible under Farmers Home Administration programs for grants and low-interest loans under the following programs.

When conventional financing for purchasing, constructing, repairing, or rehabilitating a home in a rural area cannot be obtained,

---

[41] *Id.* § 12742(b).
[42] *Id.* § 12743.
[43] *Id.* § 12803.
[44] *Id.* § 12804.
[45] 56 Fed. Reg. 14,436 (1991).

low-interest long-term loans (up to 33 years) may be available to low- and middle-income individuals under the Section 502 program.[46] A town is deemed rural if it has a population of no more than 10,000, is rural in character, and is not closely associated with an urban area. Residents of a town may also be eligible if the town's population is between 10,000 and 20,000 persons and it is outside an SMSA. Applicants living in suburbs are eligible.

The maximum loan varies depending on the state of the housing market in the particular area. The rate of interest is adjusted to reflect the applicant's economic circumstances.

An owner-occupant of a home in a rural area who does not have the financial resources to qualify for a loan under the Section 502 Rural Housing program may be eligible for a Section 504 loan, grant, or combined loan and grant to repair his home to make it a decent, safe, and sanitary place to live.[47] The loans and grants under this program are, however, fairly small. Eligible individuals may receive a loan no greater than $7,500. If the eligible individual is more than 62 years old, a grant of up to $5,000 is available. Appropriations for the Section 502 programs were approximately $1.31 billion for FY 1990 and $1,276 billion for FY 1991, and $1.62 billion for FY 1992. For the Section 504 loan program, approximately $11.2 million, $11.3 million, and $11.3 million were appropriated for fiscal years 1990, 1991, and 1992 respectively. Appropriations for the Section 504 grant program were $12.5 million for each of fiscal years 1990, 1991, and 1992.

Under the Rural Rental Housing and Loan Program, loans may be awarded or insured for the purchase, construction, or rehabilitation of rental or cooperative housing in rural areas for elderly or handicapped persons, families of low or moderate income, or other persons and families of low income.[48] Direct loans are available to private nonprofit corporations, consumer cooperatives, and Native American tribes. These entities, as well as individuals, profit-making corporations, associations, trusts, and partnerships, are eligible for loan insurance. The type of project usually funded is multiple-unit or cooperative housing. The loans may not exceed the development costs or the value of the security, whichever is less, and are available for a maximum term of 50 years.

On a smaller scale, the Farmers Home Administration extends direct long-term loans (up to 40 years) to construct, enlarge, expand, or rehabilitate existing community facilities.[49] Facilities must be located in rural areas or in towns with populations of no more than 20,000. The public use facility must be one which provides an essential service, such as a library, hospital, fire station, transportation center, or community building

---

[46] 42 U.S.C.A. §§ 1471, 1472 (West 1978 & Supp. 1991).

[47] *Id.* § 1474.

[48] *Id.* § 1485.

[49] 7 C.F.R. § 1942.1-.20 (1990).

providing social, cultural, or recreational benefits. Eligible applicants for the loans include nonprofit organizations and units of local governments, including special purpose districts such as school districts. Housing grants are also available for rehabilitation of housing in rural areas. The grants may be used to rehabilitate existing single-family housing that is owned by low- and very low-income persons and families or rental properties or cooperative housing serving low- and very low-income occupants, if the cooperative has a membership resale structure that enables it to maintain affordability for persons of low income. Private nonprofit organizations, Indian tribes, general units of local government, counties, states, and consortia of other eligible grantees may apply for such grants.[50]

4.1.8 Access to Credit

Many preservation projects require access to credit. Unfortunately, credit has not always been forthcoming for neighborhood revitalization, often because banks have been reluctant to make loans for projects in rundown neighborhoods.

For this reason federal laws were enacted to monitor the availability of funds for projects in these credit-starved neighborhoods. The federal role in this regard is carried out through the Community Reinvestment Act (CRA).[51] Under the CRA, a lender must help to meet the credit needs of all the neighborhoods in its community, including moderate- and low-income neighborhoods. Agencies which exercise supervisory responsibilities over financial institutions, such as the Federal Reserve Board, the Federal Deposit Insurance Corporation, the Comptroller of the Currency, and the Federal Home Loan Bank Board must consider a financial institution's credit and investment practices in the community when the bank or other lending institution applies for a new branch, relocation of a home or branch office, bank corporate reorganization (such as merger or consolidation with another financial institution) or charter. If the financial institution is found to be "redlining"—that is, uniformly denying credit to applicants in particular neighborhoods—the agency can deny the lender's application.

Where neighborhoods have been "disinvested" by lending institutions, these laws can provide a valuable tool to end this discriminatory practice. In Richmond, Virginia, the threat of using Community Reinvestment Act sanctions helped bring bank executives to the negotiating table. The result was a commitment to improve credit policies in neighborhoods where investments had not occurred. The bank promised to lend 20 percent of the dollar amount of mortgages and rehab loans for the entire city to disinvested neighborhoods, to advertise the availability of this credit

---

[50] 42 U.S.C.A. § 1490m (West Supp. 1991); 7 C.F.R. § 1944.651–.690 (1990).

[51] 12 U.S.C.A. §§ 2901–05 (West 1989).

to residents of the targeted areas, and to sell $5 million worth of tax-exempt bonds annually through state and city housing authorities, with proceeds to go to prospective homebuyers in the most distressed areas.

4.1.9 Financing for Commercial Projects

The Small Business Administration (SBA) provides direct and guaranteed/insured loans to low-income persons or small businesses which cannot acquire business financing through normal lending channels.[52] This program does not have as its primary intent the rehabilitation of historic and old buildings, yet many of these buildings are suitable for small business use and are located in areas of high unemployment. Thus, these funds could be used to serve rehabilitation purposes. Although federal funding for this program continues, there has been an effort to shift its emphasis away from providing any direct loans and toward providing assistance exclusively in the form of loan guarantees or insurance. Applicants for SBA loans must apply directly to commercial banks.

Once an important source of rehabilitation funds, the development programs of the Economic Development Administration that could be used for rehabilitation activities have now been all but eliminated. Several years ago the Department of Commerce's economic development and public works programs provided a broad package of financial assistance to aid rehabilitation projects. The programs sought projects that produced jobs and contributed to a community's economic development, and were used across the country to revitalize communities, and to acquire and renovate all types of old buildings, including factories, warehouses, courthouses, and hotels. A description of these programs follows, but as in other areas it must be noted that appropriations generally have been severely slashed or are nonexistent.

Public Works and Development Facilities grants and loans[53] are directed toward economic revitalization and improving employment opportunities. To achieve the aim of long-term economic expansion, projects that will attract business or will recycle old industrial and commercial facilities are favored. Rehabilitation of public service facilities and downtown revitalization projects are such eligible activities. States, counties, and towns, and public and private nonprofit organizations may apply for assistance for these projects.[54]

Special Economic Development and Adjustment Assistance grants, known as Title IX grants,[55] are available to assist state and local governments in reversing declining economic conditions in their areas. Regions of the country facing long-term economic deterioration are aided

---

[52] 15 U.S.C.A. § 636 (West 1976 & Supp. 1991).

[53] 42 U.S.C.A. §§ 3131–44 (West 1977 & Supp. 1991).

[54] Funding availability and selection criteria as described at 51 Fed. Reg. 3144 (1986).

[55] 42 U.S.C.A. §§ 3241–45 (West 1977 & Supp 1991).

by grants to plan activities, including recycling of land and structures, which will assist in the creation of jobs. Preservation and rehabilitation projects are quite compatible with the program's aims. Funds may be used to develop plans to revitalize aging downtown districts or residential neighborhoods. Grants may be used to establish a revolving fund for these purposes, as well as for specific preservation activities. Economic development grants may be available for rehabilitation projects in areas that are designated as redevelopment areas, or in areas that have a substantial need for such assistance.[56]

States, cities, and counties, public and private nonprofit corporations, and Native American groups are eligible. The funding level of the grants is based on the community's economic needs.

4.1.10 Special Purpose Funding

Those seeking financial aid should consider all possible relationships between the work that has to be accomplished and the wide range of subjects that government programs touch. As previously noted, in most instances the major purpose of these governmental programs is something other than rehabilitation or development, but a rehabilitation project can be structured to take advantage of the funding which the programs provide. For example, the Department of Transportation (DOT) may not seem to be a likely source of preservation funds, but if a project pertains to old public transportation facilities or structures, assistance from DOT may be available.

Consider the Amtrak Improvement Act of 1974.[57] In this program, administered by DOT, federal funds are provided for adaptive reuse of old railroad stations that are listed or eligible for listing on the National Register. Many communities have such stations, which are often run-down and abandoned. Frequently they are located in the heart of the town's downtown area, so that rehabilitation of the railroad depot can be an important step in revitalizing the entire downtown. The Amtrak Improvement Act does require that after renovation the station be used for a transportation function, such as a mass transit station for bus, subway, or light railroad. Nevertheless, whether the station is placed back into service to the community as a transportation center or station with help from this act or as a private commercial establishment with the support of other programs, preservation objectives have been furthered.

Another illustration of a program that could be exploited is one established by the Surface Transportation Act of 1978.[58] This act authorizes the identification of bridges of historical significance by DOT, with the assistance of the State Historic Preservation Office, and provides grants

---

[56] *Id.* § 3151.
[57] 49 U.S.C.A. app. § 1653(i) (West 1991).
[58] 23 U.S.C.A. § 144 (West 1990).

for rehabilitation or replacement of these bridges. Most of the grants so far have been used to fund replacement rather than rehabilitation, but the program need not be so limited.

Other funding opportunities exist as well. It may be helpful to analyze a rehabilitation project in terms of the many smaller discrete tasks of which it is composed. Thus, although the Department of Energy will not make funds available to underwrite full rehabilitation projects, it will assist with the portion of rehabilitation that involves windows and insulation.[59] Other portions of the rehabilitation project may involve the jurisdiction of other departments and agencies. The National Endowment for the Arts supports activities in the fields of architecture, urban design and planning, landscape architecture and other related areas.[60] Under the Design Arts Program, for example, activities such as adaptive use studies and district revitalization planning are eligible for grants.

Similarly, the National Endowment for the Humanities, whose purpose is to further research, education and projects in the humanities, assists programs related to history.[61] Preservation projects that further public understanding of history, whether of a geographic area or a conceptual area such as architecture, may find funding support here. Funding may also be available under the Coastal Zone Management Act for the "rehabilitation of historic buildings and structures" along the nation's coastline.[62]

4.2 PUBLIC FINANCING: STATE AND LOCAL AID

As with regulatory protection for historic sites, many important programs relating to preservation funding are carried out at the nonfederal level. This is largely due to the federal government's delegation of many of the decisions and much of the administration of its programs to nonfederal levels of government, which has caused a number of communities to create local funding sources.

The types of funding available at the state and local level are wide-ranging. Particularly popular is the revolving fund (discussed more fully later in this chapter), because of its ability to regenerate itself for further preservation activities through repayment of the loans it awards. Many states, local governments, and nonprofit corporations have developed revolving funds to obtain maximum benefit from their scarce resources.

Other strategies include direct loan programs or loan guarantees or subsidies, as well as seed grants to get projects started. Indirect financing through income and property tax relief, as discussed in **Chapter Five**, has

---

[59] *See, e.g.*, 42 U.S.C.A. § 8231 (West 1983).
[60] Statutory authority for these grants is found at 20 U.S.C.A. § 954 (West 1990 & Supp. 1991).
[61] Statutory authority for these grants is found at 20 U.S.C.A. § 956 (West 1990 & Supp. 1991).
[62] 16 U.S.C.A. § 1455a(c)(2)(B) (West 1985).

also worked successfully and is available in a number of areas. Even those areas which have found it impossible to make funds available directly because of budgetary constraints, can and do provide in-kind aid through, for example, expert architectural, survey, historical, and design assistance and advice.

4.2.1 Funding Sources

State and local governments wishing to support preservation activities must first determine how to raise necessary funding. Many communities which have not already allocated tax revenues for preservation and rehabilitation financing may find it politically difficult to raise taxes or implement new taxes or special assessments for preservation activity. The ability to utilize tax revenues will vary depending on the community and on the degree of public awareness of the benefits that can accrue to the community from preservation programs.

Another source of revenue for preservation activities is the sale of municipal bonds. Such bonds are attractive to investors because the interest is tax-free, thus allowing the municipality to sell them at an interest rate lower than that for taxable bonds. Several types of bonds are typically used: revenue bonds, to be paid from the earnings of the projects which they support; general obligation bonds, to be paid back from general tax revenues; and special assessment bonds, to be paid back from anticipated specific revenue sources.

The 1986 Act imposed significant new restrictions on the use of tax-exempt bonds that reduce the availability of such bonds to finance historic preservation projects. With certain exceptions, the new restrictions apply to bonds issued after August 15, 1986. The new rules are complex, and only some of the more generally applicable requirements will be discussed here.

The 1986 Act created a new category consisting of "private activity" bonds.[63] A bond is a private activity bond if (1) more than 10 percent of its proceeds are used in the trade or business of an entity other than a state or local government and (2) more than 10 percent of its debt service is attributable (either directly or indirectly) to such a private use.[64] If the private business use is not related or disproportionate to the governmental use, even more stringent rules apply. A bond is also considered a private activity bond if more than 5 percent of $5 million of its proceeds are used to make loans to nongovernmental persons or to acquire nongovernmental output property.[65] Once a bond is categorized as a private activity bond, certain limitations apply in order for bond interest to be tax exempt. For example, at least 95 percent of net proceeds must be

---

[63] I.R.C. § 141 (West Supp. 1991).
[64] *Id.* § 141(b).
[65] *Id.* § 141(c),(d).

used to pay qualified project costs. Moreover, the volume of tax exempt private activity bonds that may be issued within each state on an annual basis is limited to $75 per resident or $200 million, whichever is greater, through 1987; thereafter, the volume cap is the greater of $50 per resident or $150 million.[66] All 50 states were allowed to issue a total maximum of $21.3 billion in private activity bonds in 1987. According to an analysis by the Public Securities Association, this amount is nearly 60 percent less than the states' actual bond volume in 1984.[67]

Private activity bonds can be used only for a limited number of qualified purposes. Multifamily rental housing bonds can be issued if new and stringent low-income occupancy requirements are met.[68] Single-family mortgage revenue bonds and mortgage credit certificates (MCCs) may be issued until June 30, 1992, provided that target requirements on home purchase prices are met, that 95 percent of borrowers are first-time home buyers, and that the purchasers' income levels do not exceed a ceiling set by law.[69] Interest on qualified redevelopment bonds is tax exempt if at least 95 percent of the proceeds are used for redevelopment purposes in designated blighted areas.[70]

One category of bonds qualifying for tax exemption are those for qualified rehabilitation loans. These may be extended to purchasers of property to be rehabilitated, or to the first resident of property after rehabilitation. A qualified rehabilitation is one which takes place at least 20 years after a building is first used, which involves expenditures of at least 25 percent of the mortgagor's adjusted basis in the property, and which meets the retention of walls requirements discussed in § **1.2.5**.[71]

In 1979, Alabama enacted legislation allowing communities to set up local historic preservation authorities to issue tax- exempt industrial revenue bonds.[72] The revenue generated by the sale of these bonds can be utilized to acquire and renovate buildings listed in the National Register. These properties are then leased to developers who pay the debt service on the bonds. When the bonds are paid off, the developer gets title for a nominal fee and an agreement to maintain and insure the properties. The program has been successful: In Montgomery alone, 20 buildings were renovated by early 1983.

Maine, New York, and Rhode Island issued bonds to protect historic properties. A $2 million bond issue in Maine helped restore National Register listed properties, owned by the government or nonprofit organizations, which are open to the public. In New York, a portion of the

---

[66] *Id.* § 146(d).

[67] [14 Current Developments] Hous. & Dev. Rep. (BNA) 858 (March 9, 1987).

[68] I.R.C. § 142(d) (West Supp. 1991).

[69] *Id.* § 143, *amended by* Tax Extension Act of 1991, Pub. L. No 102–227 (1991).

[70] *Id.* § 144(c).

[71] *Id.* § 143(k)(5).

[72] Ala. Code §§ 41-10-137, -141(11), -142, -147 (1991).

$250 million allocated to acquire forest and park land, and for historic preservation, was available to support municipal and not-for-profit historic preservation projects.[73] In Rhode Island, $5.5 million of bond was issued to restore the State House. Another $9 million bond issue supported historic and natural resources, at least $2 million of which was allocated to a revolving loan fund for historic rehabilitation projects.[74]

4.2.2 Funding Entities

Many states have created quasi-public corporate entities to finance and undertake development projects by issuing tax-exempt bonds or through other mechanisms. While the projects undertaken by these organizations are rarely targeted at historic preservation directly, economic development programs in older urban areas often serve that goal.

One model of such an entity is the New York State Urban Development Corporation (UDC).[75] The UDC was established to provide a more effective means of dealing with problems of physical deterioration, economic stagnation, unemployment, shortage of housing, and lack of civic facilities in the state. To combat these problems, it is authorized to plan and implement projects to supply housing for low- and moderate-income families, to assist in the industrial and commercial development of areas of high unemployment or economic blight, and to provide needed educational, cultural, community, or other civic facilities. The UDC may finance projects in support of these purposes by issuing tax-exempt bonds and notes as required.

Many of the UDC's projects have involved rehabilitation of old and historic property. In one instance, UDC funding was instrumental in the renovation of the nineteenth-century Customs House in lower Manhattan. A current large-scale UDC project, the revitalization of Forty-Second Street and the Times Square area of Manhattan, is described in detail in **Chapter Eight**.

4.3 NONCONVENTIONAL SOURCES FOR FINANCING REHABILITATION

Even in the best of times, financing a preservation project can be difficult. Conventional sources for construction financing are often wary of what they perceive as the high risk associated with the rehabilitation of older buildings, which may be compounded when the buildings are located in older, more neglected areas which are less obviously capable

---

[73] Environmental Quality Bond Act of 1986, N.Y. Envtl. Conserv. Law § 52-0103(2) (McKinney Supp. 1992).

[74] 4 *Preservation L. Rep.* 1108–09 (1985).

[75] N.Y. Unconsol. Laws §§ 6251–6286 (McKinney 1979 & Supp. 1992).

of yielding a satisfactory return on investment. Accordingly, preservationists and rehabilitators may be well advised to look at some or all of the following as potential revenue sources.

4.3.1 Revolving Funds

When financing in the form of public funding or bank loans is difficult to obtain, a revolving fund can provide an alternative source of capital. This method of financing takes its name from the characteristics that make it distinctive and give it value and flexibility as an alternative financing source. Generally, moneys from a fund are used to purchase threatened historic property, or are loaned to individuals or groups to engage in preservation projects. Through acquisition and subsequent resale with protective covenants, the property may be preserved and the fund replenished. Sometimes the property is rehabilitated prior to resale, while on other occasions agreement may be reached to sell a building as is for subsequent rehabilitation by the new owner. The money that is received from the resale of the property renews the fund, and its availability for subsequent reinvestment provide a continuing source of preservation financing assistance in a community.

The characteristic of recycling funds makes this financing technique particularly suitable for certain projects, such as multiple-building or large multiple-phase developments. In such projects, the limited capital available to complete one phase can generate enough capital to finance the next phase, and so on until the project is completed.

4.3.2 Operation and Administration

Revolving funds have been administered by both public and private entities. While there may be advantages and disadvantages to each, private control has generally been found preferable.[76] Public administration of revolving funds is often hampered by unpredictable budgetary strings, and maintaining a sufficient level of appropriations has proven difficult. Private entities have greater flexibility and can adapt more quickly to changing circumstances without the encumbrances of state or local laws and regulations.

Although other legal entities can be used to administer private revolving funds, they are most often organized as nonprofit, tax-exempt corporations. This requires both incorporation under the appropriate provisions of state law and certification by the IRS of tax-exempt status.[77] Such status provides dual tax benefits: It relieves the organization itself of tax

---

[76] HCRS, *Historic Preservation Fund Grants: Potential Source for Local and Statewide Revolving Funds* (HCRS Supplement 11593, October 1978).

[77] For additional information on tax-exempt status, *see* B. Hopkins, *The Law of Tax Exempt Organizations* (1983).

liability, and permits donors to deduct their contributions for income tax purposes. Moreover, nonprofit status may be necessary to qualify for certain financial assistance. This legal form is most appropriate when the money used to purchase and resell the buildings will be solicited from private donors and charitable foundations. On the other hand, when a major portion of the fund will be composed of public general revenue or block grant funds, it may be necessary to organize a public or quasipublic organization.

A variety of preservation goals may be served by revolving funds, and the objectives of a particular fund should be clearly defined. Revolving funds have been used to save single buildings, limited areas, and entire neighborhoods. Both residential and commercial buildings can be restored, depending upon the needs of the local community.

Next, the fund should formulate an operational plan, with immediate and long-term objectives and procedures to achieve them. Responsibilities should be assigned and coordinated, and the talents of those involved in organizing the revolving fund should be assessed to determine if outside assistance will be required. The purpose of the fund will dictate the responsibilities of its administrators. Functions that will need to be performed include finance (auditing of funds spent and received), construction (planning, architectural design, supervision, and execution of restoration activities), marketing (promotion and sale of restored properties), purchasing, fund-raising, and community and government liaison.

The distribution of authority in the Lafayette Square, St. Louis, Restoration Committee is instructive.[78] The purchase and sale of property must be approved by a 13-member board of directors. The power to grant approval of expenditures for ongoing rehabilitation activities and the responsibility for implementation is held by the vice president for redevelopment. The general membership must approve proposed loans from the revolving fund. When a purchased house has been rehabilitated and is ready for resale, the housing committee chairperson is authorized to sign the contract of sale, after its review and approval by both the redevelopment vice president and the full board.

4.3.3 Funding

A revolving fund must generate a corpus of working capital sufficient to finance basic activities and to insure that the fund never becomes so depleted that its programs must be suspended or terminated. Because sales, rents, and loan repayments will often recoup an amount less than that invested in a property, an effective fund management will require continuing fundraising efforts and the development of financial management strategies to maintain the fund. It should be remembered, however,

---

[78] See Coffey, *Revolving Funds for Neighborhood Preservation: Lafayette Square, St. Louis* 5, 12 (National Trust for Historic Preservation 1977).

that the purpose of the fund is not preservation of a large bank balance, but preservation of historic resources. In some cases, a worthwhile project may not return to the fund all that had been invested. To achieve the fund's aims, its administrators must be sensitive to the fact that not every project can break even, and that requiring every project to do so may jeopardize a fund's ultimate effectiveness.

Initial seed money for a fund may be obtained in the form of grants, gifts, or loans. Government programs, private organizations, foundations, corporations, membership dues, or individual contributions, and in some cases tax revenues[79] are all potential sources of funds. In particular, a number of government programs described earlier can be used to support a revolving fund, including the Urban Development Action Grants, Community Development Block Grants, and Special Economic Development and Adjustment Assistance (Title IX).

Reduced levels of appropriations for these government programs, however, mean that revolving fund administrators, like sponsors of other preservation activities, will increasingly have to look elsewhere for financial support. Because of the localized nature of most revolving fund efforts, fund-raisers should give particular consideration to foundations, corporations, and individuals with an interest in the community to be benefited. These potential sources are discussed later in this chapter.

4.3.4 Preservation Strategies

Depending on the circumstances, the revolving fund may purchase historic property for resale or, on occasion, for rental. The fund may rehabilitate a property itself prior to resale or rental, or may require the purchaser or tenant to commit to rehabilitating the building for reuse. In other instances, it may wish to acquire options to be used to hold property off the market. A revolving fund may also serve as a lender when other sources of loan funds are unavailable. In this capacity, it may provide direct loans, loan guarantees, or participate in the lending of money with other financial institutions.

Resale of unrestored property should be accompanied by restrictions in the deed, and by an agreement for rehabilitation or restoration. The Galveston, Texas, Historical Foundation, for example, uses these two basic legal instruments to protect the property it resells after acquiring it with revolving fund money.[80] Its deed restrictions require that no demolition, exterior changes, or new construction occur without Foundation approval, and that the owner maintain the building exterior and

---

[79] In 1975, New Orleans voters levied a special tax on real property within a targeted area to establish a fund to allocate $200,000 for historic preservation activity over a 2-year period.

[80] Brink, *Commercial Area Revolving Funds for Preservation* 8 (National Trust for Historic Preservation 1976).

its structural soundness. These restrictions bind all subsequent owners of the property. In the written contract, the purchaser agrees to restore the exterior in an appropriate manner and to invest an agreed-upon sum of money to renovate the interior for active use.

A fund should be cognizant of the psychological impact of preservation activities, and use it to full financial and other advantage. Purchases, for instance, should be made quietly lest property prices soar with the disclosure that an area has been targeted for preservation activity. On the other hand, early sales may be made publicly and even at significant loss, to ignite a flurry of preservation activity and to create a positive and exciting atmosphere that may spur further investment. After the anchor projects are set in motion, however, a fund must emphasize recovery of costs to remain financially sound.

4.3.5 Private Foundations

Foundations are a potentially fruitful source of preservation funding. There are thousands of foundations in the United States, so the initial task is to identify those that will look favorably on a request for funds for preservation purposes. Foundation interests can be determined by looking at current funding patterns. Many foundations limit their giving to particular subject areas and geographic locations. Based on these considerations, the would-be recipient should develop a list of foundations with a funding history in the area.

The thousands of foundations generally fall into one of five types:

1. *General purpose foundations.* These are the smallest in number but have the greatest assets and make grants on a broad basis (though usually in accordance with set priorities) to health, education, social welfare, and international activities, among others.
2. *Special purpose foundations.* These give in a specific area of interest and/or restrict their giving to a particular geographic area.
3. *Family foundations.* These are by far the largest in number but are generally much smaller in assets, and are usually concerned with the personal philanthropic interests of the family.
4. *Corporate foundations.* These are the instruments through which corporations make their contributions. They are, in theory, largely independent of the corporations, although in practice they are generally governed by the corporation's officers and directors.
5. *Community foundations.* These entities, committed to the improvement of particular communities, may be especially helpful in supporting local preservation activities. There are more than 250 community foundations in the United States, with total assets of $2.5 billion. They exist in most large cities, but their resources vary considerably. Some small community foundations have no more than a

few thousand dollars. At the other extreme are groups such as the San Francisco Foundation with assets of more than $350 million.

Community foundations are composed of large numbers of individual trusts managed by one "parent" foundation. The donor specifies what, if any, restrictions are to be placed on the trust. The foundation provides professional management of its assets, and a governing board of directors and a professional staff administer its funds.

Community foundations are public charities and thereby offer donors tax benefits not available through other types of foundations. Because their boards and staff are involved in funding other civic activities and projects, they can provide more than money. They can help to negotiate aid from local interests, may serve as a catalyst for other funding sources, and can provide valuable contracts and technical assistance.

Foundation grants can be particularly helpful as seed money for revolving funds. In 1971, a $15,000 grant from the Putnam Foundation started the Historic Preservation Loan Fund of the New Hampshire Charitable Fund. This modest financial beginning has been the catalyst for the fund's participation in the financing of a number of projects. In 1974, for instance, it loaned $40,000 for the adaptive reuse of the 1823 Belknap Mill to convert it into an arts center and office, gallery, and meeting space for the community. Among the many other preservation projects that this fund has participated in was the preservation of the home of Robert Frost.

The job of locating those foundations that may be willing to part with their money is made easier by a number of guides to foundations. A vital resource in this regard is the Foundation Center, a nonprofit educational organization dedicated to providing information to assist those searching for grants.[81] The *Foundation Directory,* and *Grants Index* are two of many publications, reports, and other works published by the Foundation Center or contained in its libraries in a number of cities across the country. These works are helpful in identifying which foundations are giving grants, whom they are supporting, and for what purposes.

A new potential source of both funding and nonmonetary aid is an initiative officially begun on January 1, 1988, by the World Wildlife Fund and The Conservation Foundation. This program, called "Innovation Grants," is intended to "spur new approaches to conservation and sustainable development" and provide local innovation and grassroots conservation organizations. On the financial end, World Wildlife Fund awards grants in the neighborhood of $5,000 to local nonprofit organizations involved in projects with both significant local impact and an innovative character of wider significance. In 1989, 1990, and 1991, the World Wildlife Fund made grants totalling $70,000,

---

[81] The Foundation Center's central library is located at 79 Fifth Avenue, New York, NY 10003. To learn if one of its area libraries is near you, call 800-424-9836.

$75,000 and $75,000, respectively. In 1992, World Wildlife Fund plans to increase funding three-fold and expand the program to support the establishment of conservation areas. The World Wildlife Fund also publishes a book called *Creating Successful Communities: A Guidebook to Growth Management Strategies*. The program considers itself distinctive because it focuses on both cultural and natural assets, so communities should be able to use it as a resource to further historic preservation.[82]

Another particularly valuable tool of the Foundation Center is the COMSEARCH PRINT OUT, a computer-produced guide to foundation giving. Organized by state, the list gives the foundation name and location, the amount it contributed and the recipient, a description of the project, and a source to contact for further information. Moreover, foundation activities are broken down into subject categories. Microfiche file #50 for 1983, for example, is entitled, "Architecture, Historical Preservation/Historical Society." Its scope includes 319 grants with a total value of $12,284,493, made *inter alia* to historical societies, architectural associations, cultural organizations, and governmental and community development organizations for capital support, general operating support, renovations and restorations, and conversion of historic structures into facilities for present-day use. In addition to the Foundation Center publications, the fund-raiser can learn more about funding sources from a foundation's annual report and from IRS information returns, which are available for all private foundations.

4.3.6 Corporate Donations

Private corporations may also be willing to support preservation activities. Their donations are often funneled through corporate foundations set up for the purpose of making charitable contributions. As a general rule, corporations prefer to give their money to activities in communities where they have a presence, such as a headquarters, factory, or regional office. A company with facilities in a particular location has a stake in the development of that community, both for its own economic viability and as a pleasant place for its employees to work.

For example, the Brown-Forman Distillers Corporation donated $100,000 to two neighborhood organizations in Louisville, Kentucky, to rehabilitate property in the residential area near its plant. Similarly, the Atlantic Richfield Company (ARCO) contributed $300,000 to the National Trust to fund inner-city rehabilitation projects in the company's seven regional and headquarter cities—Houston, Denver, Louisville, Philadelphia, Chicago, Dallas, and Los Angeles. Standard Oil of Ohio (SOHIO) has made similar contributions. Another example is corporate support for the revolving fund that the Galveston Historical Foundation has

---

[82] Information supplied by representatives of Innovation Grants, and by a brochure entitled "Innovation Grants," published by the World Wildlife Foundation.

operated since 1973 to restore a historic downtown area known as the Strand. That revolving fund was, in fact, started with grants from the Moody Foundation ($200,000) and from the Kempner Fund ($15,000), both run by companies located in Galveston.

The Foundation Directory, the same basic text as is used in researching foundation grants, is also a good resource for corporate donations. This book can provide answers to questions that arise after a group seeking funding has identified corporations to solicit. For example, it will specify the individuals who make decisions on grant requests, and the guidelines on which those decisions are based. Corporations differ on whether these decisions are made at the headquarters or locally, and knowing whom to approach is useful information for the funding applicant.

4.3.7 National Nonprofit Organizations

Perhaps the most significant sources of nonpublic support for preservation are the programs of the National Trust for Historic Preservation.

The National Trust currently operates four grant and loan programs on an ongoing basis.[83] The Preservation Services Fund provides matching grants to enable nonprofit organizations and public agencies to begin preservation projects.[84] Average grants range between $1,000 and $1,500; the maximum amount awarded under the program is $5,000. Funds may be used to retain consultants, to provide educational programs, to conduct feasibility studies and to plan the reuse of historic buildings. The initial attorneys fees for one of the early historic preservation court victories, *Save the Courthouse Committee v. Lynn*,[85] came from this fund.

The National Preservation Loan Fund provides low-interest loans, loan guarantees, and lines of credit "to assist organizations in creating or expanding preservation revolving funds or initiating real estate development projects to preserve historic buildings, sites, and districts;" assistance provided by the fund may be used "for acquisition, rehabilitation and related capital costs for projects involving historic properties."[86] Loans typically range from $25,000 to $150,000.

The Critical Issues Fund provides matching grants "to nonprofit groups, public agencies and national organizations for research or model projects that address widespread, pressing preservation problems."[87] Matching grants range from $5,000 to $50,000.

---

[83] These programs are administered under authority granted by 16 U.S.C.A. §§ 470a–470h.
[84] Most information in this section was provided by "Grant and Loan Programs," an information sheet issued by the representatives of the National Trust for Historic Preservation.
[85] 408 F. Supp. 1323 (S.D.N.Y. 1975).
[86] "Grant and Loan Programs," *supra* note 84.
[87] *Id.*

The Inner-City Ventures Fund was established "to help community organizations revitalize their historic neighborhoods for the benefit of low- and moderate-income residents, especially minorities" through a combination of grants, loans, and technical assistance for houses and commercial rehabilitation programs.[88] The Fund is not currently accepting applications and is considering revising the program, although its goals remain the same. Interested parties may contact the National Trust to be placed on a mailing list to receive information with respect to the Fund.

In addition to its grant and loan programs, the National Trust operates other programs, including the National Main Street Center. The Center has the goal of revitalizing downtowns in towns and cities of all sizes. More than 600 communities in 31 states have participated in the program since its inception in 1980. The program considers the presence of historic resources in connection with its promotion of downtowns.

4.3.8 Private Fund-Raising and Individual Donors

Finally, preservationists should not overlook the possibility of raising funds through direct contributions from individual donors. By far the largest share of money given to nonprofit organizations in general comes from individual donations, and there is no reason why this source cannot be tapped to support rehabilitation of historic properties.

To encourage donations, fund-raisers should always seek to give contributors a sense of personal involvement in the projects undertaken with their support. One ingenious illustration is provided by New York's Polonia Restoration Company, which sold stone pieces from the walls of the Brooklyn Bridge to raise funds for its restoration. The stones came from a part of a wall being excavated for a new entryway, and thus their removal did not affect the integrity of the bridge.

In seeking private contributions, as well as support from corporations and foundations, the legal status of the preservation organization may be important. Contributors generally prefer to give to groups if their donations will qualify for a charitable deduction for federal and state income tax purposes. For this reason, as just noted, it is advantageous for the recipient organization, if it qualifies, to obtain recognition of its tax-exempt status from the IRS. The IRS recently issued a tax-exemption ruling in favor of a historic preservation organization that was formed exclusively for the purpose of "preserving the historic and architectural character of a community through the acquisition and occasional restoration of historically or architecturally significant properties, and subsequent disposition of these properties subject to restrictive covenants. . . ."[89]

---

[88] *Id.*

[89] *See* Rev. Rul. 86-49, 1986-1 C.B. 243.

Five

State and Local Incentives for Rehabilitation

Complementing the federal tax incentives discussed in **Chapter One** is a broad array of state and local programs designed to encourage rehabilitation of historic buildings. Because state and local regulation affects historic structures in more direct and diverse ways than does federal regulation, the range of preservation programs at those levels is far broader. The approaches generally adopted, like the federal program, rarely involve affirmative financial or other support for preservation activities. Rather, rehabilitated buildings are given special status and treatment under tax and regulatory programs which might otherwise make rehabilitation undesirable or uneconomic.

This chapter discusses those steps taken by state and local government entities to encourage historic preservation in three basic areas—property taxation, building codes, and zoning regulation. Local property taxes often create a major disincentive to the continued use of old buildings, and many states and municipalities have enacted special provisions to ease that burden. Reconciling the health and safety requirements of local building codes with preservation of the aesthetic and architectural integrity of historic structures is often difficult, but a number of constructive legislative efforts have been made to integrate these sometimes conflicting sets of social objectives. Finally, local zoning laws may encourage the demolition of historic buildings in favor of more lucrative uses of property, and many cities have experimented with transfer of development rights programs to ameliorate the problem.

5.1 PROPERTY TAXES

The property tax system, a major source of revenue at the local level, can pose a serious threat to the continued existence of income-producing historic structures. Property taxes are typically assessed on both the value of the underlying land on which a building sits and the value of any improvements (including buildings) that are made on the property. Historic structures are often situated either in downtown areas or in desirable outlying neighborhoods. In either event, land values are likely to be comparatively high, and a substantial return from current uses of a building may be necessary to offset property tax liabilities. Yet historic buildings, by virtue of scale and structure, may not be amenable to high-return uses, and the temptation to replace them with buildings generating greater income may be strong. In addition, rehabilitation of historic buildings increases their value, leading to higher assessed values and tax bills, without necessarily producing a greater income stream.

State and local governments have implemented a wide variety of tax incentives to help save historic structures. Basically, the incentives can be classified either as direct relief from property taxes or as measures that are designed to reduce assessments on historic properties. These programs can have an important effect on the economics of a rehabilitation by both increasing and accelerating projected cash flow.

The tax provisions adopted by different states vary both in the nature and magnitude of the tax benefits they provide.[1] This section will examine a number of state and local tax incentive programs, and highlight the range of provisions that have been adopted. No attempt is made to provide a complete categorization of all the state and local tax incentives that have been implemented; rather, the chapter describes both the typical measures and some innovative approaches that have been developed in a number of jurisdictions.

5.1.1 Exemptions from Real Property Taxation

While a large number of states grant total exemption from property taxes to historic structures, exemptions are generally allowed only in very restricted circumstances.

Thus, some states exempt historic properties from taxation but limit the exemption to specific geographic areas. Puerto Rico has enacted legislation that grants exemption to property owners of rehabilitated historic buildings located in the Old San Juan historic District.[2] An applicant who desires the exemption submits to the Secretary of the Treasury a

---

[1] *See* Powers, "Tax Incentives for Historic Preservation: A Survey, Case Studies and Analysis," 12 *Urb. Law.* 103 (1980), for an extremely useful typology of state property tax incentives. *See also* D. Listokin, *Landmarks Preservation and the Property Tax* (1982).

[2] P.R. Laws Ann. tit. 13, § 551 (1977 & Supp. 1988).

total property tax exemption plan that details the rehabilitation and restoration work to be performed. If the Secretary approves the plans, the site is granted either a 10-year (for complete renovation) or a 5-year (for partial renovation) exemption from taxation. Once the initial exemption expires, the Secretary can extend the exemption provided that the Institute of Puerto Rican Culture certifies that (1) the property has not been substantially altered in its original design; (2) the property deserves to be preserved as part of Puerto Rico's cultural heritage for its historic or architectonic value; and (3) upon conclusion of the work pursuant to the requirements of the Institute, the property will be in equal or better condition than that presented when its first total restoration was carried out. In addition, any proceeds received from leasing a designated building are exempt from income tax.[3]

Tennessee exempts the value of improvements or restoration of a historic structure[4] from property taxes so long as the owner agrees to restore the property under the guidelines that are set out in the statute. Essentially, the restoration must either be part of an official government program or the plan must be approved by a historic properties review board. The exemption lasts for 10 years in the case of a partial restoration and 15 years in the case of a full restoration. At the end of the applicable period, the structure is assessed at its full market value. However, if the structure is significantly altered or demolished during the exemption period, the property owner is immediately liable for the difference between the taxes paid and the tax that would have been due if the structure was assessed at its full market value.[5]

The Tennessee statute is subject to two limitations. First, the law only applies to counties with a population exceeding 200,000.[6] Second, the provisions of the statute only come into effect under the governing body of either the county or a municipality within the county ratifies them by a majority vote.[7]

Another method that has been employed to fully exempt certain properties from taxation is contained in New York City's Historic Landmarks

---

[3] *Id.* A similar tax incentive was enacted as part of the Louisiana State Constitution. Art. XIV, § 22A (until its repeal in 1974 by Art. VII, § 18(C)) created the Vieux Carre Commission and gave it the responsibility of preserving the architecture of the New Orleans Old French Quarter. The New Orleans City Council was authorized to exempt from municipal and parochial taxation buildings which the commission designated as having historic or architectural value.

[4] "Historic structure" is defined as structures on the Tennessee or National Register or approved by a historic properties review board. The board is to designate as historic (1) any structure over 175 years old; (2) any structure over 125 years old unless it is established as nonhistoric; and (3) any structure over 75 years old subject to an individual review. Tenn Code Ann. § 67-5-218(a)(3)(1989).

[5] *Id.* § 67-5-218(a)(4)(B).

[6] *Id.* § 67-5-218(b).

[7] *Id.* § 67-5-218(c).

Act.[8] An owner of a historic structure can file an application with the Landmarks Preservation Commission to demolish or alter the structure if it is not capable of earning a reasonable return. In response, the Commission has two alternatives. First, it can approve the property owner's plan. Second, it can develop a plan which allows a property owner to obtain a reasonable return by granting a full or partial tax exemption and/or remission. If the Board of Estimate approves the tax exemption and/or remission, the Commission can then deny a certificate of appropriateness for alteration or demolition, thereby preserving a building the return on which would otherwise be so low that the Commission would be required to grant such a certificate.[9]

Hawaii grants a property tax exemption to property owners who dedicate their land to public uses.[10] To apply, a landowner petitions the director of taxation. The application sets out the exact area of land that is to be dedicated, states how the land shall be used, and agrees that the land shall be used, improved, and maintained for the sole purpose of furthering the dedicated use. The director must approve the plan and grant the tax exemption, if he or she finds that the use of the dedicated land will have a benefit to the public that is at least as great as the value of the real property taxes for the land.

Once the plan is approved, the owner of the property is granted a tax exemption and forfeits the right to change the use of the land for a period of 10 years. The exemption and the accompanying limitation on the use of the property are automatically renewable indefinitely, subject to the right of either the owner or the director to cancel the exemption by giving 5 years' notice any time after the fifth year of the dedication. Failure to observe the restrictions on the use of the land subjects the owner to cancellation of the exemption. The owner is then liable for the difference between the taxes paid and the taxes that would have been due if there had been no exemption, plus an interest payment of 5 percent per year from the dates that the payments would have been due.[11]

Finally, a number of states provide for tax exemption for historic sites that are owned by historic associations that operate as not-for-profit corporations. For example, New York provides an exemption from taxation for any incorporated historical society that holds a historic site for nonbusiness purposes provided that the society does not hold more than six acres in any one locality.[12] New Jersey exempts from

---

[8] The enabling legislation for this provision is N.Y. Gen. Mun. Law § 96-a (McKinney 1986).
[9] New York City Admin. Code § 25-309 (1986). Note that this procedure is instituted by the Landmark Preservation Commission and not by the owner of the historic property. The provision contains a procedure that will save the building from demolition even if the owner rejects the plan. *See* Section 7.4.5.
[10] Haw. Rev. Stat. § 246-34(a),(b)(1985).
[11] *Id.* § 246-34(d).
[12] N.Y. Not-for-Profit Corp. Law § 1408 (McKinney 1970 & Supp. 1992).

taxation any building that has been certified as a historic site by the Commission of Conservation and Economic Development and that is owned by a nonprofit corporation even if the property is not being used directly for charitable purposes.[13] Ohio exempts historic buildings and sites from taxation when the property is not held for profit and when the site or building is dedicated to public use.[14]

5.1.2 Credit or Deduction Against Real Property Taxes

Another way to provide an incentive for historic preservation is to grant owners of historic property either a tax credit or a tax deduction when they undertake preservation activities.

Maryland has passed a statute that provides tax incentives for historic preservation.[15] The statute enables counties to grant tax credits against local property taxes to help property owners offset the expense of the restoration or preservation of their historic structures. The statute applies to historic structures located in designated historic districts. It allows counties and municipalities to provide property owners with a credit against the local property tax of up to 10 percent of the cost of renovating or restoring qualifying structures. Additionally, it allows counties and municipalities to provide a tax credit of up to 5 percent of the cost of the construction of architecturally compatible new structures in a designated area. Any tax credit earned in any given year can be carried forward for up to five subsequent tax years. A county or municipality can provide further conditions which must be satisfied in order for a property owner to qualify for a tax credit.[16]

New Mexico's tax credit provisions create personal and corporate tax credits for up to half the cost of restoration, to a maximum of $25,000.[17]

5.1.3 Abatement Through a Lower Tax Rate

A number of states have passed statutes that promote the preservation of historic property by taxing the property at a lower rate than other property.

---

[13] N.J. Stat. Ann. § 54:4-3.52 (West 1986). See Town of Morrison v. Women's Club of Morristown, 592 A.2d 216 (N.J. 1991) (ruling that New Jersey's tax provision did not violate the state constitution because the exemption serves a valid public purpose, and a rational basis exists for distinguishing between for-profit and nonprofit organizations).

[14] Ohio Rev. Code Ann. § 5709-18 (Anderson 1991). See also Conn. Gen. Stat. § 12-81(7) (West 1983) (providing property tax exemption for property owned by Connecticut corporations that are organized exclusively for scientific, educational, literary, historical, or charitable purposes so long as the property is being used for these purposes).

[15] Md. Tax-Prop. Code Ann. § 9-204 (1986 & Supp. 1991).

[16] Id.

[17] N.M. Stat. Ann. §§ 7-2-18.2, 7-2A-8.6 (Michie 1991). For a discussion of this and other tax-incentive programs recently enacted in South Carolina and Colorado, see 9 Preservation L. Rep. 1086 (1990).

North Carolina provides for a 50-percent abatement of the property taxes of structures, sites, or landmarks that are designated as historic. Properties can be designated as historic by the passage of a local ordinance; once designated the property is taxed at 50 percent of its true value.[18] The difference between the taxes paid and the taxes that would have been paid without the special classification becomes a lien on the property. The lien is carried in the records of the taxing unit as deferred taxes. If the property loses its designation (except through fire or natural disaster), the additional taxes for the fiscal year that begins in the calendar year in which the disqualification occurs, the additional taxes for the three preceding fiscal years, and the interest that is due on unpaid taxes, all immediately become due.[19]

In Arizona, a property owner may apply to the county assessor to have the property classified as historic for the purposes of taxation.[20] Historic property is defined as real property that is listed in the National Register, and that meets the minimum standards of maintenance established by rules of the State Parks Board.[21] It does not include property on which any business or enterprise is conducted with the intent of earning a profit. The county assessor refers the application to the state historic preservation officer (SHPO), who may view the premises and approve or disapprove the application. If the preservation officer finds that the property is historic, he cannot disapprove the application because of the potential loss of revenue that may result. If the application is disapproved, the property owner can appeal to the tax court.[22]

If approved, the property is classified as historic property indefinitely, subject to declassification initiated by either the taxpayer or the SHPO.[23] Classified property is taxed at the rate of 5 percent of full cash value. This compares with a rate of 30 percent of full cash value for mining and timber property and property used for local telecommunications or for utilities, 25 percent of full cash value for other commercial and industrial property, 16 percent of full cash value for most agricultural property, and 10 percent of full cash value for most private use residential property.[24]

If the historic property becomes disqualified (except by transfer to an exempt organization, by fire or by act of God) a penalty is levied. The penalty is the lesser of 50 percent of the amount that the property taxes were reduced during the current term in which the property has been classified as historic, or 50 percent of the market value of the property.

---

[18] N.C. Gen. Stat. § 105-278(a) (1989).

[19] *Id.* § 105-278(b).

[20] Ariz. Rev. Stat. Ann. § 42-164(A) (1991).

[21] *Id.* § 42-161.

[22] *Id.* § 42-164(B), (E).

[23] *Id.* § 42-164(F).

[24] *Id.* §§ 42-162, 42-227 (Supp. 1991).

An additional penalty of 15 percent of the base penalty is levied if the property owner fails to notify the assessor of the disqualification.[25]

5.1.4 Abatement for Rehabilitation or Renovation

A number of states provide a property tax abatement to help preserve historic property which is renovated or rehabilitated.

South Dakota provides an 8-year "moratorium on the taxation of increased valuation due to restoration or rehabilitation" of qualifying historic property.[26] To qualify, property must either (1) be on the state historic register and have received federal restoration grant-in-aid assistance, (2) have been substantially renovated with financing from the historic preservation loan fund, or (3) have been renovated with private funds with the approval of the state historical society board of trustees. In addition, the property owner must sign a covenant which requires that he, or any subsequent owner, perform maintenance which preserves the restored portions of the property.

Washington State has enacted a special valuation law that excludes the actual cost of rehabilitation projects (the cost of which equals at least 25 percent of the assessed value of the historical property, exclusive of land, prior to rehabilitation) completed within 24 months prior to the filing of an application for such special valuation. The special valuation assessment is valid for 10 consecutive years. Eligible property is historic property that falls within a class of property determined to be eligible by the local legislative authority.[27]

5.1.5 Assessment Based on Current Use of Property

Generally, property is taxed based on its highest and best use. This taxing scheme penalizes owners of historic property because their property often cannot be utilized to its maximum capability. Recognizing this problem, a number of states have enacted statutes that reduce taxes on historic property by valuing the property based on its current use.

California has provisions applying to "qualified historic property." Qualified historic property is private property that is not exempt from taxation and which is visually accessible to the public. In addition, the property must be (1) a registered California historic landmark,[28] (2) a property listed on the National Register, or (3) a property listed on a city or county historic register or inventory. For categories (1) and (2), the

---

[25] *Id.* § 42-165.

[26] S.D. Codified Laws Ann. §§ 1-19A-20, 1-19A-21 (1985 & Supp. 1991).

[27] Wash. Rev. Code Ann. § 84.26 (West 1991).

[28] For landmarks up until Register No. 769, the landmark site must conform to the existing criteria of the California Historic Landmarks Advisory Committee or the State Historic Resources Commission. Cal. Pub. Res. Code § 5031(a) (West 1984).

property must also be either (a) the "first, last, only, or most significant historic property of its type," (b) "associated with an individual or group having a profound influence on the history of California," or (c) "a prototype of, or an outstanding example of a period, style, architecture movement, or construction or . . . one of the more notable works, or the best surviving work in a region of a pioneer architect, designer, or master builder."[29] A city or county, acting on the application of an owner of a qualified historic property, may create a historic zone. The city or county may then contract with the owner of the qualified historic property located within the historic zone. The contract must restrict the use of the property to maintenance of its historically significant character, and must last for a minimum of 10 years.[30] The city or county legislature can cancel the contract after holding a public hearing, if the owner breaches one of the contract's provisions.[31] Finally, the city, county, or any other landowner can bring a court action to enforce the contract.[32]

"Qualified historic property" subject to a historical property contract described in the preceding paragraph is "restricted historical property" which is valued by a complicated capitalization of income method. This contrasts to the normal method of valuing property by evaluation of sales data from comparable properties.[33]

The District of Columbia has enacted a far simpler statute.[34] It applies to land and improvements that have been designated as a historic building by the Joint Committee on Landmarks of the National Capital. This property is assessed on the basis of the current use of the building, if this is less than the building's highest and best use. The District of Columbia can also require property owners to enter into a contract of at least 20 years' duration, that contains reasonable assurances that the property will be used and maintained to encourage the building's preservation. If the contract is violated, the city can collect the back taxes that would have been due if the property had not qualified under this provision, plus interest.

Some states provide for current use assessment for open space lands that include historic sites. The state of Washington, for example, defines open space land to include "any land area, the preservation of which in its present use would . . . preserve historic sites."[35] An owner of a historic site must apply to the county legislative authority, which decides, based on broad general criteria, whether or not to approve the application for

---

[29] *Id.* § 42-161.

[30] Cal. Gov't Code §§ 50280–50281 (West 1983 & Supp. 1991).

[31] *Id.* §§ 50284, 50285. If canceled the owner must pay a penalty equal to 12½ percent of the full value of the property when the contract was canceled. *Id.* § 50286.

[32] *Id.* § 50287.

[33] Cal. Rev. & Tax. Code §§ 439–439.4 (West 1987). Note that § 439.2 provides for different capitalization rates for owner-occupied single-family dwellings and for all other buildings.

[34] D.C. Code Ann. §§ 47-842 to 47-844 (1990).

[35] Wash. Rev. Code Ann. § 84.34.020(1)(b) (West 1991).

classification as open space land. Approval can be conditioned on the owner's meeting specified conditions. If the application is approved, the value of the land for property taxes purposes is determined by the current use of the land and improvements; other potential uses of the property will not be considered. Once approved, a site retains its special status until the owner notifies the county assessor of his intent to withdraw the property from the classification. However, a classified site cannot be applied to another use for at least 10 years. Failure to use the site for the purpose specified in the application results in a penalty equal to 120 percent of the tax that would have been due if the property had not been specially classified.[36]

Nevada also provides for current use assessment for open spaces that include historic sites.[37] Open-space use includes the utilization of land that will preserve historic sites that have been designated by the division of preservation and archaeology of the State Department of Conservation and Natural Resources.[38] An owner of real property can apply to the county assessor for an open-space use assessment. The application is referred to the board of county commissioners (and additionally, if applicable, to the governing body of the city). If the application is approved, the assessed value of the property is determined by calculating 35 percent of the value of the property's open-space use.[39]

5.1.6 Assessment Based on Restricted Property Use

Historic property is often subject to restrictions as to its use. Many states have enacted statutes that attempt to take these restrictions into account by reducing the assessed value of historic properties that are subject to encumbrances.

In Virginia, either individual sites or entire districts can be designated as historic by the Board of Historic Resources.[40] The Board can then obtain a contract with the landowner to limit the use of the landmark in order to perpetuate and preserve its historic character. In addition, the easement must be recorded in the clerk's office of the county or city, and assessments for local taxation must reflect any resulting change in the market value of the property.

West Virginia has a similar procedure. Any county or municipality may create a historic landmark commission that has the power to designate historic landmarks and historic districts.[41] The commission may contract

---

[36] *Id.* §§ 84.34.020-.108.

[37] Nev. Rev. Stat. §§ 361A.040, 361A.220 (1989).

[38] *Id.* § 361A.050

[39] *Id.* §§ 361A.190, 361A.200, 361A.220.

[40] Va. Code Ann. §§ 10.1-2200 to -2207 (1989).

[41] W. Va. Code § 8-26A (1990). A similar tax incentive plan has been adopted by South Dakota. *See* S.D. Codified Laws Ann. § 1-19B-20 to -25 (1985).

with the historic property owner to limit the property's use so as to perpetuate and preserve the features that led to its landmark designation. Once a historic district has been established, the commission must notify the tax assessor and specify the historic sites and the restrictions that the commission has obtained with regard to the sites. The assessor shall then take these factors into consideration when assessing the property.

In Connecticut, a municipality may acquire by any method (including purchase, condemnation, gift, devise, or lease) an interest in an area designated as open-space land which includes land used for historic and scenic preservation.[42] This interest can include outright purchase, easement, or restrictive covenant. The owner of an encumbered property may apply to the assessor, who shall value the property (during the next assessment) to reflect the existence of the encumbrance. An owner who is unhappy with the assessor's evaluation can appeal the determination to the board of tax review and from there to the superior court.

Kentucky also defines open-space land to include "land in an area which is provided or preserved for . . . historic or scenic purposes."[43] Its statute provides for acquisition of any interest in open-space land by local legislative bodies, through any means except eminent domain. Where a local legislature has obtained an encumbrance, the assessment of open-space property must reflect the change in the market value of the land that results from the encumbrance.[44]

In Illinois, municipal authorities have the power to provide for landmark designation of land and structures that have a historical interest or value.[45] In connection with this power, the authority may promulgate regulations that limit the construction, alteration, demolition, or use of the designated properties. Alternatively, the authority can acquire an interest in the land to achieve the same objectives. Any depreciation of designated property that occurs because of encumbrances or restrictions imposed by the corporate authorities shall be deducted from the valuation of the property for property tax purposes.

Finally, New York enacted enabling legislation in 1980 that grants municipalities broad powers to regulate historic sites, districts, or buildings in the interest of preserving their historical, cultural, or aesthetic value. Where necessary to achieve these purposes, a locality may acquire by any appropriate means a "fee or any other lesser interest, development right, easement, covenant, or other contractual right . . . to historical or cultural property within its jurisdiction."[46] The effect of the acquisition of property rights under these provisions "shall be taken into account" in valuing the property for real estate tax purposes.

---

[42] Conn. Gen. Stat. Ann. §§ 7-131b, 7-131c (West 1989 & Supp. 1991).
[43] Ky. Rev. Stat. Ann. §§ 65.410 (Michie/Bobbs-Merrill 1980).
[44] *Id.* §§ 65.440, 65.450, 65.460.
[45] Ill. Ann. Stat. ch. 24, ¶¶ 11-48.2-2, 11-48.2-6 (Smith-Hurd 1990).
[46] N.Y. Gen. Mun. Law § 119-dd (McKinny 1986).

5.1.7 Frozen Assessments

Finally, one state—Oregon—has enacted a statute that has proven quite effective in fostering rehabilitation. Oregon law provides a tax incentive for historic preservation by freezing the value of qualifying historic property for the purpose of the property tax assessment.[47] Historic property is defined as any property that is currently listed in the National Register of Historic Places, that is open to the public for sightseeing for at least one day for each calendar year, and that is maintained in accordance with the standards established by the state historic preservation officer.[48]

In order to be granted the special assessment, the owner of a historic property must submit an application to the county assessor and agree that the SHPO and the members of the state advisory committee on historic preservation can personally inspect the property. Upon receipt, the county assessor forwards the application to the state historic preservation officer. He reviews the application, with the assistance of the state advisory committee on historic preservation. If the property is properly classified as a historic property, the application cannot be denied solely on the grounds that the approval will result in a loss of revenue.[49]

If the SHPO approves the application he notifies both the applicant and the county assessor. The county assessor then classifies the property as historic property. For the 15 consecutive assessment years following the calendar year in which the application was made, he values the property at the true cash value of the property at the time that the application was approved. If the preservation officer denies the application, the property owner has an opportunity for administrative and judicial review.

Historic property can be disqualified by written notice from the property owner to the assessor, sale or transfer of the property to a tax-exempt organization, or discovery (instituted by the county assessor and carried out by the preservation officer) that the property no longer qualifies as historic property. If the property becomes disqualified, a penalty is levied that is equal to the amount that the tax would have increased if the property had not been designated as historic multiplied by the number of years that the assessment was frozen, plus an additional 15 percent (unless the property owner personally notifies the assessor that the property no longer qualifies). The penalty is waived if the property is sold to a tax-exempt organization or if the property is destroyed by fire or an act of God.[50]

---

[47] Or. Rev. Stat. §§ 358.475–.565 (1989).
[48] *Id.* § 358.480.
[49] *Id.* §§ 358.485–.490.
[50] *Id.* §§ 358.515, 358.525.

5.2 LOCAL BUILDING CODES

The rehabilitation of older structures is often complicated by the application of state and local building codes. These codes have traditionally been written with new buildings in mind, and their requirements may be unduly onerous when applied to historic buildings undergoing restoration. Moreover, prescriptive provisions of building codes designed to protect health and safety may necessitate measures that jeopardize character-defining features of historic structures.

A number of different problems can be raised by the application of modern building codes to historic rehabilitation work. The expense of meeting code requirements can sometimes tip the balance away from renovating an existing building and toward construction of a new one. If an older building undergoing rehabilitation is subject to code provisions applicable to new buildings, it may be simpler and cheaper to demolish the existing structure and build a new one instead.

Code requirements may also disrupt or destroy a historic building's texture, architectural details, or even structure. Materials mandated for use in new construction may be incompatible with historic materials. External modifications required for fire egress or handicapped access may impair the appearance or historical integrity of a building facade, as may internal renovations to meet electrical, mechanical, ventilation, or fire detection standards.

In addition, entire building assemblies used in the construction of older buildings but no longer extant may have been dropped from building codes. This may make it impossible for local officials to determine whether outmoded materials or techniques continue to meet safety requirements, or what steps need to be taken to bring them up to acceptable levels. Instead, wholesale replacement may be ordered. Code provisions frequently do permit officials to sanction use of alternative technologies or methods that will achieve the same results as those prescribed.[51] However, a lack of technical basis for determining interchangeability, or simply a resistance to innovation, may make recourse to such provisions difficult to obtain in practice.

An owner contemplating rehabilitation should first determine whether the local building code in his jurisdiction will become applicable as a result of the anticipated work, and if so, to what extent. If code requirements will apply and are likely to be difficult to meet, owners should

---

[51] For example, Section 103.2 of the *Building Officials and Code Administrators International (BOCA) Basic/National Existing Structures Code* (1984) provides the following:

Modifications. When there are practical difficulties involved in carrying out structural or mechanical provisions of this code or of any approved rule, the code official may vary or modify such provision upon application of the owner or the owner's representative, provided that the spirit and intent of the law shall be observed and public welfare and safety assured.

explore whether exceptions or variances are obtainable. Finally, special provisions of local codes, or entirely separate state or local provisions, may apply to historic structures, partially or totally in lieu of general building standards. Sample code provisions are cited here to illustrate typical approaches, but developers must refer to local codes applicable to particular projects.

Local codes may prove especially problematic for developers who anticipate receiving a 20-percent investment tax credit for rehabilitation work. Code provisions may require alterations that cannot be accomplished in conformity with the Secretary of the Interior's Standards for Rehabilitation, which in turn must be complied with to qualify for the 20-percent credit. A project sponsor who plans to seek such a credit at the completion of the project, and who intends to structure financing on that basis, should review building code requirements at an early stage to determine whether it will be possible to undertake a certified rehabilitation within building code strictures.

5.2.1 Applicability to Existing Structures

Typically, building code provisions become applicable to existing structures when they are substantially altered or when they undergo a change in use. An illustration of this general approach is the New York State Uniform Fire Prevention and Building Code (UFPBC), which applies in every municipality in the state that has not enacted an equivalent or more stringent code.[52] The UFPBC becomes applicable when the occupancy or use classification of an existing building changes (as for example, from single-family to multifamily, or from residential to commercial). The regulations regarding building construction contained in the UFPBC become applicable to an existing building when its occupancy or use classification changes (for example, from single-family to multifamily or from residential to commercial) or when it is moved.[53] The building construction regulations also apply to alterations, additions, and repairs made to an existing building, and to an entire existing building "when the cost of any alterations, additions or repairs made within any six-month period exceed 50 percent of the cost of replacement of the build at the beginning of the period."[54] Repairs "for the purpose of maintenance, preservation or restoration," however, may be made "with like or similar materials," provided that they are made in a "safe and sanitary manner" and provided that their cost, when added to the costs of additions and alterations, does not exceed the limit described in the preceding sentence.[55] Historic buildings may be repaired

---

[52] N.Y. Exec. Law §§ 373, 379 (McKinney 1982 & Supp. 1992).

[53] N.Y. Comp. Codes R. & Regs. tit. 9, §§ 1233.1, 1233.2. The UFPBC is reprinted in *id.* §§ 600–1400.

[54] *Id.* § 1231.3(a), (b).

[55] *Id.* §§ 606.3(a)(156), 1231.3(c).

"for the purpose of historical preservation or restoration" without conforming to the UFPBC (except provisions regarding facilities for the physically handicapped), provided the existing use is continued and the repairs are deemed safe by the appropriate local authority.[56]

A new approach has been taken by the Building Officials and Code Administrators International (BOCA), an organization which produces the Basic Building Code, one of the three widely used model codes in the United States.[57] In 1984, BOCA adopted a new Article 25 to its model building code, entitled, "Repair, Alteration, Addition, and Change of Use of Existing Buildings." The new section allows individual code requirements to be waived, so long as the overall degree of safety is equivalent to that under the provisions of the code which apply to new construction. In addition, the new provisions use a numerical rating system to provide an objective evaluation process for determining when minor code deficiencies can be compensated for through alternative methods which exceed other code requirements. Article 25 now appears as Article 32 in a 1987 revision to the Basic Building Code.

Also in 1984, BOCA published the first edition of the Basic/National Existing Structures Code, designed to apply to existing buildings in lieu of new construction codes. The Existing Structures Code provides an independent set of requirements, and specifies that alterations or repairs "may be made to any structure without requiring the existing structure to comply with all the requirements of the code for new construction provided such work conforms to that required by this code."[58] The code is based upon the "Code Enforcement Guidelines for Rehabilitation of Existing Structures" issued by the Department of Housing and Urban Development in 1980, and it remains to be seen how widely accepted this approach will be.

If a local housing code is determined to apply to an existing structure, or to become applicable as a result of a rehabilitation project, it may be possible to appeal the determination of a local building official that onerous work must be undertaken to meet code standards. The BOCA Existing Structures Code, for example, creates an appeals board, and permits appeal by "[a]ny person affected by any notice which has been issued in connection with the enforcement of any provision of this code."[59]

New York law, as part of the implementation of the UFPBC, requires the secretary of state to establish

---

[56] *Id.* § 1233.1.

[57] The Basic Building Code, now retitled the National Building Code, is in general use in the North and Midwest. The other model building codes are the Standard Building Code, used in the South, and the Uniform Building Code, used in the West. Although these model codes are not official documents, they frequently serve as the technical basis for codes promulgated by states and localities.

[58] BOCA Basic/National Existing Structures Code § 102.1 (1984).

[59] *Id.* § 111.1.

a procedure whereby any provision or requirement of the uniform code may be varied or modified in cases where strict compliance with such provision or requirement would entail practical difficulties or unnecessary hardship or would otherwise be unwarranted. Such procedure shall be designed to insure that any such variance or modification shall not substantially affect adversely provisions for health, safety and security, and that equally safe and proper alternatives may be prescribed. Requests for a variance shall be resolved within sixty days of the date of application unless a longer period is required for good cause shown. . . .[60]

5.2.2 Historic Building Provisions

Special building code provisions may exist at the state or local level whose applicability is restricted to historic structures. In some cases, these may be incorporated within new construction codes of general applicability and may restrict or withdraw entirely the application of a code to historic buildings. The UFPBC, for instance, provides that

> [b]uildings which are officially designated as historic buildings, because of historical or architectural importance, shall be permitted to be repaired for the purpose of historical preservation or restoration without conforming to the requirements of the code, provided that the existing use is continued and the repairs are acceptable to and deemed safe by the local authority having jurisdiction, except that requirements for facilities for the physically handicapped shall remain applicable.[61]

The benefits of this provision are somewhat more limited than they might at first appear. "Historic buildings" are defined to include those specifically designated as historically significant at the state or local level, which are listed in the National Register or which are determined by the Secretary of the Interior to be eligible for listing. Thus, for example, buildings eligible for certified rehabilitation as contributing to the significance of a historic district would not be deemed historic for building code purposes. In addition, the provision does not apply if the use of the building is to be changed, often the case in adaptive reuse of older buildings. Moreover, the historic buildings exception only applies to repairs, not to more extensive alterations.

California has taken a different approach, adopting an entire State Historical Building Code (SHBC).[62] The SHBC sets out alternative building regulations which may be applied when a "qualified historical building or structure" is to undergo repairs, alterations, or change in occupancy which would normally bring it within the purview of the local building code of general applicability. "Qualified historical buildings or

---

[60] N.Y. Exec. Law § 381(1)(f) (McKinney 1982).
[61] N.Y. Comp. Codes R. & Regs. tit. 9, § 1233.1 (1985).
[62] Cal. Code Regs. tit. 24, §§ 8-100 to 8-1403 (1987).

structures" are defined as those "deemed of importance to the history, architecture, or culture of an area by an appropriate local, state or federal government jurisdiction."[63]

Among other provisions, the SHBC permits the alteration or repair of historic buildings using original materials, providing no life-threatening hazards are thereby created.[64] It also sets out standards that can be met when it would be impossible for a historic building to conform to general building code requirements without impairing the historic fabric of the building. With respect to handicapped access, for example, the SHBC permits the local enforcement authority to use alternatives to strict compliance with access provisions so long as "reasonably equivalent" access is assured.[65] In "extreme conditions" exemption from the access provisions may be possible, but only if the historical fabric or aspect of the building would be destroyed by meeting access requirements, and equivalent services for the handicapped are offered in a nonexempt location.

Until July 1, 1985, provisions of the SHBC were permissive, not mandatory, and cities or counties in California could choose to apply its provisions as a whole, or to utilize any combination of regular and alternative building code provisions.[66] After that date, however, the alternate provisions of the SHBC became mandatory on state agencies and local building departments. On January 1, 1991, the SHBC again becomes permissive under the statute now in effect.

5.3 TRANSFERABLE DEVELOPMENT RIGHTS

Transferable Development Rights (TDRs) are a land-use technique through which the unused development potential of one piece of property is severed from that property and transferred to an area or site deemed capable of accommodating the increased density. TDRs assist in the preservation of a landmark or other low-density use (such as a theater) by mitigating the economic burden imposed on the landmark's owner.

A property's excess development "rights" consist of the difference between the actual size of the landmark and the larger building size allowed under the zoning law. The unutilized development rights can, under varying forms of restrictions, be purchased by a developer who will be permitted to construct a building on another site that is larger than the zoning regulations governing that site would otherwise allow.

TDR provisions attempt to mitigate economic burdens imposed on the landmark owner who may be unable to exercise the full bundle of development opportunities available under generally applicable zoning rules.

---

[63] *Id.* § 8-302.
[64] *Id.* § 8-1006.
[65] *Id.* § 8-1303.
[66] Cal. Health & Safety Code § 18954 (West 1984 & Supp. 1991).

There can be financial and preservation benefits for the municipality as well. TDRs prevent a loss of tax revenue to the city because the purchasers of the development rights pay taxes based on the increased value of their property attributable to its enhanced development potential. In addition, TDRs are a preservation technique that requires minimal expenditure of public funds. And, because they prevent the current use value of the landmark property from being lost to the owner, they may help to counter opposition to designating a site as a landmark.

The favorable eye cast by the Supreme Court in *Penn Central Transportation Co. v. New York City*[67] on the opportunity to transfer development rights above Grand Central Terminal suggests that a locality might be wise to include TDRs or a comparable mechanism in its preservation ordinance. The majority view, and the better reading of the *Penn Central* decision, holds that conferring landmark status and thereby restricting alteration or demolition of a structure is a legitimate exercise of the police power and does not in itself constitute a compensable taking of property rights.[68] Thus, in most cases, a TDR program should not be deemed essential to assure the constitutional validity of a well-drafted landmarks program. Nevertheless, particularly in localities whose landmark provisions are advisory only and do not bar alteration or demolition of historic structures, TDRs may, as a practical matter, be critical to a successful preservation program.

Moreover, in those communities where the use of TDRs is appropriate, the technique has often gained widespread community support. In Denver, for example, a city zoning provision expanding the transfer and sale of unused development rights from adjoining lots to other locations passed the city council unanimously after receiving broad support from local property owners, civic organizations, and city agencies.[69]

TDRs may not, however, be suitable for all communities. The value of a TDR program is dependent on the availability of a market for the transferable development rights. In some cities no purchasers may be interested in those rights, making a TDR plan at best a symbolic gesture.

Objections to TDRs have been raised on fairness grounds. Some claim that those who work or live in the area that receives the transfer must bear the cost of the more dense environment, while those who work or live adjacent to the landmark enjoy the benefits. This is a concern that should be addressed in determining the size of the transfer district.

---

[67] 438 U.S. 104 (1978).

[68] *But see* Fred F. French Investing Co. v. City of New York, 350 N.E.2d 381, *cert. denied*, 429 U.S. 990 (1976) (holding a taking of property unconstitutional even where the opportunity to transfer development rights is available).

[69] Denver, Colo., Zoning Ordinance §§ 59-364(b)(3), 59-380(b)(1)c (1991). The Denver Zoning Administration has advised that revisions to the language of these sections are currently under consideration.

TDR is a flexible tool, and municipalities can adopt different strategies for its use according to the community's needs. These differences regulate which properties are eligible, where the development rights can be transferred, how much can be transferred, and when transfer can be made. Each city must decide the boundaries of the transferor and receiving zones. Zoning requirements also differ, and this will affect the operation of a TDR program. § **5.3.1** illustrates different approaches taken by several municipalities which have adopted TDR plans.

5.3.1 Eligible Property

The first step in drafting a TDR provision is to define the category of property which the program is designed to protect. A number of definitions, of varying degrees of liberality, can be applied: Federally or locally designated landmarks, Register-listed or eligible properties, or buildings contributing to the significance of historic districts are illustrative of possible classifications. The chosen definition must balance the specific goal of protecting historic properties against the more general zoning goal of controlling the type and density of land use within a municipality or particular target areas (including historic districts), an objective that could be undermined by an overly broad TDR program.

The New York City TDR provision applies generally to "landmark buildings," which are defined to include "any structure designated as a landmark by the Landmarks Preservation Commission and the Board of Estimate" pursuant to the procedures established by the city's preservation ordinance.[70] The New York City Zoning Resolution also has a special provision relating to the Special Theatre Subdistrict, created to preserve New York's well-known Broadway theaters. In that subdistrict, the TDR program applies not only to landmark buildings but to buildings whose interiors are designated as landmarks as well.[71] This could bring many of the theaters, which are currently being considered for interior (but not exterior) landmark status, within the protection of the program.

The applicability of the Dallas TDR ordinance to a given property also depends upon the area in which the property is located. In the central business district, a building's development rights may be transferred if it is a designated historic landmark. In the city's West End Historic District, however, the program applies to any building which "is a contributing structure listed in the National Register of Historic Places."[72]

As amended in 1990, the San Francisco program has the broadest and most elaborate provisions on TDR eligibility.[73] A parcel may qualify as a

---

[70] N.Y.C. Zoning Resolution § 74-79 (1991).

[71] *Id.* § 81-747.

[72] Dallas, Tex., City Code § 51A-4.501(d)(2) (1991).

[73] City and County of San Francisco, Cal., Planning Code art. 1.2, § 128(a) (1990).

"Preservation Lot" from which rights may be transferred if it contains either (1) a "Significant" or "Contributing" building as defined in the Code, (2) a designated landmark, or (3) other eligible structures as set forth in the Code.

5.3.2 Transfer Zone

Perhaps the most significant issue in determining the viability of a TDR program is the size of the transfer zone, the area to which development rights may be transferred. The size of the transfer zone is important because it must include areas suitable for denser development and large enough to provide a sufficient number of potential receiver sites to absorb the transferred rights. Those downtown areas that would typically provide the strongest market for sellers of TDRs are also likely to be the areas in greatest danger of overcrowding. Again, a municipality may be forced into a delicate balancing of zoning and preservation objectives.

Seattle's ordinance, one of the most restrictive, permits transfer only between adjacent properties and properties located across an abutting alley.[74] New York City is slightly more liberal; its TDR provisions also limit transfers to adjacent lots, but define the term adjacent to include contiguous properties, properties across the street from each other, or properties fronting onto the same intersection.[75] Somewhat broader transfer is permitted in particular commercial districts. In those districts, an adjacent lot may be one across the street from a property which is part of a series of properties which includes the lot on which the landmark building is located, all of which are under common ownership. A similar provision applies in the Special Theater Subdistrict.[76]

Some cities do not impose such rigid proximity restriction on TDRs, on the theory that the purposes of the program are better served by allowing transfer to a broader, though still homogeneous, area. Denver, for example, allows unused development rights to be transferred anywhere within the same zoning district.[77] Recipient properties under the Dallas ordinance can be situated anywhere within the city's central business district.[78] San Francisco permits TDRs to be transferred not only to recipient properties but also to intermediary individuals or organizations who may in turn "hold them for subsequent transfer to other persons, firms, entities or to the owners of a Development Lot or Lots" where they may be used.[79]

---

[74] Seattle, Wash., Municipal Code § 24.46.110A (1981).
[75] N.Y.C. Zoning Resolution § 74-79 (1991).
[76] *Id.* § 81-747.
[77] Denver Zoning Ordinance §§ 59-364(b)(3), 59-380(b)(1)c.
[78] Dallas City Code § 51A-4.501(d)(4).
[79] San Francisco City Planning Code art. 1.2, § 128(g).

5.3.3 Rights That Can Be Transferred

To prevent TDR transactions from wreaking havoc with carefully formulated zoning regulations, most programs impose some limitations on the amount of development rights that an individual transferee site can receive. Because of these limitations, it may be impossible to transfer the full bundle of unused development rights from a landmark site to a single receiver site. This handicap can, to a large degree, be ameliorated by permitting TDRs from a single landmark site to be subdivided and transferred to more than one receiver site.

Under New York's TDR program, for example, the size of a building (measured in floor area) which is allowable on an adjacent lot to which development rights are transferred cannot be increased by more than 20 percent, except in certain sections of midtown Manhattan.[80] Unused development rights can, however, be transferred from the site of a landmark building to any number of lots, so long as all transferee lots satisfy the proximity requirements. Once completed, the transfer irrevocably reduces the amount of floor space which can be developed on the site occupied by the landmark. The reduction continues to apply to the lot even if the landmark is demolished, has its landmark designation withdrawn, or is enlarged or redeveloped.

The Dallas ordinance specifies that the maximum floor area ratio (the ratio between the allowable square footage of floor space of a building on a site and the square footage of the site itself) of a receiving site in the central business district cannot be increased by more than 4 to 1 and a site in the West End Historic District cannot be increased by more than 8 to 1.[81] A minimum of 20,000 square feet may be transferred under the terms of the ordinance.[82] In Denver, the permissible enlargement depends upon the location of the transferee site. In the central business district, development rights can be transferred up to 25 percent of the "basic maximum gross floor area" allowed on the transferee site; in the lower downtown district, under certain conditions, a structure may be enlarged by up to 50 percent of the "supplementary maximum gross floor area."[83]

5.3.4 Conditions of Transfer

Finally, TDR programs may require that certain conditions be satisfied before development rights can be transferred. Most commonly, these pertain to restoration of the transferor landmark. Denver, for instance,

---

[80] N.Y.C. Zoning Resolution § 74-792(2)(d) (1985).
[81] Dallas City Code § 51A-4.501(d)(1), (5).
[82] *Id.* § 51A-4.501(d)(1).
[83] Denver Zoning Ordinance §§ 59-364(b)(3), 59-380(b)(1)c.

bars any transfer until the landmark has been renovated.[84] Dallas has a more elaborate provision, which requires that the landmark have been renovated within the past five years and that the total value of improvements exceed 50 percent of the assessed value of the building prior to restoration.[85] Moreover, in making that calculation, only restoration performed pursuant to an appropriate building permit may be counted.

The New York Zoning Resolution does not expressly require that renovation have occurred prior to a TDR transaction. An application to transfer rights, however, must include a "program for the continuing maintenance of the landmark."[86] In addition, before approving a transfer, the City Planning Commission must make the following findings:

1. The permitted transfer will not unduly increase the bulk of a new development, or the density of population or intensity of use in any city block to the detriment of occupants of nearby buildings.
2. Any disadvantages to the neighborhood from reduced access to light and air will be more than offset by the advantages of preserving the landmark.
3. The program for continuing maintenance will result in the preservation of the landmark.[87]

In the case of government-owned landmark sites, the commission must also condition the transfer on the owner's providing a major improvement of the public pedestrian circulation or transportation system in the area. In the Special Theater Subdistrict, when rights are to be transferred to a noncontiguous site, the commission must additionally find that any intervening lots are and will continue to be used as legitimate theaters or for other theater supportive uses such as rehearsal

---

[84] *Id.*

[85] Dallas City Code § 51A-4.501(d)(2)(C).

[86] N.Y.C. Zoning Resolution § 74-791 (1985).

[87] *Id.* § 74-792(5). An example of the City Planning Commission's authority in reviewing proposed development rights transfers is the recent case of 383 Madison Assoc. v. City of New York, No. 23621/89 (N.Y. Sup. Ct. Aug. 8, 1991). In this case the New York Supreme Court, a trial level court, upheld the Commission's denial of permission to use development rights from the Grand Central Terminal to construct a 74-story building in a congested area of mid-town Manhattan. The developers argued that the property to which the development rights were to be transferred was an adjacent lot by virtue of a chain of ownership that existed between the lot and Grand Central at the time the so-called "chain amendment" to the city ordinance became effective. The Court, however, upheld the Commission's finding that the lots were not adjacent, ruling that adjacent status was to be determined at the time of transfer. Moreover, the Court rejected the argument that subsurface tax lots conferred adjacent status because transferable development rights related to surface rights totally unrelated to tax lots. Finally, the Court upheld the Commission's finding that the proposed 74-story building was more than twice the as-of-right bulk in the area, and therefore was not in compliance with the zoning ordinance.

space, recording facilities, or theater costume rental facilities.[88] The purpose of this provision is to preserve the integrity and homogeneity of the subdistrict as a focal point for the performing arts.

An even more far-reaching proposal for New York City was offered by the city's Theater Advisory Council, established to recommend modifications to local zoning and other regulations to help preserve the Broadway theaters.[89] The council proposed that existing contiguity requirements no longer apply to TDR transfers from the theaters and that unused development rights from parcels containing Broadway theaters be transferable to a much larger receiving zone than is now available under the Special Theater Subdistrict. In exchange for this liberalization, however, an owner of a theater seeking to exercise these transfer rights would be required to agree to two conditions. First, the owner would be obliged to pay over a portion of the receipts from the sale of unused rights to a newly created New York City Theater Trust Fund. The Trust Fund would use these funds, among other purposes, to purchase any Broadway theater threatened with demolition or discontinued use as a legitimate theater, or to provide funding to forestall demolition or change in use in other ways. Second, the owner would be required to enter into a covenant, binding upon all subsequent owners of the property, barring demolition of the theater and requiring its continued use as a legitimate theater. Through this approach, use of TDRs would be contingent upon conditions which would contribute to the unique cultural character of the theater district.[90]

---

[88] N.Y.C. Zoning Ordinance § 81-747 (1991).

[89] Theater Advisory Council, *To Preserve the Broadway Theatre: Report to the Planning Commission of the City of New York on Theater Preservation* (June 1984).

[90] For a comparison of this approach with another alternative (a theater development bonus, or TDB) that was considered by the Theater Advisory Council, *see* Schneider, "Broadway's Newest Hit: Incentive Zoning for Preserving Legitimate Theaters," 3 *Cardozo Arts & Entertainment L.J.* 377 (1984). Neither the Advisory Council's TDR proposal nor its TDB alternative was accepted by the Planning Commission.

Six

Federal and State Statutory Protection for Historic Buildings

A number of federal laws are designed to encourage the preservation of the country's historic resources. Chief among these are the National Historic Preservation Act of 1966 (NHPA), which has as its central focus the protection of historic resources, and the National Environmental Policy Act (NEPA), which encompasses such resources within the broadly defined environmental resources it is intended to protect. In addition, many states have enacted analogs to these federal laws that are intended to bolster the protection available to historic structures.

Unlike the local landmark laws discussed in **Chapter Seven**, which circumscribe the actions of private owners of historic properties, the statutes discussed in this chapter are not enacted in the exercise of the police power, which enables local governments to regulate the actions of their citizens in the interest of public health, safety, or general welfare. Rather, these statues are addressed to the decision-making procedures of federal and state governments and their instrumentalities. Both the NHPA Section 106 and the NEPA procedures described next (as well as their state analogs) are designed to ensure, not that individual structures are preserved, but that the impacts of proposed federal (or state) actions on historic resources are fully considered before potentially adverse action is taken. By requiring federal and state officials to be fully informed of the historic (and, more generally, the environmental) impacts of their actions, and to consider these impacts before acting, these statutes seek to foster their goal of governmental action that enhances, rather than destroys, the nation's historic resources.

In 1986, the Advisory Council promulgated revised regulations governing Section 106 review under the National Historic Preservation Act.[1] The new regulations institute significant changes which are reflected in the discussion that follows. The changes include greater emphasis on consultation between the State Historic Preservation Officer and the federal agency, less emphasis on mandatory Council participation, increased public involvement, and a streamlined review process.

6.1 THE NATIONAL HISTORIC PRESERVATION ACT

The National Historic Preservation Act (NHPA)[2] sets forth a national policy that "maximum encouragement" should be given to the preservation[3] of historic property.[4] From its investigation prior to enactment of the NHPA, Congress concluded that "historic properties significant to the Nation's heritage are being lost or substantially altered, often inadvertently, with increasing frequency."[5] The principal limitation of the NHPA's predecessor, the Historic Sites, Buildings, and Antiquities Act of 1935,[6] was that it could only protect historic resources of national significance.[7] It provided no protection to historic resources of state or local significance, a serious limitation since most of the historic sites in the country are of local or state rather than national importance. As discussed in **Chapter Two**,[8] the NHPA authorizes the Secretary of Interior to expand the country's inventory of historically significant properties, the National Register of Historic Places, to include structures and sites important on the state and local, as well as national, level.

---

[1] *See* 51 Fed. Reg. 31,118 (1986) (codified at 36 C.F.R. Part 800).

[2] 16 U.S.C.A. §§ 470 to 470w-6 (West 1985 & Supp. 1991).

[3] The NHPA defines "preservation" or "historic preservation" as including identification, evaluation, recordation, documentation, curation, acquisition, protection, management, rehabilitation, restoration, stabilization, maintenance, and reconstruction, or any combination of the foregoing activities. *Id.* § 470w(8).

[4] The NHPA defines "historic property" or "historic resource" to mean "any prehistoric or historic district, site, building, structure, or object included in, or eligible for inclusion on, the National Register; such term includes artifacts, records, and remains which are related to such a district, site, building, structure, or object." *Id.* § 470w(5).

[5] *Id.* § 470(b)(3).

[6] *Id.* §§ 461–67 (West 1985 & Supp. 1991).

[7] *See* "Preservation of Historic American Sites, Buildings, Objects, and Antiquities of National Significance: Hearings on H.R. 6670 and H.R. 6734 before the Subcommittee on Public Lands of the House Committee on Interior and Insular Affairs," 74th Cong., 1st Sess. 4-8 (1975) (testimony of Secretary Ickes).

[8] *See* § **2.1**.

The NHPA complemented its expanded effort to catalog resources in the National Register with provisions to protect these resources from federal actions that threaten their integrity.

Where a federal undertaking[9] may cause changes in the character or use of historic properties that are listed on or eligible for the National Register (other than national historic landmarks), federal agencies are encouraged "to seek ways to avoid or reduce the effects on historic properties."[10] Where the federal undertaking may adversely affect a national historic landmark, the head of the responsible agency must, "to the maximum extent possible, undertake such planning and actions as may be necessary to minimize harm" to such landmark.[11]

If the federal undertaking will adversely affect a property listed or eligible for listing on the National Register, the responsible agency must notify the Advisory Council on Historic Preservation (Council), created under the NHPA.[12] It must also consult with the state historic preservation officer (SHPO), also created under the NHPA, to seek ways to avoid or reduce such adverse effects.[13] Either the agency official or the SHPO may ask the Council to participate in that consultation process. The Council may also participate on its own initiative.

The 1976 and 1980 amendments to the NHPA incorporated many of the requirements of Executive Order 11593,[14] which had expanded the duties of federal agencies under the original 1966 Act. As amended, the NHPA imposes responsibilities on the heads of all federal agencies for the preservation of historic properties which are owned or controlled by those agencies.[15] Moreover, every agency is required to establish a program to locate and nominate any properties it owns or controls which appear to qualify for inclusion in the National Register. The amendments also apply the NHPA's protections to Register-eligible, as well as listed, properties.[16] The rationale for the latter provision is that the NHPA implements the public policy of protecting all historic structures worthy of preservation.

As explained in **Chapter Two**,[17] an owner may veto the listing of property on the National Register. The fact that the owner does so, however,

---

[9] An "undertaking" consists of any project, activity, or program which (1) is under the direct or indirect jurisdiction of a federal agency, or is licensed or assisted by a federal agency, and which (2) can result in changes in the character or use of any historic properties that may be located in an area of potential effects. 36 C.F.R. § 800.2(o) (1991). See § **6.1.2**. An "area of potential effects" is the geographic area within which an undertaking may cause changes in the character or use of historic properties, if any such properties exist. 36 C.F.R. § 800.2(c).

[10] 36 C.F.R. § 800.5(e); see also id. § 800.3(a).

[11] Id. § 800.10.

[12] Id. § 800.5(e).

[13] Id.

[14] 36 Fed. Reg. 8921 (1971).

[15] 16 U.S.C.A. § 470h-2.

[16] Id. § 470f.

[17] See § **2.1.4**.

should not, and under the 1980 amendments does not, mean that such unlisted property is unprotected from the impacts of proposed government action.

The NHPA is the central federal law enacted to reflect the national policy of encouraging preservation. While the NHPA provides no certainty that a historic property will in fact be preserved, a federal agency must consult with the SHPO, and must consider the Council's comments in arriving at its decision. Failure to properly comply with these requirements may form the basis for an injunction prohibiting federal action until the requirements are met. When the property in question is a national historic landmark,[18] the agency is subject to additional requirements. First, the Council must participate with the agency in the consultation process, and report its comments to the President, the Congress, and the Secretary of Interior.[19] Second, the agency must "to the maximum extent possible, undertake such planning and actions as may be necessary to minimize harm" to the structure.[20] This more rigorous standard further restricts agency discretion.[21]

In January 1991, Senator Wyche Fowler introduced a bill that, if passed, would amend the NHPA and substantially strengthen the national preservation program. The proposed bill is set forth in **Appendix L**. As described in **§ 6.1.4**, the bill would effectively enhance the power of the NPS to monitor undertakings by federal agencies. It would also require the Secretary of the Interior to make periodic reports to the President and Congress regarding threats to property included or eligible for inclusion in the National Register and permit the Secretary to delegate additional authority to SHPOs under certain conditions. The bill also provides for the establishment of a comprehensive preservation training and education program, creates a process pursuant to which American Indian tribes can perform the function of SHPOs with respect to tribal lands, increases the flexibility of the Secretary of the Interior in awarding grants to states and the National Trust, and requires that a federal agency deny assistance to an applicant for a grant relating to historic property in the event the applicant, at any time prior to the making of the grant, has "adversely affected" the property.

---

[18] 36 C.F.R. § 65.5 defines designation criteria for national historic landmarks.

[19] 36 C.F.R. § 800.10(c).

[20] *See* 16 U.S.C.A. § 470h-2(f); 36 C.F.R. § 800.10.

[21] *See* Mayes, "Protection of Nationally Significant Historic Structures Under Federal Law," 4 *Preservation L. Rep.* 2010, 2013-14 (1985) (a two-tier standard of review is established under the NHPA's 1980 amendments which affords national historic landmarks more protection than National Register listed and eligible properties); *see also* H.R. Rep. No. 96-1457, 96th Cong., 2d Sess. (1980), *reprinted in* 1980 U.S.C.C.A.N. 6401 (discussing higher standard for landmarks).

6.1.1 Section 106 Review

A property that is listed, or eligible for listing,[22] on the National Register is afforded certain protections under Section 106 of the NHPA.[23] Section 106 requires the federal agency that proposes to engage in an undertaking potentially affecting a listed or eligible property to consult with the SHPO and other interested persons during the early stages of planning.[24] This consultation process seeks to accommodate historic preservation concerns with the needs of federal undertakings by identifying potential conflicts and resolving such conflicts in the public interest.[25] The Section 106 consultation process must be completed prior to the expenditure of any federal funds on the undertaking, and prior to the issuance of any license or permit. However, nondestructive planning is permissible.[26]

The agency with jurisdiction over the undertaking has an affirmative duty to identify and evaluate historic properties in the project's area of potential effects.[27] Historic properties are defined as all properties listed on or eligible for the National Register.[28] The agency cannot "passively rely on other agencies to satisfy its responsibilities under the NHPA."[29]

---

[22] This includes properties eligible but not listed on the National Register because of owner objection. Moreover, under the proposed regulations governing the National Register, see § 2.1, federal agencies, with the concurrence of the SHPO, will be permitted to "consider properties eligible for the National Register solely for purposes of complying with section 106 . . . without seeking a formal determination of eligibility from the Keeper." 51 Fed. Reg. 28,206 (1986).

[23] 16 U.S.C.A. § 470f. Hereafter the statutory provision will be referred to by its popular name: Section 106 review. The section provides that:

> The head of any Federal agency having direct or indirect jurisdiction over a proposed Federal or federally assisted undertaking in any State and the head of any Federal department or independent agency having authority to license any undertaking shall, prior to the approval of the expenditure of any Federal funds on the undertaking or prior to the issuance of any license, as the case may be, take into account the effect of the undertaking on any district, site, building, structure, or object that is included in or eligible for inclusion in the National Register. The head of any such Federal agency shall afford the Advisory Council on Historic Preservation established under Sections 470i to 470v of this title a reasonable opportunity to comment with regard to such undertaking.

[24] 36 C.F.R. § 800.3(c).

[25] *Id.* § 800.1(b).

[26] *Id.* § 800.3(c).

[27] *Id.* § 800.4(a).

[28] *Id.* § 800.2(e). This includes national historic landmarks; see also Indiana Coal Council, Inc. v. Lujan, 774 F. Supp. 1385, 1403 (D.D.C. 1991) (federal Office of Surface Mining failed to comply with NHPA § 106 requirements by allowing optional rather than mandatory historical preservation reviews under its regulations governing state permitting operations).

[29] Hough v. Marsh, 557 F. Supp. 74, 87-88 (D. Mass. 1982); see also Indiana Coal Council, Inc. v. Lujan, 774 F. Supp. 1385, 1403 (D.D.C. 1991) (Federal Office of Surface Mining failed to comply with NHPA § 106 requirements by allowing optional rather than mandatory historical preservation reviews under its regulations governing state permitting operations).

Telephone calls to the Council and to the State Historical Commission to ascertain whether a property is listed on the National Register are insufficient to satisfy the agency's affirmative duty. Indeed, the agency cannot limit its search only to properties previously determined to be eligible for listing. In *Hough v. Marsh*, the court found that "eligible property" is that which actually meets the National Register criteria, not that which has been determined to meet the criteria.[30]

The identification process must be comprehensive. The agency must make a "reasonable and good faith effort" to identify properties that might be affected by the undertaking and collect "sufficient information to evaluate the eligibility of these properties for the National Register."[31] It must first review existing material describing the area of potential effects, including sources that might pinpoint previously unidentified properties and historically significant archeological resources. It must then seek input from the SHPO, local governments, public and private organizations, Native American Indian tribes, and other parties likely to possess information about properties of historic significance in the area.[32] Once this basic information has been gathered, the agency must determine whether any further information or analysis, "such as field studies and predictive modeling," would be necessary to identify such properties.[33] The regulations provide that, throughout the identification process, the agency should follow the "Standards and Guidelines for Archeology and Historic Preservation" promulgated by the Secretary of the Interior.[34]

Based on a review of the information gathered, the agency and SHPO might agree that no property within the area of potential effects is eligible for the National Register. If that is the case, the requirements of the NHPA are normally satisfied and the agency may proceed with its undertaking. Agreement will be presumed if the agency determines that no eligible properties are at issue, and the SHPO does not "provide views."[35] If, however, the agency and SHPO disagree, the regulations require that the Secretary of the Interior be requested to make a final eligibility determination.[36] Even when there is no disagreement, the Council or Secretary of the Interior can request that certain properties be submitted directly to the Secretary of the Interior for such a determination.[37]

Once it is determined that the undertaking may affect listed or eligible properties, the focus of the Section 106 process shifts to an assessment

---

[30] *Id.; see also* 36 C.F.R. § 800.2(e).
[31] 36 C.F.R. § 800.4(b).
[32] *Id.* § 800.4(a)(1).
[33] *Id.* § 800.4(a)(2).
[34] 48 Fed. Reg. 44,716 (1983).
[35] 36 C.F.R. § 800.4(c)(5).
[36] *Id.* § 800.4(c)(4).
[37] *Id.*

of the nature of that effect. The regulations require that the agency consult with the SHPO[38] and that it "consider" the Council's comments in reaching a final decision on the proposed undertaking.[39] The agency may not take lightly its responsibility to assess the effects on historic properties. Perfunctory consideration is not sufficient to meet the requirements of the NHPA. The language of the NHPA is "mandatory and the scope is broad."[40]

6.1.2 Federal Agencies and Undertakings Affected

Section 106 review applies only to projects in which the federal government is involved. State, county, or local activity that threatens historic or architectural resources does not trigger the process, nor will the activity of private entities.

It appears that the term "federal agency" will be broadly construed in determining whether the Section 106 process is to be undertaken. In *Committee to Save the Fox Building v. Birmingham Branch of the Federal Reserve Bank*,[41] for example, the court found that the regional Federal Reserve bank which was planning to demolish a historic building was a "federal agency" under the NHPA.

In analyzing whether an action proposed by a federal agency is subject to review under Section 106, it must next be determined whether the action constitutes a federal or federally assisted "undertaking."

Federal regulations define "undertaking" broadly:

> "Undertaking" means any project, activity, or program that can result in changes in the character or use of historic properties, if any such historic properties are located in the area of potential effects. The project, activity, or program must be under the direct or indirect jurisdiction of a Federal agency or licensed or assisted by a Federal agency. Undertakings include new and continuing projects, activities, or programs and any of their elements not previously considered under Section 106.[42]

Courts have also taken a broad view of the parameters of an undertaking. Undertakings have been deemed to include direct federal

---

[38] *Id.* § 800.5(c).

[39] *Id.* § 800.6(c)(2).

[40] United States v. 162.20 Acres of Land, 639 F.2d 299, 302 (5th Cir. 1981), *cert. denied*, 454 U.S. 828 (1981).

[41] 497 F. Supp. 504 (N.D. Ala. 1980). *But see* Vieux Carre Property Owners v. Brown, 875 F.2d 453 (5th Cir. 1989), *cert. denied*, 493 U.S. 1020 (1990) (historic building preservation group could not maintain action against local commissions or other defendants involved in developing or authorizing a project that were not federal agencies).

[42] 36 C.F.R. § 800.2(o).

government acts, federal construction programs,[43] and military operations.[44] But government involvement need not be so direct. The federal government has also been deemed to be sufficiently involved with a project when it has granted its imprimatur by various means such as funding,[45] permitting,[46] or providing approval for a project when that approval was a condition of its initiation.[47]

The determination as to whether a federal undertaking is present is based on the exercise of federal discretionary authority, regardless of who the ultimate actor is or where the action occurs. Thus a federal undertaking may involve actions by nonfederal governmental units and private parties, when those actions are authorized, delegated, or supported by the federal government.[48] And Section 106 review may be triggered even when the action occurs on land which is not federally owned or controlled. On the other hand, merely acquiring title to historically significant property through filing a declaration of condemnation has been declared a neutral act vis-à-vis the NHPA and not to be subject to Section 106 review.[49]

6.1.3 Effects of a Federal Undertaking

Once it has been determined that a federal undertaking is involved, the next threshold question is whether that undertaking will have an "effect" on the Register-listed or Register-eligible property sufficient to require Section 106 review procedures. In general, the issue turns on whether the undertaking causes or may cause any change in the characteristics which qualify the property for the National Register.[50] Because what may be significant in the case of a historic battlefield may not be significant with regard to a mansion (i.e., location will certainly be crucial for the battlefield, but may or may not be for the mansion), "effect" must be

---

[43] Puerto Rico v. Muskie, 507 F. Supp. 1035, 1061 (D.P.R.), *vacated on other grounds sub nom.*, Marquez-Colon v. Reagan, 668 F.2d 611 (1st Cir. 1981).

[44] Romero-Barcelo v. Brown, 643 F.2d 835, 858–60 (1st Cir. 1981), *rev'd on other grounds*, 456 U.S. 305 (1982).

[45] National Ctr. for Preservation Law v. Landrieu, 496 F. Supp. 716 (D.S.C. 1980), *aff'd*, 635 F.2d 324 (4th Cir. 1980); Ely v. Velde, 497 F.2d 252 (4th Cir. 1974); Save the Courthouse Comm. v. Lynn, 408 F. Supp. 1323, 1339 (S.D.N.Y. 1975).

[46] Coalition for Responsible Regional Dev. v. Coleman, 555 F.2d 398 (4th Cir. 1977); Weintraub v. Rural Electrification Admin., 457 F. Supp. 78, 92–93 (M.D. Pa. 1978).

[47] *See* Weintraub v. Provident Nat'l Bank, No. 78-1577 (E.D. Pa. May 11, 1978).

[48] *See* McMillan Park Comm. v. National Capital Planning Comm'n, 759 F. Supp. 908 (D.D.C. 1991) (section 106 review required when proposed amendments to the District of Columbia's Comprehensive Plan would have allowed development of McMillan Park); *Indiana Coal Council*, 774 F. Supp. at 1401 (federal Office of Surface Mining oversight of operation of state permitting programs constitutes federal undertaking).

[49] United States v. 162.20 Acres of Land, 639 F.2d at 304–05.

[50] 36 C.F.R. § 800.9(a).

evaluated in the context of the historic, architectural, archeological, or cultural significance possessed by the particular property.

The agency may conclude that the undertaking will have no effect, or that it will have an adverse effect. No effect is found when the undertaking will not alter characteristics of the property that would qualify the property for inclusion in the National Register. If the federal agency, in consultation with the SHPO and interested persons, concludes that the proposed action will have no effect on Register-listed or Register-eligible property, the agency is required to provide notice of its determination, document its findings, and make the findings public.[51] No further action is required under Section 106 unless the SHPO objects. If that occurs, the regulations treat the undertaking as if it had been determined to have some effect.[52]

When the federal agency in the first instance determines that the undertaking will have an effect, or if the SHPO objects, the next step is a determination of whether any effect will be "adverse." The agency, in consultation with the SHPO, must measure the effects of the undertaking against regulating standards. An adverse effect is found when the undertaking may "diminish the integrity of the property's location, design, setting, materials, workmanship, feeling, or association."[53] Among the effects that are deemed to be adverse are the following:

1. Physical destruction, damage, or alteration of all or part of the property
2. Isolation of the property from or alteration of the character of the property's setting when that character contributes to the property's qualification for the National Register
3. Introduction of visual, audible, or atmospheric elements that are out of character with the property or alter its setting
4. Neglect of property resulting in its deterioration or destruction; and
5. Transfer, lease, or sale of the property.[54]

This list is not exhaustive, and it may be argued that any action resulting in a deleterious change to the property constitutes an adverse effect. Note, however, that these criteria are to be applied with reference only to those characteristics of the property that would contribute to its listing on the National Register.

There are three explicit exceptions to the general guidelines for finding adverse effect. Adverse effect need not be found (1) when the property is valuable only for its potential contribution to archeological, historical, or

---

[51] *Id.* § 800.5(b).
[52] *Id.*
[53] *Id.* § 800.9(b).
[54] *Id.*

architectural research and that value can be substantially preserved through the conduct of appropriate professional research, (2) when the undertaking is limited to rehabilitation of buildings and structures according to the Secretary of the Interior's Standards for Rehabilitation and Guidelines for Rehabilitating Historic Buildings, and (3) when a transfer, lease, or sale includes a restriction or condition adequate to preserve the property's historic features.[55]

If, using the assessment criteria described, the agency finds that the undertaking will not have an adverse effect, it must seek Advisory Council review. It can submit summary documentation if the SHPO concurs in its finding. Otherwise, the agency must submit more extensive documentation, including a statement of why the criteria for assessment of adverse effect were found inapplicable.[56] Notice of that submission must be provided to the SHPO.[57] Once submitted, further review is unnecessary if the Council fails to object within 30 days.[58] The same result is obtained if the Council proposes specific conditions designed to ameliorate aspects of the undertaking which are undesirable, and the agency accepts those conditions.[59] If, however, the Council objects and any proposed conditions are not accepted, the Section 106 review process continues.

The process would necessarily continue if the agency itself determined that the undertaking would have an adverse effect.

6.1.4 The Consultation Process

Once it is established that an undertaking will cause an adverse effect, the next step is consultation between the agency and SHPO "to seek ways to avoid or reduce the effects on historic properties."[60] While not required to participate unless the property is a national historic landmark, the Council can be asked to participate in the consultation process by either party, or can participate on its own initiative.[61] Under the regulations, the consultation process must, in certain circumstances, include interested parties who request an opportunity to participate.[62] The entire process must be supported by adequate notice and documentation.[63]

The goal of consultation is to reach an agreement that enables the undertaking to proceed in a manner that will avoid or reduce any adverse

---

[55] *Id.* § 800.9(c).
[56] *Id.* § 800.5(d)(1).
[57] *Id.*
[58] *Id.* § 800.5(d)(2).
[59] *Id.*
[60] *Id.* § 800.5(e).
[61] *Id.*
[62] *Id.* § 800.5(e)(1).
[63] *Id.* § 800.5(e)(2) and (3).

effects on historic properties. The participants are to persist in achieving this goal "to the fullest extent practicable."[64]

However, when it appears that further consultation would not be productive, the agency, SHPO, or Council, if participating, may terminate the process. At that point, comment by the Council replaces agreement. The federal agency must provide the Council with adequate documentation, and additional information as requested, to facilitate such comments. The Council must then comment within 60 days.[65] The federal agency must consider, but is not bound by, those comments when reaching a final decision on the proposed undertaking.[66] In contrast, the NHPA amendment proposed by Senator Fowler would require an agency to determine that the implementation of the Council's recommendations with respect to the undertaking "is not feasible and prudent" prior to any approval of the undertaking by the agency head.

6.1.5 Memorandum of Agreement

The product of successful consultation is a memorandum of agreement (MOA) between the federal agency and the SHPO. If the Council has already participated in the consultation, it will also have signed the MOA. If, however, it did not participate, the MOA must be submitted to the Council for review and comment. Failure to provide the Council with a reasonable opportunity to comment on the MOA at this or any other stage is a serious default.[67] Once the MOA is submitted, the Council must decide to accept it, suggest changes that would make it acceptable, or comment on the undertaking.[68] If the agency official, SHPO, and Council each find the MOA acceptable, they sign the document. The carrying out of the undertaking by the agency official in accordance with the terms of the MOA becomes final evidence that the Section 106 process has been fulfilled.[69] Interested parties that participated in the consultation process may be invited to concur in the MOA.[70]

---

[64] *Id.* § 800.5(e)(6).
[65] *Id.* § 800.6(b).
[66] *Id.* § 800.6(c)(2).
[67] *Id.* § 800.6(d).
[68] *Id.* § 800.6(a)(1). In Walsh v. U.S. Army Corps of Engineers, 757 F. Supp. 781 (W.D. Tex. 1990), the district court upheld the Corps' issuance of a conditional permit approving project construction before the Corps had signed a Programmatic MOA that it was finally negotiating with the Council. (A Programmatic MOA is sometimes used with respect to projects that have many aspects that would trigger the Section 106 review process.) The permit required the permittee to comply with the final MOA and provided other safeguards to protect historic properties in the project area. Accordingly, the court concluded that, even though the Corps' permit had been issued prior to completion of the Section 106 review process, the Council had been afforded a reasonable opportunity to comment. *See* 9 *Preservation L. Rep.* 1081 (1990) for a discussion of the case.
[69] 36 C.F.R. § 800.6(c)(1).
[70] *Id.* § 800.5(e)(4).

The agency must comply with the terms of the MOA.[71] If it fails to do so or modifies its proposed undertaking, the agency must again seek the Council's comments based on its new action. And as before, while the renewed commenting process proceeds, the agency must suspend actions that would lead to an adverse effect or that would foreclose the Council's consideration of modifications or alternatives to the proposed undertaking that could avoid or mitigate the adverse effect.

The MOA may also be amended. If the Council is a signatory, the consent of the agency, SHPO, and Council are needed. If the Council is not a signatory, or the agency and SHPO cannot agree on proposed changes in the agency's plan, the amendment must be submitted to the Council for comment.[72]

Several courts have reviewed the legal enforceability of the MOA. While it is not a settled question, it appears that a nongovernmental party can force compliance with the terms of the MOA.[73]

It should be noted that the requirements outlined are derived from the Council's regulations implementing Section 106. Those regulations, however, may not control in all cases. Federal agencies are empowered to enact "counterpart regulations," which would provide an alternative route to satisfying the duties placed on agencies by Section 106. When a counterpart regulation has been adopted by another federal agency and concurred in by the Council, it replaces the Council's regulations.[74] However, when a federal agency has not adopted its own procedures, or when the Council has not concurred in proposed counterpart regulations, the agency remains bound by Council regulations. The Council may, in addition, delegate Section 106 responsibilities to a state, provided that the review process is at least as effective as, and no more burdensome than, the Council's own regulations.[75] When a state review procedure goes into effect, a federal agency may comply either with Council or state regulations.[76]

6.1.6 Phased Development

There is some controversy as to whether Section 106 requirements must be complied with through every stage of a continuing federal undertaking. The better view holds that as long as the agency retains discretionary authority over a project, Section 106 must be observed, and the Council

---

[71] *Id.* § 800.6(c)(1).

[72] *Id.* § 800.5(e)(5).

[73] Courts have implicitly suggested that an MOA, in appropriate circumstances, would be enforceable. *See* United States v. 162.20 Acres of Land, 733 F.2d 377 (5th Cir. 1984), *cert. denied*, 469 U.S. 1158 (1985); Don't Tear It Down, Inc. v. Pennsylvania Ave. Dev. Corp., 642 F.2d 527 (D.C. Cir. 1980).

[74] 36 C.F.R. § 800.15.

[75] *Id.* § 800.7.

[76] *Id.* § 800.7(b)(1).

retains review jurisdiction over continuing federal actions.[77] This problem often arises in connection with projects involving highway construction[78] and urban development.[79] In *WATCH v. Harris*,[80] the Second Circuit held that Section 106 requirements "apply until the agency has finally approved the expenditure of funds at each stage of the undertaking," but the court there acknowledged that a different conclusion had been reached in other cases. More recently, the Third Circuit concluded that the "NHPA is applicable to an ongoing project at any stage where a Federal agency has authority to approve or disapprove Federal funding and to provide meaningful review of both historic preservation and community development goals. . . ."[81] Moreover, an undertaking cannot be severed into stages without each stage of development being subjected to Section 106 review. If this were not true, Section 106 could be effectively circumvented by any project that was extensive in time or geography.

An agency is not obligated, however, to undertake a comprehensive review of all effects at the inception of a phased project. The regulations expressly provide that they shall not be construed to "prohibit phased compliance at different stages of planning."[82] At the same time, the agency should "ensure that the Section 106 process is initiated early in the planning stages of the undertaking, when the widest feasible range of alternatives is open for consideration."[83]

When it appears likely that the undertaking's area of potential effects will contain eligible properties that cannot be identified until work commences, the agency must plan for such discoveries during the initial Section 106 process.[84] When such contingency planning has not occurred and new properties, or additional adverse impacts against known properties, are discovered, the agency must afford the Council an opportunity to comment.[85] Council comment is not required, however, if the property is principally of archeological value. In that case, the agency may proceed so long as it complies with the Archeological and Historic Preservation Act and implementing regulations.[86] That act[87] was intended to provide for the preservation of historical and archaeological data that are threatened by

---

[77] Morris County Trust for Historic Preservation v. Pierce, 714 F.2d 271, 279–81 (3d Cir. 1983); WATCH v. Harris, 603 F.2d 310 (2d Cir.), *cert. denied*, 444 U.S. 995 (1979).

[78] *See* Thompson v. Fugate, 347 F. Supp. 120 (E.D. Va. 1972).

[79] *See* WATCH v. Harris, 603 F.2d at 310.

[80] *Id.* at 319.

[81] *Morris County Trust*, 714 F.2d at 280; *see also Save the Courthouse Comm.*, 408 F. Supp. at 1334.

[82] 36 C.F.R. § 800.3(c).

[83] *Id.*

[84] *Id.* § 800.11(a).

[85] *Id.* § 800.11(b)(2).

[86] *Id.* § 800.11(b)(2)(iii).

[87] 16 U.S.C.A. §§ 469 to 469c-1 (West 1985).

dam construction or terrain alteration resulting from a federal or federally licensed project or program. Its principal requirements involve notification of the Secretary of the Interior in all cases involving dam construction and whenever a federal agency discovers that its actions could irrevocably harm significant data.[88]

In certain emergency circumstances, a federal undertaking may not be subject to Section 106 review.[89] These include disasters declared by the President or a state governor. However, each agency should develop plans for taking historic properties into account during emergency operations. Moreover, the exception applies only to undertakings implemented within 30 days of the disaster or emergency.

6.1.7 Enforcement of Section 106 Requirements

Litigation under Section 106 usually entails the claim that the agency did not initiate the review process when it should have or that after beginning the process it did not follow proper procedures—that it did not seek comments from the Advisory Council or did not take its comments into account. The regulations explicitly make a responsible official's failure to act reviewable as agency action by courts or administrative tribunals under the Administrative Procedures Act and under other applicable law.[90] However, if the purposes of the NHPA are substantially achieved, courts will not block an undertaking because of technical procedural noncompliance. In one case, while "there [was] no doubt" that the agency failed to confer with the SHPO prior to issuing a permit, "the fact of actual concurrence by the SHPO in the issuance of the permit, together with the imposition of mitigating measures the SHPO requested, satisfied the statutory requirement and its intent."[91] Executive Order 11,593 provides a second prong of attack on agency actions, by allowing plaintiffs to claim violation of both the statute and the order in appropriate cases.[92] If the agency has not given the Advisory Council an opportunity to comment, then an action for injunctive relief preventing the federal agency from taking further action is the appropriate remedy.

If the Section 106 process has resulted in an MOA that has not been complied with, then an action sounding in contract and seeking specific performance, a declaratory judgment or mandamus may be appropriate.

---

[88] *Id.* §§ 469a, 469a-1.

[89] 36 C.F.R. § 800.12.

[90] 40 C.F.R. § 1508.18 (1991).

[91] Sierra Club v. Clark, 774 F.2d 1406, 1410 (9th Cir. 1985); *see also* 36 C.F.R. § 800.3(b) (indicating that procedures set out in regulations can be implemented in a flexible manner so long as the purposes of Section 106 are met).

[92] Aluli v. Brown, 437 F. Supp. 602 (D. Haw. 1977), *rev'd on other grounds*, 602 F.2d 876 (9th Cir. 1979); *Save the Courthouse Comm.*, 408 F. Supp. at 1336.

As just mentioned, however,[93] whether a private party can force the agency to comply with the terms of the MOA is not a settled legal question.

6.1.8 Section 106 Litigants

Actions to enforce Section 106 may be brought by private citizens[94] or by groups.[95] The Advisory Council has the authority to institute suits to challenge compliance, but an aversion to public airing of interagency disputes greatly diminishes the likelihood of its doing so. Instead, the Advisory Council is more often brought into a suit by the citizen-plaintiff. Other groups or individuals are also potential defendants: The acting federal agency and the SHPO are the most obvious. If federal powers are delegated or benefits conferred to nonfederal levels of government or private individuals, these parties should also be considered as possible defendants in the action.[96]

The traditional standing test of injury-in-fact,[97] requiring a "personal stake in the controversy" demonstrated by the suffering of a "distinct and palpable injury,"[98] is utilized by the courts to determine who has standing to bring an action under the NHPA.[99] A citizen need not be the owner of the historic property or allege economic harm to show injury-in-fact allowing him to bring suit.[100] Generally, any resident or owner of property proximate to the property in question will have standing. Some courts have expanded this standard so that the test is not merely one of proximity. Under this view, residents of a town are considered "users" of the property and beneficiaries of the environment that its unchanged character produces. Legal interest in preserving the property thereby accrues to each of the residents.[101]

In a Sixth Circuit case, the court held that a plaintiff deprived of enjoyment of an aesthetic resource has standing even if the plaintiff is not a resident of the neighborhood in which the building is located.[102]

---

[93] See § **6.1.5**.

[94] See Aluli v. Brown, 437 F. Supp. at 609. *Contra,* Carson v. Alvord, 487 F. Supp. 1049 (N.D. Ga. 1980).

[95] See, e.g., Neighborhood Dev. Corp. v. Advisory Council on Historic Preservation, 632 F.2d 21 (6th Cir. 1980); *Save the Courthouse Comm.,* 408 F. Supp. at 1332.

[96] See, e.g., Biderman v. Morton, 497 F.2d 1141, 1147 (2d Cir. 1974); *Save the Courthouse Comm.,* 408 F. Supp. at 1344. *But see* Woonsocket Historical Soc'y v. Woonsocket, 387 A.2d 530 (R.I. 1978).

[97] Sierra Club v. Morton, 405 U.S. 727 (1972).

[98] Warth v. Seldin, 422 U.S. 490, 498–99, 502 (1975).

[99] See Neighborhood Dev. Corp., 632 F.2d 21 at 21.

[100] See id. at 24.

[101] Edwards v. First Bank of Dundee, 393 F. Supp. 680, 682 (N.D. Ill. 1975), *rev'd on other grounds,* 534 F.2d 1242 (7th Cir. 1976); River v. Richmond Metro. Auth., 359 F. Supp. 611, 625 (E.D. Va.), *aff'd,* 481 F.2d 1280 (4th Cir. 1977).

[102] *Neighborhood Dev. Corp.,* 632 F.2d at 24.

The court stated that "[t]he deprivation of the use of an aesthetic resource is not merely an abstract injury. . . . By alleging 'use' of the building's aesthetic and architectural value, plaintiffs met the Sierra Club standard [of injury-in-fact]."[103] The court went on to assert, "We do not believe that injury-in-fact is suffered only by residents of the neighborhood in which the historically and architecturally significant buildings are located." Nor, it stated, is "standing . . . to be denied because the alleged injury is commonly shared."

A "nonprofit membership organization devoted to protection of the built environment, with a specific interest in preservation of buildings of architectural and historic value in the District of Columbia" was granted standing in another case.[104] So, too, was a historical association with some of its members residing in the vicinity of a National Register building.[105] In a third case, the plaintiff, a concerned group of citizens organized as an unincorporated association whose members claimed interest in architecturally and historically significant buildings in that city was allowed to bring suit, because "a showing by plaintiff of the imminent demolition of a building listed on the National Register of Historic Places is sufficient to establish plaintiff's standing to sue.[106] That was held by the court to be a sufficient showing of prospective injury.

SHPOs also have standing to sue to enjoin demolition of historic buildings.[107]

Another possible basis of standing would be as a claimed third-party beneficiary of a MOA. Such status may, however, be difficult to establish.[108]

6.1.9 Procedural Issues in Section 106 Litigation

Federal subject matter jurisdiction in Section 106 suits may be claimed under the Administrative Procedure Act (APA).[109] The Supreme Court has held that under the provisions of the APA, a federal district court will generally have jurisdiction to review a federal agency action.[110] The exception to this is where a defendant can show by clear and convincing evidence that Congress intended to restrict judicial review under the

---

[103] *Id.* at 23–24.

[104] *See* Don't Tear It Down, Inc. v. Pennsylvania Ave. Dev. Corp., 642 F.2d 527, 531 (D.C. Cir. 1980).

[105] *See* Wicker Park Historic Dist. Preservation Fund v. Pierce, 565 F. Supp. 1066 (N.D. Ill. 1982).

[106] *Committee to Save the Fox Bldg.* 497 F. Supp. at 509.

[107] Weintraub v. Rural Electrification Admin., 457 F. Supp. at 88.

[108] *See* Citizens Comm. for Envtl. Protection v. U.S. Coast Guard, 456 F. Supp. 101, 115–16 (D.N.J. 1978).

[109] 5 U.S.C.A. §§ 701–706 (West 1977).

[110] Abbott Lab. v. Gardner, 387 U.S. 136, 140 (1967).

specific substantive statute governing the agency's action.[111] However, a number of courts have held or implicitly found that a federal district court has the power to decide disputes relating to agency action or inaction with respect to the requirements of the NHPA.[112]

A federal district court also has subject matter jurisdiction under the general federal question jurisdiction statute, 28 U.S.C. § 1331. The grant of federal question jurisdiction for issues arising under the NHPA has been called "incontrovertible."[113]

Notwithstanding the subject matter jurisdiction federal courts generally have over NHPA issues, the Third Circuit recently held that it lacked jurisdiction to entertain a Section 106 challenge to activities that the Environmental Protection Agency (EPA) planned to conduct under the Comprehensive Environmental Response, Compensation and Liability Act of 1980 (CERCLA).[114] The EPA intended to conduct studies, including a Remedial Investigation and Feasibility Study (RI/FS) on land designated as a Superfund site in order to assess and remedy the risk that hazardous waste would be released on the land. The land contained significant Indian artifacts, and the owner filed suit to prevent the EPA from taking further action with respect to the land until it had complied with Section 106 of the NHPA. The Third Circuit, in affirming the district court decision, held that Section 113(h) of CERCLA generally deprived federal courts of jurisdiction to consider challenges to EPA's pre-cleanup related activities at hazardous waste sites.[115] The owner's NHPA challenge clearly did not fall within the limited exceptions to this provision that are enumerated in Section 113(h).

Although the Court recognized the owner's right under the NHPA to bring the challenge, it concluded that CERCLA prevented judicial review in the federal courts. As discussed in **Chapter Eight**, the case represents one of the first instances in which provisions of CERCLA and the NHPA were considered together and reflects the conflict between historic preservation goals and the need to effect thorough and prompt clean up of hazardous sites. One unanswered question posed by the court's decision is whether the result would have been different if the plaintiff had sued in state court.

It may be necessary to exhaust administrative remedies prior to seeking judicial review of controversies relating either to National Register listings or to proposed federal undertakings. A federal court in New York, for instance, dismissed a complaint seeking removal of a National Register listing because plaintiffs failed to exhaust the administrative

---

[111] *Id.*; Citizens Comm. for Hudson Valley v. Volpe, 425 F.2d 97, 101 (2d Cir.), *cert. denied*, 400 U.S. 949 (1970).

[112] *Save the Courthouse Comm.*, 408 F. Supp at 1330–31, and cases cited therein.

[113] *Id.* at 1331.

[114] 42 U.S.C.A. §§ 9601–9675 (West 1983 & Supp. 1991).

[115] Boarhead Corp. v. Erickson, 923 F.2d 1011 (3d Cir. 1991).

procedure established by the regulations.[116] Moreover, litigants may be denied a forum if a challenge to an agency's determination is not ripe for adjudication. One decision held that claims by several resident groups challenging a harbor project under the NHPA were "premature," where the Council had not yet issued final comments.[117]

Decisions of the Advisory Council are likely to be difficult to overturn in court. As the agency created to administer Section 106, the Advisory Council's determinations "are owed great deference unless those determinations are clearly in error."[118] This is consistent with the general principle that an agency action made in accordance with prescribed procedures will not be overturned under the Administrative Procedures Act unless it is found to be arbitrary, capricious, an abuse of discretion, or otherwise not in accordance with law.[119] It has been held that factual determinations of federal agencies that are approved by the Council are subject to review under an arbitrary and capricious standard.[120]

The 1980 amendments to the NHPA authorize the awarding of litigation costs—attorney's fees, expert witness fees, and other related costs—to any person who brings an action to enforce the NHPA and "substantially prevails."[121] The court may award the costs of litigation in an amount it deems reasonable. Legislative history suggests a congressional purpose of encouraging actions which might not otherwise be brought because of the expense of litigation.[122] One court, discussing the legislative history of this provision of the NHPA, noted that "Congress has framed the amendment in very broad terms . . . without any limitations as to which defendants are liable for fees."[123]

6.1.10 Other Federal Agency Responsibilities Under the NHPA

The NHPA creates other responsibilities for federal agencies in addition to compliance with Section 106. Section 206 of the 1980 amendments[124] makes federal agencies responsible for preserving historic buildings under their ownership or control. There is, moreover, a general responsibility to engage in historic preservation activities to the extent consistent

---

[116] White v. Shull, 520 F. Supp. 11 (S.D.N.Y. 1981).

[117] Enos v. Marsh, 616 F. Supp. 32, 69 (D. Haw. 1984), *aff'd*, 769 F.2d 1363 (9th Cir. 1985).

[118] National Trust for Historic Preservation v. U.S. Army Corp of Eng'rs, 552 F. Supp. 784, 791 (S.D. Ohio 1982).

[119] Aertsen v. Landrieu, 488 F. Supp. 314, 318 (D. Mass.), *aff'd*, 637 F.2d 12 (1st Cir. 1980) (quoting 5 U.S.C. § 706(2)(A)).

[120] *Id.*

[121] 16 U.S.C.A. § 470w-4.

[122] H.R. Rep. No. 1457, 96th Cong., 2d Sess., *reprinted in* 1980 U.S.C.C.A.N. 6378.

[123] WATCH v. Harris, 535 F. Supp. 9, 13 (D. Conn. 1981).

[124] 16 U.S.C.A. § 470h-2(a)(1).

with program objectives.[125] Guidelines to assist agencies in complying with this and other responsibilities under Section 110 of the NHPA have been issued effective February 17, 1988. The Section 110 Guidelines set forth 10 basic requirements federal agencies must meet under the NHPA, describes the agencies that must comply with each requirement, advises on how the requirement may be met, and lists publications that may be helpful.[126]

6.1.11 Section 110(f) (National Historic Landmarks)

Resources of national importance may also be designated as national historic landmarks.[127] Such designation results in both listing on the National Register and inclusion in the National Historic Landmarks Program, and hence in protection under both Sections 106 and 110(f) of the NHPA.[128] Section 110(f), in language similar to that of Section 106, requires federal agencies to minimize harm to national landmarks from federal undertakings.

6.2 SECTION 4(f) OF THE DEPARTMENT OF TRANSPORTATION ACT

Similar in intent to Section 106 is the statutory requirement commonly known as Section 4(f) of the Department of Transportation (DOT) Act of 1966, although it is now recodified elsewhere.[129] Section 4(f) is Congress' response to the growing concern over preservation of our nation's parklands, recreation areas, wildlife and waterfowl refuges, and historic sites.[130] The provision bars any federal transportation program from using land from a historic site of national, state, or local significance unless "(1) there is no feasible and prudent alternative to the use of such land, and (2) such program includes all possible planning to minimize harm to such . . . historic site resulting from such use." The Supreme Court has held that Section 4(f)'s language is a "plain and explicit bar" to the use of federal funds for construction of highways through properties falling within the Section's protection (Section 4(f)

---

[125] *Id.* § 470h-2(d).

[126] 53 Fed. Reg. 4727 (1988); *see* 7 *Preservation L. Rep.* 1017 (1988).

[127] 16 U.S.C.A. § 462(b). National historic landmarks are properties "which possess exceptional value as commemorating or illustrating the history of the United States." 36 C.F.R. § 65.1(b)(1). They must pertain "to the development of the Nation as a whole rather than to a particular State or locality." *Id.* § 65.2.

[128] 16 U.S.C § 470h-2(f). Properties listed in the National Historic Landmarks Program were incorporated into the National Register in 1966. *See* 36 C.F.R. § 65.2.

[129] *See* 49 U.S.C.A. § 303 (West Supp. 1991); 23 U.S.C.A. § 138 (West Supp. 1990).

[130] Druid Hills Civic Ass'n v. Federal Highway Admin., 772 F.2d 700, 713-14 (11th Cir. 1985).

properties) and that "only the most unusual situations are exempted."[131] While the section is conventionally raised in the context of highway projects funded by the Federal Highway Administration, it may also apply to airport expansions funded or approved by the Federal Aviation Administration, to mass transit projects funded by the Urban Mass Transportation Administration, and to bridge projects approved by the Coast Guard, since each of these agencies is also within DOT.

The Secretary of Transportation must determine the applicability of Section 4(f) in the early stages of planning, when alternatives to the proposed action are under consideration.[132] In making such a determination, the Secretary of Transportation must consult with the SHPO and local officials to identify properties on or eligible for the National Register.[133] A historic site is significant for purposes of Section 4(f) only if it is "on or eligible for the National Register, unless the Administration determines that the application of section 4(f) is otherwise appropriate."[134]

Section 4(f) limits the "use" of land associated with significant historic sites. The term applies both to direct use of such lands and to constructive uses when "the off-site activities of the proposed project [would] impair substantially the value of the site in terms of its environmental, ecological or historical significance."[135]

Once the applicability of Section 4(f) is established, the Secretary of Transportation must determine whether there is any feasible and prudent alternative to the use of protected lands.[136] At this stage of the inquiry, only alternatives that do not impact on parks and historic sites are considered. An alternative is feasible if it can be built as a matter of sound engineering.[137] An alternative is prudent if it serves the project's purpose, does not present uniquely difficult problems, and would not

---

[131] Citizens to Preserve Overton Park, Inc. v. Volpe, 401 U.S. 402, 411 (1971). *See* National Trust for Historic Preservation v. Dole, 828 F.2d 776 (D.C. Cir. 1987) (holding construction of suicide prevention barriers not a "transportation program or project" requiring use of 4(f) land). In Hickory Neighborhood Defense League v. Skinner, 893 F.2d 58 (4th Cir. 1990), the Fourth Circuit vacated a district court judgment that the Secretary of Transportation had complied with Section 4(f) of the DOT with respect to the proposed widening of a highway, about three blocks of which would occur in the Claremont Historic District in Hickory, North Carolina. The Fourth Circuit remanded the case for findings of whether the Secretary had determined that alternatives to the widening were not prudent and whether the facts supported such a determination. The Fourth Circuit later affirmed the district court's findings that the Secretary had determined that alternatives were not prudent and that the circumstances supported the determination. 910 F.2d 159 (4th Cir. 1990).

[132] 23 C.F.R. § 771.135(b).

[133] *Id.* § 771.135(e).

[134] *Id.*

[135] Citizen Advocates for Responsible Expansion v. Dole, 770 F.2d 423, 441 (5th Cir. 1985); *see* Coalition Against a Raised Expressway, Inc. v. Dole, 835 F.2d 803 (11th Cir. 1988) (finding impacts from a raised expressway sufficient to constitute constructive use of nearby historic sites).

[136] 23 C.F.R. § 771.135(a)(1)(i).

[137] *Citizens to Preserve Overton Park*, 401 U.S. at 411.

cause an extraordinary amount of community disruption.[138] A no-build alternative may be feasible and prudent if the need for the project has not been established.[139]

If the Secretary of Transportation concludes that no feasible and prudent alternative exists, and that the project must pass through Section 4(f) property, the Secretary of Transportation must then undertake all possible planning to minimize harm to such property. At this stage, the relative harm caused by each alternate route within Section 4(f) areas must be assessed, and the option that causes the least harm overall must be selected. "[T]he quantum of harm to the park or historic site caused by [each route]" must be the focus of this second inquiry.[140]

Any evaluation of alternatives must be supported by data disclosed in or with a draft environmental impact statement (DEIS), if one is required under the National Environmental Policy Act. Normally, such an evaluation is annexed to the DEIS as a separate document called a "Section 4(f) Statement." If a DEIS is not required, a Section 4(f) Statement must still be provided. That statement must also be provided for coordination and comment to the official having jurisdiction over the Section 4(f) property, to the Department of the Interior, and, as appropriate, to the Department of Agriculture and Department of Housing and Urban Development.[141]

An abbreviated Section 4(f) review has been adopted for highway projects that have only a minor involvement with Section 4(f) property.[142] This procedure is intended for use where a project necessitates the use of a minor strip of land next to an existing highway in order to broaden the road. The project must not involve the removal or alteration of the historic site. In this type of situation, the project may proceed if the Federal Highway Administration Division Administrator and the SHPO agree that there are no feasible and prudent alternatives, the project includes all possible planning to minimize harm, and that the project qualifies as one with only minor involvement with Section 4(f) property.

Sometimes historic properties are discovered for the first time during construction of the project. If an archaeological site is discovered, it is normally subject to the requirements of Section 4(f), although an evaluation of feasible and prudent alternatives at that point must take account of the level of investment already made, and be shortened as appropriate. If the site is chiefly important for the information it contains, and the archaeological structures themselves have minimal value

---

[138] *Id.* at 413; *see also* 23 C.F.R. § 771.135(a)(2).

[139] *Cf.* Stop H-3 Ass'n v. Dole, 740 F.2d 1442, 1455 n. 21 (9th Cir. 1984), *cert. denied*, 471 U.S. 1108 (1985).

[140] *Druid Hills Civic Ass'n*, 772 F.2d at 716.

[141] 23 C.F.R. § 771.135(i).

[142] 52 Fed. Reg. 31,111 (1987).

for preservation, Section 4(f) does not apply. However, it may be possible for data recovery to precede construction of the project.[143]

If a property is otherwise deemed "significant" after a proposed action has already begun, that action may proceed without Section 4(f) review only if the government acquired its property interest in the lands for transportation purposes prior to the determination of significance, and an adequate effort was made, prior to the onset of the project, to identify properties protected by Section 4(f).[144]

A Section 4(f) determination is subject to judicial review under the Administrative Procedure Act.[145] While the Secretary of Transportation's decision is entitled to a presumption of regularity, that presumption "does not shield [the determination] from a thorough, probing, in-depth review."[146]

The court must examine several facets of the Secretary of Transportation's decision. First, it must determine whether the Secretary of Transportation acted within the scope of his or her authority. That is, it must determine whether Section 4(f) review properly focused on the issue of feasible and prudent alternatives, and whether the Secretary of Transportation could reasonably have believed that no such alternatives existed.[147] Second, it must determine whether the ultimate decision was arbitrary, capricious, or an abuse of discretion. That is, the court must assess whether the decision was based on consideration of relevant factors and whether there has been a clear error of judgment.[148] Finally, the court must determine if necessary procedural requirements were followed.[149]

The administrative record must contain adequate information to conduct such a review. If the record is inadequate, the decision must be remanded for additional findings.[150]

Other federal laws affect the use of historic properties which are federally owned. These restrict both the demolition and, in certain circumstances, the transfer of such properties to nonfederal entities, and also require the General Services Administration and other federal agencies to acquire and use historic properties to the greatest extent possible in carrying out their programs.[151]

---

[143] 23 C.F.R. § 771.135(g)(2); *see also* Belmont v. Dole, 766 F.2d 28, 31 (1st Cir. 1985), *cert. denied*, 474 U.S. 1055 (1986).

[144] 23 C.F.R. § 771.135(h).

[145] *Citizens to Preserve Overton Park*, 401 U.S. at 410.

[146] *Id.* at 415.

[147] *Druid Hills Civic Ass'n*, 714 F.2d at 714.

[148] *Id.*

[149] *Id.*

[150] *Id.* at 716–17.

[151] *See* 40 U.S.C.A. §§ 304a-2, 484(k)(3)(A), 601a (West 1986); 16 U.S.C.A. § 470h-2(a)(1).

6.3 THE NATIONAL ENVIRONMENTAL POLICY ACT

In general, the National Environmental Policy Act (NEPA)[152] requires the federal government to consider the impact on the environment of proposed federal actions. Section 102 of NEPA provides that, before taking "major Federal actions significantly affecting the quality of the human environment," all federal agencies must, "to the fullest extent possible" prepare a "detailed statement" (known as an environmental impact statement or EIS) which analyzes the environmental impact of the proposed action.[153] The statute also makes it the "continuing responsibility of the Federal Government to use all practicable means, consistent with other essential considerations of national policy," to preserve and enhance the environment, including the "historic, cultural, and natural aspects of our national heritage."[154]

Thus, NEPA permits broad review of the effect of federal activities on both the environment in general and on historic resources in particular. The agency must consider direct, indirect, and cumulative impacts[155] of its proposed action. The NHPA amendment proposed by Senator Fowler would permit a federal agency to follow the procedures it has in place to comply with NEPA in lieu of NHPA procedures in the event that the Council found that the agency's procedures provided adequate consideration for cultural resources.

The protection provided under NEPA is similar to that of the NHPA in that both establish procedural requirements. Both statutes impose a duty on the agency to consider the adverse impact, but not necessarily to avoid it.[156] By requiring such consideration, the statute aims to produce governmental action informed by intelligent review of environmental concerns, not to dictate a particular result in any given case.[157]

---

[152] 42 U.S.C.A. §§ 4321–4347 (west 1977 & Supp. 1991).

[153] *Id.* § 4332.

[154] *Id.* § 4331(b).

[155] Northwest Indian Cemetery Protective Ass'n v. Peterson, 764 F.2d 581, 583 (9th Cir. 1985) (environmental impact statement inadequate because it did not adequately discuss cumulative effects of project), *aff'd in relevant part on reh'g*, 795 F.2d 688 (9th Cir. 1986), *rev'd on other grounds*, 485 U.S. 349 (1988); Fritiofson v. Alexander, 772 F.2d 1225, 1245 (5th Cir. 1985):

A meaningful cumulative effects study must identify: (1) the area in which effects of the proposed project will be felt; (2) the impacts that are expected in that area from the proposed project; (3) other actions past, proposed, and reasonably foreseeable that have had or are expected to have impacts in the same area; (4) the impacts or expected impacts from these other actions; and (5) the overall impact that can be expected if the individual impacts are allowed to accumulate.

But see C.A.R.E. Now, Inc. v. Federal Aviation Admin., 844 F.2d 1569 (11th Cir. 1988) (upholding limited analysis of cumulative impacts in light of limited direct and indirect effects of project).

[156] Preservation Coalition, Inc. v. Pierce, 667 F.2d 851, 859 (9th Cir. 1982).

[157] Weinberger v. Catholic Action, 454 U.S. 139, 143 (1981) (the purpose of NEPA is twofold: "to inject environmental considerations into the federal agency's decision-making process

6.3.1 Major Federal Action

Several factors must be analyzed to determine whether a proposed project involves a "major federal action." Whether an action is major is determined by its effect.[158] An act such as a demolition may itself be a large, involved, significant project, but that is not the crucial consideration and that alone does not make the action major. The focus of the inquiry is on how great an impact that project will have on the surrounding physical environment.

A difficult problem arises when a federal permit or license affecting only a small portion of a project is a "but for" condition without which the entire project cannot proceed. In deciding whether the federal action involved is major, the permitting agency must determine whether to consider the entire project or only that portion subject to the permit. Several courts have indicated that the proper resolution of this question depends upon three factors: (1) the degree of discretion exercised by the federal agency over the federal portion of the project, (2) whether the federal government has given any direct financial aid to the project, and (3) whether overall federal involvement is "sufficient to turn essentially private action into federal action."[159] Generally, only if an agency has legal control, as opposed to factual control, of an entire project is project-wide environmental review likely to be required.[160] At the same time, when a pending project and other proposed projects are "so interdependent that it would be unwise or irrational to complete one without the others," the impact of all such projects must be considered in the EIS.[161]

A major action is federal when it is "potentially subject to Federal control and responsibility."[162] If a federal entity holds discretionary power over the outcome of a project or its involvement enables the project to proceed, then it is likely that the project will be characterized as a federal action.[163]

Regulations of the Council on Environmental Quality (CEQ) identify a number of categories of federal actions. These include:

---

by requiring an agency to prepare an EIS" and "to inform the public that the agency has considered environmental concerns in its decision-making process").

[158] 40 C.F.R. § 1508.18. The term "major" reinforces but does not have a meaning independent of "significantly." *Id.* § 1508.18. Actions include a responsible official's failure to act. *Compare* Sierra Club v. Hodel, 848 F.2d 1068, 1090–91 (10th Cir. 1988), *and* Bunch v. Hodel, 793 F.2d 129, 135–36 (6th Cir. 1986), *with* Defenders of Wildlife v. Andrus, 627 F.2d 1238 (D.C. Cir. 1980), *and* Alaska v. Andrus, 591 F.2d 537 (9th Cir. 1979). *Contra*, Alaska v. Andrus, 429 F. Supp. 958 (D. Alaska. 1977), *aff'd* 591 F.2d 537 (9th Cir. 1979).

[159] Winnebago Tribe v. Ray, 621 F.2d 269 (8th Cir.), *cert. denied*, 449 U.S. 836 (1980), and cases cited therein.

[160] *Id.*

[161] Webb v. Gorsuch, 699 F.2d 157 (4th Cir. 1983).

[162] 40 C.F.R. § 1508.18.

[163] Ely v. Velde, 451 F.2d 1130, 1137 (4th Cir. 1971).

1. Adoption of official policy, such as rules, regulations, and interpretations adopted pursuant to the Administrative Procedure Act, 5 U.S.C. 551 *et seq.*; treaties and international conventions or agreements; formal documents establishing an agency's policies which will result in or substantially alter agency programs.
2. Adoption of formal plans, such as official documents prepared or approved by federal agencies which guide or prescribe alternative uses of federal resources, upon which future agency actions will be based.
3. Adoption of programs, such as a group of concerted actions to implement a specific policy or plan; systematic and connected agency decisions allocating agency resources to implement a specific statutory program or executive directive.
4. Approval of specific projects such as construction or management activities located in a defined geographic area. Projects include actions approved by permit or other regulatory decision as well as federal and federally assisted activities.[164]

"Actions" include new and continuing activities, including projects and programs entirely or partly financed, assisted, conducted, regulated, or approved by federal agencies. New or revised agency rules, regulations, plans, policies or procedures, and legislative proposals can also be actions. Actions do not include funding assistance solely in the form of general revenue sharing funds, distributed under the State and Local Fiscal Assistance Act with no federal agency control over the subsequent use of those funds.[165]

Federal action may be present in a variety of transactions affecting historic buildings. For example, HUD approval of the sale of a National Register property has been determined to be a major federal action,[166] as has the federally funded construction of a medical center for prisoners in a historically significant area.[167] It has also been held that a demolition undertaken by a municipal redevelopment authority as part of a larger urban renewal project undertaken jointly with HUD is a major federal action requiring NEPA compliance.[168] In that situation, the reviewing court stated, "HUD cannot meet its statutory responsibility by ignoring demolition and other site clearance work performed by one clearly acting in partnership with the federal government nor can it shut its eyes to the demolition activity and look only to the environmental consequences of new construction which HUD is financing."[169]

---

[164] 40 C.F.R. § 1508.18(b).

[165] *Id.* § 1508.18(a).

[166] Hart v. Denver Urban Renewal Auth., 551 F.2d 1178 (10th Cir. 1977).

[167] Ely v. Velde, 451 F.2d at 1136.

[168] Aertsen v. Harris, 467 F. Supp. 117 (D. Mass. 1979), *aff'd*, 637 F.2d 12 (1st Cir. 1980).

[169] *Id.* at 120.

Other cases, not all specifically in the context of historic preservation, suggest the range of actions by federal agencies that may trigger NEPA review. They include the lease of government-owned buildings,[170] construction by a federal agency,[171] construction by a nonfederal entity supported by federal funds,[172] construction supported by federal mortgage insurance and interest guarantees,[173] and permitting[174] and licensing[175] by a federal agency.

In considering whether an action is federal, a court may consider the relative extent of federal, as opposed to state and local, involvement. If the degree of federal involvement is relatively insubstantial, a federal environmental impact statement may not be required.[176] Moreover, the mere fact that an action is undertaken by a federally empowered entity such as a bank with a federal charter, may not be sufficient to make the action federal if no other federal involvement is present.[177] It is well-established, however, that judicial power to enforce NEPA includes injunctions against private parties where "nonfederal action cannot lawfully begin or continue without the approval of a federal agency," since action without prior federal approval would be unlawful.[178]

Manipulation of the federal role to avoid EIS review of some or all of a project will generally not be countenanced by the courts. For example, segmenting federal and nonfederal funds for this purpose[179] or diverting federal funds from one project to another and replacing them with state funds[180] are both practices rejected by the courts. Similarly, the federal government cannot avoid its NEPA responsibilities by abdicating ongoing supervision and control over a project in an attempt to transform the project into state action.[181] However, if state and federal projects are not interdependent, but rather serve complementary but distinct functions,

---

[170] S.W. Neighborhood Assembly v. Eckard, 445 F. Supp. 1195 (D.D.C. 1978).

[171] City of Rochester v. U.S. Postal Serv., 541 F.2d 967 (2d Cir. 1976).

[172] Ely v. Velde, 451 F.2d at 1136.

[173] Wilson v. Lynn, 372 F. Supp. 934 (D. Mass. 1974).

[174] Conservation Council v. Constanzo, 398 F. Supp. 653 (E.D.N.C.), *aff'd*, 528 F.2d 250 (4th Cir. 1975).

[175] Greene County Planning Bd. v. Federal Power Comm'n, 455 F.2d 412 (2d Cir.), *cert. denied*, 409 U.S. 849 (1972).

[176] Edwards v. First Bank of Dundee, 534 F.2d 1242 (7th Cir. 1976).

[177] *Committee to Save the Fox Bldg.*, 497 F. Supp. at 511.

[178] Foundation on Economic Trends v. Heckler, 756 F.2d 143, 155 (D.C. Cir. 1985).

[179] Named Individual Members of San Antonio Conservation Soc'y v. Texas Highway Dep't, 446 F.2d 1013 (5th Cir. 1971), *cert. denied*, 406 U.S. 933 (1972).

[180] Ely v. Velde, 497 F.2d at 256.

[181] Bunch v. Hodel, 793 F.2d at 135. *But see* Village of Los Ranchos De Albuquerque v. Barnhart, 906 F.2d 1477 (10th Cir. 1990) (federal EIS not required when federal involvement limited to monetary and staff support for the preparation of an EIS, and state and city elected after completion of the EIS to finance the project with state and local money rather than pursue federal funding).

an EIS may not be required for the state action.[182] Factors indicating that state action does not have a federal component that would bring it within the scope of NEPA include complete state rather than federal funding and control.[183] Proposed actions or parts of those actions which are in effect so closely related as to be a single course of action must be evaluated in one EIS.[184]

If a proposed agency action is likely to be characterized as a major federal action, a full NEPA review is required if it is determined that the action will "significantly [affect] the quality of the human environment."[185]

The large majority of courts have recognized that alteration of the features of a historic building or demolition of a historic area or building affect the human environment.[186] But frequently the adverse effect is more indirect and therefore harder to categorize. Adverse change may pertain to the physical characteristics[187] or the aesthetics[188] of a neighborhood. It may also involve a change in the neighborhood's population[189] or traffic density.[190] To determine whether the action's effect on the environment is "significant" its context and intensity must be considered.[191] By "context" the regulations mean that an action's significance may vary with its setting. "Intensity" refers to the severity of the impact. Factors that should be considered in evaluating intensity include the "degree to which the action may adversely affect National Register eligible or listed properties or other significant scientific, cultural or historic resources."

6.3.2 The EIS Process

Each agency must adopt procedures to implement NEPA and ensure that decisions are made in accordance with NEPA's goals and comply with its procedural requirements.[192]

The procedures must be designed to determine whether preparation of an EIS is required and, if so, the procedures to be followed in its

---

[182] Enos v. Marsh, 769 F.2d 1363, 1371 (9th Cir. 1985).

[183] *Id.* at 1372.

[184] 40 C.F.R. § 1502.4(a).

[185] 42 U.S.C.A. § 4332(2)(C).

[186] WATCH v. Harris, 603 F.2d at 326; Hanly v. Mitchell, 460 F.2d 640 (2d Cir.), *cert. denied,* 409 U.S. 990 (1972); Aluli v. Brown, 437 F. Supp. at 607. *Contra,* St. Joseph Historical Soc'y v. Land Clearance for Redevelopment Auth., 366 F. Supp. 605 (W.D. Mo. 1973); *Citizen Advocates for Responsible Expansion,* 770 F.2d at 438.

[187] Goose Hollow Foothills League v. Romney, 334 F. Supp. 877 (D. Or. 1971).

[188] Maryland-National Capital Park & Planning Comm'n v. U.S. Postal Serv., 487 F.2d 1029 (D.C. Cir. 1973).

[189] *Goose Hollow Foothills League,* 334 F. Supp. at 879.

[190] City of Rochester v. U.S. Postal Serv., 541 F.2d 967 (2d Cir. 1976).

[191] 40 C.F.R. § 1508.27.

[192] *Id.* § 1507.1.

preparation. The EIS process is designed to provide a full and fair discussion of significant environmental impacts and to inform the public of the reasonable alternatives which would avoid or minimize adverse impacts or enhance the quality of the environment.[193] It is a planning tool, not merely a disclosure document, a means of assessing the environmental impact of proposed actions, rather than a document to justify decisions already made.

6.3.3 When Is an EIS Required?

Unless the project falls within a categorical exclusion,[194] the first step in the NEPA process is an agency's preparation of an environmental assessment. Based on the information acquired in preparing this public document, an agency determines whether an EIS is required. If, however, it is clear from the beginning that an EIS will be required, the agency may initiate that process immediately without first preparing an environmental assessment.

Based on the environmental assessment, the agency may decide that the action is not a major federal action or will not significantly affect the quality of the human environment. In either case, it would conclude that an EIS is not required and prepare a "Finding of No Significant Impact."[195] An agency has an affirmative duty to prepare a reviewable administrative record if such a finding is made.[196] The record must demonstrate that adequate consideration was given to the same factors that would have been considered in a full-scale EIS. "[M]ere perfunctory or conclusory language will not be deemed to constitute an adequate record and cannot serve to support [an] agency's decision not to prepare an EIS."[197] A determination that a full EIS is not required does not end an agency's duties under NEPA. The agency must demonstrate continuing sensitivity to environmental considerations in its actions, and must develop a system of decision-making which ensures the consideration of environmental values. It must adopt an interdisciplinary approach to ensure that nonagency interests are considered, particularly when there is a dispute over resource use. And the agency must continue to generate less environmentally intrusive alternatives to the proposed federal action. The record must show that the agency took a "hard look" at the project's impacts and

---

[193] *Id.* § 1502.1

[194] *Id.* § 1508.4.

[195] *Id.* § 1508.13.

[196] *Citizen Advocates for Responsible Expansion*, 770 F.2d at 433; Runway 27 Coalition v. Engen, 679 F. Supp. 95, 101–02 (D. Mass. 1987).

[197] *Citizen Advocates for Responsible Expansion*, at 434; *see also* Foundation on Economic Trends v. Weinberger, 610 F. Supp. 829, 841 (D.D.C. 1985) (finding that an environmental assessment was inadequate and conclusory when it made no mention of critical factors at issue and did not directly address the question of whether an EIS was required).

that it identified the relevant areas of environmental concern; it must convincingly establish that all impacts were insignificant, or if there was an impact of true significance, that changes in the project sufficiently reduced it to a minimum.[198]

If, however, the agency finds that the threshold requirements are satisfied, it must prepare an EIS.

6.3.4 Participants

Generally, the agency proposing the undertaking is responsible for preparing the EIS. In projects involving a number of agencies, a lead agency is designated to take primary responsibility for preparing the EIS.[199] But while one agency may bear that primary responsibility, a number of other federal agencies, state and local governments, and even private individuals may contribute to its preparation before the process is completed.

Other federal, state, and local agencies may become cooperating agencies in the preparation of the EIS. A cooperating agency is one that is requested to participate by the lead agency.[200] It is appropriate for a lead agency to delegate responsibility to another federal agency to draft portions of the EIS when a portion of the project falls within that agency's jurisdiction or when that agency brings special expertise to the issue.

The lead agency must solicit comments from other federal agencies which because of their jurisdiction or special expertise are able to highlight any of the environmental consequences that can be anticipated, and those agencies have a duty to comment.[201] Also having a duty to comment are agencies created to develop and enforce environmental standards. For example, in historic preservation matters, the Department of Interior and the Advisory Council have special expertise and must comment on projects that may impact on historic resources.

Under some circumstances, a federal agency may also delegate responsibility for preparing an EIS to a state entity.[202] As a rule, federal agencies whose chief responsibility is funding of state projects (for example, the Federal Highway Administration) may rely upon an EIS prepared by a state agency. Federal entities with permitting responsibilities (for example, the Army Corps of Engineers) must undertake

---

[198] National Resources Defense Council v. Herrington, 768 F.2d 1355, 1430 (D.C. Cir. 1985); *Foundation on Economic Trends,* 610 F. Supp. at 838; Public Citizen v. National Highway Traffic Safety Admin., 848 F.2d 256, 266–67 (D.C. Cir. 1988); Coalition on Sensible Transp. v. Dole, 826 F.2d 60, 66–67 (D.C. Cir. 1987).

[199] 40 C.F.R. § 1501.5(c). This decision is hammered out by the agencies involved.

[200] *Id.* § 1501.6.

[201] *Id.* § 1503.2.

[202] 42 U.S.C.A. § 4332(2)(D).

independent analyses, and reliance upon state efforts is not acceptable.[203] In any event, the federal agency retains ultimate responsibility for compliance with NEPA.

Under the Urban Development Action Grant program discussed in **Chapter Four,** the Secretary of HUD was authorized to delegate environmental review procedures to local governments as grant applicants.[204] The applicant's request for a release of UDAG funds was accompanied by a certification that the applicant had fully carried out its responsibilities under NEPA, and the Secretary's approval of that certification was deemed to satisfy his NEPA responsibilities.[205] As discussed in § **4.1.3,** FY 1989 was the last year that the UDAG program was funded.

The regulations provide for public involvement at several steps in the EIS process. Citizen participation must be invited at the environmental assessment stage and with regard to both the draft and final versions of the EIS.[206] To facilitate this participation, hearings must be held and relevant documents made available for public review.

6.3.5 Timing

The EIS is intended to aid in an agency's decision-making process.[207] Preparation of the EIS must commence as close as possible to the time the agency begins developing its proposal so that it is completed in time to be part of any recommendation or report on the proposal. For example, with respect to an action directly undertaken by a federal agency, such as demolition of a historic site for a highway project through a historic district, the EIS must be prepared at the feasibility (go/no go) stage. Where the federal agency must pass on an application of another entity that would affect a historic building (such as an application for federal funds for new construction in a historic district), the EIS must be prepared before granting the application.

6.3.6 Contents of the EIS

There are three main elements to the EIS.[208] It must describe the environment that will be affected, the proposed action and any alternatives, and the environmental consequences of the proposed action and its alternatives.

---

[203] Sierra Club v. U.S. Army Corps of Eng'rs, 701 F.2d 1011, 1037–39 (2d Cir. 1983).

[204] 42 U.S.C.A. § 5304(g).

[205] Crosby v. Young, 512 F. Supp. 1363 (E.D. Mich. 1981); cf. Colony Fed. Sav. & Loan Ass'n v. Harris, 482 F. Supp. 296 (W.D. Pa. 1980); National Ctr. for Preservation Law v. Landrieu, 496 F. Supp. 716 (D.S.C.), aff'd, 635 F.2d 324 (4th Cir. 1980).

[206] 40 C.F.R. § 1506.6.

[207] Id. § 1502.5.

[208] Id. §§ 1502.14–1502.16.

The purpose of describing the affected environment is to assist in understanding the effects of the proposed action and its alternatives. The agency, in satisfying this requirement, must keep its description and supporting data clear and concise to aid understanding, rather than cloud it in unnecessary verbiage.

A clear description of the proposed action and adequate discussion of the alternatives is critical. The discussion should be comparative and analytical. It should "rigorously explore and objectively evaluate" all reasonable[209] alternatives, including the alternative of no action at all, in detail.[210] The issues must be sharply defined and provide a clear basis for choosing among the options based on an evaluation of their comparative merits. The agency should indicate in the EIS which alternatives it prefers. The scope of the discussion of alternatives is determined by looking at the nature and scale of the proposed project and includes reasonable alternatives not within the jurisdiction of the lead agency.

The regulations delineate what the section on environmental consequences should discuss.[211] Most significant for historic preservation purposes is the requirement that this section discuss: "urban quality, historic and cultural resources, and the design of the built environment, including the reuse and conservation potential of various alternatives and mitigation measures."[212] It must discuss direct and indirect impacts of the action and its alternatives. Any unavoidable adverse effects of the proposal must be made clear. A federal agency has a continuing duty to gather and evaluate new information relevant to the environmental impact of its actions even after release of an EIS.[213] If an agency makes substantial changes in the proposed action that are relevant to environmental concerns or if there are significant new circumstances or information relevant to environmental concerns which bear on the proposed action or its impacts, it must supplement its EIS.[214] An agency determination not to supplement an EIS and in light of new information will be upheld only if the agency makes a fair and independent determination that newly discovered information does not require additional public disclosure and comment.[215]

---

[209] *Id.* § 1502.14(a); Keith v. Volpe, 352 F. Supp. 1324, 1336 (C.D. Cal. 1972), *aff'd*, 506 F.2d 696 (9th Cir. 1974), *cert. denied*, 420 U.S. 908 (1975). *Cf.* Natural Resources Defense Council, Inc. v. Morton, 458 F.2d 827, 838 (D.C. Cir. 1972) (speculative alternatives are not required in the EIS).

[210] The level of detail required depends on the "nature and scope of the proposed action." Northwest Coalition for Alternatives to Pesticides v. Lyng, 844 F.2d 588, 592 (9th Cir. 1988) (quoting California v. Block, 690 F.2d 753, 761 (9th Cir. 1982)).

[211] 40 C.F.R. § 1502.16.

[212] *Id.* § 1502.16(g).

[213] *Stop H-3 Ass'n*, 740 F.2d at 1463.

[214] 40 C.F.R. § 1502.9(c).

[215] Action for Rational Transit v. West Side Highway Project, 536 F. Supp. 1225, 1253 (S.D.N.Y. 1982), *aff'd*, 699 F.2d 614 (2d Cir. 1983).

6.3.7 Judicial Review Under NEPA

NEPA goals are substantive, but the rights it creates are only procedural.[216] Since the statute does not require a particular result or demand the preservation of a resource, a court is likely to defer to the discretion of the agency. Consequently, a claim disputing the substance of an agency's decision is not likely to succeed. A court is likely to limit its review to ensuring that all procedural requirements have been met and that the nature and extent of the environmental impact have been considered.[217]

However, CEQ's interpretation of NEPA in its regulations, which spell out agencies' procedural duties in great detail, is entitled to "substantial deference" from the courts.[218] This suggests that a challenge to the scope of the agency's deliberation may be more fruitful than a substantive challenge to the results of that deliberation. For example, the agency decision not to prepare an EIS based on its determination that no significant adverse environmental consequence will occur may be challenged as being inadequately considered.[219] Or the EIS itself may be attacked for neglecting to address necessary considerations such as direct or cumulative effects or reasonable alternatives.

The federal courts of appeals have utilized two different standards in reviewing challenges to the substance of agency decisions under NEPA. Several have held that NEPA determinations should be overturned only if they are shown to be "arbitrary and capricious."[220] Others apply a somewhat more rigorous test, and examine agency NEPA decisions to see if they meet a standard of reasonableness.[221] In both cases, the outcome will turn largely on the sufficiency of the information that the agency had available when it reached its decision.[222] In practice, it is difficult to set

---

[216] Strycker's Bay Neighborhood Council, Inc. v. Karlen, 444 U.S. 223, 227 (1980).

[217] Vermont Yankee Nuclear Power Corp. v. Natural Resources Defense Council, Inc., 435 U.S. 519, 548 (1978).

[218] Andrus v. Sierra Club, 442 U.S. 347, 358 (1979).

[219] Preservation Coalition, Inc. v. Pierce, 667 F.2d 851, 855 (9th Cir. 1982), and cases cited therein.

[220] *E.g.* Nucleus of Chicago Homeowners Ass'n v. Lynn, 524 F.2d 225, 229–30 (7th Cir. 1975), *cert. denied*, 424 U.S. 967 (1976); Hanly v. Kleindienst, 471 F.2d 823, 828–30 (2d Cir. 1972), *cert. denied*, 412 U.S. 908 (1973).

[221] Goodman Group, Inc. v. Dishroom, 679 F.2d 182, 186 (9th Cir. 1982); Minnesota Public Interest Research Group v. Butz, 498 F.2d 1314, 1320 (8th Cir. 1974) (en banc); Wyoming Outdoor Coordinating Council v. Butz, 484 F.2d 1244, 1249 (10th Cir. 1973); Save Our Ten Acres v. Kreger, 472 F.2d 463, 465–66 (5th Cir. 1973).

[222] The courts are also divided as to the appropriate standard for reviewing an agency's decision not to prepare an EIS. *See generally* Shea, "The Judicial Standard for Review of Environmental Impact Statement Threshold Decisions," 9 Env. Aff. L. Rev. 63 (1980). *Compare* North Carolina v. Hudson, 665 F. Supp. 428, 436 (E.D.N.C. 1987) *and Foundation on Economic Trends*, 756 F.2d at 151 (arbitrary and capricious standard) *with C.A.R.E. Now*, 844 F.2d at 1569 *and Citizen Advocates for Responsible Expansion*, 770 F.2d at 432 (reasonableness standard). Some courts have noted that, in practice, there is little difference

aside an agency determination under either standard, and it is not enough to show that a better result might have been reached. Indeed, the fact that the court, upon de novo review, might not agree with the substance of an agency's determination on a NEPA question may well be immaterial to the outcome of a legal challenge.[223]

When a NEPA violation is found, however, courts may enjoin the government action pending the preparation of an adequate EIS. Some courts have held that irreparable damage flows directly from the failure of the federal agency to evaluate thoroughly the proposed federal action.

The premise for relaxing the equitable tests in NEPA cases is that irreparable damage may be implied from the failure of responsible authorities to evaluate thoroughly the environmental impact of a proposed federal action.[224]

The purpose of granting such an injunction is to preserve the decision-maker's choice among alternatives before an irretrievable commitment of resources has occurred. Similarly, an injunction may be imposed under the same standard to ensure that an adequate environmental assessment is filed.

The discussion of federal court jurisdiction to hear claims arising under the NHPA,[225] is fully applicable to NEPA as well.

6.4 COORDINATING NEPA AND THE NHPA FOR MAXIMUM FEDERAL STATUTORY PROTECTION

Both the NHPA and NEPA provide protection for historic, archaeological, and cultural resources. But the applicability of NEPA is not precisely coextensive with that of the NHPA. Like the NHPA, NEPA applies to federal agencies but not to their counterparts at other levels of government. Nor are private actions subject to regulation by either law.[226] Unlike the NHPA, though, the protection provided by NEPA may extend to historic property even if it has not been determined to be eligible for listing on the National Register.[227] In this respect, NEPA complements the NHPA, and expands federal statutory protection for historic resources.

Similarly, the NHPA may apply in some instances where NEPA does not. Because NEPA's threshold—requiring a major federal action significantly

---

between the two standards. *See, e.g.,* Alexandria v. Federal Highway Admin., 756 F.2d 1014, 1017 (4th Cir. 1985); River Road Alliance, Inc. v. Army Corps of Eng'rs, 764 F.2d 445, 449 (7th Cir. 1985), *cert. denied*, 475 U.S. 1055 (1986).

[223] Aertsen v. Landrieu, 637 F.2d 12, 19 (1st Cir. 1980).

[224] American Motorcyclist Ass'n v. Watt, 714 F.2d 962, 966 (9th Cir. 1983). *See* Save the Yaak Committee v. Block, 840 F.2d 714, 722 (9th Cir. 1988).

[225] *See* § **6.1.9**.

[226] However, both laws do apply to the activities of these nonfederal or nongovernmental actors when their actions are subject to federal activity.

[227] Boston Waterfront Residents Ass'n v. Romney, 343 F. Supp. 89 (D. Mass. 1972).

affecting the quality of the human environment—is higher than for the NHPA, there may be federal actions that are subject to review under the NHPA, but not NEPA.

Where the procedures of the two statutes overlap and steps taken to comply with one are the same steps required to comply with the other, the regulations attempt to avoid unnecessary duplication and expense by requiring that the procedures be integrated to the extent possible. Thus surveys, studies, and analyses prepared under the NHPA are incorporated into the EIS.[228] However, compliance with the NHPA does not assure compliance with the requirements of NEPA[229] and vice versa.[230] The requirements of each must be shown to have been met independently of the other.

6.5 STATE STATUTORY PROTECTION

Many states have sought to supplement the statutory protection available under both the NHPA and NEPA by adopting similar statutes that are applicable to the actions of state and, sometimes, local agencies. Typically, these state enactments seek to encourage protection of historic and cultural resources by establishing a State Register, requiring governmental agencies to adhere to restrictions designed to protect these resources, and establishing an environmental review procedure.

6.5.1 State Historic Preservation Statutes

A number of states have enacted constitutional provisions, statutes, or administrative orders that offer direct protection to historical sites which exceeds that provided by federal law. These statutes often expand the scope of protection of the NHPA by imposing direct preservation duties upon state and often local government activities. A state may also create its own register of historic sites to complement the National Register, affording listed resources protection against state financed or licensed projects.

In New York State, the Historic Preservation Act of 1980[231] authorizes the creation of a Register of Sites and Structures "significant in the history, architecture, archaeology, or culture of the state, its communities or the nation."[232] The criteria for listing on the New York State

---

[228] 40 C.F.R. § 1502.25(a).

[229] *Preservation Coalition*, 667 F.2d at 859.

[230] Stop H-3 Ass'n v. Coleman, 533 F.2d 434, 444–45 (9th Cir.), *cert. denied*, 429 U.S. 999 (1976).

[231] N.Y. Parks Rec. & Hist. Preserv. Law § 14.01-14.09 (McKinney 1984). Regulations implementing the Historic Preservation Act of 1980 are found at N.Y. Comp. Codes R. & Regs. tit. 9, §§ 426.1–428.16 (1991).

[232] *2Id.* § 14.07(1)(a).

Register mirror those for the National Register. This is in contrast to a number of states, which utilize eligibility criteria that are less stringent than those of the National Register.

The consequence of a listing in the New York State Register is that a state agency and, in some cases, local agencies, may not engage in any action that effects the listed property without considering the impact of its activity and taking steps to conserve the property. The statute makes it "the responsibility of every state agency . . . to avoid or mitigate adverse impacts to registered property or property determined eligible for listing" on the state register of historic places.[233]

The state of California has enacted legislation[234] that creates a State Historical Resources Commission to designate state historical landmarks.[235] This commission consists of members with broadly relevant expertise in the areas of history, architecture, and archaeology. The criteria used to designate property as state landmarks vary somewhat from those established in local ordinances and under the NHPA. Review and approval of a nomination are based on a finding of the presence of at least one of the following:

1. The property is the first, last, only, or most significant historic property of its type in the region.
2. The property is associated with an individual or group having a profound influence in California.
3. The property is an outstanding example of a particular architectural movement or architect.
4. The property is listed on the National Register.

These statutes are illustrative of state efforts to protect historic properties on their own initiative. Like the federal statutes just discussed, they do not guarantee the preservation of historic structures, but they do signal an increasing commitment by states to consider the impacts of agency action on their cultural heritage and to require property owners and developers seeking state assistance to cooperate in this review.

6.5.2 State Environmental Protection Statutes

A majority of states have enacted environmental protection statutes which parallel the requirements of NEPA. As with their federal counterpart, it is the purpose of these state acts to mandate a full consideration of the environmental implications of planned state and, in some cases, local actions. Because NEPA's application is limited to federal actions,

---

[233] *Id.* § 14.09(2).
[234] Cal. Pub. Res. Code §§ 5020–26 (West 1984 & Supp. 1992).
[235] This commission also evaluates nominations to the National Register. *Id.* § 5020.4(a).

the role these statutes play in the preservation process is an important one particularly because a great number of actions which touch on land use are initiated at the state and local, rather than the federal, level.

The language of many state statutes is substantially similar to NEPA and their procedures are essentially the same. The New York State Environmental Quality Review Act (SEQRA)[236] is one example. It requires that state agencies prepare an EIS for any action they undertake which will have a significant effect on the environment. New York defines "environment" to include "physical conditions . . . including . . . resources of . . . archaeological, historic or aesthetic significance . . . [and] existing community or neighborhood character."[237] The agency must take the further step of choosing alternative actions which, to the extent practicable, minimize or avoid such adverse impacts. The "extent practicable" is influenced by a number of considerations including social and economic factors. The agency must choose a course of action based on findings reflecting consideration of these factors.

The SEQRA regulations identify two categories of actions for purposes of indicating the level of environmental scrutiny required. Type I actions are those that presumptively have a significant effect on the environment, and for which an EIS is likely to be required.[238] For all Type I actions, an EIS will be required unless the lead agency issues a determination that the specific action proposed will not have a significant effect on the environment (a so-called negative declaration), based upon a more limited Environmental Assessment Form that must be prepared in all cases. Type I actions include actions "occurring wholly or partially within, or contiguous to, any facility or site listed on the National Register of Historic Places, or any historic building, structure or site, or prehistoric site, that has been proposed by the Committee on the Registers for consideration by the New York State Board on Historic Preservation" for inclusion in the National Register.[239]

Type II actions are those that have been generically determined not to have a significant effect on the environment.[240] They include such things as repaving of existing highways, construction of minor accessory facilities, and renewal of licenses or permits involving no material change in allowable activities. Neither an Environmental Assessment Form nor an EIS must be prepared for a Type II action.

---

[236] N.Y. Envtl. Conserv. Law §§ 8.0101 to 8.0117 (McKinney 1984 & Supp. 1992).

[237] N.Y. Comp. Codes R. & Regs. tit. 6, § 617.2(l) (1987).

[238] *Id.* § 617.12.

[239] *See, e.g.,* McKelvey v. White, 565 N.Y.S.2d 428 (Sup. Ct. 1991) (annulling the N.Y. Department of Transportation's decision to replace the Mitchell Road Bridge, a bridge built in 1911 as part of the Barge Canal System, because the Department failed to consider the environmental significance of the project as required by SEQRA).

[240] N.Y. Comp. Codes R. & Regs. tit. 6, § 617.13.

The regulations also permit a local agency to designate as a "critical environmental area (CEA)" an area that has exceptional or unique character with respect to "social, cultural, historic, archaeological, recreational, or educational values."[241] Any unlisted action located in a CEA must be treated as a Type I action by any involved agency.[242]

The California Environmental Quality Act (CEQA)[243] expresses the legislative intent that state agencies encourage activities of private citizens which enhance the environment, including historic resources. The statute expresses the state's policy that it is every citizen's responsibility to preserve and enhance the environment. The purpose of the CEQA is to prevent significant avoidable damage to the environment by requiring changes in projects through mitigation measures.

Any state agency must prepare an environmental impact report (EIR) when its activity will have a significant effect on the environment. In addition to ensuring that agencies assess all reasonable alternatives, the EIR is intended to inform the public and other agencies of the environmental impact of the project.

The concept of "project" is quite broad.[244] In addition to including direct governmental activities and discretionary projects such as zoning ordinances and variances, it also includes actions in which a public entity considers a permit, license, lease, certificate, or other entitlement for a private action that may potentially change the environment. The CEQA is similar to many other statutes in distinguishing between discretionary and ministerial actions and applying only to discretionary ones. Whether an agency has discretionary or ministerial control over a project depends on the authority granted by the law which gives the agency control over the activity.[245] A discretionary project is one that requires the exercise of judgment, deliberation, or decision on the part of the public agency or body in the process of approving or disapproving a particular activity. In contrast, a ministerial project, as a general rule, includes those activities which are undertaken or approved by a governmental agency which entail a decision which a public officer or public agency makes upon a given set of facts in a prescribed manner in obedience to the mandate of legal authority. With these projects, the officer or agency must act upon the given facts without regard to his own judgment or opinion concerning the propriety or wisdom of the act. Similar projects may, then, be subject to

---

[241] *Id.* §§ 617.2(i), 617.4(h)(1)(ii).

[242] *Id.* §§ 617.2(i), 617.4(h).

[243] Cal. Pub. Res. Code §§ 21000–21177 (West 1986 & Supp. 1992); *see* Cal. Code Regs. tit. 14, §§ 15000–15387 (1990). The CEQA applies to governmental agencies at all levels. State, regional, county, and local agencies must develop standards and procedures to protect environmental quality.

[244] *See* Cal. Pub. Res. Code § 21065.

[245] Cal. Code Regs. tit. 14, §§ 15357, 15369 (1990).

discretionary controls and environmental review requirements—in one city or county and only ministerial controls—and no such review in another.

A project "significantly" affects the environment when it will potentially cause a substantial adverse change.[246] The "environment" is defined to mean the physical conditions that exist within the area which will be affected by the proposed project, including objects of historic and aesthetic significance.[247]

All reasonable alternatives to an agency's proposed project must be considered. This includes the alternative of not going forward with the project at all, and alternatives outside the expertise of the agency or which may require implementing legislation.[248] The California Supreme Court has stated, "Obviously if the adverse consequences to the environment can be mitigated, or if feasible alternatives are available, the proposed activity . . . should not be approved." However, the CEQA does not mandate the choice of the environmentally best feasible project.[249] For example, the California Supreme Court recently reversed a lower court decision and upheld an EIR conducted by the County of Santa Barbara for a major resort development on Haskell's Beach.[250] The project will have adverse impacts on several Native American burial grounds and the habitat of several environmentally sensitive species, including the Monarch Butterfly. Nevertheless, the EIR was upheld because alternate sites were adequately explored, and the evidence supported the finding that the alternative sites were infeasible because of their impact on existing residential areas, the unavailability of urban services, and high seismic ratings.

Significantly, some states provide substantive as well as procedural protection to historic resources by means of their environmental review statutes. These states create a binding protection that is much stronger than NEPA and other review laws that impose only procedural duties upon the agencies and which, even if complied with, may still result in the loss of the resource. The state of Washington is an example of one which imposes a substantive requirement.[251] Its State Environmental Protection Act (SEPA)[252] has been found to confer on localities the discretionary right to deny a building permit based on an EIS which concluded that an adverse environmental impact would result. The

---

[246] Cal. Pub. Res. Code § 21068.

[247] Cal. Code Regs. tit. 14, § 15360 (1990).

[248] Resident Ad Hoc Stadium Comm. v. Board of Trustees of Cal. State Univ., 89 Cal. App. 3d 274 (1979).

[249] Friends of Mammoth v. Board of Supervisors, 502 P.2d 1049, 1059 n.8 (Cal. 1972). This was legislatively ratified in 1976 amendments.

[250] Citizens of Goleta Valley v. Board of Supervisors, 801 P.2d 1161 (Cal. 1990).

[251] *See* Polygon Corp. v. City of Seattle, 578 P.2d 1309 (Wash. 1978) (en banc).

[252] Wash. Rev. Code §§ 43.21C.010 to .21C.914 (1983 & Supp. 1991).

Minnesota Environmental Rights Act[253] has been interpreted to require the protection of resources unless the owner could show that there was no way that the resource could be preserved while meeting his needs.[254]

The purpose of the state environmental statute is to provide the fullest possible protection of the environment. To achieve this, the agencies and the courts must give its language the broadest interpretation.[255] Courts have, for instance, drawn assistance from NEPA cases in interpreting the CEQA. Thus, the more expansive case law developed under NEPA may be treated as persuasive authority in analyzing parallel state provisions.[256]

It is worthwhile for a state to make efforts to keep state requirements from duplicating those of federal law, in both the environmental and preservation contexts. New York is one state that has taken steps in this area. The state's Environmental Conservation Law provides that when a state agency is required to prepare or participate in preparing a federal EIS, any submissions required by state law "shall be coordinated with and made in conjunction with federal requirements in a single environmental reporting procedure."[257] Where both Section 106 review under the NHPA and state historic preservation review requirements coincide (that is, where both federal and state agency action is involved), the Section 106 process must be used to satisfy state law, and the procedures of Section 14.09 do not apply.[258] Nevertheless, the agency's substantive obligations continue, and it must still minimize or avoid adverse impacts to historic resources, and explore prudent and feasible alternatives that avoid such impacts.

---

[253] Minn. Stat. §§ 116B.01–116B.13 (1987).

[254] State by Powderly v. Erickson, 285 N.W.2d 84 (Sup. Ct. Minn. 1979).

[255] People *ex rel.* Younger v. Local Agency Formation Comm'n, 81 Cal. App. 3d 464 (1978); Bozung v. Local Agency Formation Comm'n, 529 P.2d 1017, 1024 (Cal. 1975).

[256] Wildlife Alive v. Chickering, 553 P.2d 537, 543 (Cal. 1976).

[257] N.Y. Envtl. Conserv. Law § 8-0111(1) (McKinney 1984).

[258] N.Y. Parks Rec. & Hist. Preserv. Law § 14.09(2) (McKinney 1984).

Seven

Local Regulation of Historic Buildings

Local regulation plays an increasingly important role in preservation law. Neither federal nor state laws prohibit actions that are adverse to the integrity of a historic structure. Rather, as explained in detail in **Chapter Six**, they require government agencies to identify the potential impacts which a proposed action may have on historic resources, identify alternatives to an action that may have an adverse impact on such resources, and consider steps to mitigate the potential damage. Once these procedural steps are completed, the governmental agency may still proceed to take or allow the action which will adversely affect the historic resources. In contrast, local ordinances may provide direct protection for historic resources by regulating their maintenance, alteration, and demolition. It is not surprising, then, that approximately 1,200 communities throughout the United States have enacted local ordinances to provide additional protection for their built heritage.[1]

In general terms, the local preservation ordinance establishes the preservation framework for the community. Typically, the ordinance itself does not designate specific sites as landmarks. Instead, it articulates substantive and procedural standards to guide the community in

---

[1] Boasberg, Coughlin, & Miller, 11 *Historic Preservation Law & Taxation: Real Estate Transactions* (Supp. 1989); *A Handbook on Historic Preservation Law* 59 (Christopher J. Duerksen, ed., Conservation Found., et al. 1983) [hereinafter *Handbook*]; *see* Nat'l Trust for Historic Preservation, *Directory of American Preservation Commissions* (Stephen N. Dennis, ed., 1981) [hereinafter *Directory*]. For a listing of local ordinances in New York State, see National Ctr. for Preservation Law, *A Primer on Preservation Law in the State of New York* at app. A (Berle, Kass & Case, 1985).

identifying and protecting historic and architectural resources. The preservation ordinance may provide for the designation of individual structures as landmarks or of entire areas as historically, culturally, or aesthetically significant districts, or may do both. Since the purpose of a landmark ordinance is to provide a framework within which such decisions may be made, the ordinance must be flexible enough to be applied in a wide variety of circumstances and sufficiently specific to provide guidance in making individual designations.[2]

This chapter is intended to assist communities which are drafting their own preservation ordinances, as well as building owners, developers, lawyers, architects, and citizens who appear before local preservation commissions.[3] The New York City ordinance, found in **Appendix K**, is an example of an ordinance which allows the designation of individual structures as well as districts. While specific reference is made to that ordinance at various places throughout this chapter, readers are encouraged to review it thoroughly and to consider its relative merits with regard to the needs of their own communities. Certification of a local ordinance by the Department of the Interior is often a necessary prerequisite to the rehabilitation tax credit discussed in **Chapter One**. Consequently, the final part of this chapter explains the process by which local ordinances are certified by state and federal agencies.

It should be noted that, unless expressly provided to the contrary, a preservation ordinance does not supersede or modify previously enacted zoning laws. Rather it is an overlay on existing land use regulation which focuses primarily on the preservation of existing buildings rather than the location, size, and use of new buildings.

7.1 STRUCTURAL PROVISIONS OF LOCAL PRESERVATION ORDINANCES

Local preservation ordinances share many common provisions. However, their precise language varies widely because each jurisdiction has tailored its ordinance to meet its own specific needs, preservation

---

[2] *See generally* Duerksen, "Drafting and Administering Historic District Ordinances," *in Handbook, supra* note 1. For further guidance in drafting preservation ordinances, see generally Beaumont, "Local Ordinances: The Major Tool for Protecting Historic Places," *in Landmark Yellow Pages* (Nat'l Trust for Historic Preservation 1992); R. Roddewig, *Preparing a Historic Preservation Ordinance* (1983).

[3] The Supreme Court has noted the concerns that give rise to these legislative efforts. *See* Penn Central Transp. Co. v. City of New York, 438 U.S. 104, 108 (1978). Rhode Island has recently enacted an enabling statute that requires local governments to create comprehensive development plans. R.I. Gen. Laws § 45-22.1-1 to -6 (1991). Under the new statute, each town is required to create growth and development plans that reflect the state's planning goals, including the preservation of historical and cultural resources.

goals, and political realities. Each ordinance also reflects the scope of authority that the locality can exercise both under its state's enabling statute and the case law in its jurisdiction. Though ordinances will vary, much can be learned by surveying those features that are common and studying how various municipalities have approached the drafting of their ordinances. The discussion that follows outlines the provisions most commonly included in preservation ordinances throughout the country. Relevant examples are provided from a variety of local ordinances, in addition to the ordinance included in the appendix. Where appropriate, cases that interpret the language of these provisions are also surveyed.

7.1.1 Statement of Purpose

One of the most important provisions of the ordinance is its statement of purpose, a statement of public policy. Generally this provision will contain two components: a reference to the municipality's authority to use the police power in furtherance of the public welfare, and a statement of the interests the community seeks to protect. Together, these elements provide the legal basis upon which the ordinance rests.[4]

The public welfare interests advanced by the preservation ordinance should be stated as broadly as possible. Too often ordinances cite only the obvious cultural, historic, and aesthetic reasons for preservation and thereby miss the opportunity to place preservation in a broader context. It is now widely recognized that preservation may further education, commercial, and economic interests as well, and the statement of purpose should reflect the full range of public benefits which may be realized.

After the ordinance has been enacted, the statement of purpose will assist the local landmarks commission in interpreting other provisions of the ordinance. The purposes set forth in the statement will be considered by the commission and guide its deliberations. Moreover, the statement of purpose is one of the benchmarks against which courts of review can evaluate whether the commission has acted within the scope of its authority and has decided a particular case in accordance with the mandate of

---

[4] Reference to the public or general welfare should be included even though no court has yet struck down an ordinance solely for an inadequate statement of purpose. *See Handbook, supra* note 1, at 64. *See also* Berman v. Parker, 348 U.S. 26, 33 (1954); Figarsky v. Historic Dist. Comm'n, 368 A.2d 163 (Conn. 1976); Bohannan v. City of San Diego, 30 Cal. App. 3d 416 (1973). The articulation of the statement of purpose is particularly vital in view of the Supreme Court's recent decision in Nollan v. California Coastal Comm'n, 483 U.S. 825 (1987). In *Nollan*, the Court invalidated a permit condition on the grounds that there was an insufficient nexus between the condition and the public purposes asserted for its justification. *See* § **7.4.5**. This decision underscores the importance of stating a valid public purpose and connecting it precisely with the method used for its advancement and can appropriately be applied in the context of drafting preservation ordinances.

the ordinance.[5] Invoking a broad range of objectives to be served by the protection of qualifying properties provides a stronger basis for preservation activities, and may make it more likely that the ordinance will withstand judicial review, for the subjective nature of determinations which are solely aesthetic in nature has been a source of concern for some lower courts.[6]

The purposes clause should be drafted with reference not only to the U.S. Constitution but also the state constitution, case law relating to other preservation ordinances within the state and zoning and other forms of land use regulation.

---

[5] An example of a comprehensive Statement of Purpose is found in New York City's Ordinance:

Purpose and declaration of public policy.

a. The council finds that many improvements, as herein defined, and landscape features, as herein defined, having a special character or a special historical or aesthetic interest or value and many improvements representing the finest architectural products of distinct periods in the history of the city, have been uprooted, notwithstanding the feasibility of preserving and continuing the use of such improvements and landscape features, and without adequate consideration of the irreplaceable loss to the people of the city of the aesthetic, cultural and historic values represented by such improvements and landscape features. In addition distinct areas may be similarly uprooted or may have their distinctiveness destroyed, although the preservation thereof may be both feasible and desirable. It is the sense of the council that the standing of this city as a worldwide tourist center and world capital of business, culture and government cannot be maintained or enhanced by disregarding the historical and architectural heritage of the city and by countenancing the destruction of such cultural assets.

b. It is hereby declared as a matter of public policy that the protection, enhancement, perpetuation and use of improvements and landscape features of special character or a special historical or aesthetic interest or value is a public necessity and is required in the interest of the health, prosperity, safety and welfare of the people. The purpose of this chapter is to (a) effect and accomplish the protection, enhancement and perpetuation of such improvements and landscape features and of districts which represent or reflect elements of the city's cultural, social, economic, political and architectural history; (b) safeguard the city's historic, aesthetic and cultural heritage, as embodied and reflected in such improvements, landscape features and districts; (c) stabilize and improve property values in such districts; (d) foster civic pride in the beauty and noble accomplishments of the past; (e) protect and enhance the city's attractions to tourists and visitors and the support and stimulus to business and industry thereby provided; (f) strengthen the economy of the city; and (g) promote the use of historic districts, landmarks, interior landmarks and scenic landmarks for the education, pleasure and welfare of the people of the city.

N.Y.C. Admin. Code § 25-301 (1986).

[6] See 21 A.L.R.3d 1222 (1968 & Supp. 1991) for cases stating judicial concern about aesthetics being forwarded as the sole rationale for regulation. In some cases, state grounds (constitutional and statutory) have been invoked to strike down ordinances based on aesthetic objectives alone. Note, however, that cases which hold that zoning ordinances based on aesthetic criteria are invalid are not analogous to those involving ordinances designed to preserve historic architectural style. See A-S-P Assocs. v. City of Raleigh, 258 S.E.2d 444, 450 (N.C. 1979), and cases cited therein.

7.1.2 Definitions

The definitions section which often follows the statement of purpose is a key section of the ordinance because the commission and the courts will refer to it to interpret the language, and thereby to determine the scope of the ordinance.[7]

The primary terms to be defined may include, inter alia:

Historic district
Landmark
Alteration
Maintenance
Improvement
Reasonable return

One example of a set of definitions for these terms can be found in the New York City Landmark and Historic District Ordinance.

Each definition should specify the word's meaning in the clearest possible terms. This will not only facilitate the administration of the ordinance, but is essential to its constitutionality, since due process requires that those subject to a law's regulation be able to understand it.[8] Persons with widely differing perspectives and backgrounds will be working with the ordinance, and it should be comprehensible to all. Unnecessary legal and technical terms should be avoided; a definitions section that relies too heavily on legal and technical terms may be clear to a developer's attorney but incomprehensible to the small property owner who does not often read ordinances.[9]

While definitions should be drafted with precision, they should not be too narrow or rigid. The ordinance must be sufficiently flexible to be useful in the vast range of contexts in which it will be applied over time.

7.1.3 Establishing the Administrative Body

The local preservation commission designated by the ordinance bears overall responsibility for ongoing preservation planning and activities in the community. In addition to playing the key role in regulating the alteration or demolition of historic structures, its responsibilities may range from conducting surveys by which historic properties are identified and designated, to ensuring that other municipal agencies consider the goals of preservation in conducting their activities, to providing information to other levels of government in their preservation activities, such as nominations of properties to the National Register.

---

[7] *See* South of Second Assocs. v. Georgetown, 580 P.2d 807 (Colo. 1978).
[8] Rose v. Locke, 423 U.S. 48, 49–50 (1975).
[9] Dennis, "Do's and Don'ts in Drafting a Preservation Ordinance," *in Reusing Old Buildings: Preservation Law and the Development Process* 315 (Conservation Found., et al. 1982).

7.1.4 Creation and Makeup

The administrative bodies created by preservation ordinances are called a variety of names, including landmarks preservation commissions and boards of architectural review.[10] Whatever the administrative body is called (in this chapter, it will be called the commission), the ordinance usually provides for the appointment of its members by the community's mayor or by an elected body such as the city council.

Sometimes the composition of the commission is mandated in the state enabling law; in most cases it is left to the discretion of the locality. Although some communities opt to use existing municipal bodies, such as the planning board, most ordinances require the creation of a separate board composed of experts in relevant fields. Frequently the ordinance specifies the professions or interests to be represented, such as a local historian, architect, urban planner, lawyer, real estate professional, preservation group officer, or community resident.[11] Composition specifications should reflect the nature of the ordinance and of the tasks to be performed by the commission, some of which may require specialized skills. For example, the Palo Alto Historic Resources Board consists of five members who must include an owner-occupant of a designated historic structure or historic district; at least three architects, landscape architects, building designers, or other design professionals; one member with relevant academic or practical experience.[12]

Such diversity of perspective and expertise enhances the likelihood of a full airing of the issues and thorough consideration of the implications of approving a designation, alteration, or demolition. Courts have observed that a broad-based commission membership "curb[s] the possibility for abuse,"[13] and tends to protect a commission's decision from the allegation of arbitrary enforcement.[14] In addition, as noted, representation on the commission of a broad spectrum of relevant expertise is required if the local ordinance is to qualify for certification to receive federal funding.[15]

In small communities which do not have residents with the specialized skills needed for the commission, it may be possible to pool resources with neighboring communities and establish an intermunicipal commission.

---

[10] *See generally Directory, supra* note 1.

[11] For an illustration of such a provision, see "Recommended Model Provisions for a Preservation Ordinance with Annotations," § 54.10.2, *in Handbook, supra* note, 1, at app. A [hereinafter Model Preservation Ordinance].

[12] Palo Alto, Cal., Municipal Code ch. 16.49.030(d) (1989).

[13] Maher v. City of New Orleans, 516 F.2d 1051, 1062 (5th Cir. 1975), *cert. denied*, 426 U.S. 905 (1976).

[14] *See South of Second Assocs.*, 580 P.2d at 808–09 n.1.

[15] 16 U.S.C.A. § 470w(13) (West 1985).

In addition to specifying the categories of individuals to serve as the members of the commission and the method of their selection, the ordinance should establish procedures for their appointment and specify the length of their terms and amount of compensation, if any.

7.1.5 Scope of Authority

The authority which the ordinance grants to the administrative body will depend on two factors: first, the extent of authority granted to the locality in the state enabling statute and case law interpreting that statute; and second, the preservation goals of the community. Since 1976, every state has had enabling legislation for local preservation ordinances.[16] Under these empowering statutes, a municipality may choose whether or not to establish a commission to advance preservation purposes. Once it does choose to establish one, however, its discretion as to the methods and the standards by which the ordinance is to be administered may be limited by the enabling statute.[17] Consequently, in drafting its preservation ordinance, a municipality should pay careful attention to the scope of the enabling legislation. Furthermore, a local law may have to be amended to conform with new state legislation. New Jersey, for example, passed comprehensive amendments to the New Jersey Municipal Land Use Law in January 1986. As a result of this action, which was aimed at integrating the protection of historic sites and structures into the zoning process, the legal status of many local preservation commissions was thrown into question. Most of these commissions were established when New Jersey did not yet have comprehensive enabling legislation, and their authority had been grounded in the traditional police power. Since the local ordinances had necessarily been drafted before the state legislation was passed, some of their provisions were not in compliance with the terms of the state law and the preservation commissions had to be reauthorized.[18]

Enabling legislation may limit a municipality's ability to control the manner in which historic property may be owned or held, or to impose an affirmative duty of restoration. In one decision, the New York Court of Appeals, the highest state court, held that nothing in the state's zoning enabling or historic preservation laws, or in a city's landmark preservation law, enacted thereunder, empowered a city to mandate the form of ownership of a historic property. It also held that a city could

---

[16] *National Trust Guide to State Historic Preservation Programs* (1976). *See, e.g.*, N.Y. Gen. Mun. Law §§ 96-a, 119-dd (McKinney 1986).

[17] *See A-S-P Assocs.*, 258 S.E.2d at 452.

[18] In Estate of Neuberger v. Township of Middletown, 521 A.2d 1336 (N.J. App. Div. 1987), Middletown's preservation ordinance was invalidated. The court concluded, after a review of the New Jersey Municipal Land Use Law, that only the planning board and board of adjustment had the authority to protect historic sites. While praising the state's goal of unifying control over planning and zoning, the court remarked that "with very little modification, [the town] can bring its ordinances within the statutory delegation." 521 A.2d at 1342.

not impose the costs of rehabilitation (as opposed to maintenance) of that property on the owner, or on purchasers of properties neighboring the site.[19]

If there is no state enabling statute specifically relating to preservation, or if the statute is not sufficiently encompassing for the locality's purposes, authority may be found elsewhere. In some states, the state constitution or a statute grants localities broad home rule powers. Alternatively, the general zoning power of localities may serve as a basis for preservation ordinances,[20] although assertions of authority based on the general zoning power may be viewed with less favor by the courts than those based on specific state enabling statutes.[21]

Once the enabling law has been studied to determine the extent of the authority delegated to the municipality, it must be determined whether the municipality wishes to exercise the full extent of the power available to it. Since a landmark ordinance generally provides the framework within which decisions will be made, there is only one reason for a community not to reserve for itself the full range of power it can claim: It may be politically unfeasible to gain passage of the stronger ordinance, because of fear of this additional and to some, unfamiliar form of regulation. Nonetheless, given the benefits to be gained from an effective preservation effort, local legislators often decide to enact an ordinance that grants to the commission the broadest possible authority to protect historic resources.

As outlined in more detail in this chapter, the commission's powers should include the destination of landmarks, districts, or sites (after nomination by a third party or on the commission's own initiative) and the review of applications for proposed physical changes—that is, alterations, demolitions, or new construction. The commission should also have the power to ensure maintenance of landmarks and, when necessary, to acquire property rights, particularly easements, to ensure that preservation goals are achieved. Typically, the ordinance also will grant the commission the power to adopt and amend the rules of procedure under which it will work.

7.1.6 Administrative Structure

The administrative structure required to carry out a landmark ordinance can be tailored to fit the needs of the particular community. For example, in some communities, the landmarks commission is responsible for designation and alteration determinations, but its decisions are subject to review by another city agency or legislative body. In New York

---

[19] FGL & L Property Corp. v. City of Rye, 485 N.E.2d 986 (N.Y. 1985).

[20] *See* City of Santa Fe v. Gamble-Skogmo, Inc., 389 P.2d 13, 17 (1964).

[21] *See* Tierney v. Norwalk Planning & Zoning Comm'n, 3 *Preservation L. Rep.* 3016 (Conn. 1984).

City, for example, the Board of Estimate has the power to modify or disapprove a landmark designation made by the Landmarks Preservation Commission.[22]

In other cities, the commission may be advisory only, and will report and make recommendations to another municipal official, board, or legislature.[23] In Washington, DC, for instance, preservation proceedings are conducted by the mayor or by a designated agent with the advice of the Historic Preservation Review Board. If the permit application affects a landmark in the Old Georgetown District, it is subject to review by the Commission of Fine Arts and may be referred to the Historic Preservation Review Board for recommendation.

7.2 THE HISTORIC RESOURCES INVENTORY

The duties of the commission should include identifying the historic resources of the community and maintaining an inventory of them. Compiling a survey of the community's historical resources serves several purposes. This inventory is the groundwork upon which the community can base its preservation planning and justify its actions. For example, surveying properties in the community for their historic and architectural value, plotting them on a map, photographing them, and recording their significance may reveal clusters of properties that are worthy of inclusion in a historic district. Exhaustive recordkeeping will assist in formulating the boundaries of the historic district and in justifying the choices made should a dispute arise. The survey can also serve as a data base for nominations to the National Register, identification of properties that may be eligible for protection under environmental review statutes, and projects to promote public awareness through publications, tours, or historical identification plaques.

Finally, the survey should lead to the development of a comprehensive preservation plan which sets forth the community's goals and proposes actions to be undertaken to achieve them.[24]

---

[22] N.Y.C. Admin. Code § 25-303 (1986).

[23] District of Columbia Historic Landmark and Historic District Protection Act of 1978, D.C. Code Ann. § 5-1003(c) (1988). *See e.g.*, San Francisco, Cal., Planning Code art. 10 (limiting the authority of the landmarks board to nomination and review activities for the purpose of presenting recommendations to the planning commission).

[24] The Massachusetts Historical Commission has published *Preservation Planning Manual*, an extremely helpful manual for local historical commissions that discusses the items that should be included in a community's plan. It is worth quoting from pages 50–51:

> A Preservation Plan is a formal document that analyzes the preservation issues confronting a community and presents recommendations for the resolution of those issues. It is generally published and distributed throughout the community to all local decision makers so that it can be incorporated into the community's overall planning efforts. The Plan serves as the local commission's goal statement and sets out a series of

A community may also wish to conduct a historical analysis to aid it in identifying how its physical resources reflect its heritage. The emphasis of the analysis should be to trace the forces that shaped the development of the area and gave it its essential character.[25] To a large extent, the inventory of historically prominent properties may be developed from such a historical analysis.

tasks for the commission to undertake, along with priorities and a time frame for completion of those tasks. A formal Preservation Plan is an excellent means of disseminating information about the commission's goals and purpose, and of strengthening the commission's image as a competent and professional planning body.

Generally, Preservation Plans include some combination of the following elements:

—A summary history of the growth and development of the community;

—An analysis of all the architectural styles represented in the community;

—A survey of the significant structures and areas in the community . . . ;

—A map showing all cultural resources surveyed (except archaeological sites);

—A statement of the local commission's preservation policy and overall objectives;

—Recommendations for preservation measures for specific properties or areas (these might include but are not limited to the following: National Register nomination, local historic district designation, scenic road designation, acquisition of preservation restrictions, and amendment of zoning ordinances);

—Identification of funding sources for preservation projects in the community (these might include Massachusetts Preservation Projects Fund grants, Housing and Urban Development Community Block Grant funds, National Endowment for the Arts grants, and Architectural Conservation Trust for Massachusetts revolving fund assistance);

—Recommendations for the integration of preservation goals and objectives into the community planning process.

[25] Some possible elements that may have contributed to a community's historical development include

1. Geological formations, geographical features, and the natural environment.
2. Prehistoric life.
3. Historic Indian tribes and their culture.
4. The arrival of people from abroad, including explorers, missionaries, traders, early settlers, and later immigrants.
5. The reasons and incentives for settlement, such as land grants, mill sites, and mineral resources.
6. The patterns of transportation development, including rivers, canals, railroads, roads, and street patterns.
7. Military and political history, including the French and Indian War, American Revolution, War of 1812, local rebellions, impact of the Civil War, and later foreign wars.
8. Economic factors such as water power, technological inventions, turnpike, canal or railroad construction, war industries, mineral resources, recreation, and periods of boom and depression.
9. Social and cultural trends such as religious sects, reform movements, education, art, architecture, music, and literature.
10. Individuals or groups that played a part in shaping the character of the community, including farmers, industrialists, merchants, bankers, religious figures, judges, architects, and statesmen.

State of New York Div. for Historic Preservation, *Historic Resources Survey Manual* 27–28 (rev. ed., Albany, New York: New York State Office of Parks and Recreation 1974).

The identification of a community's historic resources is a critical first step in a local preservation program. The failure to gather information pertaining to potential landmarks can undermine later efforts to save threatened buildings.[26] Moreover, the process can be time consuming; starting it after a building or historic area is directly threatened may well be too late. For example, a neighborhood of Revolutionary war-era homes in Cambridge, Massachusetts, completed a 2-year battle for approval as a historic district when the area was officially declared the Half Crown Neighborhood Conservation District. Residents had sought to preserve the area in the face of severe development pressures from the Harvard Square area, adjacent to the neighborhood. While this 2-year effort was in progress, nearby development included two office buildings, a hotel, a bank building, and more than 100 condominiums. The value of land in the area rose to as much as $1 million an acre.[27] In an even more extreme example, the filing of an application nominating Pittsburgh's Syria Mosque for designation as a historical landmark *two hours* after a demolition permit was issued was insufficient to prevent the mosque's destruction.[28]

Some states have passed legislation to enhance cooperation of state and local governments with respect to the preservation of historic resources. For example, the Florida Division of Historical Resources must cooperate with local governments in conducting a survey of historic resources and must assist local governments to accelerate and expand their historic *preservation* programs.[29]

7.3 THE DESIGNATION PROCESS

7.3.1 Nomination

Most communities allow a nomination for designation as a landmark or historic district to be made by any of several methods. For example, in Boston, any ten registered voters, the mayor, or any Landmarks Commission member may submit a petition to the commission asking that a property be considered for designation.[30] A slightly different

---

[26] *See* Committee to Save the Fox Bldg. v. Birmingham Branch of the Fed. Reserve Bank, 497 F. Supp 504 (N.D. Ala. 1980); Life of the Land, Inc. v. City Council of Honolulu, 606 P.2d 866, 899–901 (Haw. 1980).

[27] *Boston Globe*, Apr. 15, 1984, at 34.

[28] Committee to Save the Syria Mosque v. National Dev. Corp., No. GD91-08228 (Pa. Ct. Comm. Pleas June 25, 1991).

[29] Fla. Stat. §§ 267.061 (West 1991).

[30] Acts of 1975 ch. 772, § 4, Mass. Gen. Laws. In DGM Partners-Rye v. City of Rye, Index No. 4609/85 (N.Y. Sup. Ct. July 10, 1985), the New York Supreme Court rejected the plaintiff's claim that the Rye, NY, Landmarks Ordinance violated the U.S. Constitution's equal protection clause. The ordinance required owner consent for the landmark designation of properties that are not listed on or nominated for the National Register. Consent was not

approach is taken by the Town of Pound Ridge, New York, which will initiate its process upon request from affected property owners or upon the commission's own motion.[31] Palo Alto, California, provides the broadest avenue for initiating the designation procedure. There, any individual or group may propose designation of a landmark building or district.[32]

By providing a variety of methods by which a property can be proposed for designation, a community takes a large step toward ensuring that no building that is potentially worthy of protection is overlooked.

7.3.2 Designation Standards

A local preservation ordinance should articulate clear standards for the designation of a structure or site as a landmark. These standards sometimes track the criteria provided in the enabling statute; if the statute is silent, they may be developed in the first instance for the ordinance. Other ordinances delegate the task of formulating designation standards to the commission, whose members can bring their expertise to bear on the question. Clear designation standards will provide fair notice to the owner or potential buyer of property as to the characteristics that may lead to designation. The owners can thereby better anticipate possible limitations upon alteration or development of the property. Carefully drafted standards will also serve as guidelines for the commission's deliberations. Finally, they provide a benchmark against which a reviewing court may judge whether the commission's actions were well-grounded, arbitrary, or discriminatory.

7.3.3 General Criteria

Many communities, such as Rye, New York, adopt the list of characteristics that a structure, site, or area must possess to be included on the Department of Interior's National Register of Historic Places.[33] Other

---

required for listed or eligible properties. The court concluded that the classifications were rationally related to the purpose of the ordinance and to public policy and were thus valid.

[31] Pound Ridge, NY, Local Law No. 4-1976 art. III § 17-8A (1988).

[32] Palo Alto, Cal., Municipal Code ch. 16.49.040 (1986).

[33] No Preservation District or Protected Site or Structure, as the case may be, shall be designated unless it is found to possess one or more of the following characteristics:
   1. Association with persons or events of historic significance to the city, region, state or nation.
   2. Illustrative of historic growth and development of the city, region, state, or nation.
   3. In the case of structures: embodying distinctive characteristics of a type, period, or method of construction or representing the work of a master, or possessing unique architectural and artistic qualities, or representing a significant and distinguishable entity whose components may lack individual distinction.

jurisdictions, such as Seattle, Washington, have drafted their own standards for identifying structures and districts of historical, cultural, geographic, or archaeological importance.[34]

While the ordinance should be precise enough to provide adequate guidance to the commission and owners alike, language that is unreasonably and rigidly specific may preclude the designation of buildings that the community may wish to protect. The commission will be called on to

4. In the case of districts, possessing a unique overall quality of architectural scale, texture, form, and visual homogeneity, even though certain structures within the district may lack individual distinction.
5. In the case of interiors, possessing one or more of the characteristics enumerated in (1), (2) or (3) above and, in addition, embodying distinctive characteristics of architectural scale, form, and visual homogeneity, which are an integral part of the character of the structure in which the space is contained.

Rye, NY, Code § 117-5(B) (1984).

[34] Standards for Designation of Structures and Districts for Preservation. A structure, group of structures, site, or district may be designated for preservation as a landmark or landmark district if it has—

Historical, Cultural Importance

1. Has significant character, interest or value, as part of the development heritage; or
2. Is the site of a historic event with a significant effect upon society; or
3. Exemplifies the cultural, political, economic, social or historic heritage of the community; or

Architectural, Engineering Importance

4. Portrays the environment in an era of history characterized by a distinctive architectural style; or
5. Embodies those distinguishing characteristics of an architectural-type or engineering specimen; or
6. Is the work of a designer whose individual work has significantly influenced the development of Seattle; or
7. Contains elements of design, detail, materials or craftsmanship which represent a significant innovation; or

Geographic Importance

8. By being part of or related to a square, park or other distinctive area, should be developed or preserved according to a plan based on a historic, cultural or architectural motif; or
9. Owing to its unique location or singular physical characteristic, represents an established and familiar visual feature of the neighborhood, community or city; or

Archaeological Importance

10. Has yielded, or may be likely to yield, information important in pre-history or history.

Seattle, Wash. Landmarks Ordinance No. 102229 § 6. Seattle, Wash. Landmarks Ordinance No. 102229, referred to in **Ch. 7**, *see id.* and *infra* notes 67, 82, 138, 151, and accompanying text, has been repealed and replaced with Landmarks Preservation Ordinance No. 106348. Many provisions of the old ordinance have been omitted in the new ordinance, and many requirements regarding buildings within a historic district (e.g., maintenance) are contained in the ordinances designating specific historic districts. References to the old ordinance are retained in this chapter to serve as examples of possible approaches to drafting of local preservation laws.

apply the language of the ordinance in a wide range of situations, and the language must be sufficiently flexible to allow the commission to fulfill its task. It should also be noted that unless explicitly precluded, the property protected by a designation extends to structures and grounds which are necessary for the integrity of the landmark, but which may not be independently significant and worthy of protection.[35]

7.3.4 Historic Districts

The designation of boundaries of historic districts can present special difficulties. Frequently, the architectural or historical "theme" with which the buildings in an area may be associated pertains more strongly to some buildings than to others. Often, for example, the buildings in a proposed historic district will not be architecturally uniform. And while some buildings may not be worthy of individual designation, they may contribute significantly to the overall architectural or historical significance of a neighborhood. Accordingly, when defining boundaries, a commission must consider the unifying qualities of the structures to be included in the district. It should also evaluate the inclusion of structures and/or open space on the periphery of the district that are necessary to protect its historic properties. In addition, boundaries should be clear and, where possible, should follow existing natural or mapped features.[36]

As a general matter, however, certain types of boundaries should be avoided. It is typically not a good idea, for example, to run the boundary of a historic district down the middle of a street. Doing so could result in incompatible building designs and facades on opposite sides, since construction and alteration on one side would be regulated while on the other it would not.

---

[35] See A-S-P Assocs., 258 S.E.2d at 450–51.

[36] The Massachusetts Historical Commission has identified these factors to assist in evaluating historic district boundaries:

> EVALUATION FOR SELECTION OF BOUNDARIES. In determining the boundaries of the historic district(s), the Study Committee should consider:
> a. the significance of the architectural characteristics of each building and structure within the district and the degree to which they are visible from the public ways;
> b. the buildings and structures on the edges of the district which are an asset, as part of the setting or as protection to historic properties, or which are a detriment, because of incongruity of style, mass, use, condition;
> c. the amount of open space within and on the edges of the district which can be justified as historic or necessary for protection to historic properties;
> d. the distance up side street which district boundaries should extend to provide protection;
> e. the amount of open space visible from the main public ways within the district;
> f. the immediate surroundings of the district and the view into the district from the approaches to it.

Recent editions of the Commission's *Establishing Local Historic Districts*, in which these factors were listed, contain less detailed language.

In order to reduce the potential for subjectivity in setting district boundaries, the ordinance should refer to the overall consistency of the proposed area and explicitly recognize that all buildings within the district may not be of the same significance. For example, the Rye ordinance refers to districts "possessing a unique overall quality of architectural scale, texture, form, and visual homogeneity, even though certain structures within the District may lack individual distinction." Other ordinances use such language as "congruity" or "consistency" in describing the relationship between the buildings in a district.

Generally, a court will uphold a commission's designation if it is based on clearly articulated standards.[37] In determining whether the discretion of the commission is limited, courts have gone fairly far to find that the commission acted under limiting factors.[38] Nevertheless, vague or nonexistent standards may result in a court invalidating the designation.[39] One court has said that discretion is sufficiently limited by a contextual standard found in the "readily identifiable, . . . predominant architectural style" of Victorian architecture in the district. This gave meaning to the general standard of "incongruity" in the ordinance.[40] Another court found that standards were provided to guide the commission in determining the effect of new construction on the character of a historic district when specific criteria to be considered, such as the architectural style of the new construction, texture, and material, were provided in the ordinance. The court found that such narrowing standards were "objective and easily discernible."[41]

For this reason, the standards section of a local ordinance assumes great importance. If the standards are found to be adequate, a court will be disinclined to substitute its judgment for that of the commission when it applies those standards to determine whether a particular building or district should be designated. Instead, the traditional deference extended by courts to the assumed expertise of administrative boards is reflected in the broad discretion allowed a commission in its designation determinations. Some states have provided that a threshold number of voters owning property in an area must favor designation of that area as a historic district before such designation can occur. In Connecticut, for example, there is a statutory requirement that an

---

[37] See, e.g., Society for Ethical Culture v. Spatt, 416 N.Y.S.2d 246, 249–50 (App. Div. 1979), aff'd, 415 N.E.2d 922 (1980).

[38] See e.g., A-S-P Assocs., 258 S.E.2d at 453 (documents incorporated by reference in ordinance provide sufficient standards).

[39] See Historic Green Springs, Inc. v. Bergland, 497 F. Supp. 839 (E.D. Va. 1980); South of Second Assoc. v. Georgetown, 580 P.2d 807 (Colo. 1978); Texas Antiquities Comm'n v. Dallas County Community College Dist., 554 S.W.2d 924 (Tex. 1977).

[40] A-S-P Assocs., 258 S.E.2d at 454.

[41] South of Second Assocs., 580 P.2d at 810.

affirmative vote of two thirds of the owners of property in a proposed district be attained before a historic district can be established.[42]

Moreover, in establishing boundaries, it is important that a commission indicate, as part of the record of its proceedings, legally defensible reasons for deciding what to include within a district, based on relevant architectural and historic factors. This should reduce the chances of a successful challenge to the boundaries by property owners seeking to avoid historic preservation requirements.[43]

7.3.5 Procedural Standards

Proper procedural standards in the preservation context follow traditional constitutional and administrative law principles for agency decision making. The purpose of these standards is to ensure fairness in the decision-making process and to provide a structural check on potential abuse of discretion by the commission.[44] Adequate procedural standards will include notice to the owner of the nominated property, an opportunity for the owner to present his views to the commission and the requirement that any decision include findings and embody a conclusion that is supported by the record. In addition to basic constitutional standards (derived from both the United States and applicable state constitutions), further procedural requirements may be found in a state's enabling act or administrative procedure act.

Designations have often been challenged on procedural grounds.[45] As one court stated in requiring a city to rescind a landmark designation because of inadequate notice, rules concerning public notice, hearing, and procedure must be "spelled out and followed."[46] But while precise drafting is in the interests of due process, "[t]o satisfy due process,

---

[42] Conn. Gen. Stat. Ann. § 7-147b(i) (West 1989); Gentry v. City of Norwalk, 494 A.2d 1206 (Conn. 1985).

[43] *See* Portsmouth Advocates v. Portsmouth, 587 A.2d 600 (N.H. 1991) (affirming city council's action taken pursuant to request by individual landowner adjusting historic district boundaries in order to remove buildings lacking historical significance).

[44] *Maher,* 516 F.2d at 1062-63.

[45] *See, e.g.,* Shubert Organization, Inc. v. Landmarks Preservation Comm'n, 570 N.Y.S.2d 504 (App. Div.), *appeal dismissed,* 580 N.E.2d 1059, *appeal denied,* 79 N.Y.2d 751 (1991) (dismissing a challenge against the process used in the designation of the interiors and exteriors of 22 Broadway Theaters because the commission conducted preliminary analyses, made exhaustive reports, conducted the decision making over the course of several years, and held three days of hearings providing a meaningful opportunity for public comment).

[46] St. James United Methodist Church v. Kingston (N.Y. Ulster Cty. Sup. Ct. March 11, 1977). *Compare* Assheton v. Planning Board, No. 47624 (N.Y. Sup. Ct. Apr. 3, 1991) (upholding Coopertown ordinance against a facial challenge to its constitutionality due to plaintiff's failure to establish that the law was unconstitutional beyond a reasonable doubt, but expressing concern over lack of process in the exercise of the commission's power expanding the historic district, including the failure to conduct inventories or studies, lack of formal process for designating structures of historical significance, and failure to provide advance notice to property owners).

guidelines to aid a commission charged with implementing a public zoning purpose need not be so rigidly drawn as to prejudge the outcome in each case, precluding reasonable administrative discretion."[47]

7.3.6 Notice

As noted earlier, many ordinances allow the designation process to be initiated by someone other than the owner of the property. To allow the process to continue without providing an opportunity for the owner's input would be fundamentally unfair. Since designation as a landmark may place restrictions on the use of the property and even impose affirmative duties on the owner, it seems beyond question that before any property is designated, due process requires notice which is "reasonably calculated, under all the circumstances to apprise the interested parties of the pendency of the action and afford them an opportunity to present their objections."[48] Procedural due process was found to have been provided in one case when, although a zoning ordinance prohibited a particular use of property, the owners "had actual notice of the introduction of the ordinance, appeared at the hearing proceeding its adoption, and availed themselves of the opportunity to argue against its adoption."[49]

The question remains open whether in the context of landmark designation personal notice or notice by publication is required. Although it is not a settled matter, a community would be well advised to provide personal notice by certified mail any time the number of property owners affected is not so large as to make that method impractical or economically prohibitive.

In circumstances where personal notice is appropriate, adequate notice should include a copy of the application, the time and location of the hearing, and either a copy of the rules and procedures that the commission will use or an explanation of where this can be obtained. Notice should be provided sufficiently in advance of the public hearing to allow proper preparation of testimony.

The designation of a site may affect a number of parties in addition to the applicant or property owner. These other parties may include adjoining landowners, tenants, preservation organizations, and relevant business organizations. Interested parties such as these should have the opportunity to have their views heard by the commission and the commission should encourage their participation by identifying them and by providing them with notice of hearing as well.[50]

---

[47] *Maher*, 516 F.2d at 1062.

[48] Mullane v. Central Hanover Bank & Trust Co., 339 U.S. 306, 314 (1950). See Volkswagenwerk Aktiengesellschaft v. Schlunk, 486 U.S. 694, 706–07 (1988); Tulsa Professional Collection Serv. v. Pope, 485 U.S. 478, 484 (1988).

[49] Schafer v. City of New Orleans, 743 F.2d 1086, 1089 (5th Cir. 1984).

[50] However, notice to these interested parties may not be required by the U.S. Constitution. *See* Zartman v. Reisem, 399 N.Y.S.2d 506, 510 (App. Div. 1977).

7.3.7 Prehearing

After the designation of an individual building or district has been proposed, the commission must begin to develop the information which will be included in the record in support of its decision either to make or reject the designation. Participants in the designation process should determine what practices the commission and its staff, if any, follow in evaluating the properties or districts prior to the hearing.

For example, in Boston the significance of a nominated property is evaluated in a formal study report which is prepared prior to the public hearing.[51] When a single landmark is proposed, the commission staff is responsible for preparing the study. In contrast, when a historic district is proposed, the study is performed by five of the nine commission members and six persons who have a "demonstrated interest in the district" and have been appointed by the mayor and confirmed by the City Council. The resulting report is made available three weeks prior to a public hearing on a proposed landmark designation and 60 days prior to a proposed district designation. The study, which makes recommendations as to the proposed designation, serves as an important reference document in all further deliberations of the Boston Commission.

7.3.8 Hearing

The due process clause of the Fifth Amendment of the U.S. Constitution generally requires the opportunity for a hearing prior to the deprivation of a constitutionally protected interest, such as a property right,[52] but it need not be analogous to a formal trial with cross-examination and a verbatim record. Instead, the hearing may be informal, more similar to a legislative hearing than a trial. At a minimum, however, some adjudicative procedure must be provided.

Most jurisdictions utilize the legislative hearing format rather than the trial-like setting of the judicial approach. The municipality's ordinance will normally specify which is to be used. If the ordinance is silent on this point, counsel should refer to the jurisdiction's administrative procedures act which governs general agency procedures.[53] It is important that all parties involved with a designation proceeding be familiar with applicable procedural requirements.

Both proponents and opponents, if any, of the proposed designation should identify the particular concerns of the commission with regard to the property at issue and determine how best to satisfy these concerns. A number of methods may be helpful, including presenting

---

[51] Boston, Mass., Landmarks Ordinance § 4.

[52] *See* Board of Regents v. Roth, 408 U.S. 564, 570 n.7 (1972).

[53] *See Society for Ethical Culture*, 416 N.Y.S.2d at 250.

testimony by experts, offering demonstrative evidence such as slides, and presenting a comparative analysis of prior approvals and denials and describing how the proposal under consideration fits into that broader context.

7.3.9 Decision

The commission should develop a comprehensive written record upon which it can base its decision. The record should include written submissions, transcripts of oral testimony, and whatever documents the staff or the commission itself has produced. Based on this record, the commission should issue a written statement of its findings of fact and its determination and should include an explanation of how the designation relates to the standards set forth in the ordinance. A decision based on a repetition of the language of the ordinance and the mere conclusory statement that these requirements have been met may well not be found to be sufficient if the decision is challenged judicially.[54]

The ordinance should require that notice of a designation be given to the owner, published generally, and provided to the municipal agencies with an interest in the outcome, such as those administering taxes and building permits. Notice to other municipal agencies is critical to the effective administration of the ordinance. The buildings department, for example, must know which buildings are subject to special procedures in connection with the grant of demolition or alteration permits by virtue of their status as landmarks. The designation should also be recorded in the appropriate title records so that any potential buyer of the property is on notice that it is subject to regulation under the ordinance.

7.3.10 Appeal

An ordinance should provide a mechanism for appealing a decision by the commission. Some ordinances allow review of the decision by another municipal body such as the city council. Others provide for immediate judicial review.

The question of standing—that is, of who may bring the appeal—should be dealt with in this section of the ordinance. In some communities only the owner of the designated property may appeal the decision. In other cases, standing is extended to any member of the community in recognition of the interest which each may have in preserving the community's historic resources.

---

[54] See, e.g., Historic Green Springs, 497 F. Supp. at 850–51; Don't Tear it Down, Inc. v. D.C. Dep't of Hous. & Community Dev., 428 A.2d 369 (D.C. 1981); Broadview Apartments Co. v. Commission for Historical & Architectural Preservation, 433 A.2d 1214 (Md. Ct. Spec. App. 1981).

7.4 APPLICATIONS RELATING TO ALTERATION, NEW CONSTRUCTION, AND DEMOLITION

7.4.1 Alteration and New Construction

The fundamental provision of the local ordinance is the requirement that the commission review and approve proposed alterations to any individual landmark or building in a historic district. This is the heart of the ordinance's substantive protection. Under the typical alterations section, no building permit for physical change to a designated landmark or property in a historic district can be issued without approval of the commission evidenced by its issuance of a certificate of appropriateness.

The authority of the commission to restrict alterations is found in the police power.[55] This authority extends to all changes to the building's exterior and, in some instances, interior.[56] In a historic district, the commission has the power to approve or deny proposed changes not only to historic buildings but to all of the property within the district.[57] This would include nonhistoric buildings, and new construction on undeveloped lots. It is necessary that the commission's authority encompass all property within the district (it would be impossible to protect the integrity of the district if unregulated development of any property were allowed), and extend to review of subdivision plans that affect historic properties[58] and to the use of building materials that would be inconsistent with the character of a historic district.[59] If necessary, emergency provisions may be enacted to maintain the status quo and protect historic structures within the municipality until a more fully developed local ordinance is enacted. The City of Pasadena, California, for example, passed an ordinance that imposed a 90-day moratorium throughout the city on the alteration, removal, or relocation of fixtures from structures more than 50 years old.[60]

Some municipalities have extended the reach of their regulations still further to protect scenic views. Austin, Texas, for example, enacted

---

[55] *See* § **7.1.1**.

[56] For example, the inside of Radio City Music Hall in New York City is protected interior space.

[57] *See, e.g.,* Sleeper v. Old King's Highway Regional Historic Dist. Comm'n, 417 N.E.2d 987, 989 (Mass. App. Ct. 1981); Faulkner v. Town of Chestertown, 428 A.2d 879 (Md. 1981).

[58] *See* Smith v. Zoning Board of Appeals, No. D.N. CV89-0101333-S, 1991 Conn. Super. LEXIS 771 (Conn. Super. Ct. Apr. 10, 1991) (upholding Zoning Board of Appeals' denial of a subdivision proposal for a property located in the Mill Pond Historic District based, *inter alia*, on recommendations by the Historic District Commission opposing the subdivision).

[59] *See* Coscan Washington, Inc. v. Maryland-National Capital Park and Planning Comm'n, 590 A.2d 1080 (Md. Ct. Spec. App. 1991) (upholding Planning Commission's specification of building materials as within the Commission's statutory authority).

[60] 1 *Preservation L. Rep.* 1066 (1985); *see also, Schafer,* 743 F.2d at 1088 (90-day moratorium on fast-food restaurants passed to preserve status quo pending further study).

zoning ordinances to protect important views of the Texas State Capitol by establishing a series of "Capitol View Corridor Overlay Zones."[61] Other methods of accomplishing the same goal include implementing a Visual Resource Overlay District, as recommended for Guilford, Connecticut, and creating conservation easements, a method recommended by a Georgia study.[62] Massachusetts recently passed legislation that prohibits construction of new buildings or additions to existing buildings that would cast new shadows on the Boston Commons or the Lynn Commons in Lynn, Massachusetts.[63] The statute makes an exception for structures that cast *de minimis* shadows, such as antennas, flag poles, fences, or signs. Recognizing the adverse impact higher traffic speeds and necessary road modifications have on historic districts, the Rhode Island Legislature recently passed a law authorizing the Department of Transportation to reduce speed limits in such areas.[64]

A commission's authority to restrict alterations may result in conflicts with other land use requirements. In one of the first cases of its kind, a New York Court in *Sanzone v. City of Rome*[65] resolved such a conflict in favor of historic preservation. Sanzone filed a petition with the City of Rome Historic and Scenic Preservation Commission for permission to build two on-site parking lots next to a church that was located in a historic district but was being converted into professional office space. When the Commission denied the petition on aesthetic grounds, Sanzone petitioned the Zoning Board of Appeals to obtain a variance from off-street parking requirements. When ZBA denied the variance, Sanzone brought suit challenging both decisions. A trial court annulled both decisions, and the Commission and ZBA appealed. On review, the appellate court reversed the trial court and upheld the Commission's denial of approval for the parking lots, finding that the Commission had properly exercised its aesthetic judgement. However, the court annulled the ZBA determination. Finding that strict compliance with the off-street parking ordinance would result in practical and economic difficulties for Sanzone (particularly since the court had upheld the Commission's action), the Court held that the ZBA must grant a variance absent a showing of harm to public health, safety, and welfare. Because there was no evidence that the granting of a variance would result in a detriment to the essential character of the neighborhood, or an increase in the parking problem, and because Sanzone's hardship was not self-created, the Court reversed the ZBA decision.

---

[61] Austin, Tex., Zoning Ordinances Nos. 840802-T and 841220-CC.

[62] *See Preservation L. Update* (Nat'l Ctr. for Preservation Law, Washington, D.C.), Mar. 25, 1987.

[63] "Massachusetts Adopts Shadow Legislation," 9 *Preservation L. Rep.* 1015 (1991).

[64] R.I. Gen. Laws § 31-14-4.1 (1991).

[65] 565 N.Y.S.2d 666 (App. Div.), *appeal dismissed*, 575 N.E.2d 397 (1991).

7.4.2 Standards

A clear definition of the term "alteration" is crucial to the effective administration of the ordinance. The definition should assist the property owner in distinguishing between routine maintenance, which does not require review by the commission, and alterations, which do. An ordinance that does not make this distinction clear may create confusion regarding the scope of the commission's authority and ultimately undermine public support for the ordinance.

Prior to the commencement of any proposed change, the owner should be required to submit all plans and related materials to the commission.[66] This information must be sufficient to allow the commissioners to determine the compatibility of the change with the existing structure or district. Determining compatibility can be problematic, since it necessarily involves some element of subjectivity. To circumscribe the subjectivity, the ordinance should establish criteria for review. Many ordinances instruct commissioners to look for compatibility, consistency, or appropriateness in the relationship between the existing landmark or district and the proposed change in such factors as mass, material, color, proportions, architectural style, and detailing.[67] Alternatively, when a change within an architecturally uniform district, rather than a single landmark, is proposed, the "observable character of the district"[68] can guide the commission.

---

[66] The preservation ordinance of Dallas, Texas, for example, requires the owner to submit "copies of all plans and other documents relating to the work." Dallas, Tex., City Code § 51A-4.501(b)(3)(1991).

[67] New York City's Admin. Code Section 25-307(b)(1) and (2) (1986) is an example:
1. In making [the] determination [as to whether the proposed work would be appropriate for and consistent with the effectuation of the purposes of this chapter] with respect to any such application for a permit to construct, reconstruct, alter or demolish an improvement in a historic district, the commission shall consider (a) the effect of the proposed work in creating, changing, destroying or affecting the exterior architectural features of the improvement upon which such work is to be done and (b) the relationship between the results of such work and the exterior architectural features of other, neighboring improvements in such district.
2. In appraising such effects and relationship, the commission shall consider, in addition to any other pertinent matters, the factors of aesthetic, historical and architectural values and significance, architectural style, design, arrangement, texture, material and color.

In Seattle the Board must consider
> among other things, the purposes of this ordinance, the historical and architectural value and significance of the landmark or landmark district, the texture, material and color of the building or structure in question or its appurtenant fixtures, including signs and the relationship of such features to similar features of other buildings within a landmark district, and the position of such building or structure in relation to the street or public way and to other buildings and structures.

Seattle, Wash., Landmark Preservation Ordinance No. 102229, § 8(c).

[68] Town of Deering *ex rel.* Bittenbender v. Tibbetts, 202 A.2d 232, 235 (N.H. 1964).

Some ordinances contain specific formulas. For example, the Boston ordinance contains a provision devoted to the historic integrity of the doorways found on Beacon Hill.[69] Others, such as the Madison, Wisconsin, ordinance are more encompassing but contain less detail than the Boston ordinance. The Madison ordinance requires *inter alia*:

> (d) The proportions and relationships between doors and windows in the street facade(s) should be visually compatible with the buildings and environment with which it is visually related. . . .
>
> (1) All street facade(s) should blend with other buildings via directional expression. When adjacent buildings have a dominant horizontal or vertical expression, this expression should be carried over and reflected.[70]

Drafters of preservation ordinances should pay close attention to the case law in their state to ensure that the criteria adhere to minimum levels of explicitness. Likewise, federal constitutional standards of explicitness must be satisfied. The articulated standards governing alterations must "provide structure and guidelines" to the administrative body charged with enforcing them, and prevent unreviewable, unfettered authority from being exercised by that agency. Applying this standard, a Fifth Circuit decision held that a provision of a Dallas City Ordinance, regulating the appropriateness of a building's facade, permitted the city to prohibit painting on natural brick.[71]

New construction, like alterations, can be designed to be compatible with a historic building or district and therefore may be found to be appropriate. It is generally recognized that good "contemporary architecture per se is not incompatible with historic buildings. . . ."[72] For example, the U.S. Supreme Court in *Penn Central* noted that the New York City Landmarks Preservation Commission had approved construction of a new building which, "though completely modern in idiom, respects the qualities of its surroundings and will enhance the Brooklyn Heights Historic District. . . ."[73] Standards that regulate the uses of property in a historic district may also be established to maintain the uniform character of the district. Charleston, South Carolina, for example, passed an ordinance that regulates "bed and breakfast" uses within Charleston's Old and Historic District.[74] Atlanta, Georgia, passed an ordinance prohibiting the placement of advertising signs, such as billboards, within 300 feet of certain designated historic properties if the signs are

---

[69] Acts of 1955 ch. 616, § 1, Mass. Gen. Laws, *as amended*.

[70] Madison, Wis., General Ordinances § 33.01 (6)(d), 2.1 (1985).

[71] Mayes v. City of Dallas, 747 F.2d 323, 325 (5th Cir. 1984).

[72] *Handbook, supra* note 1, at A-71; *see also* Hayes v. Smith, 167 A.2d 546, 549–50 (R.I. 1961).

[73] 438 U.S. 104, 118 n. 18 (1978).

[74] Charleston, S.C., Code § 54-12(11)(1984). Amendments to the ordinance are currently under consideration.

visible from such properties.[75] However, competing societal interests may come into play, and special exceptions may be granted. Thus the Board of Zoning Appeals in Indianapolis, Indiana, allowed a group home for mentally retarded adults to be sited in a historic district, a decision that was upheld by the courts as a valid exercise of discretion.[76]

7.4.3 Certificate of Appropriateness

In contrast to the standards for designation which must be written into the ordinance itself, the standards to be applied when considering certificates of appropriateness may also be developed as separate detailed guidelines to be adopted by the commission.[77] While commission action taken without the benefit of narrowing guidelines is generally looked upon with disfavor by the courts, decisions based on incorporated materials have been upheld. These materials may include, inter alia, city and historic documents.[78] A building within a historic district does not itself have to be historically significant to be subject to certificate of appropriateness requirements. A Connecticut court upheld the application of certificate of appropriateness regulations to such a nonsignificant property after it determined that the enabling statute and the standards for appropriateness were not constitutionally defective.[79]

The commission considering an application for a certificate of appropriateness should take care to establish an adequate record, make findings, and base its conclusion on those findings. Typically, a public hearing is held to receive oral and written testimony from the owner and any opponents to the alteration or new construction. When reviewing the decision of a commission that has failed to take these steps, a court may remand the case with an order that this be done.[80]

---

[75] Corey Outdoor Advertising v. Board of Zoning, 327 S.E.2d 178 (Ga.), *appeal dismissed*, 474 U.S. 802 (1985).

[76] Metropolitan Bd. of Zoning Appeals v. Gunn, 477 N.E.2d 289 (Ind. Ct. App. 1985).

[77] Dennis, *supra* note 9, at 315.

[78] *Maher*, 516 F.2d at 1063; *A-S-P Assocs.*, 258 S.E. 2d at 453 n.4, 454.

[79] Vincino v. Wethersfield Historic Dist. Comm'n, 4 *Preservation L. Rep.* 3008 (1985).

[80] *See Assheton*, No. 47624 (N.Y. Sup. Ct. Apr. 3, 1991) (reversing Planning Board's decision denying application to install vinyl siding on building in historic district and ordering Board to issue permit because the Board failed to make explicit findings regarding the property's historic significance or the reasons for its decision in contravention of the standards contained within the ordinance); Fout v. Frederick Historic Dist. Comm'n, Misc. No. 4005 (Md. Cir. Ct. Feb. 5, 1980); Equitable Funding Corp. v. Spatt, No. 12832/77 (N.Y. Sup. Ct. Feb. 8, 1978). *Compare* Tourkow v. City of Fort Wayne, 563 N.E.2d 151 (Ind. Ct. App. 1990) (upholding Fort Wayne Historic Preservation Review Board's denial of an application for a certificate of appropriateness to replace "insul-brick siding" on a house located in the city's west central historic district with vinyl siding because of the review board's long-standing practice of denying applications to install artificial siding; failure to include findings of fact in its notice of decision "harmless error" because the findings of facts were included in the review board's minutes).

Although local commissions have the authority to deny certificates of appropriateness,[81] this is not the only action the commission may take. The ordinance may grant the commission the power to modify or amend an unacceptable proposal pending the applicant's agreement to such modification. If the modification is not acceptable to the property owner, then the effective result of the commission's decision would be a denial of the application. The ordinance may also permit the commission to suspend final action to allow the owner to make his proposal more consistent with the ordinance.[82]

7.4.4 Demolition

The presence of a landmark on a parcel of property can prevent the property from being used as the site of a new, larger, and presumably more economic building. Particularly in dense urban environments, this can create severe pressure to demolish the landmark to make way for a building capable of generating greater income to its owner.

Accordingly, to preserve the integrity of landmarks and districts, the ordinance should provide protection against demolition. The authority of landmark commissions to prohibit demolitions is settled.[83] Many communities make full use of this authority by granting their commission the power to refuse a permit for a landmark's demolition. However, some ordinances only allow the commission to comment prior to demolition. To the extent that the commission's authority to block demolition is decreased, protection of the city's landmarks is dramatically weakened.

An example of one city's approach is the Austin, Texas, preservation ordinance, which grants the commission the power to prohibit demolition:

> If an application is received for demolition or removal of a designated historic landmark, the building official shall immediately forward the application to the Landmark Commission. The Landmark Commission shall hold a public hearing on the application within thirty (30) days after the application is initially filed with the building official. The applicant shall be given ten (10) days written notice of the hearing. The Landmark Commission shall consider the state of repair of the building, the reasonableness of the cost of restoration or repair, the existing and/or potential usefulness, including economic usefulness, of the building, the purpose behind preserving the structure as a historic landmark, the character of the neighborhood, and all other factors it finds appropriate. If the Landmark Commission

---

[81] *See* Penn Central Transp. Co. v. New York City, 438 U.S. 104 (1978).

[82] For example, the Seattle, Wash., Ordinance states:
> In the event of a determination to deny a Certificate of Approval, the Board shall request consultation with the owner for a period not to exceed 90 days for the purpose of considering means of preservation in keeping with the criteria.

Seattle, Wash., Ordinance no. 102229 § 8(d).

[83] *See, e.g., Maher*, 516 F.2d at 1066.

determines that in the interest of preserving historical values, the structure should not be demolished or removed, it shall notify the building official that the application has been disapproved, and the building official shall so advise the applicant within five (5) days therefrom."[84]

This ordinance is a good example of one attempt to provide a commission with guidelines to aid in the difficult task of evaluating the economic impact of the restriction on demolition. This ordinance also indicates the relationship between the restrictions on demolition and other legal considerations. Although an owner does not have the right to receive the highest possible economic return from the use of his property, he must be able to make some economically viable use of his property. As discussed more fully in the following section on Economic Hardship,[85] a commission must consider whether denial of a demolition permit precludes any reasonable economic return. Thus, the demolition provision of the ordinance should be considered in relation to the ordinance's economic hardship clause.

Demolition may also be considered in conjunction with applications for certificates of appropriateness for new construction, if local ordinances so provide. Ordinances in the District of Columbia, Philadelphia, and San Antonio, for example, empower their respective preservation commissions to review plans for new construction when deciding whether to permit demolition.[86] Local preservation commissions that are not now expressly authorized to consider together demolition permit applications and applications for a certificate of appropriateness for new construction may wish to pursue an amendment to their ordinances, as at least one court has declined to find such authority when it was not clearly indicated in the local ordinance.[87]

Typically, a commission only has jurisdiction to consider applications to permit demolition of designated historic buildings or buildings within historic districts. Thus, unless the community has identified and

---

[84] City of Austin, Tex., Ordinance No. 740307-A § 45-51.

[85] *See* § **7.4.5**.

[86] *See Preservation L. Update* (Nat'l Ctr. for Preservation L., Washington, D.C.), July 18, 1988. The New York Appellate Division recently rejected a claim that such an Albany, New York, ordinance is facially invalid because it constitutes an unconstitutional taking of private property. The ordinance conditions the issuance of a permit to demolish a structure located in a historic district upon the submission to and approval by the Albany Historic Resources Commission of plans for new development. Historic Albany Found., Inc. v. Coyne, 558 N.Y.S.2d 986 (App. Div. 1990). (See § **7.4.5** for a discussion of takings cases). The court also upheld the application of the ordinance in a case in which the demolition of a building as "involuntary" because the building was structurally unsound and dangerous; the court noted that the plaintiff, by failing to submit plans, did not afford the Commission an opportunity to grant a waiver or variance so that new, approved development would yield a fair return. Lemme v. Dolan, 558 N.Y.S.2d 991 (App. Div. 1990). For a discussion of these cases, *see* 9 *Preservation L. Rep.* 1094 (1990).

[87] *See* Wolk v. Reisem, 413 N.Y.S.2d 60 (App. Div. 1979).

designated significant buildings in the first instance, the effectiveness of the demolition provision will be curtailed. Since the designation process can be very time consuming, a number of ordinances ban demolition (or alteration) until the designation process has been completed.[88]

Least effective from the standpoint of preservation goals are ordinances which only delay demolition for a period of time while alternatives are considered. If this approach is employed, the length of the delay period should be sufficient to allow meaningful negotiations to occur between the property owner, the commission, and other interested parties in an attempt to arrange an alternative to demolition.[89] Judicial interpretation of a provision granting a commission the power to delay has indicated that the power to grant a demolition permit implies the power to deny that permit.[90] Accordingly, an ordinance which by its terms only authorized a demolition delay was interpreted to give the commission authority to deny the permit if during that period a feasible alternative to demolition was found. Despite this ruling, however, the property in question, San Diego's Melville/Klauber House, was demolished while the case was being appealed. Moreover, some courts have strictly interpreted preservation legislation to limit the scope of its protection. For example, a Massachusetts court has held that demolition protection afforded to individual landmarks in the local ordinance did not apply to properties in an architectural conservation district.[91] The lesson of this case is that the power to deny demolition, if desired, should be explicitly granted in the ordinance.

7.4.5 Economic Hardship Clause

By requiring that landmark buildings be retained and maintained, preservation regulations have a direct economic impact on the owners of such property. If the economic burden imposed is too severe, the ordinance may be challenged on the grounds that the landmarked property has been constructively confiscated without just compensation. To prevent such a challenge, the local ordinance should contain a hardship clause.

A claim that property has been taken unlawfully may rest on several alternative bases. Both the federal Constitution[92] and many state constitutions[93] prohibit the taking of private property without just compensation

---

[88] *See, e.g.,* Berkeley, Cal., Ordinance § 15; District of Columbia Historic Landmark and Historic District Protection Act of 1978, D.C. Code Ann. § 5-1004 (1988).

[89] *See Handbook, supra* note 1, at A106; Dunbar High School Alumni Ass'n v. Department of Hous. & Urban Dev., Civ. No. 8911-75 (D.C. Sup. Ct. April 1, 1977).

[90] San Diego Trust & Sav. Bank v. Friends of Gill, 121 Cal. App. 3d 203 (1981). *But see* Conn. Gen. Stat. Ann. § 29-406(b) (West 1990) (enabling municipalities to adopt a delay of not more than 90 days before granting demolition permits), *cited in* 4 *Preservation L. Rep.* 2033 (1985).

[91] Southland Corp. v. City of Boston, 4 *Preservation L. Rep.* 3041 (1985).

[92] U.S. Const. amend. V.

[93] *See, e.g.,* N.Y. Const. art. 1, § 7.

to the owner. It is clear that a taking may occur without any physical invasion of the property. A regulation that interferes with the owner's use, possession or enjoyment of property, or his right to dispose of it freely, may constitute a taking.[94] In practice, however, such a de facto taking is extremely difficult to demonstrate. Courts do not deem it adequate to show that the value of property has been reduced, even drastically reduced, to make out a constitutional violation.[95] Rather, the owner is generally required to show that he or she has been denied any economically viable use of his land before a taking will be found.[96]

In the 1986 Term, the Supreme Court decided three cases that concerned takings of private property. Although these cases, *First English Evangelical Lutheran Church of Glendale v. Los Angeles*,[97] *Keystone Bituminous Coal Ass'n v. DeBenedictis*,[98] and *Nollan v. California Coastal Commission*[99] received a great deal of publicity when they were decided, their effect on landmarks designations has thus far been limited. In the context of historic preservation, it is probably most important to understand their potential relevance to drafting preservation ordinances.

In *First English*, the Court held that a temporary regulatory taking of all use of property would entitle the owner to just compensation. Because of the procedural posture of the case and the issue presented, however, the Court never reached the question of whether the regulation at issue constituted a taking: For the purposes of the case, the opinion addressed only the issue of the property owner's entitlement to compensation, assuming there had been a taking. This case arose from the following facts. In 1957, the church purchased a 21-acre parcel of land in a canyon along the banks of a creek in the Angeles National Forest. The church operated the site, which it called Lutherglen, as a campground, a retreat center and a recreational area for handicapped children. In July 1977, a forest fire denuded the upstream hills, and in February 1978, a flash flood destroyed the church's buildings in Lutherglen. In July 1979, in response to the flood, the County of Los Angeles adopted an interim ordinance, which was later repealed, prohibiting all construction or reconstruction of any building along the banks of the creek.

---

[94] *See, e.g., Penn Central*, 438 U.S. at 124; City of Buffalo v. J.W. Clement Co., 269 N.E.2d 895, 902-03 (N.Y. 1971).

[95] Federal courts have declined to find takings when government regulation has reduced the value of property by as much as 90 percent. *See* Park Ave. Tower Assocs. v. City of New York, 746 F.2d 135, 139–40 (2d Cir. 1984), *cert. denied*, 470 U.S. 1087 (1985).

[96] Agins v. Tiburon, 447 U.S. 255, 260 (1980). *See Shubert Organization*, 570 N.Y.S.2d at 508 (holding that the New York landmark law serves a legitimate purpose of saving historic landmarks, and that the designation of the interiors and exteriors of 22 Broadway theaters was not an unconstitutional taking without just compensation since the owners receive economic benefit from the continued use of the buildings as theaters, and from transferable development rights).

[97] 482 U.S. 304 (1987).

[98] 480 U.S. 470 (1987).

[99] 483 U.S. 825 (1987).

The church sued the county for damages, asserting among other claims that the county had deprived it of all use of Lutherglen for a period of time without compensation. The California courts denied the church's claim, relying on the California Supreme Court decision in *Agins v. Tiburon*,[100] which held that a landowner may not maintain an inverse condemnation suit based on a regulatory taking. The U.S. Supreme Court's decision in *Agins* did not affect the portion of the California court's opinion that held that compensation is not required until the challenged regulation or ordinance has been held excessive in an injunctive proceeding. For purposes of the appeal to the Supreme Court, the allegation in the complaint that the church was seeking damages for an uncompensated taking was accepted as true, so the Court considered only the question of whether the Constitution requires the government to pay for temporary regulatory takings.

The Court began by stating the recognized principles that a regulation can work a taking, citing *Pennsylvania Coal v. Mahon*,[101] and that temporary takings are compensable.[102] While *First English* is the first case in which the Supreme Court has decided the precise issue of the compensability of temporary, regulatory takings, the result followed from the Court's decisions in prior takings cases. The Court held "that where the government's activities have already worked a taking of all use of property, no subsequent action by the government can relieve it of the duty to provide compensation for the period during which the taking was effective."[103] Thus "amendment of the regulation, withdrawal of the invalidated regulation, or exercise of eminent domain,"[104] which are still available options, do not eliminate the government's liability for the owner's losses.[105]

Many questions were left unanswered by *First English*. The Court emphasized, for example, that it was limiting its holding to the facts presented, which were accepted as involving a denial of *all* use of property. In *First English*, the Court explicitly excluded "the case of normal delays in obtaining building permits, change in zoning ordinances, variances, and the like,"[106] but did not elaborate on the scope of the standard that it applied. The Court recognized that "our present holding will undoubtedly lessen to some extent the freedom and flexibility of land-use planners and governing bodies of municipal corporations when enacting land-use regulations."[107] While the opinion does increase the importance

---

[100] 598 P.2d 25 (Cal. 1979), *aff'd on other grounds*, 447 U.S. 255 (1980).

[101] 260 U.S. 393 (1922).

[102] Kimball Laundry Co. v. United States, 338 U.S. 1 (1949) (wartime seizures).

[103] 482 U.S. at 321.

[104] *Id.*

[105] This holding invalidates the rules in New York, *see* Fred F. French Investing Co. v. City of New York, 350 N.E.2d 381, *cert. denied*, 429 U.S. 990 (1976), and in California, which had allowed the government to avoid compensating the owner by rescinding the rule.

[106] 482 U.S. at 321.

[107] *Id.*

of careful legislative drafting, however, it is unclear to what extent it will actually hamper land use regulation.

In *Keystone* and *Nollan*, the Court did address the issue of what constitutes a taking under the fifth amendment. Keystone rejected a challenge by certain coal companies to Pennsylvania's Bituminous Mine Subsidence and Land Conservation Act, which requires that 50 percent of the coal beneath certain structures be kept in place to provide surface support. Emphasizing the strong state interest in protecting the public health, safety, and general welfare, and the limited extent of the taking, the Court distinguished *Pennsylvania Coal v. Mahon*,[108] and found that the Act did not work an unconstitutional taking of the coal companies' property.

Because plaintiffs made no showing or allegation that the Act rendered it commercially impractical to continue any mining operations, they failed to sustain their burden of establishing an unconstitutional deprivation of property. A prohibition against mining on certain portions of their land was an insufficient limitation for this purpose:

> "Taking" jurisprudence does not divide a single parcel into discrete segments and attempt to determine whether rights in a particular segment have been entirely abrogated. In deciding whether a particular governmental action has effected a taking, this Court focuses rather both on the character of the action and on the nature of the interference with rights *in the parcel as a whole*.[109]

As the court noted, "our test for regulatory taking requires us to compare the value that has been taken from the property with the value that remains in the property" overall.[110] An additional consequence of plaintiffs' not having alleged or proved any specific injuries caused by the enforcement of the Act was that their cause of action was limited to a facial challenge to the Act, which also narrowed the scope of the Court's review of their taking claim.

In *Nollan*, by contrast, the Court upheld the property owners' claim. There, the landowner's application for a building permit in a coastal zone had been issued subject to a condition of public access to part of their property parallel to their beach, which was located between two public beaches. The Court held that the condition worked an unconstitutional taking, reasoning that an easement requirement imposing the same condition independent of a permit application would be a taking, and that the formal difference between an easement and a permit condition should not determine whether or not governmental action constitutes a taking.[111]

---

[108] 260 U.S. 393 (1922).

[109] 480 U.S. at 497 (quoting *Penn Central*, 436 U.S. at 130–31).

[110] *Id.*

[111] 483 U.S. at 831–32.

The Court based its findings that there had been a taking on its determination that the permit condition was not sufficiently related to the public purposes asserted, which were to protect the public's ability to see the beach, to assist the public in overcoming a perceived "psychological" barrier to using the public beach, and to prevent beach congestion. The Court did not reach the issue of the validity of those ends, assuming for the purposes of the case that the claimed ends were legitimate municipal goals. In assessing the standard to apply to the nexus required between the asserted purposes and the imposed condition, the Court stated that its precedents "describe the condition for abridgment of property rights through the police power as a *substantial* advanc[ing]' of a legitimate State interest,"[112] adding that its choice of the adjective was particularly significant "where the actual conveyance of property is made a condition to the lifting of a land use restriction, since in that context there is heightened risk that the purpose is avoidance of the compensation requirement, rather than the stated police power objective."[113] The Court had noted earlier, however, that it could have used any nexus requirement in this case because it did not find that the case met "even the most untailored standards."[114]

Following *Nollan*, municipalities were well advised to be particularly careful in articulating both the public purpose intended to be served by their land use conditions and requirements, and in demonstrating the manner in which conditions imposed advance those purposes.[115] Despite the Court's use of the term "substantial" in describing the nexus requirement, however, it is not entirely clear whether the Court would necessarily apply so stringent a standard to a determination of the validity of all land use requirements and conditions.[116] Until subsequent decisions clarify this issue, however, it would be prudent to define the public purpose and connect it to the substantive regulation as precisely as possible.[117]

---

[112] *Id.* at 841.

[113] *Id.*

[114] *Id.* at 838.

[115] *See* Naegele Outdoor Advertising v. City of Durham, 844 F.2d 172 (4th Cir. 1988) (distinguishing *Nollan* in finding an adequate aesthetic justification for an ordinance banning certain billboards).

[116] See § **7.4.10** for a discussion of free exercise claims raised in connection with takings claims.

[117] In DGM Partners-Rye v. City of Rye, Index No. 4609/85 (N.Y.S. Ct. May 31, 1989), *aff'd*, 575 N.Y.S.2d 330 (App. Div. 1991), *appeal dismissed*, No. 172-SSD-13 (N.Y. Ct. App. Feb. 25, 1992), the New York Supreme Court upheld the landmark designation of a carriage house and view way located on the John Jay family estate under Section 117-5(B) of the Rye landmarks ordinance (set forth in note 28 of this chapter) against the plaintiff's challenge that the designation constituted an unconstitutional taking under *Nollan*. The court rejected the plaintiff's arguments that the necessary nexus between the designation of these properties and Section 117-5(B) of the Rye ordinance was missing given the allegedly limited historical significance of the properties and the inability of the public to view fully the carriage house.

Despite the U.S. Supreme Court's *Penn Central* decision upholding the constitutionality of New York City's Landmark Preservation Law, a 1991 Pennsylvania Supreme Court decision under the Pennsylvania State Constitution once again raised the question whether historic preservation regulations are a legitimate exercise of a state's police power. In *United Artists Theater Circuit, Inc. v. City of Philadelphia*,[118] the Pennsylvania Supreme Court held that the Philadelphia historic preservation ordinance violated the state constitution.[119] A four-member majority held that the designation of the interior of the Boyd Theater without the consent of the property owner was an unlawful taking of property without just compensation. The majority held that, in assuming control over the Boyd Theater, Philadelphia was forcing the owner to bear a public burden which should have been borne by the general public. The Court rejected an argument that historic preservation values are explicitly embodied in the state constitution,[120] and therefore a valid exercise of police power. Instead, the Court relied on a 1954 Pennsylvania Supreme Court decision in which the Court held that, in the zoning context, "neither aesthetic reasons nor the conservation of property values or the stabilization of economic values . . . are, singly or combined, sufficient to promote the health or the morals or the safety or the general welfare of the . . . inhabitants or property owners."

The Court did not expressly find historic preservation to be an unlawful use of the state police power. However, the majority quoted a dissent in *First Presbyterian Church v. City Council of the City of York*,[121] in which Judge Harry Kramer expressed his concern over the gradual erosion of basic private property rights due to the application of zoning laws and urban development laws. In addition, the Court relied on Chief Justice William Rehnquist's dissent in *Penn Central*, in which the then-Associate Justice Rehnquist argued that designations of individual landmarks are unconstitutional because there is no "reciprocity of advantage," as there is in general zoning ordinances which place all owners in a designated area under the same restrictions "not only for the benefit of the municipality as a whole but for the mutual benefit of one another."

A three justice minority concurred in the result of the court's decision, but disagreed with the majority's interpretation of the Pennsylvania

---

[118] 595 A.2d 6 (Pa. 1991).

[119] Article 1, section 10 of the Pennsylvania Constitution provides: "nor shall private property be taken or applied to public use, without authority of law and without just compensation being first made or secured."

[120] Article 1, section 27 of the Pennsylvania Constitution provides:

> The people have a right to clean air, pure water, and to the preservation of the natural scenic, historic and esthetic values of the environment. Pennsylvania's natural resources are the common property of all the people, including generations yet to come. As trustee of these resources, the Commonwealth shall conserve and maintain them for the benefit of all the people.

[121] 260 A.2d 257 (Pa. 1976).

Constitution. Justice Cappy noted that the majority did not reconcile its holding with the decision in *Penn Central*, in which the U.S. Supreme Court held, *inter alia*, that the New York City Landmark's Preservation Law, which is similar to the Philadelphia law, did not constitute a "taking" under the U.S. Constitution. Justice Cappy noted that, while *Penn Central* was decided under the federal constitution and *United Artists* was decided under the state constitution, "I do not believe that the language of our state constitution necessarily mandates a different outcome on the issue of 'taking.'" Instead, the three concurring Justices would have decided the case on the statutory grounds that the city did not have the authority to designate the interior of the Boyd Theater under the plain meaning of the statute.

The effect of the *United Artists* decision is not yet clear. The Court did not address the constitutionality of historic designations with owner consent, or the constitutionality of historic preservation districts. What is clear, however, is that the Pennsylvania ruling is in direct conflict with the U.S. Supreme Court's analysis in *Penn Central* and with the great weight of state court authority as well. A petition for rehearing by the City of Philadelphia, supported by the National Trust for Historic Preservation, the American Planning Association, and U.S. Conference of Mayors, the National League of Cities, the American Institute of Architects, and the National Center for Preservation Law, was granted on August 31, 1991 and re-argued on October 23, 1991. A decision is expected in 1992. Even if the Pennsylvania Court adopts the position of Justice Cappy's concurrence (thus avoiding a conflict with *Penn Central*), similar challenges may now be expected to historic preservation laws under other state constitutions.

The U.S. Supreme Court will, however, have the opportunity to review the "takings" issue again in the near future. On October 15, 1991, the Supreme Court granted *certiorari* in the case of *Yee v. City of Escondido*,[122] in which the California Court of Appeals had held that the joint operation of a state and local regulation of mobile homes did not constitute a taking without compensation. California State law compels mobile home park owners to accept the purchaser of an existing mobile home as a new tenant. As a result, existing tenants in rent-controlled mobile home parks could charge a premium for their homes equal to the value of the right to occupy the mobile home at the reduced rate. In *Yee*, a California Court rejected an argument by an association of mobile home park owners that the combined operation of the state and local laws constituted a compensable taking because it essentially transferred a monetary interest from park owners—an interest which the owners would normally capture through rent increases—to departing tenants. On April 1, 1992, the Supreme Court affirmed the California decision, finding, in an opinion by Justice

---

[122] 224 Cal. App. 3d 1349, *cert. granted*, 112 S. Ct. 294 (1991).

O'Connor, that the California laws did not constitute a physical taking of the park owners' properties, despite their transfer of economic value to park tenants.[123] Justice O'Connor declined to address the tenants' claims that the statutory scheme also constituted a "regulatory taking" and a denial of substantive due process since neither of these issues was properly before the Court.

On November 18, 1991, the Supreme Court also granted *certiorari* in a case involving the operation of a state law designed to protect the beach and dune system of the South Carolina coast. In *Lucas v. South Carolina Coastal Council*,[124] the South Carolina Supreme Court had held that the state's Beachfront Management Act, which prevented the owner of two vacant beachfront lots from constructing any permanent structures except a small deck or walkway, did not constitute a compensable taking. Relying on the *Keystone* decision, the majority held that, since the state was regulating the use of beachfront property to prevent serious public harm pursuant to its police power, there was no "taking" for which compensation was due. In dissent, two justices disputed the majority's characterization of the public purpose being served. The dissent argued that the regulation's primary purpose was not the prevention of a "nuisance." Instead, in the dissent's view, the regulation deprived the owner of "all economically viable use" of his property and therefore amounted to a compensable taking.

On June 29, 1992, the Supreme Court reversed the South Carolina decision (1992 U.S. Lexis 4537). In an opinion by Justice Scalia, the Court held that, regardless of the legitimacy of the Beachfront Management Act, the state may not deprive a property owner of all economically viable use of his property without compensation unless the prohibited uses constitute a nuisances under the state's background principles of property law, as reflected in its common law. The Supreme Court therefore remanded the case to the South Carolina courts to determine whether Lucas' proposed use of his lots constituted such a common law nuisance, observing that, while this seemed unlikely, the record was undeveloped on this point. Justice Kennedy concurred in the result; Justices Blackmun and Stevens dissented; and Justice Souter voted to dismiss the appeal as improvidently granted.

As was evident from their opinions in *Lucas*, Justices Blackmun and Stevens and, to a lesser extent, Justice Kennedy have a very different understanding of "property rights" than Justice Scalia and the Court's majority, who appear to view such rights as a fixed and inflexible concept hallowed by time and the common law. Justices Blackmun and Stevens would permit an owner's rights to be redefined to reflect major changes in social values, from a recognition of the evil of slavery to a comparable recognition of the impropriety of destroying the community's environment. Justice Kennedy, while less amenable to imposing

---

[123] 112 S. Ct. 1552, 60 U.S.L.W. 4301 (1992).
[124] 404 S.E.2d 895 (S.C. 1991), *cert. granted*, 60 U.S.L.W. 3374 (1991).

the cost of changing social mores on individual property owners, recognizes that reasonable investment-backed expectations may also be expected to reflect those changes, with a consequent evolution in the public's understanding of property rights.

While *Lucas* provided an interesting opportunity for this exchange of views, it did not, as Justice Souter observed, provide an adequate factual predicate for informed analysis of these issues. Thus neither the majority's nor the dissenters' dicta in *Lucas* is likely to have a significant effect on contemporary landmarks practice, which, as discussed in § 7.4.5, already affords "hardship" relief from landmarking controls for owners denied all economic use of their property. Not only is Lucas' situation rare (very few environmental regulations impose virtually total use restrictions) but, as Justice Souter noted, the nuisance exception contemplated by the majority is rarer still. For these reasons, the *Lucas* decision is likely to have relatively little application in practice. Indeed, as the dissenters pointed out, it is possible that, on remand, the majority's assumption that Lucas' land was rendered valueless may prove unwarranted in that case as well.

In the context of historic preservation, a taking claim may also be based upon the state enabling legislation, which empowers local government entities to preserve historic buildings and to restrict their alteration or demolition. New York's Town Law, for example, authorizes town boards to enact measures that provide for the preservation and protection of historic buildings. The enabling provision, however, stipulates that "[a]ny such measures, if adopted in the exercise of the police power, shall be reasonable and appropriate to the purpose, or if constituting a taking of private property, shall provide for due compensation, which may include the limitation or remission of taxes."[125]

While a hardship clause may not be constitutionally required, it will help to provide flexibility where needed to prevent the application of the ordinance from unjustly burdening a particular property owner. If the owner can establish that the denial of a certificate of appropriateness (and the demolition or alteration it would have allowed) prevents realization of a given economic return, considering all possible alternatives including selling or leasing the property, then the clause may authorize the commission to devise a plan under which an appropriate return can be achieved. This may include tax relief or approval of a limited construction project.

The legal standard in the ordinance is usually expressed as one of reasonableness. In the District of Columbia, the mayor cannot issue a permit to demolish a designated landmark unless "failure to issue a permit will result in unreasonable economic hardship to the owner."[126] In some cases, the ordinance itself will define "reasonable." For example, in New York City, a reasonable annual rate of return is defined as 6 percent

---

[125] N.Y. Town Law § 64(17-a) (McKinney 1987).

[126] D.C. Code Ann. § 5-1004(e) (1988); MB Assoc. v. D.C. Dep't of Licenses, Investigation & Inspection, 456 A.2d 344 (D.C. 1982).

of the valuation of the building and its site, including a depreciation allowance of 2 percent of the assessed value of improvements or the amount deducted for depreciation on the owner's latest federal tax return, whichever is less.[127] When the ordinance supplies a definition of reasonableness, the commission's inquiry in a given case can be limited largely to the economic situation of the particular building.[128]

When the party seeking alteration or demolition of its building is a charitable organization, use of the "reasonable rate of return" standard is not appropriate. Nor is the tax relief provided under many hardship provisions an ameliorative measure for tax-exempt institutions, which often enjoy tax-exempt status under local property tax statutes. Recognizing that the use of charitable property cannot be judged on the same basis as commercial property, the court may, instead of evaluating the availability of a reasonable return, ask whether the restrictions imposed by the ordinance prevent or seriously interfere with the organization's charitable purpose.[129] This approach is likely to be employed with respect to buildings used for religious purposes as well.[130]

The application of a hardship provision should be quite narrow, and the argument that the property could be put to a higher economic use should, by itself, be inadequate to secure relief.[131] Moreover, to further preservation purposes, the ordinance should contain the broadest possible array of alternatives for the commission to explore prior to permitting undesirable alteration or demolition of a historic building. The New York City ordinance is a good illustration.[132] If the commission determines that alteration of a given building would not be appropriate and that absent alteration a reasonable return cannot be obtained, it has several options. First, it must "endeavor to devise" a plan which would serve preservation goals and provide a reasonable return on the property. The plan may include tax exemption, tax remission, or authorization for appropriate alterations or construction. Once the plan is approved by the commission after public hearings, the property owner has the option to accept or reject it. If the owner accepts, and if the plan includes tax exemption or remission, the city tax commission must grant the approved tax relief upon the owner's application.

---

[127] *See* N.Y.C. Admin. Code § 25-302(v) (1986).

[128] For one set of factors to be considered in relation to economic hardship, see Model Preservation Ordinance, *supra* note 11, § 54.10.29.

[129] *See Society for Ethical Culture*, 415 N.E.2d at 922; Trustees of Sailors' Snug Harbor v. Platt, 288 N.Y.S.2d 314, 316 (App. Div. 1968).

[130] Lutheran Church v. City of New York, 316 N.E.2d 305 (N.Y. 1974).

[131] *See Society for Ethical Culture*, 415 N.E.2d at 926; Manhattan Club v. Landmarks Preservation Comm'n, 273 N.Y.S.2d 848 (Sup. Ct. 1966).

[132] N.Y.C. Admin. Code § 25-309 (1986). For a general discussion of the application of the New York City landmark ordinance to buildings owned by nonprofit organizations, see "Constitutional Standards for Hardship Relief Eligibility for Nonprofit Landowners Under New York City's Historic Preservation Law," 21 *Colum. J.L. & Soc. Probs.* 163 (1988).

If the owner rejects the plan, the commission may recommend to the mayor that the city acquire a "specified appropriate protective interest" in the property, which would compensate the owner for his inability to undertake the work necessary to achieve a reasonable return. If the city does not take steps to condemn and acquire the recommended interest within ninety days, the commission must issue a notice to proceed with the proposed work.

A separate provision applies when an owner establishes that he can no longer economically use a property for the purposes to which it has been devoted, and seeks a certificate of appropriateness for alterations which are essential to enable him to enter into a contract of sale or long-term lease of the property. In that case, the commission must attempt to find a purchaser or tenant who will agree to take the property without the work for which the certificate of appropriateness is required. If a purchaser or tenant is found who will accept the property on "reasonably equivalent terms and conditions" as in the owner's original proposal, the certificate of appropriateness will be denied. If not, the previously outlined procedure will be followed: The city must either condemn an appropriate protective interest, or the commission must issue the notice to proceed.

7.4.6 Maintenance

Issues relating to the maintenance of old buildings are growing in importance with the increase in the number of buildings which are landmarked and kept in active use for longer than had typically been the case in the past. Indeed, one commentator suggested in 1980 that in New York City issues relating to maintenance will be "[t]he greatest challenge facing the Landmarks Commission over the next twenty years."[133] A similar challenge will face preservation commissions of many other cities.

It is well settled that government has the constitutional authority to require owners to take affirmative steps to keep their landmarks in a state of good repair. *Maher v. City of New Orleans*[134] is the seminal case which upheld as constitutional a local ordinance's requirement that to achieve the legitimate end of preserving a landmark, "an owner may incidentally be required to make out-of-pocket expenditures" for the building's upkeep.

While *Maher* and other cases have upheld ordinances designed to prevent deterioration of historical structures, local governments do not have unfettered authority to require an owner to bear unlimited maintenance costs, or to require payment of maintenance costs at all absent

---

[133] Gray, "Landmarks Preservation Comes of Age," *N.Y. Affairs*, Nov. 3, 1980, at 52.
[134] 516 F.2d 1051, 1067 (5th Cir. 1975), *cert. denied*, 426 U.S. 905 (1976).

statutory authority.[135] In considering whether a commission has exceeded its authority, courts are likely to utilize a balancing test in which the public interest in preserving the landmark is weighed against the reasonableness of the economic burden to the owner.[136] Some communities draft their maintenance provision in general terms while others specify the level of work which will be deemed to constitute adequate minimum upkeep. An example of a general minimum maintenance standard is the ordinance of the Town of Yorktown, New York, which states simply, "Every owner of property in a preservation district or a designated landmark shall keep it in good repair."[137] In contrast, the ordinance of Seattle, Washington, enumerates specific and quite detailed maintenance requirements, and a historic building is deemed "substandard" if it is permitted to deteriorate to the point at which occupant or public safety is endangered.[138]

---

[135] See FGL & L Property Corp., 485 N.E.2d at 988.
[136] City of Chicago v. Kutil, 357 N.E.2d 200 (Ill. App. Ct. 1976).
[137] Yorktown, N.Y., Code § 60-20.
[138] Section 6A of the Seattle Landmark Ordinance provides the following:

Minimum Maintenance Standards. The City Council finds that in order to accomplish the purposes of this ordinance, buildings and structures in the Historic District must be preserved against decay and deterioration occasioned by neglect. Any building or portion thereof or any structure appurtenant thereto in which there exists any of the following conditions to the degree that the preservation of the building or structure or the safety of its occupants, the occupants of adjacent buildings, or the public, is endangered is hereby declared for the purposes of this ordinance to be a "substandard historic district building":

A. Structural defects or hazards, including but not limited to the following:

1. Footings or foundations which are weakened, deteriorated, insecure or inadequate or of insufficient size to carry imposed loads with safety;

2. Floorings or floor supports which are defective, deteriorated, or of insufficient size or strength to carry imposed loads with safety;

3. Members of walls, partitions, or other vertical supports that split, lean, list, buckle, or are of insufficient size or strength to carry imposed loads with safety;

4. Members of ceilings, roofs, ceilings and roof supports, or other horizontal members which sag, split, buckle, or are of insufficient size or strength to carry imposed loads with safety;

5. Fireplaces or chimneys which list, bulge, settle, or are of insufficient size or strength to carry imposed loads with safety;

6. Exterior cantilever walls, or parapets, or appendages attached to or supported by an exterior wall of a building located adjacent to a public way or to a way set apart for exit from a building or passage of pedestrians, if such cantilever walls, parapets or appendages are not so constructed, anchored or braced as to remain wholly in their original position in the event of an earthquake or wind capable of producing a lateral force equal to 0.2 of gravity;

7. Any exterior wall (or element thereof such as arches, keystones, lintels, etc.) located adjacent to a public way or to a way set apart for exit from a building or passage of pedestrians, if such wall is not so constructed, anchored or braced as to remain wholly in its original position in event of an earthquake or wind capable of producing a lateral force equal to 0.2 of gravity;

New York City's landmarks ordinance establishes fairly general maintenance standards, but contains separate provisions depending upon the nature of the landmark. Persons "in charge of" historic buildings in historic districts must keep in good repair all exterior portions of the buildings, and all interior portions which, if not maintained, could cause the exterior portions to "deteriorate, decay or become damaged or otherwise to fall into a state of disrepair." Persons controlling interior landmarks must keep those interior portions in good repair, as well as any other portions which, if not maintained, could cause damage of any kind to the interior landmark.[139]

Some communities provide financial assistance to property owners who face financial hardship caused by the requirement that certain repairs be made. For example, some ordinances establish a revolving fund for this purpose. Others allow the municipality to undertake directly maintenance which an owner fails to provide and to impose a lien against the property for the costs. When a municipality is unable adequately to enforce maintenance requirements, neighboring owners may bring a nuisance action to enjoin neglect of the property.[140]

7.4.7 Exclusion for Routine Maintenance

It is important that ordinances distinguish between routine maintenance, which can be undertaken without commission approval, and repair work and alterations, which may require such review and approval. Ordinances which impose unduly burdensome approval procedures on

---

    8. Any structure, chimney, flashing, antenna, air conditioner, or other appendage attached to or located on a roof of a building that is not so attached thereto so as to remain wholly in its original position in event of an earthquake or windstorm capable of producing a lateral force equal to 0.2 of gravity or an uplift force equal to the weight of the object plus gravity.
  B. Defective or inadequate weather protection, including but not limited to the following:
    1. Crumbling, broken, loose, or falling interior wall or ceiling covering;
    2. Broken or missing doors and windows;
    3. Deteriorated, ineffective, or lack of waterproofing of foundations or floors;
    4. Deteriorated, ineffective, or lack of exterior wall covering, including lack of paint or other approved protective coating;
    5. Deteriorated, ineffective, or lack of roof covering;
    6. Broken, split, decayed or buckled exterior wall or roof covering;
    7. Gutters and downspouts which have deteriorated.
  C. Defects increasing the hazards of fire or accident, including, but not limited to the following:
    1. Accumulations of rubbish and debris;
    2. Any condition as to cause a fire of explosion or to provide a ready fuel to augment the spread or intensity of fire or explosion arising from any cause.
Seattle, Wash., Ordinance No. 102229 § 6A.

[139] N.Y.C. Admin. Code § 25-311 (1986).

[140] *See* Kelly v. Boys' Club, Inc., 588 S.W.2d 254 (Mo. App. 1979).

owners who wish to undertake relatively minor maintenance will discourage the end they seek.

New York City's ordinance distinguishes among three types of work, each of which is subject to a difficult level of review. "Ordinary repairs and maintenance,"[141] for which no approval from the landmarks commission is required, is defined as:

> (1) work done on any improvement; or (2) replacement of any part of an improvement; for which a permit issued by the department of buildings is not required by law, where the purpose and effect of such work or replacement is to correct any deterioration or decay of or damage to such improvement or any part thereof and to restore same, as nearly as may be practicable, to its condition prior to the occurrence of such deterioration, decay or damage.

A second category, "minor work," consists of somewhat more extensive projects undertaken with respect to historic buildings, although still not so major as to require a building permit. Minor work includes "any change in, addition to or removal from the parts, elements or materials comprising an improvement including, but not limited to, the exterior architectural features or interior architectural features thereof . . ." The Landmarks Commission is authorized to incorporate by regulation within this category the "surfacing, resurfacing, painting, renovating, restoring, or rehabilitating of the exterior architectural features or interior architectural features or the treating of the same in any manner that materially alters their appearance. . . ."[142] Minor work may only be performed in accordance with a permit issued by the commission.[143]

The third and most intrusive category of work under the New York City ordinance, "alteration," includes "[a]ny of the acts defined as an alteration by the building code of the city."[144] Alterations may not be undertaken without the issuance of a certificate of no effect, certificate of appropriateness, or a notice to proceed.

The ordinance should also contain a provision for undertaking work necessary to remedy dangerous conditions relating to historic buildings on an emergency basis, without the issuance of a certificate of appropriateness or permit. The New York City ordinance permits essential steps to be taken, without commission approval, to remedy "conditions determined to be dangerous to life, health or property," if the work has been ordered by the Department of Buildings, the Fire Department, the Health Service Administration, or by a court upon application of any of those agencies.[145]

---

[141] N.Y.C. Admin. Code § 25-302(r) (1986).
[142] Id. § 25-302(q).
[143] Id. § 25-310(a)(1).
[144] Id. § 25-302(a). See also Model Preservation Ordinance, supra note 11, § 54.10.21.
[145] N.Y.C. Admin. Code § 25-312 (1986).

7.4.8 Compliance Inspections

The authority of local governments to require that affirmative steps be taken by the owner of a landmark to maintain the property suggests a corresponding right to evaluate the owner's diligence in doing so. However, Fourth-Amendment issues relating to the government's right to search private property are implicated when a landmark commission attempts to detect compliance through a schedule of periodic inspections. Therefore, an ordinance's program of inspections must meet certain minimum constitutional standards or risk successful challenge in court. In Camara v. Municipal Court,[146] for example, the Supreme Court held that a warrant based on probable cause was required prior to an administrative inspection.[147]

Establishing probable cause for purposes of an administrative inspection, however, does not require concrete evidence that a violation of a city ordinance exists. Rather, it is sufficient to show that "reasonable legislative or administrative standards for conducting an . . . inspection are satisfied" in order to obtain a warrant to inspect.[148] If the preservation ordinance or regulations adopted by the commission outline a "general administrative plan" for enforcement of the ordinance's maintenance requirements, based upon "neutral" and nondiscriminatory principles, that should provide an adequate basis for the issuance of warrants.[149]

In addition to, or in lieu of, inspections to verify that routine maintenance is being performed, a municipality may wish to monitor work being done pursuant to a permit or certificate of appropriateness issued by the commission.[150] Permission for such inspections could be made a condition of issuance of the permit or certificate, thus avoiding any constitutional complications. In addition, it may be advisable, bureaucratic considerations permitting, to vest total or primary responsibility for inspection of historic buildings in the city buildings department, which will already have a trained inspection staff and an established program.[151] If this is done the commission must make sure the building inspectors are trained to identify those particular maintenance problems which are peculiar to historic preservation of buildings, as opposed to more general health and safety considerations.

7.4.9 Publicly Owned Property

Historical buildings are often publicly owned. Nevertheless, it should be noted that the extent to which a higher level of government, particularly a

---

[146] 387 U.S. 523 (1967).
[147] *Id.* at 538.
[148] Marshall v. Barlow's, Inc., 436 U.S. 307, 320 (1978).
[149] *Id.* at 321.
[150] *See* Model Preservation Ordinance, *supra* note 11, at § 54.10.31-.32.
[151] *Id.* § 54.10.31; Seattle Landmark Ordinance § 6B.

county, must comply with a local ordinance remains an unsettled question.[152] The use of state-owned property by state agencies is not generally within the jurisdiction of local preservation ordinances. A New York court has held that the State University Construction Fund is not required to comply with a local historic preservation ordinance before it can demolish an existing structure on a state college campus as part of a construction project.[153] It has been held that a city's police power may not extend to the designation of state-owned buildings as landmarks.[154]

Even if the commission cannot control the use of historic buildings that are publicly owned, it should have the power to participate in decisions which affect such buildings. New York City's ordinance requires all agencies to refer to the landmarks commission plans for construction, reconstruction, alteration, or demolition of any buildings, owned by the city or situated on land owned by the city, which are landmarks themselves or are located within historic districts. No agency or official can approve such plans until the commission has had the opportunity to prepare a report detailing its views on the proposed work.[155] This procedure does not permit the commission to veto a project, but does insure that preservation concerns will be considered before irreversible action is taken. A state agency may, however, be subject to state preservation laws meant to preserve state-owned historic property. In a suit brought by a nonprofit preservation organization against a state agency that demolished a historic structure, an Indiana court ordered the state agency to reconstruct the facade of the structure, retrieve and safeguard the original building materials, submit plans for the reconstruction of the building facade which would conform to the guidelines for reconstruction of historic structures issued by the Secretary of the Interior, and restore a historic canal on the property adjacent to the building if acquired by the agency.[156]

7.4.10 Religious Structures

It is becoming more common for religious organizations to claim that the application of landmark laws to buildings they own violates the First Amendment's free exercise clause. However, preservationists believe that two 1990 Supreme Court decisions significantly weaken the

---

[152] *Compare* City of Ithaca v. County of Tompkins, 355 N.Y.S.2d 275 (Sup. Ct. 1974) *and* Mayor of Annapolis v. Anne Arundel County, 316 A.2d 807 (Md. 1974) (county property subject to city landmark ordinance) *with* Texas Antiquities Comm'n v. Dallas County Community College Dist., 554 S.W.2d 924 (Tex. 1977) (county property not subject to local regulations).

[153] Ebert v. N.Y. State Office of Parks, Recreation, and Historic Preservation, 505 N.Y.S.2d 470 (App. Div. 1986).

[154] *See, e.g.,* City of Santa Fe v. Armijo, 634 P.2d 685 (N.M. 1981); State v. City of Seattle, 615 P.2d 461 (Wash. 1980).

[155] N.Y.C. Admin. Code § 25-318(b)(1)(1986).

[156] Indiana *ex rel.* Historic Landmark Found. v. White River Dev. Comm'n, 5 *Preservation L. Rep.* 3005 (1986).

strength of these claims.[157] Two recent actions by the Supreme Court, both on March 4, 1991, appear to confirm this belief, as discussed next.[158]

Even before the U.S. Supreme Court sustained the constitutionality of New York City's Landmarks Preservation Law in *Penn Central*, the New York courts had wrestled with the application of zoning laws to property owned by religious institutions. In a 1968 decision involving the Westchester Reform Temple in Scarsdale,[159] the New York Court of Appeals, the state's highest court, had held that, while a local zoning ordinance was not facially invalid because it applied to religious properties, it could not be used to prevent the Temple's expansion in violation of that ordinance absent a showing that the expansion would have "a direct and immediate adverse effect upon the health, safety or welfare of the community." Writing for a unanimous court, Judge Keating said, "Religious structures enjoy a constitutionally protected status which severely curtails the permissible extent of governmental regulation in the name of the police powers . . . ." Moreover, he emphasized that when an "irreconcilable conflict" arises between the First Amendment right to build a religious structure in a residential area and the community's legitimate zoning interests, the religious interest must prevail.[160]

The *Westchester Reform* decision had not used the term "strict scrutiny." Nevertheless, its holding made clear that, where religious properties were involved, the neutral application of otherwise valid and rational land-use regulations was not sufficient. Absent a direct and immediate threat to the public, such regulations must, at least in the zoning context, yield to religious liberty.

In view of *Penn Central*'s equation of landmarking with zoning, it might have been reasonable to expect the New York courts to apply this test to the landmarking of religious properties as well. However, the courts did not follow this course. After an initial false start in a case involving the Lutheran Church,[161] the Court of Appeals made clear, in *Society for Ethical Culture v. Spatt*,[162] that religious organizations were to be treated like other non-profit owners of landmarks when they wished to develop their properties. In *Ethical Culture*, the Society (a religious organization) argued that the landmarking of its meeting house was both a confiscatory taking of its property and an abridgement of its free exercise rights. Noting that the landmark designation

---

[157] *See, e.g.,* "Supreme Court's *Swaggart* Decision Flowers into Bloom," *Preservation L. Update,* (Nat'l Ctr. for Preservation L., Washington, D.C.), March 29, 1990; "No Peyote for Religious Purposes in Oregon," *id.,* April 18, 1990.

[158] For a contemporary analysis of these developments, see Kass & Gerrard, "God, Mammon and Historic Preservation," N.Y.L.J., Apr. 23, 1991, at 7, from which the text analysis is drawn.

[159] *Westchester Reform Temple v. Brown*, 239 N.E.2d 891 (N.Y. 1968).

[160] *Id.* at 896.

[161] *See* Lutheran Church v. City of New York, 316 N.E.2d 305 (1974).

[162] 415 N.E.2d 922 (1980).

was clearly supported by the record, the Court of Appeals held that the Society's taking claim must be rejected "so long as [the designation] does not physically or financially prevent, or seriously interfere with the carrying out of the charitable purpose."[163] On the facts before it, the Court found that "there is no genuine complaint that elemosynary activities within the landmark are wrongfully disrupted, but rather the complaint is instead that the landmark stands as an effective bar against putting the property to its most lucrative use."[164]

The Society's free exercise claim, based squarely on the Court's earlier decision in *Westchester Reform Temple*, was rejected for the same reason. "[R]ather than argue its desire to modify the structure to accommodate . . . religious activities, the Society has suggested that it is improper to restrict its ability to develop the property to permit rental to nonreligious tenants. . . . Although the Society is concededly entitled to First Amendment protection as a religious organization, this does not entitle it to immunity from reasonable government regulation when it acts in purely secular matters."[165]

Ethical Culture thus set forth twin tests for evaluating taking and free exercise claims by religious organizations: for taking purposes, an otherwise reasonable landmark designation is valid so long as it does not physically or financially prevent (or seriously interfere with) the organization's charitable purpose; for free exercise purposes, reasonable landmark designation is valid where its principal effect is on "purely secular matters," including revenues from potential development of the landmarked property.

In a subsequent decision, *Church of St. Paul and St. Andrew v. Barwick*,[166] the Court of Appeals also held (by a 4 to 3 margin) that judicial challenges on either of these grounds are not ripe until the religious organization has first applied for and been denied a certificate of appropriateness from the City's Landmarks Preservation Commission. In the absence of such a denial, said the Court's majority, there is no basis to find that the organization cannot carry out its religious activities despite its landmark designation. That, said the Court, "will require a careful examination of facts not yet developed pertaining to plaintiff's financial situation and to whatever action the Commission takes with respect to plaintiff's rebuilding program." The fact that the Church's claim had "incidental First Amendment overtones . . . is simply not germane to the ripeness issue here."[167]

Both the *Ethical Culture* and *St. Paul and St. Andrew* cases had been decided by the New York Court of Appeals. It was not until the case of *Rector, Wardens and Members of the Vestry of St. Bartholomew's Church*

---

[163] *Id.* at 925.
[164] *Id.* at 926.
[165] *Id.*
[166] 496 N.E.2d 183 (N.Y.), *cert. denied*, 479 U.S. 985 (1986).
[167] *Id.* at 192.

v. City of New York[168] that both taking and free exercise claims were raised in the federal courts. St. Bartholomew's desired to replace its community house (a designated landmark) with an office tower that would both provide additional space for the Church's charitable activities and generate significant funds for the church. St. Bartholomew's first sought a certificate of appropriateness from the Landmarks Preservation Commission for a 59-story tower and, when that was denied on architectural grounds, for a 47-story tower, which was also denied. The Church than sought approval for its 47-story tower on hardship grounds, which was denied following extensive public hearings by the Commission on the continued suitability of the community house for its charitable purposes, the costs of necessary repairs to the community house and the church and the overall condition of the Church's finances.

Having thus demonstrated the ripeness of its claim, St. Bartholomew's contended in federal District Court that the City's Landmarks Preservation Law was, among other things, facially unconstitutional on both free exercise and equal protection grounds and, as applied, a taking of the Church's property, an abridgement of its free exercise rights and a violation of the First Amendment's establishment clause (because of the Commission's allegedly intrusive review of the Church's internal affairs).

Each of these claims was rejected by the District Court. The Court first rejected the claim that landmarking was, by itself, a violation of St. Bartholomew's free exercise rights. "[T]he mere possibility that a church may at some time want to make a different use of its landmarked property creates no more than an incidental burden on the practice of religion that does not 'require the state to come forward with a compelling reason justifying its actions.'"[169] Nor did the Commission's need to inquire into the Church's finances constitute an establishment of religion where its purpose was to determine the Church's entitlement to hardship relief. Turning to St. Bartholomew's claims that the Commission's actions in denying the requested permits amounted to a taking of its property and an abridgement of its free exercise rights, the Court adopted the *Ethical Culture* standard of the New York Court of Appeals (that is, whether the landmark designation would prevent or seriously interfere with the Church's charitable purposes), noting that it served equally well for both claims.

The Court then conducted a de novo review of the record before the Commission "in an effort to determine if plaintiff has proved by a preponderance of the evidence that it can no longer carry out its charitable purpose in its existing facilities."[170] The Court found that St. Bartholomew's witnesses and documentary evidence were not credible with respect to either the continued usefulness of its community house

---

[168] 728 F. Supp. 958 (S.D.N.Y. 1989), *aff'd*, 914 F.2d 348 (2d Cir. 1990), *cert. denied*, 111 S. Ct. 1103 (1991).

[169] *Id.* at 963.

[170] *Id.* at 967.

for charitable activities, the cost of repairing the community house, church and adjacent terrace or the sources of funding reasonably available to it to meet these needs. (The court observed, in this regard, that St. Bartholomew's had already spent more than $1.6 million on the office tower project.) Since the Church had failed to demonstrate that it could no longer conduct its charitable activities or carry out its religious mission in the existing facilities, its claims were dismissed.

In affirming the District Court decision, the Second Circuit held that "no First Amendment violation has occurred absent a showing of discriminatory motive, coercion in religious practice or the Church's inability to carry out its religious mission in its existing facilities."[171] The Court found the Landmarks Law to be facially neutral and generally applicable and found no evidence that it was intended, or had been applied, to discriminate against or impinge upon religious belief. While it recognized that St. Bartholomew's capacity to raise money was "drastically restricted" by its inability to build an office tower, the Court agreed with the District Court that neither this fact nor the evidence relating to the Church's current facilities was adequate to demonstrate that St. Bartholomew's had been prevented by the Commission from performing its religious mission.

The Second Circuit also rejected the Church's claim that the denial of the requested permits amounted to an unconstitutional taking. The Church could continue to use its property for religious purposes, and, on the facts as analyzed by the District Court, alternative sources of funds were available to it to maintain that property. Since St. Bartholomew's use of its property was not for commercial purposes, its inability to earn a reasonable return was irrelevant.

As a result of the District Court and Second Circuit decisions in *St. Bartholomew's,* the standard announced in *Ethical Culture* has been adopted by the Second Circuit, placing on religious organizations the burden of demonstrating (after first exhausting administrative remedies) that landmarking effectively deprives them of their ability to carry out their religious mission in their current facilities. To meet this burden, as the District Court demonstrated, churches and synagogues must be prepared for a searching administrative and judicial examination of their internal affairs and finances, including alternative sources of funds.

In the context of more conventional religious activities affected by landmarking, at least two courts have applied the strict scrutiny standard applied by the New York Court of Appeals in its *Westchester Reform Temple* decision. In *Society of Jesus v. Boston Landmarks Commission,*[172] the Supreme Judicial Court of Massachusetts recently invalidated the landmark designation of the Jesuit Church of the Immaculate Conception in Boston, which had commenced a renovation plan to convert its main

---

[171] 914 F.2d 348, 355 (2d Cir. 1990), *cert. denied,* 111 S. Ct. 1103 (1991).
[172] 564 N.E.2d 571 (Mass. 1990).

church (which was larger than required for religious services) into office, counseling and residential space. Upon its landmarking, the Church became subject to Commission approval for its renovation plan, which the Massachusetts court viewed as inseparable from the Church's religious activities ("the church interior is so freighted with religious meaning that it must be considered part and parcel of the Jesuits' religious practices"). Applying the highly protective Massachusetts Constitutional prohibition on religious restraints, the Supreme Judicial Court concluded that the designation restrained freedom of worship without justification on grounds of either public safety or the religious worship of others and was therefore invalid. It did not reach the Church's First Amendment claims.

But the Washington Supreme Court did. In *First Covenant Church v. City of Seattle*[173] it considered, as a matter of first impression, a First Amendment challenge both to the Seattle Landmarks Preservation Board's designation of the church as a landmark and to the Seattle Landmarks Preservation Ordinance as applied to churches generally. After first holding that the designation itself presented an issue that was ripe for adjudication (thus adopting the minority view rejected by the New York Court of Appeals in *St. Paul and St. Andrew*), the Washington Court phrased the issue before it as "whether the law should prefer religious freedom or an exercise of the police power to maintain the architectural and cultural interests associated with landmark preservation."[174]

Citing Thomas Jefferson's "wall of separation" letter to the Danbury Baptist Association, the Court decided that religious interests should prevail. It also noted that, even under a liturgical exception contained in the Seattle Ordinance, the Church was required to submit plans for its proposed facade alteration (not a development project) and to explore with the Landmarks Board alternative proposals that would preserve the designated features of the facade. The Court found this obligation, as well as the broader approval of alterations required if the liturgical exception were not available to the Church, to constitute "governmental interference in religious matters" that simply was not justified by the state's interest in maintaining "the aesthetic and cultural features of a community." The Court therefore invalidated the Seattle Ordinance both generally with respect to religious structures and as applied to the First Covenant Church.

Taken together, the Massachusetts and Washington decisions suggested that, where the issue is the alteration of religious property (whether interior or exterior) for purposes related to "traditional" church or synagogue activities and concerns, the state has a heavy, and perhaps unsupportable, burden to demonstrate that the public interest requires landmark controls. Historic preservation alone is not sufficient, at least in this context, to meet that burden, just as traffic

---

[173] 787 P.2d 1352 (Wash. 1990), *vacated*, 111 S. Ct. 1097 (1991).
[174] *Id.* at 1356.

congestion and property values were not sufficient to sustain zoning restrictions in *Westchester Reform Temple*.

Preservationists concerned by *First Covenant Church* found relief in unexpected quarters. Several months after the Washington decision, the U.S. Supreme Court decided *Employment Division, Department of Human Resources of Oregon v. Smith*,[175] in which it held that, notwithstanding the free exercise clause, Oregon could prohibit sacramental use of peyote by members of the Native American Church and could, as a result, deny unemployment benefits to members discharged for such use. In reaching this result, the Court explicitly declined to apply the compelling state interest standard it had previously used in reviewing laws burdening religious conduct. Instead, the Court held that the free exercise clause does not exempt compliance with neutral and generally applicable laws that do not purport to regulate religious beliefs, even if such laws forbid acts that are themselves compelled by religious beliefs.

Smith was met by criticism from the civil liberties community, including the American Civil Liberties Union.[176] The ACLU launched a major effort to reverse its broad holding through legislation, and Representative Solarz (D-N.Y.) and others introduced a bill (H.R. 2797) to this effect in Congress in June, 1991. The Solarz bill would prohibit all federal, state and local governments from restricting any person's "free exercise of religion" even if the burden results from a rule of general applicability, unless the restriction is "essential to further a compelling governmental interest" and the "least restrictive means" of furthering that interest. The Solarz bill was not acted on in 1991, and its future prospects are modest at best.[177]

It was against this background that the Supreme Court acted on March 4, 1991. In a *per curiam* decision, the Court vacated the judgment of the Washington Supreme Court in *First Covenant Church* and remanded the case "for further consideration in light of" *Smith*. This action portends the reversal of that portion of the *First Covenant Church* decision that invalidated Seattle's landmark ordinance as applied to religious properties generally. In all likelihood, *Smith* will also require reversal of the entire *First Covenant* decision, with the result that landmark churches, synagogues and other religious structures in Seattle and elsewhere will continue to be subject to administrative review for alteration plans that are unrelated to "secular" development projects such as that proposed by St. Bartholomew's.[178]

There are, however, a number of reasons for preservationists to be cautious in praising *Smith*. There are probably limits to what preservationist

---

[175] 494 U.S. 872 (1990).

[176] *See* Strossen, "Michigan Department of State Police v. Sitz," 42 *Hastings L.J.* 285, 381 (1991).

[177] H.R. 2797 is currently under consideration in the House Judiciary Committee.

[178] The case on remand was argued in November, 1991 and is now (February, 1992) awaiting decision by the Washington Supreme Court.

would accept in the regulation of religious properties (for example, the right of one sect to remove from a church religious symbols used by a previous denomination that conflict with the beliefs of the new congregation). More fundamentally, the extraordinary architectural heritage of the nation's religious institutions is itself a reflection of the diversity of thought and practice that has flourished under the protection of the First Amendment. To condone significant restrictions on that liberty in the name of historic preservation could undermine both preservation and liberty.

Historic preservation has done well under the strict scrutiny standard and there is no reason to believe the social values it represents are not adequately protected by the *Ethical Culture* test against "secular" activities by religious organizations. Where truly religious beliefs or activities come into conflict with preservationist goals, society should be willing to accept some alteration of a number of church interiors (or even, in some cases, exteriors) in order to preserve the religious diversity that gave birth to a significant share of the nation's architectural heritage.

This is not to suggest, as the Washington court did in *First Covenant Church*, that landmark designation of religious property is improper *per se* or that an owner of such property should be exempt from normal certificate of appropriateness or hardship procedures. Rather, in applying hardship standards, the purpose of a proposed alteration should be relevant to a local commission or a court. If a church, synagogue or mosque can show, for example, that its on-site liturgical practice, educational programs or religious beliefs are compromised by the denial of a certificate of appropriateness, this could constitute a permissible basis for hardship relief without the kind of searching engineering and financial inquiry conducted by the District Court in evaluating St. Bartholomew's hardship claim. For such religious activities, the Court of Appeals standard in *Westchester Reform Temple* may continue to provide better guidance than *Ethical Culture*. Thus irreconcilable conflicts between religious practices and landmark designation would, at least in the absence of compelling public interests to the contrary, be resolved in favor of religious liberty. Where "secular" activities are involved, the *Ethical Culture* test would continue to apply, as it did in *St. Bartholomew's*. While the line between religious and secular activities will at times be difficult to draw, the New York cases to date suggest that distinguishing one from the other should, in most cases, be feasible.

7.4.11 Penalties

A city should provide the commission with the means to enforce its actions. Most ordinances provide for penalties to be imposed against those who violate their provisions. For example, in Syracuse, New York, those who fail to comply with the provisions of the preservation ordinance are subject to a penalty of $100 a day. Willful violators are subject to fines of

$150 per day or up to 15 days' imprisonment.[179] New York City's ordinance provides varying penalties for those who violate its alteration and demolition provisions or its repair and minor work provisions, and those who withhold information or make false statements to the commission. It also provides for injunctive relief.[180]

The District of Columbia requires that any person who demolishes, alters, or constructs a structure in violation of the act must restore the property and its site to its appearance prior to the violation.[181] This remedy is, in practice, designed to be an economic deterrent to the destruction of historic property, since damage to a historic property is often irremediable.

A city should also decide whether penalties should apply to subsequent purchasers of historic property. The Maryland Court of Appeals, the highest state court, recently decided that a penal provision of a Baltimore historic preservation ordinance did not apply to an innocent purchaser of a property that was in violation of prior agreement to make certain alterations.[182] The purchaser had completed a title search and obtained a lien report that gave no indication of the violation. Since the purchaser had no knowledge of the violation and did not do any of the acts referred to in the ordinance, the Court held that the penal provisions did not apply. This suggests that cities should be careful to establish procedures for recording violations of certificates of appropriateness so that purchasers have actual, or at least record, notice of any outstanding violations.

7.5 CERTIFICATION OF LOCAL STATUTES AND HISTORIC DISTRICTS

In order to survive court challenges to the designation of historic districts and buildings, it is important that communities incorporate the appropriate substantive provisions in their preservation statutes, and abide by the processes just outlined in making designations. There is, however, an important additional reason for complying with these requirements: Such compliance may determine whether local property owners are eligible for the federal tax incentives for historic preservation discussed in **Chapter One**.

As explained in **Chapter Two**, to qualify for certain preservation tax benefits, a structure must either be listed individually on the National Register or located within a registered historic district. A district can achieve that status in only two ways. First, it may itself be listed on the

---

[179] Syracuse, N.Y., General Ordinance No. 11 § IX(A) (1975).

[180] N.Y.C. Admin. Code § 25-317 (1986).

[181] District of Columbia Historic Landmark and Historic District Protection Act of 1978, D.C. Code Ann. § 5-1010(b) (1988).

[182] Belman v. State, 586 A.2d 1291 (Md. 1991).

National Register as a historic district. Alternatively, the district must be designated under a state or local statute which has been certified by the Secretary of the Interior as containing criteria which will substantially achieve the purpose of preserving and rehabilitating buildings of significance to the district,[183] and be certified as meeting the same requirements as applying to listing of districts on the National Register. Only when the locality has complied with this two-step certification process can individual building owners benefit from the federal tax incentive program.

7.5.1 Certification of Statutes

The National Park Service (NPS) will review requests for certification of state or local statutes only at the request of the chief elected official of the enacting jurisdiction or that official's authorized representative. A private citizen, therefore, cannot go directly to the federal government seeking certification of a local ordinance; he must prevail upon the local government to initiate the process. In evaluating the adequacy of a local statute, the NPS will decide whether the statute "contain[s] criteria which will substantially achieve the purpose of preserving and rehabilitating properties of historic significance to the district." The regulations specify only two additional requirements: The statute must designate a landmarks review board or commission, and that entity must be empowered to review proposed alterations to historic structures within any districts designated under the statute.[184]

Past certification decisions indicate additional criteria which the NPS applies in reviewing local statutes.[185] Statutes have been deemed not to achieve preservation purposes if they permit owners to veto landmark designation of their own property. This power, according to the NPS, could threaten the integrity of a historic district, by withholding protection from important properties within it. For similar reasons, the NPS refused to certify a statute providing for review of alterations only to listed structures within a district, rather than to all structures. These "patchwork" concerns also led to denial of certification for a statute which excluded from landmark review any district structures less than 100 years old.

Conversely, however, the NPS has certified statutes which provide for district-wide review of designation. These have contained provisions that a majority of property owners within a proposed historic district must agree to designation, or even that 2/3 of such owners must consent to

---

[183] 36 C.F.R. § 67.8(a) (1991).

[184] Id.

[185] See "Certification of State and Local Statutes," in *Reusing Old Buildings, supra* note 9, at 346–49.

designation in writing. The NPS has indicated that even 100 percent owner occurrence would be acceptable.

Moreover, before the NPS will review local ordinances enacted under the authority of state enabling legislation, the empowering state law must itself be certified. The NPS generally will not review state enabling laws in isolation, unless those laws actually designate historic districts without the need for local action. Rather, state laws, when submitted to the NPS, must be accompanied by local statutes that implement them and carry out their purposes. If the state enabling legislation does not satisfy the intent of federal law, then no local statutes enacted under its authority will be certified.

7.5.2 Certification of Historic Districts

Once the enabling statute is certified, the district itself must also be certified before individual buildings can be certified for tax incentive purposes. Although designation under a state or local ordinance is an alternative to listing in the National Register, direct certification depends upon a determination by the NPS that the locally created district "substantially" meets the requirements for district certification.[186] Thus, it is imperative that the local ordinance provide for full and reasoned consideration of district designations by the local commission, so that its ultimate decisions will survive NPS scrutiny.

Again, the certification request must come from an official of the relevant governmental entity, not from an individual property owner. The certification request should include the following documentation:

1. A description of the physical or historical qualities which define the district, an explanation of the choice of boundaries, and a description of the typical architectural styles and types of buildings;
2. A statement explaining why the district has significance and substantially meets the National Register criteria;
3. A definition of what types of properties contribute and do not contribute to the significance of the district, and an estimate of the percentage of properties that do not;
4. A map showing all properties, preferably identifying contributing and noncontributing structures; and
5. Photographs of typical areas and properties in the district.

Once a district itself is certified, individual property owners within it are eligible to begin the certification process for rehabilitation to their own buildings.

---

[186] 36 C.F.R. § 67.9(a). The National Register criteria are found in 36 C.F.R. Part 60. *See* **Appendix I**.

Eight

Asbestos and Other Hazardous Substances

During the past decade, the remediation of hazardous conditions on real property has become a focus of both national and state laws. As a result, the rehabilitation of historic properties has acquired a new dimension of risk. It is therefore important to understand the applicable laws and take prudent steps to identify and abate such conditions. This chapter provides sponsors of rehabilitation projects with an introduction to the applicable federal laws and regulations relating to asbestos and other hazardous materials. It also helps sponsors ask the right kinds of questions during the planning stages of a project. However, with the vast increase in the number, scope, and complexity of environmental laws in force today, it is essential that a sponsor seek sound legal and technical advice to ascertain the requirements applicable to a proposed project and, equally important, the history and current conditions of the property in question. The discussion that follows is intended to identify the principal area of concern for sponsors and others involved in a rehabilitation project, but is not intended to be a complete analysis of any of these subjects.

8.1 ASBESTOS

Asbestos is a naturally occurring mineral whose fine, strong and flexible fibers can be spun into materials that are resistant to fire, moisture, and mold, are stable when exposed to acids and alkalis, and provide electrical resistance and sound absorption. Valued for centuries for these properties, asbestos production began in earnest in the late nineteenth century and into the twentieth century, with the most extensive use of asbestos occurring during the period from 1940 to 1980. An estimated 30 million tons of the fiber is incorporated into U.S. building materials used in public, commercial, and residential structures.[1] Asbestos may be found sprayed onto walls, ceilings, and internal beams for insulation, in wraparound insulation on pipes, boilers, and other similar building equipment, in gypsum wall board, interior drywall, or external facade joint compound, in textured paint, and in floor, ceiling, and roofing tiles. Asbestos may also be found in household appliances such as ovens, woods stoves, dishwashers, and refrigerators and in fireproof drapes, curtains, and other furnishings.

The beneficial properties of asbestos do not come without a price. As long as asbestos fibers remain intact and are left undisturbed, there is apparently no health risk involved. However, airborne and waterborne asbestos fibers have been linked to serious illness, including lung cancer and abdominal cancer. The exact level of risk associated with asbestos exposure is not known, and one commentator has stated that there may not be any safe level of asbestos exposure.[2] Whatever the final resolution of this issue, asbestos has become the subject of complex regulatory controls that have particular relevance to older and historic properties.

Asbestos fibers become airborne when material containing asbestos becomes dry and crumbly (a condition known as "friable") and are disturbed by movement or touch. This can often occur during the renovation or demolition of older buildings. It is therefore essential for sponsors to be aware of the legal requirements for the removal and disposal of asbestos before beginning a rehabilitation project.

8.1.1 National Emission Standards for Hazardous Air Pollution

Under the Clean Air Act's National Emission Standards for Hazardous Air Pollution (NESHAP) program,[3] Congress gave the U.S. Environmental Protection Agency (EPA) the power to establish emission standards for the release of hazardous air pollutants. In 1973, asbestos was added to the list of such hazards.[4] The asbestos NESHAP standards for demolition or renovation apply to "any person who owns, leases, operates, controls, or supervises" the facility being demolished or renovated, thereby binding both

---

[1] *See* Arlene Fickler, "Asbestos in Buildings: An Overview," *in Indoor Pollution and Toxic Torts* 53, 55 (Law Journal Seminars Press, 1987).
[2] *See* City of Greenville v. W.R. Grace & Co., 827 F.2d 975, 980 (4th Cir. 1987).
[3] 42 U.S.C.A. § 7412 (West Supp. 1991).
[4] *See* 38 Fed. Reg. 8820 (1973). The asbestos NESHAP regulations are located at 40 C.F.R. §§ 61.140–61.156 (1991).

building owners and asbestos removal contractors.[5] The NESHAP regulations do not apply to residential buildings having four or fewer dwelling units.[6] However, as discussed below, other requirements may apply to such buildings.

The NESHAP regulations distinguish between "friable" and "nonfriable" asbestos. Friable asbestos material is any asbestos-containing material (ACM) with more than 1 percent asbestos that, when dry, can be crumbled, pulverized, or reduced to powder by hand pressure. Nonfriable ACM is divided into two categories.[7] Category I nonfriable ACM includes packings, gaskets, resilient floor coverings, and asphalt roofing products containing more than 1 percent asbestos.[8] Category II nonfriable ACM is any material (excluding Category I material) that, when dry, cannot be crumbled, pulverized, or reduced to powder by hand pressure.[9] The NESHAP regulations apply to regulated ACM (RACM), which includes friable ACM, Category I nonfriable ACM that has become friable or has been subjected to sanding, grinding, cutting, or abrading, and Category II nonfriable ACM that has become, or has a high probability of becoming, crumbled, pulverized, or reduced to powder during the course of demolition or renovation.[10]

Under the asbestos NESHAP, before a demolition or renovation project is begun, the owner or operator must conduct an asbestos survey in the affected area to determine the presence of friable and Category I and II nonfriable ACM. The removal and disposal requirements apply if the survey reveals 260 linear feet of RACM on pipes, 160 square feet on other components, or 35 cubic feet on off-facility components where the length or area cannot be measured.[11] Because the presence of asbestos is often difficult to detect, it is recommended that an experienced licensed asbestos inspector conduct the investigation and develop a written asbestos audit report. All asbestos testing should be conducted by authorized laboratories.

If the minimum threshold of RACM is discovered, the owner or operator must notify EPA of the operation at least ten working days before the renovation or demolition begins, and must keep EPA appraised of changes in the schedule.[12] Renovation or demolition may begin *only* on the date indicated in the notice to EPA.[13]

---

[5] 40 C.F.R. § 61.141.
[6] *Id.*
[7] *Id.*
[8] *Id.*
[9] *Id.*
[10] *Id.*
[11] *Id.* § 61.145(a)(1).
[12] *Id.* § 61.145(b)(3)(i).
[13] *Id.* § 61.145(b)(3)(iv)(C).

Owners and operators of the project must remove all RACM from a building being demolished or renovated before any activity that would break up, dislodge, or disturb the material, or preclude access to the material is undertaken.[14] Removal is not required if the material is Category I ACM in good condition and not friable, is encased in concrete and adequately wetted (where exposed), or is not accessible for testing and cannot be removed safely, or is Category II nonfriable ACM and is not likely to become crumbled, pulverized, or reduced to powder during demolition.[15] As building components that contain or are covered with RACM are removed, they must be adequately wetted and carefully lowered to the floor without disturbing the RACM.[16] RACM must also be adequately wetted during stripping operations, unless certain conditions are met and prior approval is obtained from EPA.[17] No removal or stripping may take place unless a person trained in the provisions of the asbestos NESHAP standards is present on site during the operation.[18]

The asbestos NESHAP standards also specify requirements for the transportation and disposal of asbestos.[19] The owner or operator must either discharge no visible emissions to the outside air during the collection, processing, packaging, or transportation of any ACM, or must comply with emission control and waste treatment procedures outlined in the regulations.[20] These procedures include adequately wetting and packaging the ACM in labeled and leak-tight containers or wrapping, processing the ACM into nonfriable pellets or other shapes, or an alternate method approved by EPA. ACM that is not removed because it is exempted from the removal requirements may be transported and disposed of in bulk without complying with the packaging requirements.[21] The regulations do not apply to Category I and II nonfriable ACM that is not crumbled, pulverized, or reduced to powder during demolition or removal.[22]

Finally, the removed ACM must be transported in marked vehicles and disposed of at an approved waste disposal site.[23] The owner or operator generating the ACM must maintain waste shipment records for two years.[24] A waste shipment record must accompany the waste to the disposal site. If the generator does not receive a copy of the record signed by

---

[14] *Id.* § 61.145(c)(1).
[15] *Id.*
[16] *Id.* § 61.145(c)(2).
[17] *Id.* § 61.145(c)(3).
[18] *Id.* § 61.145(c)(8).
[19] *Id.* § 61.150.
[20] *Id.* § 61.150(a).
[21] *Id.* § 61.150(a)(3).
[22] *Id.* § 61.150(a)(5).
[23] *Id.* § 61.150(b), (c).
[24] *Id.* § 61.150(d).

the disposal site operator within 35 days, the generator must contact the transporter or disposal site operator to determine the status of the shipment. If the signed record is not received within 45 days, the generator must send written notice to EPA.

EPA has broad powers to enforce the NESHAP standards. Courts have generally found owners and operators of buildings strictly liable for violations of the NESHAP standards.[25] The EPA may seek civil sanctions and penalties of up to $25,000 per day for each violation.[26] For knowing violations, EPA may seek criminal penalties of an additional fine or imprisonment for up to 5 years, or both.[27] Any person who knowingly makes a false report to EPA, or fails to report or notify EPA as required, may be subject to fines and imprisonment for up to two years. Anyone who knowingly releases asbestos into the air and places another person in imminent danger of death or serious bodily injury may be fined and imprisoned for up to 15 years. Organizations who are knowingly responsible for endangering others may be fined up to $1 million. Negligent releases that endanger others may subject the responsible party to a fine and up to one year in prison.

8.1.2 Occupational Health and Safety Act

Pursuant to its authority under the Occupational Health and Safety Act (OSH Act),[28] the Occupational Health and Safety Administration (OSHA) regulates occupational exposure to asbestos. In 1986, OSHA promulgated its Revised General Industry Asbestos Standard (General Standard),[29] which applies to all industries covered by the OSH Act except construction, and its Revised Construction Industry Asbestos Standard (Construction Standard),[30] which applies to the construction industry. The Standards do not apply directly to building owners as such. However, they may apply to building owners as employers before, during, and after a rehabilitation project. The employer of an operation and maintenance (O&M) staff may have to comply with the General Standard's initial air monitoring and notice requirements, and compliance with the General Standard's exposure levels and other requirements may be required when O&M staff become involved in or come into contact with an abatement action.[31] The Construction Standard would apply to workers involved in

---

[25] *See* United States v. Hugo Key & Son, Inc., 731 F. Supp 1135 (D.R.I. 1989) (contractor held strictly liable for violation of asbestos NESHAP); United States v. Ben's Truck & Equip., Inc., 25 Env't Rep. Cas. (BNA) 1295 (E.D. Cal. 1986).

[26] 42 U.S.C.A. § 7413(b) (West Supp. 1991).

[27] *Id.* § 7413(c). 6

[28] 29 U.S.C.A. §§ 651–678 (West 1985 & Supp. 1991).

[29] 29 C.F.R. § 1910.1001 (1991).

[30] 29 C.F.R. § 1929.58 (1991).

[31] 51 Fed. Reg. 22,678 (1986).

conducting an abatement action, and workers involved in renovation or demolition in areas where asbestos may be present.[32]

Under the General Standard, employers must ensure that employees are not exposed to airborne asbestos concentrations greater than the permissible exposure level (PEL) of 0.2 fibers per cubic centimeter (f/cc) of air as an eight-hour time-weighted average, or greater than the "excursion limit" of 1.0 f/cc as averaged over a sampling period of 30 minutes.[33] If either the PEL or excursion limit is exceeded, the employer must establish regulated areas to reduce employee exposure. The employer must demarcate the area, restrict access, provide respirators and prohibit certain activities within the regulated area.[34] Under the Construction Standard, the employer must also establish a negative-pressure enclosure around the restricted area before renovation or demolition may begin.[35] However, such an enclosure is not required for small-scale short-duration operations such as pipe repair, valve replacement, the installation of electrical conduits or drywall, roofing, or other general building maintenance or renovation.

Both the General Standard and the Construction Standard establish an action level of 0.1 f/cc based on an 8-hour time weighted average airborne concentration.[36] Employers must perform initial monitoring of areas where employees may reasonably be expected to be exposed to airborne concentrations above the action level or excursion level.[37] Initial monitoring is not required if asbestos is not capable of being released.[38] If airborne concentrations of asbestos exceed the action level, the employer must continue periodic monitoring until the airborne concentrations drop below the threshold level. However, monitoring must resume whenever there has been a change in the production, process, control equipment, personnel, or work practices that may result in new or additional exposure above the action level or excursion limit.[39] Employers must notify employees of all monitoring results, and maintain accurate records of all monitoring operations and employee medical surveillance for 30 years.[40]

The Construction Standard requires training of all asbestos workers, including inspectors and abatement workers.[41] Training programs must be approved by EPA and may be conducted by the employer, or other government or private agency. While the OHSA standards do not provide

---

[32] 29 C.F.R. § 1926.58(a).
[33] 29 C.F.R. § 1910.1001(c).
[34] *Id.* § 1910.1001(e).
[35] *Id.* § 1926.58(e)(6).
[36] *Id.* § 1910.1001(b); *id.* § 1926.58(b).
[37] *Id.* § 1910.1001(d)(2); *id.* § 1926.58(f)(2).
[38] *Id.* § 1910.1001(d)(2)(iii); *id.* § 1926.58(f)(2)(ii).
[39] *Id.* § 1910.1001(d)(4)-(5); *id.* § 1926.58(f)(4).
[40] *Id.* § 1910.1001(d)(7), (m); *id.* § 1926.58(f)(6), (n).
[41] *Id.* § 1926.58(b), (e)(6)(iii).

for a licensing or accreditation program, regulations under other statutes do. As a result, asbestos workers must be licensed before abatement work may be undertaken.

In order to enforce the standards, OSHA has the power to inspect facilities and issue citations and penalties for violations.[42] Civil penalties of up to $70,000 may be imposed for willful or repeated violations, or of up to $7,000 for less serious violations. In addition, criminal penalties of up to $10,000 and imprisonment of up to six months may be assessed for willful violations that cause the death of an employee.

8.1.3 Asbestos Hazard Emergency Response Act

In 1986, Congress, concerned about schoolchildren's exposure to friable asbestos, enacted the Asbestos Hazard Emergency Response Act (AHERA)[43] to regulate asbestos in schools. The AHERA regulations apply to any school building operated by any public or private local education agency (LEA).[44]

The AHERA regulations require that all LEAs inspect school premises for the existence of friable or nonfriable asbestos and implement appropriate asbestos management plans. The LEA must designate a responsible employee to ensure that the regulations are complied with, use accredited asbestos inspectors, and train O&M personnel who may come into contact with friable or nonfriable asbestos. Notification of parent, teacher, and employee organizations is required at various stages in the management program.

LEAs have discretion to decide whether asbestos should be removed from school premises, unless friable and damaged asbestos is found. The method for abatement of friable and damaged asbestos depends on the location of the material. If an abatement action is undertaken, it must be conducted in compliance with the OSHA standards discussed above. A response action is considered completed when airborne asbestos concentrations within the affected area equal levels outside the affected area, or for abatement actions involving less than 160 square feet or 260 linear feet of asbestos-containing building material, when airborne levels are 0.01 f/cc or less.[45]

Employees who conduct asbestos inspections, prepare a management plan, or design or conduct response actions must be accredited through a state program at least as stringent as the federal model.[46] These training standards are useful for training asbestos personnel in other contexts beyond AHERA compliance.

---

[42] 29 U.S.C.A. § 666.
[43] 15 U.S.C.A. §§ 2641–2656 (West Supp. 1991).
[44] *Id.* § 2642.
[45] 40 C.F.R. § 763.90(i)(3).
[46] 15 U.S.C.A. § 2646.

LEAs that fail to comply with AHERA requirements may be liable for civil penalties of up to $5,000 for each day the violation continues.[47] Criminal penalties of up to $25,000 per day, or up to one year in prison may be assessed for knowing or willful violations.[48] Furthermore, EPA may seek injunctive relief if the presence of friable asbestos-containing materials in school poses an imminent and substantial endangerment to human health or the environment.[49] Citizens may also file a complaint with EPA or the governor of the state in which the school is located with respect to asbestos-containing material in a school building.[50] EPA has established an Asbestos Ombudsman who can answer questions or receive complaints from concerned citizens. The Ombudsman may be contacted at (800) 368-5888.

8.1.4 Comprehensive Environmental Response, Compensation, and Liability Act

The Comprehensive Environmental Response, Compensation, and Liability Act (CERCLA),[51] also known as the Superfund law, governs the release of hazardous substances into the general environment. Friable asbestos is designated as a hazardous substance under CERCLA.[52]

CERCLA imposes strict liability on both the owner and operator of a facility where a hazardous substance is located, and on the generator and transporter of a hazardous substance, for any release that causes removal or clean up costs.[53] Hazardous substance generators, transporters, and facility owners and operators are jointly and severally liable for all costs incurred in response to a release.[54] CERCLA's liability provision are thus extremely broad, imposing full liability on many of the parties who come into contact with the hazardous substance before or during their release, regardless of relative fault or degree of contribution. Fault and contribution do, however, become relevant in apportioning liability among those responsible parties who are solvent.

Under CERCLA, the National Response Center [(800) 424-8802] must be notified if at least one pound of friable asbestos is released into the environment in any 24-hour period.[55] The actual weight of asbestos in asbestos-containing material must be calculated to determine if a reportable

---

[47] *Id.* § 2647.

[48] *Id.* § 2615.

[49] *Id.* § 2648(b).

[50] *Id.* § 2647(d).

[51] 42 U.S.C.A. §§ 9601–9675 (West 1983 & Supp. 1991).

[52] 40 C.F.R. § 302.4 (1991).

[53] 42 U.S.C.A. § 9607.

[54] *See* United States v. Monsanto, 858 F.2d 160 (4th Cir. 1988), *cert. denied*, 490 U.S. 1106 (1990); United States v. Chem-Dyne Corp., 572 F. Supp. 802 (S.D. Ohio 1983).

[55] *Id.* § 9603(a); 40 C.F.R. § 302.6.

amount has been released. "Environment" is defined as any surface water, ground water, drinking water supply, land surface, subsurface strata, or ambient air within the United States, or ocean waters under U.S. jurisdiction.[56] Penalties for a knowing failure to report include fines or imprisonment for up to three years, and up to five years for repeated failures to notify.[57] Because of the broad scope of CERCLA's liability provisions, a building owner may be liable for the release of asbestos by a transporter or from the facility to which the material was sent for disposal. It is recommended that the shipment and disposal of asbestos be documented in a fashion similar to that provided by NESHAP.

The enforcement of CERCLA's abatement provisions may be accomplished in one of several ways. EPA may clean up a release itself. Private parties may also clean up a release and then sue other potentially liable parties for contribution for costs incurred. In contribution suits, courts have rejected liability for asbestos manufacturers or previous building owners. In such cases, courts generally find that the sale and use of asbestos-containing building materials is not a "disposal" of hazardous substances within the meaning of CERCLA, and that CERCLA was not intended to provide a remedy for asbestos removal or to target the legitimate manufacturers or sellers of useful products.[58] However, CERCLA does provide for recovery from such parties of the cost of removal of asbestos found buried on a property,[59] or released onto the property from an off-site source.[60] Governments or landfill owners and operators may also theoretically recover response costs from building owners and others who disposed of asbestos at landfills where releases of asbestos into air or water have been discovered.

8.1.5 Hazardous Materials Transportation Act

The transportation of asbestos is governed by the Hazardous Materials Transportation Act (HMTA).[61] The regulations apply to both generators and transporters of friable asbestos.[62]

Under the HMTA regulations, the generator of more than one pound of asbestos must provide shipping papers that describe the material,[63]

---

[56] 40 U.S.C.A. § 9601(8).

[57] *Id.* § 9603(b).

[58] *See* Dayton Indep. School Dist. v. U.S. Mineral Prods., 906 F.2d 1059, 1064–66 (5th Cir. 1990) (no CERCLA claim for removal costs available against manufacturer of asbestos-containing building materials); *see also* 3550 Stevens Creek Assocs. v. Barclays Bank, 915 F.2d 1355 (9th Cir. 1990), *cert. denied*, 111 S. Ct. 2014 (1991) (no CERCLA claim for removal costs available against previous building owner).

[59] *See* United States v. Nicolet, Inc., 712 F. Supp. 1193 (E.D. Pa. 1989).

[60] *See* United States v. Metate Asbestos Corp., 584 F. Supp. 1143 (D. Ariz. 1984).

[61] 49 U.S.C.A. §§ 1801–1819 (West 1976 & Supp. 1991); 49 C.F.R. § 172.101 app. (1990).

[62] 49 C.F.R. § 172.3(a).

[63] *Id.* §§ 172.202–172.203.

and each package must be labeled to indicate it contains asbestos and marked with other warning symbols.[64] The carrier must immediately notify the Department of Transportation of releases occurring during transport that result in any death or hospitalization, the evacuation of the general public for an hour or more, the shut down of a major transportation artery or facility for an hour or more, or the alteration of a routine flight plan of an airplane.[65] A detailed report of any release must be filed with the Department within 30 days.[66]

Civil penalties for knowing violations of the HMTA regulations include fines of up to $25,000 per violation per day.[67] Criminal penalties of fines or imprisonment of up to five years may be imposed on persons who knowingly alter, remove, deface, destroy, or otherwise tamper with any label required by the regulations, or any package used for the transportation of hazardous materials.[68]

8.1.6 State Regulation of Asbestos

In addition to the federal laws governing the treatment of asbestos, a variety of state and local laws may apply as well. Many states also set strict requirements for the training and licensing of asbestos abatement workers. New York State, for example, requires that asbestos contractors meet state training and licensing requirements.[69]

Many states also impose additional restrictions on the transportation and disposal of ACM. New York State requires that ACM transporters obtain state permits.[70] California defines asbestos as a hazardous waste subject to the disposal requirements of the state Hazardous Waste Control Act.[71] Some states also require that owners and operators disclose the presence of asbestos in buildings. New York requires sponsors of condominium offering plans to make an asbestos report available.[72] California requires owners of property to disclose the presence of asbestos to employees, tenants, and contractors.[73] Landlords and tenants in nonresidential property must disclose to each other the presence of asbestos and other hazardous materials discovered on the property.[74]

[64] *Id.* § 172.324.
[65] *Id.* § 171.15(a).
[66] *Id.* § 171.16(a).
[67] 49 U.S.C.A. § 1809(a).
[68] *Id.* § 1809(b).
[69] N.Y. Lab. Law § 902 (McKinney 1988 & Supp. 1992).
[70] N.Y. Envtl. Conserv. Law § 27-0305 (McKinney 1984 & Supp. 1992).
[71] Cal. Health & Safety Code §§ 25100–25249 (West 1984 & Supp. 1992).
[72] N.Y. Comp. Codes R. & Regs. tit. 13, §§ 18.7, 20.7(ac), 21.7 (1991).
[73] Cal. Health & Safety Code §§ 25915–25924 (West Supp. 1992).
[74] § 25359.7 (West Supp. 1992).

Many local jurisdictions also have their own asbestos requirements. New York City's Asbestos Control Program,[75] among the most rigorous in the nation, includes comprehensive procedures for reporting, air and bulk sampling, monitoring and analysis, workplace practices, and worker training and certification. The City also has specific regulations for the storage and disposal of asbestos wastes.[76] Under the New York regulations, the asbestos requirements go into effect whenever a building owner or operator applies for a demolition permit or certain plumbing permits,[77] or before the alteration, renovation, or modification of a building.[78] Asbestos inspections must be conducted by a City-certified asbestos investigator, who must maintain records of such inspections for 30 years.[79]

Because of the variety and complexity of regulations governing asbestos removal and disposal, it is critical that the sponsor of a rehabilitation project seek advice on applicable federal, state, and local laws, as applied to specific projects, before work begins.

8.2 OTHER HAZARDOUS SUBSTANCES

In addition to asbestos, there are a variety of other hazardous substances subject to federal, state, and local regulation that may be present on properties being considered for historic preservation or rehabilitation projects. The presence of old electrical transformers, underground storage tanks, and other hazardous materials each presents special health risks and disposal problems to the rehabilitation project. Failure to comply with the complex regulatory schemes designed for different hazardous substances may result in unavoidable, and often astronomical, clean-up costs, and possibly civil and criminal penalties.

8.2.1 PCB Regulation Under the Toxic Substance Control Act

Polychlorinated biphenyls (PCBs) are a group of 200 fire-resistant compounds that can be found in electrical components and waste oil supplies. If improperly disposed of, they can seep into ground water supplies, vaporize into the air, or attach to dust particles. When absorbed into the body, PCBs accumulate in fat cells. Acute short-term exposure to PCBs can cause headaches, fatigue, skin eruptions, nausea, and digestive, liver,

---

[75] Rules of New York City tit. 15, §§ 1-01 to 1-170 (1991).
[76] *See id.* tit. 16, §§ 8-01 to 8-10 (1991).
[77] *Id.* tit. 15, § 1-52.
[78] *Id.* § 1-53.
[79] *Id.* § 1-58(d).

and reproductive problems. Long-term exposure can cause cancer and low birth weight.

The Toxic Substance Control Act (TSCA),[80] which provided for the phase out of PCB production by 1979, directs EPA to prescribe methods for the proper disposal of PCBs. The regulations do not require the removal of electrical components from service earlier than would normally be the case.[81] However, once they are removed, their disposal must comply with the regulatory requirements.

The regulations distinguish between PCBs and PCB articles. "PCB" is any chemical that contains PCB alone or in combination with other chemicals.[82] "PCB articles" are any manufactured article that contains and whose surfaces have been in direct contact with PCBs. Electric transformers are one of the PCB articles commonly found in old and historic buildings. Expert guidance should be sought to identify equipment that may be subject to the regulations.

PCBs in concentrations greater than 50 parts per million (ppm) must be incinerated at a facility in compliance with the regulations. Mineral oil dielectric fluid from PCB-contaminated electric equipment and other liquids with PCB concentrations of over 50 ppm may also be incinerated, or disposed of in a special chemical waste facility, not in a municipal landfill. PCB contaminated soil, rags, other debris may be incinerated or disposed of in a chemical waste facility. Dredged materials with 50 ppm or greater may be similarly treated or disposed of by an alternate method approved by EPA.[83]

PCB articles are treated slightly differently. Transformers and large, high-or low-voltage capacitors containing PCBs in concentrations of 500 ppm or more may be incinerated or disposed of in a chemical waste landfill.[84] Capacitors are subject to certain container requirements before disposal. Hydraulic machines such as die casting machines containing PCBs in concentration of 50 ppm or more may be disposed of as municipal solid waste or salvaged as long as any liquid is drained off. If the liquids had PCB concentrations of 1000 ppm or more, the machine must also be flushed. PCB-contaminated electrical equipment and other equipment containing PCBs in concentrations of 500 ppm or more may also be drained, if necessary, and incinerated or disposed of in a chemical waste landfill.

The TSCA regulations also describe procedures for PCB spill clean up. To the extent that the regulations overlap with requirements under other statutes, the stricter standard applies.[85] Spills of PCBS in concentrations

---

[80] 15 U.S.C.A. §§ 2601–2671 (West 1982 & Supp. 1991).
[81] See the note before 40 C.F.R. § 761.60 (1991).
[82] *Id.* § 761.3.
[83] *Id.* § 761.60(a).
[84] *Id.* § 761.60(b).
[85] *Id.* § 761.120(e).

of 50 ppm or more must be reported to EPA within 24 hours. This reporting requirement is in addition to reporting requirement under the Clean Water Act or CERCLA. Under CERCLA, for example, PCB spills of 10 pounds or more by weight must be reported to the National Response Center (NRC). For spills under one pound, clean up is subject to specific decontamination requirements, and must be completed within 48 hours.[86] Clean-up documentation for small spills must be kept for five years. For larger spills, notice must be provided to EPA and NRC, the affected area must be cordoned off, the size and area of the spill must be documented, and clean-up of soils and hard-surfaces must be initiated, all within 48 hours.[87] Once clean up is completed, all clean-up debris and materials must be properly disposed of, and the site subjected to post clean-up sampling requirements.[88]

The transport of PCBs and PCB articles containing PCB concentrations of 50 ppm or more for disposal is subject to a manifest system similar to that required for the disposal of asbestos materials.[89] Furthermore, the generator must confirm that the commercial storage or disposal facility actually received the waste.[90]

Civil penalties for violations of the regulations may be assessed for up to $25,000 per violation per day.[91] A fine of up to $25,000 per day and up to one year in prison may be imposed for willful or knowing violations.[92]

8.2.2 Control of Hazardous Substances Under Federal and State Laws

In response to growing concerns over the risk hazardous waste landfills and contaminated sites pose to public health and the environment, Congress and several states have adopted programs to clean up hazardous substances already released, and to prevent their release into the environment in the future. Because these programs generally have broad liability provisions, it is important that potential liabilities be explored before commitments are made to purchase or lease property.

The primary federal law regulating the clean up of prior contaminations is CERCLA. In order to accomplish this purpose, CERCLA created the Hazardous Substance Response Trust Fund, later named the Hazardous Substance Superfund (Superfund).[93] Whenever any hazardous

---

[86] *Id.* § 761.125(b).
[87] *Id.* § 761.125(c).
[88] *See id.* § 761.130.
[89] *See id.* § 761.207.
[90] *Id.* § 761.208(a)(4).
[91] 15 U.S.C.A. § 2615(a).
[92] *Id.* § 2615(b).
[93] *See* 42 U.S.C.A. § 9611.

substance is released (or there is a substantial threat of release) into the environment, EPA may act pursuant to the National Contingency Plan (NCP) to remove the hazard or remediate the site.[94] Hazardous substances are those that present a substantial danger to public health or the environment and include any chemicals designated pursuant to certain provision of the Clean Water Act, the Clean Air Act, TSCA, or the Resource Conservation and Recovery Act (RCRA).[95] In addition to asbestos and PCBs, as previously discussed, EPA has listed numerous other substances as hazardous.[96] However, petroleum, crude oil, and natural gas are not subject to regulation as hazardous substances, unless contaminated with other substances qualifying as hazardous. "Release" is also broadly defined, and EPA is not required to show actual harm to establish a release.

In order to prioritize abatement actions, EPA established a National Priorities List (NPL).[97] When undertaking an abatement action, EPA has several options. The preferred course is to negotiate a consent decree with the parties involved, shifting the conduct of the clean up and payment for costs upon the private parties.[98] Failing this, EPA can order responsible private parties to clean up the site, or clean up the site itself, using Superfund money to pay for response costs, and then recover the costs from any or all of the potentially responsible parties (PRPs).[99]

As previously discussed, CERCLA imposes strict, joint, and several liability on PRPs,[100] which include past and current owners and operators of a site at which a release occurs, and all hazardous substance generators and transporters associated with the release.[101] This means that EPA can recover response costs from virtually anyone associated with the site since the original release, regardless of relative degrees of contribution or fault. The defenses to liability under CERCLA are narrow and extremely limited.[102] Even innocent purchasers and mortgagees must undertake appropriate inquiry before acquiring the site (or making a loan) in order to avoid liability. Often the only recourse for a PRP who has been held liable for response costs by the government is to sue other PRPs for contribution.[103] In such a contribution action, the courts will apportion costs based on equitable factors such as the volume of hazardous substance contributed, the toxicity of the substance, the degree of involvement with the site, the degree of care

---

[94] *Id.* § 9604(a).
[95] *Id.* § 9601(14).
[96] *See* 40 C.F.R. § 302.4 (1991).
[97] 42 U.S.C.A. § 9605(a).
[98] *See id.* § 9604(a)(1).
[99] *See id.* §§ 9604, 9606, 9607.
[100] *See supra* note 54 and accompanying text.
[101] 42 U.S.C.A. § 9607(a).
[102] *Id.* § 9607(b).
[103] *Id.* § 9613(f).

exercised, and the extent to which the PRP cooperated with the government's response actions.[104]

In 1991, the Third Circuit Court of Appeals had the opportunity to consider how CERCLA and the National Historic Preservation Act (NHPA)[105] function together. In *Boarhead Corp. v. Erickson*,[106] a conflict between the two statutes arose when EPA conducted a preclean-up study on a superfund site that was also eligible to be listed as a historic place under the NHPA. The owner of a farm, on which Indian remains and artifacts could be found (but on which the owner had himself deposited toxic wastes) brought suit to stay EPA-ordered preclean-up activities under CERCLA until EPA conducted a Section 106 review pursuant to the NHPA. In affirming the district court's dismissal of the action, the Third Circuit found that it did not have subject matter jurisdiction to review the case. Under CERCLA, no federal court has jurisdiction under federal law to review EPA's preclean-up administrative orders, except in exceptional circumstances. Since NHPA Section 106 review was not one of those exceptions, the court found it did not have jurisdiction to decide Boarhead's claim, even though based on an independent federal law.

The court did note in a footnote that EPA was still required to comply with its own regulations under the NHPA and to consider the impact of preclean-up activities on the Indian burial sites located on the Boarhead farm. Moreover, because Boarhead had failed to demonstrate the EPA would fail to comply with its CERCLA regulations, the court did not "reach the troubling questions of whether judicial review would be available if Boarhead could show that [EPA] failed to comply with the regulations the EPA has promulgated pursuant to CERCLA or whether Boarhead would have standing to bring such a suit."[107]

It remains to be seen whether federal agencies will seek to circumvent their Section 106 obligations by inducing EPA to order demolitions of historic structures or sites as part of preclean-up administrative orders. If so, one may expect courts to revisit the issues raised in *Boarhead*, where the plaintiff had himself contaminated the property and appeared to have no genuine interest in its Indian artifacts.

In addition to CERCLA, many states have adopted their own state Superfund programs to supplement federal efforts. New York, for example, maintains a registry of inactive hazardous waste disposal sites pursuant to the Remedial Treatment of Inactive Hazardous Waste Sites Act.[108] While similar to the federal program, this New York superfund

---

[104] *See* Amoco Oil Co. v. Borden, Inc., 889 F.2d 664, 672-73 (5th Cir. 1989).

[105] 16 U.S.C.A. §§ 470 to 470w-6 (West 1985 & Supp. 1991). See § **6.1** for a complete discussion of the NHPA.

[106] 923 F.2d 1011 (3d Cir. 1991).

[107] *Id.* at 1022 n. 17.

[108] N.Y. Envtl. Conserv. Law §§ 27-1301 to -1321 (McKinney 1984 & Supp. 1992). For a more detailed discussion of the New York Superfund, *see* Mark A. Izeman, "New York Superfund

program has some significant differences. First, there is no "innocent" landowner defense, although several attempts have been made in the state legislature to amend the law to include one.[109] Second, the New York law only applies to "hazardous wastes," a category narrower than the federal "hazardous substances" category.[110] Third, the state registry separates sites into six classes, the two most common of which are Class 2a and Class 2 sites. Class 2a is a temporary classification of sites for which there is inadequate or insufficient evidence about the presence of hazardous wastes to assign a more definitive classification. Class 2 sites are those on which the presence of hazardous wastes present a significant threat to public health or the environment for which action is required. Sites listed as Class 2a are subject to preliminary investigations to determine whether the site should be upgraded to Class 2 or delisted. An owner wishing to conduct the preliminary investigation must negotiate a consent order with the Department of Environmental Conservation (DEC). Class 2 sites are subject to formal remediation procedures similar to those followed under CERCLA. Unlike the federal government (which, as discussed previously, can issue nonreviewable administrative orders to compel private parties to clean up a site), clean-up orders by the DEC are subject to administrative hearings.[111]

New Jersey's Environmental Cleanup Responsibility Act (ECRA)[112] requires that, before certain industrial facilities are transferred or sold, they must be investigated for possible remediation actions.[113] California's Superfund law, the Carpenter-Presley-Tanner Hazardous Substance Account Act,[114] parallels the federal CERCLA, but with several distinctive features. California's procedure for listing is more complex, allowing for consideration of whether a responsible party has entered into an enforceable agreement to remediate the site, and whether the site has been adequately characterized before listing.[115] The California law also provides for a preliminary allocation of responsibility among responsible parties, allows for binding arbitration to apportion obligations, and allows discharge of subsequent civil liabilities on completion of a successful arbitration.[116]

Enforcement Strategies," *Envtl. L. in N.Y.*, Jan. 1992, at 1; Mark A. Izeman, "The Evolution and Status of New York's Superfund Program," *Envtl. L. in N.Y.*, Oct. 1991, at 1; James J. Periconi, "State Superfund: Cleaning Up Sites on New York State's Hazardous Waste Registry," *Envtl. L. in N.Y.*, Aug. 1989, at 1.

[109] *See* N.Y. Envtl. Conserv. Law § 27-1313(3)(a).

[110] *See id.* § 27-1301(1).

[111] *Id.* § 27-1313(3), (4).

[112] N.J. Stat. Ann. §§ 13:1K-6 to -35 (West 1991).

[113] *Id.* § 13:1K-9.

[114] Cal. Health & Safety Code §§ 25300–25395 (West 1984 & Supp. 1992).

[115] *Id.* § 25356.

[116] *Id.* §§ 25356.1(d), 25356.3, 25356.6.

The primary federal mechanism for preventing the release of hazardous wastes is the Hazardous Waste Management program created by the Resource Conservation and Recovery Act (RCRA).[117] The central feature of RCRA is a "cradle-to-grave" manifesting systems designed to track hazardous waste from generation to disposal. However, the class of "hazardous wastes" regulated by RCRA is narrower than the class of hazardous substances regulated by CERCLA. Under RCRA, a hazardous waste is a solid, liquid, semi-solid, or contained gas waste that may cause death or serious injury, or present a substantial or potential hazard to human health or the environment if improperly disposed of, transported, or stored.[118] A solid waste is a hazardous waste under RCRA if it appears on a list of specific chemicals, published by the EPA ("listed wastes") or if it possesses the characteristics of ignitability, corrosivity, reactivity, or toxicity, as determined by testing procedures specified by EPA ("characteristic wastes").[119]

The generator of a hazardous waste must comply with specific procedures for proper disposal. First, the generator must prepare a manifest that lists the contents of a hazardous waste shipment and shows that the shipment is sent via a licensed transporter to a licensed storage or disposal site.[120] Second, the generator must package, label, and mark the waste before shipment according to Department of Transportation regulations applicable to hazardous substances.[121] Finally, the generator must provide copies of the manifest for each transporter, and storage and disposal facility operator, and must keep a signed copy of the manifest received from the designated facility that accepted the waste for three years.[122]

For violations of RCRA requirements, EPA may give notice of a violation to a state enforcement agency authorized to enforce a hazardous waste program, or EPA may issue its own compliance orders and assess civil penalties of up to $25,000 per day per violation against present owners or operators.[123] Knowing violations of the requirements and regulations are subject to criminal penalties of up to $50,000 per day or imprisonment for up to two years.[124] Knowing endangerment of another person is subject to criminal penalties of up to $250,000 or up to 15 years in prison.[125] EPA may also bring action against any present or past operator, owner, or generator if their treatment of a hazardous waste

---

[117] 42 U.S.C.A. §§ 6901–6992k (West 1983 & Supp. 1991).

[118] *Id.* § 6903(5), (27).

[119] 40 C.F.R. § 261.11 (1991).

[120] *Id.* § 262.20.

[121] *Id.* §§ 262.30–262.34.

[122] *Id.* §§ 262.23, 262.40.

[123] 42 U.S.C.A. § 6928(a), (c), (g).

[124] *Id.* § 6928(d).

[125] *Id.* § 6928(e).

presents an "imminent and substantial endangerment" to public health or the environment.[126] If EPA fails to act within 60 days after written notice of violation, individual citizens may bring citizen suits against anyone who violates a RCRA permit, standard, or regulation, or any person whose past or present activity poses an imminent and substantial danger to health or the environment.[127]

In addition to the federal requirements, individual states have implemented their own solid and hazardous waste management statutes.[128] These state requirements should be consulted to determine the extent to which they overlap with and establish requirements beyond the federal laws.

8.2.3 Underground Storage Tanks

Amendments in 1984 and 1986 to RCRA established a federal program for the regulation of underground storage tanks (USTs).[129] USTs are defined as tanks with 10 percent or more volume below ground.[130] Exempted from this regulation (but often subject to other rules) are hazardous waste tanks, wastewater treatment tanks regulated under the Clean Water Act, equipment or machinery containing regulated substances for operational facilities (such as hydraulic lift tanks and electrical equipment tanks) tanks with capacities of 110 gallons or less, and USTs with *de minimis* concentrations of regulated substances. Other types of tanks, such as USTs containing radioactive materials, airport hydrant fuel distribution systems, and USTs with field-constructed tanks, are subject to interim regulations.

EPA regulations specify procedures and requirements for the design, construction, and installation of USTs.[131] In addition, general operating requirements, notification to EPA, release detection and reporting procedures, and so on are established. A Leaking Underground Storage Tank Trust Fund (known as the LUST Fund) for EPA clean up of leaking USTs provides for reimbursement of response costs from suit against responsible parties.[132] It is important to note that the statute requires registration of all USTs and notification to EPA if a UST is taken out of service.[133]

---

[126] *Id.* § 6973(a).

[127] *Id.* § 6972.

[128] *See, e.g.,* California Hazardous Waste Control Act, Cal. Health & Safety Code §§ 25100–25249.100 (West 1984 & Supp. 1992); New Jersey Solid Waste Management Act, N.J. Stat. Ann. §§ 13:1E-1 to -207 (West 1991); Pennsylvania Solid Waste Management Act, 35 Pa. Cons. Stat. §§ 6018.101–.1003 (Supp. 1990). The hazardous waste laws of every state are discussed in *Environmental Law Practice Guide,* Michael B. Gerrard, ed. (Matthew Bender 1991).

[129] *See* 42 U.S.C.A. §§ 6991–6991i.

[130] *Id.* § 6991(1).

[131] 40 C.F.R. §§ 280.10–.112 (1991).

[132] 42 U.S.C.A. § 6991b(h).

[133] *Id.* § 6991a(a)(2)(A).

To enforce the UST regulations, EPA may seek compliance orders and civil penalties of up to $25,000 per day.[134] Failure to register, false reporting, or violation of standards are subject to penalties of up to $10,000 per day.[135] In addition, violations may be enforced through the RCRA citizen suit provisions discussed previously.[136]

Some states supplement the federal program with UST programs of their own. For example, New York has five distinct programs for the regulation of petroleum storage tanks, major petroleum bulk storage facilities, chemical bulk storage tanks, nonhazardous liquid waste storage tanks, and hazardous waste storage tanks.[137]

8.3 ASBESTOS AND OTHER HAZARDOUS SUBSTANCES IN REHABILITATION PROJECTS: AVOIDING LIABILITY

Because of the increasingly complex environmental regulations applicable to real property, the seller, sponsor, contractor, lender or even buyer of a rehabilitation project should not only be aware of the potential liabilities involved, but should also act to avoid assuming unknown risks or, at the very least, to reduce the uncertainty now associated with such transactions.[138]

8.3.1 Potential Liabilities

As discussed above, almost everyone involved in the sale, acquisition, rehabilitation, and operation of a historic preservation project can be subject to a variety of liabilities if hazardous conditions exist on the site. This section will briefly outline the potential problems that each of these parties will wish to consider.

The *seller* or *sponsor* of a historic property is subject to several potential liabilities. The mere presence of a hazardous condition on a historic property may reduce the value of property due to the costs associated with clean up. Furthermore, lenders are particularly reluctant, for reasons discussed below, to lend money for the rehabilitation of a property that contains a known or potential environmental hazard. As a result, a seller or sponsor may be forced to clean up a dangerous condition before

---

[134] *Id.* § 6991e(a).
[135] *Id.* § 6991e(d).
[136] *Id.* § 6972; *see also supra* note 127 and accompanying text.
[137] For a more detailed discussion of New York and federal programs, *see* Stephen L. Kass & Michael B. Gerrard, "Storage Tanks Underground and Aboveground," N.Y.L.J., May 16, 1990, at 3.
[138] For a general discussion of environmental risks and real estate transactions, *see* Jennifer L. Machlin & Tomme R. Young, *Managing Environmental Risk: Real Estate and Business Transaction* (Clark Boardman 1991); Joel S. Moskowitz, *Environmental Liability and Real Property Transactions: Law and Practice* (John Wiley & Sons 1989).

attempting to place the property on the market or even to secure financing for its rehabilitation.

The seller or sponsor may also be required to disclose certain environmental conditions to either the prospective purchaser, the government, or both. As discussed in § **8.1.6**, some states require sellers to disclose the presence of asbestos on a property. Others, such as New Jersey's ECRA, require that certain properties be investigated for the presence of hazardous substances and, if necessary, remediated before the property may be sold. Under federal and state securities laws (discussed in §§ **3.3** and **3.4**), certain sales of contaminated property to limited or general partnerships or to home buyers may also be subject to the disclosure requirements of such statutes, including material information concerning clean up costs or agency enforcement actions.[139] In addition to statutory disclosure requirements, common law principles of fraud and misrepresentation may apply to transactions where the seller or sponsor fails to disclose hazardous conditions on the property.[140]

The *purchaser* of historic property should also be concerned with potential liability for the clean-up bill. The application of federal and state Superfund laws may result in a landowner's liability for all response costs incurred by the government, regardless of contribution, fault, or due diligence in investigating the site before purchase. In addition, the common law imposes obligations on a building owner to protect tenants, occupants, and the public from unreasonable dangers that the building owner knows or should have known about.

Lessees of a rehabilitated property may have similar obligations. For example, CERCLA would hold a net lessee liable, as an "operator" of the facility, for response costs associated with a remediation action. As an employer, a lessee would also be obligated to observe OSHA requirements regarding asbestos in the workplace.

Finally, *lending institutions* can also be liable, under certain conditions, for a project's clean up costs. In 1985, in *United States v. Mirabile*,[141] a U.S. district court found that a bank officer's frequent visits to a site and his insistence on certain manufacturing practices and personnel might make the bank an "operator" and therefore liable under CERCLA for the site's cleanup. In *United States v. Maryland Bank & Trust Co.*,[142] the foreclosure and subsequent purchase of a property at the foreclosure sale established the bank as an "owner" under CERCLA. In *United States v. Fleet Factors Corp.*,[143] the court found that a bank might even be liable if

---

[139] *See, e.g.*, Levine v. NL Indus., Inc., 926 F.2d 199 (2d Cir. 1991).

[140] *See, e.g.*, State Dep't of Envtl. Protection v. Ventron Corp., 468 A.2d 150 (1983) (allowing recovery on misrepresentation/failure to disclose claim for failure to disclose presence of hazardous substance on property).

[141] 15 Envtl. L. Rep. (Envtl. L. Inst.) 20994 (E.D. Pa. 1985).

[142] 632 F. Supp. 573 (D. Md. 1986).

[143] 901 F.2d 1550 (11th Cir. 1990), *cert. denied*, 111 S. Ct. 752 (1991).

it did not foreclose but became so involved in the day-to-day operations of the facility "sufficient . . . to support the inference that it could affect hazardous waste disposal decisions if it so chose." Extending liability beyond hazardous wastes, a federal court in Rhode Island in *O'Neil v. Q.L.C.R.I.*[144] held the mortgagee of a 33-unit residential subdivision potentially liable for a failed septic system where the mortgagee bank had permitted the borrower to engage in fraudulent activities. As a result of these decisions, many lenders have become far more cautious about mortgage loans on real property that might be contaminated and now require, as a condition of a loan, one or more of the protective steps discussed next.[145]

8.3.2 Avoiding Liability: Indemnification and Hold Harmless Provisions

Seller and lenders concerned with potential liabilities under environmental statutes often require indemnification and "hold harmless" provisions in the sale or loan documents. Under CERCLA, such provisions do not avoid liability to the government or third parties.[146] However, these provisions do provide for a useful means of apportioning ultimate liability among the parties to the agreement. Indemnification provisions should be drafted with care and explicitly refer to environmental liability relating to hazardous substances. The provision should use a broad definition of hazardous substances to cover both CERCLA and other non-CERCLA liabilities. The indemnification should also be crafted to survive transfer of the property (for sellers) or payment of the debt (for lenders) and be secured by the mortgage. If possible, the indemnification should be designed to run with the land, although this may not always be enforceable against subsequent purchasers of the property. The provision should also include liability for expenses of consultants, counsel, laboratories, and expert witness, and should reserve to the seller or lender the right to settle claims with the government or third parties and to carry out remediation to settle claims. Finally, the seller or lender may require the borrower to covenant to comply with all federal, state, and local laws and regulations, provide notification of all hazardous releases, send copies of environmental notices and complaints, and even commit to not use the land for some uses.

---

[144] 750 F. Supp. 551 (D.R.I. 1990).

[145] For a more detailed discussion of lender liability and methods for avoiding it, *see* Stephen L. Kass & Michael B. Gerrard, "Minimizing Lender Liability," N.Y.L.J., Dec. 27, 1991, at 3.

[146] *See* 42 U.S.C.A. § 9607(e)(1); *see also* Jones-Hamilton Co. v. Kop-Coat, Inc., 750 F. Supp. 1022 (N.D. Cal. 1990), *aff'd in relevant part,* 1992 U.S. App. LEXIS 3924 (1992), and cases cited therein.

8.3.3 Environmental Audits

Although indemnification clauses can be helpful, the safest approach to a limiting potential liabilities for sellers, sponsors, contractors, buyers, and lenders is to conduct an environmental audit of the property before the sale, loan, or other transaction is completed or even completely negotiated. An environmental audit is a study of overall compliance with environmental laws and regulations. The results of such an audit should give the parties an idea of the environmental risks involved, and provide a basis for apportioning liabilities by agreement. Furthermore, such an exercise is essential if a purchaser or lender wishes to take advantage of the elusive "appropriate inquiry" defense under Section 101(35)(B) of CERCLA.[147] Another more limited review, a site assessment, looks for contamination at the site, but does not review other practices and activities of the previous owner. While such an approach is certainly less expensive, it may not provide the level of due diligence required to avoid liability.

A good place to start an environmental audit is to request the seller to make representations regarding the existence of hazardous conditions, and the presence of asbestos, PCBs, USTs, and so on the property. The sponsor, purchaser, or lender may also seek representations that no government or third party litigation or administrative procedures have been undertaken against the property, and that the prior owner is in possession of all required permits.

Next, the prior owner should be asked to complete a questionnaire regarding all current and past uses and practices. Significant omission or evasions in both the questionnaire and the representations can alert the auditor to potential problem areas. (False answers may also be helpful in fraud cases.)

Once the preliminary questionnaire is complete, the environmental audit moves on-site. Generally, an environmental audit should proceed in two phases. A Phase I audit, which is usually relatively inexpensive, is a site visit in which the inspector makes a preliminary survey of the property for hazardous conditions, and examines applicable documents, including public records concerning prior uses, the presence of USTs and the like. If the results of the Phase I audit indicate that further investigation is required, a Phase II audit should be undertaken. In a Phase II audit, limited on-site sampling and chemical testing of soils, groundwater, and building materials is conducted. A full Phase II review can be expensive, sometimes running to tens of thousands of dollars.

Once the audit results are in, the parties are in a better position to fairly assess their potential liabilities, decide whether the project should go forward, identify (and carry out) those clean-up activities required by law or otherwise necessary for a successful project, and apportion responsibilities if government or third party claims arise in the future. Moreover, as

---

[147] *See* 42 U.S.C.A. § 9601(35)(B).

indicated above, proper audits can be essential for purchasers, sponsors and lenders to demonstrate that they have made "due inquiry" before acquiring an interest in the property (and are thus entitled to protection against third party claims). Audits are also likely to be required with increasing frequency by both individual buyers and regulatory authorities, including state officials who must approve condominium or cooperative offering plans.

The environmental audit is becoming, and is likely to remain, an essential part of the rehabilitation process. As discussed, there are sound reasons for this caution, and the project sponsor is well-advised to include the costs of either a Phase I or Phase II audit, as well as any necessary remediation, in the project's financial projections.

Nine

A Rehabilitation Sampler

By its nature, each rehabilitation or preservation project is unique; there is no single formula for success. Nevertheless, there are common issues that arise in the course of rehabilitation efforts, and an understanding of these issues is important to virtually all preservation projects. Objectives must be defined, properties identified and inspected, proposed uses evaluated, financing obtained, applicable laws and regulations satisfied, and the project carried out and operated as planned. The preceding chapters have identified the major considerations that the sponsor or coordinator of a rehabilitation project must address. When the property to be rehabilitated is historic, the project takes on additional levels of complexity but, as previously mentioned, offers additional rewards as well.

The first portion of this chapter outlines an overall program for the rehabilitation of a historic property. The framework it provides is skeletal; it does not purport to describe all of the decisions that will confront those who undertake historic rehabilitations, nor will the issues necessarily arise in the order presented. It is intended to illustrate the breadth and complexity of the tasks which may be involved in a preservation project, and the range of expertise which may be required. No single individual should expect to possess all of the skills required to carry out a project of any significant size, and outside assistance—whether legal, financial, architectural, or otherwise—should be brought in as necessary.

The second portion of the chapter describes four preservation projects that illustrate both the common elements and the extraordinary diversity of the rehabilitation process. They are also examples of rehabilitation successfully undertaken with preservation objectives in mind and demonstrate greatly varying approaches to the challenge of adapting historic structures to contemporary use.

9.1 THE REHABILITATION PROGRAM

This section is intended to assist an individual or organization wishing to embark upon a preservation project that has not yet been defined in detail. The following discussion identifies the principal steps that must be taken on the path from initial project plan to completion. It must be emphasized, however, that this description is not exhaustive, and that the preservationist should obtain outside expertise as appropriate to insure that all components of the project are properly in place.

9.1.1 Identifying the Property

The first step in any project is to locate the historic structure or structures to be preserved. In some cases, this will be obvious: An organization may have been formed for the precise purpose of restoring a particular local landmark, designated or otherwise. In others, a project sponsor may have a certain objective in mind—creating new residential units, for example—but may not yet have identified a property which will serve that purpose.

In either event, a number of characteristics of the property should be analyzed. The condition of the property will determine the extent and cost of the required renovation. These in turn may affect eligibility for the rehabilitation tax credit, which is available only for a "substantial" rehabilitation—one whose cost must generally exceed the owner's basis in the building. At the same time, if tax credits are desired, a rehabilitated building must meet the requirements regarding the retention of external walls and internal structural features that are described in § **1.2.5**.

Eligibility for the tax credit will depend on other building characteristics as well. Except under the transition rules discussed in § **1.2.9**, a building must have been first placed in service before 1936 to qualify for the 10 percent credit. As described in § **1.2.1**, a property must be a certified historic structure to qualify for the 20 percent credit. Certified historic structures include National Register properties, which ordinarily must be at least 50 years old.[1] If the building is located in a National Register historic district, federal restrictions may govern the type of rehabilitation work which can be undertaken. Unless certified as not contributing to the significance of the district, a building within a historic district must undergo a certified rehabilitation for the tax credit to be available. If the structure is a locally designated landmark or situated within a locally created district, provisions of the local

---

[1] 36 C.F.R. 60.4 (1991).

preservation ordinance may dictate the extent and nature of alterations which can be carried out under any circumstances.

In choosing a property for rehabilitation, then, the prospective developer should establish that the property can be adapted to its intended use in conformity with applicable federal and local regulations. In making this determination, he or she may wish to consult with an architect or structural engineer familiar with historic preservation work, or with the staffs of the local preservation commission, the state historic preservation office, or (particularly in states that do not participate in the certification process) the office of the National Park Service which administers the certification program.

9.1.2 Planning the Project

Having selected an appropriate property or properties, the next step is to formulate a plan for carrying out the rehabilitation project. In most cases, this will involve hiring an architect to design the project and, at a later date, to prepare the required plans for submission to governmental authorities and financing sources. It may also be useful at this point to retain an attorney experienced in preservation law (and other relevant fields) to identify, as early as possible in project planning, the likely regulatory reviews and legal standards to which the project will be subject. As indicated in preceding chapters, a complex rehabilitation project may require one or more levels of environmental and historic review and involve legal issues such as code compliance; zoning regulations; local, state, and federal preservation and environmental regulations; and the tax, securities, and partnership matters discussed in earlier portions of this book. A clear understanding of the impact of these issues on a particular project is an essential component of successful advance planning.

Once an overall project plan has been completed, the architect can proceed with the detailed drawings and plans. After the architect's plans have been completed, they will have to be submitted to local building authorities, who must certify that they comply with applicable building code standards. Depending upon the nature of the project, it may be necessary to take advantage of special building code provisions pertaining to historic buildings in order to achieve compliance without significantly violating the building's historic character; in some cases, where these do not exist or are not adequate, a project sponsor may wish to seek a variance or exemption from code requirements.

The architect should also prepare a zoning analysis to determine the permissible building size and configuration under local zoning ordinances. If the structure to be renovated does not utilize all of the available building bulk for the site on which it is located, the owner should explore its eligibility for the transfer of development rights to another site or sites, a step that could help raise funds to finance the project.

The architect should also prepare an estimated construction budget for the project. This will serve as the basis for the overall financing package discussed next. If the property to be rehabilitated is a federally or locally designated landmark or located within a federally or locally designated historic district, additional reviews may be required beyond that of local building authorities. If the building is a local landmark, construction plans will typically have to be submitted to the landmarks preservation commission in order to obtain a certificate of appropriateness permitting alteration.

If the building is federally designated or within a federally certified district, and the owner intends to take a rehabilitation tax credit, the appropriate certification procedures must be followed. If the building is located within a federally designated district, and no rehabilitation credit is desired, the owner must first obtain a certification that the building does not contribute to the significance of that district. This may enable him to claim the 10 percent tax credit if the building was first placed in service before 1936. Absent such certification, or in the case of a National Register landmark, a certified rehabilitation will be necessary if *any* tax credit is desired. In such cases it may also be useful, although not essential, to request preliminary certification of the rehabilitation plans, to provide some assurance to the owner and other potential investors that the benefits of the tax credit will be forthcoming when the project is completed. If a certified rehabilitation is to be undertaken, the project sponsor would be well advised to retain the services of an architect or other consultant who is well versed in the certification process.

9.1.3 Structuring the Financing Package

Once the overall cost of the project has been estimated, the sponsor must determine how it is to be financed. The simplest methods, which may be adequate for small-scale projects, involve self-financing of some or all project costs, with the remainder to be provided as a construction or mortgage loan from a bank or other lending institution. However, most preservation projects can benefit from financial aid targeted or available for historic preservation activities. Such aid may come from public or private sources, may be provided in the form of loans or grants, and may constitute either direct assistance or indirect benefits which have the effect of lowering project costs.

The latter category, consisting of a variety of tax incentives for rehabilitation, is potentially the most beneficial and should generally be explored first. The most powerful incentive is the rehabilitation tax credit, which, as just discussed, can offset 10 or 20 percent of qualifying project costs. If a project can be structured to take advantage of one of these credits, it is generally advisable to do so. In addition, a number of approaches are available under the tax laws for depreciating project costs. Different depreciation formulas may be most beneficial in different instances, and the optimal combination of tax credits and depreciation deductions will depend upon the specifics of the project. The sponsor should seek tax advice from either an attorney or a financial adviser to determine the best possible utilization of such tax incentives.

An additional offset to project costs may be achieved, in certain instances, through the donation of a facade easement (technically, a qualified conservation contribution) on the building to be renovated. By agreeing not to alter the facade, the owner may be entitled to a tax deduction equal to the amount by which that restriction reduces the value of the building. The possibility of benefiting from such a donation should be explored. Finally, a variety of state and local tax incentives may also be available. These will generally take the form of a partial or total exemption from, or abatement of, property taxes for projects that meet specified criteria.

The advantages of using these cost offsets, however, depend upon the existence of a tax liability to offset. If the entity undertaking the rehabilitation cannot use tax credits or deductions at all (for example, if it is a nonprofit, tax-exempt organization), or if the entity or individual cannot make full use of the amount of tax benefits that will be generated by the project, it will probably be desirable to include other investors in financing the project, and to offer a portion of the tax savings as an incentive for them to invest. This is an additional advantage of syndication and is discussed in this chapter.

In addition to those tax provisions, there may be other programs of direct governmental assistance for preservation. The federal government funds programs which can be used to facilitate preservation involving adaptive reuse, as, for example, through Community Development Block Grants, or Federal Housing Administration loans. Other programs, such as those of the National Trust for Historic Preservation, may not typically provide direct project support but can provide technical assistance and other services. States and localities, either directly or through quasi-public corporations, may be able to issue tax-exempt bonds, the revenue from which can be devoted to certain kinds of rehabilitation or conversion projects. This may be especially helpful for large-scale commercial or residential projects with significant public benefits.

Private sources of funding may also exist. Many communities have revolving funds that will lend money to finance a portion of the cost of rehabilitating older buildings. Foundations, particularly community foundations, with a commitment to economic development and civic improvement in a particular locale, may also offer financial assistance. All of these potential funding sources should be explored in putting together a construction funding package.

A final method of obtaining financing, though by no means a last resort, involves putting together a syndicate to finance the rehabilitation. This may be desirable if the sources of public and private funding just discussed will not cover project costs; if sufficient bank financing cannot be obtained or is prohibitively expensive; if the sponsor wishes to share the risk of a project (as well as the potential benefits) with others;

or if the project will produce tax savings of which the sponsor cannot take full advantage.

A project sponsor may wish to obtain the services of a professional syndicator to assist in structuring financing and securing investors.[2] On the basis of information provided by the developer of the project, the syndicator will typically prepare a proposal letter indicating the amount of equity he believes can be raised for the renovation and the terms on which solicitations for investment should be made. If the proposal is acceptable, the syndicator will put together a more comprehensive syndication agreement. This will specify the guarantees which the sponsor will be required to provide, such as a construction completion guarantee, a promise to repurchase investor interests in the event completion is not achieved, or even a price adjustment provision if the project ultimately does not qualify for an investment tax credit. The agreement will also outline the form of syndication, usually a limited partnership, the requirements and timetable for capital contributions from the limited partners, the apportioning of partnership items (income, loss, credits, and so on) among the general and limited partners, and the obligation of the developer to assume other costs associated with the project.

If the agreement is acceptable to the developer, the next step is to prepare a partnership agreement, which will contain a more detailed set of rules for the conduct of partnership business. In most instances, a private placement memorandum or prospectus will also be prepared and, depending upon relevant state requirements, submitted to state officials for a review of compliance with securities regulations. This document will describe the project, particularly its financial aspects, and will identify any risks associated with the project of which potential investors should be aware.

In particular, the memorandum or prospectus will usually contain a *pro forma* projection of financial data relating to the project for the duration of a prospective limited partner's investment. It will itemize the anticipated expenses of the project over time, as well as the sources of funds to meet rehabilitation and other project costs. The memorandum will also break down projected cash flow from the project by category, including direct income from the rental, sale, or use of the rehabilitated property, and indirect returns in the form of tax benefits. Finally, it will project the annual capital contributions that will be required of potential investors, and indicate the expected return of capital and tax benefits that will be allocated to each limited partnership share on an annual basis. While these projections cannot be made with certainty, and will be accompanied by appropriate disclaimers, they do provide a basis to help investors evaluate the merits of a proposed investment. **Appendix G** contains an illustration of such a *pro*

---

[2] *See* Oldham, "The Equity Syndication Process," *in Historic Preservation Law: Tax Planning for Old and Historic Buildings* 371 (American Law Institute 1984).

forma projection for a typical rehabilitation project. Once the appropriate disclosure document has been approved, it will be used as the basis for soliciting the participation of limited partners.

When sufficient funds have been raised for a project through the methods just described, and after all required permits and approvals have been secured, the project can begin. However, as with any construction project, the hiring of a competent and knowledgable contractor is essential to the successful completion of rehabilitation work. If historic features of the building are to be preserved, it may be necessary to find a contractor or subcontractor particularly skilled in restoration. Depending upon the scale of the project, it may also be desirable to employ a supervisor to oversee the entire project, and to make sure the work is completed as planned, on time, and as close to budget as possible. The project's architect may be willing to provide this construction supervision.

Once the renovated building is placed in service in its new (or rejuvenated) function, the partnership agreement should govern the allocation of revenues among investors, as well as the ultimate disposition of the building. In some cases, it will be retained as an income-producing asset; in others, it will be sold when rehabilitation is finished to generate an immediate cash flow. If the project is eligible for the 20-percent investment tax credit, it will be necessary to seek certification of the completed work, regardless of whether preliminary certification was sought or obtained.

9.2 REHABILITATION PROJECTS

The foregoing discussion outlines the basic elements which must come together for a successful rehabilitation project. The remainder of this chapter describes four widely varying rehabilitation projects that have combined these elements in different, but ultimately successful, ways. These illustrations are not intended as models for undertaking historic preservation work, nor will the financing packages used to underwrite these projects necessarily be appropriate in other circumstances. Nevertheless, each of these projects demonstrates the range of benefits possible, as well as the leadership and perseverance required, in the rehabilitation field and the need for project sponsors both to assemble a completed project team and to be familiar with the essential components of real estate development and finance. The detailed financial feasibility analysis that must be undertaken before initiating a project is beyond the scope of this book.[3]

---

[3] A number of useful publications are available to the prospective sponsor of a rehabilitation project, which will help in analyzing the investment prospects of a particular project and in choosing among various financing options. Among those worth consulting are

9.2.1 Small Residential Building (78 Hudson Street, Providence, Rhode Island)

Small-scale rehabilitation projects are often undertaken for reasons that are not solely financial, and in those cases a range of nonprofit and governmental entities may have to work together to make the projects feasible. An example of this type of project is the rehabilitation of a 2½ story building within the Broadway-Armory National Register Historic District in Providence, Rhode Island.[4] Although the project resulted in the creation of only four apartments, it was thought important as a catalyst to further rehabilitation activity in the district, and money from several sources, including a revolving fund, was made available to supplement the funds obtained from private investors.

The costs associated with the creation of a limited partnership and the sale of the limited partnership interests may cast doubt on the advisability of a partnership syndication in situations, such as this one, where the amount raised from the limited partners is relatively small. However, there are often situations in which other forms of financial assistance are not available unless private funds are committed, or where the nonprofit and public funds are not sufficient. If preservation rather than profit alone is the objective, and the limited funds available from the syndication are critical, the costs of the syndication may be necessary transaction costs. In any event, the structure of this transaction can serve as a useful model for the rehabilitation of buildings that are more expensive to acquire or rehabilitate, and which therefore require more substantial capital contributions from the limited partners.

The Armory District, part of the Broadway-Armory National Register Historic District, is five minutes from downtown Providence. The district is a neighborhood of late nineteenth- and early twentieth-century homes constructed in a variety of Victorian styles, which have sheltered successive influxes of new Americans, including most recently Hispanic and Southeast Asian immigrants.

The character of the neighborhood has reflected the changing economic climate of Providence; the last few decades have not been kind to the district. Large-scale migration from the city has led to disinvestment, and a 1980 study revealed a 16-percent vacancy rate in the district. At the time this project was initiated, the district contained a number of abandoned properties and many others in varying states of disrepair.

J. Canestaro, *Real Estate Financial Feasibility Analysis Handbook: A Guide to Project Cost-Benefit Evaluation* (Virginia Polytechnic Institute and State University, 1982); A. Ring and J. Dasso, *Real Estate: Principles and Practices* (1981); R. Lifton, *Practical Real Estate: Legal, Tax and Business Strategies* (1979).

[4] The information in this section is taken primarily from an offering memorandum for limited partnership interests in Hudson Street Associates, dated June 30, 1982, generously provided by the Providence Preservation Society Revolving Fund.

Nonetheless, the neighborhood's housing stock escaped the large-scale clearance and demolition activities of the urban renewal programs of the 1960s, and its rows of predominantly two- and three-family wood-frame houses have remained basically unchanged. With the renewed popularity of urban residential areas, these buildings are becoming more attractive, and there have recently been signs of reinvestment by both new and older residents of the area. To this end, neighborhood residents have established a variety of organizations to assist in improving housing conditions in the district. The city of Providence has also lent its support. The city's Community Development Office has funded a program to provide financial assistance to district property owners for home improvements. The city has also planted 300 trees around the perimeter of the Dexter Training Field, a park that is a focal point of the neighborhood.

By early 1985, the character of the district had been substantially upgraded as a result of the rehabilitation of over 30 properties in the area, including the residential structure located at 78 Hudson Street. This building is a Second Empire house built in 1875, apparently as a two-family dwelling with servants' quarters in the basement and on the top floor. This large, 2½ story wood-frame, mansard-roofed structure has retained most of its unusually fine exterior detailing. The acquisition and rehabilitation of 78 Hudson Street was coordinated by the Providence Preservation Society Revolving Fund, Inc. (Fund), a non-profit organization incorporated in 1980 as an affiliate of the Providence Preservation Society. The society set up the Fund to work in areas where urban blight threatens buildings of historic significance, and to undertake projects of high visibility in an effort to spur other neighborhood revitalization efforts.

Hudson Street Associates, a limited partnership, was created to help finance and carry out the project. The general partner, who is responsible for the administration of the partnership and management of the property, is a former carpenter who has refitted large sailing yachts and worked on a variety of construction projects, including two rehabilitation projects within the Armory District. He also has experience in managing an apartment building in Providence.

The rehabilitation of 78 Hudson Street consisted of restoring the exterior of the building, part of which had been damaged by fire, to its original condition and converting the interior to four residential units. New heating, electrical, and plumbing systems were installed. Through the use of paint scrapings, the original colors of the building's exterior were approximated and the entire building was repainted. Clapboards that had been custom-shaped to duplicate the originals were installed, and deteriorated wooden detail was replaced.

The total purchase and rehabilitation effort cost approximately $90,000, of which $56,673 qualified for the 25-percent investment tax credit available at that time. Funds were obtained from several sources.

The general partner borrowed $25,000 from a commercial lending institution to purchase the property and to finance a portion of the rehabilitation. The loan is secured by a first mortgage on the property. The general partner then conveyed the property to the partnership, subject to the bank loan and first mortgage. He remained personally liable on the loan.

The Fund loaned the partnership $15,000, secured by a second mortgage on the property. This loan, made possible by funds loaned to the Fund by the National Trust for Historic Preservation, was in turn partially secured by the Fund's assignment of its second mortgage to the National Trust. The Fund also loaned the partnership an additional $15,000 from its own resources for renovation work undertaken prior to the receipt of revenues from the partnership's planned syndication.

The Providence Office of Community Development and the West Broadway Incentive Corporation provided a grant of approximately $8,200 to be applied to the exterior renovation of the building. The remainder of the financing came from an offering of 10 limited partnership shares of $2,700 each. Under the agreement, the limited partners are to share 98 percent of the profits, losses, and tax credits from normal operation of the partnership, with the remaining 2 percent to go to the general partner. The partners shared the 25-percent investment tax credit of $14,168 and also shared losses, which were expected to total $11,629 during 1983–87. In addition, they shared a charitable deduction based on the appraised value of a historic easement granted to the Fund. Under the terms of this easement, without the authorization of the Fund, no construction or modification may be undertaken that would affect the appearance or structural integrity of the building's exterior, alter the composition of the exterior surfaces, or increase the building's height. The easement agreement specifies that the building's exterior is to be maintained in its restored condition in perpetuity and that the building shall contain no more than four dwelling units. The amount of the deduction available as a result of the donation of this easement to a charitable organization was expected to be about 12 to 15 percent of the unrestricted fair market value of the renovated property.

For its services and expenses in organizing the partnership and preparing the offering memo, the Fund received a fee of $5,000 upon admission of the limited partners. The general partner, for his work in managing the construction and rehabilitation work, as well as actually doing much of the construction, received $225 per week during the year-long construction period. In addition, the general partner receives a management fee equal to the rent for the apartment he occupies within the building, plus 2 percent of the net cash flow from the apartment rentals.

Upon the sale of the property, and after the limited partners recover their capital contributions, the general partner will be reimbursed for his capital contribution and for the loans he made to the partnership to help finance the rehabilitation. The Fund will then receive 10 percent of the balance for its services as the representative of the limited partners. Of the remainder, 55 percent will go to the general partner and 45 percent will be distributed among the limited partners.

In addition, the general partner received a 2-year option, to begin 5 years after the completion of rehabilitation, to purchase the building for its fair market value, so long as that price is sufficient to satisfy the debts of the partnership and to repay the limited partners' capital contributions. The general partner also received a right of first refusal should the partnership choose to sell the property at any time between 5 and 15 years after the completion of rehabilitation.

In January 1989, the general partner bought out the limited partners in Hudson Street Associates for a purchase price based on a valuation of the partnership property (not including the value of the easement discussed above) at approximately $145,000. Accordingly, the limited partners received, for each share of limited partnership interest, $1,640 plus $2,700 in return for their initial investment. In addition, the limited partners benefited from the tax credit, charitable deduction based on the easement donation, and real estate loss deduction to which they were entitled as a result of their investment in the partnership.

The momentum created by 78 Hudson Street, and buildings like it, in the Broadway Armory National Register District has continued to foster the rehabilitation and preservation of historic structures. Forty-five major restorations have now been completed within the community.

In August 1990, a local historic district near (but not including) 78 Hudson Street was formed and made subject to the city's "Historic District Zoning" provisions (Article VI-A of Chapter 544 of the Ordinances of the City of Providence). The Providence Historic District Commission has authority to review all permits for construction, alteration, substantial repair, moving, or demolition of a structure within the district. The controls apply to the exterior features of the properties. In assessing proposals by property owners which would affect the historic value of the building or area, the Historic District Commission is required, whenever possible, to work with owners to develop an economically feasible plan for preservation of the structure. It also reviews alterations and repairs to structures for consistency with their original architectural design and style.

One of the concerns of the Fund and the community has been to ensure that low- and moderate-income families are protected from the pressures of increasing property values within the area. This has presented difficulty for low income renters in the area, as investors have moved into the Providence market. In order to protect low- and moderate-income families from displacement incident to historic restoration in the district, the Fund has included a provision in its purchase and sale agreement that gives it the right to repurchase the property, if resold, with an appreciation cap of 5 percent per year on the repurchase price. In addition, the purchase and sale agreement includes a provision requiring that at least

51 percent of the rental units must be rented to low- and moderate-income families.

Additionally, a homeowners' association has been formed that includes a neighborhood loan committee. This committee reviews loans to be made from the Fund to prospective owners of Fund properties to ensure each owner's commitment to the community.[5]

9.2.2 Low-Income Housing (Kensington Square, New Haven, Connecticut)

Large-scale low-income housing projects generally involve governmental assistance at the federal, state, and local levels, as well as support from nonprofit organizations. These projects, which have been notoriously complex, have become even more difficult over the past few years since the forms of government assistance available for low-income housing projects have been in a state of flux. Some of the types of financial assistance used for the Kensington Square project described later in this chapter (most notably Section 8 rent guarantees) are no longer available. Nevertheless, since this project was undertaken new programs, such as the HOME program described in **Chapter Four**, have been created. Developers should be aware of all of the funding sources available at any given time and combine them as creatively as possible.

Dwight-Edgewood is a neighborhood of single-family and small multi-family buildings, many of which are 50 to 100 years old.[6] It is situated two blocks from the western edge of the Yale University campus in New Haven, Connecticut. These residences range in condition from well maintained to newly rehabilitated to badly deteriorated; several commercial properties are intermingled among them. A major retail district is located a few blocks away.

A local nonprofit group, Neighborhood Housing, Inc. (NHI), was designated by the city of New Haven to redevelop the neighborhood. NHI was organized in 1971 by a group of area residents who gathered together local architects, bankers, lawyers, and builders to discuss the problems of substandard housing in the neighborhood and to create home ownership opportunities for low- and moderate-income families. The city chose NHI for this project (which was to include the rehabilitation and rental to low-income tenants of 225 housing units in more than 40 scattered sites under the Neighborhood Strategies Area program administered by HUD) because the group had previously developed some 86 dwelling units

---

[5] Information and materials graciously provided by B. Clarkson Schoettle, Executive Director of the Providence Preservation Society Revolving Fund, Inc.

[6] The information in both this section and § **9.2.3** is taken, with the permission of Preservation Action, from Deborah Dunning & Nellie Longsworth, *Another Revolution in New England: A Case Study of the Historic Rehabilitation Tax Incentives*, (Boston: Preservation Action and Boston University Preservation Studies Program).

under a "buy, rehabilitate, and sell" program, it was an established grass-roots organization with broad community support, and it had a highly respected board of directors.

In order to avoid jeopardizing the tax-exempt status of NHI, a new organization called Neighborhood Housing Developers, Inc. (NHDI) was formed to serve as the cogeneral partner of NHP Kensington Square Associates, the limited partnership formed for this project. The other general partner was the Washington, DC-based National Housing Partnership (NHP), which in turn has as its general partner the National Corporation for Housing Partnerships (NCHP). Both the NCHP and the NHP are private, profit-making organizations created by Congress in 1968. The purpose of each is to encourage the widest possible participation by private enterprise in the provision of housing for low- and moderate-income families. The NHP and the NCHP were initially capitalized in 1970 by means of a public securities offering that raised over $42 million. The NHP thus brought to the project the financial strength to enable it to offer, among other guarantees, to repurchase each investor's interest if rehabilitation were not completed or if the project did not qualify for the anticipated government assistance by the date of final closing.

Because its aim was the creation of low-income housing, the project received government assistance at the federal, state, and local levels. This assistance included a Section 8 rental payment guarantee for 20 years, as well as tax-exempt financing through the state public housing agency and mortgage loan insurance from the Federal Housing Administration (FHA). In addition, the city of New Haven granted a 15-year freeze on property tax assessments and helped to secure the federal commitment to provide assistance under Section 8. Despite this backing, and the availability at that time of 60-month depreciation for low-income housing under Section 167(k) of the Internal Revenue Code, plans for the project were complicated by higher-than-anticipated cost projections until the 25-percent investment tax credit provided the possibility of substantial additional tax benefits, the precise amount of which depends upon the number of buildings certified as contributing to the historic district in which they are located.

The 21 buildings (120 units overall) included in the project consist of 2½- and 3-story structures, some are wood-frame buildings with wood siding, others have masonry bearing walls with brick or masonry exterior finishes. Some were constructed during New Haven's carriage building boom of the early and mid-nineteenth century; others date from the city's era of industrial prosperity during the late nineteenth and early twentieth century. They are all located within what, in September 1983, became the Dwight Street National Register Historic District.

The bulk of the project financing came from tax-exempt construction loan notes and from mortgage revenue bonds issued by the Kensington Square Housing Development Corporation, created by the Connecticut

State Housing Authority. All proceeds from the sale of the tax-exempt securities were held by the Connecticut Bank and Trust Company (CBT) as trustee. A mortgage loan from the development corporation to the partnership is evidenced by a note in the amount of $5,738,900 from the partnership to CBT. The note is secured by a mortgage on the properties that constitute the project, a security interest in all personal property to be used in connection with the properties and an assignment to CBT, effective in the event of a default, of all tenant leases and all subsidy payments to be received by the partnership under the Section 8 program. The NHP was also required by HUD to post both a working capital letter of credit (to secure performance of the partnership's obligations during the construction period and unanticipated costs of equipping the properties, rent-up expenses, taxes, mortgage insurance premiums, and hazard insurance premiums) and a debt service letter of credit as additional security for the bonds issued by the corporation.

The partnership's agreement with the general contractor provided for liquidated damages for each day of delay beyond a specified date for the completion of construction. Under the partnership's agreement with HUD, as well as the Section 8 program, the partnership was required to deposit monthly payments in a reserve fund for replacements, beginning upon initial occupancy of the properties. Whenever rents are increased in future years by a HUD-established annual automatic adjustment factor, the amount of the monthly deposit is to be increased by the same factor.

Since the project's estimated costs amounted to more than $7 million, it was necessary to supplement the $5.7 million tax-exempt bond issue through the sale of limited partnership interests. Thirty such partnership interests, valued at $74,400 each, were sold to raise a total of $2,232,000. Together with the tax-exempt bond proceeds, this covered the project's anticipated $7.9 million cost.

To assist the partnership offering, the NHP offered to repurchase each investor's interest in the partnership if the rehabilitation of the properties was not completed by the date scheduled for final closing, or if the properties failed to qualify for rent subsidy or other contemplated government assistance. The NHP also agreed that, if the partnership were unable to cover costs of construction, the NHP or the NCHP would advance or lend the amounts necessary to complete rehabilitation within the required time (or the NHP would repurchase the investors' interests at cost). The purchase price for each investment unit included a $3,720 fee for providing this construction completion/repurchase guarantee. The NHP provided a similar guarantee, for the first several years of operation, with respect to operating expenditures and debt service payments, at a cost of $5,207 per unit.

Since the purchase price for each investment unit was based upon the assumption that 17 of the buildings involved in this project would be certified by the Department of the Interior and hence eligible for the rehabilitation tax credit, the NHP offered to reduce by $84 the cost of each investment unit for every dwelling unit that did not qualify for the tax credit. The NHP could also, in the event some buildings were not certified, elect to repurchase all units at the investors' cost. (In fact, 19 buildings were ultimately submitted for certification.)

Each partner was to be allocated partnership losses incurred after his or her acquisition of an interest in the partnership. The 25-percent investment tax credit was also allocated among the partners. The tax losses of the partnership are expected to decline over time and, unless the properties are sold or otherwise disposed of, after 16 years the partnership is expected to generate income in excess of capital returned to the investors.

Plans are underway for a second Kensington Square project.

9.2.3 Commercial Building (Hildreth Building, Lowell, Massachusetts)

The key role that the investment tax credits can play in conjunction with industrial development bonds is indicated in the following example, which focuses on the rehabilitation of an office building in Lowell, Massachusetts, for commercial use. New Internal Revenue Code limits on the amount of industrial development bonds that states are authorized to issue on a tax-free basis may make such transactions more difficult in certain states in the future. However, the Lowell project also emphasizes the importance of a building's facade, not simply as a conspicuous architectural feature, but as a potential financing source through either direct restoration grants or tax deductions for the donation of facade easement to a qualifying organization.

Lowell, Massachusetts, is located 33 miles northwest of Boston, on the banks of the Merrimack River. It is one of the many New England riverside mill towns that enjoyed their commercial heyday before this century began. The Hildreth Building, a product of that era of growth and vitality, is one of the largest buildings in Lowell's old, and in parts deteriorated, commercial and retail center. It lies within the Merrimack-Middle Street National Register Historic District. Because the building, which has suffered from some deferred maintenance, was found to contribute to the historic significance of the district, federal tax incentives were available for a rehabilitation that conformed to the Secretary of the Interior's standards.

In September 1980, Ted Trivers, a Lowell native and area businessman, was looking for space to relocate a family retail clothing store when he became interested in the Hildreth Building, in which both F.W. Woolworth and S.S. Kresge stores were located. Trivers was impressed with the building's architecture, low vacancy rate, central location, and the potential income from its four floors of office space and the retail space on the ground floor. The city was also eager to see the building rehabilitated, if possible by a local resident, and both the city manager, B. Joseph Tully, and then-Massachusetts Senator Paul Tsongas threw their weight behind the project. The Lowell Historic Preservation Commission also let its support, and in March 1981, the building's owner agreed to sell the property.

Financing the rehabilitation proved problematic since interest rates were high. A financial consultant, New England Communities, Inc. (NEC), was brought in to oversee the project and structure its financing. Trivers, NEC, and NEC president Mark Slotnick became general partners of Hildreth Associates, a limited partnership created to undertake the project.

The initial rehabilitation work involved only the facade, lobby, and common areas, allowing many existing tenants to remain and providing a needed income stream throughout construction. Although a Boston syndicator was approached, initial efforts to syndicate the project to raise the necessary equity proved unsuccessful. And, notwithstanding the support of the city and the Lowell Historic Preservation Commission, local financial institutions showed limited interest in providing industrial revenue bond financing. In the midst of these difficulties, however, Congress passed the Economic Recovery Tax Act (ERTA) of 1981. The 25-percent investment tax credit for certified historic rehabilitations provided by ERTA suddenly made the project salable to limited partner investors and, as a result, financially feasible.

In an effort to expedite the project, a request for the Secretary of the Interior to certify that the Hildreth Building contributed to the character of the historic district was submitted immediately upon closing. In preparing this application, the partners and their architect worked closely with the Lowell Historic Preservation Commission, the technical staff of the National Park Service, and the review director at the State Historical Commission, all to ensure that the plans submitted could be approved as consistent with the historic character of the structure and the district.

The bulk of the project's financing was provided by a consortium of nine local banks, which purchased $1,250,000 worth of industrial revenue bonds issued by the Lowell Industrial Development Finance Agency. The proceeds of that sale were loaned to the partnership at an interest rate of 11.5 percent for the first four years. A variable rate of 75 percent of a local bank's prime rate, with a floor of 11.5 percent and a ceiling of 17 percent, applies to the remaining 21 years of the loan. The partners, with the help of the Lowell Historic Preservation Commission, also secured a $75,000, 25-year loan from the Lowell Development Financing Corporation at an interest rate of 6.5 percent for the first four years, adjusted semiannually to 40 percent of a Boston bank's prime rate, with a floor of 5 percent. Grants totaling $28,000 for the rehabilitation of the building's facade were obtained from the preservation commission and from the Lowell Planning and Development Department (under the terms of the commission's grant, the partnership must maintain the historic character of the facade for at least 15 years). The last major piece of the financing came from the project's 15 limited partners, each of whom paid $50,000 per unit (for a total of $750,000). As a result of these efforts, a total financing package amounting to some $2.1 million was successfully assembled.

With financing in place, actual rehabilitation could begin. A photograph of the Hildreth Building taken in 1884 revealed that the upper stories of the structure had changed little over the past century. Routine repointing and stabilizing of some decorative elements were necessary. The retail ground level and main entry, however, had been completely changed during 1930 and 1963 renovations. Most of the nineteenth-century columns, piers, and ornaments on the ground floor had been removed, and very little of the original lobby survived. Many of the offices in the building were partially or totally renovated in the 1950s and 1960s.

The missing ground floor elements were replaced and painted wooden storefronts replaced, including signs and awnings. Several original features were uncovered when paneling, floor tiles, and the hung ceiling were removed from the lobby. The uncovered plaster ceiling was repaired, the wall replastered, and the floor and walls retiled. Columns were cast in place, with original capitals recreated in metal.

In the upper story offices, many original features were also found hidden behind newer wall panels. The original wooden doors were reused and wood trim preserved. For the facade of the upper stories, a matching mortar formula was developed for spot pointing. A bay window on the second floor was removed, and the original arched windows it had replaced were restored. Rotted window sashes were replaced with wood rather than with more modern materials.

The cost of this work amounted to some $883,440 and yielded an investment tax credit of $220,860. It is expected that income from the building will provide a rate of return on equity of over 23 percent, including tax benefits.[7]

Complying with the Secretary of the Interior's Standards for Rehabilitation added somewhat to the construction costs of the project. Whether the incremental costs of such compliance exceeded the marginal 5-percent difference between the 25-percent certified rehabilitation credit and the 20-percent tax credit for a noncertified rehabilitation is difficult to determine. The owners did, of course, consider the latter option, but decided that there was little likelihood that the Interior Department would

---

[7] This rate of return would be slightly different were this project begun now, after the passage of the Tax Equity and Financial Responsibility Act of 1982 (TEFRA). This difference seems sufficiently small, however, that it would not mandate any different structure for the transaction. The rate of return and the tax benefits, other than the 25-percent investment tax credit, would be slightly smaller under TEFRA. The gain on the sale of the building, however, would be slightly greater.

decertify the building, a prerequisite where, as here, the structure is situated in a historic district. In addition, they believed their own rehabilitation standards and the requirements of the preservation commission grant would meet or exceed the mandated standards, and that a first-class renovation would give them a significant marketing advantage.

The techniques used to rehabilitate the Hildreth Building have proven to be broadly adaptable to other projects in Lowell, and dozens of older buildings have been rehabilitated using similar techniques. These include both downtown commercial buildings and a number of the massive old mills that once fueled Lowell's economy along the city's canals. These rehabilitated mills have been revived as homes for high-tech industry—Lowell's recently acquired source of economic strength and a major new source of employment for its residents.

Lowell's historic rehabilitation was accompanied by a boom in new construction. In 1983, new building permits were issued for projects valued at almost $70 million, an increase of 169 percent over 1982. Lowell's young people, who once left the city in search of jobs, now tend to remain in an area that is presently considering plans to bus in workers to remedy a labor shortage. In summary, Lowell experienced a dramatic and successful turnaround, and one in which the rehabilitation of its remarkable architectural and industrial heritage played a major role. The rebirth of Lowell progressed during the mid-1980s. From 1984 to 1987, the Lowell Historic Preservation Commission grant-aided facade restoration on 26 projects representing an aggregate investment of $10,486,035 from private sources. This figure does not include the $1,523,960 obtained in grants or the $780,000 in loans for that period. It is also in addition to the close to $170 million in public and private funds that had been invested in historic preservation and rehabilitation, public improvements, commercial development, and industrial expansion projects during the 10-year period prior to 1984.

Unfortunately, Lowell's boom ended in 1988, just before the onset of the recession that engulfed the northeast two years later. Because of a general downturn in the local economy, there has been little new rehabilitation work undertaken since 1987. Although grant funds remain available for qualifying projects, private rehabilitation work has ceased. However, public investment in preservation and park infrastructure development continues.[8]

One major project has managed to progress in spite of the current economic slump. In early 1985, several community interests developed a proposal for turning the Lowell Canal System into a major urban amenity.[9] The proposal establishes several goals related to recreation, development,

---

[8] *Revitalization Through Partnerships: Public and Private Sector Investment in Lowell, Massachusetts* (1984). Current statistics provided by Chuck Parrott, Lowell Historical Preservation Commission.

[9] *The Canalway: A Proposal, Draft Report of the Canalway Task Force* (June 1985).

preservation, and the canalway itself. In the preservation area, focus will be on two types of ownership and responsibilities: the canal structures owned by the Department of Environmental Management, and the adjacent land and buildings owned by various firms and individuals. A detailed map will be developed showing locations where historic canal elements need rehabilitation and where incompatible land uses exist. Areas of critical preservation needs will be identified.

In order to undertake the historic preservation of the canal system, the proposal seeks to establish a permanent, joint working party consisting of representatives of all major interested groups (City of Lowell, Department of Environmental Management, National Park Service, Lowell Historic Preservation Commission, Lowell Development and Financial Corporation, Lowell Plan, and the private sector). This joint working party is to coordinate preservation, interpretation, development, and maintenance efforts, and to "present a consistent voice during the budgetary process at federal, state, and municipal levels." Finally, the task force seeks to develop objective design standards to guide governmental agencies and departments, which are exempt from review by the Lowell Historic Board, and "to supplement that Board's standards to acknowledge the significance of building elevations facing the Canalway."

"Canalways," the revitalization of the Canal System in Lowell, is now underway. On October 16, 1987, the President signed federal legislation authorizing the extension of the project for an additional seven years. The project has been funded, and design and construction are underway with a proposed completion date of 1995.[10]

Other rehabilitation projects have not weathered the economic downturn as successfully as Canalways. On a smaller scale, New England Communities, Inc., planned to continue its preservation activities by the development of the Bon Marche building, with the assistance of a $300,000 loan from the Lowell Historic Preservation Commission and a historic grant from the City of Lowell. The renovation included facade improvements. However, when the building's tenant moved out at the end of the lease, the bank foreclosed. The preservation commission does not expect to recover the loan.[11]

In addition, major rehabilitation of two major textile mill complexes has been adversely affected by the recession. A Boston area developer made a purchase and sale commitment for one of these complexes, the Massachusetts Mills. This development is the largest rehabilitation project undertaken in Lowell, with three phases of subsidized housing: 160 units in the first phase, 120 in the second, and the balance in the third. So far, the first two phases have been completed. Phase three is currently on hold because of the economic downturn. The other project,

---

[10] Information provided by Chuck Parrott at the Lowell Historic Preservation Commission.

[11] Information was provided by Don Markson of New England Communities, Inc., and Chuck Parrott, Lowell Historical Preservation Commission.

Boot Mills, did not fare as well. The developer completed phase one of the project, the rehabilitation of office space, before the economic downturn. However, the lender recently foreclosed on the property and the project has ceased.

9.2.4 Comprehensive Public Development Project (Forty-Second Street Development Project, New York, New York)

At one time comprehensive public development projects were generally urban renewal programs that entailed the wholesale clearance of inner-city areas. In the past few years, however, there has been increased sensitivity to the importance of retaining structures of historic or architectural merit and integrating them into projects designed to revitalize their surrounding areas. Given the scope and complexity of such projects, they often require active participation by several governmental bodies, as well as major commitments of private capital.

The presence of government actors in the rehabilitation process brings with it the possibility of utilizing powers, such as eminent domain, property tax abatements, and zoning or building code exemptions, which are not available to private entities. At the same time, this requires that the environmental and historic review processes that are triggered by government activities be satisfied. The Forty-Second Street Development Project, jointly undertaken by the State and City of New York, illustrates the complexities of area-wide redevelopment which includes the preservation and restoration of historic structures in a major downtown area.

The Forty-Second Street Development Project is a collaborative undertaking of the City of New York and the New York State Urban Development Corporation (UDC) that is intended to eliminate the persistent blight which has characterized West Forty-Second Street near Times Square, and to return the area to productive use.[12] The project proposes to rehabilitate and redevelop West Forty-Second Street between Broadway and Eighth Avenue with a mix of major office buildings, a hotel, a wholesale mart, restaurants and other retail uses, major subway improvements and, as a centerpiece for the development, ten renovated theaters. Most of these theaters have been used for "action" (violence), pornographic, and occasional first-run movies, as well as for cut-rate retail and fast food outlets. The theaters occupy nine separate buildings, constructed between 1899 and 1918, that once formed the heart of New York's theater district. Despite their recent use and the "exotic seediness"

---

[12] For a comprehensive description and analysis of the Forty-Second Street Development Project, see the Final Environmental Impact Statement issued by the UDC in August, 1984, from which much of the information contained in this section is drawn. The authors' law firm served as environmental counsel to UDC in the preparation of the Impact Statement.

of their surroundings, the theaters have been remarkably well preserved because, apart from movies, no alternative use has appeared economically viable in the context of Forty-Second Street's current condition.

The theaters included within the project are as follows:

New Amsterdam Theater. Built in 1902 and listed on the National Register of Historic Places (as well as a New York City landmark), this is one of the few public structures in the United States designed entirely in the Art Nouveau style. The New Amsterdam is most famous as the home of the Ziegfeld Follies; the careers of Fannie Brice, Ed Wynn, Will Rogers, Eddie Cantor, and Marilyn Miller were also launched there. In addition to the main theater, the New Amsterdam includes a smaller rooftop theater once used for private shows by Florenz Ziegfield.

Harris Theater. Built along with the Candler Building, an office structure, this theater is well-known as the site of John Barrymore's *Hamlet*, which played there in 1922.

Liberty Theater. Designed at the same time as the New Amsterdam and by the same firm, this theater's facade makes a strong contribution to the Forty-Second Street streetscape; its interior still contains a grand proscenium, carved arches, boxes, and an unusual printed asbestos curtain. George M. Cohan and Fred Astaire both played there.

Empire Theater. Built in 1912, the 80-foot facade of this theater is one of the most distinctive elements on Forty-Second Street. It housed the Eltinge Follies, a burlesque, from its inception until 1930.

Victory. Designed in 1899 for Oscar Hammerstein, the Victory is the oldest of Forty-Second Street's theaters, though its splendid interior is extremely well-preserved. Its most famous play was *Abie's Irish Rose*, whose record of 2,327 performances was only recently broken.

Lyric Theater. Built shortly after 1900, this theater specialized in musical comedy until 1925 (when the Marx Brothers appeared in *Coconuts*). Its 119-foot Beaux Arts Facade on Forty-Third Street, of red and white brick and terra cotta, is largely intact.

Times Square and Apollo Theaters. The 100-foot common facade of these two theaters, with its 3-story colonnade, is a major architectural feature on Forty-Second Street. The Times Square was first constructed in 1910 for movies and vaudeville and was later reconstructed and joined to the new Apollo Theater.

The Selwyn Theater. In its 15 years as a legitimate theater, the Selwyn housed plays by Rudolph Friml, Cole Porter, Noel Coward, and George S. Kaufman. Its Beaux Arts facade is largely intact.

In addition to the Forty-Second Street theaters, the project area includes the 24-story Candler Building, an office structure constructed in 1912 that is rich in decorative detail and clad in white terra cotta with a stepped-back roof tower. Like the New Amsterdam Theater, the Candler Building is listed on the National Register. The area also contains the former Times Tower (now known as One Times Square), which is widely known for its New Year's Eve celebrations and for its electric news sign which brought New Yorkers news of both V–E Day and V–J Day in 1945. The original facade of the Times Tower was completely stripped in 1965, and as a consequence the building lost much of its architectural character. However, the site is still regarded as important by many, and continues to serve as a visual focal point for the southern end of Times Square.

Committed to restoring the Forty-Second Street theaters to legitimate theater, theater-related, and upgraded retail use, the city joined forces with the UDC in 1980 to develop a comprehensive redevelopment plan which relied almost entirely on private investment. Not only were the individual theaters to be preserved and renovated, but the low scale of Forty-Second Street's mid-blocks was to be maintained and the area revitalized as an entertainment area attractive to a broad cross-section of New Yorkers and tourists. In addition, the city was eager to overcome the blight and crime that have plagued West Forty-Second Street for many years and deterred many visitors (and New Yorkers) from patronizing the area. Finally, the city sought to carry out this development in a way which would contribute to the city's long-term tax revenues, help finance needed subway improvements, and be a positive influence on the neighboring garment center, the Clinton residential area, and the Broadway theater district.

With these objectives in mind, the city and the UDC undertook an economic feasibility study of the overall development plan (of which the project area theaters were to be a part) and commenced a detailed analysis of the architectural and historic significance of each of the theaters. In addition, the project team carried out a careful assessment of land use, social and street conditions, traffic, mass transit, pedestrian, air quality, waste disposal, and other characteristics of the project area. As part of these studies, the project team, with assistance from outside consultants, also reviewed the eligibility of each of the theaters for inclusion on both the National and New York State Registers of Historic Places, as well as their eligibility for local landmark designation. From these studies grew a series of specific guidelines for both the use and exterior and interior treatment of each theater.

After completing this review, the city and the UDC concluded that it would be possible to carry out the project (including acquisition and renovation of the theaters) by "transferring the theaters" unused development rights to the intersections of Forty-Second Street with Broadway (on the east) and Eighth Avenue (on the west). These corner sites were judged to be appropriate for large-scale commercial development, which could in turn generate sufficient revenues to pay for both the theaters' acquisition and renovation and significant subway improvements. After extensive discussion of this concept with local officials and civic and business organizations, the city and the UDC requested developer proposals for four separate office towers to be located at the Forty-Second Street/Broadway intersection and a hotel and wholesale mart to be located at the Forty-Second Street/Eighth Avenue intersection. At the same time, the city and the UDC sought developers to renovate and operate the theaters (with initial financial assistance from the commercial developers, who would also be required to pay for the renovation of the Times Square subway station). Under the plan, the Candler Building was to be left in private ownership as part of the renovated mid-block and the former Times Tower modified to enhance its visual contribution to the redeveloped southern end of Times Square.

Since the project's economic feasibility studies had shown that it would be necessary, in order to preserve both the theaters and the low scale of the Forty-Second Street midblocks, to "transfer" unused development potential from the midblocks to the corner development sites, an appropriate technique had to be identified to effect that transfer. As noted in **Chapter Five**, New York City's zoning and landmark regulations authorize only limited transfers of unused development rights within the city's special theater subdistrict. Moreover, to make the project economically feasible, it would be necessary for the sponsoring agency to proceed by eminent domain in completing assembly of the complex project site and, once site assembly had been completed, to offer phased property tax abatements to the developers designated to carry out individual components of the project. For these reasons, among others, the city requested the UDC to join in carrying out the project. Under the New York State Urban Development Corporation Act (UDC Act), the UDC has the power to acquire all necessary sites, to hold the acquired sites free of local property taxes and to construct the project in accordance with its project plan without being bound by local zoning requirements.

Use of the UDC to implement the project meant that the UDC would have "lead agency" status under New York's State Environmental Quality Review Act (SEQRA) and State Historic Preservation Act (SHPA), both of which are discussed in **Chapter Six**. It also meant that the project would be subject to review and approval under the UDC Act and under the State's Eminent Domain Procedure Law (EDPL). On the other hand, the project would not be subject to the city's Uniform Land Use Review Procedure, which governs approval of privately sponsored development projects within the city.

Just as NEPA and the NHPA (both discussed in **Chapter Six**) require comprehensive environmental and historic reviews for proposed federal actions, SEQRA and the SHPA require a comparable review of the environmental and historic impacts of actions by state agencies, including the UDC, likely to have significant impacts on their surroundings. In addition, SEQRA, the UDC Act and the EDPL each required public hearings, followed by specific statutory findings by the UDC with respect to the project's purpose and impacts. In August 1981, the UDC held its first public hearings on the project, after which the agency commenced (with the cooperation of the city) an exhaustive environmental review process that drew upon not only the UDC's and the city's own staffs, but independent experts in the relevant disciplines, including historic preservation, as well as special environmental and preservation counsel. This process included extensive consultation with the state commissioner of parks, recreation, and historic preservation under the SHPA and the city's Landmarks Preservation Commission under SEQRA.

All this culminated in the issuance, in February 1984, of a draft environmental impact statement for the entire project, after which extensive public hearings were again held on the project's likely impacts and public benefits. A final environmental impact statement, containing more than 1,000 pages, was then issued by the UDC in August 1984. Following yet another round of pubic comments, the UDC formally approved the project in October 1984, and the city's Board of Estimate took similar action in November 1984.

As originally approved, the project plan contemplated that the Lyric, Apollo, Selwyn, Harris, and New Amsterdam theaters would be used for "legitimate" musical or dramatic productions, the Victory and, possibly, the Liberty theaters would be used as nonprofit "institutional theaters" and the Times Square and Empire (and, possibly, the Liberty) would be used for upgraded restaurant, retail, or mart-related uses. These uses of the theaters were broadened in 1991 to permit a fuller range of art and entertainment-related activities, rather than simply live theater; at least two of the structures must still be used for nonprofit theater.

In accordance with the project's original objective, the cost of acquiring and renovating these theaters will be born largely by developers of the project's commercial sites.

Following its approval by UDC and the city, the Forty-Second Street Development Project was challenged in 42 separate legal proceedings, including claims under the New York State Environmental Quality Review Act, the State Historic Preservation Act, the Federal Clean Air Act, the First Amendment, the federal anti-trust laws, and New York's Eminent Domain Procedure Law. All legal challenges proved unsuccessful,[13] and in mid-1990 UDC acquired title to the initial portions of the project area, including the historic theaters and the office tower sites. Funds for acquisition of all theaters within the project and for rehabilitation of the nonprofit theaters have been committed by the developer of the project's office towers.

A separate not-for-profit corporation has been established by UDC to develop and implement an operating plan for both the nonprofit and commercial theaters included within the project. That plan is expected to be released by the nonprofit management corporation during 1992 after it has completed its review of applications for the use of such theaters from both commercial and nonprofit applicants.

---

[13] The authors' law firm represented UDC in a majority of these proceedings.

If the Development Project succeeds in restoring Forty-Second Street, it will be in significant part because the city and the UDC succeeded in structuring their efforts in a way which combined public condemnation powers, property tax abatements, and exemption from local zoning controls with private funding, comprehensive historic, environmental and economic impact analyses, and a concerted effort to integrate the project's historic resources into an overall redevelopment plan for Forty-Second Street and the Times Square area.

9.2.5 Combined Historic Rehabilitation and Low-Income Housing Credits (706–712 Huntington Avenue, Boston, Massachusetts)

A new opportunity created by the Tax Reform Act of 1986 involves the combined use of the rehabilitation tax credit (for historic or nonhistoric properties) and the low-income housing credit. Obviously, the two credits represent a package that will not be appropriate for all, or even most, rehabilitation projects. The low-income housing credit imposes many restrictions on the use of rehabilitated property that may not be compatible with other project goals. Nevertheless, the financing advantages of using both credits should be explored where feasible, and are illustrated by the rehabilitation for residential rental use of a building on Huntington Avenue in Boston, Massachusetts.

The building at 706–712 Huntington Avenue was built in 1885, with an addition constructed in 1910. A four- and five-story building, it was once operated as the Hotel Helvetia. It is located in the Mission Hill section of Boston, in an area characterized by institutional and residential uses. Within close proximity of the building are Brigham & Womens Hospital, the Harvard Institute of Public Health, and Harvard Medical School, as well as other such facilities.

Concern about the loss of housing to institutional expansion motivated neighborhood groups to look for opportunities to protect and expand residential uses. In the early 1980s, a local group, Mission Hill Neighborhood Housing Services, Inc. (Mission Hill) focused on returning the Huntington Avenue property, then vacant for a number of years, to active rental use. The building had been owned by Brigham Hospital since 1961, and Mission Hill approached the Hospital seeking to acquire the building for renovation. In response, the Hospital issued a Request For Proposals to rehabilitate the property, and selected Mission Hill's proposal to convert it to low- and moderate-income housing. The project was given an additional boost when it was determined to be compatible with an overall "affordable housing" policy adopted by newly elected Boston Mayor Raymond Flynn. Finally, in April 1985, the Hospital and Mission Hill signed an option to purchase the property, which was soon amended to set a nominal purchase price of $10.00.

After concluding the option, Mission Hill first set about putting together a project team, consisting of financial consultants, lawyers and architects. (Historic property consultants were brought in later when the decision to seek the rehabilitation credit was made.) Zoning approval for the project, which involved the variance of parking requirements, was obtained. Mission Hill then proceeded to seek government financing for the project, and succeeded in structuring a package of four separate components of varying amounts and with varying terms.

The Massachusetts Housing Finance Agency (MHFA) provided a mortgage loan of $2,466,281 for construction and permanent financing. MHFA also agreed to provide additional aid in the form of a State Housing Assistance for Rental Production (SHARP) loan with a maximum annual amount of $103,303 over 15 years. This was to serve as back-up financing, and because it was subject to continuing appropriation by the state legislature, its availability could not be guaranteed. A condition of the SHARP loan was that 25 percent of the units in the project be set aside for low-income residents.

The project also received Housing Development Grant (HODAG) financing of $203,193 from the Department of Housing and Urban Development (through the City of Boston). As a final piece, the Boston Public Facilities Department Neighborhood Development Fund agreed to provide a loan of $298,569.

Despite the public financing thus provided, the financial consultants advised that the project would not be economically feasible without some additional source of support. Because the building was located in the Mission Hill Triangle Architectural Conservation District, it was potentially eligible for the 20-percent rehabilitation tax credit, and the decision was made to undertake a certified rehabilitation. Revising the plans to accommodate certification requirements raised the cost of the project somewhat. The building's existing windows were repaired rather than replaced. Both of the existing interior staircases (rather than just one, as originally planned) had to be retained, resulting in the loss of two units in the project. And more interior finish work was required by the National Park Service than had been contemplated. Nevertheless, the value of the credit more than offset these additional expenses.

After passage of the Tax Reform Act of 1986, Mission Hill decided to take advantage of the newly available low-income housing credit as well. Because the MHFA loan was financed from the proceeds of tax-exempt bonds, the project qualified for the low-income credit independent of the state cap. Mission Hill chose to qualify as a project in which 20 percent of the units would be rented to tenants with incomes of no more than 50 percent of the area's median (25 percent of the units were already set aside for low-income tenants under the terms of the SHARP loan). Under a special transition rule included in the 1986 Act, because of the project's SHARP funding, all of its units (not only the low-income units) could be included in the qualified basis amount on which the tax credit would be figured. Because of the project's federal subsidies, however, it could qualify only for the 30-percent present value credit.

A syndicated offering was then prepared by CDC Investment Corporation to solicit investors who could benefit from the tax credits and other financial aspects of the project. CDC structured a partnership in which CDC Equity Corporation, an affiliate of CDC Investment Corporation, and 706 Huntington Inc. (Huntington), a wholly-owned subsidiary of Mission Hill, would act as general partners. Huntington would serve as managing general partner, with responsibility for completion of the project, and would guarantee its eligibility for the tax credits.

The offering sought to raise a total of $1,246,000 in 35 units with a capital contribution of $35,600 each. The limited partnership shares were offered to accredited investors, as well as to a limited number (no more than 35) of nonaccredited investors meeting certain suitability requirements relating to net worth, ability to bear the risks of the investment, and other matters. The Offering Memorandum also stated that investors would generally not be deemed suitable if they had (or expected to have within an 11-year period) an adjusted gross income in excess of $200,000, since such investors would not be able to make full (or perhaps any) use of the rehabilitation or low-income housing credits.

Construction of the project began in June 1987, and was completed in September 1988. Rent-up took place in October. Huntington is now fully renovated, and the building contains 37 rental units, 10 of them low-income, and 1,640 square feet of commercial space.

Huntington is currently fully occupied and continues to operate successfully. Low-income housing is not an easy venture in the current era of little direct governmental support, but the Huntington project illustrates the creative use of those federal and state subsidies that are available, coupled with the incentives to private investment provided by the rehabilitation and low-income housing credits.

9.2.6 Preserving the John Jay Estate (Rye, New York)

Preservationists, elected officials and prominent judges gathered on May 17, 1992, to recall the life of John Jay and to celebrate the successful culmination of a 10-year struggle to preserve Alansten, the 23-acre estate in Rye, New York, where Jay was raised. That struggle began in 1981 with a requested zoning change before the Rye City Council and followed a tortuous path through the local Planning Commission and Board of Architectural Review, the Westchester County Board of Legislators, New York State's Office of Parks, Recreation and Historic Preservation, the State's Department of Environmental Conservation, the Keeper of the National Register of Historic Places, the Secretary of the Interior, a dozen state court proceedings, a federal action in which the District Court judge recused himself because of his own passionate efforts to honor Jay and, finally, an agreement by the County to acquire the entire parcel, with help from the State and a commitment from the non-profit Jay Coalition to rehabilitate and maintain Alansten's 1838 mansion and early 20th Century carriage house.[14]

Jay was an extraordinary figure, a lawyer who was a model for all seasons. We know him principally as the first Chief Justice of the United States. He was also the first Chief Justice of New York State, the State's Governor, President of the Continental Congress, principal negotiator of both the Treaty of Paris (which recognized the independence of the new nation) and Jay's Treaty (which preserved it) and, with Hamilton and Madison, one of the principal authors of the Federalist Papers, which helped persuade a reluctant state and nation to ratify the Constitution. He was the only one of our nation's founders to serve in all three branches of its government. While we rightly associate judicial review of constitutional questions with his successor, John Marshall, we often forget that it was an early Jay opinion, contained in a 1792 letter to President Washington in the *Invalid Pension Cases*,[15] that laid the foundation for Marshall's opinion in *Marbury v. Madison*.[16]

Jay's boyhood home is also exceptional. Together with the adjacent Rye Marshlands and Jay Family Cemetery (where Jay is buried), both of which formed part of the original estate, Alansten is one of Westchester's last major undeveloped parcels on Long Island Sound. The property includes a Greek Revival mansion constructed in 1838 by Jay's son, Peter, and a complementary carriage house built in 1912. The Marshlands (donated to Westchester County for conservation purposes) attracts many thousands of visitors and students to study its rich array of plant and bird life, which has been sheltered by the Jay property from the rapid pace of suburban development along the Boston Post Road.

It was this unusual combination of historical, architectural and environmental values that made the Jay campaign so attractive to a coalition of preservationists, ecologists and students of American history. Like Jay's own career, the effort to save Alansten reached across the spectrum of federal and state laws and ended with a dramatic public commitment (in this case land acquisition, not a new constitution) intended to bridge sharply competing interests. Along the way, the effort also led to important developments in New York land-use law and practice. The historic, architectural and environmental values of Alansten were themselves related, and the manner in which the City of Rye and the courts

[14]The authors' firm served as counsel to the Jay Coalition and its members in the administrative proceedings and litigation discussed in this column. This account of the Coalition's victory is also described in Stephen L. Kass and Michael B. Gerrard, "Preservation of the Jay Estate," N.Y. Law J., June 1, 1992 at 3:1.
[15]See Extract of the Minutes of the Circuit Court for New York and letter, dated April 10, 1792, from John Jay, William Cushing and James Duane to President Washington, 1 American State Papers, Miscellaneous 49–50 (Washington, 1834).
[16]5 U.S. (1 Cranch) 137 (1803).

sought to balance these interests against the rights of a private developer indicates the extent to which landmarks preservation, environmental review, zoning and public land acquisition have begun to merge into an integrated system of land-use management.

9.2.7 Initial Landmarking

The Jay estate, including the mansion and Marshlands, remained in the Jay family until the early years of this century. The property was eventually acquired by the Deveraux family, which conveyed the Marshlands to Westchester County and Alansten, including the mansion and carriage house, to the Methodist Conference. (The adjacent cemetery continues to be owned by the Jay family.) In 1981, the Conference, eager to sell a portion of the site to a commercial developer, applied for approval to subdivide its property, with six acres to be used for a religious conference center and 17 acres to be used for development. This application was denied, and the Conference contracted to sell the entire parcel to a developer, FGL&L Properties Corp. FGL&L then applied to rezone the parcel for campus-style office use and construct some 220,000 square feet of office space on the site. This provoked intense opposition from a group of neighbors in the adjacent Greenhaven neighborhood, from Marshlands supporters and from a handful of local preservationists, who urged that Alansten be landmarked because of its historical and architectural significance and that, in any event, it be restricted to residential use.

There was a problem with landmarking. Like many New York communities, the City of Rye had adopted a landmarks ordinance pursuant to the state enabling act.[17] However, while the *Penn Central* decision had upheld the constitutionality of landmarking without owner consent, the Rye City Code required such consent for all landmark properties, and the developer was explicit that such consent would not be forthcoming. A further problem was also perceived by the City Council: what assurance would the City have that the deteriorating mansion would be properly restored and maintained even if landmarked, especially if Alansten were sold to individual homeowners? Faced with the concerns and the need for owner consent, the Council was reluctant to consider landmarking the site.

The early opponents did, however, score two important successes. The first resulted directly from the requirement of the State Environmental Quality Review Act (SEQRA)[18] that the Rye City Council prepare an environmental impact statement (EIS) for FGL&L's proposed office development. The public hearing on the draft EIS for the office proposal generated such intense opposition that the Council, in its role as

---

[17]New York General Municipal Law § 96-a and Article 5-K.
[18]New York Environmental Conservation Law Article 8.

lead agency under SEQRA, determined that the final EIS would consider only residential alternatives for Alansten and that no further office or nonresidential use would be considered.

The second success occurred in a different arena, or so it seemed at the time. While the rezoning proposal was pending, the Rye Landmarks Advisory Committee recommended that Alansten, together with the Marshlands, the Jay Cemetery and two adjacent parcels also containing historic properties, be nominated to the National Register of Historic Places as a new "Boston Post Road Historic District." This National Register nomination moved forward through New York State's Office of Parks, Recreation and Historic Preservation (OPRHP) and, ultimately, to the U.S. Department of the Interior's Keeper of the National Register, who agreed that the entire District, including Alansten, qualified for such listing. This appeared to some as a largely symbolic act since the principal effect of National Register listing was to require detailed historic and environmental review of proposed *federal* actions affecting listed properties and no such action was contemplated for Alansten.

Yet the National Register listing proved decisive. As the EIS process continued, the City Council came to recognize the historic and architectural significance of Alansten, as well as its environmental sensitivity. Unwilling to amend the landmarks ordinance to eliminate the owner consent requirement, the City Council instead created a special *zoning* district (known as the Alansten Landmarks Preservation District) that, among other things, identified a protected "viewway" from the mansion to the rear property line (thus protecting the vista over the Marshlands to Long Island Sound and from the Marshlands to the mansion), stipulated that the parcel must remain in single ownership (and all residential units held in condominium form) and required the owner not only to maintain but to restore the mansion and carriage house.

The developer promptly challenged the new zoning district on both constitutional and statutory grounds. Avoiding constitutional issues, the New York Court of Appeals held, in *FGL&L Property Corp. v. City of Rye*,[19] that neither the state's zoning enabling act nor its landmarks counterpart authorized the City to regulate the form of ownership of Alansten or to require the developer to rehabilitate, as opposed to maintain, the mansion. Although *FGL&L* has likely been the most widely cited decision to emerge from the Jay dispute, it had little practical effect on the outcome of the controversy. What was of greater long term interest was the Court's willingness to analyze *both* zoning and landmarks enabling laws, as well as Rye's landmarks ordinance, in determining whether the challenged zoning provisions were authorized.

As the *FGL&L* litigation was proceeding, the City Council was also reconsidering the wisdom of owner consent for all landmarks. In December, 1983, the landmarks ordinance was amended to eliminate the

---

[19] 66 N.Y.2d 111, 495 N.Y.S.2d 321, 485 N.E.2d 986 (1985).

owner consent requirement for National Register properties. In July, 1984, the entire Alansten site, including the "viewway" and the mansion and carriage house exteriors, was landmarked without such consent.

This immediately led to further litigation, with FGL&L's successor (DGM Partners-Rye, which had the same managing partner as FGL&L) challenging the different treatment afforded National Register properties as a violation of the Equal Protection and Due Process clauses of the 14th Amendment. In the most significant single decision during this extended struggle, Justice Marbach (Supreme Court, Westchester County) held that the differing levels of protection afforded National Register and other potential landmark properties were rationally related to the purpose of the landmarks ordinance, despite the fact that Rye's Landmarks Advisory Committee also applied National Register criteria in proposing local landmarks.[20] The importance attached to National Register listing by the National Parks Service, said the Court, was sufficient to merit landmark designation without owner consent. Moreover, the City Council was under no obligation to landmark all National Register properties within its jurisdiction. The Court noted that the City Council "must use its discretion in making the final determination of local landmark designation, and must be guided by considerations of zoning, planning and economics which go beyond mere historic considerations."[21]

Justice Marbach's decision upholding the new landmarks ordinance was not, however, the end of even that phase of the dispute. DGM had also alleged that, as applied to it, the landmark designation effected a compensable "taking," a claim that was to be repeated often as the dispute continued. Justice Marbach held that, before that claim could be decided by the courts, DGM was required to exhaust its administrative remedies by applying to Rye's Board of Architectural Review (BAR) for hardship relief. DGM then did so. In January, 1986, the BAR denied DGM's request to demolish the mansion and carriage house, finding, after lengthy hearings, that DGM had failed to establish that it could not earn a "reasonable return" on its investment by offering the landmarked property for sale.

After this decision was affirmed by the City Council, DGM challenged it in an Article 78 proceeding, which was ultimately dismissed by the Appellate Division, Second Department. In its unanimous 1989 decision,[22] the Appellate Division held that the BAR had properly looked at the developer's potential return from the entire landmark site, not merely from the improvements (the mansion and carriage house) that it sought to demolish.

---

[20]DGM Partners-Rye v. City of Rye, Index No. 4609/85 (Sup. Ct. Westchester County, July 10, 1985).
[21]*Id.*, slip op. at 5.
[22]DGM Partners-Rye v. Board of Architectural Review of City of Rye, 148 A.D.2d 608, 539 N.Y.S.2d 74 (2d Dep't 1989).

9.2.8 Subdivision and SEQRA Review

While the landmarking process (and associated litigation) was proceeding, the developer was also applying for approval from the Rye Planning Commission for a residential subdivision on Alansten. The original SEQRA process had led the City Council to create the special Alansten zoning district that the developer had successfully challenged in *FGL&L*. As a result, the property reverted to its original one-half acre residential zoning, consistent with that of the adjacent Greenhaven neighborhood. Nevertheless, the SEQRA process had served, despite numerous deficiencies, to alert the community not only to the historic and architectural values of Alansten and its viewway, but also to the fragile ecology of the adjacent Marshlands and the surrounding neighborhood, which experienced repeated flooding following storms. As a result, when DGM applied to the Planning Commission for subdivision approval, it was faced with a body informed about the site and prepared to ask the developer to shape its plans so as to minimize adverse impacts to both Alansten and its surroundings.

After extensive hearings and public review, in June 1986 the Planning Commission granted preliminary subdivision approval for a residential development of approximately 33 units on Alansten (compared to the 53 units permitted by the special zoning district that FGL&L had successfully challenged in the Court of Appeals). The Planning Commission's approval was, however, subject to 17 different conditions, which were promptly challenged by the developer in yet another Article 78 proceeding. The project's opponents, now swelled beyond the original group of preservationists, neighbors and Marshlands supporters to include members of the Jay family and more than 60 environmental organizations throughout the state, also sued, alleging that the Planning Commission's procedures and conditions violated SEQRA. Both of these proceedings were ultimately dismissed, with the great bulk of the contested conditions upheld by the courts.[23]

This was not the end of the subdivision process either. Because Alansten was a landmark site, the subdivision plan also required a certificate of appropriateness from the BAR. In December, 1988, DGM submitted its proposed plan to the BAR, having first satisfied itself that its new proposal met the Planning Commission conditions that DGM was continuing to challenge in court. In January, 1989, after another round of public hearings, the BAR (also functioning as an "involved agency" under SEQRA) denied the requested certificate and set forth additional conditions, beyond those imposed by the Planning Commission, which it believed necessary to satisfy the requirements of the

---

[23] *See* DGM Partners-Rye v. Rye City Planning Comm'n, 148 A.D.2d 607, 539 N.Y.S.2d 73 (2d Dep't 1989); Peter Jay Heritage Coalition v. Planning Comm'n of City of Rye, NYLJ, April 4, 1988, at 18:2 (Sup. Ct. Westchester County 1988).

landmarks ordinance. These conditions were likely to reduce further the number of residential units that could be constructed. The BAR conditions were, unsurprisingly, also challenged by DGM on the ground that they too effected a taking of its property.

This led to a circumstance that, to all except land-use lawyers, can only be described as anomalous: at the same time that one Westchester court was considering DGM's claim that the BAR conditions were unconstitutional because they lacked a proper "nexus" to the historic significance of the property and deprived DGM of its use, another court was deciding DGM's claim, originally brought before Justice Marbach in 1985, that the landmark designation itself was unconstitutional because of the absence of a proper nexus with the goals of the ordinance and the state enabling act. In June, 1989, Judicial Hearing Officer Zeck (sitting with the consent of the parties) found, after trial and site visit, that the designation was indeed supported by such a nexus to the goals of the ordinance and sustained its constitutionality.[24] In October, 1989, Justice Silverman (Supreme Court, Westchester County) found that, while DGM had failed to exhaust its administrative remedies before challenging the BAR conditions, a hearing was nevertheless appropriate to consider whether those conditions (as opposed to the significance of the mansion, carriage house and viewway) had a sufficient nexus to the site's historic features or deprived the developer of economically viable use of its property.[25] Both decisions were affirmed by the Appellate Division, Second Department, in October, 1991.[26]

9.2.9 Public Acquisition

The subdivision plans that were emerging from the Planning Commission and BAR satisfied neither DGM, which claimed they were confiscatory, nor the expanding Jay Coalition, which believed that any development of Alansten would destroy its historic character and threaten the Marshlands. Indeed, the Jay Coalition had, from its inception, urged public acquisition of the entire parcel so that the mansion and carriage house could be restored and the site preserved in a manner compatible with the Marshlands. As the subdivision review went forward, the Coalition approached the state's OPRHP and DEC, as well as Westchester County, in an effort to secure public funds for this purpose. If such funds were available, the Coalition promised, it would raise the funds

---

[24]DGM Partners-Rye v. City of Rye, NYLJ, June 5, 1989, at 26:6 (Sup. Ct. Westchester County 1989).
[25]DGM Partners-Rye v. Board of Architectural Review of City of Rye, NYLJ, Oct. 18, 1989, at 21 (Sup. Ct. Westchester County 1989).
[26]DGM Partners-Rye v. City of Rye, 575 N.Y.S.2d 330 (2d Dep't 1991); DGM Partners-Rye v. Board of Architectural Review of City of Rye, 575 N.Y.S.2d 346 (2d Dep't 1991), *appeal dismissed*, 79 N.Y.2d 914, 581 N.Y.S.2d 666 (1992).

necessary to rehabilitate the mansion and carriage house and commit to maintain those structures on a continuing basis.

The Coalition proposal enjoyed wide support within the environmental and preservation communities, and OPRHP and DEC were able to identify some $4 million that they could contribute to the site's acquisition, if the County would provide the remaining funds and a number of other conditions were satisfied. For its part, the County, which already owned the Marshlands, expressed interest in the proposed acquisition but was reluctant to assume open-ended risks in connection with either the condemnation or maintenance of the parcel.

DGM initially opposed acquisition of the entire Alansten site, offering instead to sell a portion of the site to the County if DGM could be assured of subdivision approval for a smaller project on the balance of the site. This proposal was opposed by the Jay Coalition and, ultimately, the County Board of Legislators on the ground that it involved the expenditure of public funds for a "compromise" that would destroy Alansten's historic character. The Jay Coalition also indicated that it could not finance the rehabilitation and maintenance of the mansion and carriage house under such a plan.

In 1990, DGM changed its position. Perhaps stimulated by a declining real estate market, DGM indicated that it would not oppose acquisition of the entire parcel by the County if the parties could agree on fair market value. The County, however, was not yet ready to act without firmer assurances from OPRHP and DEC as to the availability of state funds, from the Jay Coalition as to its rehabilitation and maintenance commitments, and from its own experts as to the County's possible exposure in any condemnation proceeding. Negotiations on these subjects proved time-consuming and frustrating for all sides.

Frustrated by the delay, DGM commenced another legal action, this one in federal court against the County, Rye and the Jay Coalition alleging an "inverse condemnation" of DGM's property by the defendants. (The claims against the Jay Coalition were quickly withdrawn by DGM after the Coalition indicated it would move to dismiss.) The action was assigned to United States District Judge Gerard Goettel, who, it happened, was not only a contributor to the Jay Coalition but also a student of John Jay's life. In fact, Judge Goettel indicated, he had corresponded with both the Chief Justice of the United States and the U.S. Judicial Conference in support of the Coalition's unsuccessful effort to have the Boston Post Road Historic District also designated a National Historic Landmark (a largely symbolic classification for which a small percentage of National Register properties qualify). Judge Goettel felt obliged to recuse himself, and the matter was reassigned in April, 1991.[27]

---

[27] *See* DGM Partners-Rye v. County of Westchester, No. 90 Civ. 8261 (GLG) (S.D.N.Y. Apr. 16, 1991).

A more important development was also occurring at this time: sharply increased political support, evidenced both in repeated editorials in the local media and in county-wide legislative elections in November, 1991, for public acquisition of the entire Jay parcel. Buoyed by this support, the County's new legislative leaders renewed discussions with DGM and, in April, 1992, announced an agreement for the County to acquire all of Alansten at a market value to be determined by appraisal procedures agreed to by both the County and DGM. (The agreement also provides that, under certain circumstances, DGM may withdraw entirely.) Although it is not a component of the agreement, it is also expected that OPRHP and DEC will make available the $4 million they had earlier pledged to the acquisition effort. The Jay Heritage Center, a nonprofit corporation established by the Coalition, is also expected to acquire the mansion and carriage house directly from DGM so that it can undertake its long-planned rehabilitation program, which is expected to cost at least $2 million.

If implemented, the 1992 agreement between the County and DGM promises a successful conclusion, for all parties, of the most significant historic preservation battle in New York since the St. Bartholomew's Church dispute. Unlike that controversy (which centered on church-state issues and the definition of "hardship" for nonprofit organizations), the campaign to save Alansten brought into play virtually all elements (other than wetlands permitting) of contemporary land-use controls. Although time-consuming and expensive, the zoning, subdivision, preservation and acquisition processes triggered by DGM's applications ultimately produced a consensus as to the most appropriate, and fairest, manner in which to utilize this exceptional property. Although both state and federal courts were called upon to oversee these procedures at virtually every step of the way, the decisions summarized above provided the ground rules under which the relevant public agencies were able to exercise their discretion to achieve a lawful and wise result.

Appendix A

National Historic Preservation Act

16 U.S.C. § § 470-470w-6

§ 470. [NHPA § 1]   Short title; Congressional finding and declaration of policy
§ 470-1. [NHPA § 2]   Declaration of policy of the Federal Government
§ 470a. [NHPA § 101]   Historic preservation program
    (a) National Register of Historic Places; designation of properties as historic landmarks; properties deemed included; criteria; nomination of properties by states, local governments or individuals; regulations
    (b) Regulations for State Historic Preservation Programs; periodic evaluations and fiscal audits of state programs; administration of state programs; contracts and cooperative agreements with nonprofit or educational institutions; treatment of state programs as approved programs
    (c) Certification of local governments by State Historic Preservation Officer; transfer of portion of grants; certification by Interior Secretary; nomination of properties by local governments for inclusion in National Register
    (d) Matching grants-in-aid to states for programs and projects; matching grants-in-aid to National Trust for Historic Preservation in the United States; program of direct grants for preservation of properties included in National Register; grants or loans to Indian tribes and ethnic or minority groups for preservation of cultural heritage
    (e) Prohibition of use of funds for compensation of intervenors in preservation program
    (f) Guidelines for federal agency responsibility for agency-owned or controlled historic properties
    (g) Professional standards for preservation of federally owned or controlled historic properties
    (h) Dissemination of information concerning professional methods and techniques for preservation of historic properties
§ 470a-1.   World Heritage Convention
    (a) United States participation

(b) Nomination of property to World Heritage Committee
(c) Nomination of nonfederal property to World Heritage Committee

§ 470a-2. Federal undertakings outside United States; mitigation of adverse effects
§ 470b. [NHPA § 102] Requirements for awarding of grant funds
§ 470b-1. Grants to National Trust for Historic Preservation
    (a) Authority of Secretary of Housing and Urban Development; renovation or restoration costs; terms and conditions; amounts
    (b) Authorization of appropriations
§ 470c. [NHPA § 103] Appropriation of grant funds; reapportionment
§ 470d. [NHPA § 104] Loan insurance program for preservation of property included in National Register
    (a) Establishment
    (b) Loan qualifications
    (c) Limitation on amount of unpaid principal balance of loans
    (d) Assignability of insurance contracts; contracts as obligation of United States; contestability
    (e) Conditions and methods of payment as result of loss
    (f) Protection of financial interests of federal government
    (g) Conveyance to governmental or nongovernmental entity of property acquired by foreclosure
    (h) Assessment of fees in connection with loans
    (i) Treatment of loans as nonfederal funds
    (j) Authorization of appropriations for payment of losses
    (k) Eligibility of debt obligation for purchase, etc., by Federal Financing Bank
§ 470e. [NHPA § 105] Required record keeping by recipients of assistance
§ 470f. [NHPA § 106] Effect of federal undertakings upon property listed in National Register; comment by Advisory Council on Historic Preservation
§ 470g. [NHPA § 107] White House, United States Supreme Court Building and United States Capitol not included in program for preservation of historic properties
§ 470h. [NHPA § 108] Historic Preservation Fund; establishment; appropriations; source of revenue
§ 470h-1. [NHPA § 109] Acceptance of privately donated funds by Interior Secretary
    (a) Authorization; use of funds
    (b) Consideration of factors respecting expenditure of funds
    (c) Transfer of unobligated funds
§ 470h-2. [NHPA § 110] Historic properties owned or controlled by federal agencies
    (a) Responsibilities of federal agencies; program for location, inventory and nomination
    (b) Records on historic properties to be altered or demolished; deposit in Library of Congress or other appropriate agency
    (c) Agency Preservation Officer; responsibilities; qualifications
    (d) Agency programs and projects
    (e) Review of plans of transferees of surplus federally owned historic properties
    (f) Planning and actions to minimize harm to National Historic Landmarks

(g) Costs of preservation as eligible project costs
(h) Annual preservation awards program
(i) Environmental impact statement
(j) Waiver of provisions in event of natural disaster or imminent threat to national security

§ 470h-3. [NHPA § 111]   Lease or exchange of historic property
  (a) Authorization; consultation with Advisory Council on Historic Preservation
  (b) Proceeds of lease for administration, etc., of property; deposit of surplus proceeds into Treasury
  (c) Contracts for management of historic property

§ 470i. [NHPA § 201]   Advisory Council on Historic Preservation
  (a) Establishment; membership; chairman
  (b) Designation of substitutes
  (c) Term of office
  (d) Vacancies; term of office of members already appointed
  (e) Designation of Vice Chairman
  (f) Quorum

§ 470j. [NHPA § 202]   Functions of council; annual report to president and Congress; recommendations

§ 470k. [NHPA § 203]   Cooperation between council and instrumentalities of executive branch of federal government

§ 470l. [NHPA § 204]   Compensation of members of council

§ 470m. [NHPA § 205]   Administration
  (a) Executive director of council; appointment; functions and duties
  (b) General counsel; appointment; functions and duties
  (c) Appointment and compensation of officers and employees
  (d) Appointment and compensation of additional personnel
  (e) Expert and consultant services; procurement
  (f) Financial and administrative services; Interior Department
  (g) Use of funds, personnel, facilities and services of council members

§ 470n. [NHPA § 206]   International Centre for Study of Preservation and Restoration of Cultural Property; United States participation; council recommendations; authorization of appropriations

§ 470o. [NHPA § 207]   Transfer of personnel, property, etc., by Interior Department to council; time limit

§ 470p. [NHPA § 208]   Rights, benefits and privileges of transferred employees

§ 470q. [NHPA § 209]   Operations of council; exemption

§ 470r. [NHPA § 210]   Transmittal of legislative recommendations, testimony or comments to president, Office of Management and Budget and congressional committees; prohibition

§ 470s. [NHPA § 211]   Rules and regulations; participation by local governments

§ 470t. [NHPA § 212]   Budget; authorization of appropriations

§ 470u. [NHPA § 213]   Report by Interior Secretary to council

§ 470v. [NHPA § 214]   Exemption for federal programs or undertakings; regulations

§ 470w. [NHPA § 301]   Definitions

§ 470w-1. [NHPA § 302]   Authorization for expenditure of appropriated funds

§ 470w-2. [NHPA § 303]   Donations and bequests of money, personal property and less than fee interests in historic property

§ **470w-3.** [NHPA § 304] Information relating to location or character of historic resources, disclosure to public
§ **470w-4.** [NHPA § 305] Attorneys' fees and costs to prevailing parties in civil actions
§ **470w-5.** [NHPA § 306] National Museum for the Building Arts
 (a) Cooperative agreement between Interior Secretary, administrator of General Services Administration and Committee for National Museum of the Building Arts; purposes
 (b) Provisions of cooperative agreement
 (c) Matching grants-in-aid to committee; limitation on amounts
 (d) Renovation of site
 (e) Annual committee report to secretary and administrator
 (f) Definition of "building arts"
§ **470w-6.** [NHPA § 307] Effective date of regulations
 (a) Copy to Congress prior to publication in Federal Register; effective date of final regulations
 (b) Effective date of final regulation in case of emergency
 (c) Disapproval of regulation by resolution of Congress
 (d) Failure of Congress to adopt resolution of disapproval of regulation
 (e) Sessions of Congress
 (f) Congressional inaction or rejection of resolution of disapproval not deemed approval of regulation

§ 470. Short title; Congressional finding and declaration of policy

(a) Sections 470 to 470a, 470b, and 470c to 470w-6 of this title may be cited as the "National Historic Preservation Act".

(b) The Congress finds and declares that—

(1) the spirit and direction of the Nation are founded upon and reflected in its historic heritage;

(2) the historical and cultural foundations of the Nation should be preserved as a living part of our community life and development in order to give a sense of orientation to the American people;

(3) historic properties significant to the Nation's heritage are being lost or substantially altered, often inadvertently, with increasing frequency;

(4) the preservation of this irreplaceable heritage is in the public interest so that its vital legacy of cultural, educational, aesthetic, inspirational, economic, and energy benefits will be maintained and enriched for future generations of Americans;

(5) in the face of ever-increasing extensions of urban centers, highways, and residential, commercial, and industrial developments, the present governmental and nongovernmental historic preservation programs and activities are inadequate to insure future generations a genuine opportunity to appreciate and enjoy the rich heritage of our Nation;

(6) the increased knowledge of our historic resources, the establishment of better means of identifying and administering them, and the encouragement of their preservation will improve the planning and execution of Federal and federally assisted projects and will assist economic growth and development; and

(7) although the major burdens of historic preservation have been borne and major efforts initiated by private agencies and individuals, and both should continue to play a vital role, it is nevertheless necessary and appropriate for the Federal Government to accelerate its historic preservation programs and activities, to give maximum encouragement to agencies and individuals undertaking preservation by private means, and to assist State and local governments and the National Trust for Historic Preservation in the United States to expand and accelerate their historic preservation programs and activities.

§ 470-1. Declaration of policy of the Federal Government

It shall be the policy of the Federal Government, in cooperation with other nations and in partnership with the States, local governments, Indian tribes, and private organizations and individuals to—

(1) use measures, including financial and technical assistance, to foster conditions under which our modern society and our prehistoric and historic resources can exist in productive harmony and fulfill the social, economic, and other requirements of present and future generations;

(2) provide leadership in the preservation of the prehistoric and historic resources of the United States and of the international community of nations;

(3) administer federally owned, administered, or controlled prehistoric and historic resources in a spirit of stewardship for the inspiration and benefit of present and future generations;

(4) contribute to the preservation of nonfederally owned prehistoric and historic resources and give maximum encouragement to organizations and individuals undertaking preservation by private means;

(5) encourage the public and private preservation and utilization of all usable elements of the Nation's historic built environment; and

(6) assist State and local governments and the National Trust for Historic Preservation in the United States to expand and accelerate their historic preservation programs and activities.

§ 470a. Historic preservation program—National Register of Historic Places; designation of properties as historic landmarks; properties deemed included; criteria; nomination of properties by States, local governments or individuals; regulations

(a) (1) (A) The Secretary of the Interior is authorized to expand and maintain a National Register of Historic Places composed of districts, sites, buildings, structures, and objects significant in American history, architecture, archeology, engineering, and culture.

(B) Properties meeting the criteria for National Historic Landmarks established pursuant to paragraph (2) shall be designated as "National Historic Landmarks" and included on the National Register, subject to the requirements of paragraph (6). All historic properties included on the National Register on December 12, 1980 shall be deemed to be included on the National Register as of their initial listing for purposes of sections 470 to 470a, 470b to 470w-6 of this title. All historic properties listed in the Federal Register of February 6, 1979, as "National Historic Landmarks" or thereafter prior to the effective date of this Act are declared by Congress to be National Historic Landmarks of national historic significance as of their initial listing as such in the Federal Register for purposes of sections 470 to 470a, 470b, and 470c to 470w-6 of this title and the Act of August 21, 1935; except that in cases of National Historic Landmark districts for which no boundaries have been established, boundaries must first be published in the Federal Register and submitted to the Committee on Energy and National Resources of the United States Senate and to the Committee on Interior and Insular Affairs of the United States House of Representatives.

(2) The Secretary in consultation with national historical and archaeological associations, shall establish or revise criteria for properties to be included on the National Register and criteria for National Historic Landmarks, and shall also promulgate or revise regulations as may be necessary for—

(A) nominating properties for inclusion in, and removal from, the National Register and the recommendation of properties by certified local governments;

(B) designating properties as National Historic Landmarks and removing such designation;

(C) considering appeals from such recommendations, nominations, removals, and designations (or any failure or refusal by a nominating authority to nominate or designate);

(D) nominating historic properties for inclusion in the World Heritage List in accordance with the terms of the Convention concerning the Protection of the World Cultural and Natural Heritage;

(E) making determinations of eligibility of properties for inclusion on the National Register; and

(F) notifying the owner of a property, any appropriate local governments, and the general public, when the property is being considered for inclusion on the National Register, for designation as a National Historic Landmark or for nomination to the World Heritage List.

(3) Subject to the requirements of paragraph (6), any State which is carrying out a program approved under subsection (b) of this section, shall nominate to the Secretary properties which meet the criteria promulgated under subsection (a) of this section for inclusion on the National Register. Subject to paragraph (6), any property nominated under this paragraph or under section 470h-2 (a) (2) of this title shall be included on the National Register on the date forty-five days after receipt by the Secretary of the nomination and the necessary documentation, unless the Secretary disapproves such nomination within such forty-five day period or unless an appeal is filed under paragraph (5).

(4) Subject to the requirements of paragraph (6) the Secretary may accept a nomination directly from any person or local government for inclusion of a property on the National Register only if such property is located in a State where there is no program approved under subsection (b) of this section. The Secretary may include on the National Register any property for which such a

nomination is made if he determines that such property is eligible in accordance with the regulations promulgated under paragraph (2). Such determination shall be made within ninety days from the date of the nomination unless the nomination is appealed under paragraph (5).

(5) Any person or local government may appeal to the Secretary a nomination of any historic property for inclusion on the National Register and may appeal to the Secretary the failure or refusal of a nominating authority to nominate a property in accordance with this subsection.

(6) The Secretary shall promulgate regulations requiring that before any property or district may be included on the National Register or designated as a National Historic Landmark, the owner or owners of such property, or a majority of the owners of the properties within the district in the case of an historic district, shall be given the opportunity (including a reasonable period of time) to concur in, or object to, the nomination of the property or district for such inclusion or designation. If the owner or owners of any privately owned property, or a majority of the owners of such properties within the district in the case of an historic district, object to such inclusion or designation, such property shall not be included on the National Register or designated as a National Historic Landmark until such objection is withdrawn. The Secretary shall review the nomination of the property or district where any such objection has been made and shall determine whether or not the property or district is eligible for such inclusion or designation, and if the Secretary determines that such property or district is eligible for such inclusion or designation, he shall inform the Advisory Council on Historic Preservation, the appropriate State Historic Preservation Officer, the appropriate chief elected local official and the owner or owners of such property, of his determination. The regulations under this paragraph shall include provisions to carry out the purposes of this paragraph in the case of multiple ownership of a single property.

(7) The Secretary shall promulgate, or revise, regulations—

(A) ensuring that significant prehistoric and historic artifacts, and associated records, subject to section 470h-2 of this title, the Act of June 27, 1960, and the Archaeological Resources Protection Act of 1979 are deposited in an institution with adequate long-term curatorial capabilities;

(B) establishing a uniform process and standards for documenting historic properties by public agencies and private parties for purposes of incorporation into, or complementing, the national historical architectural and engineering records within the Library of Congress; and

(C) certifying local governments, in accordance with subsection (c)(1) of this section and for the allocation of funds pursuant to section 470c (c) of this title.

Regulations for State Historic Preservation Programs; periodic evaluations and fiscal audits of State programs; administration of State programs; contracts and cooperative agreements with nonprofit or educational institutions; treatment of State programs as approved programs

(b) (1) The Secretary, in consultation with the National Conference of State Historic Preservation Officers and the National Trust for Historic Preservation, shall promulgate or revise regulations for State Historic Preservation Programs. Such regulations shall provide that a State program submitted to the Secretary under this section shall be approved by the Secretary if he determines that the program—

    (A) provides for the designation and appointment by the Governor of a "State Historic Preservation Officer" to administer such program in accordance with paragraph (3) and for the employment or appointment by such officer of such professional qualified staff as may be necessary for such purposes;

    (B) provides for an adequate and qualified State historic preservation review board designated by the State Historic Preservation Officer unless otherwise provided for by State law; and

    (C) provides for adequate public participation in the State Historic Preservation Program, including the process of recommending properties for nomination to the National Register.

(2) Periodically, but not less than every four years after the approval of any State program under this subsection, the Secretary shall evaluate such program to make a determination as to whether or not it is in compliance with the requirements of sections 470 to 470a, 470b, and 470c to 470w-6 of this title. If at any time, the Secretary determines that a State program does not comply with such requirements, he shall disapprove such program, and suspend in whole or in part assistance to such State under subsection (d)(1) of this section, unless there are adequate assurances that the program will comply with such requirements within a reasonable period of time. The Secretary may also conduct periodic fiscal audits of State programs approved under this section.

(3) It shall be the responsibility of the State Historic Preservation Officer to administer the State Historic Preservation Program and to—

    (A) in cooperation with Federal and State agencies, local governments, and private organizations and individuals, direct and conduct a comprehensive statewide survey of historic properties and maintain inventories of such properties;

    (B) identify and nominate eligible properties to the National Register and otherwise administer applications for listing historic properties on the National Register;

    (C) prepare and implement a comprehensive statewide historic preservation plan;

    (D) administer the State program of Federal assistance for historic preservation within the State;

    (E) advise and assist, as appropriate, Federal and State agencies and local governments in carrying out their historic preservation responsibilities;

    (F) cooperate with the Secretary, the Advisory Council on Historic Preservation, and other Federal and State agencies, local governments, and organizations and individuals to ensure that historic properties are taken into consideration at all levels of planning and development;

    (G) provide public information, education, and training and technical assistance relating to the Federal and State Historic Preservation Programs; and

(H) cooperate with local governments in the development of local historic preservation programs and assist local governments in becoming certified pursuant to subsection (c) of this section.

(4) Any State may carry out all or any part of its responsibilities under this subsection by contract or cooperative agreement with any qualified nonprofit organization or educational institution.

(5) Any State historic preservation program in effect under prior authority of law may be treated as an approved program for purposes of this subsection until the earlier of —

(A) the date on which the Secretary approves a program submitted by the State under this subsection, or

(B) three years after December 12, 1980.

Certification of local governments by State Historic Preservation Officer; transfer of portion of grants; certification by Secretary; nomination of properties by local governments for inclusion on National Register

(c) (1) Any State program approved under this section shall provide a mechanism for the certification by the State Historic Preservation Officer of local governments to carry out the purposes of section 470 to 470a, 470b, and 470c to 470w-6 of this title and provide for the transfer, in accordance with section 470c (c) of this title, of a portion of the grants received by the States under sections 470 to 470a, 470b, and 470c to 470w-6 of this title, to such local governments. Any local government shall be certified to participate under the provisions of this section if the applicable State Historic Preservation Officer, and the Secretary, certifies that the local government —

(A) enforces appropriate State or local legislation for the designation and protection of historic properties;

(B) has established an adequate and qualified historic preservation review commission by State or local legislation;

(C) maintains a system for the survey and inventory of historic properties that furthers the purposes of subsection (b) of this section;

(D) provides for adequate public participation in the local historic preservation program, including the process of recommending properties for nomination to the National Register; and

(E) satisfactorily performs the responsibilities delegated to it under sections 470 to 470a, 470b, and 470c to 470w-6 of this title.

Where there is no approved State program, a local government may be certified by the Secretary if he determines that such local government meets the requirements of subparagraphs (A) through (E); and in any such case the Secretary may make grants-in-aid to the local government for purposes of this section.

(2) (A) Before a property within the jurisdiction of the certified local government may be considered by the State to be nominated to the Secretary for inclusion on the National Register, the State Historic Preservation Officer shall notify the owner, the applicable chief local elected official, and the local historic preservation commission. The commission, after reasonable opportunity for public comment, shall prepare a report as to whether or not such property, in its opinion, meets the criteria of the National Register. Within sixty days of notice from the

State Historic Preservation Officer, the chief local elected official shall transmit the report of the commission and his recommendation to the State Historic Preservation Officer. Except as provided in subparagraph (B), after receipt of such report and recommendation, or if no such report and recommendation are received within sixty days, the State shall make the nomination pursuant to subsection (a) of this section. The State may expedite such process with the concurrence of the certified local government.

(B) If both the commission and the chief local elected official recommend that a property not be nominated to the National Register, the State Historic Preservation Officer shall take no further action, unless within thirty days of the receipt of such recommendation by the State Historic Preservation Officer an appeal is filed with the State. If such an appeal is filed, the State shall follow the procedures for making a nomination pursuant to subsection (a) of this section. Any report and recommendations made under this section shall be included with any nomination submitted by the State to the Secretary.

(3) Any local government certified under this section or which is making efforts to become so certified shall be eligible for funds under the provisions of section 470c (c) of this title, and shall carry out any responsibilities delegated to it in accordance with such terms and conditions as the Secretary deems necessary or advisable.

Matching grants-in-aid to States for programs and projects; matching grant-in-aid to National Trust for Historic Preservation in the United States; program of direct grants for preservation of properties included on National Register; grants or loans to Indian tribes and ethnic or minority groups for preservation of cultural heritage

(d) (1) The Secretary shall administer a program of matching grants-in-aid to the States for historic preservation projects, and State historic preservation programs, approved by the Secretary and having as their purpose the identification of historic properties and the preservation of properties included on the National Register.

(2) The Secretary shall administer a program of matching grant-in-aid to the National Trust for Historic Preservation in the United States, chartered by Act of Congress approved October 26, 1949 for the purposes of carrying out the responsibilities of the National Trust.

(3) (A) In addition to the programs under paragraphs (1) and (2), the Secretary shall administer a program of direct grants for the preservation of properties included on the National Register. Funds to support such program annually shall not exceed 10 per centum of the amount appropriated annually for the fund established under section 470h of this title. These grants may be made by the Secretary, in consultation with the appropriate State Historic Preservation Officer—

(i) for the preservation of National Historic Landmarks which are threatened with demolition or impairment and for the preservation of historic properties of World Heritage significance,

(ii) for demonstration projects which will provide information concerning professional methods and techniques having application to historic properties,

(iii) for the training and development of skilled labor in trades and crafts, and in analysis and curation, relating to historic preservation; and

(iv) to assist persons or small businesses within any historic district included in the National Register to remain within the district.

(B) The Secretary may also, in consultation with the appropriate State Historic Preservation Officer, make grants or loans or both under this section to Indian tribes and to nonprofit organizations representing ethnic or minority groups for the preservation of their cultural heritage.

(C) Grants may be made under subparagraph (A) (i) and (iv) only to the extent that the project cannot be carried out in as effective a manner through the use of an insured loan under section 470d of this title.

Prohibition of use of funds for compensation of intervenors in preservation program

(e) No part of any grant made under this section may be used to compensate any person intervening in any proceeding under sections 470 to 470a, 470b, and 470c to 470w-6 of this title.

Guidelines for Federal agency responsibility for agency-owned historic properties

(f) In consultation with the Advisory Council on Historic Preservation, the Secretary shall promulgate guidelines for Federal agency responsibilities under section 470h-2 of this title.

Professional standards for preservation of Federally owned or controlled historic properties

(g) Within one year after December 12, 1980, the Secretary shall establish, in consultation with the Secretaries of Agriculture and Defense, the Smithsonian Institution, and the Administrator of the General Services Administration, professional standards for the preservation of historic properties in Federal ownership or control.

Dissemination of information concerning professional methods and techniques for preservation of historic properties

(h) The Secretary shall develop and make available to Federal agencies, State and local governments, private organizations and individuals, and other nations and international organizations pursuant to the World Heritage Convention, training in, and information concerning, professional methods and techniques for the preservation of historic properties and for the administration of the historic preservation program at the Federal, State, and local level. The Secretary shall also develop mechanisms to provide information concerning historic preservation to the general public including students.

§ 470a-1. World Heritage Convention—United States participation

(a) The Secretary of the Interior shall direct and coordinate United States participation in the Convention Concerning the Protection of the World Cultural and Natural Heritage, approved by the Senate on October 26, 1973, in cooperation with the Secretary of State, the Smithsonian Institution, and the Advisory Council on Historic Preservation. Whenever possible, expenditures incurred in carrying out activities in cooperation with other nations and international organizations shall be paid for in such excess currency of the country or area where the expense is incurred as may be available to the United States.

Nomination of property to World Heritage Committee

(b) The Secretary of the Interior shall periodically nominate properties he determines are of international significance to the World Heritage Committee on behalf of the United States. No property may be so nominated unless it has previously been determined to be of national significance. Each such nomination shall include evidence of such legal protections as may be necessary to ensure preservation of the property and its environment (including restrictive covenants, easements, or other forms of protection). Before making any such nomination, the Secretary shall notify the Committee on Interior and Insular Affairs of the United States House of Representatives and the Committee on Energy and Natural Resources of the United States Senate.

Nomination of non-Federal property to World Heritage Committee

(c) No non-Federal property may be nominated by the Secretary of the Interior to the World Heritage Committee for inclusion on the World Heritage List unless the owner of the property concurs in writing to such nomination.

§ 470a-2. Federal undertakings outside United States; mitigation of adverse effects

Prior to the approval of any Federal undertaking outside the United States which may directly and adversely affect a property which is on the World Heritage List or on the applicable country's equivalent of the National Register, the head of a Federal agency having direct or indirect jurisdiction over such undertaking shall take into account the effect of the undertaking on such property for purposes of avoiding or mitigating any adverse effects.

§ 470b. Requirements for awarding of grant funds

(a) No grant may be made under sections 470 to 470a, 470b, and 470c to 470w-6 of this title—
    (1) unless application therefor is submitted to the Secretary in accordance with regulations and procedures prescribed by him.

(2) unless the application is in accordance with the comprehensive statewide historic preservation plan which has been approved by the Secretary after considering its relationship to the comprehensive statewide outdoor recreation plan prepared pursuant to the Land and Water Conservation Fund Act of 1965 (78 Stat. 897);

(3) for more than 50 per centum of the aggregate cost of carrying out projects and programs specified in section 470a (d) (1) and (2) of this title in any one fiscal year, except that for the costs of State or local historic surveys or inventories the Secretary shall provide 70 per centum of the aggregate cost involved in any one fiscal year;

(4) unless the grantee has agreed to make such reports, in such form and containing such information as the Secretary may from time to time require;

(5) unless the grantee has agreed to assume, after completion of the project, the total cost of the continued maintenance, repair, and administration of the property in a manner satisfactory to the Secretary; and

(6) until the grantee has complied with such further terms and conditions as the Secretary may deem necessary or advisable.

Except as permitted by other law, the State share of the costs referred to in paragraph (3) shall be contributed by non-Federal sources. Notwithstanding any other provision of law, no grant made pursuant to sections 470 to 470a, 470b, and 470c to 470w-6 of this title shall be treated as taxable income for purposes of the Internal Revenue Code of 1954.

(b) The Secretary may in his discretion waive the requirements of subsection (a), paragraphs (2) and (5) of this section for any grant under sections 470 to 470b and 470c to 470t of this title to the National Trust for Historic Preservation in the United States, in which case a grant to the National Trust may include funds for the maintenance, repair, and administration of the property in a manner satisfactory to the Secretary.

(c) Repealed. Pub.L. 96-515, Title II, § 202 (c), Dec. 12, 1980, 94 Stat. 2993.

(d) No State shall be permitted to utilize the value of real property obtained before October 15, 1966, in meeting the remaining cost of a project for which a grant is made under sections 470 to 470b and 470c to 470t of this title.

§ 470b-1. Grants to National Trust for Historic Preservation—
Authority of Secretary of Housing and Urban Development; renovation or restoration costs; terms and conditions; amounts

(a) The Secretary of Housing and Urban Development is authorized to make grants to the National Trust for Historic Preservation, on such terms and conditions and in such amounts (not exceeding $90,000 with respect to any one structure) as he deems appropriate, to cover the costs incurred by such Trust in renovating or restoring structures which it considers to be of historic or architectural value and which it has accepted and will maintain (after such renovation or restoration) for historic purposes.

Authorization of appropriations

(b) There are authorized to be appropriated such sums as may be necessary for the grants to be made under subsection (a) of this section.

§ 470c. Apportionment of grant funds; reapportionment

(a) The amounts appropriated and made available for grants to the States for comprehensive statewide historic surveys and plans under sections 470 to 470b and 470c to 470t of this title shall be apportioned among the States by the Secretary on the basis of needs as determined by him.

(b) The amounts appropriated and made available for grants to the States for projects and programs under sections 470 to 470a, 470b, and 470c to 470w-6 of this title for each fiscal year shall be apportioned among the States by the Secretary in accordance with needs as disclosed in approved statewide historic preservation plans.

The Secretary shall notify each State of its apportionment under this subsection within thirty days following the date of enactment of legislation appropriating funds under sections 470 to 470a, 470b, and 470c to 470w-6 of this title. Any amount of any apportionment that has not been paid or obligated by the Secretary during the fiscal year in which such notification is given, and for two fiscal years thereafter, shall be reapportioned by the Secretary in accordance with this subsection.

(c) A minimum of 10 per centum of the annual apportionment distributed by the Secretary to each State for the purposes of carrying out sections 470 to 470a, 470b, and 470c to 470w-6 of this title shall be transferred by the State, pursuant to the requirements of sections 470 to 470a, 470b, and 470c to 470w-6 of this title, to local governments which are certified under section 470a (c) of this title for historic preservation projects or programs of such local governments. In any year in which the total annual apportionment to the States exceeds $65,000,000, one half of the excess shall also be transferred by the States to local governments certified pursuant to section 470a (c) of this title.

(d) The Secretary shall establish guidelines for the use and distribution of funds under subsection (c) of this section to insure that no local government receives a disproportionate share of the funds available, and may include a maximum or minimum limitation on the amount of funds distributed to any single local government. The guidelines shall not limit the ability of any State to distribute more than 10 per centum of its annual apportionment under subsection (c) of this section, nor shall the Secretary require any State to exceed the 10 per centum minimum distribution to local governments.

§ 470d. Loan insurance program for preservation of property included on National Register—Establishment

(a) The Secretary shall establish and maintain a program by which he may, upon application of a private lender, insure loans (including loans made in accordance with a mortgage) made by such lender to finance any project for the preservation of a property included on the National Register.

Loan qualifications

(b) A loan may be insured under this section only if—

(1) the loan is made by a private lender approved by the Secretary as financially sound and able to service the loan property;

(2) the amount of the loan, and interest rate charged with respect to the loan, do not exceed such amount, and such a rate, as is established by the Secretary, by rule;

(3) the Secretary has consulted the appropriate State Historic Preservation Officer concerning the preservation of the historic property;

(4) the Secretary has determined that the loan is adequately secured and there is reasonable assurance of repayment;

(5) the repayment period of the loan does not exceed the lesser of forty years or the expected life of the asset financed;

(6) the amount insured with respect to such loan does not exceed 90 per centum of the loss sustained by the lender with respect to the loan; and

(7) the loan, the borrower, and the historic property to be preserved meet other terms and conditions as may be prescribed by the Secretary, by rule, especially terms and conditions relating to the nature and quality of the preservation work.

The Secretary shall consult with the Secretary of the Treasury regarding the interest rate of loans insured under this section.

Limitation on amount of unpaid principal balance of loans

(c) The aggregate unpaid principal balance of loans insured under this section and outstanding at any one time may not exceed the amount which has been covered into the Historic Preservation Fund pursuant to section 470h of this title and subsections (g) and (i) of this section, as in effect on December 12, 1980, but which has not been appropriated for any purpose.

Assignability of insurance contracts; contract as obligation of United States; contestability

(d) Any contract of insurance executed by the Secretary under this section may be assignable, shall be an obligation supported by the full faith and credit of the United States, and shall be incontestable except for fraud or misrepresentation of which the holder had actual knowledge at the time it became a holder.

Conditions and methods of payment as result of loss

(e) The Secretary shall specify, by rule and in each contract entered into under this section, the conditions and method of payment to a private lender as a result of losses incurred by the lender on any loan insured under this section.

Protection of financial interests of Federal Government

(f) In entering into any contract to insure a loan under this section, the Secretary shall take steps to assure adequate protection of the financial interests of the Federal Government. The Secretary may—

(1) in connection with any foreclosure proceeding, obtain, on behalf of the Federal Government, the property securing a loan insured under sections 470a, 470b, and 470c to 470h-3 of this title, and

(2) operate or lease such property for such period as may be necessary to protect the interest of the Federal Government and to carry out subsection (g) of this section.

Conveyance to governmental or nongovernmental entity of property acquired by foreclosure

(g) (1) In any case in which a historic property is obtained pursuant to subsection (f) of this section, the Secretary shall attempt to convey such property to any governmental or nongovernmental entity under such conditions as will ensure the property's continued preservation and use; except that if, after a reasonable time, the Secretary, in consultation with the Advisory Council on Historic Preservation, determines that there is no feasible and prudent means to convey such property and to ensure its continued preservation and use, then the Secretary may convey the property at the fair market value of its interest in such property to any entity without restriction.

(2) Any funds obtained by the Secretary in connection with the conveyance of any property pursuant to paragraph (1) shall be covered into the historic preservation fund, in addition to the amounts covered into such fund pursuant to section 470h of this title and subsection (i) of this section, and shall remain available in such fund until appropriated by the Congress to carry out the purposes of sections 470 to 470a, 470b, and 470c to 470w-6 of this title.

Assessment of fees in connection with loans

(h) The Secretary may assess appropriate and reasonable fees in connection with insuring loans under this section. Any such fees shall be covered into the Historic Preservation Fund, in addition to the amounts covered into such fund pursuant to section 470h of this title and subsection (g) of this section, and shall remain available in such fund until appropriated by the Congress to carry out purposes of sections 470 to 470a, 470b, and 470c to 470w-6 of this title.

Treatment of loans as non-Federal funds

(i) Notwithstanding any other provision of law, any loan insured under this section shall be treated as non-Federal funds for the purposes of satisfying any requirement of any other provision of law under which Federal funds to be used for any project or activity are conditioned upon the use of non-Federal funds by the recipient for payment of any portion of the costs of such project or activity.

Authorization of appropriations for payment of losses

(j) Effective after the fiscal year 1981 there are authorized to be appropriated, such sums as may be necessary to cover payments incurred pursuant to subsection (e) of this section.

Eligibility of debt obligation for purchase, etc., by Federal Financing Bank

(k) No debt obligation which is made or committed to be made, or which is insured or committed to be insured, by the Secretary under this section shall be eligible for purchase by, or commitment to purchase by, or sale or issuance to, the Federal Financing Bank.

§ 470e. Required record keeping by recipients of assistance

The beneficiary of assistance under sections 470 to 470b and 470c to 470n of this title shall keep such records as the Secretary shall prescribe, including records which fully disclose the disposition by the beneficiary of the proceeds of such assistance, the total cost of the project or undertaking in connection with which such assistance is given or used, and the amount and nature of that portion of the cost of the project or undertaking supplied by other sources, and such other records as will facilitate an effective audit.

§ 470f. Effect of Federal undertakings upon property listed in National Register; comment by Advisory Council on Historic Preservation

The head of any Federal agency having direct or indirect jurisdiction over a proposed Federal or federally assisted undertaking in any State and the head of any Federal department or independent agency having authority to license any undertaking shall, prior to the approval of the expenditure of any Federal funds on the undertaking or prior to the issuance of any license, as the case may be, take into account the effect of the undertaking on any district, site, building, structure, or object that is included in or eligible for inclusion in the National Register. The head of any such Federal agency shall afford the Advisory Council on Historic Preservation established under sections 470i to 470t of this title a reasonable opportunity to comment with regard to such undertaking.

§ 470g. White House, United States Supreme Court building, and United States Capitol not included in program for preservation of historical properties

Nothing in sections 470 to 470b and 470c to 470n of this title shall be construed to be applicable to the White House and its grounds, the Supreme Court Building and its grounds, or the United States Capitol and its related buildings and grounds.

§ 470h. Historic Preservation Fund; establishment; appropriations; source of revenue

To carry out the provisions of this subchapter, there is hereby established the Historic Preservation Fund (hereafter referred to as the "fund") in the Treasury of the United States.

There shall be covered into such fund $24,400,000 for fiscal year 1977, $100,000,000 for fiscal year 1978, $100,000,000 for fiscal year 1979, $150,000,000 for fiscal year 1980, and $150,000,000 for fiscal year 1981 and $150,000,000 for each of fiscal years 1982 through 1992, from revenues due and payable to the United States under the Outer Continental Shelf Lands Act (67 Stat. 462, 469), as amended (43 U.S.C., 1338), and/or under section 7433(b) of Title 10, notwithstanding any provision of law that such proceeds shall be credited to miscellaneous receipts of the Treasury. Such moneys shall be used only to carry out the purposes of this subchapter and shall be available for expenditure only when appropriated by the Congress. Any moneys not appropriated shall remain available in the fund until appropriated for said purposes: Provided, That appropriations made pursuant to this paragraph may be made without fiscal year limitation.

§ 470h-1. Acceptance of privately donated funds by Secretary—Authorization; use of funds

(a) In furtherance of the purposes of sections 470 to 470b and 470c to 470t of this title, the Secretary may accept the donation of funds which may be expended by him for projects to acquire, restore, preserve, or recover data from any district, building, structure, site, or object which is listed on the National Register of Historic Places established pursuant to section 470a of this title, so long as the project is owned by a State, any unit of local government, or any nonprofit entity.

Consideration of factors respecting expenditure of funds

(b) In expending said funds, the Secretary shall give due consideration to the following factors: the national significance of the project; its historical value to the community; the imminence of its destruction or loss; and the expressed intentions of the donor. Funds expended under this subsection shall be made available without regard to the matching requirements established by section 470b of this title, but the recipient of such funds shall be permitted to utilize them to match any grants from the Historic Preservation Fund established by section 470h of this title.

Transfer of unobligated funds

(c) The Secretary is hereby authorized to transfer unobligated funds previously donated to the Secretary for the purposes of the National Park Service, with the consent of the donor, and any funds so transferred shall be used or expended in accordance with the provisions of sections 470 to 470b and 470c to 470t of this title.

§ 470h-2. Historic properties owned or controlled by Federal agencies—
Responsibilities of Federal agencies; program for location, inventory and
nomination

(a) (1) The heads of all Federal agencies shall assume responsibility for the
preservation of historic properties which are owned or controlled by such agency.
Prior to acquiring, constructing, or leasing buildings for purposes of carrying out
agency responsibilities, each Federal agency shall use, to the maximum extent feasible, historic properties available to the agency. Each agency shall undertake, consistent with the preservation of such properties and the mission of the agency and
the professional standards established pursuant to section 470a (f) of this title, any
preservation, as may be necessary to carry out this section.

(2) With the advice of the Secretary and in cooperation with the State
historic preservation officer for the State involved, each Federal agency shall establish a program to locate, inventory, and nominate to the Secretary all properties
under the agency's ownership or control by the agency, that appear to qualify for
inclusion on the National Register in accordance with the regulations promulgated
under section 470a (a) (2) (A) of this title. Each Federal agency shall exercise
caution to assure that any such property that might qualify for inclusion is not
inadvertently transferred, sold, demolished, substantially altered, or allowed to
deteriorate significantly.

Records on historic properties to be altered or demolished; deposit in Library of Congress or other appropriate agency

(b) Each Federal agency shall initiate measures to assure that where, as a result of Federal action or assistance carried out by such agency, an historic property
is to be substantially altered or demolished, timely steps are taken to make or have
made appropriate records, and that such records then be deposited, in accordance
with section 470a (a) of this title, in the Library of Congress or with such other
appropriate agency as may be designated by the Secretary, for future use and
reference.

Agency Preservation Officer; responsibilities; qualifications

(c) The head of each Federal agency shall, unless exempted under section
470v, designate a qualified official to be known as the agency's "preservation
officer" who shall be responsible for coordinating that agency's activities under
sections 470 to 470a, 470b, and 470c to 470w-6 of this title. Each Preservation
Officer may, in order to be considered qualified, satisfactorily complete an appropriate training program established by the Secretary under section 470a (g) of
this title.

Agency programs and projects

(d) Consistent with the agency's missions and mandates, all Federal agencies
shall carry out agency programs and projects (including those under which any

Rehabilitating Older and Historic Buildings

Federal assistance is provided or any Federal license, permit, or other approval is required) in accordance with the purposes of sections 470 to 470a, 470b, and 470c to 470w-6 of this title and, give consideration to programs and projects which will further the purposes of sections 470 to 470a, 470b, and 470c to 470w-6 of this title.

Review of plans of transferees of surplus federally owned historic properties

(e) The Secretary shall review and approve the plans of transferees of surplus federally owned historic properties not later than ninety days after his receipt of such plans to ensure that the prehistorical, historical, architectural, or culturally significant values will be preserved or enhanced.

Planning and actions to minimize harm to National Historic Landmarks

(f) Prior to the approval of any Federal undertaking which may directly and adversely affect any National Historic Landmark, the head of the responsible Federal agency shall, to the maximum extent possible, undertake such planning and actions as may be necessary to minimize harm to such landmark, and shall afford the Advisory Council on Historic Preservation a reasonable opportunity to comment on the undertaking.

Costs of preservation as eligible project costs

(g) Each Federal agency may include the costs of preservation activities of such agency under sections 470 to 470a, 470b, and 470c to 470w-6 of this title as eligible project costs in all undertakings of such agency or assisted by such agency. The eligible project costs may also include amounts paid by a Federal agency to any State to be used in carrying out such preservation responsibilities of the Federal agency under sections 470 to 470a, 470b, and 470c to 470w-6 of this title, and reasonable costs may be charged to Federal licensees and permittees as a condition to the issuance of such license or permit.

Annual preservation awards program

(h) The Secretary shall establish an annual preservation awards program under which he may make monetary awards in amounts of not to exceed $1,000 and provide citations for special achievement to officers and employees of Federal, State, and certified local governments in recognition of their outstanding contributions to the preservation of historic resources. Such program may include the issuance of annual awards by the President of the United States to any citizen of the United States recommended for such award by the Secretary.

Environmental impact statement

(i) Nothing in sections 470 to 470a, 470b, and 470c to 470w-6 of this title shall be construed to require the preparation of an environmental impact statement where such a statement would not otherwise be required under the National Environment Policy Act of 1969, and nothing in sections 470 to 470a, 470b, and 470c to 470w-6 of this title shall be construed to provide any exemption from any requirement respecting the preparation of such a statement under such Act.

Waiver of provisions in event of natural disaster or imminent threat to national security

(j) The Secretary shall promulgate regulations under which the requirements of this section may be waived in whole or in part in the event of a major natural disaster or an imminent threat to the national security.

§ 470h-8. Lease or exchange of historic property—Authorization; consultation with Advisory Council on Historic Preservation

(a) Notwithstanding any other provision of law, any Federal agency may, after consultation with the Advisory Council on Historic Preservation, lease an historic property owned by the agency to any person or organization, or exchange any property owned by the agency with comparable historic property, if the agency head determines that the lease or exchange will adequately insure the preservation of the historic property.

Proceeds of lease for administration, etc., of property; deposit of surplus proceeds into Treasury

(b) The proceeds of any lease under subsection (a) of this section may, notwithstanding any other provision of law, be retained by the agency entering into such lease and used to defray the costs of administration, maintenance, repair, and related expenses incurred by the agency with respect to such property or other properties which are on the National Register which are owned by, or are under the jurisdiction or control of, such agency. Any surplus proceeds from such leases shall be deposited into the Treasury of the United States at the end of the second fiscal year following the fiscal year in which such proceeds were received.

Contracts for management of historic property

(c) The head of any Federal agency having responsibility for the management of any historic property may, after consultation with the Advisory Council on Historic Preservation, enter into contracts for the management of such property. Any such contract shall contain such terms and conditions as the head of such agency deems necessary or appropriate to protect the interests of the United States and insure adequate preservation of the historic property.

§ 470i. Advisory Council on Historic Preservation—Establishment; membership; chairman

(a) There is established as an independent agency of the United States Government an Advisory Council on Historic Preservation (hereinafter referred to as the "Council") which shall be composed of the following members:

    (1) a Chairman appointed by the President selected from the general public;

    (2) the Secretary of the Interior;

    (3) the Architect of the Capitol;

    (4) the Secretary of Agriculture and the heads of four other agencies of the United States (other than the Department of the Interior) the activities of which affect historic preservation, appointed by the President;

    (5) one Governor appointed by the President;

    (6) one mayor appointed by the President;

    (7) the President of the National Conference of State Historic Preservation Officers;

    (8) the Chairman of the National Trust for Historic Preservation;

    (9) four experts in the field of historic preservation appointed by the President from the disciplines of architecture, history, archeology, and other appropriate disciplines; and

    (10) three at-large members from the general public, appointed by the President.

Designation of substitutes

(b) Each member of the Council specified in paragraphs (2) through (8) (other than (5) and (6)) of subsection (a) of this section may designate another officer of his department, agency, or organization to serve on the Council in his stead, except that, in the case of paragraphs (2) and (4), no such officer other than an Assistant Secretary or an officer having major department-wide or agency-wide responsibilities may be so designated.

Term of office

(c) Each member of the Council appointed under paragraph (1), and under paragraphs (9) and (10) of subsection (a) of this section shall serve for a term of four years from the expiration of his predecessor's term; except that the members first appointed under that paragraph shall serve for terms of one to four years; as designated by the President at the time of appointment, in such manner as to insure that the terms of not more than two of them will expire in any one year. The members appointed under paragraphs (5) and (6) shall serve for the term of their elected office but not in excess of four years. An appointed member may not serve more than two terms. An appointed member whose term has expired shall serve until that member's successor has been appointed.

Vacancies; term of office of members already appointed

(d) A vacancy in the Council shall not affect its powers, but shall be filled, not later than sixty days after such vacancy commences, in the same manner as the original appointment (and for the balance of any unexpired terms). The members of the Advisory Council on Historic Preservation appointed by the President under sections 470 to 470a, 470b, and 470c to 470w-6 of this title as in effect on the day before December 12, 1980 shall remain in office until all members of the Council, as specified in this section, have been appointed. The members first appointed under this section shall be appointed not later than one hundred and eighty days after December 12, 1980.

Designation of Vice Chairman

(e) The President shall designate a Vice Chairman, from the members appointed under paragraph (5), (6), (9), or (10). The Vice Chairman may act in place of the Chairman during the absence or disability of the Chairman or when the office is vacant.

Quorum

(f) Nine members of the Council shall constitute a quorum.

§ 470j. Functions of Council; annual report to President and Congress; recommendations

(a) The Council shall—
  (1) advise the President and the Congress on matters relating to historic preservation; recommend measures to coordinate activities of Federal, State, and local agencies and private institutions and individuals relating to historic preservation; and advise on the dissemination of information pertaining to such activities;
  (2) encourage, in cooperation with the National Trust for Historic Preservation and appropriate private agencies, public interest and participation in historic preservation;
  (3) recommend the conduct of studies in such areas as the adequacy of legislative and administrative statutes and regulations pertaining to historic preservation activities of State and local governments and the effects of tax policies at all levels of government on historic preservation;
  (4) advise as to guidelines for the assistance of State and local governments in drafting legislation relating to historic preservation;
  (5) encourage, in cooperation with appropriate public and private agencies and institutions, training and education in the field of historic preservation;
  (6) review the policies and programs of Federal agencies and recommend to such agencies methods to improve the effectiveness, coordination, and consistency of those policies and programs with the policies and programs carried out under sections 470 to 470a, 470b, and 470c to 470w-6 of this title; and

(7) inform and educate Federal agencies, State and local governments, Indian tribes, other nations and international organizations and private groups and individuals as to the Council's authorized activities.

(b) The Council shall submit annually a comprehensive report of its activities and the results of its studies to the President and the Congress and shall from time to time submit such additional and special reports as it deems advisable. Each report shall propose such legislative enactments and other actions as, in the judgment of the Council, are necessary and appropriate to carry out its recommendations and shall provide the Council's assessment of current and emerging problems in the field of historic preservation and an evaluation of the effectiveness of the programs of Federal agencies, State and local governments, and the private sector in carrying out the purposes of sections 470 to 470a, 470b, and 470c to 470w-6 of this title.

§ 470k. Cooperation between Council and instrumentalities of Executive Branch of Federal government

The Council is authorized to secure directly from any department, bureau, agency, board, commission, office, independent establishment or instrumentality of the executive branch of the Federal Government information, suggestions, estimates, and statistics for the purpose of sections 470i to 470n of this title; and each such department, bureau, agency, board, commission, office, independent establishment or instrumentality is authorized to furnish such information, suggestions, estimates, and statistics to the extent permitted by law and within available funds.

§ 470l. Compensation of members of Council

The members of the Council specified in paragraphs (2), (3), and (4) of section 470i (a) of this title shall serve without additional compensation. The other members of the Council shall receive $100 per diem when engaged in the performance of the duties of the Council. All members of the Council shall receive reimbursement for necessary traveling and subsistence expenses incurred by them in the performance of the duties of the Council.

§ 470m. Administration—Executive Director of Council; appointment; functions and duties

(a) There shall be an Executive Director of the Council who shall be appointed in the competitive service by the Chairman with the concurrence of the Council. The Executive Director shall report directly to the Council and perform such functions and duties as the Council may prescribe.

General Counsel; appointment; functions and duties

(b) The Council shall have a General Counsel, who shall be appointed by the Executive Director. The General Counsel shall report directly to the Executive

Director and serve as the Council's legal advisor. The Executive Director shall appoint such other attorneys as may be necessary to assist the General Counsel, represent the Council in courts of law whenever appropriate, including enforcement of agreements with Federal agencies to which the Council is a party, assist the Department of Justice in handling litigation concerning the Council in courts of law, and perform such other legal duties and functions as the Executive Director and the Council may direct.

Appointment and compensation of officers and employees

(c) The Executive Director of the Council may appoint and fix the compensation of such officers and employees in the competitive service as are necessary to perform the functions of the Council at rates not to exceed that now or hereafter prescribed for the highest rate for grade 15 of the General Schedule under section 5332 of Title 5: *Provided,* however, That the Executive Director, with the concurrence of the chairman, may appoint and fix the compensation of not to exceed five employees in the competitive service at rates not to exceed that now or hereafter prescribed for the highest rate of grade 17 of the General Schedule under section 5332 of Title 5.

Appointment and compensation of additional personnel

(d) The Executive Director shall have power to appoint and fix the compensation of such additional personnel as may be necessary to carry out its duties, without regard to the provisions of the civil service laws and chapter 51 and subchapter III of chapter 53 of Title 5.

Expert and consultant services; procurement

(e) The Executive Director of the Council is authorized to procure expert and consultant services in accordance with the provisions of section 3109 of Title 5.

Financial and administrative services; Department of Interior

(f) Financial and administrative services (including those related to budgeting, accounting, financial reporting, personnel and procurement) shall be provided the Council by the Department of the Interior, for which payments shall be made in advance, or by reimbursement, from funds of the Council in such amounts as may be agreed upon by the Chairman of the Council and the Secretary of the Interior: *Provided,* That the regulations of the Department of the Interior for the collection of indebtedness of personnel resulting from erroneous payments (section 5514 (b) of Title 5) shall apply to the collection of erroneous payments made to or on behalf of a Council employee, and regulations of said Secretary for the administrative control of funds (section 665 (g) of Title 31) shall apply to appropriations of the Council:

Use of funds, personnel, facilities, and services of Council members

(g) The members of the Council specified in paragraphs (2) through (4) of section 470i (a) of this title shall provide the Council, with or without reimbursement as may be agreed upon by the Chairman and the members, with such funds, personnel, facilities, and services under their jurisdiction and control as may be needed by the Council to carry out its duties, to the extent that such funds, personnel, facilities, and services are requested by the Council and are otherwise available for that purpose. To the extent of available appropriations, the Council may obtain, by purchase, rental, donation, or otherwise, such additional property, facilities, and services as may be needed to carry out its duties and may also receive donations of moneys for such purpose, and the Executive Director is authorized, in his discretion, to accept, hold, use, expend, and administer the same for the purposes of sections 470 to 470a, 470b, and 470c to 470w-6 of this title.

§ 470n. International Centre for Study of Preservation and Restoration of Cultural Property; United States participation; Council recommendations; authorization of appropriations

(a) The participation of the United States as a member in the International Centre for the Study of the Preservation and Restoration of Cultural Property is hereby authorized.

(b) The Council shall recommend to the Secretary of State, after consultation with the Smithsonian Institution and other public and private organizations concerned with the technical problems of preservation, the members of the official delegation which will participate in the activities of the Centre on behalf of the United States. The Secretary of State shall appoint the members of the official delegation from the persons recommended to him by the Council.

(c) For the purposes of this section there is authorized to be appropriated an amount equal to the assessment for United States membership in the Centre for fiscal years 1979, 1980, 1981, and 1982: *Provided,* That no appropriation is authorized and no payment shall be made to the Centre in excess of 25 per centum of the total annual assessment of such organization. Authorization for payment of such assessments shall begin in fiscal year 1981, but shall include earlier costs.

§ 470o. Transfer of personnel, property, etc., by Department of Interior to Council; time limit

So much of the personnel, property, records, and unexpended balances of appropriations, allocations, and other funds employed, held, used, programed, or available or to be made available by the Department of the Interior in connection with the functions of the Council, as the Director of the Office of Management and Budget shall determine, shall be transferred from the Department to the Council within 60 days of the effective date of this Act.

§ 470p. Rights, benefits, and privileges of transferred employees

Any employee in the competitive service of the United States transferred to the Council under the provisions of this section shall retain all the rights, benefits, and privileges pertaining thereto held prior to such transfer.

§ 470q. Operations of Council; exemption

The Council is exempt from the provisions of the Federal Advisory Committee Act (86 Stat. 770), and the provisions of subchapter II of chapter 5 and chapter 7 of Title 5 shall govern the operations of the Council.

§ 470r. Transmittal of legislative recommendations, or testimony, or comments to President, Office of Management and Budget, and congressional committees; prohibition

No officer or agency of the United States shall have any authority to require the Council to submit its legislative recommendations, or testimony, or comments on legislation to any officer or agency of the United States for approval, comments, or review, prior to the submission of such recommendations, testimony, or comments to the Congress. In instances in which the Council voluntarily seeks to obtain the comments or review of any officer or agency of the United States, the Council shall include a description of such actions in its legislative recommendations, testimony, or comments on legislation which it transmits to the Congress.

§ 470s. Rules and regulations; participation by local governments

The Council is authorized to promulgate such rules and regulations as it deems necessary to govern the implementation of section 470f of this title. The Council shall, by regulation, establish such procedures as may be necessary to provide for participation by local governments in proceedings and other actions taken by the Council with respect to undertakings referred to in section 470f of this title which affect such local governments.

§ 470t. Budget; authorization of appropriations

(a) The council shall submit its budget annually as a related agency of the Department of the Interior. There are authorized to be appropriated up to $2,500,000 million in each fiscal year 1990 through 1994.

(b) Whenever the Council submits any budget estimate or request to the President or the Office of Management and Budget, it shall concurrently transmit copies of that estimate or request to the House and Senate Appropriations Committees and the House Committee on Interior and Insular Affairs and the Senate Committee on Energy and Natural Resources.

§ 470u. Report by Secretary to Council.

To assist the Council in discharging its responsibilities under sections 470 to 470a, 470b, and 470c to 470w-6 of this title, the Secretary at the request of the Chairman, shall provide a report to the Council detailing the significance of any historic property, describing the effects of any proposed undertaking on the affected property, and recommending measures to avoid, minimize, or mitigate adverse effects.
Pub. L. 89-665, Title II, § 213, as added Pub. L. 96-515, Title III, § 302 (a), Dec. 12, 1980, 94 Stat. 3000.

§ 470v. Exemption for Federal programs or undertakings; regulations

The Council, with the concurrence of the Secretary, shall promulgate regulations or guidelines, as appropriate, under which Federal programs or undertakings may be exempted from any or all of the requirements of sections 470 to 470a, 470b, and 470c to 470w-6 of this title when such exemption is determined to be consistent with the purposes of sections 470 to 470a, 470b, and 470c to 470w-6 of this title, taking into consideration the magnitude of the exempted undertaking or program and the likelihood of impairment of historic properties.
Pub.L. 89-665, Title II, § 214, as added Pub.L. 96-515, Title III, § 302 (a), Dec. 12, 1980, 94 Stat. 3000.

§ 470w. Definitions

As used in sections 470 to 470a, 470b, and 470c to 470w-6 of this title, the term—

(1) "Agency" means agency as such term is defined in section 551 of Title 5, except that in the case of any Federal program exempted under section 470v of this title, the agency administering such program shall not be treated as an agency with respect to such program.

(2) "State" means any State of the United States, the District of Columbia, the Commonwealth of Puerto Rico, Guam, the Virgin Islands, American Samoa, the Commonwealth of the Northern Mariana Islands, and the Trust Territories of the Pacific Islands.

(3) "Local government" means a city, county, parish, township, municipality, or borough, or any other general purpose political subdivision of any State.

(4) "Indian tribe" means the governing body of any Indian tribe, band, nation, or other group which is recognized as an Indian tribe by the Secretary of the Interior and for which the United States holds land in trust or restricted status for that entity or its members. Such term also includes any Native village corporation, regional corporation, and Native Group established pursuant to the Alaska Native Claims Settlement Act.

(5) "Historic property" or "historic resource" means any prehistoric or historic district, site, building, structure, or object included in, or eligible for inclusion on the National Register; such term includes artifacts, records, and remains which are related to such a district, site, building, structure, or object.

(6) "National Register" or "Register" means the National Register of Historic Places established under section 470a of this title.

(7) "Undertaking" means any action as described in section 470f of this title.

(8) "Preservation" or "historic preservation" includes identification, evaluation, recordation, documentation, curation, acquisition, protection, management, rehabilitation, restoration, stabilization, maintenance and reconstruction, or any combination of the foregoing activities.

(9) "Cultural park" means a definable urban area which is distinguished by historic resources and land related to such resources and which constitutes an interpretive, educational, and recreational resource for the public at large.

(10) "Historic conservation district" means an urban area of one or more neighborhoods and which contains (A) historic properties, (B) buildings having similar or related architectural characteristics, (C) cultural cohesiveness, or (D) any combination of the foregoing.

(11) "Secretary" means the Secretary of the Interior except where otherwise specified.

(12) "State historic preservation review board" means a board, council, commission, or other similar collegial body established as provided in section 470a (b) (1) (B) of this title—

>   (A) the members of which are appointed by the State Historic Preservation Officer (unless otherwise provided for by State law),
>
>   (B) a majority of the members of which are professionals qualified in the following and related disciplines: history, prehistoric and historic archaeology, architectural history, and architecture, and
>
>   (C) which has the authority to—
>
>> (i) review National Register nominations and appeals from nominations;
>>
>> (ii) review appropriate documentation submitted in conjunction with the Historic Preservation Fund;
>>
>> (iii) provide general advice and guidance to the State Historic Preservation Officer, and
>>
>> (iv) perform such other duties as may be appropriate.

(13) "Historic preservation review commission" means a board, council, commission, or other similar collegial body which is established by State or local legislation as provided in section 470a (c) (1) (B) of this title, and the members of which are appointed, unless otherwise provided by State or local legislation, by the chief elected official of the jurisdiction concerned from among—

>   (A) professionals in the disciplines of architecture, history, architectural history, planning, archaeology, or related disciplines, to the extent such professionals are available in the community concerned, and
>
>   (B) such other persons as have demonstrated special interest, experience, or knowledge in history, architecture, or related disciplines, and as will provide for an adequate and qualified commission.

§ 470w-1. Authorization for expenditure of appropriated funds

Where appropriate, each Federal agency is authorized to expend funds appropriated for its authorized programs for the purposes of activities carried out pursuant to sections 470 to 470a, 470b, and 470c to 470w-6 of this title, except to the extent appropriations legislation expressly provides otherwise.

§ 470w-2. Donations and bequests of money, personal property and less than fee interests in historic property

(a) The Secretary is authorized to accept donations and bequests of money and personal property for the purposes of sections 470 to 470a, 470b, and 470c to 470w-6 of this title and shall hold, use, expend, and administer the same for such purposes.

(b) The Secretary is authorized to accept gifts or donations of less than fee interests in any historic property where the acceptance of such interests will facilitate the conservation or preservation of such properties. Nothing in this section or in any provision of sections 470 to 470a, 470b, and 470c to 470w-6 of this title shall be construed to affect or impair any other authority of the Secretary under other provision of law to accept or acquire any property for conservation or preservation or for any other purposes.

§ 470w-3. Information relating to location or character of historic resources, disclosure to public

The head of any Federal agency, after consultation with the Secretary, shall withhold from disclosure to the public, information relating to the location or character of historic resources whenever the head of the agency or the Secretary determines that the disclosure of such information may create a substantial risk of harm, theft, or destruction to such resources or to the area or place where such resources are located.

§ 470w-4. Attorneys' fees and costs to prevailing parties in civil actions

In any civil action brought in any United States district court by any interested person to enforce the provisions of sections 470 to 470a, 470b, and 470c to 470w-6 of this title, if such person substantially prevails in such action, the court may award attorneys' fees, expert witness fees, and other costs of participating in such action, as the court deems reasonable.

§ 470w-5. National Museum for the Building Arts—Cooperative agreement between Secretary, Administrator of General Services Administration and Committee for National Museum of the Building Arts; purposes

(a) In order to provide a national center to commemorate and encourage the building arts and to preserve and maintain a nationally significant building which exemplifies the great achievements of the building arts in the United States, the Secretary and the Administrator of the General Services Administration are authorized and directed to enter into a cooperative agreement with the Committee for a National Museum of the Building Arts, Incorporated, a nonprofit corporation organized and existing under the laws of the District of Columbia, or its successor, for the operation of a National Museum for the Building Arts in the Federal Building located in the block bounded by Fourth Street, Fifth Street, F Street, and G Street, Northwest in Washington, District of Columbia. Such museum shall—

(1) collect and disseminate information concerning the building arts, including the establishment of a national reference center for current and historic documents, publications, and research relating to the building arts;

(2) foster educational programs relating to the history, practice and contribution to society of the building arts, including promotion of imaginative educational approaches to enhance understanding and appreciation of all facets of the building arts;

(3) publicly display temporary and permanent exhibits illustrating, interpreting and demonstrating the building arts;

(4) sponsor or conduct research and study into the history of the building arts and their role in shaping our civilization; and

(5) encourage contributions to the building arts.

Provisions of cooperative agreement

(b) The cooperative agreement referred to in subsection (a) of this section shall include provisions which—

(1) make the site available to the Committee referred to in subsection (a) of this section without charge;

(2) provide, subject to available appropriations, such maintenance, security, information, janitorial and other services as may be necessary to assure the preservation and operation of the site; and

(3) prescribe reasonable terms and conditions by which the Committee can fulfill its responsibilities under sections 470 to 470a, 470b, and 470c to 470w-6 of this title.

Matching grants-in-aid to Committee; limitation on amounts

(c) The Secretary is authorized and directed to provide matching grants-in-aid to the Committee referred to in subsection (a) of this section for its programs related to historic preservation. The Committee shall match such grants-in-aid in a manner and with such funds and services as shall be satisfactory to the Secretary, except that no more than $500,000 may be provided to the Committee in any one fiscal year.

Renovation of site

(d)   The renovation of the site shall be carried out by the Administrator with the advice of the Secretary. Such renovation shall, as far as practicable—
   (1)   be commenced immediately,
   (2)   preserve, enhance, and restore the distinctive and historically authentic architectural character of the site consistent with the needs of a national museum of the building arts and other compatible use, and
   (3)   retain the availability of the central court of the building, or portions thereof, for appropriate public activities.

Annual Committee report to Secretary and Administrator

(e)   The Committee shall submit an annual report to the Secretary and the Administrator concerning its activities under this section and shall provide the Secretary and the Administrator with such other information as the Secretary may, from time to time, deem necessary or advisable.

Definition of "building arts"

(f)   For purposes of this section, the term "building arts" includes, but shall not be limited to, all practical and scholarly aspects of prehistoric, historic, and contemporary architecture, archaeology, construction, building technology and skills, landscape architecture, preservation and conservation, building and construction, engineering, urban and community design and renewal, city and regional planning, and related professions, skills, and trades, and crafts.

§470w-6. Effective date of regulations—Copy to Congress prior to publication in Federal Register; effective date of final regulations

(a)   At least thirty days prior to publishing in the Federal Register any proposed regulation required by sections 470 to 470a, 470b, and 470c to 470w-6 of this title, the Secretary shall transmit a copy of the regulation to the Committee on Interior and Insular Affairs of the House of Representatives and the Committee on Energy and Natural Resources of the Senate. The Secretary also shall transmit to such committees a copy of any final regulation prior to its publication in the Federal Register. Except as provided in subsection (b) of this section, no final regulation of the Secretary shall become effective prior to the expiration of thirty calendar days after it is published in the Federal Register during which either or both Houses of Congress are in session.

Effective date of final regulation in case of emergency

(b)   In the case of an emergency, a final regulation of the Secretary may become effective without regard to the last sentence of subsection (a) of this section if the

Secretary notified in writing the Committee on Interior and Insular Affairs of the United States House of Representatives and the Committee on Energy and Natural Resources of the United States Senate setting forth the reasons why it is necessary to make the regulation effective prior to the expiration of the thirty-day period.

Disapproval of regulation by resolution of Congress

(c)   Except as provided in subsection (b) of this section, the regulation shall not become effective if, within ninety calendar days of continuous session of Congress after the date of promulgation, both Houses of Congress adopt a concurrent resolution, the matter after the resolving clause of which is as follows: "That Congress disapproves the regulation promulgated by the Secretary dealing with the matter of   , which regulation was transmitted to Congress on   ," the blank spaces therein being appropriately filled.

Failure of Congress to adopt resolution of disapproval of regulation

(d)   If at the end of sixty calendar days of continuous session of Congress after the date of promulgation of a regulation, no committee of either House of Congress has reported or been discharged from further consideration of a concurrent resolution disapproving the regulation, and neither House has adopted such a resolution, the regulation may go into effect immediately. If, within such sixty calendar days, such a committee has reported or been discharged from further consideration of such a resolution, the regulation may go into effect not sooner than ninety calendar days of continuous session of Congress after its promulgation unless disapproved as provided for.

Sessions of Congress

(e)   For the purposes of this section—
   (1)   continuity of session is broken only by an adjournment sine die; and
   (2)   the days on which either House is not in session because of an adjournment of more than three days to a day certain are excluded in the computation of sixty and ninety calendar days of continuous session of Congress.

Congressional inaction or rejection of resolution of disapproval not deemed approval of regulation

(f)   Congressional inaction on or rejection of a resolution of disapproval shall not be deemed an expression of approval of such regulation.

Appendix B

National Park Service, "Historic Preservation Certification," Final Rule, 36 C.F.R. Part 67

PART 67—HISTORIC PRESERVATION CERTIFICATIONS PURSUANT TO SEC. 48(g) AND SEC. 170(h) OF THE INTERNAL REVENUE CODE OF 1986

- § 67.1 Sec. 48(g) and Sec. 170(h) of the Internal Revenue Code of 1936.
- § 67.2 Definitions.
- § 67.3 Introduction to certifications of significance and rehabilitation and information collection.
- § 67.4 Certifications of historic significance.
- § 67.5 Standards for Evaluating Significance within Registered Historic Districts.
- § 67.6 Certifications of rehabilitation.
- § 67.7 Standards for Rehabilitation.
- § 67.8 Certifications of statutes.
- § 67.9 Certifications of state or local historic districts.
- § 67.10 Appeals.
- § 67.11 Fees for processing rehabilitation certification requests.

Authority: Sec. 101(a)(1) of the National Historic Preservation Act of 1966, 16 U.S.C. 470a-1(a)(170 ed.), as amended; Sec. 48(g) of the Internal Revenue Code of 1986 (90 Stat. 1519, as amended by 100 Stat. 2085) 26 U.S.C. 48(g); and Sec. 170(h) of the Internal Revenue Code of 1986 (94 Stat. 3204) 26 U.S.C. 170(h).

Source: 54 FR 6771, Feb. 26, 1990, unless otherwise noted.

§ 67.1 Sec. 48(g) and Sec. 170(h) of the Internal Revenue Code of 1986.

(a) Sec. 48(g) of the Internal Revenue Code of 1986, 90 Stat. 1519, as amended by 100 Stat. 2085, and Sec. 170(h) of the Internal Revenue Code of 1986, 94 Stat. 3204, require the Secretary to make certifications of historic district statutes and of State and local districts, certifications of significance, and certifications of rehabilitation in connection with certain tax incentives involving historic preservation. These certification responsibilities have been delegated to the National Park Service (NPS); the following five regional offices issue certifications for the States listed below them.

Alaska Regional Office, National Park Service, 2525 Gambell Street, Room 107, Anchorage, Alaska 99503:
Alaska

Mid-Atlantic Regional Office, National Park Service, U.S. Customs House, Second Floor, Second and Chestnut Streets, Philadelphia, Pennsylvania 19106:

Connecticut	New Jersey
Delaware	New York
District of Columbia	Ohio
Indiana	Pennsylvania
Maine	Rhode Island
Maryland	Vermont
Massachusetts	Virginia
Michigan	West Virginia
New Hampshire	

Rocky Mountain Regional Office, National Park Service, 12795 West Alameda Parkway, P.O. Box 25287, Denver, Colorado 80225:

Colorado	New Mexico
Illinois	North Dakota
Iowa	Oklahoma
Kansas	South Dakota
Minnesota	Texas
Missouri	Utah
Montana	Wisconsin
Nebraska	Wyoming

Southeast Regional Office, National Park Service, 75 Spring Street SW, Atlanta, Georgia 30303:

Alabama	Mississippi
Arkansas	North Carolina
Florida	Puerto Rico
Georgia	South Carolina
Kentucky	Tennessee
Louisiana	Virgin Islands

Western Regional Office, National Park Service, 450 Golden Gate Avenue, P.O. Box 36063, San Francisco, California 94102:

Arizona	Nevada
California	Oregon
Hawaii	Washington
Idaho	

(b) The Washington office of the NPS establishes program direction and considers appeals of certification denials. The procedures for obtaining certifications are set forth below. It is the responsibility of owners wishing certifications to provide sufficient documentation to the Secretary to make certification decisions. These procedures, upon their effective date, are applicable to future and pending certification requests, except as otherwise provided herein.

(c) States receiving Historic Preservation Fund grants from the Department participate in the review of requests for certification, through recommendations to the Secretary by the State Historic Preservation Officer (SHPO). The SHPO acts on behalf of the State in this capacity and, therefore, the NPS is not responsible for any actions, errors or omissions of the SHPO.

(1) Requests for certifications and approvals of proposed rehabilitation work are sent by an owner first to the appropriate SHPO for review. State comments are recorded on National Park Service Review Sheets (NPS Forms 10-168 (d) and (e)) and are carefully considered by the Secretary before a certification decision is made. Recommendations of States with approved State programs are generally followed, but by law, all certification decisions are made by the Secretary, based upon professional review of the application and related information. The decision of the Secretary may differ from the recommendation of the SHPO.

(2) A State may choose not to participate in the review of certification requests. States not wishing to participate in the comment process should notify the Secretary in writing of this fact. Owners from such nonparticipating States may request certifications by sending their applications directly to the appropriate NPS regional office listed above. In all other situations, certification requests are sent first to the appropriate SHPO.

(d) The Internal Revenue Service is responsible for all procedures, legal determinations, and rules and regulations concerning the tax consequences of the historic preservation provisions described in this part. Any certification made by the Secretary pursuant to this part shall not be considered as binding upon the Internal Revenue Service or the Secretary of the Treasury with respect to tax consequences under the Internal Revenue Code. For example, certifications made by the Secretary do not constitute determinations that a structure is of the type subject to the allowance for depreciation under section 167 of the Code.

§ 67.2 Definitions.

As used in these regulations:

Certified Historic Structure means a building (and its structural components) which is of a character subject to the allowance for depreciation provided in section 167 of the Internal Revenue Code of 1986 which is either:

(a) Individually listed in the National Register; or

(b) Located in a registered historic district and certified by the Secretary as being of historic significance to the district.

Portions of larger buildings, such as single condominium apartment units, are no [sic] independently considered certified historic structures. Rowhouses, even with abutting or party walls, are considered as separate buildings. For purposes of the certification decisions set forth in this part, a certified historic structure encompasses the historic building and its site, landscape features, and environment, generally referred to herein as a "property" as defined below. The

NPS decision on listing a property in the National Register of Historic Places, including boundary determinations, does not limit the scope of review of the rehabilitation project for tax certification purposes. Such review will include the entire historic property as it existed prior to rehabilitation and any related new construction. For purposes of the charitable contribution provisions only, a certified historic structure need not be depreciable to qualify; may be a structure other than a building; and may also be a remnant of a building such as a facade, if that is all that remains. For purposes of the other rehabilitation tax credits under section 48(g) of the Internal Revenue Code, any property located in a registered historic district is considered a certified historic structure so that other rehabilitation tax credits are not available; exemption from this provision can generally occur only if the Secretary has determined, prior to the rehabilitation of the property, that it is not of historic significance to the district.

Certified Rehabilitation means any rehabilitation of a certified historic structure which the Secretary has certified to the Secretary of the Treasury as being consistent with the historic character of the certified historic structure and, where applicable, with the district in which such structure is located.

Duly Authorized Representative means a State or locality's Chief Elected Official or his or her representative who is authorized to apply for certification of State/local statutes and historic districts.

Historic District means a geographically definable area, urban or rural, that possesses a significant concentration, linkage or continuity of sites, buildings, structures or objects united historically or aesthetically by plan or physical development. A district may also comprise individual elements separated geographically during the period of significance but linked by association or function.

Inspection means a visit by an authorized representative of the Secretary or a SHPO to a certified historic structure for the purposes of reviewing and evaluating the significance of the structure and the ongoing or completed rehabilitation work.

National Register of Historic Places means the National Register of districts, sites, buildings, structures, and objects significant in American history, architecture, archeology, engineering, and culture that the Secretary is authorized to expand and maintain pursuant to section 101(a)(1) of the National Historic Preservation Act of 1966, as amended. The procedures of the National Register appear in 36 CFR part 60 *et seq*.

Owner means a person, partnership, corporation, or public agency holding a fee-simple interest in a property or any other person or entity recognized by the Internal Revenue Code for purposes of the applicable tax benefits.

Property means a building and its site and landscape features.

Registered Historic District means any district listed in the National Register or any district which is:

(a) Designated under a State or local statute which has been certified by the Secretary as containing criteria which will substantially achieve the purpose of preserving and rehabilitating buildings of significance to the district, and

(b) Certified by the Secretary as meeting substantially all of the requirements for the listing of districts in the National Register.

Rehabilitation means the process of returning a building or buildings to a state of utility, through repair or alteration, which makes possible an efficient use while preserving those portions and features of the building and its site and environment which are significant to its historic, architectural, and cultural values as determined by the Secretary.

Secretary means the Secretary of the Interior or the designee authorized to carry out his responsibilities.

Standards for Rehabilitation means the Secretary's Standards for Rehabilitation set forth in section 67.7 hereof.

State Historic Preservation Officer means the official within each State designated by the Governor or a State statute to act as liaison for purposes of administering historic preservation programs within that State.

State or Local Statute means a law of a State or local government designating, or providing a method for the designation of, a historic district or districts.

§ 67.3 Introduction to certifications of significance and rehabilitation and information collection.

(a) Who may apply:

(1) Ordinarily, only the fee simple owner of the property in question may apply for the certifications described in §§ 67.4 and 67.6 hereof. If an application for an evaluation of significance or rehabilitation project is made by someone other than the fee simple owner, however, the application must be accompanied by a written statement from the fee simple owner indicating that he or she is aware of the application and has no objection to the request for certification.

(2) Upon request of a SHPO the Secretary may determine whether or not a particular property located within a registered historic district qualifies as a certified historic structure. The Secretary shall do so, however, only after notifying the fee simple owner of record of the request, informing such owner of the possible tax consequences of such a decision, and permitting the property owner a 30-day time period to submit written comments to the Secretary prior to decision. Such time period for comment may be waived by the fee simple owner.

(3) The Secretary may undertake the certifications described in §§ 67.4 and 67.6 on his own initiative after notifying the fee simple owner and the SHPO and allowing a comment period as specified in § 67.3(a)(2).

(4) Owners of properties which appear to meet National Register criteria but are [sic] yet listed in the National Register or which are located within potential historic districts may request preliminary determinations from the Secretary as to whether such properties may qualify as certified historic structures when and if the properties or the potential historic districts in which they are located are listed in the National Register. Preliminary determinations may also be requested for properties outside the period or area of significance of registered historic districts as specified in § 67.5(c). Procedures for obtaining these determinations shall be the same as those described in § 67.4. Such determinations are preliminary only and are not binding on the Secretary. Preliminary determinations of significance will become final as of the date of the listing of the individual property or district in the National Register. For properties outside the period or area of significance of a registered historic district, preliminary determinations of significance will become final, except as provided below, when the district documentation on file with the NPS is formally amended.

If during review of a request for certification of rehabilitation, it is determined that the property does not contribute to the significance of the district because of changes which occurred after the preliminary determination of significance was made, certified historic structure designation will be denied.

(5) Owners of properties not yet designated certified historic structures may obtain determinations from the Secretary on whether or not rehabilitation proposals meet the Secretary's Standards for Rehabilitation. Such determinations will be made only when the owner has requested a preliminary determination of the significance of the property as described in paragraph (a)(4) of this section and such request for determination has been acted upon by the NPS. Final certifications of rehabilitation will be issued only to owners of certified historic structures. Procedures for obtaining these determinations shall be the same as those described in sec. 67.6.

(b) How to apply:

(1) Requests for certifications of historic significance and of rehabilitation shall be made on Historic Preservation Certification Applications (NPS Form No. 10-168). Normally, two copies of the application are required; one to be retained by the SHPO and the other to be forwarded to the NPS. The information collection requirements contained in the application and in this part have been approved by the Office of Management and Budget under 44 U.S.C. 3507 and assigned clearance number 1024-0009. Part 1 of the application shall be used in requesting a certification of historic significance or nonsignificance and preliminary determinations, while part 2 of the application shall be used in requesting an evaluation of a proposed rehabilitation project or, in conjunction with a Request for Certification of Completed Work, a certification of a completed rehabilitation project. Information contained in the application is required to obtain a benefit. Public reporting burden for this form is estimated to average 2.5 hours per response including the time for reviewing instructions, gathering and maintaining data, and completing and reviewing the form. Direct comments regarding this burden estimate or any aspect of this form may be made to the Chief, Administrative Services Division, National Park Service, P.O. Box 37127, Washington, DC 20013-7127 and to the Office of Management and Budget, Paperwork Reduction Project Number 1024-0009, Washington, DC 20503.

(2) Application forms are available from NPS regional offices or the SHPOs.

(3) Requests for certifications, preliminary determinations, and approvals of proposed rehabilitation projects shall be sent to the SHPO in participating States. Requests in nonparticipating States shall be sent directly to the appropriate NPS regional office.

(4) Generally reviews of certification requests are concluded within 60 days of receipt of a complete, adequately documented application, as defined § 67.4 and § 67.6 (30 days at the State level and 30 days at the Federal level). Where a State has chosen not to participate in the review process, review by the NPS generally is concluded within 60 days of receipt of a complete, adequately documented application. Where adequate documentation is not provided, the owner will be notified of the additional information needed to undertake or complete review. The time periods in this part are based on the receipt of a complete application; they will be adhered to as closely as possible and are defined as calendar days. They are not, however, considered to be

mandatory, and the failure to complete review within the designated periods does not waive or alter any certification requirement.

(5) Approval of applications and amendments to applications is conveyed only in writing by duly authorized officials of the NPS acting on behalf of the Secretary. Decisions with respect to certifications are made on the basis of the descriptions contained in the application form and other available information. In the event of any discrepancy between the application form and other, supplementary material submitted with it (such as architectural plans, drawings, specifications, etc.), the applicant shall be requested to resolve the discrepancy in writing. In the event the discrepancy is not resolved, the description in the application form shall take precedence. Falsification of factual representations in the application is subject to criminal sanctions of up to $10,000 in fines or imprisonment for up to five years pursuant to 18 U.S.C. 1001.

(6) It is the owner's responsibility to notify the Secretary if application reviews are not completed within the time periods specified above. The Secretary in turn will consult with the appropriate office to ensure that the review is completed in as timely manner as possible in the circumstances.

(7) Although certifications of significance and rehabilitation are discussed separately below, owners must submit Part 1 of the Historic Preservation Certification Application prior to, or with, part 2. Part 2 of the application will not be processed until an adequately documented part 1 is on file and acted upon unless the property is already a certified historic structure. Reviews of rehabilitation projects will also not be undertaken if the owner has objected to the listing of the property in the National Register.

§ 67.4 Certifications of historic significance.

(a) Requests for certifications of historic significance should be made by the owner to determine—

(1) That a property located within a registered historic district is of historic significance to such district; or

(2) That a property located within a registered historic district is not of historic significance to such district; or

(3) That a property not yet on the National Register appears to meet National Register criteria; or

(4) That a property located within a potential historic district appears to contribute to the significance of such district.

(b) To determine whether or not a property is individually listed or is part of a district in the National Register, the owner may consult the listing of National Register properties in the Federal Register (found in most large libraries), or contact the appropriate SHPO for current information.

(c) If a property is located within the boundaries of a registered historic district and the owner wishes the Secretary to certify whether the property contributes or does not contribute to the historic significance of the district or if the owner is requesting a preliminary determination of significance in accordance with § 67.3(a)(4), the owner must complete part 1 of the Historic Preservation Certification Application according to instructions accompanying the application. Such documentation includes but is not limited to:

(1) Name and mailing address of owner;

(2) Name and address of property;

(3) Name of historic district;

(4) Current photographs of property; photographs of the building and its site and landscape features prior to alteration if rehabilitation has been completed; photograph(s) showing the property along with adjacent properties and structures on the street; and photographs of interior features and spaces adequate to document significance;

(5) Brief description of appearance including alterations, distinctive features and spaces, and date(s) of construction;

(6) Brief statement of significance summarizing how the property does or does not reflect the values that give the district its distinctive historical and visual character, and explaining any significance attached to the property itself (i.e., unusual building techniques, important event that took place there, etc.).

(7) Sketch map clearly delineating property's location within the district; and

(8) Signature of fee simple owner requesting or concurring in a request for evaluation.

(d) If a property is individually listed in the National Register, it is generally considered a certified historic structure and no further certification is required. More specific considerations in this regard are as follows:

(1) If the property is individually listed in the National Register and the owner believes it has lost the characteristics which caused it to be nominated and therefore wishes it delisted, the owner should refer to the delisting procedures outlined in 36 CFR part 60.

(2) Some properties individually listed in the National Register include more than one building. In such cases, the owner must submit a single part 1 application, as described in paragraph (c) of this section, which includes descriptions of all the buildings within the listing. The Secretary will utilize the Standards for Evaluating Significance within Registered Historic Districts (§ 67.5) for the purpose of determining which of the buildings included within the listing are of historic significance to the property. The requirements of this paragraph are applicable to certification requests received by the SHPOs (and the NPS regional offices in the case of nonparticipating States only) upon the effective date of these regulations.

(e) Properties containing more than one building where the buildings are judged by the Secretary to have been functionally related historically to serve an overall purpose, such as a mill complex or a residence and carriage house, will be treated as a single certified historic structure, whether the property is individually listed in the National Register or is located within a registered historic district, when rehabilitated as part of an overall project. Buildings that are functionally related historically are those which have functioned together to serve an overall purpose during the property's period of significance. In the case of a property within a registered historic district which contains more than one building where the buildings are judged to be functionally related historically, an evaluation will be made to determine whether the component buildings contribute to the historic significance of the property and whether the property contributes to the significance of the historic district as in § 67.4(i). For questions concerning demolition of separate structures as part of an overall rehabilitation project, see § 67.6.

(f) Applications for preliminary determinations for individual listing must show how the property individually meets the National Register Criteria for

Evaluation. An application for a property located in a potential historic district must document how the district meets the criteria and how the property contributes to the significance of that district. An application for a preliminary determination for a property in a registered historic district which is outside the period or area of significance in the district documentation on file with the NPS must document and justify the expanded significance of the district and how the property contributes to the significance of the district or document the individual significance of the property. Applications must contain substantially the same level of documentation as National Register nominations, as specified in 36 CFR part 60 and National Register Bulletin 16, "Guidelines for Completing National Register of Historic Places Forms" (available from SHPOs and NPS regional offices). Applications must also include written assurance from the SHPO that the district nomination is being revised to expand its significance or, for certified districts, written assurance from the duly authorized representative that the district documentation is being revised to expand its significance, or that the SHPO is planning to nominate the property or the district. Owners should understand that confirmation of intent to nominate by a SHPO does not constitute listing in the National Register, nor does it constitute a certification of significance as required by law for Federal tax incentives. Owners should further understand that they are proceeding at their own risk. If the property or district is not listed in the National Register for procedural, substantive or other reasons; if the district documentation is not formally amended; or if the significance of the property has been lost as a result of alterations or damage, these preliminary determinations of significance will not become final. The SHPO must nominate the property or the district or the SHPO for National Register districts and the duly authorized representative in the case of certified districts must submit documentation and have it approved by the NPS to amend the National Register nomination or certified district or the property or district must be listed before the preliminary certification of significance can become final.

(g) For purposes of the other rehabilitation tax credits under sec. 48(g) of the Internal Revenue Code, properties within registered historic districts are presumed to contribute to the significance of such districts unless certified as nonsignificant by the Secretary. Owners of nonhistoric properties within registered historic districts, therefore, must obtain a certification of nonsignificance in order to qualify for those investment tax credits. If an owner begins or completes a substantial alteration (within the meaning of sec. 167(n) of the Internal Revenue Code) of a property in a registered historic district without knowledge of requirements for certification of nonsignificance, he or she may request certification that the property was not of historic significance to the district prior to substantial alteration in the same manner as stated in sec. 67.4(c). The owner should be aware, however, of the requirements under sec. 48(g) of the Internal Revenue Code that the taxpayer must certify to the Secretary of the Treasury that, at the beginning of such substantial alteration, he or she in good faith was not aware of the certification requirement by the Secretary of the Interior.

(h) The Secretary discourages the moving of historic buildings from their original sites. However, if a building is to be moved as part of a rehabilitation for which certification is sought, the owner must follow different procedures depending on whether the building is individually listed in the National Register or is within a registered historic district. When a building is moved, every effort should be made to re-establish its historic orientation, immediate setting, and general environment. Moving a building may result in removal of the property from the National Register or, for buildings within a registered historic district, denial or revocation of a certification of significance; consequently, a moved building may, in certain circumstances, be ineligible for rehabilitation certification.

(1) Documentation must be submitted that demonstrates:

(i) The effect of the move on the building's integrity and appearance (any proposed demolition, proposed changes in foundations, etc.);

(ii) Photographs of the site and general environment of the proposed site;

(iii) Evidence that the proposed site does not possess historical significance that would be adversely affected by the moved building;

(iv) The effect of the move on the distinctive historical and visual character of the district, where applicable; and

(v) The method to be used for moving the building.

(2) For buildings individually listed in the National Register, the procedures contained in 36 CFR part 60 must be followed prior to the move, or the building will be removed from the National Register, will not be considered a certified historic structure, and will have to be renominated for listing. The owner may submit a part 1 application in order to receive a preliminary determination from the NPS of whether a move will cause the property to be removed from the National Register. However, preliminary approval of such a part 1 application does not satisfy the requirements of 36 CFR part 60. The SHPO must follow the remaining procedures in that regulation so that the NPS can determine that the moved building will remain listed in the National Register and retain its status as a certified historic structure.

(3) If an owner moves (or proposes to move) a building into a registered historic district or moves (or proposes to move) a building elsewhere within a registered historic district, a part 1 application containing the required information described in paragraph (h)(1) of this section must be submitted. The building to be moved will be evaluated to determine if it contributes to the historic significance of the district both before and after the move as in § 67.4(i).

(i) Properties within registered historic districts will be evaluated to determine if they contribute to the historic significance of the district by application of the Secretary's Standards for Evaluating Significance within Registered Historic Districts as set forth in § 67.5.

(j) Once the significance of a property located within a registered historic district or a potential historic district has been determined by the Secretary, written notification will be sent to the owner and the SHPO in the form of a certification of significance or nonsignificance.

(k) Owners shall report to the Secretary through the SHPO any substantial damage, alteration or changes to a property that occurs after issuance of a certification of significance and prior to a final certification of rehabilitation. The Secretary may withdraw a certification of significance, upon thirty days notice to the owner, if a property has been damaged, altered or changed effective as of the date of the occurrence. The property may also be removed from the National Register, in accordance with the procedures in 36 CFR part 60. A revocation of certification of significance pursuant to this part may be appealed under § 67.10. For damage, alteration or changes caused by unacceptable rehabilitation work, see § 67.6(f).

§ 67.5 Standards for Evaluating Significance within Registered Historic Districts.

(a) Properties located within registered historic districts are reviewed by the Secretary to determine if they contribute to the historic significance of the district by applying the following Standards for Evaluating Significance within Registered Historic Districts.

(1) A building contributing to the historic significance of a district is one which by location, design, setting, materials, workmanship, feeling and association adds to the district's sense of time and place and historical development.

(2) A building not contributing to the historic significance of a district is one which does not add to the district's sense of time and place and historical development; or one where the location, design, setting, materials, workmanship, feeling and association have been so altered or have so deteriorated that the overall integrity of the building has been irretrievably lost.

(3) Ordinarily buildings that have been built within the past 50 years shall not be considered to contribute to the significance of a district unless a strong justification concerning their historical or architectural merit is given or the historical attributes of the district are considered to be less than 50 years old.

(b) A condemnation order may be presented as evidence of physical deterioration of a building but will not of itself be considered sufficient evidence to warrant certification of nonsignificance for loss of integrity. In certain cases it may be necessary for the owner to submit a structural engineer's report to help substantiate physical deterioration and/or structural damage. Guidance on preparing a structural engineer's report is available from the appropriate SHPO or NPS regional office.

(c) Some properties listed in the National Register, primarily districts, are resources whose concentration or continuity possesses greater historical significance than many of their individual component buildings and structures. These usually are documented as a group rather than individually. Accordingly, this type of National Register documentation is not conclusive for the purposes of this part and must be supplemented with information on the significance of the specific property. Certifications of significance and nonsignificance will be made on the basis of the application documentation, existing National Register documentation, and other available information as needed. The Keeper may amend the National Register documentation by issuing a supplementary record if the application material warrants such an amendment. If a certification request is received for a property which is not yet listed on the National Register or which is outside a district's established period or area of significance, a preliminary determination of significance will be issued only if the request includes adequate documentation and if there is written assurance from the SHPO that the SHPO plans to nominate the property or district or that the district nomination in question is being revised to expand its significance or for certified districts, written assurance from the duly authorized representative that the district documentation is being revised to expand the significance. Certifications will become final when the property or district is listed or when the district documentation is officially amended unless the significance of the property has been lost as a result of alteration or damage. For procedures on amending listings to the National Register and additional information on the use of National Register documentation and the supplementary record which is contained in National

Register Bulletin 19, "Policies and Procedures for Processing National Register Nominations," consult the appropriate SHPO or NPS regional office.

(d) Where rehabilitation credits are sought, certifications of significance will be made on the appearance and condition of the property before rehabilitation was begun.

(e) If a nonhistoric surface material obscures a facade, it may be necessary for the owner to remove a portion of the surface material prior to requesting certification so that a determination of significance or nonsignificance can be made. After the material has been removed, if the obscured facade has retained substantial historic integrity and the property otherwise contributes to the historic district, it will be determined to be a certified historic structure. However, if the obscuring material remains when a determination of nonsignificance is requested under § 67.4(a)(2), the property will be presumed to contribute to the historic significance of the district, if otherwise qualified, and, therefore, not eligible for the other tax credits under section 48(g) of the Internal Revenue Code.

(f) Additional guidance on certifications of historic significance is available from SHPOs and NPS regional offices.

§ 67.6 Certifications of rehabilitation.

(a) Owners who want rehabilitation projects for certified historic structures to be certified by the Secretary as being consistent with the historic character of the structure, and, where applicable, the district in which the structure is located, thus qualifying as a certified rehabilitation, shall comply with the procedures listed below. A fee, as described in § 67.11, for reviewing all proposed, ongoing, or completed rehabilitation work is charged by the Secretary. No certification decisions will be issued on any application until the appropriate remittance is received.

(1) To initiate review of a rehabilitation project for certification purposes, an owner must complete part 2 of the Historic Preservation Certification Application according to instructions accompanying the application. These instructions explain in detail the documentation required for certification of a rehabilitation project. The application may describe a proposed rehabilitation project, a project in progress, or a completed project. In all cases, documentation, including photographs adequate to document the appearance of the structure(s), both on the exterior and on the interior, and its site and environment prior to rehabilitation must accompany the application. The social security or taxpayer identification number(s) of all owners must be provided in the application. Other documentation, such as window surveys or cleaning specifications, may be required by reviewing officials to evaluate certain rehabilitation projects. Plans for any attached, adjacent, or related new construction must also accompany the application. Where necessary documentation is not provided, review and evaluation may not be completed and a denial of certification will be issued on the basis of lack of information. Owners are strongly encouraged to submit part 2 of the application prior to undertaking any rehabilitation work. Owners who undertake rehabilitation projects without prior approval from the Secretary do so strictly at their own risk. Because the circumstances of each rehabilitation project are unique to the particular certified historic structure involved, certifications that may have been granted to other rehabilitations are not specifically applicable and may not be relied on by owners as applicable to other projects.

(2) A project does not become a certified rehabilitation until it is completed and so designated by the NPS. A determination that the completed rehabilitation of a property not yet designated a certified historic structure meets the Secretary's Standards for Rehabilitation does not constitute a certification of rehabilitation. When requesting certification of a completed rehabilitation project, the owner shall submit a Request for Certification of Completed Work (NPS Form 10-168c) and provide the project completion date and a signed statement that the completed rehabilitation project meets the Secretary's Standards for Rehabilitation and is consistent with the work described in part 2 of the Historic Preservation Certification Application. Also required in requesting certification of a completed rehabilitation project are costs attributed to the rehabilitation, photographs adequate to document the completed rehabilitation, and the social security or taxpayer identification number(s) of all owners.

(b) A rehabilitation project for certification purposes encompasses all work on the interior and exterior of the certified historic structure(s) and its site and environment, as determined by the Secretary, as well as related demolition, new construction or rehabilitation work which may affect the historic qualities, integrity or site, landscape features, and environment of the certified historic structure(s). More specific considerations in this regard are as follows:

(1) All elements of the rehabilitation project must meet the Secretary's ten Standards for Rehabilitation (§ 67.7); portions of the rehabilitation project not in conformance with the Standards may not be exempted. In general, an owner undertaking a rehabilitation project will not be held responsible for prior rehabilitation work not part of the current project, or rehabilitation work that was undertaken by previous owners or third parties.

(2) However, if the Secretary considers or has reason to consider that a project submitted for certification does not include the entire rehabilitation project subject to review hereunder, the Secretary may choose to deny a rehabilitation certification or to withhold a decision on such a certification until such time as the Internal Revenue Service, through a private letter ruling, has determined, pursuant to these regulations and applicable provisions of the Internal Revenue Code and income tax regulations, the proper scope of the rehabilitation project to be reviewed by the Secretary. Factors to be taken into account by the Secretary and the Internal Revenue Service in this regard include, but are not limited to, the facts and circumstance [sic] of each application and (i) whether previous demolition, construction or rehabilitation work irrespective of ownership or control at the time was in fact undertaken as part of the rehabilitation project for which certification is sought, and (ii) whether property conveyances, reconfigurations, ostensible ownership transfers or other transactions were transactions which purportedly limit the scope of a rehabilitation project for the purpose of review by the Secretary without substantially altering beneficial ownership or control of the property. The fact that a property may still qualify as a certified historic structure after having undergone inappropriate rehabilitation, construction or demolition work does not preclude the Secretary or the Internal Revenue Service from determining that such inappropriate work is part of the rehabilitation project to be reviewed by the Secretary.

(3) Conformance to the Standards will be determined on the basis of the application documentation and other available information by evaluating the property as it existed prior to the commencement of the rehabilitation project, regardless of when the property becomes or became a certified historic structure.

(4) For rehabilitation projects involving more than one certified historic structure where the structures are judged by the Secretary to have been functionally related historically to serve an overall purpose, such as a mill complex or a residence and carriage house, rehabilitation certification will be issued on the merits of the overall project rather than for each structure or individual component. For rehabilitation projects where there is no historic functional relationship among the structures, the certification decision will be made for each separate certified historic structure regardless of how they are grouped for ownership or development purposes.

(5) Demolition of a building as part of a rehabilitation project involving multiple buildings may result in denial of certification of the rehabilitation. In projects where there is no historic functional relationship among the structures being rehabilitated, related new construction which physically expands one certified historic structure undergoing rehabilitation and, therefore, directly causes the demolition of an adjacent structure will generally result in denial of certification of the rehabilitation unless a determination has been made that the building to be demolished is not a certified historic structure as in § 67.4(a). In rehabilitation projects where the structures have been determined to be functionally related historically, demolition of a component may be approved, in limited circumstances, when:

(i) The component is outside the period of significance of the property, or

(ii) The component is so deteriorated or altered that its integrity has been irretrievably lost; or

(iii) The component is a secondary one that generally lacks historic, engineering, or architectural significance or does not occupy a major portion of the site and persuasive evidence is present to show that retention of the component is not technically or economically feasible.

(6) In situations involving rehabilitation of a certified historic structure in a historic district, the Secretary will review the rehabilitation project first as it affects the certified historic structure and second as it affects the district and make a certification decision accordingly.

(7) In the event that an owner of a portion of a certified historic structure requests certification for a rehabilitation project related only to that portion, but there is or was a larger related rehabilitation project(s) occurring with respect to the certified historic structure, the Secretary's decision on the requested certification will be based on review of the overall rehabilitation project(s) for the certified historic structure.

(8) For rehabilitation projects which are to be completed in phases over the alternate 60-month period allowed in section 48(g) of the Internal Revenue Code, the initial part 2 application and supporting architectural plans and specifications should identify the project as a 60-month phased project and describe the number and order of the phases and the general scope of the overall rehabilitation project. If the initial part 2 application clearly identifies the project as a phased rehabilitation, the NPS will consider the project in all its phases as a single rehabilitation. If complete information on the rehabilitation work of the later phases is not described in the initial part 2 application, it may be submitted at a later date but must be clearly identified as a later phase of a 60-month phased project that was previously submitted for review. Owners are cautioned that work undertaken in a later phase of a 60-month phased project that does not meet the Standards for Rehabilitation, whether or not submitted for review, will result in a

denial of certification of the entire rehabilitation with the tax consequences of such a denial to be determined by the Secretary of the Treasury. Separate certifications for portions of phased rehabilitation projects will not be issued. Rather the owner will be directed to comply with Internal Revenue Service regulations governing late certifications contained in 26 CFR 1.48-12.

(c) Upon receipt of the complete application describing the rehabilitation project, the Secretary shall determine if the project is consistent with the Standards for Rehabilitation. If the project does not meet the Standards for Rehabilitation, the owner shall be advised of that fact in writing and, where possible, will be advised of necessary revisions to meet such Standards. For additional procedures regarding rehabilitation projects determined not to meet the Standards for Rehabilitation, see § 67.6(f).

(d) Once a proposed or ongoing project has been approved, substantive changes in the work as described in the application must be brought promptly to the attention of the Secretary by written statement through the SHPO to ensure continued conformance to the Standards; such changes should be made using a Historic Preservation Certification Application Continuation/Amendment Sheet (NPS Form 10-168b). The Secretary will notify the owner and the SHPO in writing whether the revised project continues to meet the Standards. Oral approvals of revisions are not authorized or valid.

(e) Completed projects may be inspected by an authorized representative of the Secretary to determine if the work meets the Standards for Rehabilitation. The Secretary reserves the right to make inspections at any time up to five years after completion of the rehabilitation and to revoke a certification, after giving the owner 30 days to comment on the matter, if it is determined that the rehabilitation project was not undertaken as represented by the owner in his or her application and supporting documentation, or the owner, upon obtaining certification, undertook further unapproved project work inconsistent with the Secretary's Standards for Rehabilitation. The tax consequences of a revocation of certification will be determined by the Secretary of the Treasury.

(f) If a proposed, ongoing, or completed rehabilitation project does not meet the Standards for Rehabilitation, an explanatory letter will be sent to the owner with a copy to the SHPO. A rehabilitated property not in conformance with the Standards for Rehabilitation and which is determined to have lost those qualities which caused it to be nominated to the National Register, will be removed from the National Register in accord with Department of the Interior regulations 36 CFR part 60. Similarly, if a property has lost those qualities which caused it to be designated a certified historic structure, it will be certified as noncontributing (see § 67.4 and § 67.5). In either case, the delisting or certification of nonsignificance is considered effective as of the date of issue and is not considered to be retroactive. In these situations, the Internal Revenue Service will be notified of the substantial alterations. The tax consequences of a denial of certification will be determined by the Secretary of the Treasury.

§ 67.7 Standards for Rehabilitation.

(a) The following Standards for Rehabilitation are the criteria used to determine if a rehabilitation project qualifies as a certified rehabilitation. The intent of the Standards is to assist the long-term preservation of a property's significance through the preservation of historic materials and features. The

Standards pertain to historic buildings of all materials, construction types, sizes, and occupancy and encompass the exterior and the interior of historic buildings. The Standards also encompass related landscape features and the building's site and environment, as well as attached, adjacent, or related new construction. To be certified, a rehabilitation project must be determined by the Secretary to be consistent with the historic character of the structure(s) and, where applicable, the district in which it is located.

(b) The following Standards are to be applied to specific rehabilitation projects in a reasonable manner, taking into consideration economic and technical feasibility. (The application of these Standards to rehabilitation projects is to be the same as under the previous version so that a project previously acceptable would continue to be acceptable under these Standards.)

(1) A property shall be used for its historic purpose or be placed in a new use that requires minimal change to the defining characteristics of the building and its site and environment.

(2) The historic character of a property shall be retained and preserved. The removal of historic materials or alteration of features and spaces that characterize a property shall be avoided.

(3) Each property shall be recognized as a physical record of its time, place, and use. Changes that create a false sense of historical development, such as adding conjectural features or architectural elements from other buildings, shall not be undertaken.

(4) Most properties change over time; those changes that have acquired historic significance in their own right shall be retained and preserved.

(5) Distinctive features, finishes, and construction techniques or examples of craftsmanship that characterize a historic property shall be preserved.

(6) Deteriorated historic features shall be repaired rather than replaced. Where the severity of deterioration requires replacement of a distinctive feature, the new feature shall match the old in design, color, texture, and other visual qualities and, where possible, materials. Replacement of missing features shall be substantiated by documentary, physical, or pictorial evidence.

(7) Chemical or physical treatments, such as sandblasting, that cause damage to historic materials shall not be used. The surface cleaning of structures, if appropriate, shall be undertaken using the gentlest means possible.

(8) Significant archeological resources affected by a project shall be protected and preserved. If such resources must be disturbed, mitigation measures shall be undertaken.

(9) New additions, exterior alterations, or related new construction shall not destroy historic materials that characterize the property. The new work shall be differentiated from the old and shall be compatible with the massing, size, scale, and architectural features to protect the historic integrity of the property and its environment.

(10) New additions and adjacent or related new construction shall be undertaken in such a manner that if removed in the future, the essential form and integrity of the historic property and its environment would be unimpaired.

(c) The quality of materials and craftsmanship used in a rehabilitation project must be commensurate with the quality of materials and craftsmanship of the historic building in question. Certain treatments, if improperly applied, or certain materials by their physical properties, may cause or accelerate physical deterioration of historic buildings. Inappropriate physical treatments include, but are not limited to: improper repointing techniques; improper exterior masonry cleaning methods; or improper introduction of insulation where damage to historic fabric would result. In almost all situations, use of these materials and treatments will result in denial of certification. Similarly, exterior additions that duplicate the form, material, and detailing of the structure to the extent that they compromise the historic character of the structure will result in denial of certification. For further information on appropriate and inappropriate rehabilitation treatments, owners are to consult the Guidelines for Rehabilitating Historic Buildings published by the NPS. "Preservation Briefs" and additional technical information to help property owners formulate plans for the rehabilitation, preservation, and continued use of historic properties consistent with the intent of the Secretary's Standards for Rehabilitation are available from the SHPOs and NPS regional offices. Owners are responsible for procuring this material as part of property planning for a certified rehabilitation.

(d) In certain limited cases, it may be necessary to dismantle and rebuild portions of a certified historic structure to stabilize and repair weakened structural members and systems. In such cases, the Secretary will consider such extreme intervention as part of a certified rehabilitation if:

(1) The necessity for dismantling is justified in supporting documentation;

(2) Significant architectural features and overall design are retained; and

(3) Adequate historic materials are retained to maintain the architectural and historic integrity of the overall structure.

Section 48(g) of the Internal Revenue Code of 1986 exempts certified historic structures from meeting the physical test for retention of external walls and internal structural framework specified therein for other rehabilitated buildings. Nevertheless, owners are cautioned that the Standards for Rehabilitation require retention of distinguishing historic materials of external and internal walls as well as structural systems. In limited instances, rehabilitations involving removal of existing external walls, i.e., external walls that detract from the historic character of the structure such as in the case of a nonsignificant later addition or walls that have lost their structural integrity due to deterioration, may be certified as meeting the Standards for Rehabilitation.

(e) Prior approval of a project by Federal, State, and local agencies and organizations does not ensure certification by the Secretary for Federal tax purposes. The Secretary's Standards for Rehabilitation take precedence over other regulations and codes in determining whether the rehabilitation project is consistent with the historic character of the property and, where applicable, the district in which it is located.

(f) The qualities of a property and its environment which qualify it as a certified historic structure are determined taking into account all available information, including information derived from the physical and architectural attributes of the building; such determinations are not limited to information contained in National Register or related documentation.

§ 67.8 Certifications of statutes.

(a) *State or local statutes which will be certified by the Secretary.* For the purpose of this regulation, a State or local statute is a law of the State or local government designating, or providing a method for the designation of, a historic district or districts. This includes any by-laws or ordinances that contain information necessary for the certification of the statute. A statute must contain criteria which will substantially achieve the purpose of preserving and rehabilitating properties of historic significance to the district. To be certified by the Secretary, the statute generally must provide for a duly designated review body, such as a review board or commission, with power to review proposed alterations to structures of historic significance within the boundaries of the district or districts designated under the statute except those owned by governmental entities which, by law, are not under the jurisdiction of the review body.

(b) When the certification of State statutes will have an impact on districts in specific localities, the Secretary encourages State governments to notify and consult with appropriate local officials prior to submitting a request for certification of the statute.

(c) State enabling legislation which authorizes local governments to designate, or provides local governments with a method to designate, a historic district or districts will not be certified unless accompanied by local statutes that implement the purposes of the State law. Adequate State statutes which designate specific historic districts and do not require specific implementing local statutes will be certified. If the State enabling legislation contains provisions which do not meet the intent of the law, local statutes designated under the authority of the enabling legislation will not be certified. When State enabling legislation exists, it must be certified before any local statutes enacted under its authority can be certified.

(d) Who may apply. Requests for certification of State or local statutes may be made only by the Chief Elected Official of the government which enacted the statute or his or her authorized representative. The applicant shall certify in writing that he or she is authorized by the appropriate State or local governing body to apply for certification.

(e) Statute certification process. Requests for certification of State or local statutes shall be made as follows:

(1) The request shall be made in writing from the duly authorized representative certifying that he or she is authorized to apply for certification. The request should include the name or title of a person to contact for further information and his or her address and telephone number. The authorized representative is responsible for providing historic district documentation for review and certification prior to the first certification of significance in a district unless another responsible person is indicated including his or her address and telephone number. The request shall also include a copy of the statute(s) for which certification is requested, including any by-laws or ordinances that contain information necessary for the certification of the statute. Local governments shall also submit a copy of the State enabling legislation, if any, authorizing the designation of historic districts.

(2) Requests shall be sent to the SHPO in participating States and directly to appropriate NPS regional offices in nonparticipating States.

(3) The Secretary shall review the statute(s) and assess whether the statute(s) and any by-laws or ordinances that contain information necessary for the certification of the statute contain criteria which will substantially achieve the purposes of preserving and rehabilitating properties of historic significance to the district(s) based upon the standards set out above in § 67.8(a). The SHPO

shall be given a 30-day opportunity to comment upon the request. Comments received from the SHPO within this time period will be considered by the Secretary in the review process. If the statute(s) contain such provisions and if this and other provisions in the statute will substantially achieve the purpose of preserving and rehabilitating properties of historic significance to the district, the Secretary will certify the statute(s).

(4) The Secretary generally provides written notification within 30 days of receipt by the NPS to the duly authorized representative and to the SHPO when certification of the statute is given or denied. If certification is denied, the notification will provide an explanation of the reason(s) for such denial.

(f) Amendment or repeal of statute(s). State or local governments, as appropriate, must notify the Secretary in the event that certified statutes are repealed, whereupon the certification of the statute (and any districts designated thereunder) will be withdrawn by the Secretary. If a certified statute is amended, the duly authorized representative shall submit the amendment(s) to the Secretary, with a copy to the SHPO, for review in accordance with the procedures outlined above. Written notification of the Secretary's decision as to whether the amended statute continues to meet these criteria will be sent to the duly authorized representative and the SHPO within 60 days of receipt.

(g) The Secretary may withdraw certification of a statute (and any districts designated thereunder) on his own initiative if it is repeal or amended to be inconsistent with certification requirements after providing the duly authorized representative and the SHPO 30 days in which to comment prior to the withdrawal of certification.

§ 67.9 Certifications of state or local historic districts.

(a) The particular State or local historic district must also be certified by the Secretary as substantially meeting National Register criteria, thereby qualifying it as a registered historic district, before the Secretary will process requests for certification of individual properties within a district or districts established under a certified statute.

(b) The provision described herein will not apply to properties within a State or local district until the district has been certified, even if the statute creating the district has been certified by the Secretary.

(c) The Secretary considers the duly authorized representative requesting certification of a statute to be the official responsible for submitting district documentation for certification. If another person is to assume responsibility for the district documentation, the letter requesting statute certification shall indicate that person's name, address, and telephone number. The Secretary considers the authorizing statement of the duly authorized representative to indicate that the jurisdiction involved wishes not only that the statute in question be certified but also wishes all historic districts designated by the statute to be certified unless otherwise indicated.

(d) Requests shall be sent to the SHPO in participating States and directly to the appropriate NPS regional office in nonparticipating States. The SHPO shall be given a 30-day opportunity to comment upon an adequately documented request. Comments received from the SHPO within this time period will be considered by the Secretary in the review process. The guidelines in National Register Bulletin 16, "Guidelines for Completing National Register of Historic Places Forms," provide information on how to document historic districts for the National Register. Each request should include the following documentation:

(1) A description of the general physical or historical qualities which make this a district; and [sic] explanation for the choice of boundaries for the district; descriptions of typical architectural styles and types of buildings in the district.

(2) A concise statement of why the district has significance, including an explanation of the areas and periods of significance, and why it meets National Register criteria for listing (see 36 CFR part 60); the relevant criteria should be identified (A, B, C, and D).

(3) A definition of what types of properties contribute and do not contribute to the significance of the district as well as an estimate of the percentage of properties within the district that do not contribute to its significance.

(4) A map showing all district properties with, if possible, identification of contributing and noncontributing properties; the map should clearly show the district's boundaries.

(5) Photographs of typical areas in the district as well as major types of contributing and noncontributing properties; all photographs should be keyed to the map.

(e) Districts designated by certified State or local statutes shall be evaluated using the National Register criteria (36 CFR part 60) within 30 days of the receipt of the required documentation by the Secretary. Written notification of the Secretary's decision will be sent to the duly authorized representative or to the person designated as responsible for the district documentation.

(f) Certification of statutes and districts does not constitute certification of significance of individual properties within the district or of rehabilitation projects by the Secretary.

(g) Districts certified by the Secretary as substantially meeting the requirements for listing will be determined eligible for listing in the National Register at the time time [sic] of certification and will be published as such in the Federal Register.

(h) Documentation on additional districts designated under a State or local statute the [sic] has been certified by the secretary should be submitted to the secretary for certification following the same procedures and including the same information outlined in the section above.

(i) State or local governments, as appropriate, shall notify the Secretary if the certified district designation is amended (including boundary changes) or repealed. If a certified district designation is amended, the duly authorized representative shall submit documentation describing the change(s) and, if the district has been increased in size, information on the new areas as outlined in § 67.9. A revised statement of significance for the district as a whole shall also be included to reflect any changes in overall significance as a result of the addition or deletion of areas. Review procedures shall follow those outlined in § 67.9 (d) and (e). The Secretary will withdraw certification of repealed or inappropriately amended certified district designations, thereby disqualifying them as registered historic districts.

(j) The Secretary may withdraw certification of a district on his own initiative if it ceases to meet the National Register Criteria for Evaluation after providing the duly authorized representative and the SHPO 30 days in which to comment prior to withdrawal of certification.

(k) The Secretary urges State and local review boards of commissions to become familiar with the Standards used by the Secretary of the Interior for certifying the rehabilitation of historic properties and to consider their adoption for local design review.

§ 67.10 Appeals.

(a) An appeal by the owner, or duly authorized representative as appropriate, may be made from any of the certifications or denials of certification made pursuant to this part or any decisions made pursuant to § 67.6(f). Such appeals must be in writing and received by the Chief Appeals Officer, Cultural Resources, National Park Service, U.S. Department of the Interior, P.O. Box 37127, Washington, DC 20013-7127, within 30 days of receipt of the decision which is the subject of the appeal. The appellant may request an opportunity for a meeting to discuss the appeal but all information the owner wishes the Chief Appeals Officer to consider must be submitted in writing. The SHPO will be notified that an appeal is pending. The Chief Appeals Officer will consider the record of the decision in question, any further written submissions by the owner, and other available information and shall provide the appellant a written decision as promptly as circumstances permit. Such appeals constitute an administrative review of the decision appealed from and are not conducted as an adjudicative proceeding.

(b) The denial of a preliminary determination of significance for an individual property may not be appealed by the owner because the denial itself does not exhaust the administrative remedy that is available. The owner instead must seek recourse by undertaking the usual nomination process (36 CFR part 60). Similarly, the denial of preliminary certification for a rehabilitation for a rehabilitation [sic] project for a property that is not a certified historic structure may not be appealed. The owner must seek a final certification of significance as the next step, rather than appealing the denial of rehabilitation certification. Administrative reviews in these circumstances may be performed at the discretion of the Chief Appeals Officer. The decision to undertaken [sic] an administrative review will be made on a case-by-case basis, depending on particular facts and circumstances and the Chief Appeals Officer's schedule, the expected date for nomination, and the nature of the rehabilitation project (proposed, ongoing, or completed). Administrative reviews of rehabilitation projects will not be undertaken if the owner has objected to the listing of the property in the National Register.

(c) In considering such appeals or administrative reviews, the Chief Appeals Officer shall take in account alleged errors in professional judgment or alleged prejudicial procedural errors by NPS officials. The Chief Appeals Officer's decision may:

(1) Reverse the appealed decision;

(2) Affirm the appealed decision;

(3) Resubmit the matter to the appropriate Regional Director for further consideration; or

(4) Where appropriate, withhold a decision until issuance of a ruling from the Internal Revenue Service pursuant to § 67.6(b)(2).

The Chief Appeals Officer may base his decision in whole or part on matters or factors not discussed in the decision appealed from. The Chief Appeals Officer is authorized to issue the certifications discussed in this part only if he considers that the requested certification meets the applicable statutory standard upon application of the Standards set forth herein or he considers that prejudicial procedural error by a Federal official legally compels issuance of the requested certification.

(d) The decision of the Chief Appeals Officer shall be the final administrative decision on the appeal. No person shall be considered to have exhausted his or her administrative remedies with respect to the certifications or decisions described in this part until the Chief Appeals Officer has issued a final administrative decision pursuant to this section.

§ 67.11 Fees for processing rehabilitation certification requests.

(a) Fees are charged for reviewing rehabilitation certification requests in accordance with the schedule below.

(b) Payment shall not be made until requested by the NPS regional office according to instructions accompanying the Historic Preservation Certification Application. All checks shall be made payable to: *National Park Services*. A certification decision will not be issued on an application until the appropriate remittance is received. Fees are nonrefundable.

(c) The fee for review of proposed or ongoing rehabilitation projects for projects over $20,000 is $250. The fees for review of completed rehabilitation projects are based on the dollar amount of the costs attributed solely to the rehabilitation of the certified historic structure as provided by the owner in the Historic Preservation Certification Application, Request for Certification of Completed Work (NPS Form 10-168c), as follows:

Fee	Size of Rehabilitation
$1,500	20,000 to $99,999
$1,800	100,000 to $499,999
$1,500	500,000 to $999,999
$2,500	1,000,000 or more

If review of a proposed or ongoing rehabilitation project had been undertaken by the Secretary prior to submission of Request for Certification of Completed Work, the initial fee of $250 will be deducted from these fees. No fee will be charged for rehabilitations under $20,000.

(d) In general, each rehabilitation of a separate certified historic structure will be considered a separate project for purposes of computing the size of the fee.

(1) In the case of a rehabilitation project which includes more than one certified historic structure where the structures are judged by the Secretary to

have been functionally related historically to serve an overall purpose, the fee for preliminary review is $250 and the fee for final review is computed on the basis of the total rehabilitation costs.

    (2)   In the case of multiple building projects where there is no historic functional relationship amont [sic] the structures and which are under the same ownership; are located in the same historic district; are adjacent or contiguous; are of the same architectural type (e.g., rowhouses, loft buildings, commercial buildings); and are submitted by the owner for review at the same time, the fee for preliminary review is $250 per structure to a maximum of $2,500 and the fee for final review is computed on the basis of the total rehabilitation costs of the entire multiple building project to a maximum of $2,500. If the $2,500 maximum fee was paid at the time of review of the proposed or ongoing rehabilitation project, no further fee will be charged for review of a Request for Certification of Completed Work.

Appendix C

National Park Service, Historic Preservation Certification Application Form

Application forms and instructions may be obtained by contacting the Preservation Assistance Division, National Park Service, P.O. Box 37127, Washington, D.C. 20013-7127, at (202) 343-9573.

Rehabilitating Older and Historic Buildings

350

Form 10-168
Rev. 12/90

UNITED STATES DEPARTMENT OF THE INTERIOR
NATIONAL PARK SERVICE

OMB Approved
No. 1024-0009

HISTORIC PRESERVATION CERTIFICATION APPLICATION
PART 1 — EVALUATION OF SIGNIFICANCE

NPS Office Use Only
NRIS No: _____

NPS Office Use Only
Project No: _____

Instructions: Read the instructions carefully before completing application. No certification will be made unless a completed application form has been received. Type or print clearly in black ink. If additional space is needed, use continuation sheets or attach blank sheets.

1. Name of property: _____

    Address of property: Street _____

    City _____ County _____ State _____ Zip _____

    Name of historic district: _____

    ☐ National Register district   ☐ certified state or local district   ☐ potential historic district

2. Check nature of request:

    ☐ certification that the building contributes to the significance of the above-named historic district (or National Register property) for the purpose of rehabilitation.
    ☐ certification that the structure or building and, where appropriate, the land area on which such a structure or building is located contributes to the significance of the above-named historic district for a charitable contribution for conservation purposes.
    ☐ certification that the building does not contribute to the significance of the above-named district.
    ☐ preliminary determination for individual listing in the National Register.
    ☐ preliminary determination that a building located within a potential historic district contributes to the significance of the district.
    ☐ preliminary determination that a building outside the period or area of significance contributes to the significance of the district.

3. Project contact:

    Name _____

    Street _____ City _____

    State _____ Zip _____ Daytime Telephone Number _____

4. Owner:

    I hereby attest that the information I have provided is, to the best of my knowledge, correct, and that I own the property described above. I understand that falsification of factual representations in this application is subject to criminal sanctions of up to $10,000 in fines or imprisonment for up to five years pursuant to 18 U.S.C. 1001.

    Name _____ Signature _____ Date _____

    Organization _____

    Social Security or Taxpayer Identification Number _____

    Street _____ City _____

    State _____ Zip _____ Daytime Telephone Number _____

NPS Office Use Only

The National Park Service has reviewed the "Historic Preservation Certification Application — Part 1" for the above-named property and hereby determines that the property:

☐ contributes to the significance of the above-named district (or National Register property) and is a "certified historic structure" for the purpose of rehabilitation.
☐ contributes to the significance of the above-named district and is a "certified historic structure" for a charitable contribution for conservation purposes in accordance with the Tax Treatment Extension Act of 1980.
☐ does not contribute to the significance of the above-named district.

Preliminary Determinations:

☐ appears to meet the National Register Criteria for Evaluation and will likely be listed in the National Register of Historic Places if nominated by the State Historic Preservation Officer according to the procedures set forth in 36 CFR Part 60.
☐ does not appear to meet the National Register Criteria for Evaluation and will likely not be listed in the National Register.
☐ appears to contribute to the significance of a potential historic district, which will likely be listed in the National Register of Historic Places if nominated by the State Historic Preservation Officer.
☐ appears to contribute to the significance of a registered historic district but is outside the period or area of significance as documented in the National Register nomination or district documentation on file with the NPS.
☐ does not appear to qualify as a certified historic structure.

Date _____ National Park Service Authorized Signature _____ National Park Service Office/Telephone No: _____

☐ See Attachments

Appendix C

HISTORIC PRESERVATION CERTIFICATION APPLICATION—PART 1

NPS Office Use Only

Property Name: _____

Project Number: _____

Property Address: _____

5. Description of physical appearance:

Date of Construction: _____ Source of Date: _____

Date(s) of Alteration(s): _____

Has building been moved? ☐ yes ☐ no. If so, when? _____

6. Statement of significance:

7. Photographs and maps.

Attach photographs and maps to application.

Continuation sheets attached: ☐ yes ☐ no

Rehabilitating Older and Historic Buildings 352

Form 10-168a
Rev. 12/90

UNITED STATES DEPARTMENT OF THE INTERIOR
NATIONAL PARK SERVICE

OMB Approved
No. 1024-0009

HISTORIC PRESERVATION CERTIFICATION APPLICATION
PART 2 — DESCRIPTION OF REHABILITATION

NPS Office Use Only

NRIS No: _____

NPS Office Use Only

Project No: _____

Instructions: Read the instructions carefully before completing application. No certification will be made unless a completed application form has been received. Type or print clearly in black ink. If additional space is needed, use continuation sheets or attach blank sheets. A copy of this form may be provided to the Internal Revenue Service. The decision by the National Park Service with respect to certification is made on the basis of the descriptions in this application form. In the event of any discrepancy between the application form and other, supplementary material submitted with it (such as architectural plans, drawings and specifications), the application form shall take precedence.

1. **Name of property:** _____

   Address of property: Street _____

   City _____ County _____ State _____ Zip _____

   ☐ Listed individually in the National Register of Historic Places; give date of listing: _____

   ☐ Located in a Registered Historic District; specify: _____

   Has a Part 1 Application (Evaluation of Significance) been submitted for this project? ☐ yes ☐ no

   If yes, date Part 1 submitted: _____ Date of certification: _____ NPS Project Number: _____

2. **Data on building and rehabilitation project:**

   Date building constructed: _____   Total number of housing units before rehabilitation _____

   Type of construction: _____   Number that are low-moderate income: _____

   Use(s) before rehabilitation: _____   Total number of housing units after rehabilitation: _____

   Proposed use(s) after rehabilitation: _____   Number that are low-moderate income: _____

   Estimated cost of rehabilitation: _____   Floor area before rehabilitation: _____

   This application covers phase number _____ of _____ phases   Floor area after rehabilitation: _____

   Project/phase start date (est.): _____   Completion date (est.) _____

3. **Project contact:**

   Name _____

   Street _____ City _____

   State _____ Zip _____ Daytime Telephone Number _____

4. **Owner:**

   I hereby attest that the information I have provided is, to the best of my knowledge, correct, and that I own the property described above. I understand that falsification of factual representations in this application is subject to criminal sanctions of up to $10,000 in fines or imprisonment for up to five years pursuant to 18 U.S.C.1001.

   Name _____ Signature _____ Date _____

   Organization _____

   Social Security or Taxpayer Identification Number _____

   Street _____ City _____

   State _____ Zip _____ Daytime Telephone Number _____

NPS Office Use Only

The National Park Service has reviewed the "Historic Certification Application — Part 2" for the above-named property and has determined:

☐ that the rehabilitation described herein is consistent with the historic character of the property or the district in which it is located and that the project meets the Secretary of the Interior's "Standards for Rehabilitation." This letter is a preliminary determination only, since a formal certification of rehabilitation can be issued only to the owner of a "certified historic structure" after rehabilitation work is completed.

☐ that the rehabilitation or proposed rehabilitation will meet the Secretary of the Interior's "Standards for Rehabilitation" if the attached conditions are met.

☐ that the rehabilitation or proposed rehabilitation is not consistent with the historic character of the property or the district in which it is located and that the project does not meet the Secretary of the Interior's "Standards for Rehabilitation." A copy of this form will be provided to the Internal Revenue Service.

Date _____   National Park Service Authorized Signature _____   National Park Service Office/Telephone No. _____

☐ See Attachments

Appendix C

**HISTORIC PRESERVATION
CERTIFICATION APPLICATION—
PART 2**

NPS Office Use Only

Property Name _____

Project Number: _____

Property Address _____

5. DETAILED DESCRIPTION OF REHABILITATION/PRESERVATION WORK—Includes site work, new construction, alterations, etc. Complete blocks below.

| NUMBER 1 | Architectural feature _____ | Describe work and impact on existing feature: |

Approximate date of feature _____

Describe existing feature and its condition:

Photo no. _____ Drawing no. _____

| NUMBER 2 | Architectural feature _____ | Describe work and impact on existing feature: |

Approximate date of feature _____

Describe existing feature and its condition:

Photo no. _____ Drawing no. _____

| NUMBER 3 | Architectural feature _____ | Describe work and impact on existing feature: |

Approximate date of feature _____

Describe existing feature and its condition:

Photo no. _____ Drawing no. _____

| NUMBER 4 | Architectural feature _____ | Describe work and impact on existing feature: |

Approximate date of feature _____

Describe existing feature and its condition:

Photo no. _____ Drawing no. _____

Rehabilitating Older and Historic Buildings

354

Form 10-168c
Rev. 12/90

UNITED STATES DEPARTMENT OF THE INTERIOR
NATIONAL PARK SERVICE

OMB Approval
No. 1024-0009

HISTORIC PRESERVATION CERTIFICATION APPLICATION
REQUEST FOR CERTIFICATION OF COMPLETED WORK

NPS Office Use Only:

NRIS No: _____

Instructions: Upon completion of the rehabilitation, return this form with representative photographs of the completed work (both exterior and interior views) to the appropriate reviewing office. If a Part 2 application has not been submitted in advance of project completion, it must accompany this Request for Certification of Completed Work. A copy of this form will be provided to the Internal Revenue Service. Type or print clearly in black ink. The decision by the National Park Service with respect to certification is made on the basis of the descriptions in this application form. In the event of any discrepancy between the application form and other, supplementary material submitted with it (such as architectural plans, drawings and specifications), the application form shall take precedence.

1. Name of property: _____

   Address of property: Street _____

   City _____ County _____ State _____ Zip _____

   Is property a certified historic structure? ☐ yes ☐ no   If yes, date of certification by NPS: _____

   or date of listing in the National Register: _____

2. **Data on rehabilitation project:**

   National Park Service assigned rehabilitation project number: _____

   Project starting date: _____

   Rehabilitation work on this property was completed and the building placed in service on: _____

   Estimated costs attributed solely to the rehabilitation of the historic structure: $ _____

   Estimated costs attributed to new construction associated with the
   rehabilitation, including additions, site work, parking lots, landscaping: $ _____

3. **Owner:** (space on reverse for additional owners)

   I hereby apply for certification of rehabilitation work described above for purposes of the Federal tax incentives. I hereby attest that the information provided is, to the best of my knowledge, correct, and that in my opinion the completed rehabilitation meets the Secretary's "Standards for Rehabilitation" and is consistent with the work described in Part 2 of the Historic Preservation Certification Application. I also attest that I own the property described above. I understand that falsification of factual representations in this application is subject to criminal sanctions of up to $10,000 in fines or imprisonment for up to five years pursuant to 18 U.S.C. 1001.

   Name _____ Signature _____ Date _____

   Organization _____

   Social Security or Taxpayer Identification Number _____

   Street _____ City _____

   State _____ Zip _____ Daytime Telephone Number _____

NPS Office Use Only

The National Park Service has reviewed the "Historic Preservation Certification Application — Part 2" for the above-listed "certified historic structure" and has determined:

☐ that the completed rehabilitation meets the Secretary of the Interior's "Standards for Rehabilitation" and is consistent with the historic character of the property or the district in which it is located. Effective the date indicated below, the rehabilitation of the "certified historic structure" is hereby designated a "certified rehabilitation." A copy of this certification has been provided to the Department of the Treasury in accordance with Federal law. This letter of certification is to be used in conjunction with appropriate Internal Revenue Service regulations. Questions concerning specific tax consequences or interpretations of the Internal Revenue Code should be addressed to the appropriate local Internal Revenue Service office. Completed projects may be inspected by an authorized representative of the Secretary to determine if the work meets the "Standards for Rehabilitation." The Secretary reserves the right to make inspections at any time up to five years after completion of the rehabilitation and to revoke certification, if it is determined that the rehabilitation project was not undertaken as presented by the owner in the application form and supporting documentation, or the owner, upon obtaining certification, undertook unapproved further alterations as part of the rehabilitation project inconsistent with the Secretary's "Standards for Rehabilitation."

☐ that the rehabilitation is not consistent with the historic character of the property or the district in which it is located and that the project does not meet the Secretary of the Interior's "Standards for Rehabilitation." A copy of this form will be provided to the Internal Revenue Service.

Date _____   National Park Service Authorized Signature _____   National Park Service Office/Telephone No. _____

☐ See Attachments

Appendix C

REQUEST FOR CERTIFICATION OF COMPLETED WORK, *continued*

NPS Project No. _____

Additional Owners:

Name _____
Street _____
City _____ State _____ Zip _____
Social Security or Taxpayer Identification Number: _____

Name _____
Street _____
City _____ State _____ Zip _____
Social Security or Taxpayer Identification Number: _____

Name _____
Street _____
City _____ State _____ Zip _____
Social Security or Taxpayer Identification Number: _____

Name _____
Street _____
City _____ State _____ Zip _____
Social Security or Taxpayer Identification Number: _____

Name _____
Street _____
City _____ State _____ Zip _____
Social Security or Taxpayer Identification Number: _____

Name _____
Street _____
City _____ State _____ Zip _____
Social Security or Taxpayer Identification Number: _____

Appendix D

The Secretary's Guidelines for Rehabilitating Historic Buildings and Interpretations of the Secretary of the Interior's Standards for Rehabilitation

In addition to establishing standards and guidelines for rehabilitating historic buildings, the National Park Service, U.S. Department of the Interior, also publishes technical information on appropriate preservation techniques, including Preservation Briefs, case studies, and Preservation Tech Notes. A catalogue of Historic Preservation Publications may be obtained by writing to Preservation Assistance Division, Technical Preservation Service, P.O. Box 37127, Washington, D.C. 20013-7127.

The Secretary's Guidelines for Rehabilitating Historic Buildings are reproduced on pages 357 to 408.

As further guidance in applying the Standards for Rehabilitation, the National Park Service periodically published a bulletin entitled *Interpreting the Secretary of the Interior's Standards for Historic Preservation Projects*. While the Bulletins have been discontinued, they are still relevant. A number of the major bulletins are reproduced on pages 409 to 427.

GUIDELINES FOR REHABILITATING HISTORIC BUILDINGS

The Guidelines were initially developed in 1977 to help property owners, developers, and Federal managers apply the Secretary of the Interior's "Standards for Rehabilitation" during the project planning stage by providing general design and technical recommendations. Unlike the Standards, the Guidelines are *not* codified as program requirements. Together with the "Standards for Rehabilitation" they provide a model process for owners, developers, and Federal agency managers to follow.

It should be noted at the outset that the Guidelines are intended to assist in applying the Standards to projects generally; consequently, they are not meant to give case-specific advice or address exceptions or rare instances. For example, they cannot tell an owner or developer which features of their own historic building are important in defining the historic character and must be preserved—although examples are provided in each section—or which features could be altered, if necessary, for the new use. This kind of careful case-by-case decisionmaking is best accomplished by seeking assistance from qualified historic preservation professionals in the planning stage of the project. Such professionals include architects, architectural historians, historians, archeologists, and others who are skilled in the preservation, rehabilitation, and restoration of historic properties.

The Guidelines pertain to historic buildings of all sizes, materials, occupancy, and construction types; and apply to interior and exterior work as well as new exterior additions. Those approaches, treatments, and techniques that are consistent with the Secretary of the Interior's "Standards for Rehabilitation" are listed in the "**Recommended**" column on the left; those approaches, treatments, and techniques which could adversely affect a building's historic character are listed in the "**Not Recommended**" column on the right.

To provide clear and consistent guidance for owners, developers, and federal agency managers to follow, the "Recommended" courses of action in each section are listed in order of historic preservation concerns so that a rehabilitation project may be successfully planned and completed—one that, first, assures the preservation of a building's important or "character-defining" architectural materials and features and, second, makes possible an efficient contemporary use. Rehabilitation guidance in each section begins with protection and maintenance, that work which should be maximized in every project to enhance overall preservation goals. Next, where some deterioration is present, repair of the building's historic materials and features is recommended. Finally, when deterioration is so extensive that repair is not possible, the most problematic area of work is considered: replacement of historic materials and features with new materials.

To further guide the owner and developer in planning a successful rehabilitation project, those complex design issues dealing with new use requirements such as alterations and additions are highlighted at the end of each section to underscore the need for particular sensitivity in these areas.

Identify, Retain, and Preserve

The guidance that is basic to the treatment of all historic buildings—***identifying, retaining, and preserving*** the form and detailing of those architectural materials and features that are important in *defining the historic character*—is always listed first in the "Recommended" column. The parallel "Not Recommended" column lists the types of actions that are most apt to cause the diminution or even loss of the building's historic character. It should be remembered, however, that such loss of character is just as often caused by the cumulative effect of a series of actions that would seem to be minor interventions. Thus, the guidance in *all* of the "Not Recommended" columns must be viewed in that larger context, e.g., for the total impact on a historic building.

Protect and Maintain

After identifying those materials and features that are important and must be retained in the process of rehabilitation work, then ***protecting and maintaining*** them are addressed. Protection generally involves the least degree of intervention and is preparatory to other work. For example, protection includes the maintenance of historic material through treatments such as rust removal, caulking, limited paint removal, and re-application of protective coatings; the cyclical cleaning of roof gutter systems; or installation of fencing, protective plywood, alarm systems and other temporary protective measures. Although a historic building will usually require more extensive work, an overall evaluation of its physical condition should always begin at this level.

Repair

Next, when the physical condition of character-defining materials and features warrants additional work ***repairing*** is recommended. Guidance for the repair of historic materials such as masonry, wood, and architectural metals again begins with the least degree of intervention possible such as patching, piecing-in, splicing, consolidating, or otherwise reinforcing or upgrading them according to recognized preservation methods. Repairing also includes the limited replacement in kind—or with compatible substitute material—of extensively deteriorated or missing *parts* of features when there are surviving prototypes (for example, brackets, dentils, steps, plaster, or portions of slate or tile roofing). Although using the same kind of material is always the preferred option, substitute material is acceptable if the form and design as well as the substitute material itself convey the visual appearance of the remaining parts of the feature and finish.

Replace

Following repair in the hierarchy, guidance is provided for ***replacing*** an entire character-defining feature with new material because the level of deterioration or damage of materials precludes repair (for example, an exterior cornice; an interior staircase; or a complete porch or storefront). If the essential form and detailing are still evident so that the physical evidence can be used to re-establish the feature as an integral part of the rehabilitation project, then its replacement is appropriate. Like the guidance for repair, the preferred option is always replacement of the entire feature in kind, that is, with the same material. Because this approach may not always be technically or economically feasible, provisions are made to consider the use of a compatible substitute material.

It should be noted that, while the National Park Service guidelines recommend the replacement of an entire character-defining feature under certain well-defined circumstances, they *never* recommend removal and replacement with new material of a feature that—although damaged or deteriorated—could reasonably be repaired and thus preserved.

Design for Missing Historic Features

When an entire interior or exterior feature is missing (for example, an entrance, or cast iron facade; or a principal staircase), it no longer plays a role in physically defining the historic character of the building unless it can be accurately recovered in form and detailing through the process of carefully documenting the historical appearance. Where an important architectural feature is missing, its recovery is always recommended in the guidelines as the *first* or preferred, course of action. Thus, if adequate historical, pictorial, and physical documentation exists so that the feature may be accurately reproduced, and if it is desireable to re-establish the feature as part of the building's historical appearance, then designing and constructing a new feature based on such information is appropriate. However, a *second* acceptable option for the replacement feature is a new design that is compatible with the remaining character-defining features of the historic building. The new design should always take into account the size, scale, and material of the historic building itself and, most importantly, should be clearly differentiated so that a false historical appearance is not created.

Alterations/Additions to Historic Buildings

Some exterior and interior alterations to the historic building are generally needed to assure its continued use, but it is most important that such alterations do not radically change, obscure, or destroy character-defining spaces, materials, features, or finishes. Alterations may include providing additional parking space on an existing historic building site; cutting new entrances or windows on secondary elevations; inserting an additional floor; installing an entirely new mechanical system; or creating an atrium or light well. Alteration may also include the selective removal of buildings or other features of the environment or building site that are intrusive and therefore detract from the overall historic character.

The construction of an exterior addition to a historic building may seem to be essential for the new use, but it is emphasized in the guidelines that such new additions should be avoided, if possible, and considered *only* after it is determined that those needs cannot be met by altering secondary, i.e., non character-defining interior spaces. If, after a thorough evaluation of interior solutions, an exterior addition is still judged to be the only viable alternative, it should be designed and constructed to be clearly differentiated from the historic building and so that the character-defining features are not radically changed, obscured, damaged, or destroyed.

Additions to historic buildings are referenced within specific sections of the guidelines such as Site, Roof, Structural Systems, etc., but are also considered in more detail in a separate section, NEW ADDITIONS TO HISTORIC BUILDINGS.

Health and Safety Code Requirements; Energy Retrofitting

These sections of the rehabilitation guidance address work done to meet health and safety code requirements (for example, providing barrier-free access to historic buildings); or retrofitting measures to conserve energy (for example, installing solar collectors in an unobtrusive location on the site). Although this work is quite often an important aspect of rehabilitation projects, it is usually not part of the overall process of protecting or repairing character-defining features; rather, such work is assessed for its potential negative impact on the building's historic character. For this reason, particular care must be taken not to radically change, obscure, damage, or destroy character-defining materials or features in the process of rehabilitation work to meet code and energy requirements.

Specific information on rehabilitation and preservation technology may be obtained by writing to the National Park Service, at the addresses listed below:

Preservation Assistance Division
National Park Service
P.O. Box 37127
Washington, D.C. 20013-7127

National Historic Preservation
 Programs
Western Regional Office
National Park Service
450 Golden Gate Ave.
Box 36063
San Francisco, CA 94102

Division of Cultural Resources
Rocky Mountain Regional Office
National Park Service
655 Parfet St.
P.O. Box 25287
Denver, CO 80225

Preservation Services Division
Southeast Regional Office
National Park Service
75 Spring St. SW., Room 1140
Atlanta, GA 30303

Office of Cultural Programs
Mid-Atlantic Regional Office
National Park Service
Second and Chestnut Streets
Philadelphia, PA 19106

Cultural Resources Division
Alaska Regional Office
National Park Service
2525 Gambell St.
Anchorage, AK 99503

BUILDING EXTERIOR

Masonry: Brick, stone, terra cotta, concrete, adobe, stucco and mortar

Masonry features (such as brick cornices and door pediments, stone window architraves, terra cotta brackets and railings) as well as masonry surfaces (modelling, tooling, bonding patterns, joint size, and color) may be important in defining the historic character of the building. It should be noted that while masonry is among the most durable of historic building materials, it is also the most susceptible to damage by improper maintenance or repair techniques and by harsh or abrasive cleaning methods. Most preservation guidance on masonry thus focuses on such concerns as cleaning and the process of repointing.

Recommended

Identifying, retaining, and preserving masonry features that are important in defining the overall historic character of the building such as walls, brackets, railings, cornices, window architraves, door pediments, steps, and columns; and joint and unit size, tooling and bonding patterns, coatings, and color.

Protecting and maintaining masonry by providing proper drainage so that water does not stand on flat, horizontal surfaces or accumulate in curved decorative features.

Cleaning masonry only when necessary to halt deterioration or remove heavy soiling.

Not Recommended

Removing or radically changing masonry features which are important in defining the overall historic character of the building so that, as a result, the character is diminished.

Replacing or rebuilding a major portion of exterior masonry walls that could be repaired so that, as a result, the building is no longer historic and is essentially new construction.

Applying paint or other coatings such as stucco to masonry that has been historically unpainted or uncoated to create a new appearance.

Removing paint from historically painted masonry.

Radically changing the type of paint or coating or its color.

Failing to evaluate and treat the various causes of mortar joint deterioration such as leaking roofs or gutters, differential settlement of the building, capillary action, or extreme weather exposure.

Cleaning masonry surfaces when they are not heavily soiled to create a new appearance, thus needlessly introducing chemicals or moisture into historic materials.

Recommended	*Not Recommended*
Carrying out masonry surface cleaning tests after it has been determined that such cleaning is necessary. Tests should be observed over a sufficient period of time so that both the immediate effects and the long range effects are known to enable selection of the gentlest method possible.	Cleaning masonry surfaces without testing or without sufficient time for the testing results to be of value.
Cleaning masonry surfaces with the gentlest method possible, such as low pressure water and detergents, using natural bristle brushes.	Sandblasting brick or stone surfaces using dry or wet grit or other abrasives. These methods of cleaning permanently erode the surface of the material and accelerate deterioration.
	Using a cleaning method that involves water or liquid chemical solutions when there is any possibility of freezing temperatures.
	Cleaning with chemical products that will damage masonry, such as using acid on limestone or marble, or leaving chemicals on masonry surfaces.
	Applying high pressure water cleaning methods that will damage historic masonry and the mortar joints.
Inspecting painted masonry surfaces to determine whether repainting is necessary.	Removing paint that is firmly adhering to, and thus protecting, masonry surfaces.
Removing damaged or deteriorated paint only to the next sound layer using the gentlest method possible (e.g., handscraping) prior to repainting.	Using methods of removing paint which are destructive to masonry, such as sandblasting, application of caustic solutions, or high pressure waterblasting.
Applying compatible paint coating systems following proper surface preparation.	Failing to follow manufacturers' product and application instructions when repainting masonry.
Repainting with colors that are historically appropriate to the building and district.	Using new paint colors that are inappropriate to the historic building and district.

Recommended	Not Recommended
Evaluating the overall condition of the masonry to determine whether more than protection and maintenance are required, that is, if repairs to the masonry features will be necessary.	Failing to undertake adequate measures to assure the preservation of masonry features.
Repairing masonry walls and other masonry features by repointing the mortar joints where there is evidence of deterioration such as disintegrating mortar, cracks in mortar joints, loose bricks, damp walls, or damaged plasterwork.	Removing nondeteriorated mortar from sound joints, then repointing the entire building to achieve a uniform appearance.
Removing deteriorated mortar by carefully hand-raking the joints to avoid damaging the masonry.	Using electric saws and hammers rather than hand tools to remove deteriorated mortar from joints prior to repointing.
Duplicating old mortar in strength, composition, color, and texture.	Repointing with mortar of high portland cement content (unless it is the content of the historic mortar). This can often create a bond that is stronger than the historic material and can cause damage as a result of the differing coefficient of expansion and the differing porosity of the material and the mortar.
	Repointing with a synthetic caulking compound.
	Using a "scrub" coating technique to repoint instead of traditional repointing methods.
Duplicating old mortar joints in width and in joint profile.	Changing the width or joint profile when repointing.
Repairing stucco by removing the damaged material and patching with new stucco that duplicates the old in strength, composition, color, and texture.	Removing sound stucco; or repairing with new stucco that is stronger than the historic material or does not convey the same visual appearance.
Using mud plaster as a surface coating over unfired, unstabilized adobe because the mud plaster will bond to the adobe.	Applying cement stucco to unfired, unstabilized adobe. Because the cement stucco will not bond properly, moisture can become entrapped between materials, resulting in accelerated deterioration of the adobe.

Recommended

Repairing masonry features by patching, piecing-in, or consolidating the masonry using recognized preservation methods. Repair may also include the limited replacement in kind—or with compatible substitute material—of those extensively deteriorated or missing parts of masonry features when there are surviving prototypes such as terra-cotta brackets or stone balusters.

Applying new or non-historic surface treatments such as water-repellent coatings to masonry only after repointing and only if masonry repairs have failed to arrest water penetration problems.

Replacing in kind an entire masonry feature that is too deteriorated to repair—if the overall form and detailing are still evident—using the physical evidence to guide the new work. Examples can include large sections of a wall, a cornice, balustrade, column, or stairway. If using the same kind of material is not technically or economically feasible, then a compatible substitute material may be considered.

Not Recommended

Replacing an entire masonry feature such as a cornice or balustrade when repair of the masonry and limited replacement of deteriorated or missing parts are appropriate.

Using a substitute material for the replacement part that does not convey the visual appearance of the surviving parts of the masonry feature or that is physically or chemically incompatible.

Applying waterproof, water-repellent, or non-historic coatings such as stucco to masonry as a substitute for repointing and masonry repairs. Coatings are frequently unnecessary, expensive, and may change the appearance of historic masonry as well as accelerate its deterioration.

Removing a masonry feature that is unrepairable and not replacing it; or replacing it with a new feature that does not convey the same visual appearance.

The following work is highlighted to indicate that it represents the particularly complex technical or design aspects of rehabilitation projects and should only be considered after the preservation concerns listed above have been addressed.

Design for Missing Historic Features

Designing and installing a new masonry feature such as steps or a door pediment when the historic feature is completely missing. It may be an accurate restoration using historical, pictorial, and physical documentation; or be a new design that is compatible with the size, scale, material, and color of the historic building.

Creating a false historical appearance because the replaced masonry feature is based on insufficient historical, pictorial, and physical documentation.

Introducing a new masonry feature that is incompatible in size, scale, material and color.

Wood: Clapboard, weatherboard, shingles, and other wooden siding and decorative elements

Because it can be easily shaped by sawing, planing, carving, and gouging, wood is the most commonly used material for architectural features such as clapboards, cornices, brackets, entablatures, shutters, columns and balustrades. These wooden features—both functional and decorative—may be important in defining the historic character of the building and thus their retention, protection, and repair are of particular importance in rehabilitation projects.

Recommended

Identifying, retaining, and preserving wood features that are important in defining the overall historic character of the building such as siding, cornices, brackets, window architraves, and doorway pediments; and their paints, finishes, and colors.

Protecting and maintaining wood features by providing proper drainage so that water is not allowed to stand on flat, horizontal surfaces or accumulate in decorative features.

Not Recommended

Removing or radically changing wood features which are important in defining the overall historic character of the building so that, as a result, the character is diminished.

Removing a major portion of the historic wood from a facade instead of repairing or replacing only the deteriorated wood, then reconstructing the facade with new material in order to achieve a uniform or "improved" appearance.

Radically changing the type of finish or its color or accent scheme so that the historic character of the exterior is diminished.

Stripping historically painted surfaces to bare wood, then applying clear finishes or stains in order to create a "natural look."

Stripping paint or varnish to bare wood rather than repairing or reapplying a special finish, i.e., a grained finish to an exterior wood feature such as a front door.

Failing to identify, evaluate, and treat the causes of wood deterioration, including faulty flashing, leaking gutters, cracks and holes in siding, deteriorated caulking in joints and seams, plant material growing too close to wood surfaces, or insect or fungus infestation.

365

Recommended

Applying chemical preservatives to wood features such as beam ends or outriggers that are exposed to decay hazards and are traditionally unpainted.

Retaining coatings such as paint that help protect the wood from moisture and ultraviolet light. Paint removal should be considered only where there is paint surface deterioration and as part of an overall maintenance program which involves repainting or applying other appropriate protective coatings.

Inspecting painted wood surfaces to determine whether repainting is necessary or if cleaning is all that is required.

Removing damaged or deteriorated paint to the next sound layer using the gentlest method possible (handscraping and handsanding), then repainting.

Using with care electric hot-air guns on decorative wood features and electric heat plates on flat wood surfaces when paint is so deteriorated that total removal is necessary prior to repainting.

Using chemical strippers primarily to supplement other methods such as handscraping, handsanding and the above-recommended thermal devices. Detachable wooden elements such as shutters, doors, and columns may—with the proper safeguards—be chemically dip-stripped.

Applying compatible paint coating systems following proper surface preparation.

Repainting with colors that are appropriate to the historic building and district.

Not Recommended

Using chemical preservatives such as creosote which can change the appearance of wood features unless they were used historically.

Stripping paint or other coatings to reveal bare wood, thus exposing historically coated surfaces to the effects of accelerated weathering.

Removing paint that is firmly adhering to, and thus, protecting wood surfaces.

Using destructive paint removal methods such as a propane or butane torches, sandblasting or waterblasting. These methods can irreversibly damage historic woodwork.

Using thermal devices improperly so that the historic woodwork is scorched.

Failing to neutralize the wood thoroughly after using chemicals so that new paint does not adhere.

Allowing detachable wood features to soak too long in a caustic solution so that the wood grain is raised and the surface roughened.

Failing to follow manufacturers' product and application instructions when repainting exterior woodwork.

Using new colors that are inappropriate to the historic building or district.

Recommended

Evaluating the overall condition of the wood to determine whether more than protection and maintenance are required, that is, if repairs to wood features will be necessary.

Repairing wood features by patching, piecing-in, consolidating, or otherwise reinforcing the wood using recognized preservation methods. Repair may also include the limited replacement in kind—or with compatible substitute material—of those extensively deteriorated or missing parts of features where there are surviving prototypes such as brackets, moldings, or sections of siding.

Replacing in kind an entire wood feature that is too deteriorated to repair—if the overall form and detailing are still evident—using the physical evidence to guide the new work. Examples of wood features include a cornice, entablature or balustrade. If using the same kind of material is not technically or economically feasible, then a compatible substitute material may be considered.

Not Recommended

Failing to undertake adequate measures to assure the preservation of wood features.

Replacing an entire wood feature such as a cornice or wall when repair of the wood and limited replacement of deteriorated or missing parts are appropriate.

Using substitute materials for the replacement part that does not convey the visual appearance of the surviving parts of the wood feature or that is physically or chemically incompatible.

Removing an entire wood feature that is unrepairable and not replacing it; or replacing it with a new feature that does not convey the same visual appearance.

The following work is highlighted because it represents the particularly complex technical or design aspects of rehabilitation projects and should only be considered after the preservation concerns listed above have been addressed.

Design for Missing Historic Features

Designing and installing a new wood feature such as a cornice or doorway when the historic feature is completely missing. It may be an accurate restoration using historical, pictorial, and physical documentation; or be a new design that is compatible with the size, scale, material, and color of the historic building.

Creating a false historic appearance because the replaced wood feature is based on insufficient historical, pictorial, and physical documentation.

Introducing a new wood feature that is incompatible in size, scale, material, and color.

Architectural Metals: Cast iron, steel, pressed tin, copper, aluminum, and zinc

Architectural metal features—such as cast-iron facades, porches, and steps; sheet metal cornices, roofs, roof cresting and storefronts; and cast or rolled metal doors, window sash, entablatures, and hardware—are often highly decorative and may be important in defining the overall historic character of the building. Their retention, protection, and repair should be a prime consideration in rehabilitation projects.

Recommended

Identifying, retaining, and preserving architectural metal features such as columns, capitals, window hoods, or stairways that are important in defining the overall historic character of the building; and their finishes and colors.

Protecting and maintaining architectural metals from corrosion by providing proper drainage so that water does not stand on flat, horizontal surfaces or accumulate in curved, decorative features.

Cleaning architectural metals, when necessary, to remove corrosion prior to repainting or applying other appropriate protective coatings.

Not Recommended

Removing or radically changing architectural metal features which are important in defining the overall historic character of the building so that, as a result, the character is diminished.

Removing a major portion of the historic architectural metal from a facade instead of repairing or replacing only the deteriorated metal, then reconstructing the facade with new material in order to create a uniform, or "improved" appearance.

Radically changing the type of finish or its historical color or accent scheme.

Failing to identify, evaluate, and treat the causes of corrosion, such as moisture from leaking roofs or gutters.

Placing incompatible metals together without providing a reliable separation material. Such incompatibility can result in galvanic corrosion of the less noble metal, e.g., copper will corrode cast iron, steel, tin, and aluminum.

Exposing metals which were intended to be protected from the environment.

Applying paint or other coatings to metals such as copper, bronze, or stainless steel that were meant to be exposed.

Recommended

Identifying the particular type of metal prior to any cleaning procedure and then testing to assure that the gentlest cleaning method possible is selected or determining that cleaning is inappropriate for the particular metal.

Cleaning soft metals such as lead, tin, copper, terneplate, and zinc with appropriate chemical methods because their finishes can be easily abraded by blasting methods.

Using the gentlest cleaning methods for cast iron, wrought iron, and steel—hard metals—in order to remove paint buildup and corrosion. If handscraping and wire brushing have proven ineffective, low pressure dry grit blasting may be used as long as it does not abrade or damage the surface.

Applying appropriate paint or other coating systems after cleaning in order to decrease the corrosion rate of metals or alloys.

Repainting with colors that are appropriate to the historic building or district.

Applying an appropriate protective coating such as lacquer to an architectural metal feature such as a bronze door which is subject to heavy pedestrian use.

Evaluating the overall condition of the architectural metals to determine whether more than protection and maintenance are required, that is, if repairs to features will be necessary.

Not Recommended

Using cleaning methods which alter or damage the historic color, texture, and finish of the metal; or cleaning when it is inappropriate for the metal.

Removing the patina of historic metal. The patina may be a protective coating on some metals, such as bronze or copper, as well as a significant historic finish.

Cleaning soft metals such as lead, tin, copper, terneplate, and zinc with grit blasting which will abrade the surface of the metal.

Failing to employ gentler methods prior to abrasively cleaning cast iron, wrought iron or steel; or using high pressure grit blasting.

Failing to re-apply protective coating systems to metals or alloys that require them after cleaning so that accelerated corrosion occurs.

Using new colors that are inappropriate to the historic building or district.

Failing to assess pedestrian use or new access patterns so that architectural metal features are subject to damage by use or inappropriate maintenance such as salting adjacent sidewalks.

Failing to undertake adequate measures to assure the preservation of architectural metal features.

Recommended

Repairing architectural metal features by patching, splicing, or otherwise reinforcing the metal following recognized preservation methods. Repairs may also include the limited replacement in kind—or with a compatible substitute material—of those extensively deteriorated or missing parts of features when there are surviving prototypes such as porch balusters, column capitals or bases; or porch cresting.

Replacing in kind an entire architectural metal feature that is too deteriorated to repair—if the overall form and detailing are still evident—using the physical evidence to guide the new work. Examples could include cast iron porch steps or steel sash windows. If using the same kind of material is not technically or economically feasible, then a compatible substitute material may be considered.

Not Recommended

Replacing an entire architectural metal feature such as a column or a balustrade when repair of the metal and limited replacement of deteriorated or missing parts are appropriate.

Using a substitute material for the replacement part that does not convey the visual appearance of the surviving parts of the architectural metal feature or that is physically or chemically incompatible.

Removing an architectural metal feature that is unrepairable and not replacing it; or replacing it with a new architectural metal feature that does not convey the same visual appearance.

The following work is highlighted to indicate that it represents the particularly complex technical or design aspects of rehabilitation projects and should only be considered after the preservation concerns listed above have been addressed.

Design for Missing Historic Features

Designing and installing a new architectural metal feature such as a sheet metal cornice or cast iron capital when the historic feature is completely missing. It may be an accurate restoration using historical, pictorial and physical documentation; or be a new design that is compatible with the size, scale, material, and color of the historic building.

Creating a false historic appearance because the replaced architectural metal feature is based on insufficient historical, pictorial, and physical documentation.

Introducing a new architectural metal feature that is incompatible in size, scale, material, and color.

Roofs

The roof—with its shape; features such as cresting, dormers, cupolas, and chimneys; and the size, color, and patterning of the roofing material—can be extremely important in defining the building's overall historic character. In addition to the design role it plays, a weathertight roof is essential to the preservation of the entire structure; thus, protecting and repairing the roof as a "cover" is a critical aspect of every rehabilitation project.

Recommended

Identifying, retaining, and preserving roofs—and their functional and decorative features—that are important in defining the overall historic character of the building. This includes the roof's shape, such as hipped, gambrel, and mansard; decorative features such as cupolas, cresting, chimneys, and weathervanes; and roofing material such as slate, wood, clay tile, and metal, as well as its size, color, and patterning.

Protecting and maintaining a roof by cleaning the gutters and downspouts and replacing deteriorated flashing. Roof sheathing should also be checked for proper venting to prevent moisture condensation and water penetration; and to insure that materials are free from insect infestation.

Providing adequate anchorage for roofing material to guard against wind damage and moisture penetration.

Not Recommended

Radically changing, damaging, or destroying roofs which are important in defining the overall historic character of the building so that, as a result, the character is diminished.

Removing a major portion of the roof or roofing material that is repairable, then reconstructing it with new material in order to create a uniform, or "improved" appearance.

Changing the configuration of a roof by adding new features such as dormer windows, vents, or skylights so that the historic character is diminished.

Stripping the roof of sound historic material such as slate, clay tile, wood, and architectural metal.

Applying paint or other coatings to roofing material which has been historically uncoated.

Failing to clean and maintain gutters and downspouts properly so that water and debris collect and cause damage to roof fasteners, sheathing, and the underlying structure.

Allowing roof fasteners, such as nails and clips to corrode so that roofing material is subject to accelerated deterioration.

Recommended

Protecting a leaking roof with plywood and building paper until it can be properly repaired.

Repairing a roof by reinforcing the historic materials which comprise roof features. Repairs will also generally include the limited replacement in kind—or with compatible substitute material—of those extensively deteriorated or missing parts of features when there are surviving prototypes such as cupola louvers, dentils, dormer roofing; or slates, tiles, or wood shingles on a main roof.

Replacing in kind an entire feature of the roof that is too deteriorated to repair—if the overall form and detailing are still evident—using the physical evidence to guide the new work. Examples can include a large section of roofing, or a dormer or chimney. If using the same kind of material is not technically or economically feasible, then a compatible substitute material may be considered.

Not Recommended

Permitting a leaking roof to remain unprotected so that accelerated deterioration of historic building materials—masonry, wood, plaster, paint and structural members—occurs.

Replacing an entire roof feature such as a cupola or dormer when repair of the historic materials and limited replacement of deteriorated or missing parts are appropriate.

Using a substitute material for the replacement part that does not convey the visual appearance of the surviving parts of the roof or that is physically or chemically incompatible.

Removing a feature of the roof that is unrepairable, such as a chimney or dormer, and not replacing it; or replacing it with a new feature that does not convey the same visual appearance.

The following work is highlighted to indicate that it represents the particularly complex technical or design aspects of rehabilitation projects and should only be considered after the preservation concerns listed above have been addressed.

Design for Missing Historic Features

Designing and constructing a new feature when the historic feature is completely missing, such as a chimney or cupola. It may be an accurate restoration using historical, pictorial and physical documentation; or be a new design that is compatible with the size, scale, material, and color of the historic building.

Creating a false historical appearance because the replaced feature is based on insufficient historical, pictorial, and physical documentation.

Introducing a new roof feature that is incompatible in size, scale, material, and color.

Recommended

Alterations/Additions for the New Use

Installing mechanical and service equipment on the roof such as air conditioning, transformers, or solar collectors when required for the new use so that they are inconspicuous from the public right-of-way and do not damage or obscure character-defining features.

Designing additions to roofs such as residential, office, or storage spaces; elevator housing; decks and terraces; or dormers or skylights when required by the new use so that they are inconspicuous from the public right-of-way and do not damage or obscure character-defining features.

Not Recommended

Installing mechanical or service equipment so that it damages or obscures character-defining features; or is conspicuous from the public right-of-way.

Radically changing a character-defining roof shape or damaging or destroying character-defining roofing material as a result of incompatible design or improper installation techniques.

Windows

A highly decorative window with an unusual shape, or glazing pattern, or color is most likely identified immediately as a character-defining feature of the building. It is far more difficult, however, to assess the importance of repeated windows on a facade, particularly if they are individually simple in design and material, such as the large, multi-paned sash of many industrial buildings. Because rehabilitation projects frequently include proposals to replace window sash or even entire windows to improve thermal efficiency or to create a new appearance, it is essential that their contribution to the overall historic character of the building be assessed together with their physical condition before specific repair or replacement work is undertaken.

Recommended

Identifying, retaining, and preserving windows—and their functional and decorative features—that are important in defining the overall historic character of the building. Such features can include frames, sash, muntins, glazing, sills, heads, hoodmolds, panelled or decorated jambs and moldings, and interior and exterior shutters and blinds.

Protecting and maintaining the wood and architectural metal which comprise the window frame, sash, muntins, and surrounds through appropriate surface treatments such as cleaning, rust removal, limited paint removal, and re-application of protective coating systems.

Not Recommended

Removing or radically changing windows which are important in defining the overall historic character of the building so that, as a result, the character is diminished.

Changing the number, location, size or glazing pattern of windows, through cutting new openings, blocking-in windows, and installing replacement sash which does not fit the historic window opening.

Changing the historic appearance of windows through the use of inappropriate designs, materials, finishes, or colors which radically change the sash, depth of reveal, and muntin configuration; the reflectivity and color of the glazing; or the appearance of the frame.

Obscuring historic window trim with metal or other material.

Stripping windows of historic material such as wood, iron, cast iron, and bronze.

Failing to provide adequate protection of materials on a cyclical basis so that deterioration of the windows results.

Recommended	Not Recommended
Making windows weathertight by recaulking and replacing or installing weatherstripping. These actions also improve thermal efficiency.	Retrofitting or replacing windows rather than maintaining the sash, frame, and glazing.
Evaluating the overall condition of materials to determine whether more than protection and maintenance are required, i.e. if repairs to windows and window features will be required.	Failing to undertake adequate measures to assure the preservation of historic windows.
Repairing window frames and sash by patching, splicing, consolidating or otherwise reinforcing. Such repair may also include replacement in kind of those parts that are either extensively deteriorated or are missing when there are surviving prototypes such as architraves, hoodmolds, sash, sills, and interior or exterior shutters and blinds.	Replacing an entire window when repair of materials and limited replacement of deteriorated or missing parts are appropriate.
	Failing to reuse serviceable window hardware such as brass lifts and sash locks.
	Using a substitute material for the replacement part that does not convey the visual appearance of the surviving parts of the window or that is physically or chemically incompatible.
Replacing in kind an entire window that is too deteriorated to repair—if the overall form and detailing are still evident—using the physical evidence to guide the new work. If using the same kind of material is not technically or economically feasible, then a compatible substitute material may be considered.	Removing a character-defining window that is unrepairable and blocking it in; or replacing it with a new window that does not convey the same visual appearance.

The following work is highlighted to indicate that it represents the particularly complex technical or design aspects of rehabilitation projects and should only be considered after the preservation concerns listed above have been addressed.

Design for Missing Historic Features

Designing and installing new windows when the historic windows (frame, sash and glazing) are completely missing. The replacement windows may be an accurate restoration using historical, pictorial, and physical documentation; or be a new design that is compatible with the window openings and the historic character of the building.	Creating a false historical appearance because the replaced window is based on insufficient historical, pictorial, and physical documentation.
	Introducing a new design that is incompatible with the historic character of the building.

Recommended

Alterations/Additions for the New Use

Designing and installing additional windows on rear or other-non character-defining elevations if required by the new use. New windows openings may also be cut into exposed party walls. Such design should be compatible with the overall design of the building, but not duplicate the fenestration pattern and detailing of a character-defining elevation.

Providing a setback in the design of dropped ceilings when they are required for the new use to allow for the full height of the window openings.

Not Recommended

Installing new windows, including frames, sash, and muntin configuration that are incompatible with the building's historic appearance or obscure, damage, or destroy character-defining features.

Inserting new floors or furred-down ceilings which cut across the glazed areas of windows so that the exterior form and appearance of the windows are changed.

Entrances and Porches

Entrances and porches are quite often the focus of historic buildings, particularly when they occur on primary elevations. Together with their functional and decorative features such as doors, steps, balustrades, pilasters, and entablatures, they can be extremely important in defining the overall historic character of a building. Their retention, protection, and repair should always be carefully considered when planning rehabilitation work.

Recommended

Identifying, retaining, and preserving entrances—and their functional and decorative features—that are important in defining the overall historic character of the building such as doors, fanlights, sidelights, pilasters, entablatures, columns, balustrades, and stairs.

Protecting and maintaining the masonry, wood, and architectural metal that comprise entrances and porches through appropriate surface treatments such as cleaning, rust removal, limited paint removal, and re-application of protective coating systems.

Evaluating the overall condition of materials to determine whether more than protection and maintenance are required, that is, if repairs to entrance and porch features will be necessary.

Not Recommended

Removing or radically changing entrances and porches which are important in defining the overall historic character of the building so that, as a result, the character is diminished.

Stripping entrances and porches of historic material such as wood, iron, cast iron, terra cotta, tile and brick.

Removing an entrance or porch because the building has been re-oriented to accommodate a new use.

Cutting new entrances on a primary elevation.

Altering utilitarian or service entrances so they appear to be formal entrances by adding panelled doors, fanlights, and sidelights.

Failing to provide adequate protection to materials on a cyclical basis so that deterioration of entrances and porches results.

Failing to undertake adequate measures to assure the preservation of historic entrances and porches.

Recommended

Repairing entrances and porches by reinforcing the historic materials. Repair will also generally include the limited replacement in kind—or with compatible substitute material—of those extensively deteriorated or missing parts of repeated features where there are surviving prototypes such as balustrades, cornices, entablatures, columns, sidelights, and stairs.

Replacing in kind an entire entrance or porch that is too deteriorated to repair—if the form and detailing are still evident—using the physical evidence to guide the new work. If using the same kind of material is not technically or economically feasible, then a compatible substitute material may be considered.

Not Recommended

Replacing an entire entrance or porch when the repair of materials and limited replacement of parts are appropriate.

Using a substitute material for the replacement parts that does not convey the visual appearance of the surviving parts of the entrance and porch or that is physically or chemically incompatible.

Removing an entrance or porch that is unrepairable and not replacing it; or replacing it with a new entrance or porch that does not convey the same visual appearance.

The following work is highlighted to indicate that it represents the particularly complex technical or design aspects of rehabilitation projects and should only be considered after the preservation concerns listed above have been addressed.

Design for Missing Historic Features

Designing and constructing a new entrance or porch if the historic entrance or porch is completely missing. It may be a restoration based on historical, pictorial, and physical documentation; or be a new design that is compatible with the historic character of the building.

Creating a false historical appearance because the replaced entrance or porch is based on insufficient historical, pictorial, and physical documentation.

Introducing a new entrance or porch that is incompatible in size, scale, material, and color.

Alterations/Additions for the New Use

Designing enclosures for historic porches when required by the new use in a manner that preserves the historic character of the building. This can include using large sheets of glass and recessing the enclosure wall behind existing scrollwork, posts, and balustrades.

Enclosing porches in a manner that results in a diminution or loss of historic character such as using solid materials such as wood, stucco, or masonry.

Recommended

Designing and installing additional entrances or porches when required for the new use in a manner that preserves the historic character of the building, i.e., limiting such alteration to non-character-defining elevations.

Not Recommended

Installing secondary service entrances and porches that are incompatible in size and scale with the historic building or obscure, damage, or destroy character-defining features.

Storefronts

Storefronts are quite often the focus of historic commercial buildings and can thus be extremely important in defining the overall historic character. Because storefronts also play a crucial role in a store's advertising and merchandising strategy to draw customers and increase business, they are often altered to meet the needs of a new business. Particular care is required in planning and accomplishing work on storefronts so that the building's historic character is preserved in the process of rehabilitation.

Recommended

Identifying, retaining, and preserving storefronts—and their functional and decorative features—that are important in defining the overall historic character of the building such as display windows, signs, doors, transoms, kick plates, corner posts, and entablatures.

Protecting and maintaining masonry, wood, and architectural metals which comprise storefronts through appropriate treatments such as cleaning, rust removal, limited paint removal, and reapplication of protective coating systems.

Not Recommended

Removing or radically changing storefronts—and their features—which are important in defining the overall historic character of the building so that, as a result, the character is diminished.

Changing the storefront so that it appears residential rather than commercial in character.

Removing historic material from the storefront to create a recessed arcade.

Introducing coach lanterns, mansard overhangings, wood shakes, nonoperable shutters, and small-paned windows if they cannot be documented historically.

Changing the location of a storefront's main entrance.

Failing to provide adequate protection to materials on a cyclical basis so that deterioration of storefront features results.

Recommended

Protecting storefronts against arson and vandalism before work begins by boarding up windows and installing alarm systems that are keyed into local protection agencies.

Evaluating the overall condition of storefront materials to determine whether more than protection and maintenance are required, that is, if repairs to features will be necessary.

Repairing storefronts by reinforcing the historic materials. Repairs will also generally include the limited replacement in kind—or with compatible substitute material—of those extensively deteriorated or missing parts of storefronts where there are surviving prototypes such as transoms, kick plates, pilasters, or signs.

Replacing in kind an entire storefront that is too deteriorated to repair—if the overall form and detailing are still evident—using the physical evidence to guide the new work. If using the same material is not technically or economically feasible, then compatible substitute materials may be considered.

Not Recommended

Permitting entry into the building through unsecured or broken windows and doors so that interior features and finishes are damaged through exposure to weather or through vandalism.

Stripping storefronts of historic material such as wood, cast iron, terra cotta, carrara glass, and brick.

Failing to undertake adequate measures to assure the preservation of the historic storefront.

Replacing an entire storefront when repair of materials and limited replacement of its parts are appropriate.

Using substitute material for the replacement parts that does not convey the same visual appearance as the surviving parts of the storefront or that is physically or chemically incompatible.

Removing a storefront that is unrepairable and not replacing it; or replacing it with a new storefront that does not convey the same visual appearance.

The following work is highlighted to indicate that it represents the particularly complex technical or design aspects of rehabilitation projects and should only be considered after the preservation concerns listed above have been addressed.

Recommended

Design for Missing Historic Features

Designing and constructing a new storefront when the historic storefront is completely missing. It may be an accurate restoration using historical, pictorial, and physical documentation; or be a new design that is compatible with the size, scale, material, and color of the historic building. Such new design should generally be flush with the facade; and the treatment of secondary design elements, such as awnings or signs, kept as simple as possible. For example, new signs should fit flush with the existing features of the facade, such as the fascia board or cornice.

Not Recommended

Creating a false historical appearance because the replaced storefront is based on insufficient historical, pictorial, and physical documentation.

Introducing a new design that is incompatible in size, scale, material, and color.

Using new illuminated signs; inappropriately scaled signs and logos; signs that project over the sidewalk unless they were a characteristic feature of the historic building; or other types of signs that obscure, damage, or destroy remaining character-defining features of the historic building.

BUILDING INTERIOR
Structural System

If features of the structural system are exposed such as loadbearing brick walls, cast iron columns, roof trusses, posts and beams, vigas, or stone foundation walls, they may be important in defining the building's overall historic character. Unexposed structural features that are not character-defining or an entire structural system may nonetheless be significant in the history of building technology; therefore, the structural system should always be examined and evaluated early in the project planning stage to determine both its physical condition and its importance to the building's historic character or historical significance. See also Health and Safety Code Requirements.

Recommended

Identifying, retaining, and preserving structural systems—and individual features of systems—that are important in defining the overall historic character of the building, such as post and beam systems, trusses, summer beams, vigas, cast iron columns, abovegrade stone foundation walls, or loadbearing brick or stone walls.

Not Recommended

Removing, covering, or radically changing features of structural systems which are important in defining the overall historic character of the building so that, as a result, the character is diminished.

Putting a new use into the building which could overload the existing structural system; or installing equipment or mechanical systems which could damage the structure.

Demolishing a loadbearing masonry wall that could be augmented and retained and replacing it with a new wall (i.e., brick or stone) using the historic masonry only as an exterior veneer.

Leaving known structural problems untreated such as deflection of beams, cracking and bowing of walls, or racking of structural members.

Utilizing treatments or products that accelerate the deterioration of structural material such as introducing urea-formaldehyde foam insulation into frame walls.

Recommended

Protecting and maintaining the structural system by cleaning the roof gutters and downspouts; replacing roof flashing; keeping masonry, wood, and architectural metals in a sound condition; and assuring that structural members are free from insect infestation.

Examining and evaluating the physical condition of the structural system and its individual features using non-destructive techniques such as X-ray photography.

Repairing the structural system by augmenting or upgrading individual parts or features. For example, weakened structural members such as floor framing can be spliced, braced, or otherwise supplemented and reinforced.

Replacing in kind—or with substitute material—those portions or features of the structural system that are either extensively deteriorated or are missing when there are surviving prototypes such as cast iron columns, roof rafters or trusses, or sections of loadbearing walls. Substitute material should convey the same form, design, and overall visual appearance as the historic feature; and, at a minimum, be equal to its loadbearing capabilities.

Not Recommended

Failing to provide proper building maintenance on a cyclical basis so that deterioration of the structural system results.

Utilizing destructive probing techniques that will damage or destroy structural material.

Upgrading the building structurally in a manner that diminishes the historic character of the exterior, such as installing strapping channels or removing a decorative cornice; or damages interior features or spaces.

Replacing a structural member or other feature of the structural system when it could be augmented and retained.

Installing a replacement feature that does not convey the same visual appearance, e.g., replacing an exposed wood summer beam with a steel beam.

Using substitute material that does not equal the loadbearing capabilities of the historic material and design or is otherwise physically or chemically incompatible.

The following work is highlighted to indicate that it represents the particularly complex technical or design aspects of rehabilitation projects and should only be considered after the preservation concerns listed above have been addressed.

Recommended	Not Recommended
Alterations/Additions for the New Use	
Limiting any new excavations adjacent to historic foundations to avoid undermining the structural stability of the building or adjacent historic buildings.	Carrying out excavations or regrading adjacent to or within a historic building which could cause the historic foundation to settle, shift, or fail; or could have a similar effect on adjacent historic buildings.
Correcting structural deficiencies in preparation for the new use in a manner that preserves the structural system and individual character-defining features.	Radically changing interior spaces or damaging or destroying features or finishes that are character-defining while trying to correct structural deficiencies in preparation for the new use.
Designing and installing new mechanical or electrical systems when required for the new use which minimize the number of cutouts or holes in structural members.	Installing new mechanical and electrical systems or equipment in a manner which results in numerous cuts, splices, or alterations to the structural members.
Adding a new floor when required for the new use if such an alteration does not damage or destroy the structural system or obscure, damage, or destroy character-defining spaces, features, or finishes.	Inserting a new floor when such a radical change damages a structural system or obscures or destroys interior spaces, features, or finishes.
	Inserting new floors or furred-down ceilings which cut across the glazed areas of windows so that the exterior form and appearance of the windows are radically changed.
Creating an atrium or a light well to provide natural light when required for the new use in a manner that assures the preservation of the structural system as well as character-defining interior spaces, features, and finishes.	Damaging the structural system or individual features; or radically changing, damaging, or destroying character-defining interior spaces, features, or finishes in order to create an atrium or a light well.

Interior: Spaces, Features, and Finishes

An interior floor plan, the arrangement of spaces, and built-in features and applied finishes may be individually or collectively important in defining the historic character of the building. Thus, their identification, retention, protection, and repair should be given prime consideration in every rehabilitation project and caution exercised in pursuing any plan that would radically change character-defining spaces or obscure, damage or destroy interior features or finishes.

Interior Spaces

Recommended

Identifying, retaining, and preserving a floor plan or interior spaces that are important in defining the overall historic character of the building. This includes the size, configuration, proportion, and relationship of rooms and corridors; the relationship of features to spaces; and the spaces themselves such as lobbies, reception halls, entrance halls, double parlors, theaters, auditoriums, and important industrial or commercial use spaces.

Not Recommended

Radically changing a floor plan or interior spaces—including individual rooms—which are important in defining the overall historic character of the building so that, as a result, the character is diminished.

Altering the floor plan by demolishing principal walls and partitions to create a new appearance.

Altering or destroying interior spaces by inserting floors, cutting through floors, lowering ceilings, or adding or removing walls.

Relocating an interior feature such as a staircase so that the historic relationship between features and spaces is altered.

Recommended

Interior Features and Finishes

Identifying, retaining, and preserving interior features and finishes that are important in defining the overall historic character of the building, including columns, cornices, baseboards, fireplaces and mantles, paneling, light fixtures, hardware, and flooring; and wallpaper, plaster, paint, and finishes such as stenciling, marbling, and graining; and other decorative materials that accent interior features and provide color, texture, and patterning to walls, floors, and ceilings.

Protecting and maintaining masonry, wood, and architectural metals which comprise interior features through appropriate surface treatments such as cleaning, rust removal, limited paint removal, and reapplication of protective coatings systems.

Not Recommended

Removing or radically changing features and finishes which are important in defining the overall historic character of the building so that, as a result, the character is diminished.

Installing new decorative material that obscures or damages character-defining interior features or finishes.

Removing paint, plaster, or other finishes from historically finished surfaces to create a new appearance (e.g., removing plaster to expose masonry surfaces such as brick walls or a chimney piece).

Applying paint, plaster, or other finishes to surfaces that have been historically unfinished to create a new appearance.

Stripping historically painted wood surfaces to bare wood, then applying clear finishes or stains to create a "natural look."

Stripping paint to bare wood rather than repairing or reapplying grained or marbled finishes to features such as doors and paneling.

Radically changing the type of finish or its color, such as painting a previously varnished wood feature.

Failing to provide adequate protection to materials on a cyclical basis so that deterioration of interior features results.

Recommended

Protecting interior features and finishes against arson and vandalism before project work begins, erecting protective fencing, boarding-up windows, and installing fire alarm systems that are keyed to local protection agencies.

Protecting interior features such as a staircase, mantel, or decorative finishes and wall coverings against damage during project work by covering them with heavy canvas or plastic sheets.

Installing protective coverings in areas of heavy pedestrian traffic to protect historic features such as wall coverings, parquet flooring and panelling.

Removing damaged or deteriorated paints and finishes to the next sound layer using the gentlest method possible, then repainting or refinishing using compatible paint or other coating systems.

Repainting with colors that are appropriate to the historic building.

Limiting abrasive cleaning methods to certain industrial or warehouse buildings where the interior masonry or plaster features do not have distinguishing design, detailing, tooling, or finishes; and where wood features are not finished, molded, beaded, or worked by hand. Abrasive cleaning should *only* be considered after other, gentler methods have been proven ineffective.

Evaluating the overall condition of materials to determine whether more than protection and maintenance are required, that is, if repairs to interior features and finishes will be necessary.

Not Recommended

Permitting entry into historic buildings through unsecured or broken windows and doors so that interior features and finishes are damaged by exposure to weather or through vandalism.

Stripping interiors of features such as woodwork, doors, windows, light fixtures, copper piping, radiators; or of decorative materials.

Failing to provide proper protection of interior features and finishes during work so that they are gouged, scratched, dented, or otherwise damaged.

Failing to take new use patterns into consideration so that interior features and finishes are damaged.

Using destructive methods such as propane or butane torches or sandblasting, to remove paint or other coatings. These methods can irreversibly damage the historic materials that comprise interior features.

Using new paint colors that are inappropriate to the historic building.

Changing the texture and patina of character-defining features through sandblasting or use of other abrasive methods to remove paint, discoloration or plaster. This includes both exposed wood (including structural members) and masonry.

Failing to undertake adequate measures to assure the preservation of interior features and finishes.

Recommended

Repairing interior features and finishes by reinforcing the historic materials. Repair will also generally include the limited replacement in kind—or with compatible substitute material—of those extensively deteriorated or missing parts of repeated features when there are surviving prototypes such as stairs, balustrades, wood panelling, columns; or decorative wall coverings or ornamental tin or plaster ceilings.

Replacing in kind an entire interior feature or finish that is too deteriorated to repair—if the overall form and detailing are still evident—using the physical evidence to guide the new work. Examples could include wainscoting, a tin ceiling, or interior stairs. If using the same kind of material is not technically or economically feasible, then a compatible substitute material may be considered.

The following work is highlighted to indicate that it represents the particularly complex technical or design aspects of rehabilitation projects and should only be considered after the preservation concerns listed above have been addressed.

Design for Missing Historic Features

Designing and installing a new interior feature or finish if the historic feature or finish is completely missing. This could include missing partitions, stairs, elevators, lighting fixtures, and wall coverings; or even entire rooms if all historic spaces, features, and finishes are missing or have been destroyed by inappropriate "renovations." The design may be a restoration based on historical, pictorial, and physical documentation; or be a new design that is compatible with the historic character of the building, district, or neighborhood.

Not Recommended

Replacing an entire interior feature such as a staircase, panelled wall, parquet floor, or cornice; or finish such as a decorative wall covering or ceiling when repair of materials and limited replacement of such parts are appropriate.

Using a substitute material for the replacement part that does not convey the visual appearance of the surviving parts or portions of the interior feature or finish or that is physically or chemically incompatible.

Removing a character-defining feature or finish that is unrepairable and not replacing it; or replacing it with a new feature or finish that does not convey the same visual appearance.

Creating a false historical appearance because the replaced feature is based on insufficient physical, historical, and pictorial documentation or on information derived from another building.

Introducing a new interior feature or finish that is incompatible with the scale, design, materials, color, and texture of the surviving interior features and finishes.

Alterations/Additions for the New Use

Recommended

Accommodating service functions such as bathrooms, mechanical equipment, and office machines required by the building's new use in secondary spaces such as first floor service areas or on upper floors.

Reusing decorative material or features that have had to be removed during the rehabilitation work including wall and baseboard trim, door moulding, panelled doors, and simple wainscoting; and relocating such material or features in areas appropriate to their historic placement.

Installing permanent partitions in secondary spaces; removable partitions that do not destroy the sense of space should be installed when the new use requires the subdivision of character-defining interior spaces.

Enclosing an interior stairway where required by code so that its character is retained. In many cases, glazed fire-rated walls may be used.

Placing new code-required stairways or elevators in secondary and service areas of the historic building.

Not Recommended

Dividing rooms, lowering ceilings, and damaging or obscuring character-defining features such as fireplaces, niches, stairways or alcoves, so that a new use can be accommodated in the building.

Discarding historic material when it can be reused within the rehabilitation project or relocating it in historically inappropriate areas.

Installing permanent partitions that damage or obscure character-defining spaces, features, or finishes.

Enclosing an interior stairway with fire-rated construction so that the stairwell space or any character-defining features are destroyed.

Radically changing, damaging, or destroying character-defining spaces, features, or finishes when adding new code-required stairways and elevators.

Recommended

Creating an atrium or a light well to provide natural light when required for the new use in a manner that preserves character-defining interior spaces, features, and finishes as well as the structural system.

Adding a new floor if required for the new use in a manner that preserves character-defining structural features, and interior spaces, features, and finishes.

Not Recommended

Destroying character-defining interior spaces, features, or finishes; or damaging the structural system in order to create an atrium or light well.

Inserting a new floor within a building that alters or destroys the fenestration; radically changes a character-defining interior space; or obscures, damages, or destroys decorative detailing.

Mechanical Systems: Heating, Air Conditioning, Electrical, and Plumbing

The visible features of historic heating, lighting, air conditioning and plumbing systems may sometimes help define the overall historic character of the building and should thus be retained and repaired, whenever possible. The systems themselves (the compressors, boilers, generators and their ductwork, wiring and pipes) will generally either need to be upgraded, augmented, or entirely replaced in order to accommodate the new use and to meet code requirements. Less frequently, individual portions of a system or an entire system are significant in the history of building technology; therefore, the identification of character-defining features or historically significant systems should take place together with an evaluation of their physical condition early in project planning.

Recommended

Identifying, retaining, and preserving visible features of early mechanical systems that are important in defining the overall historic character of the building, such as radiators, vents, fans, grilles, plumbing fixtures, switchplates, and lights.

Protecting and maintaining mechanical, plumbing, and electrical systems and their features through cyclical cleaning and other appropriate measures.

Preventing accelerated deterioration of mechanical systems by providing adequate ventilation of attics, crawlspaces, and cellars so that moisture problems are avoided.

Repairing mechanical systems by augmenting or upgrading system parts, such as installing new pipes and ducts; rewiring; or adding new compressors or boilers.

Replacing in kind—or with compatible substitute material—those visible features of mechanical systems that are either extensively deteriorated or are missing when there are surviving prototypes such as ceiling fans, switchplates, radiators, grilles, or plumbing fixtures.

Not Recommended

Removing or radically changing features of mechanical systems that are important in defining the overall historic character of the building so that, as a result, the character is diminished.

Failing to provide adequate protection of materials on a cyclical basis so that deterioration of mechanical systems and their visible features results.

Enclosing mechanical systems in areas that are not adequately ventilated so that deterioration of the systems results.

Replacing a mechanical system or its functional parts when it could be upgraded and retained.

Installing a replacement feature that does not convey the same visual appearance.

The following work is highlighted to indicate that it represents the particularly complex technical or design aspects of rehabilitation projects and should only be considered after the preservation concerns listed above have been addressed.

Recommended	Not Recommended
Alterations/Additions for the New Use	
Installing a completely new mechanical system if required for the new use so that it causes the least alteration possible to the building's floor plan, the exterior elevations, and the least damage to historic building material.	Installing a new mechanical system so that character-defining structural or interior features are radically changed, damaged, or destroyed.
Installing the vertical runs of ducts, pipes, and cables in closets, service rooms, and wall cavities.	Installing vertical runs of ducts, pipes, and cables in places where they will obscure character-defining features.
	Concealing mechanical equipment in walls or ceilings in a manner that requires the removal of historic building material.
	Installing "dropped" acoustical ceilings to hide mechanical equipment when this destroys the proportions of character-defining interior spaces.
Installing air conditioning units if required by the new use in such a manner that the historic materials and features are not damaged or obscured.	Cutting through features such as masonry walls in order to install air conditioning units.
Installing heating/air conditioning units in the window frames in such a manner that the sash and frames are protected. Window installations should be considered only when all other viable heating/cooling systems would result in significant damage to historic materials.	Radically changing the appearance of the historic building or damaging or destroying windows by installing heating/air conditioning units in historic window frames.

BUILDING SITE

The relationship between a historic building or buildings and landscape features within a property's boundaries—or the building site—helps to define the historic character and should be considered an integral part of overall planning for rehabilitation project work.

Recommended

Identifying, retaining, and preserving buildings and their features as well as features of the site that are important in defining its overall historic character. Site features can include driveways, walkways, lighting, fencing, signs, benches, fountains, wells, terraces, canal systems, plants and trees, berms, and drainage or irrigation ditches; and archeological features that are important in defining the history of the site.

Retaining the historic relationship between buildings, landscape features, and open space.

Protecting and maintaining buildings and the site by providing proper drainage to assure that water does not erode foundation walls; drain toward the building; nor erode the historic landscape.

Not Recommended

Removing or radically changing buildings and their features or site features which are important in defining the overall historic character of the building site so that, as a result, the character is diminished.

Removing or relocating historic buildings or landscape features, thus destroying the historic relationship between buildings, landscape features, and open space.

Removing or relocating historic buildings on a site or in a complex of related historic structures—such as a mill complex or farm—thus diminishing the historic character of the site or complex.

Moving buildings onto the site, thus creating a false historical appearance.

Lowering the grade level adjacent to a building to permit development of a formerly below-grade area such as a basement in a manner that would drastically change the historic relationship of the building to its site.

Failing to maintain site drainage so that buildings and site features are damaged or destroyed; or, alternatively, changing the site grading so that water no longer drains properly.

Recommended

Minimizing disturbance of terrain around buildings or elsewhere on the site, thus reducing the possibility of destroying unknown archeological materials.

Surveying areas where major terrain alteration is likely to impact important archeological sites.

Protecting, e.g. preserving in place known archeological material whenever possible.

Planning and carrying out any necessary investigation using professional archeologists and modern archeological methods when preservation in place is not feasible.

Protecting the building and other features of the site against arson and vandalism before rehabilitation work begins, i.e., erecting protective fencing and installing alarm systems that are keyed into local protection agencies.

Providing continued protection of masonry, wood, and architectural metals which comprise building and site features through appropriate surface treatments such as cleaning, rust removal, limited paint removal, and re-application of protective coating systems; and continued protection and maintenance of landscape features, including plant material.

Not Recommended

Introducing heavy machinery or equipment into areas where their presence may disturb archeological materials.

Failing to survey the building site prior to the beginning of rehabilitation project work so that, as a result, important archeological material is destroyed.

Leaving known archeological material unprotected and subject to vandalism, looting, and destruction by natural elements such as erosion.

Permitting unqualified project personnel to perform data recovery so that improper methodology results in the loss of important archeological material.

Permitting buildings and site features to remain unprotected so that plant materials, fencing, walkways, archeological features, etc. are damaged or destroyed.

Stripping features from buildings and the site such as wood siding, iron fencing, masonry balustrades; or removing or destroying landscape features, including plant material.

Failing to provide adequate protection of materials on a cyclical basis so that deterioration of building and site features results.

Recommended

Evaluating the overall condition of materials to determine whether more than protection and maintenance are required, that is, if repairs to building and site features will be necessary.

Repairing features of buildings and the site by reinforcing the historic materials. Repair will also generally include replacement in kind—with a compatible substitute material—of those extensively deteriorated or missing parts of features where there are surviving prototypes such as fencing and paving.

Replacing in kind an entire feature of the building or site that is too deteriorated to repair—if the overall form and detailing are still evident—using the physical evidence to guide the new work. This could include an entrance or porch, walkway, or fountain. If using the same kind of material is not technically or economically feasible, then a compatible substitute material may be considered.

Not Recommended

Failing to undertake adequate measures to assure the preservation of building and site features.

Replacing an entire feature of the building or site such as a fence, walkway, or driveway when repair of materials and limited replacement of deteriorated or missing parts are appropriate.

Using a substitute material for the replacement part that does not convey the visual appearance of the surviving parts of the building or site feature or that is physically or chemically incompatible.

Removing a feature of the building or site that is unrepairable and not replacing it; or replacing it with a new feature that does not convey the same visual appearance.

The following work is highlighted to indicate that it represents the particularly complex technical or design aspects of rehabilitation project work and should only be considered after the preservation concerns listed above have been addressed.

Recommended	Not Recommended
Design for Missing Historic Features	
Designing and constructing a new feature of a building or site when the historic feature is completely missing, such as an outbuilding, terrace, or driveway. It may be based on historical, pictorial, and physical documentation; or be a new design that is compatible with the historic character of the building and site.	Creating a false historical appearance because the replaced feature is based on insufficient historical, pictorial, and physical documentation.
	Introducing a new building or site feature that is out of scale or otherwise inappropriate.
	Introducing a new landscape feature or plant material that is visually incompatible with the site or that destroys site patterns or vistas.
Alterations/Additions for the New Use	
Designing new onsite parking, loading docks, or ramps when required by the new use so that they are as unobtrusive as possible and assure the preservation of character-defining features of the site.	Placing parking facilities directly adjacent to historic buildings where automobiles may cause damage to the buildings or landscape features or be intrusive to the building site.
Designing new exterior additions to historic buildings or adjacent new construction which is compatible with the historic character of the site and which preserve the historic relationship between a building or buildings, landscape features, and open space.	Introducing new construction onto the building site which is visually incompatible in terms of size, scale, design, materials, color and texture or which destroys historic relationships on the site.
Removing nonsignificant buildings, additions, or site features which detract from the historic character of the site.	Removing a historic building in a complex, a building feature, or a site feature which is important in defining the historic character of the site.

DISTRICT/ NEIGHBORHOOD

The relationship between historic buildings, and streetscape and landscape features within a historic district or neighborhood helps to define the historic character and therefore should always be a part of the rehabilitation plans.

Recommended

Identifying, retaining, and preserving buildings, and streetscape, and landscape features which are important in defining the overall historic character of the district or neighborhood. Such features can include streets, alleys, paving, walkways, street lights, signs, benches, parks and gardens, and trees.

Retaining the historic relationship between buildings, and streetscape and landscape features such as a town square comprised of row houses and stores surrounding a communal park or open space.

Protecting and maintaining the historic masonry, wood, and architectural metals which comprise building and streetscape features, through appropriate surface treatments such as cleaning, rust removal, limited paint removal, and reapplication of protective coating systems; and protecting and maintaining landscape features, including plant material.

Protecting buildings, paving, iron fencing, etc. against arson and vandalism before rehabilitation work begins by erecting protective fencing and installing alarm systems that are keyed into local protection agencies.

Not Recommended

Removing or radically changing those features of the district or neighborhood which are important in defining the overall historic character so that, as a result, the character is diminished.

Destroying streetscape and landscape features by widening existing streets, changing paving material, or introducing inappropriately located new streets or parking lots.

Removing or relocating historic buildings, or features of the streetscape and landscape, thus destroying the historic relationship between buildings, features and open space.

Failing to provide adequate protection of materials on a cyclical basis so that deterioration of building, streetscape, and landscape features results.

Permitting buildings to remain unprotected so that windows are broken; and interior features are damaged.

Stripping features from buildings or the streetscape such as wood siding, iron fencing, or terra cotta balusters; or removing or destroying landscape features, including plant material.

DISTRICT/NEIGHBORHOOD (continued)

Recommended

Evaluating the overall condition of building, streetscape and landscape materials to determine whether more than protection and maintenance are required, that is, if repairs to features will be necessary.

Repairing features of the building, streetscape, or landscape by reinforcing the historic materials. Repair will also generally include the replacement in kind—or with a compatible substitute material—of those extensively deteriorated or missing parts of features when there are surviving prototypes such as porch balustrades, paving materials, or streetlight standards.

Replacing in kind an entire feature of the building, streetscape, or landscape that is too deteriorated to repair—when the overall form and detailing are still evident—using the physical evidence to guide the new work. This could include a storefront, a walkway, or a garden. If using the same kind of material is not technically or economically feasible, then a compatible substitute material may be considered.

Not Recommended

Failing to undertake adequate measures to assure the preservation of building, streetscape, and landscape features.

Replacing an entire feature of the building, streetscape, or landscape such as a porch, walkway, or streetlight, when repair of materials and limited replacement of deteriorated or missing parts are appropriate.

Using a substitute material for the replacement part that does not convey the visual appearance of the surviving parts of the building, streetscape, or landscape feature or that is physically or chemically incompatible.

Removing a feature of the building, streetscape, or landscape that is unrepairable and not replacing it; or replacing it with a new feature that does not convey the same visual appearance.

The following work is highlighted because it represents the particularly complex technical or design aspects of rehabilitation projects and should only be considered after the preservation concerns listed above have been addressed.

Recommended	Not Recommended
Design for Missing Historic Features	
Designing and constructing a new feature of the building, streetscape, or landscape when the historic feature is completely missing, such as row house steps, a porch, streetlight, or terrace. It may be a restoration based on historical, pictorial, and physical documentation; or be a new design that is compatible with the historic character of the district or neighborhood.	Creating a false historical appearance because the replaced feature is based on insufficient historical, pictorial and physical documentation.
	Introducing a new building, streetscape or landscape feature that is out of scale or otherwise inappropriate to the setting's historic character, e.g., replacing picket fencing with chain link fencing.
Alterations/Additions for the New Use	
Designing required new parking so that it is as unobtrusive as possible, i.e., on side streets or at the rear of buildings. "Shared" parking should also be planned so that several business can utilize one parking area as opposed to introducing random, multiple lots.	Placing parking facilities directly adjacent to historic buildings which cause the removal of historic plantings, relocation of paths and walkways, or blocking of alleys.
Designing and constructing new additions to historic buildings when required by the new use. New work should be compatible with the historic character of the district or neighborhood in terms of size, scale, design, material, color, and texture.	Introducing new construction into historic districts that is visually incompatible or that destroys historic relationships within the district or neighborhood.
Removing nonsignificant buildings, additions, or streetscape and landscape features which detract from the historic character of the district or of the neighborhood.	Removing a historic building, building feature, or landscape or streetscape feature that is important in defining the overall historic character of the district or the neighborhood.

Although the work in these sections is quite often an important aspect of rehabilitation projects, it is usually *not* part of the overall process of preserving character-defining features (maintenance, repair, replacement); rather, such work is assessed for its potential negative impact on the building's historic character. For this reason, particular care must be taken not to obscure, radically change, damage, or destroy character-defining features in the process of rehabilitation work to meet new use requirements.

HEALTH AND SAFETY CODE REQUIREMENTS

As a part of the new use, it is often necessary to make modifications to a historic building so that it can comply with current health, safety and code requirements. Such work needs to be carefully planned and undertaken so that it does not result in a loss of character-defining spaces, features, and finishes.

Recommended

Identifying the historic building's character-defining spaces, features, and finishes so that code-required work will not result in their damage or loss.

Complying with health and safety code, including seismic codes and barrier-free access requirements, in such a manner that character-defining spaces, features, and finishes are preserved.

Working with local code officials to investigate alternative life safety measures or variances available under some codes so that alterations and additions to historic buildings can be avoided.

Providing barrier-free access through removable or portable, rather than permanent, ramps.

Providing seismic reinforcement to a historic building in a manner that avoids damaging the structural system and character-defining features.

Upgrading historic stairways and elevators to meet health and safety codes in a manner that assures their preservation, i.e., so that they are not damaged or obscured.

Installing sensitively designed fire suppression systems, such as a sprinkler system for wood frame mill buildings, instead of applying fire-resistant sheathing to character-defining features.

Not Recommended

Undertaking code-required alterations to a building or site before identifying those spaces, features, or finishes which are character-defining and must therefore be preserved.

Altering, damaging, or destroying character-defining spaces, features, and finishes while making modifications to a building or site to comply with safety codes.

Making changes to historic buildings without first seeking alternatives to code requirements.

Installing permanent ramps that damage or diminish character-defining features.

Reinforcing a historic building using measures that damage or destroy character-defining structural and other features.

Damaging or obscuring historic stairways and elevators or altering adjacent spaces in the process of doing work to meet code requirements.

Covering character-defining wood features with fire-resistant sheathing which results in altering their visual appearance.

Recommended

Applying fire-retardant coatings, such as intumescent paints, which expand during fire to add thermal protection to steel.

Adding a new stairway or elevator to meet health and safety codes in a manner that preserves adjacent character-defining features and spaces.

Placing a code-required stairway or elevator that cannot be accommodated within the historic building in a new exterior addition. Such an addition should be located at the rear of the building or on an inconspicuous side; and its size and scale limited in relationship to the historic building.

Not Recommended

Using fire-retardant coatings if they damage or obscure character-defining features.

Radically changing, damaging, or destroying character-defining spaces, features, or finishes when adding a new code-required stairway or elevator.

Constructing a new addition to accommodate code-required stairs and elevators on character-defining elevations highly visible from the street; or where it obscures, damages or destroys character-defining features.

ENERGY RETROFITTING

Some character-defining features of a historic building or site such as cupolas, shutters, transoms, skylights, sun rooms, porches, and plantings also play a secondary energy conserving role. Therefore, prior to retrofitting historic buildings to make them more energy efficient, the first step should always be to identify and evaluate the existing historic features to assess their inherent energy conserving potential. If it is determined that retrofitting measures are necessary, then such work needs to be carried out with particular care to insure that the building's historic character is preserved in the process of rehabilitation.

Recommended	*Not Recommended*
District/Neighborhood	
Maintaining those existing landscape features which moderate the effects of the climate on the setting such as deciduous trees, evergreen wind-blocks, and lakes or ponds.	Stripping the setting of landscape features and landforms so that the effects of the wind, rain, and the sun result in accelerated deterioration of historic materials.
Building Site	
Retaining plant materials, trees, and landscape features, especially those which perform passive solar energy functions such as sun shading and wind breaks.	Removing plant materials, trees, and landscape features, so that they no longer perform passive solar energy functions.
Installing freestanding solar collectors in a manner that preserves the historic property's character-defining features.	Installing freestanding solar collectors that obscure, damage, or destroy historic landscape or archeological features.
Designing attached solar collectors, including solar greenhouses, so that the character-defining features of the property are preserved.	Locating solar collectors where they radically change the property's appearance; or damage or destroy character-defining features.
Masonry/Wood/Architectural Metals	
Installing thermal insulation in attics and in unheated cellars and crawlspaces to increase the efficiency of the existing mechanical systems.	Applying urea of formaldehyde foam or any other thermal insulation with a water content into wall cavities in an attempt to reduce energy consumption.

Recommended	Not Recommended
Installing insulating material on the inside of masonry walls to increase energy efficiency where there is no character-defining interior moulding around the window or other interior architectural detailing.	Resurfacing historic building materials with more energy efficient but incompatible materials, such as covering historic masonry with exterior insulation.
Installing passive solar devices such as a glazed "trombe" wall on a rear or inconspicuous side of all the historic building.	Installing passive solar devices such as an attached glazed "trombe" wall on primary or other highly visible elevations; or where historic material must be removed or obscured.

Roofs

Recommended	Not Recommended
Placing solar collectors on noncharacter-defining roofs or roofs of nonhistoric adjacent buildings.	Placing solar collectors on roofs when such collectors change the historic roofline or obscure the relationship of the roof to character-defining roof features such as dormers, skylights, and chimneys.

Windows

Recommended	Not Recommended
Utilizing the inherent energy conserving features of a building by maintaining windows and louvered blinds in good operable condition for natural ventilation.	Removing historic shading devices rather than keeping them in an operable condition.
Improving thermal efficiency with weatherstripping, storm windows, caulking, interior shades, and, if historically appropriate, blinds and awnings.	Replacing historic multi-paned sash with new thermal sash utilizing false muntins.
Installing interior storm windows with airtight gaskets, ventilating holes, and/or removable clips to insure proper maintenance and to avoid condensation damage to historic windows.	Installing interior storm windows that allow moisture to accumulate and damage the window.

Recommended	Not Recommended
Installing exterior storm windows which do not damage or obscure the windows and frames.	Installing new exterior storm windows which are inappropriate in size or color, which are inoperable.
Considering the use of lightly tinted glazing on non-character-defining elevations if other energy retrofitting alternatives are not possible.	Replacing windows or transoms with fixed thermal glazing or permitting windows and transoms to remain inoperable rather than utilizing them for their energy conserving potential.
	Using tinted or reflective glazing on character-defining or other conspicuous elevations.

Entrances and Porches

Recommended	Not Recommended
Utilizing the inherent energy conserving features of a building by maintaining porches, and double vestibule entrances in good condition so that they can retain heat or block the sun and provide natural ventilation.	Enclosing porches located on character defining elevations to create passive solar collectors or airlock vestibules. Such enclosures can destroy the historic appearance of the building.

Interior Features

Recommended	Not Recommended
Retaining historic interior shutters and transoms for their inherent energy conserving features.	Removing historic interior features which play a secondary energy conserving role.

New Additions to Historic Buildings

Recommended	Not Recommended
Placing new additions that have an energy conserving function such as a solar greenhouse on non-character-defining elevations.	Installing new additions such as multistory solar greenhouse additions which obscure, damage, destroy character-defining features.

Mechanical Systems

Recommended	Not Recommended
Installing thermal insulation in attics and in unheated cellars and crawlspaces to conserve energy.	Apply urea formaldehyde foam or any other thermal insulation with a water content or that may collect moisture into wall cavities.

NEW ADDITIONS TO HISTORIC BUILDINGS

An attached exterior addition to a historic building expands its "outer limits" to create a new profile. Because such expansion has the capability to radically change the historic appearance, an exterior addition should be considered only after it has been determined that the new use cannot be successfully met by altering non-character-defining *interior* spaces. If the new use cannot be met in this way, then an attached exterior addition is usually an acceptable alternative. New additions should be designed and constructed so that the character-defining features of the historic building are not radically changed, obscured, damaged, or destroyed in the process of rehabilitation. New design should always be clearly differentiated so that the addition does not appear to be part of the historic resources.

Recommended

Placing functions and services required for the new use in non-character-defining interior spaces rather than installing a new addition.

Constructing a new addition so that there is the least possible loss of historic materials and so that character-defining features are not obscured, damaged, or destroyed.

Locating the attached exterior addition at the rear or on an inconspicuous side of a historic building; and limiting its size and scale in relationship to the historic building.

Designing new additions in a manner that makes clear what is historic and what is new.

Not Recommended

Expanding the size of the historic building by constructing a new addition when the new use could be met by altering non-character-defining interior spaces.

Attaching a new addition so that the character-defining features of the historic building are obscured, damaged, or destroyed.

Designing a new addition so that its size and scale in relation to the historic building are out of proportion, thus diminishing the historic character.

Duplicating the exact form, material, style, and detailing of the historic building in the new addition so that the new work appears to be part of the historic building.

Imitating a historic style or period of architecture in new additions, especially for contemporary uses such as drive-in banks or garages.

Recommended

Considering the attached exterior addition both in terms of the new use and the appearance of other buildings in the historic district or neighborhood. Design for the new work may be contemporary or may reference design motifs from the historic building. In either case, it should always be clearly differentiated from the historic building and be compatible in terms of mass, materials, relationship of solids to voids, and color.

Placing new additions such as balconies and greenhouses on non-character-defining elevations and limiting the size and scale in relationship to the historic building.

Designing additional stories, when required for the new use, that are set back from the wall plane and are as inconspicuous as possible when viewed from the street.

Not Recommended

Designing and constructing new additions that result in the diminution or loss of the historic character of the resource, including its design, materials, workmanship, location, or setting.

Using the same wall plane, roof line, cornice height, materials, siding lap or window type to make additions appear to be a part of the historic building.

Designing new additions such as multistory greenhouse additions that obscure, damage, or destroy character-defining features of the historic building.

Constructing additional stories so that the historic appearance of the building is radically changed.

☆U.S. GOVERNMENT PRINTING OFFICE : 1989 O - 230-394

INTERPRETING THE SECRETARY OF THE INTERIOR'S STANDARDS FOR HISTORIC PRESERVATION PROJECTS

(selected issues)

[*Note:* As distributed by the National Park Service, these publications contain copies of photographs of the buildings to which they relate, illustrating the particular features being discussed. These photographs have not been reproduced here.]

Number: 84-058

Applicable Standards

2. Retention of Distinguishing Architectural Character (nonconformance)
5. Sensitive Treatment of Distinctive Features and Craftsmanship (nonconformance)
9. Compatible Contemporary Design for New Alterations/Additions (nonconformance)

Subject: Inappropriate Size and Scale of New Exterior Additions: Loss of Historic Character

Issue: In the Secretary of the Interior's "Standards for Rehabilitation," the Department of the Interior acknowledges that a new exterior addition to a historic building (such as a fire stair, service wing, or additional story) may be essential to return the property to a state of utility for an efficient contemporary use; however, at the same time, the cumulative effect of the design and installation process of a new addition must not radically change, damage, destroy, or obscure those "portions and features of the property which are significant to its historic, architectural, or cultural values" (36 CFR 67.2).

Therefore, in evaluating the appropriateness of a new addition, it is critical that the important character-defining materials, form, features, and detailing of the historic building be properly identified so that they may be protected and preserved. This identification process will also make clear those "portions and features" of the historic property that are *not* important in defining the historic character and may thus be reasonably altered or added to in the course of rehabilitating for the new use.

Because of the difficulty in designing sensitive new additions and to clarify what constitutes a compatible new addition, the NPS has expanded its guidance in this area (see pp. 56-57, "New Exterior Additions to Historic Buildings" in the Revised Guidelines to the Standards for Rehabilitation, 1983). The advice listed first in the guidelines is to avoid constructing a new exterior addition altogether because of the potential for altering and expanding the historic form and thereby diminishing the historic character. Rather, it is recommended that services and functions required by the new use be located in non-character-defining *interior* spaces. Only after it is determined that interior spaces cannot be utilized, should a new exterior addition be considered at all. Then, the new addition should be designed so that its size and scale are limited in proportion in relationship to the historic building— and located on an inconspicuous side of a historic building to further assure that there will be no radical changes to the historic form and appearance.

The failure to recognize those qualities that comprise a building's historic character (its materials, form, features, and detailing as well as relationship to the site and the district) prior to designing and attaching a new exterior addition can result in overall changes that are inconsistent with the historic character. In consequence, Standard 2, 5, or 9 may be violated, thus jeopardizing project certification.

Application: A small late 1920s Mission Revival building of brick construction with stucco finish is primarily distinguished on the main facade by a waved parapet cap and symmetrically placed openings (see illus. 1). In rehabilitating the building for use as law offices, interior and exterior work was undertaken, including replacement of damaged plastered walls, re-stuccoing of the brick, cleaning and painting of windows, and the construction of two new exterior additions.

The first new addition consisted of enclosing existing stairs at one end of the facade for the clients' main entrance, as well as serving as handicapped access to a ground floor elevator. The second new addition was a non-functional matching wing wall at the other end of the facade which the developer felt would preserve the sense of symmetry which was so strong in the historic building (see illus. 2 and 3).

After reviewing the Part II application, the State office recommended denial of the project, citing violation of Standards 5 and 9; the regional office, completing its review, concurred with the State's assessment. In a denial letter to the owner, the regional office stated:

> The new additions, consisting of the exterior stairs enclosure at one end of the facade and the wing wall at the other end, increase the length of the facade by at least one-third, thereby altering significantly its overall mass, scale, and proportional relationships. Further, these additions extend and expand on the symmetrical historic design of the facade in a way that lends to it a degree of expansiveness ... not present in the simple design character of the structure's original design features. It is apparent that the attempt to match the color, texture, and detail of the original design and to continue its symmetry by extending the facade wall was motivated by a desire to preserve the historic character of the building. In effect, however, this matching new design is incompatible: it compounds the additions' negative

visual impacts on the original design by making contemporary and historic portions of the building indistinguishable from one another.

When the project was subsequently appealed, the Chief Appeals Officer sustained the regional office's decision that the new additions violated Standards 5 and 9, adding that "they also give the building a monumentality that, historically, it never possessed, thus changing its historic character." In consequence, the project also failed to conform to Standard 2. As part of the appeals process, the architect forwarded three drawings (schemes A, B, and C; see illus. 4, 5, and 6) for possible changes to the new additions to bring the project into conformance with the Standards and thus qualify for Federal historic preservation tax incentives. After reviewing all of the drawings, the Chief Appeals Officer concluded in his final letter to the owner:

> The only remedial action that can now be taken ... would be to follow scheme "C": insert a wide expansion joint between the historic building facade and the new stair enclosure, demolish the new wing wall, lower the parapet on the stair tower by at least one foot, and paint the new addition a different color than the original facade. These actions would make the distinction between the old and new construction clear; and would restore to the building its aspect of a modest, simplified Spanish Colonial Revival commercial structure. Demolition of the wing wall would allow one to view the continuous wavy cornice as it carries around the corner. If the final revised project fails to meet any of the above conditions, it will not meet the Standards and cannot be certified.

Prepared by: Kay D. Weeks, TPS

These bulletins are issued to explain preservation project decisions made by the U.S. Department of the Interior. The resulting determinations, based on the Secretary of the Interior's Standards for Rehabilitation, are not necessarily applicable beyond the unique facts and circumstances of each particular case.

Number: 84-059

Applicable Standards:

2. Retention of Distinguishing Architectural Character (nonconformance)
5. Sensitive Treatment of Distinctive Features and Craftsmanship (nonconformance)
6. Repair/Replacement of Deteriorated or Missing Features Based on Historical Evidence (nonconformance)

Subject: Replacing a Significant Interior Feature to Meet Health and Safety Code Requirements

Issue: To comply with health and safety codes in rehabilitation projects, the Revised Guidelines to the Secretary of the Interior's "Standards for Rehabilitation" first recommendation to owners and developers is to work with local code officials to investigate variances available under some codes or to devise creative and safe alternatives so that alterations and additions to historic buildings can be avoided completely, if possible. Because such variances or alternatives may not always be feasible, owners and developers are next advised to identify significant spaces, features, and finishes, so that they can be preserved in the process of successfully meeting code requirements (such as providing barrier-free access, upgrading historic stairways or elevators, or installing fire suppression systems).

While it is understood that owners must often undertake work necessary to meet health and safety codes, the Department of the Interior—by law—cannot approve rehabilitation projects if significant interior spaces, features, or finishes are lost as a result of such code-required work and, in consequence, the rehabilitation is not consistent with the historic character of the building. In reviewing an overall project, it is thus critical that administrators evaluate work proposals to assure that significant interior features are properly identified so that they may be protected and preserved in the process of meeting health and safety code requirements. Where a conflict exists between code requirements and the Secretary of the Interior's "Standards for Rehabilitation," it should be noted that ". . . The Secretary of the Interior's Standards take precedence over other regulations and the codes in determining whether the historic character of the building is preserved in the process of rehabilitation and should be certified." 36 CFR 67.7(d).

Application: An early 20th century commercial building was being rehabilitated for use as medical offices (see illus. 1). As a result of an inspection by a structural engineer to assure compliance with State health and safety codes, proposed rehabilitation work involved removal of a historic ornamental iron cage-type elevator that was manually operated (see illus. 2) and replacement with a modern elevator (see illus. 3) featuring automatic pushbutton operation. (The ANSI building code specifically requires an enclosed cab and hollow metal shaft doors.) Additional proposed work included removal of the ground floor elevator doors; removal of one set of the existing west-side elevator doors on floors 3 through 7; and the subsequent blocking of access to the elevator on that side due to limited passenger use after rehabilitation (see illus. 4 and 5).

When the project was initially reviewed by the SHPO, recommendation for certification was made because it was felt that loss of the elevator—although unfortunate—did not constitute a radical change to the building's interior. However, when the National Park Service evaluated the proposed work that principally involved removal of the historic elevator and replacement with a modern elevator to meet code, a final determination was made that such removal of a significant interior feature violated Standards 2, 5, and 6. The denial letter to the owner stated:

> The elevator with its highly elaborate iron grillwork and the decoratively molded elevator doors in the lobby is a significant historic feature which contributes to the historic character of this early twentieth century commercial building. The features of the elevator, particularly the decorative cab and the lobby doors are historically significant elements which should be preserved. Your rehabilitation ... will lead to the loss of a significant feature of the building, in violation of the Standards of Rehabilitation, and the rehabilitation will not be consistent with the historic character of the building. For purposes of the historic preservation tax incentives, the Standards for Rehabilitation take precedence over other regulations and codes in determining whether the historic character of the building is preserved in the process of rehabilitation and should be certified (36 CFR 67.7(d)).

The denial was subsequently appealed and, in spite of the owner's referral to ANSI codes requiring enclosure of the elevator, the NPS decision was sustained by the Chief Appeals Officer, who reiterated in the letter to the owner,". . . since a rehabilitation must preserve the historic character of a property to be certified, I have determined that this project is not consistent with the historic character of the building and does not meet the "Standards for Rehabilitation." In the same letter —in order to achieve a certifiable project—the owner was encouraged to pursue alternative means of preserving the elevator by enclosing the cab itself with fire-rated glass or by constructing a fire-rated enclosure for the elevator shaft.

Prepared by: Kay D. Weeks, TPS

These bulletins are issued to explain preservation project decisions made by the U.S. Department of the Interior. The resulting determinations, based on the Secretary of the Interior's Standards for Rehabilitation, are not necessarily applicable beyond the unique facts and circumstances of each particular case.

Number: 84-061

Applicable Standards:

2. Retention of Distinguishing Architectural Character (nonconformance)
3. Recognition of Historic Period (nonconformance)
4. Retention of Significant Later Alterations/Additions (nonconformance)
6. Repair/Replacement of Deteriorated or Missing Architectural Features Based on Historical Evidence (nonconformance)

Subject: Alterations to Non-Original 20th Century Storefronts

Issue: Storefronts on many 19th and early 20th century buildings were changed in the 1920s and 1930s, incorporating new materials and designs popular at that time and introducing trademarks of the increasing number of commercial chains. Some of these later storefronts today have no intrinsic value while others merit preservation as part of the historic structure.

As guidance in evaluating non-original storefronts, those that meet one or more of the following categories usually are worthy of retention:

1. Exhibit high quality workmanship;
2. Show evidence of being architect-designed;
3. Incorporate materials not commonly used today but are characteristic of a particular period (e.g., curved glass, Carrara glass, bronze frames);
4. Are representative of a particular architectural style;
5. Are compatible with the rest of the building in terms of design and scale and date to a historically significant period of the building and/or district.

Application: A two-story commercial building located in a historic district in the Southwest was operated until recently as part of the S. H. Kress Company store chain (see illus. 1). While the building dates to the early teens, the storefront had been altered in the late 1930s, incorporating a distinctive design which was a trademark of many Kress Company buildings. The band of transom windows, recessed entries, metal framing and large glass display windows sections created the visual image characteristic of, and historically associated with, the Kress Company chain and its buildings constructed or renovated in the 1920s and 1930s (see illus. 2 and

3). Thus, while the 50-year age criteria of the National Register was minimally met, greater significance was attached to the storefront because it was part of the nationwide Kress Company effort in storefront design. While the new owners of the building originally had intended to maintain the existing storefront, breakage of one of the large curved glass sections posed an unforseen rehabilitation problem since such glass was not readily available locally in the required safety glass. With the overall rehabilitation progressing quickly, the decision was made to replace the entire storefront with a composite design referencing features from other buildings in the historic district (see illus. 4). Regretfully, little physical or pictorial evidence of the original appearance of the building had survived. The completed rehabilitation was denied certification and the decision sustained on appeal primarily because of the loss of the intact 1930s storefront (Standard 4), but also because the new storefront was a conjectural historic design and contained inappropriate detailing (Standards 2, 3, and 6). Regarding the problem of availability of materials—curved glass sections—cost was not the major factor but rather time. Given time, companies could have been located which make such custom shapes in safety glass. Unfortunately, expedience and perhaps only mild apprecation of the historic importance of the 1930s storefront did not facilitate the careful investigation of such alternatives.

Prepared by: Charles E. Fisher, TPS

These bulletins are issued to explain preservation project decisions made by the U.S. Department of the Interior. The resulting determinations, based on the Secretary of the Interior's Standards for Rehabilitation, are not necessarily applicable beyond the unique facts and circumstances of each particular case.

Number: 84-062

Applicable Standards:

2. Retention of Distinguishing Architectural Character (conformance)
4. Retention of Significant Later Alterations /Additions (conformance)
5. Sensitive Treatment of Distinctive Features and Craftsmanship (conformance)

Subject: Replacing Altered Features of a Historic Storefront: Compatible Contemporary Design

Issue: Standards 2, 4, and 5 call for the retention of distinctive architectural features—whether original or changes that reflect the history and development of the building or the craftsmanship of its builders—and Standard 6 states that such distinctive features should be repaired rather than replaced, wherever possible. However, there may be cases where, over time, there has been a cumulative loss of historic material comprising these features and introduction of new material that neither exhibits a distinctive style nor special craftsmanship. (Examples of material loss may include decorative portions of a building such as a storefront cornice; more functional portions, such as its display windows, entrance doors, metal kick plates, or transoms; larger portions that combine structural and design roles within the overall storefront such as masonry, wood, or cast-iron pilasters between bays; or even the individual storefront bays themselves.)

If individual features of a storefront have been altered and the alterations are not "changes that have acquired significance in their own right," then the preservation and repair requirements of Standard 6 do not apply. In these cases, the nonsignificant later features may be removed and compatible replacement features designed and installed as long as the new work preserves any remaining historic material, the storefront character is preserved, and the overall rehabilitation is consistent with the historic character of the building. The option of replacing features, such as storefront doors or windows would, however, never extend to later, distinctive features that help define the storefront character.

In summary, it is cautioned that a thorough professional evaluation be made prior to removal to ascertain both the significance of individual storefront features as well as their potential for repair. Demolition of distinctive architectural features and craftsmanship can be the basis for denying an entire rehabilitation project.

Appendix D

Application: A 6-story brownstone and terra-cotta structure built in the 1890s and located in a historic district in a southeastern city was being rehabilitated for retail and office use. Proposed exterior work included removal of nonoriginal 20th century storefront infill features—transoms, double doors, glass display windows, and concrete block kick panels (see illus. 1, 2). A contemporary replacement storefront would then be installed within the original cast-iron columns, pilasters, and framing, thus retaining the three-bay division of the historic storefront. The owner's primary reason for removing much of the later storefront—those nonoriginal portions—was to integrate an additional code-required fire exit into an overall design scheme that he felt would successfully reflect the building's new use as an art gallery.

In its initial review, the SHPO recommended approval of the project work, but expressed concern over whether or not the 20th storefront infill features had acquired significance over time. In the regional review, the project was denied certification. In a letter to the owner, the reasons for denial were explained:

> We have reviewed your proposal to replace the existing storefront with a new entrance of contemporary design that would meet the code requirement of providing a second fire exit. Though not original to the building, the storefront appears to be of sufficient age and design quality to have gained significance in its own right; we feel that its removal would violate Standards 4 and 5. Although we recognize the need to install a fire exit through one of the side display windows, alternative methods were suggested to the architect by this office that would avoid damaging the significant portions of the storefront (i.e., the gridded transom windows and double doors) and which would not require replacement of the entire storefront ... In the absence of documentation demonstrating that the existing storefront is not significant in terms of its age, period, style, materials, or condition, we cannot approve its removal for the purpose of installing a modern entrance to the building.

Because the owner felt that the existing storefront needed to be altered to accommodate code; that the altered portions were not important historically; and that the contemporary storefront met Standard 9, the region's decision was appealed. Prior to appeal, the SHPO offered a final recommendation on the storefront replacement issue in a letter to the Chief Appeals Officer, supporting the owner's contention that new evidence seemed to indicate that most of the later alterations to the storefront had post-dated the 1930s:

> In our initial review of the project, much discussion occurred concerning the significance of the existing storefront. While the existing storefront, which is obviously not original, is of nice design, it is not of sufficient quality to say that the storefront has acquired special significance in its own right or that it is important to retain the storefront to show the evolution of the building through history. In addition, I have personally inspected the building and believe that the storefront is not representative of any particular stylistic period and is not an example of skilled craftsmanship or a good example of design and use of material.

On appeal, the regional decision was overturned and the project subsequently certified for preservation tax benefits. In a final letter to the owner, the Chief Appeals Officer stated:

After carefully considering information submitted by your architect concerning the construction detail and dating of the existing storefront and comments provided by the State Historic Preservation Officer, I have determined that the proposed project meets the Secretary's Standards. I share, however, some of the concerns of the regional office regarding proposed storefront design. While I have concluded that the existing storefront has not acquired special significance over time nor exhibits significant stylistic features or craftsmanship, I would encourage you to consider a contemporary design that provides greater visual distinction between the transom and the display windows. I would also encourage you to revise your design to provide for solid base panels beneath the windows and doors. These alterations would, I feel, be more in keeping with the historic character of the building and district yet would clearly "read" as new construction.

After removal of the altered, nonhistoric portions of the storefront, the compatible new infill was installed, thus retaining and preserving those original portions identified as historically significant (see illus. 3, 4).

Prepared by: Kay D. Weeks and Charles E. Fisher, TPS

These bulletins are issued to explain preservation project decisions made by the U.S. Department of the Interior. The resulting determinations, based on the Secretary of the Interior's Standards for Rehabilitation, are not necessarily applicable beyond the unique facts and circumstances of each particular case.

Number: 84-063

Applicable Standard:

7. Cleaning with Gentlest Method Possible (nonconformance)

Subject: Inappropriate Chemical Cleaning of Historic Masonry Buildings

Standard 7 of the Secretary of the Interior's Standards for Rehabilitation states that "the surface cleaning of structures shall be undertaken with the gentlest means possible. Sandblasting and other cleaning methods that will damage the historic building materials shall not be undertaken." While "the gentlest means possible" is usually interpreted to mean chemical cleaning, water, or water with the addition of detergents, it is important to realize that these methods, too, can be damaging to historic building fabric. Cleaning techniques involving water or chemicals are not infallible, and must always be tested. If carried out improperly—for instance, if the chemical mixture is too strong, if chemicals are not adequately rinsed out of the masonry, if wet cleaning methods are undertaken during cold weather or if there is still a possibility of freezing temperatures—such cleaning methods can physically abrade or otherwise visually damage historic masonry. In short, chemical cleaning may not be "the gentlest means possible." Historic masonry buildings (and brick buildings in particular) which have been chemically cleaned in a way that has resulted in damage to the visual or aesthetic qualities of the masonry, may be denied certification for tax benefits.

Application No. 1: A 1912 bank and office building constructed of brick with stone and terra cotta trim was rehabilitated for contemporary office use after being vacant for several years (see illus. 1). Located at a major downtown intersection, this nine-story building is a prominent and highly visible landmark throughout the city, towering as it does above the more modestly scaled two or three story neighboring buildings. The proposed project which was given preliminary approval by the National Park Service, and was carried out in 1982, included refurbishing of office suites on the interior, chemical cleaning of the exterior masonry, and replacement of the later 1940s storefront infill with more appropriately scaled window glass.

When the completed project was submitted to the National Park Service for final review, however, it was denied certification on the basis of the cleaning techniques which had resulted in "severe discoloration and splotching of the brick surfaces" (see illus. 2). The region's denial letter went on to say: "The brick was apparently cleaned with an inappropriate chemical cleaner which was not adequately tested before its use, contrary to the recommendations contained in the Secretary's Guidelines for Rehabilitating Historic Buildings. Although the physical damage to the brick was not documented, the region felt that the *visual* change to the brick surface was sufficient to deny the project, citing violation of Standards 7 and 2."

When the owner appealed the denial he explained that the exterior of the building had actually been cleaned *and* treated with a water repellent *two* times. Unsatisfied with the result after the first chemical cleaning, the owner required the cleaning contractor to reclean the building in what turned out to be a futile attempt to improve the appearance of the brick. During the appeal, the owner was unable to identify the type of chemicals or the methods used in the cleaning, nor did he provide any close-up photographs of the discolored brick. Consequently, it remained unknown whether the chemical cleaning had also caused physical damage to the brick.

After careful review of the project, the Chief Appeals Officer sustained the region's decision, stating that: "I concur with the regional office's finding that this treatment (cleaning of the exterior brickwork) 'has so altered the appearance of the building as to detract from its historic character.' Standard 7 permits only the gentlest means of surface cleaning. . . . Close-up photographs showing the conditions of the brick before and after this process (the second cleaning) were not submitted, nor were technical details of the cleaning methods and substances made available. Nevertheless, it is convincingly evident from the extent and degree of the persistent discoloration that the brickwork was subjected to unacceptably harsh cleaning. Accordingly, I find a violation of Standard 7."

Application No. 2: In a second case, a mid-nineteenth century brick rowhouse was rehabilitated for rental residential use (see illus. 3). A major aspect of the rehabilitation of the exterior was the removal of paint covering the brick facade. The project application stated that the building was to be chemically cleaned, generally an acceptable paint removal technique in accordance with the Secretary of the Interior's "Standards for Rehabilitation," and the proposal was given preliminary approval by the National Park Service. However, when the request for final certification was submitted, photographs showed that the "cleaned" brick appeared to have been damaged by the cleaning method (see illus. 4). When questioned, the owner revealed that the paint had been removed with sodium hydroxide, more commonly called caustic soda or lye. With the knowledge that some types of chemical cleaning may be just as damaging to historic brick as sandblasting, it was decided that an on-site inspection of the property by the National Park Service was necessary in order to determine if, indeed, the brick really had been damaged by this method of paint removal. At the project site, comparison of the cleaned brick with the painted brick of an identical row house on the same block provided evidence (see illus. 4 and 5) that the surface of the rather soft brick had been "etched" by lye.

On that basis, the project was denied certification by the National Park Service Regional office. The denial letter sent to the owner stated: "The National Park

Service has been cautioning property owners for some time about the dangers of paint removal and cleaning of soft masonry. The (State Historic Preservation Office) has been advising property owners concerning the early practice of painting many . . . rowhouses for aesthetic reasons and as a protective treatment for inherently poor quality brick. We strongly urge you to be more cautious in future projects when you consider removing paint from historic masonry, we would encourage you not to remove paint where historically such surface treatment has acquired significance over time. Where paint removal is an appropriate treatment, only the gentlest means possible, determined by careful testing, should be used. *If no method can be found which does not damage the brick or change its original visual appearance, the paint should not be removed."*

When the owner appealed this decision, the Chief Appeals Officer upheld the denial of the regional office, explaining that "as a result of the cleaning, the surface of the brick has been eroded, exposing additional folds and irregularities in the clay and creating a rougher texture to the brick. These visual and physical changes to the brick have altered the character of the masonry facade."

Prepared by: Anne E. Grimmer, TPS

These bulletins are issued to explain preservation project decisions made by the U.S. Department of the Interior. The resulting determinations, based on the Secretary of the Interior's Standards for Rehabilitation, are not necessarily applicable beyond the unique facts and circumstances of each particular case.

Number: 84-064

Standards for Evaluating Significance Within Registered Historic Districts (36 CFR 67.5 (a) (2))

Subject: Extensive Replacement of Historic Materials/Features: Loss of Integrity

Issue: In planning any rehabilitation project, it is assumed that some historic materials (masonry, wood, and metal) will be deteriorated or damaged and need repair or replacement in preparation for the new use. While a reasonable level of replacement of such deteriorated or damaged exterior and interior material is acceptable, at the same time the preservation requirements outlined in 36 CFR 67 must always be met. To receive Part 1 certification, the building, *prior* to rehabilitation, must convey historic significance through its intact features, i.e., display integrity of design, materials, and workmanship, location, feeling, and association according to the Secretary of the Interior's "Standards for Evaluating Historic Significance Within Registered Historic Districts"; and to receive Part 2 certification, the building, *after* rehabilitation, must retain those portions and features of the building that have been identified as significant prior to work, in accordance with the Secretary of the Interior's "Standards for Rehabilitation."

If, after close inspection, it becomes clear that the significant portions and features of the building cannot be retained and preserved because of the extent of physical deterioration or damage, then the building will generally not possess sufficient integrity of design, materials, and workmanship to be designated as a "certified historic structure" and, in consequence, Part 1 certification should be denied. In unusual cases where Part 1 certification has already been issued and, during the course of rehabilitation, it is discovered that the structure does not possess sufficient integrity, the Part 1 certification should be rescinded and the Part 2 application returned to the owner, unprocessed, with a letter explaining the action.

Application: A deteriorated, three-story, three-bay wide brick structure built in 1843 was certified in the Part 1 application as contributing to the significance of the registered historic district—a 13-block area of 19th century Federal and Greek Revival structures (see illus. 1, 2, 3, 4).

A Part 2 application was submitted at the same time as the Part 1 application, but a determination on Part 2 could not be given due to a lack of information concerning the below-grade storefront which the owner proposed removing as part of the work to return the building to a residential appearance. The letter from NPS, WASO requesting additional information, stated:

> Although the application material indicates that the structure was originally residential, the photographs suggest that the storefront, including the projecting bay with side entrance door and cornice, may have acquired historic significance over time. For this office to make a Part 2 assessment, however, you will have to provide information concerning the building's conversion on the lower floor to commercial use and the approximate date of the existing storefront. Photographs of the storefront showing in more detail what had survived should be submitted. When additional information and photographic documentation is received, a determination can be made as to whether the project meets the Standards for Rehabilitation.

In response, the owner submitted the requested information on the storefront in order to process the Part 2 application; this particular work component was reviewed and found to be in conformance with the Standards.

The amended application also included new photographic documentation that revealed the severely deteriorated condition of previously blocked-up portions of the rear of the building and the extent of damage and loss of both exterior and interior features. This portion of the building had not been assessed in the initial application, but was assumed to be substantially intact when Part 1 certification was issued. The newly submitted photographic documentation called into question the integrity of design, materials, and workmanship of the building, and it was decided to re-evaluate the Part 1 certification (see illus. 5, 6, 7). Following re-assessment, a second letter was sent to the owner, explaining the region's findings:

> Based on the information submitted in the original application, the National Park Service determined that the property contributed to the significance of the registered historic district in which it was located, and thus qualified (for tax benefits) as a "certified historic structure." This certification was based on the assumption that a majority of the structure was still standing and that character-giving features such as interior trim, moldings, and fireplace details would be retained.
>
> The new photographic documentation that you submitted shows that barely one-third of the building was standing at the time rehabilitation work commenced. As a result of the building's extremely deteriorated condition, significant architectural features are too deteriorated to be preserved on the remaining portion of the building. In addition, nearly all interior finishes are to be replaced and rebuilt using new materials. As a result of the new information, we have determined that No. 2 of the "Standards for Evaluating Significance Within Registered Historic Districts" has been met (e.g., the structure does *not* contribute to the significance of the district) and, therefore, the building cannot qualify as a "certified historic structure." This decision supersedes the earlier decision . . . since the building does not qualify as a "certified historic structure," in accordance with Department of Interior regulations, the project is not eligible for certification of rehabilitation.

Because the owner felt preservation tax incentives should be made available and the Part 2 processed, the project was appealed. On appeal, the region's denial of Part 1 was affirmed by the Chief Appeals Officer, who reiterated: "Similarly, I have determined that it is not a certified historic structure because the integrity of the original design, individual architectural features and spaces have been irretrievably lost through physical deterioration and structural damage . . . ."

Prepared by: Kay D. Weeks, TPS

These bulletins are issued to explain preservation project decisions made by the U.S. Department of the Interior. The resulting determinations, based on the Secretary of the Interior's Standards for Rehabilitation, are not necessarily applicable beyond the unique facts and circumstances of each particular case.

Appendix D

Number: 85-065

Applicable Standards:

1. Compatible New Use (conformance)
2. Retention of Distinguishing Architectural Character (nonconformance, conformance)
5. Sensitive Treatment of Distinctive Features and Craftsmanship (nonconformance, conformance)
6. Repair/Replacement of Deteriorated or Missing Features (conformance)
9. Compatible Design for New Alterations/Additions (nonconformance, conformance)

Subject: Alterations to Historic Auditorium Spaces

Issue: Changing the use of historic auditorium spaces, such as those in theaters, churches and schools, poses difficult design problems. Some new uses cannot be accommodated in such auditoriums without destroying character-defining spaces or features. Dividing the space, or altering or destroying its features will result in a denial of certification for noncompliance with Standards 2 and 5. However, there are cases where earlier insensitive alteration to, or extensive deterioration of, the materials comprising significant features and spaces has already resulted in loss of the historic character. In such cases, further alterations to accommodate a new use will generally not result in denial of rehabilitation certification. It is particularly important, however, that a careful professional evaluation be made of altered spaces and deteriorated features to assure that repair is, indeed, infeasible.

Applications: A small church built in 1875 in the Gothic style and located in a historic district had been purchased by a neighboring church in 1923 for use as an educational facility. During the 1960s it had been used as a theater and recreational center (see illus. 1 and 2). A proposal was made to rehabilitate the structure into residential condominiums (see illus. 3). In order to accomplish this conversion, the owner proposed to subdivide the interior space and to insert three new floor levels into the sanctuary.

The regional office denied the project preliminary certification on the basis that the "austere interior is of major importance" in defining the "ecclesiastical character of the structure." It found that inserting seven residential units into the interior would seriously impair that character. While the concept of inserting residences into the church was not ruled out, the plans as submitted were deemed unsatisfactory because they involved the "total loss of the original volume and space of the sanctuary."

Upon appeal the owner stressed the alterations made to the interior during the previous 20 years. The "austere" appearance resulted, he stated, from the gutting of the interior to provide a basketball court. The interior did not, therefore, contribute to the overall character of the building. He further stated that "the sense of volume and the ecclesiastical character of the former church will be retained in the individual apartment units. After the rehabilitation, this building will look like a church, as it does now."

In his decision upholding the denial of certification, the Chief Appeals Officer determined that changes made to the interior over the years had not seriously diminished the historic character of that space. The alterations, he said, "appear to amount to little more than removal of church furnishings." He noted that the church retains such features as the regularly spaced windows, the conspicuous roof structure and exposed scissor trusses, and that the extent and form of the space remain. Overall, he concluded, the interior still conveys a sense of the purpose for which it was designed—assembly. The interior space, therefore, was determined to be integral to the historic character of the building. Because that space would be destroyed by the insertion of apartments as planned, certification was denied.

A second case involved an 1890's brownstone, Romanesque Revival church with an octagon plan sanctuary, individually listed in the National Register, and located in a residential section of a major northeastern city. A rehabilitation was proposed to convert the building, which had been empty for fourteen years, to medical offices. The new use necessitated insertion of three floors and office partitions into the sanctuary (see illus. 4). The interior had ornate, clustered, engaged colonettes; acanthus leaf entablatures; a wooden chair rail; four arched tripartite windows; an egg-and-dart ceiling cornice; and a shallow dished ceiling. Plans called for enclosing most of the deteriorated plaster detailing on the walls with furred-out walls, and removal of the lath and plaster of the dished ceiling (see illus. 5).

The church had been converted to a synagogue in 1948, at which time the organ; organ chamber; choir, choir gate, and railing; pulpit; stained glass windows; and pendant lighting fixtures had been removed. Shortly afterward (early 1950s), an acoustical tile ceiling and recessed lighting were installed. During fourteen years of disuse, the building's attic and tower had become infested with pigeons, little maintenance had been done, the building was without heat, and had been vandalized.

The NPS regional office denied the proposal preliminary certification, citing Standards 1, 2, 5, 6, and 9. The decision was predicated on an evaluation of the sanctuary space and its elaborate ornamentation as essential to the historic character of the building. The region determined that, "although parts of the historic fabric were water-damaged and although alterations had occurred, the sanctuary had not lost its ability to convey historical associations and the damaged features were repairable." The denial letter stated that the installation of new floors and partitions that "leave no area for perception of even part of the original, grand, open plan" violates Standards 1, 2, and 9. The removal of the ceiling, enclosure of decorative detailing, and replacement of (1948) windows violates Standards 2, 5, and 6.

In appealing the regional denial, the owners stated that the dished ceiling plaster and lath (as well as the applied acoustical tile) would have to be removed, as they were soaked with water from the numerous roof leaks, and had a thick layer (as much as one foot) of pigeon excrement above. Further, due to water penetration and freeze-thaw cycles, the decorative plaster on the sanctuary walls was severely damaged and so unstable as to be unable to withstand even the slightest impact.

At the appeal meeting, close-up photographs of deteriorated plaster details were shown (see illus. 6), and the condition of the plasterwork was fully discussed. The Appeals Officer overturned the regional office denial and determined that the project was consistent with the *existing* historic character of the church. In certifying the project, he said:

> The information and photographs (as well as the physical evidence) you provided clarified for me the condition of the building ... I am convinced that the plasterwork has deteriorated to such an extent that it cannot now be repaired, and that the interior wall and ceiling finishes have lost their physical integrity and their historic character.

Church sanctuaries are often character-defining features of historic churches. The importance of these spaces, however, is not dependent on the ornateness of detailing. The first space discussed here was plain; the second was elaborate. In neither case did evaluation of the proposed project depend on the level of ornamentation. Minor changes had been made to the first church interior, but the materials and the sanctuary space had remained intact. In the second case, the sanctuary had lost its character due to extreme deterioration. Regardless of the original level of detail, if a character-defining historic interior remains largely intact, it must be retained in a rehabilitation. Subdivision or other alteration that destroys the form or features of a significant space will result in denial of certification.

Prepared by: Michael Auer and Susan Dynes, TPS

These bulletins are issued to explain preservation project decisions made by the U.S. Department of the Interior. The resulting determinations, based on the Secretary of the Interior's Standards for Rehabilitation, are not necessarily applicable beyond the unique facts and circumstances of each particular case.

Appendix E

Internal Revenue Service, Final Regulations Relating to Qualified Conservation Contributions, 26 C.F.R. Parts 1, 20, and 25

The following text is in the form of the amendments to 26 C.F.R. Parts 1, 20, and 25 that appeared in the Federal Register, Vol. 51, No. 9 on January 14, 1986. It reflects some subsequent amendments to make conforming changes and correct printing errors in the January 14 text.

PART 1—[AMENDED]

Paragraph 1. The authority for Part 1 continues to read in part: **Authority:** 26 U.S.C. 7805. * * *

§ **1.167(a)-5 [Amended]**

Par. 2. Section 1.167(a)-5 is amended by adding at the end thereof the following new sentence: "For the adjustment to the basis of a structure in the case of a donation of a qualified conservation contribution under section 170(h), see § 1.170A-14(h)(3)(iii)."

Par. 3. Section 1.170A-7 is amended as follows:

a. The first sentence of paragraph (b)(1)(ii) is amended to begin with the phrase "With respect to contributions made on or before December 17, 1980."

b. Paragraph (b)(1)(ii) is amended by adding at the end the following new sentence: "For the deductibility of a qualified conservation contribution, see § 1.170A-14."

c. A new paragraph (b)(5) is added immediately after paragraph (b)(4), as set forth below.

d. The first sentence of paragraph (c) is amended to begin with the phrase "Except as provided in § 1.170A-14."

e. Paragraph (e) is revised as set forth below.

§ 1.170A-7 Contributions not in trust of partial interests in property.

* * * *

(b) *Contributions of certain partial interests in property for which a deduction is allowed.* * * *

(5) *Qualified conservation contribution.* A deduction is allowed under section 170 for the value of a qualified conservation contribution. For the definition of a qualified conservation contribution, see § 1.170A-14.

* * * *

(e) *Effective date.* This section applies only to contributions made after July 31, 1969. The deduction allowable under § 1.170A-7(b)(1)(ii) shall be available only for contributions made on or before December 17, 1980. Except as otherwise provided in § 1.170A-14(g)(4)(ii), the deduction allowable under § 1.170A-7(b)(5) shall be available for contributions made on or after December 18, 1980.

Par. 4. A new § 1.170A-14 is added after § 1.170A-13T to read as set forth below.

§ 1.170A-14 Qualified conservation contributions.

(a) Qualified conservation contributions. A deduction under section 170 is generally not allowed for a charitable contribution of any interest in property that consists of less than the donor's entire interest in the property other than certain transfers in trust (see § 1.170A-6 relating to charitable contributions in trust and § 1.170A-7 relating to contributions not in trust of partial interests in property). However, a deduction may be allowed under section 170(f)(3)(B)(iii) for the value of a qualified conservation contribution if the requirements of this section are met. A qualified conservation contribution is the contribution of a qualified real property interest to a qualified organization exclusively for conservation purposes. To be eligible for a deduction under this section, the conservation purpose must be protected in perpetuity.

(b) *Qualified real property interest.*

(1) *Entire interest of donor other than qualified mineral interest.*

(i) The entire interest of the donor other than a qualified mineral interest is a qualified real property interest. A qualified mineral interest is the donor's interest in subsurface oil, gas, or other minerals and the right of access to such minerals.

(ii) A real property interest shall not be treated as an entire interest other than a qualified mineral interest by reason of section 170(h)(2)(A) and this paragraph (b)(1) if the property in which the donor's interest exists was divided prior to the contribution in order to enable the donor to retain control of more than a qualified mineral interest or to reduce the real property interest donated. See Treasury regulations § 1.170A-7(a)(2)(i). An entire interest in real property may consist of an undivided interest in the property. But see section 170(h)(5)(A) and the regulations thereunder (relating to the requirement that the conservation purpose which is the subject of the donation must be protected in perpetuity). Minor interests, such as rights-of-way, that will not interfere with the conservation purposes of the donation, may be transferred prior to the conservation contribution without affecting the treatment of a property interest as a qualified real property interest under this paragraph (b)(1).

(2) *Perpetual conservation restriction.* A perpetual conservation restriction is a qualified real property interest. A "perpetual conservation restriction" is a restriction granted in perpetuity on the use which may be made of real property—including, an easement or other interest in real property that under state law has attributes similar to an easement (e.g., a restrictive covenant or equitable servitude). For purposes of this section, the terms "easement," "conservation restriction," and "perpetual conservation restriction" have the same meaning. The definition of "perpetual conservation restriction" under this paragraph (b)(2) is not intended to preclude the deductibility of a donation of affirmative rights to use a land or water area under § 1.170A-13(d)(2). Any rights reserved by the donor in the donation of a perpetual conservation restriction must conform to the requirements of this section. See, e.g., paragraph (d)(4)(ii), (d)(5)(i), (e)(3), and (g)(4) of this section.

(c) *Qualified organization*

(1) *Eligible donee.* To be considered an eligible donee under this section, an organization must be a qualified organization, have a commitment to protect the conservation purposes of the donation, and have the resources to enforce the restrictions. A conservation group organized or operated primarily or substantially for one of the conservation purposes specified in section 170(h)(4)(A) will be considered to have the commitment required by the preceding sentence. A qualified organization need not set aside funds to enforce the restrictions that are the subject of the contribution. For purposes of this section, the term "qualified organization" means:

(i) A governmental unit described in section 170(b)(1)(A)(v);

(ii) An organization described in section 170(b)(1)(A)(vi);

(iii) A charitable organization described in section 501(c)(3) that meets the public support test of section 509(a)(2);

(iv) A charitable organization described in section 501(c)(3) that meets the requirements of section 509(a)(3) and is controlled by an organization described in paragraphs (c)(1)(i), (ii), or (iii) of this section.

(2) *Transfers by donee.* A deduction shall be allowed for a contribution under this section only if in the instrument of conveyance the donor prohibits the donee from subsequently transferring the easement (or, in the case of a remainder interest or the reservation of a qualified mineral interest, the property), whether or not for consideration, unless the donee organization, as

a condition of the subsequent transfer, requires that the conservation purposes which the contribution was originally intended to advance continue to be carried out. Moreover, subsequent transfers must be restricted to organizations qualifying, at the time of the subsequent transfer, as an eligible donee under paragraph (c)(1) of this section. When a later unexpected change in the conditions surrounding the property that is the subject of a donation under paragraph (b)(1), (2), or (3) of this section makes impossible or impractical the continued use of the property for conservation purposes, the requirement of this paragraph will be met if the property is sold or exchanged and any proceeds are used by the donee organization in a manner consistent with the conservation purposes of the original contribution. In the case of a donation under paragraph (b)(3) of this section to which the preceding sentence applies, see also paragraph (g)(5)(ii) of this section.

(d) *Conservation purposes*

(1) *In general.* For purposes of section 170(h) and this section, the term "conservation purposes" means—

(i) The preservation of land areas for outdoor recreation by, or the education of, the general public, within the meaning of paragraph (d)(2) of this section.

(ii) The protection of a relatively natural habitat of fish, wildlife, or plants, or similar ecosystem, within the meaning of paragraph (d)(3) of this section,

(iii) The preservation of certain open space (including farmland and forest land) within the meaning of paragraph (d)(4) of this section, or

(iv) The preservation of a historically important land area or a certified historic structure, within the meaning of paragraph (d)(5) of this section.

(2) *Recreation or education*

(i) In general. The donation of a qualified real property interest to preserve land areas for the outdoor recreation of the general public or for the education of the general public will meet the conservation purposes test of this section. Thus, conservation purposes would include, for example, the preservation of a water area for the use of the public for boating or fishing, or a nature or hiking trail for the use of the public.

(ii) Access. The preservation of land areas for recreation or education will not meet the test of this section unless the recreation or education is for the substantial and regular use of the general public.

(3) *Protection of environmental system*

(i) In general. The donation of a qualified real property interest to protect a significant relatively natural habitat in which a fish, wildlife, or plant community, or similar ecosystem normally lives will meet the conservation purposes test of this section. The fact that the habitat or environment has been altered to some extent by human activity will not result in a deduction being denied under this section if the fish, wildlife, or plants continue to exist there in a relatively natural state. For example, the preservation of a lake formed by a man-made dam or a salt pond formed by a man-made dike would meet the conservation purposes test if the lake or pond were a nature feeding area for a wildlife community that included rare, endangered, or threatened native species.

(ii) *Significant habitat or ecosystem.* Significant habitats and ecosystems include, but are not limited to, habitats for rare, endangered, or threatened species of animal, fish, or plants; natural areas that represent high quality examples of a terrestrial community or aquatic community, such as islands that are undeveloped or not intensely developed where the coastal ecosystem is relatively intact; and natural areas which are included in, or which contribute to, the ecological viability of a local, state, or national park, nature preserve, wildlife refuge, wilderness area, or other similar conservation area.

    (iii)   Access. Limitations on public access to property that is the subject of a donation under this paragraph (d)(3) shall not render the donation nondeductible. For example, a restriction on all public access to the habitat of a threatened native animal species protected by a donation under this paragraph (d)(3) would not cause the donation to be nondeductible.

  (4) *Preservation of open space*

    (i)   In general. The donation of a qualified real property interest to preserve open space (including farmland and forest land) will meet the conservation purposes test of this section if such preservation is—

      (A)   Pursuant to a clearly delineated Federal, state, or local governmental conservation policy and will yield a significant public benefit, or

      (B)   For the scenic enjoyment of the general public and will yield a significant public benefit.

An open space easement donated on or after December 18, 1980, must meet the requirements of section 170(h) in order to be deductible.

    (ii)   *Scenic enjoyment*

      (A)   *Factors.* A contribution made for the preservation of open space may be for the scenic enjoyment of the general public. Preservation of land may be for the scenic enjoyment of the general public if development of the property would impair the scenic character of the local rural or urban landscape or would interfere with a scenic panorama that can be enjoyed from a park, nature preserve, road, water body, trail, or historic structure or land area, and such area or transportation way is open to, or utilized by, the public. "Scenic enjoyment" will be evaluated by considering all pertinent facts and circumstances germane to the contribution. Regional variations in topography, geology, biology, and cultural and economic conditions require flexibility in the application of this test, but do not lessen the burden on the taxpayer to demonstrate the scenic characteristics of a donation under this paragraph. The application of a particular objective factor to help define a view as "scenic" in one setting may in fact be entirely inappropriate in another setting. Among the factors to be considered are:

        (1)   The compatibility of the land use with other land in the vicinity;

        (2)   The degree of contrast and variety provided by the visual scene;

        (3)   The openness of the land (which would be a more significant factor in an urban or densely populated setting or in a heavily wooded area);

        (4)   Relief from urban closeness;

        (5)   The harmonious variety of shapes and textures;

        (6)   The degree to which the land use maintains the scale and character of the urban landscape to preserve open space, visual enjoyment, and sunlight for the surrounding area;

(7) The consistency of the proposed scenic view with a methodical state scenic identification program, such as a state landscape inventory; and

(8) The consistency of the proposed scenic view with a regional or local landscape inventory made pursuant to a sufficiently rigorous review process, especially if the donation is endorsed by an appropriate state or local governmental agency.

(B) *Access.* To satisfy the requirement of scenic enjoyment by the general public, visual (rather than physical) access to or across the property by the general public is sufficient. Under the terms of an open space easement on scenic property, the entire property need not be visible to the public for a donation to qualify under this section, although the public benefit from the donation may be insufficient to qualify for a deduction if only a small portion of the property is visible to the public.

(iii) *Governmental conservation policy*

(A) *In general.* The requirement that the preservation of open space be pursuant to a clearly delineated federal, state, or local governmental policy is intended to protect the types of property identified by representatives of the general public as worthy of preservation or conservation. A general declaration of conservation goals by a single official or legislative body is not sufficient. However, a governmental conservation policy need not be a certification program that identifies particular lots or small parcels of individually owned property. This requirement will be met by donations that further a specific, identified conservation project, such as the preservation of land within a state or local landmark district that is locally recognized as being significant to that district; the preservation of a wild or scenic river; the preservation of farmland pursuant to a state program for flood prevention and control; or the protection of the scenic, ecological, or historic character of land that is contiguous to, or an integral part of, the surroundings of existing recreation or conservation sites. For example, the donation of a perpetual conservation restriction to a qualified organization pursuant to a formal resolution or certification by a local governmental agency established under state law specifically identifying the subject properly as worthy of protection for conservation purposes will meet the requirement of this paragraph. A program need not be funded to satisfy this requirement, but the program must involve a significant commitment by the government with respect to the conservation project. For example, a governmental program according preferential tax assessment or preferential zoning for certain property deemed worthy of protection for conservation purposes would constitute a significant commitment by the government.

(B) *Effect of acceptance by governmental agency.* Acceptance of an easement by an agency of the federal government or by an agency of a state or local government (or by a commission, authority, or similar body duly constituted by the state or local government and acting on behalf of the state or local government) tends to establish the requisite clearly delineated governmental policy, although such acceptance, without more, is not sufficient. The more rigorous the review process by the governmental agency, the more the acceptance of the easement tends to establish the requisite clearly delineated governmental policy. For example, in a state where the legislature has established an Environmental Trust to accept gifts to the state which meet certain conservation purposes and to submit the gifts to a review that requires the approval of the state's highest officials, acceptance of a gift by the Trust tends to establish the requisite clearly delineated governmental policy. However, if the Trust merely accepts such gifts without a review process, the requisite clearly delineated governmental policy is not established.

(C) *Access.* A limitation on public access to property subject to a donation under this paragraph (d)(4)(iii) shall not render the deduction nondeductible unless the conservation purpose of the donation would be undermined or frustrated without public access. For example, a donation pursuant to a governmental policy to protect the scenic character of land near a river requires visual access to the same extent as would a donation under paragraph (d)(4)(ii) of this section.

(iv) *Significant public benefit—*

(A) *Factors.* All contributions made for the preservation of open space must yield a significant public benefit. Public benefit will be evaluated by considering all pertinent facts and circumstances germane to the contribution. Factors germane to the evaluation of public benefit from one contribution may be irrelevant in determining public benefit from another contribution. No single factor will necessarily be determinative. Among the factors to be considered are:

(1) The uniqueness of the property to the area;

(2) The intensity of land development in the vicinity of the property (both existing development and foreseeable trends of development);

(3) The consistency of the proposed open space use with public programs (whether federal, state or local) for conservation in the region, including programs for outdoor recreation, irrigation or water supply protection, water quality maintenance or enhancement, flood prevention and control, erosion control, shoreline protection, and protection of land areas included in, or related to, a government approved master plan or land management area;

(4) The consistency of the proposed open space use with existing private conservation programs in the area, as evidenced by other land, protected by easement or fee ownership by organizations referred to in § 1.170A-14(c)(1), in close proximity to the property;

(5) The likelihood that development of the property would lead to or contribute to degradation of the scenic, natural, or historic character of the area;

(6) The opportunity for the general public to use the property or to appreciate its scenic values;

(7) The importance of the property in preserving a local or regional landscape or resource that attracts tourism or commerce to the area;

(8) The likelihood that the donee will acquire equally desirable and valuable substitute property or property rights;

(9) The cost to the donee of enforcing the terms of the conservation restriction;

(10) The population density in the area of the property; and

(11) The consistency of the proposed open space use with a legislatively mandated program identifying particular parcels of land for future protection.

(B) *Illustrations.* The preservation of an ordinary tract of land would not in and of itself yield a significant public benefit, but the preservation of ordinary land areas in conjunction with other factors that demonstrate significant public benefit or the preservation of a unique land area for public employment would yield a significant public benefit.

For example, the preservation of a vacant downtown lot would not by itself yield a significant public benefit, but the preservation of the downtown lot as a public garden would, absent countervailing factors, yield a significant public benefit. The following are other examples of contributions which would, absent countervailing factors, yield a significant public benefit: The preservation of farmland pursuant to a state program for flood prevention and control; the preservation of a unique natural land formation for the enjoyment of the general public; the preservation of woodland along a public highway pursuant to a government program to preserve the appearance of the area so as to maintain the scenic view from the highway; and the preservation of a stretch of undeveloped property located between a public highway and the ocean in order to maintain the scenic ocean view from the highway.

(v) *Limitation.* A deduction will not be allowed for the preservation of open space under section 107(h)(4)(A)(iii), if the terms of the easement permit a degree of intrusion or future development that would interfere with the essential scenic quality of the land or with the governmental conservation policy that is being furthered by the donation. See § 1.170A-14(e)(2) for rules relating to inconsistent use.

(vi) *Relationship of requirements*

(A) *Clearly delineated governmental policy and significant public benefit.* Although the requirements of "clearly delineated governmental policy" and "significant public benefit" must be met independently, for purposes of this section the two requirements may also be related. The more specific the governmental policy with respect to the particular site to be protected, the more likely the governmental decision, by itself, will tend to establish the significant public benefit associated with the donation. For example, while a statute in State X permitting preferential assessment for farmland is, by definition, governmental policy, it is distinguishable from a state statute, accompanied by appropriations, naming the X River as a valuable resource and articulating the legislative policy that the X River and the relatively natural quality of its surrounding be protected. On these facts, an open space easement on farmland in State X would have to demonstrate additional factors to establish "significant public benefit." The specificity of the legislative mandate to protect the X River, however, would by itself tend to establish the significant public benefit associated with an open space easement on land fronting the X River.

(B) *Scenic enjoyment and significant public benefit.* With respect to the relationship between the requirements of "scenic enjoyment" and "significant public benefit," since the degrees of scenic enjoyment offered by a variety of open space easements are subjective and not as easily delineated as are increasingly specific levels of governmental policy, the significant public benefit of preserving a scenic view must be independently established in all cases.

(C) *Donations may satisfy more than one test.* In some cases, open space easements may be both for scenic enjoyment and pursuant to a clearly delineated governmental policy. For example, the preservation of a particular scenic view identified as part of a scenic landscape inventory by a rigorous governmental review process will meet the tests of both paragraphs (d)(4)(i)(A) and (d)(4)(i)(B) of this section.

    (5) *Historic preservation*

        (i) *In general.* The donation of a qualified real property interest to preserve a historically important land area or a certified historic structure will meet the conservation purposes test of this section. When restrictions to preserve a building or land area within a registered historic district permit future development on the site, a deduction will be allowed under this section only if the terms of the restrictions require that such development conform with appropriate local, state, or Federal standards for construction or rehabilitation within the district. See also, § 1.170A-14(h)(3)(ii).

        (ii) *Historically important land area.* The term "historically important land area" includes:

        (A) An independently significant land area including any related historic resources (for example, an archaeological site or a Civil War battlefield with related monuments, bridges, cannons, or houses) that meets the National Register Criteria for Evaluation in 36 CFR 60.4 (Pub. L. 89-665, 80 Stat. 951);

        (B) Any land area within a registered historic district including any buildings on the land area that can reasonably be considered as contributing to the significance of the district; and

        (C) Any land area (including related historic resources) adjacent to a property listed individually in the National Register of Historic Places (but not within a registered historic district) in a case where the physical or environmental features of the land area contribute to the historic or cultural integrity of the property.

        (iii) *Certified historic structure.* The term "certified historic structure," for purposes of this section, means any building, structure or land area which is—

        (A) Listed in the National Register, or

        (B) Located in a registered historic district (as defined in section 48(g)(3)(B)) and is certified by the Secretary of the Interior (pursuant to 36 CFR 67.4) to the Secretary of the Treasury as being of historic significance to the district.

    A "structure" for purposes of this section means any structure, whether or not it is depreciable. Accordingly easements on private residences may qualify under this section. In addition, a structure would be considered to be a certified historic structure if it were certified either at the time the transfer was made or at the due date (including extensions) for filing the donor's return for the taxable year in which the contribution was made.

        (iv) *Access.*

        (A) In order for a conservation contribution described in section 170(h)(4)(A)(iv) and this paragraph (d)(5) to be deductible, some visual public access to the donated property is required. In the case of a historically important land area, the entire property need not be visible to the public for a donation to qualify under this section. However, the public benefit from the donation may be insufficient to qualify for a deduction if only a small portion of the property is so visible. Where the historic land area or certified historic structure which is the subject of the donation is not visible from a public way (e.g., the structure is hidden from view by a wall or shrubbery, the structure is too far from the public way, or interior characteristics and features of the structure are the subject of the easement), the terms of the easement must be such that the general public is given the opportunity on a regular basis to view the characteristics and features of the property which are preserved by the easement to the extent consistent with the nature and condition of the property.

(B) Factors to be considered in determining the type and amount of public access required under paragraph (d)(5)(iv)(A) of this section include the historical significance of the donated property, the nature of the features that are the subject of the easement, the remoteness or accessibility of the site of the donated property, the possibility of physical hazards to the public visiting the property (for example, an unoccupied structure in a dilapidated condition), the extent to which public access would be an unreasonable intrusion on any privacy interests of individuals living on the property, the degree to which public access would impair the preservation interests which are the subject of the donation, and the availability of opportunities for the public to view the property by means other than visits to the site.

(C) The amount of access afforded the public by the donation of an easement shall be determined with reference to the amount of access permitted by the terms of the easement which are established by the donor, rather than the amount of access actually provided by the donee organization. However, if the donor is aware of any facts indicating that the amount of access that the donee organization will provide is significantly less than the amount of access permitted under the terms of the easement, then the amount of access afforded the public shall be determined with reference to this lesser amount.

(v) *Examples.* The provisions of paragraph (d)(5)(iv) of this section may be illustrated by the following examples:

Example (1). A and his family live in a house in a certified historic district in the State of X. The entire house, including its interior, has architectural features representing classic Victorian period architecture. A donates an exterior and interior easement on the property to a qualified organization but continues to live in the house with his family. A's house is surrounded by a high stone wall which obscures the public's view of it from the street. Pursuant to the terms of the easement, the house may be opened to the public from 10:00 a.m. to 4:00 p.m. on one Sunday in May and one Sunday in November each year for house and garden tours. These tours are to be under the supervision of the donee and open to members of the general public upon payment of a small fee. In addition, under the terms of the easement, the donee organization is given the right to photograph the interior and exterior of the house and distribute such photographs to magazines, newsletters, or other publicly available publications. The terms of the easement also permit persons affiliated with educational organizations, professional architectural associations, and historical societies to make an appointment through the donee organization to study the property. The donor is not aware of any facts indicating that the public access to be provided by the donee organization will be significantly less than that permitted by the terms of the easement. The two opportunities for public visits per year, when combined with the ability of the general public to view the architectural characteristics and features that are the subject of the easement through photographs, the opportunity for scholarly study of the property, and the fact that the house is used as an occupied residence, will enable the donation to satisfy the requirement of public access.

Example (2). B owns an unoccupied farmhouse built in the 1840s and located on a property that is adjacent to a Civil War battlefield. During the Civil War the farmhouse was used as quarters for Union troops. The battlefield is visited year round by the general public. The condition of the farmhouse is such that the safety of visitors will not be jeopardized and opening it to the public will not result in significant deterioration. The farmhouse is not visible from the battlefield or any public way. It is accessible only by way of a private road owned by B. B donates a conservation easement on the farmhouse to a qualified organization. The terms of the easement provide that the donee organization may open the property (via B's road) to the general public on four weekends each year from 8:30 a.m. to 4:00 p.m. The donation does not meet the public access requirement because the farmhouse is safe, unoccupied, and easily accessible to the general public who have come to the site to visit Civil War historic land areas (and related resources), but will only be open to the public on four weekends each year. However, the donation would meet the public access requirement if the terms of the easement permitted the donee organization to open the property to the public every other weekend during the year and the donor is not aware of any facts indicating that the donee organization will provide significantly less access than that permitted.

(e) *Exclusively for conservation purposes.*

(1) *In general.* To meet the requirements of this section, a donation must be exclusively for conservation purposes. See paragraphs (c)(1) and (g)(1) through (g)(6)(ii) of this section. A deduction will not be denied under this section when incidental benefit inures to the donor merely as a result of conservation restrictions limiting the uses to which the donor's property may be put.

(2) *Inconsistent use.* Except as provided in paragraph (e)(4) of this section, a deduction will not be allowed if the contribution would accomplish one of the enumerated conservation purposes but would permit destruction of other significant conservation interests. For example, the preservation of farmland pursuant to a state program for flood prevention and control would not qualify under paragraph (d)(4) of this section if under the terms of the contribution a significant naturally occurring ecosystem could be injured or destroyed by the use of pesticides in the operation of the farm. However, this requirement is not intended to prohibit uses of the property, such as selective timber harvesting or selective farming if, under the circumstances, those uses do not impair significant conservation interests.

(3) *Inconsistent use permitted.* A use that is destructive of conservation interests will be permitted only if such use is necessary for the protection of the conservation interests that are the subject of the contribution. For example, a deduction for the donation of an easement to preserve an archaeological site that is listed on the National Register of Historic Places will not be disallowed if site excavation consistent with sound archaeological practices may impair a scenic view of which the land is a part. A donor may continue a preexisting use of the property that does not conflict with the conservation purposes of the gift.

(f) *Examples.* The provisions of this section relating to conservation purposes may be illustrated by the following examples.

Example (1). State S contains many large tract forests that are desirable recreation and scenic areas for the general public. The forests' scenic values attract millions of people to the state. However, due to the increasing intensity of land development in State S, the continued existence of forest land parcels greater than 45 acres is threatened. *J* grants a perpetual easement on a 100-acre parcel of forest land that is part of one of the state's scenic areas to a qualifying organization. The easement imposes restrictions on the use of the parcel for the purpose of maintaining its scenic values. The restrictions include a requirement that the parcel be maintained forever as open space devoted exclusively to conservation purposes and wildlife protection, and that there be no commercial, industrial, residential, or other development use of such parcel. The law of State *S* recognizes a limited public right to enter private land, particularly for recreational pursuits, unless such land is posted or the landowner objects. The easement specifically restricts the landowner from posting the parcel, or from objecting, thereby maintaining public access to the parcel according to the custom of the State. *J*'s parcel provides the opportunity for the public to enjoy the use of the property and appreciate its scenic values. Accordingly, J's donation qualifies for a deduction under this section.

Example (2). A qualified conservation organization owns Greenacre in fee as a nature preserve. Greenacre contains a high quality example of a tall grass prairie ecosystem. Farmacre, an operating farm, adjoins Greenacre and is a compatible buffer to the nature preserve. Conversion of Farmacre to a more intense use, such as a housing development, would adversely affect the continued use of Greenacre as a nature preserve because of human traffic generated by the development. The owner of Farmacre donates an easement preventing any future development on Farmacre to the qualified conservation organization for conservation purposes. Normal agricultural uses will be allowed on Farmacre. Accordingly, the donation qualifies for a deduction under this section.

Example (3). *H* owns Greenacre, a 900-acre parcel of woodland, rolling pasture, and orchards on the crest of a mountain. All of Greenacre is clearly visible from a nearby national park. Because of the strict enforcement of an applicable zoning plan, the highest and best use of Greenacre is as a subdivision of 40-acre tracts. *H* wishes to donate a scenic easement on Greenacre to a qualifying conservation organization, but H would like to reserve the right to subdivide Greenacre into 90-acre parcels with no more than one single-family home allowable on each parcel. Random building on the property, even as little as one home for each 90 acres, would destroy the scenic character of the view. Accordingly, no deduction would be allowable under this section.

Example (4). Assume the same facts as in *example (3)*, except that not all of Greenacre is visible from the park and the deed of easement allows for limited cluster development of no more than five 9-acre clusters (with four houses on each cluster) located in areas generally not visible from the national park and subject to site and building plan approval by the donee organization in order to preserve the scenic view from the park. The donor and the donee have already identified sites where limited cluster development would not be visible from the park or would not impair the view. Owners of homes in the clusters will not have any rights with respect to the surrounding Greenacre property that are not also available to the general public. Accordingly, the donation qualifies for a deduction under this section.

Example (5). In order to protect State *S*'s declining open space that is suited for agricultural use from increasing development pressure that has led to a marked decline in such open space, the legislature of State *S* passed a statute authorizing the purchase of "agricultural land development rights" on open acreage. Agricultural land development rights allow the state to place agricultural preservation restrictions on land designated as worthy of protection in order to preserve open space and farm resources. Agricultural preservation restrictions prohibit or limit construction or placement of buildings except those used for agricultural purposes or dwellings used for family living by the farmer and his family and employees; removal of mineral substances in any manner that adversely affects the land's agricultural potential; or other uses detrimental to retention of the land for agricultural use. Money has been appropriated for this program and some landowners have in fact sold their "agricultural land development rights" to State S. K owns and operates a small dairy farm in state S located in an area designated by the legislature as worthy of protection. K desires to preserve his farm for agricultural purposes in perpetuity. Rather than selling the development rights to State S, K grants to a qualified organization an agricultural preservation restriction on his property in the form of a conservation easement. K reserves to himself, his heirs and assigns the right to manage the farm consistent with sound agricultural and management practices. The preservation of K's land is pursuant to a clearly delineated governmental policy of preserving open space available for agricultural use, and will yield a significant public benefit by preserving open space against increasing development pressures.

(g) *Enforceable in perpetuity.*

(1) *In general.* In the case of any donation under this section, any interest in the property retained by the donor (and the donor's successors in interest) must be subject to legally enforceable restrictions (for example, by recordation in the land records of the jurisdiction in which the property is located) that will prevent uses of the retained interest inconsistent with the conservation purposes of the donation. In the case of a contribution of a remainder interest, the contribution will not qualify if the tenants, whether they are tenants for life or a term of years, can use the property in a manner that diminishes the conservation values which are intended to be protected by the contribution.

(2) *Protection of a conservation purpose in case of donation of property subject to a mortgage.* In the case of conservation contributions made after February 13, 1986, no deduction will be permitted under this section for an interest in property which is subject to a mortgage unless the mortgagee subordinates its rights in the property to the right of the qualified organization to enforce the conservation purposes of the gift in perpetuity. For conservation contributions made prior to February 14, 1986, the requirement of section 170(h)(5)(A) is satisfied in the case of mortgaged property (with respect to which the mortgagee has not subordinated its rights) only if the donor can demonstrate that the conservation purpose is protected in perpetuity without subordination of the mortgagee's rights.

(3) *Remote future event.* A deduction shall not be disallowed under section 170(f)(3)(B)(iii) and this section merely because the interest which passes to, or is vested in, the donee organization may be defeated by the performance of some act or the happening of some event, if on the date of the gift it appears that the possibility that such act or event will occur is so remote as to be negligible. See paragraph (e) of § 1.170A-1. For example, a state's statutory requirement that use restrictions must be rerecorded every 30 years to remain enforceable shall not, by itself, render an easement nonperpetual.

(4) *Retention of qualified mineral interest.*

(i) *In general.* Except as otherwise provided in paragraph (g)(4)(ii) of this section, the requirements of this section are not met and no deduction shall be allowed in the case of a contribution of any interest when there is a retention by any person of a qualified mineral interest (as defined in paragraph (b)(1)(i) of this section) if at any time there may be extractions or removal of minerals by any surface mining method. Moreover, in the case of a qualified mineral interest gift, the requirement that the conservation purposes be protected in perpetuity is not satisfied if any method of mining that is inconsistent with the particular conservation purposes of a contribution is permitted at any time. See also § 1.170A-14(e)(2). However, a deduction under this section will not be denied in the case of certain methods of mining that may have limited, localized impact on the real property but that are not irremediably destructive of significant conservation interests. For example, a deduction will not be denied in a case where production facilities are concealed or compatible with existing topography and landscape and when surface alteration is to be restored to its original state.

(ii) *Exception for qualified conservation contributions after July 1984.*

(A) A contribution made after July 18, 1984, of a qualified real property interest described in section 170(h)(2)(A) shall not be disqualified under the first sentence of paragraph (g)(4)(i) of this section if the following requirements are satisfied.

(1) The ownership of the surface estate and mineral interest were separated before June 13, 1976, and remain so separated up to and including the time of the contribution.

(2) The present owner of the mineral interest is not a person whose relationship to the owner of the surface estate is described at the time of the contribution in section 267(b) or section 707(b), and

(3) The probability of extraction or removal of minerals by any surface mining method is so remote as to be negligible.

Whether the probability of extraction or removal of minerals by surface mining is so remote as to be negligible is a question of fact and is to be made on a case by case basis. Relevant factors to be considered in determining if the probability of extraction or removal of minerals by surface mining is so remote as to be negligible include: Geological, geophysical or economic data showing the absence of mineral reserves on the property, or the lack of commercial feasibility at the time of the contribution of surface mining the mineral interest.

(B) If the ownership of the surface estate and mineral interest first became separated after June 12, 1976, no deduction is permitted for a contribution under this section unless surface mining on the property is completely prohibited.

(iii) *Examples.* The provisions of paragraph (g)(4)(i) and (ii) of this section may be illustrated by the following examples:

Example (1). K owns 5,000 acres of bottomland hardwood property along a major watershed system in the southern part of the United States. Agencies within the Department of the Interior have determined that southern bottomland hardwoods are a rapidly diminishing resource and a critical ecosystem in the south because of the intense pressure to cut the trees and convert the land to agricultural use. These agencies have further determined (and have indicated in correspondence with K) that bottomland hardwoods provide a superb habitat for numerous species and play an important role in controlling floods and purifying rivers. K donates to a qualified organization his entire interest in this property other than his interest in the gas and oil deposits that have been identified under K's property. K covenants and can ensure that, although drilling for gas and oil on the property may have some temporary localized impact on the real property, the drilling will not interfere with the overall conservation purpose of the gift, which is to protect the unique bottomland hardwood ecosystem. Accordingly, the donation qualifies for a deduction under this section.

Example (2). Assume the same facts as in *example (1)*, except that in 1979, K sells the mineral interest to A, an unrelated person, in an arm's-length transaction, subject to a recorded prohibition on the removal of any minerals by any surface mining method and a recorded prohibition against any mining technique that will harm the bottomland hardwood ecosystem. After the sale to A, K donates a qualified real property interest to a qualified organization to protect the bottomland hardwood ecosystem. Since at the time of the transfer, surface mining and any mining technique that will harm the bottomland hardwood ecosystem are completely prohibited, the donation qualifies for a deduction under this section.

(5) *Protection of conservation purpose where taxpayer reserves certain rights.*

(i) *Documentation.* In the case of a donation made after February 13, 1986, of any qualified real property interest when the donor reserves rights the exercise of which may impair the conservation interests associated with the property, for a deduction to be allowable under this section the donor must make available to the donee, prior to the time the donation is made, documentation sufficient to establish the condition of the property at the time of the gift.

Such documentation is designed to protect the conservation interests associated with the property, which although protected in perpetuity by the easement, could be adversely affected by the exercise of the reserved rights. Such documentation may include:

(A) The appropriate survey maps from the U.S. Geological Survey, showing the property line and other contiguous or nearby protected areas;

(B) A map of the area drawn to scale showing all existing man-made improvements or incursions (such as roads, buildings, fences, or gravel pits), vegetation and identification of flora and fauna (including, for example, rare species locations, animal breeding and roosting areas, and migration routes), land use history (including present uses and recent past disturbances), and distinct natural features (such as large trees and aquatic areas);

(C) An aerial photograph of the property at an appropriate scale taken as close as possible to the date the donation is made; and

(D) On-site photographs taken at appropriate locations on the property. If the terms of the donation contain restrictions with regard to a particular natural resource to be protected, such as water quality or air quality, the condition of the resource at or near the time of the gift must be established.

The documentation, including the maps and photographs, must be accompanied by a statement signed by the donor and a representative of the donee clearly referencing the documentation and in substance saying "This natural resources inventory is an accurate representation of [the protected property] at the time of the transfer."

(ii) *Donee's right to inspection and legal remedies.* In the case of any donation referred to in paragraph (g)(5)(i) of this section, the donor must agree to notify the donee, in writing, before exercising any reserved right, for example, the right to extract certain minerals which may have an adverse impact on the conservation interests associated with the qualified real property interest. The terms of the donation must provide a right of the donee to enter the property at reasonable times for the purpose of inspection of the property to determine if there is compliance with the terms of the donation. Additionally, the terms of the donation must provide a right of the donee to enforce the conservation restrictions by appropriate legal proceedings, including but not limited to, the right to require the restoration of the property to its condition at the time of the donation.

(6) *Extinguishment*—

(i) *In general.* If a subsequent unexpected change in the conditions surrounding the property that is the subject of a donation under this paragraph can make impossible or impractical the continued use of the property for conservation purposes, the conservation purpose can nonetheless be treated as protected in perpetuity if the restrictions are extinguished by judicial proceeding and all of the donee's proceeds (determined under paragraph (g)(6)(ii) of this section) from a subsequent sale or exchange of the property are used by the donee organization in a manner consistent with the conservation purposes of the original contribution.

(ii) *Proceeds.* In case of a donation made after February 13, 1986, for a deduction to be allowed under this section, at the time of the gift the donor must agree that the donation of the perpetual conservation restriction gives rise to a property right, immediately vested in the donee organization, with a fair market value that is at least equal to the proportionate value that the perpetual conservation restriction at the time of the gift, bears to the value of the property as a whole at that time. See § 1.170A-14(h)(3)(iii) relating to the allocation of basis. For purposes of this paragraph (g)(6)(ii), that proportionate value of the donee's property rights shall remain constant. Accordingly, when a change in conditions give rise to the extinguishment of a perpetual conservation restriction under paragraph (g)(6)(i) of this section, the donee organization, on a subsequent sale, exchange, or involuntary conversion of the subject property, must be entitled to a portion of the proceeds at least equal to that proportionate value of the perpetual conservation restriction, unless state law provides that the donor is entitled to the full proceeds from the conversion without regard to the terms of the prior perpetual conservation restriction.

(h) *Valuation.*

(1) *Entire interest of donor other than qualified mineral interest.* The value of the contribution under section 170 in the case of a contribution of a taxpayer's entire interest in property other than a qualified mineral interest is the fair market value of the surface rights in the property contributed. The value of the contribution shall be computed without regard to the mineral rights. See paragraph (h)(4), *example (1),* of this section.

(2) *Remainder interest in real property.* In the case of a contribution of any remainder interest in real property, section 170(f)(4) provides that in determining the value of such interest for purposes of section 170, depreciation and depletion of such property shall be taken into account. See § 1.170A-12. In the case of the contribution of a remainder interest for conservation purposes, the current fair market value of the property (against which the limitations of § 1.17A-12 are applied) must take into account any preexisting or contemporaneously recorded rights limiting, for conservation purposes, the use to which the subject property may be put.

(3) *Perpetual conservation restriction.*

(i) *In general.* The value of the contribution under section 170 in the case of a charitable contribution of a perpetual conservation restriction is the fair market value of the perpetual conservation restriction at the time of the contribution. See § 1.170A-7(c). If there is a substantial record of sales of easements comparable to the donated easement (such as purchases pursuant to a governmental program), the fair market value of the donated easement is based on the sales prices of such comparable easements. If no substantial record of marketplace sales is available to use as a meaningful or valid comparison, as a general rule (but not necessarily in all cases) the fair market value of a perpetual conservation restriction is equal to the difference between the fair market value of the property it encumbers before the granting of the restriction and the fair market value of the encumbered property after the granting of the restriction. The amount of the deduction in the case of a charitable contribution of a perpetual conservation restriction covering a portion of the contiguous property owned by a donor and the donor's family (as defined in section 267(c)(4)) is the difference between the fair market value of the entire contiguous parcel of property before and after the granting of the restriction. If the granting of a perpetual conservation restriction after January 14, 1986, has the effect of increasing the value of any other property owned by the donor or a related person, the amount of the deduction for the conservation contribution shall be reduced by the amount of the increase in the value of the other property, whether or not such property is contiguous. If, as a result of the donation of a perpetual conservation restriction, the donor or a related person receives, or can reasonably expect to receive, financial or economic benefits that are greater than those that will inure to the general public from the transfer, no deduction is allowable under this section. However, if the donor or a related person receives, or can reasonably expect to receive, a financial or economic benefit that is substantial, but it is clearly shown that the benefit is less than the amount of the transfer, then a deduction under this section is allowable for the excess of the amount transferred over the amount of the financial or economic benefit received or reasonably expected to be received by the donor or the related person. For purposes of this paragraph (h)(3)(i), related person shall have the same meaning as in either section 267(b) or section 707(b). (See *example (10)* of paragraph (h)(4) of this section.)

(ii) *Fair market value of property before and after restriction.* If before and after valuation is used, the fair market value of the property before contribution of the conservation restriction must take into account not only the current use of the property but also an objective assessment of how immediate or remote the likelihood is that the property, absent the restriction, would in fact be developed, as well as any effect from zoning, conservation, or historic preservation laws that already restrict the property's potential highest and best use. Further, there may be instances where the grant of a conservation restriction may have no material effect on the value of the property or may in fact serve to enhance, rather than reduce, the value of property. In such instances no deduction would be allowable. In the case of a conservation restriction that allows for any development, however limited, on the property to be protected, the fair market value of the property after contribution of the restriction must take into account the effect of the development. In the case of a conservation easement such as an easement on a certified historic structure, the fair market value of the property after contribution of the restriction must take into account the amount of access permitted by the terms of the easement. Additionally, if before and after valuation is used, an appraisal of the property after contribution of the restriction must take into account the effect of restrictions that will result in a reduction of the potential fair market value represented by highest and best use but will, nevertheless, permit uses of the property that will increase its fair market value above that represented by the property's current use. The value of a perpetual conservation restriction shall not be reduced by reason of the existence of restrictions on transfer designed solely to ensure that the conservation restriction will be dedicated to conservation purposes. See § 1.170A-14(c)(3).

(iii) *Allocation of basis.* In the case of the donation of a qualified real property interest for conservation purposes, the basis of the property retained by the donor must be adjusted by the elimination of that part of the total basis of the property that is properly allocable to the qualified real property interest granted. The amount of the basis that is allocable to the qualified real property interest shall bear the same ratio to the total basis of the property as the fair market value of the qualified real property interest bears to the fair market value of the property before the granting of the qualified real property interest. When a taxpayer donates to a qualifying conservation organization an easement on a structure with respect to which deductions are taken for depreciation, the reduction required by this paragraph (h)(3)(ii) in the basis of the property retained by the taxpayer must be allocated between the structure and the underlying land.

(4) *Examples.* The provisions of this section may be illustrated by the following examples. In examples illustrating the value or deductibility of donations, the applicable restrictions and limitations of § 1.170A-4, with respect to reduction in amount of charitable contributions of certain appreciated property, and § 1.170A-8, with respect to limitations on charitable deductions by individuals, must also be taken into account.

Example (1). A owns Goldacre, a property adjacent to a state park. A wants to donate Goldacre to the state to be used as part of the park, but A wants to reserve a qualified mineral interest in the property, to exploit currently and to devise at death. The fair market value of the surface rights in Goldacre is $200,000 and the fair market value of the mineral rights is $100,000. In order to ensure that the quality of the park will not be degraded, restrictions must be imposed on the right to extract the minerals that reduce the fair market value of the mineral rights to $80,000. Under this section, the value of the contribution is $200,000 (the value of the surface rights).

Example (2). In 1984 B, who is 62, donates a remainder interest in Greenacre to a qualifying organization for conservation purposes. Greenacre is a tract of

200 acres of undeveloped woodland that is valued at $200,000 at its highest and best use. Under § 1.170A-12(b), the value of a remainder interest in real property following one life is determined under § 25.2512-5 of the Gift Tax Regulations. (See § 25.2512-9 with respect to the valuation of annuities, life estates, terms for years, remainders, and reversions transferred after December 31, 1970 and before December 1, 1983. With respect to the valuation of annuities, life estates, terms for years, remainders, and reversions transferred before January 1, 1971, see T.D. 6334, 23 FR 8904, November 15, 1958, as amended by T.D. 7077, 35 FR 18464, December 4, 1970). Accordingly, the value of the remainder interest, and thus the amount eligible for an income tax deduction under section 170(f), is $55,996 ($200,000 × .27998).

Example (3). Assume the same facts as in *example (2)*, except that Greenacre is B's 200-acre estate with a home built during the colonial period. Some of the acreage around the home is cleared; the balance of Greenacre, except for access roads, is wooded and undeveloped. See section 170(f)(3)(B)(i). However, B would like Greenacre to be maintained in its current state after his death, so he donates a remainder interest in Greenacre to a qualifying organization for conservation purposes pursuant to section 170(f)(3)(B)(iii) and (h)(2)(B). At the time of the gift the land has a value of $200,000 and the house has a value of $100,000. The value of the remainder interest, and thus the amount eligible for an income tax deduction under section 170(f), is computed pursuant to § 1.170A-12. See § 1.170A-12(b)(3).

Example (4). Assume the same facts as in *example (2)*, except that at age 62 instead of donating a remainder interest B donates an easement in Greenacre to a qualifying organization for conservation purposes. The fair market value of Greenacre after the donation is reduced to $110,000. Accordingly, the value of the easement, and thus the amount eligible for a deduction under section 170(f), is $90,000 ($200,000 less $110,000).

Example (5). Assume the same facts as in *example (4)*, and assume that three years later, at age 65, B decides to donate a remainder interest in Greenacre to a qualifying organization for conservation purposes. Increasing real estate values in the area have raised the fair market value of Greenacre (subject to the easement) to $130,000. Accordingly, the value of the remainder interest, and thus the amount eligible for a deduction under section 170(f), is $41,639 ($130,000 × .32030).

Example (6). Assume the same facts as in *example (2)*, except that at the time of the donation of a remainder interest in Greenacre, B also donates an easement to a different qualifying organization for conservation purposes. Based on all the facts and circumstances, the value of the easement is determined to be $100,000. Therefore, the value of the property after the easement is $100,000 and the value of the remainder interest, and thus the amount eligible for deduction under section 170(f), is $27,998 ($100,000 × .27998).

Example (7). C owns Greenacre, a 200-acre estate containing a house built during the colonial period. At its highest and best use, for home development, the fair market value of Greenacre is $300,000. C donates an easement (to maintain the house and Greenacre in their current state) to a qualifying organization for conservation purposes. The fair market value of Greenacre after the donation is reduced to $125,000. Accordingly, the value of the easement and the amount eligible for a deduction under section 170(f) is $175,000 ($300,000 less $125,000).

Example (8). Assume the same facts as in *example (7)* and assume that 3 years later, C decides to donate a remainder interest in Greenacre to a qualifying organization for conservation purposes. Increasing real estate values in the area have raised the fair market value of Greenacre to $180,000. Assume that because of the perpetual easement prohibiting any development of the land, the value of the house is $120,000 and the value of the land is $60,000. The value of the remainder interest, and thus the amount eligible for an income tax deduction under section 170(f), is computed pursuant to § 1.170A-12. See § 1.170A-12(b)(3).

Example (9). D owns property with a basis of $20,000 and a fair market value of $80,000. D donates to a qualifying organization an easement for conservation purposes that is determined under this section to have a fair market value of $60,000. The amount of basis allocable to the easement is $15,000 ($60,000/$80,000 = $15,000/$20,000). Accordingly, the basis of the property is reduced to $5,000 ($20,000 − $15,000).

Example (10). E owns 10 1-acre lots that are currently woods and parkland. The fair market value of each of E's lots is $15,000 and the basis of each lot is $3,000. E grants to the county a perpetual easement for conservation purposes to use and maintain eight of the acres as a public park and to restrict any future development on those eight acres. As a result of the restrictions, the value of the 8 acres is reduced to $1,000 an acre. However, by perpetually restricting development on this portion of the land, E has ensured that the two remaining acres will always be bordered by parkland, thus increasing their fair market value to $22,500 each. If the 8 acres represented all of E's land, the fair market value of the easement would be $112,000, an amount equal to the fair market value of the land before the granting of the easement (8 × $15,000 = $120,000) minus the fair market value of the encumbered land after the granting of the easement (8 × $1,000 = $8,000). However, because the easement only covered a portion of the taxpayer's contiguous land, the amount of the deduction under section 170 is reduced to $97,000 ($150,000 − $53,000), that is, the difference between the fair market value of the entire tract of land before ($150,000) and after [(8$1,000) + (2 × $22,500)]the granting of the easement.

Example (11). Assume the same facts as in *example (10).* Since the easement covers a portion of E's land, only the basis of that portion is adjusted. Therefore, the amount of basis allocable to the easement is $22,400 [(8 × $3,000)($112,000/$120,000)]. Accordingly, the basis of the 8 acres encumbered by the easement is reduced to $1,600 ($24,000 − $22,400), or $200 for each acre. The basis of the two remaining acres is not affected by the donation.

Example (12). F owns and uses as professional offices a 2 story building that lies within a registered historic district. F's building is an outstanding example of period architecture with a fair market value of $125,000. Restricted to its current use, which is the highest and best use of the property without making changes to the facade, the building and lot would have a fair market value of $100,000, of which $80,000 would be allocable to the building and $20,000 would be allocable to the lot. F's basis in the property is $50,000, of which $40,000 is allocable to the building and $10,000 is allocable to the lot. F's neighborhood is a mix of residential and commercial uses, and it is possible that F (or another owner) could enlarge the building for more extensive commercial use, which is its highest and best use. However, this would require changes to the facade. F would like to donate to a qualifying preservation organization an easement restricting any changes to the facade and promising to maintain the facade in perpetuity. The donation would qualify for a deduction under this section. The fair market value of the easement is $25,000 (the fair market value of the property before the easement, $125,000, minus the fair market value of the property after the easement, $100,000). Pursuant to § 1.170A-14(h)(3)(iii),the basis allocable to the easement is $10,000 and the basis of the underlying property (building and lot) is reduced to $40,000.

(i) *Substantiation requirement.* If a taxpayer makes a qualified conservation contribution and claims a deduction, the taxpayer must maintain written records of the fair market value of the underlying property before and after the donation and the conservation purpose furthered by the donation and such information shall be stated in the taxpayer's income tax return if required by the return or its instructions. See also § 1.170A-13T(c) (relating to substantiation requirements for deductions in excess of $5,000 for charitable contributions made after 1984), and section 6659 (relating to additions to tax in the case of valuation overstatements).

(j) *Effective date.* Except as otherwise provided in § 1.170A-14(g)(4)(ii), this section applies only to contributions made on or after December 18, 1980.

PART 20—[AMENDED]

Par. 5. The authority for Part 20 continues to read in part:
Authority: 26 U.S.C. 7805. * * *
Par. 6. Paragraph (e)(2) of § 20.2055-2 is amended as follows:
    a.   The sixth sentence of paragraph (e)(2)(i) is revised to read: "However, except as provided in paragraphs (e)(2)(ii), (iii), and (iv) of this section, for purposes of this subdivision a charitable contribution of an interest in property not in trust where the decedent transfers some specific rights to one party and transfers other substantial rights to another party will not be considered a contribution of an undivided portion of the decedent's entire interest in property."
    b.   The seventh sentence of paragraph (e)(2)(i) is revised to read; "A bequest to charity made on or before December 17, 1980, of an open space easement in gross in perpetuity shall be considered the transfer to charity of an undivided portion of the decedent's entire interest in the property."
    c.   Paragraphs (e)(2)(iv), (e)(2)(v), and (e)(2)(vi) are redesignated (e)(2)(v), (e)(2)(vi), and (e)(2)(vii), respectively.
    d.   A new paragraph (e)(2)(iv) is inserted after paragraph (e)(2)(iii) to read as set forth below.

§ 20.2055-2 Transfers not exclusively for charitable purposes.

* * * *

(e) *Limitations applicable to decedents dying after December 31, 1969.* * *
    (2) *Deductible interests.* * * *
        (iv) *Qualified conservation contribution.* The charitable interest is a qualified conservation contribution. For the definition of a qualified conservation contribution, see § 1.170A-14.

PART 25—[AMENDED]

Par. 7. The authority for Part 25 continues to read in part:
Authority: 26 U.S.C. 7805. * * *
Par. 8. Paragraph (c)(2) of § 25.2522(c) 3 is amended as follows:

    a.   The sixth sentence of paragraph (c)(2)(i) is revised to read; "However, except as provided in paragraphs (e)(2)(ii), (iii), and (iv) of this section, for purposes of this subdivision a charitable contribution of an interest in property not in trust where the decedent transfers some specific rights to one party and transfers other substantial rights to another party will not be considered a contribution of an undivided portion of the decedent's entire interest in property."

    b.   The eighth sentence of paragraph (c)(2)(i) is revised to read; "A gift to charity made on or before December 17, 1980, of an open space easement in gross in perpetuity shall be considered the transfer to charity of an undivided portion of the donor's entire interest in property."

    c.   Paragraphs (c)(2)(iv), (c)(2)(v), and (c)(2)(vi) are redesignated (c)(2)(v), (c)(2)(vi), and (c)(2)(vii), respectively.

    d.   A new paragraph (c)(2)(iv) is inserted after paragraph (c)(2)(iii), to read as set forth below.

§ 25.2522(c)-3 Transfers not exclusively for charitable, etc., purposes in the case of gifts made after July 31, 1969.

* * * *

(c) *Transfers of partial interest in property.*

    (2) *Deductible interests.* * * *

        (iv) *Qualified Conservation Contribution.* The charitable interest is a qualified conservation contribution. For the definition of a qualified conservation contribution, see § 1.170A-14.

* * * *

Appendix F

Agreement of AAA Associates Limited Partnership Formed to Conduct Real Property Rehabilitation

Dated: As of January   , 1985

TABLE OF CONTENTS

Page No.

- I. Formation
  - 1.1 Formation—Name—Office
  - 1.2 Purposes
  - 1.3 Term
- II. Capital Contributions
  - 2.1 Capital Contributions
  - 2.2 Withdrawal of Capital
  - 2.3 Interest
  - 2.4 Use of Capital Contributions
  - 2.5 Limited Partner's Liability
- III. Title to the Property of the Partnership
- IV. The General Partner; Conduct of Business; Powers; Other Activities
  - 4.1 Management
  - 4.2 Compensation
  - 4.3 Limitations on Powers
  - 4.4 Duties
  - 4.5 Exculpation
  - 4.6 Outside Interests
  - 4.7 Conflicts of Interest
- V. Accounting Provisions
  - 5.1 Fiscal Year
  - 5.2 Books and Accounts
  - 5.3 Financial and Other Reports
  - 5.4 Tax Elections
  - 5.5 Expenses
- VI. Admission of Successor Limited Partners; Transfer of a Limited Partner's Interest; Disability of a Limited Partner
  - 6.1 Admission of Successor Limited Partners
  - 6.2 Transfer of a Limited Partner's Interest
  - 6.3 Limitations on Transfers of Limited Partner's Interests

	6.4	Disability of a Limited Partner
	6.5	Rights of First Refusal
VII.	Assignment by the General Partner; Disability of the General Partner; Reconstitution of the Partnership	
	7.1	Assignment by the General Partner
	7.2	Disability of the General Partner
	7.3	Reconstitution of the Partnership
VIII.	Distribution and Allocations	
	8.1	Definitions
	8.2	Distributions of Net Cash Flow
	8.3	Allocation of Net Profits and Net Losses
	8.4	Certain Additional Allocations
	8.5	No Right to Receive Property
	8.6	Return of Distributions
	8.7	Allocations between Assignor and Assignee Partners
IX.	Liquidation and Termination of the Partnership	
	9.1	General
	9.2	Statements on Termination
	9.3	Priority on Liquidation
	9.4	Distribution of Non-Liquid Assets
	9.5	Orderly Liquidation
	9.6	Deficit upon Liquidation
	9.7	Source of Distributions
X.	Loans and Advances by Partners	
	10.1	General
XI.	Power of Attorney	
	11.1	General
	11.2	Successor Limited Partner
	11.3	Additional Power of Attorney
XII.	Indemnification	
	12.1	General
XIII.	Determination of Disputes	
	13.1	General
XIV	Miscellaneous Provisions	
	14.1	Investment Representations
	14.2	Applicable Law
	14.3	Creditors
	14.4	Oral Modification
	14.5	Notices
	14.6	Captions
	14.7	Amendments
	14.8	Binding Effect
	14.9	Construction
	14.10	Separability
	14.11	Survival of Representations, Warranties and Agreement
	14.12	Further Assurances
	14.13	Counterparts

AGREEMENT OF LIMITED PARTNERSHIP OF AAA Associates, dated as of January   , 1985, among GP Associates, a partnership consisting of [Names of Individuals], as general partner (the "General Partner") and the other persons executing this Agreement as limited partners and Class B limited partners (individually, a "Limited Partner" and collectively, the "Limited Partners"; the General Partner and the Limited Partners as constituted from time to time are hereinafter sometimes referred to individually as "Partner" or collectively as the "Partners").

WITNESSETH:

WHEREAS, the Partners wish to form a limited partnership pursuant to the Partnership Law of the State of [   ] (the "Uniform Act") for the purposes and term and upon the conditions set forth herein;

NOW, THEREFORE, in consideration of the premises and the agreements herein contained, the Partners hereby agree as follows:

I. Formation

1.1. *Formation–Name–Office.* The Partners hereby form a [State in which partnership is formed] limited partnership (the "Partnership"), under and pursuant to the Uniform Act, which partnership shall be conducted under the name of AAA Associates. The office of the Partnership shall be [Address of Office], or at such other place or places as the General Partner may from time to time designate. Each Partner shall be notified by the General Partner of any change in the office of the Partnership.

1.2. *Purposes.* The purposes for which the Partnership has been formed are—

(i) to acquire the fee estate to certain real property and the buildings (the "Buildings") and improvements situate thereon located in [Location of property] (the "Property"),

(ii) to renovate the Buildings,

(iii) to manage and operate the Property and hold the Property as the owner thereof, and

(iv) to engage in such other activities as shall be necessary or desirable in connection with or incidental to the foregoing.

1.3. *Term.* The term of the Partnership shall begin as of the date hereof, and shall end on the date which is the earlier of

(i) December 31, 2021;

(ii) the date of the disposition of all, or substantially all, of the Property and other assets of the Partnership, or

(iii) a date determined by all of the Partners.

II. Capital Contributions

2.1. *Capital Contributions.* As of the date of execution hereof, each Partner has made an initial cash contribution to the Partnership in the amount set forth opposite his name on the signature page of this agreement.

2.2. *Withdrawal of Capital.* No Partner shall have the right to withdraw any part of his capital contributions prior to the liquidation and termination of the Partnership pursuant to Article IX hereof, unless such withdrawal is provided for in this Agreement.

2.3. *Interest.* No Partner shall receive any interest on his capital contributions to the Partnership.

2.4. *Use of Capital Contributions.* The funds received by the Partnership pursuant to Section 2.1 hereof shall be held by the Partnership in trust in a special bank account or bank accounts for the benefit of the Partners, until disbursed as provided in this Agreement.

2.5. *Limited Partner's Liability.* The liability of each Limited Partner, as such, shall be limited to the amount of the capital contribution which he has made pursuant to this Article II. No Limited Partner shall have any further obligation to contribute money to or in respect of, nor shall any Limited Partner be personally liable for, any liability or other obligation to the Partnership.

III. Title to the Property of the Partnership

3.1. Title to the Property and to any other property, real or personal, owned by or leased to the Partnership shall be held in the name of the Partnership or in the name of any nominee the General Partner, in its sold discretion, may designate.

IV. The General Partner; Conduct of Business; Powers; Other Activities

4.1. *Management*

(a) The business and affairs of the Partnership shall be conducted and managed solely by the General Partner in accordance with the Uniform Act. Subject to the other provisions of this Agreement, the General Partner shall be authorized, among other things, in furtherance of the objects of the business of the Partnership to—

(i) sell, or grant options relating to a sale of, all or any portion of the Property,

(ii) incur indebtedness, secured or unsecured,

(iii) mortgage, lease or otherwise encumber the Property, whether or not the term of any such mortgage or lease shall extend beyond the date of termination of the Partnership,

(iv) enter into and perform contracts of any kind in connection with or necessary or incidental to the management and operation of the Partnership's business, including employing such persons, firms or corporations as the General Partner, in his sole discretion, deems necessary or advisable, and open accounts and maintain funds in the Partnership's name in any bank or savings and loan association, and

(v) prepare or cause to be prepared reports and other relevant information for distribution to the Partners.

(b) The Limited Partners consent to the exercise by the General Partner of the powers conferred on him by this Agreement. No Limited Partner (except one who may also be a general partner and then only in his capacity as General Partner) shall participate in or have any control over the Partnership's business or have any right or authority to act for or bind the Partnership. No grantee, lessee or mortgagee shall be required to investigate the General Partner's authority to sell, mortgage or lease the Property or any part thereof, and any deed, lease, mortgage or option executed by the General Partner shall be binding upon the Partnership. The power of the General Partner to sell the Partnership Property shall be deemed to include full authority and power in his discretion to sell or exchange the Property, or any part thereof, for all cash or for part cash and part deferred payment whether or not secured by mortgage, or wholly or partly for other property or for stock or other securities of any corporation, trust, or other entity, as the General Partner in his sole discretion, may deem advisable.

4.2. *Compensation*

(a) Except as otherwise provided in this Agreement, no Partner shall be entitled to receive any salary or other remuneration from the Partnership.

(b) Should the General Partner assume responsibility for management of the Buildings, for reconstruction or renovation of the Buildings, or for the performance of any other service to the Partnership or relating to the Buildings or the Property, the General Partner shall be entitled to compensation at a rate no more favorable than would be charged for comparable service by an unaffiliated party of comparable stature in the [Name of Locality] area.

4.3. *Limitations on Powers*

(a) The General Partner, in its conduct and management of the business and affairs of the Partnership, shall have all the powers conferred by the Uniform Act on a general partner of a limited partnership.

(b) The General Partner, with the consent of 51% in interest of the Limited Partners, may cause the Partnership to:

(i) make loans to other persons,

(ii) invest in the equity securities of other entities,

(iii) repurchase, redeem or otherwise acquire Limited Partner's interests, or

(iv) issue senior or other securities of the Partnership. However, such consent of 51% in interest of the Limited Partners shall not be required in connection with the refinancing of any of the Partnership's indebtedness.

(c) The General Partner is hereby authorized on behalf of the Partnership to execute, deliver or accept any document, agreement or instrument which shall be required in connection with and any transaction related to the acquisition of the Property and the activities referred to in Section 1.2 hereof. The execution, delivery or acceptance by the General Partner of any document, agreement or instrument related to the foregoing shall be deemed to be the act of and shall be binding upon the Partnership.

4.4. *Duties.* The General Partner shall devote only so much of its time and attention to the business and affairs of the Partnership as it in his sole discretion may deem reasonably necessary for the purposes of the Partnership.

4.5. *Exculpation.* The General Partner shall not be liable to the Partnership or to the Limited Partners for any act performed by it in good faith on behalf of the Partnership or any failure to so act, if in the sole discretion of the General Partner such action or inaction was in the best interests of the Partnership and did not constitute bad faith or willful misconduct.

4.6. *Outside Interests.* The General Partner and the two individual partners of the General Partner may engage in, invest in, participate in or otherwise enter into such other bsuiness ventures of any kind, nature and description, individually and with others, including, without limitation, the ownership of, or investment in or the operation and management of real estate, whether or not any such business venture competes with the Partnership, and neither the Partnership nor any other Partner shall have any right in or to any such activities or the income or profits derived therefrom.

4.7. *Conflicts of Interest*

(a) The General Partner may employ, on behalf of the Partnership, such persons, firms or corporations as he, in his sole judgment, shall deem advisable for the operation and management of the business of the Partnership on such terms and for such compensation, as he in his sole judgment, shall determine. Any such entity also may be employed or retained by the General Partner in connection with other business ventures of the General Partner.

(b) The fact that any partner or a member of his family is directly or indirectly interested in or connected with any person, firm or corporation employed by the Partnership or from whom the Partnership may buy merchandise, services or other property shall not prohibit the General Partner from employing, or from dealing with, such person, firm or corporation on behalf of the Partnership.

V. Accounting Provisions

5.1. *Fiscal Year.* The General Partner, in its sole discretion, shall elect, and from time to time may change, the fiscal year of the Partnership.

5.2. *Books and Accounts*

(a) Complete and accurate books and accounts shall be kept and maintained for the Partnership at the principal place of business of the Partnership. Each Partner or his duly authorized representative, at his own expense, shall at all reasonable times have access to, and may inspect such books and accounts and any other records of the Partnership.

(b) All funds received by the Partnership shall be deposited in such bank account or accounts as the General Partner may designate from time to time, and withdrawals therefrom shall be made upon the signature of the General Partner and/ or upon such other signature or signatures on behalf of the Partnership as the General Partner may designate from time to time. All deposits (including security deposits) and other funds not needed in the operation of the Partnership's business may, in the sole discretion of the General Partner, be deposited in interest-bearing bank accounts or invested in United States Government or municipal obligations, money market investments or banking certificates of deposit, or such other investments as the General Partner, in its sole discretion, may determine.

5.3. *Financial and Other Reports*

(a) The Partnership will report its operations on an accrual or a cash basis, as the General Partner in its sole discretion shall from time to time determine.

Each year, each Partner will be provided with financial statements of the Partnership. The books of account of the Partnership shall be audited on a regular basis at least annually by certified public accountants selected from time to time by the General Partner.

(b) The General Partner shall cause to be prepared and filed after the end of each fiscal year of the Partnership, all Federal and State income tax returns of the Partnership for such fiscal year and shall take all action as may be necessary to permit the Partnership to prepare timely and thereafter to file promptly such returns. A copy of each such tax return and Form 1065 (Schedule K-1) shall be transmitted to each Partner after the end of each fiscal year relating to the Partner's *pro rata* share of income, credit and deductions for such fiscal year.

5.4. *Tax Elections.* The Partnership, in the sole discretion of the General Partner, may make any election permitted under the Internal Revenue Code of 1954, as amended (the "Code"), including, without limitation, the election permitted under Section 754 of the Code.

5.5. *Expenses.* To the extent practicable, all expenses of the Partnership shall be billed directly to and be paid by the Partnership.

VI. Admission of Successor Limited Partners; Transfer of a Limited Partner's Interest; Disability of a Limited Partner

6.1. *Admission of Successor Limited Partners.* The General Partners shall have the right to admit successor limited partners to the Partnership, pursuant to the provisions of Sections 6.2 and 6.3 hereof. Upon the admission of a successor limited partner, an amendment to the Certificate of Partnership of the Partnership reflecting such admission shall be filed by the General Partner. The admission of any successor limited partner pursuant to this Section 6.1 shall not be cause for dissolution of the Partnership.

6.2. *Transfer of a Limited Partner's Interest.*

(a) Subject to the provisions of Sections 6.2(b) and 6.4 hereof, a Limited Partner may not, without the consent of the General Partner, transfer, assign, or otherwise dispose of all or any portion of his interest in the Partnership (other than an economic interest) (hereinafter, a "Transfer"). Any purported Transfer without such consent shall be void *ab initio* and shall not bind the Partnership. However, if

(i) the General Partner consents thereto,

(ii) the provisions of Section 6.3 hereof do not otherwise prohibit the Transfer, and

(iii) a duly executed and acknowledged counterpart of the instrument effecting the Transfer, in form and substance satisfactory to the Partnership's counsel, shall have been delivered to the General Partner, then the Transfer may be made; provided, however, that the assignee shall not have the right to be admitted as a successor Limited Partner unless

(A) the assignor shall have indicated such intention of substitution in the instrument effecting such Transfer and the assignee shall expressly agree to be bound by the provisions of this Agreement and assume all of the obligations imposed upon a Limited Partner hereunder;

(B) the General Partner, in its sole discretion, shall have consented in writing to such admission and,

(c) the assignor and the assignee shall have executed or delivered such other instruments as the General Partner may deem necessary or desirable to effectuate such admission. Any assignee must also agree to pay, as the General Partner shall determine, all reasonable expenses and legal fees relating to his admission as a Limited Partner, including but not limited to the cost of any required counsel's opinion and of preparing, filing, and publishing any amendment to the Partnership's Certificate of Partnership necessary to effect such admission. Any valid Transfer shall be recognized not later than the last day of the calendar month following receipt of notice of assignment and required documentation and any required amendment of the Certificate of Partnership of the Partnership shall be filed at least once every calendar quarter to reflect the admission of a substituted Limited Partner.

(b) The consent of the General Partner shall not be required to a Transfer of a Limited Partner's interest or to the substitution of an assignee as a successor limited partner if the Transfer is made

(i) to another Partner or

(ii) for no consideration to the assignor's spouse or bloodline descendant or to a trustee for the benefit of the assignor, his spouse or his bloodline descendant; provided, however, that no Transfer or substitution of a successor limited partner as provided in this Section 6.2(b) shall become effective unless the Transfer or substitution is otherwise made in accordance with and subject to the provisions of paragraph (a) of this Section 6.2.

6.3. *Limitations on Transfers of Limited Partner's Interests.* No Transfer may be made if such Transfer would result in the termination of the Partnership under the terms of any relevant section of the Code or any successor statute, and, if so attempted, such Transfer shall be void *ab initio* and shall not bind the Partnership. In making a determination of this issue, the General Partner, in its sole and absolute discretion, may require the assignee to furnish, at his expense, an opinion of counsel passing on this issue. No Transfer may be made to (and no successor limited partner shall be admitted to the Partnership who is) a person below the age of 21 years or a person who has been adjudged to be insane or incompetent, and any purported Transfer to any such person shall be void *ab initio* and shall not bind the Partnership.

As a condition of recognizing any Transfer, the General Partner may require such proof of the age and competency of the assignee as the General Partner may deem necessary.

6.4. *Disability of a Limited Partner.* The death, insanity, incompetency, bankruptcy, insolvency, dissolution or liquidation and termination (any of the foregoing being hereinafter referred to as a "Disability") of a Limited Partner shall not terminate or dissolve the Partnership. In the event of the Disability of a Limited Partner or the making of an assignment for the benefit of creditors by a Limited Partner, the executor, administrator, guardian, committee, trustee or other legal representative of such Limited Partner shall have all of the rights and liabilities of such Limited Partner, subject to the provisions of this Agreement, upon compliance with the provisions of Sections 6.2 and 6.3 hereof.

6.5. *Rights of First Refusal.* If any Limited Partner shall desire to sell his partnership interest and shall receive a bona fide offer in writing to purchase all of his interest in the Partnership ("Assigning Partner"), such Assigning Partner shall first offer, by notice in writing, to sell all of his interest to the General Partner for the same price and on the same terms and conditions of sale as set forth in the bona fide offer. Such notice or offer shall set forth the name, residence and business address of the bona fide offeror and sufficient facts concerning the bona fide offeror to enable the General Partner to arrive at an informed judgment as to the bona fides of such offer and shall contain a copy of the bona fide offer. The bona fide offer shall set forth the representations and warranties requested of the Assigning Partner and all items affecting the price. The General Partner shall have the option to purchase the interest of the Assigning Partner. The General Partner may elect to exercise the option by written notice to the Assigning Partner mailed within 30 days after the date of delivery of the notice of offer. If the option is not exercised within said 30-day period with respect to the entire interest of the Assigning Partner, then the Assigning Partner shall be free to assign his interest in the Partnership to the bona fide offeror pursuant to the terms of the bona fide offer. If such assignment to the bona fide offeror is not completed in accordance with the terms of the bona fide offer within 30 days thereafter, then the Assigning Partner shall not assign his interest in the Partnership without again offering the same to the General Partner in accordance with the procedure set forth above.

VII. Assignment by the General Partner; Disability of the General Partner; Reconstitution of the Partnership

7.1. *Assignment by the General Partner.* Except as provided in this Article VII, the General Partner may not, without the consent of the other Partners, sell, transfer, assign or otherwise dispose of all or any portion of its General Partner's interest, other than an economic interest. Any such purported sale, transfer, assignment or other disposition shall be void *ab initio* and shall not bind the Partnership unless and until a duly executed and acknowledged counterpart of the instrument effecting the same, in form and substance satisfactory to the Partnership's counsel, shall have been delivered to the Partnership's counsel; and further provided that no such sale, transfer, assignment or other disposition may be made if it would result in the termination of the Partnership under the terms of any relevant section of the Code and, if so attempted, shall be void *ab initio* and shall not bind the Partnership. No General Partner's interest shall be sold, transferred, assigned or otherwise disposed of to a person below the age of 21 years or to a person who has been adjudged to be insane or incompetent.

7.2. *Disability of the General Partner.* Upon

(a) the death, retirement, dissolution, withdrawal, insanity, incompetency, bankruptcy, or insolvency of a General Partner or the making by a General Partner of an assignment for the benefit of creditors, or

(b) the failure of a General Partner, at any time; in the opinion of the Partnership's counsel, to satisfy the provision of Section 7.3 hereof relating to the financial net worth requirements of a general partner of a limited partnership (each of the foregoing being hereinafter referred to as a "Disabling Event"), the Partnership may be reconstituted pursuant to Section 7.3 hereof.

7.3. *Reconstitution of the Partnership.* Upon the occurrence of a Disabling Event to the General Partner (the "Disabled General Partner"), the Partnership shall be dissolved, provided, however, within 90 days after the occurrence of a Disabling Event, the Partnership may be reconstituted pursuant to this Section 7.3 as a successor limited partnership upon the consent of such of the Limited Partners as may then be required by law. In reconstituting the Partnership pursuant to this Section 7.3, the Limited Partners may designate a successor general partner to serve in place of the Disabled General Partner; provided, however, no person shall be designated or admitted as a successor general partner unless, in the opinion of the Partnership's counsel, such person has a financial net worth to assure that he shall satisfy the financial net worth requirements of a general partner of a limited partnership. If the Limited Partners shall make such designation

(i) the interest of the Disabled General Partner shall be converted into and shall be deemed to be that of a limited partner with the same interest in the Partnership as the Disabled General Partner had (as a General Partner) prior to the Disabling Event (as reduced in the manner set forth below in this Section 7.3); and

(ii) if the successor general partner does not own a 1% interest in all material items of profit, loss, capital and cash flow of the Partnership, then each Limited Partner (including the person succeeding to the interest of the Disabled General Partner as a limited partner) shall transfer a *pro rata* portion of his interest to the successor general partner sufficient to give the successor general partner such 1% interest and the successor general partner shall pay to each Limited Partner (including the person succeeding to the interest of the Disabled General Partner as a limited partner), as the purchase price for his interest, an amount to be agreed upon by the successor general partner and the Limited Partners (including the person succeeding to the interest of the Disabled General Partner as a limited partner) and in the absence of such agreement the purchase price for such interest shall be determined by arbitration in accordance with the provisions of Article XIII hereof.

The successor general partner and all of the Limited Partners shall agree to be bound by the provisions of this Agreement; provided, however, that if this Agreement is amended by them, no amendment shall be made unless counsel to the Partnership shall issue an opinion that the Partnership shall continue to be treated as a partnership and not as an association taxable as a corporation, and, further provided, the amended agreement shall be as similar in form and substance to this Agreement as practicable and the new or successor partnership shall engage in the same business as this Partnership employing the assets and name of this Partnership to the extent possible.

For the purposes of this Agreement, unless the context otherwise requires, any successor general partner, upon compliance with the provisions of this Article VII and his admission as a general partner, shall be included within the meaning of the term "General Partner" and any interest of a General Partner or Disabled General Partner, unless the context otherwise requires, shall not include any Limited Partner's interests held by a General Partner, Disabled General Partner or successor general partner. Except for the purposes of Article VIII hereof, any person holding an interest held by a Disabled General Partner which has been converted into a limited partner's interest shall be included within the meaning of the term "limited Partner."

VIII. Distributions and Allocations

8.1. *Definitions.* As used in this Agreement:

(a) The term "Net Cash Flow" as used herein shall mean net cash available from the operation of the Property utilizing sound accounting practices, inclusive of proceeds derived from mortgage refinancing, new financing, condemnation, sale or insurance recoveries (a "Capital Transaction") and deducting therefrom all cash expenses in connection with the operation of the Property and other cash expenses of the Partnership, provided, however, in making such computation there shall be no deduction for depreciation or for amortization of capital improvements. Expenditures for capital improvements and mortgage amortization payments shall constitute a deduction.

(b) "Net Profits" or "Net Losses" shall mean the annual net income or net loss, respectively, of the Partnership for a fiscal year as determined by the Partnership's certified public accountant in accordance with principles applied in determining income, gains, expenses, deductions or losses, as the case may be, reported by the Partnership for Federal income tax purposes on its United States partnership tax return.

8.2. *Distributions of Net Cash Flow.* The General Partner shall, from time to time, determine the Net Cash Flow and other available proceeds which may, from time to time, be distributed to all partners, after the establishment and maintenance of appropriate reserves.

(a) Such Net Cash Flow, except that which is attributable to a Capital Transaction, shall be divided eighty (80%) percent thereof *pro rata* to the Limited Partners, fifteen (15%) percent thereof to the General Partner, and four (4%) percent and one (1%) percent to [Name of individual] and [Name of individual], respectively, as Class B Limited Partners.

(b) Such Net Cash Flow which is attributable to a Capital Transaction shall be devided eighty (80%) percent *pro rata* to the Limited Partners, fifteen (15%) percent thereof to the General Partner and four (4%) percent and one (1%) percent, respectively, to [Name of individual] and [Name of individual] as Class B Limited Partners. Provided, however, before any distribution may be made on account of the 20% aggregate shares to the General Partner and the Class B Limited Partners hereunder by reason of a sale or condemnation of the entire Property, the Partners* must have received in aggregate distributions under this subparagraph (b) from such transaction the net amount of their cash capital contributions to the Partnership.

8.3. *Allocation of Net Profits and Net Losses.*

(a) All items of Net Profits or Net Losses, other than capital gain of the Partnership, shall be allocated *pro rata* in the same proportion as provided for in paragraph 8.2 (a).

(b) All items of capital gain shall be allocated as follows: To the extent that Net Losses in excess of Net Profits have been allocated to any Partner, net capital gain shall be allocated to each such Partner whose capital account has been decreased by such excess in the proportion which such decrease bears to the total decreases until the gain allocated pursuant to this subparagraph equals the total decreases.

---

*Including the General Partner and the Class B Limited Partners with respect to any Limited Partnership interests which they may own.

(c) To the extent that any Partner has received distributions from the Partnership in excess of Partnership Net Profits allocated to him, net capital gain shall then be allocated to such Partner in the proportion which such excess bears to the total excesses until the gain allocated pursuant to this subparagraph equals such excess. For the purpose of this subparagraph, if Net Losses allocated to any Partner exceed Net Profit allocated to such Partner, the Partnership income allocated to him shall be considered equal to zero.

(d) After allocating the net capital gains to the extent provided in the preceding subparagraphs (b) and (c), the remaining net capital gains, if any, shall be allocated in the same proportion as set forth in paragraph 8.2(a).

8.4. *Certain Additional Allocations.*

(a) Upon liquidation of the Partnership pursuant to Article IX hereof, Net Profits or Net Losses realized upon such liquidation shall be allocated pursuant to Section 8.3 hereof and any asset shall be distributed in cash or in kind in accordance with the provisions of Section 9.3 hereof. With respect to assets distributed in kind to the Partners,

(i) any unrealized appreciation or unrealized depreciation in the values of such assets shall be deemed to be Net Profits or Net Losses realized by the Partnership immediately prior to the liquidation (for the purposes of this Section 8.4(a), "unrealized appreciation" or "unrealized depreciation" shall mean the difference between the appraised value of such assets (as determined pursuant to Section 9.3(b) hereof) and the Partnership's basis for such assets; and

(ii) such Net Profits or Net Losses shall be allocated to the Capital Accounts pursuant to Section 8.3 hereof and any property so distributed shall be treated as a distribution to the Partners pursuant to Section 8.4 hereof to the extent of the aforesaid appraised value less the amount of any liability related thereto. Nothing contained in this Section 8.4 or elsewhere in this Agreement is intended to treat or cause such distributions to be treated as sales for value.

(b) For income tax purposes, if the Partnership in any year incurs income or is allowed a deduction (including additional depreciation or amortization as a result of adding an item to its basis) as a result of the transfer of an interest in property to or from a Partner, the difference between the amount taken into account for tax purposes and the amount otherwise taken into account under this Agreement shall be allocated solely to such Partner.

8.5. *No Right to Receive Property.* No Partner shall have the right to demand and receive property other than cash in return for his capital contributions.

8.6. *Return of Distributions.* No Partner shall have any obligation to refund to the Partnership any amount which shall have been distributed to such Partner pursuant to this Agreement, subject, however, to the rights of any third party creditor.

8.7. *Allocations between Assignor and Assignee Partners.* In the case of a Transfer of a Partner's interest in the Partnership, the assignor and assignee shall each be entitled to receive distributions pursuant to Section 8.2 hereof or allocations of Net Profits or Net Losses pursuant to Sections 8.3, and 8.4 hereof, as follows:

(a) Unless the assignor and assignee agree to the contrary and shall so provide in the instrument effecting the assignment, distributions shall be made to the person owning the Partner's interest on the date of the distribution; and

(b) Net Profits or Net Losses shall be allocated by the number of days each person held the Partner's interest, except that if the assignor and the assignee agree to the contrary and shall so advise the General Partner in writing within ten days after the end of the fiscal year in which the assignment occurs, Net Profits or Net Losses from any Capital Transaction shall be allocated to the holder of the Partner's interest on the day the Capital Transaction occurred during such year.

IX. Liquidation and Termination of the Partnership

9.1. *General.* Upon the termination of the Partnership, the Partnership shall be liquidated in accordance with this Article IX and the Uniform Act. The liquidation shall be conducted and supervised by the General Partner or, if there be no General Partner, by a person who shall be designated for such purposes by the remaining Partners (the General Partner or such person so designated being herein referred to as the "Liquidating Agent"). The Liquidating Agent shall have all of the rights and powers with respect to the assets and liabilities of the Partnership in connection with the liquidation and termination of the Partnership that the General Partner would have with respect to the assets and liabilities of the Partnership during the term of the Partnership, and the Liquidating Agent is hereby expressly authorized and empowered to execute any and all documents necessary or desirable to effectuate the liquidation and termination of the Partnership and the transfer of any asset or liability of the Partnership. The Liquidating Agent shall have the right from time to time, by revocable powers of attorney, to delegate to one or more persons any or all of such rights and powers and such authority and power to execute documents, and, in connection therewith, to fix the reasonable compensation of each such person, which compensation shall be charged as an expense of liquidation. The Liquidating Agent is also expressly authorized to distribute the Partnership's property to the Partners subject to liens.

9.2. *Statements on Termination.* Each Partner shall be furnished with a statement prepared by the Partnership's certified public accountant which shall set forth the assets and liabilities.

9.3. *Priority on Liquidation.* The Liquidating Agent shall, to the extent feasible, liquidate the assets of the Partnership as promptly as shall be practicable. To the extent the proceeds are sufficient therefor, as the Liquidating Agent shall deem appropriate, the proceeds of such liquidation shall be applied in the following order of priority:

(a) To the payment of matured debts and liabilities of the Partnership and the costs and expenses of the dissolution and liquidation;

(b) To the setting up of any reserve which the Liquidating Agent may deem reasonably necessary for any contingent, unmatured or unforeseen liability of the Partnership; and

(c) Any balance then remaining shall be allocated among the Partners and paid and distributed in the manner provided in Sections 8.2 and 8.3 hereof.

9.4. *Distribution of Non-Liquid Assets.* Subject to the provisions of Section 8.4(a) hereof, if the Liquidating Agent shall determine that it is not feasible to liquidate all of the assets of the Partnership, then the Liquidating Agent shall cause the fair market value of the assets not so liquidated to be determined by appraisal. Such assets, as so appraised, shall be retained or distributed by the Liquidating Agent as follows:

(a) The Liquidating Agent shall retain assets having a fair market value equal to the amount by which the net proceeds of liquidated assets are insufficient to satisfy the debts and liabilities of the Partnership (other than any debt or liability for which neither the Partnership nor a Partner is personally liable), to pay the costs and expenses of the dissolution and liquidation, to establish reserves and to repay any loan or advance made by the Partners and any other debt and liability to the Partners, all subject to the provisions of Sections 8.2, 8.3 and 8.4 hereof. The foregoing notwithstanding, the Liquidating Agent shall have the right to distribute property subject to liens at the value of the Partnership's equity therein.

(b) The remaining assets (including mortgages and other receivables) shall be distributed to the Partners *pro rata* in accordance with their respective percentage interests in the Partnership. If, in the sole and absolute judgment of the Liquidating Agent, it shall not be feasible to distribute to each Partner an aliquot share of each asset, the Liquidating Agent may allocate and distribute specific assets to one or more Partners as tenants-in-common as the Liquidating Agent shall determine to be fair and equitable, taking into consideration, *inter alia*, the basis for tax purposes of each asset distributed and after crediting or charging the Capital Accounts of the Partners for any unrealized gain or loss as provided in Section 8.4(a) hereof.

9.5. *Orderly Liquidation.* A reasonable time shall be allowed for the orderly liquidation of the assets of the Partnership and the discharge of liabilities to creditors so as to minimize the losses normally attendant upon a liquidation.

9.6. *Deficit Upon Liquidation.* Upon liquidation, no Partner shall be liable to the Partnership for any deficit in his Capital Account, except to the extent provided by law with respect to third party creditors of the Partnership, nor shall such deficit be deemed an asset of the Partnership.

9.7. *Source of Distributions.* No Partner shall be personally liable for the return of the capital contributions of any other Partners, or any portion thereof, it being expressly understood that any such return shall be made solely from Partnership assets.

X. Loans and Advances by Partners

10.1. *General.* Except as expressly provided for herein, if any Partner shall loan or advance any funds to the Partnership (other than the capital contributions provided in Article II hereof), such loan or advance shall not be deemed a contribution to the capital of the Partnership and shall not in any respect increase such Partner's interest in the Partnership. Such loan or advance shall constitute an obligation and liability of the Partnership and shall not bear any interest. Unless otherwise agreed in writing between a Partner and the Partnership, no Partner shall have personal obligation or liability for the repayment of such loans and the same shall be collectible only from Partnership assets.

XI. Power of Attorney

11.1. *General.* Each Limited Partner irrevocably constitutes and appoints the General Partner, any successor general partner and the Liquidating Agent, or any one of them, the true and lawful attorney of such Limited Partner to execute, acknowledge, swear to and file any of the following:

(a) Any amendment to the Partnership Certificate of Limited Partnership pursuant to the Uniform Act;

(b) Any certificate or other instrument

(i) which may be required to be filed by the Partnership under the laws of the United States, the State of [   ] or any other State in which any of the Partners reside or

(ii) which the General Partner shall deem advisable to file;

(c) Any amendment to any certificate or other instrument referred to in paragraphs (a) and (b) of this Section 11.1;

(d) Any document which may be required to effectuate the liquidation or termination of the Partnership; and

(e) Any amendment to this Agreement or the foregoing certificates or instruments necessary to effect any change permitted under Section 14.5 hereof.

It is expressly acknowledged by each Limited Partner that the foregoing power of attorney is coupled with an interest and shall survive the death, legal incapacity or a Transfer by a Limited Partner; provided, however, if a Limited Partner shall make a Transfer of all of his interest and the assignee shall, in accordance with Section 6.3 hereof, become a successor limited partner, such power of attorney shall survive the Transfer only for the purpose of executing, acknowledging, swearing to and filing any and all instruments necessary to affectuate such substitution.

Each Limited Partner hereby agrees to execute concurrently herewith or upon 15 days' prior written notice, a special power of attorney containing the substantive provisions hereof in form satisfactory to the General Partner.

11.2. *Successor Limited Partner.* A power of attorney similar to that contained in Section 11.1 hereof shall be one of the instruments which the General Partner may require a successor limited partner to execute, acknowledge and swear to pursuant to Section 6.3 hereof.

11.3. *Additional Power of Attorney.* Upon the admission of a successor general partner pursuant to Section 7.3 hereof, or upon the liquidation or termination of the Partnership, each Limited Partner at the request of the successor general partner or the Liquidating Agent shall execute, acknowledge and swear to a new power of attorney similar to that described in Section 11.1 hereof, in favor of such successor general partner or Liquidating Agent.

XII. Indemnification

12.1. *General.*

(a) In no event shall the General Partner, or any partners of the partnership which is the initial General Partner, be subject to any personal liability to the Partnership or to any Partner for any reason whatsoever other than the bad faith or willful misconduct of such General Partner. The conduct of the General Partner in reliance upon the advice of counsel shall in all cases be deemed to be in good faith. In the event that any action or proceeding is instituted or threatened against the General Partner, or in which he may be a party, he shall be entitled to retain legal counsel and other experts at the expense of the Partnership and to be immediately reimbursed for, indemnified against and saved harmless with respect to any liabilities, costs and expenses arising out of or in connection with such action or proceeding including, but not limited to, legal fees and expenses, as and when such liabilities, costs and expenses are incurred and whether or not such General Partner is serving in such capacity as of the date that such liabilities, costs and expenses are fixed or incurred and without awaiting determination of the action or proceeding. It is understood and agreed that the reimbursement and indemnification herein provided for shall include without limitation, to the extent permitted by law, any claim based upon fraud in the inducement of this agreement, misrepresentation, violation of any securities law, syndication law or other Blue Sky law, and it is expressly agreed that all of such matters are, to the extent permitted by law, arbitrable and subject to the arbitration provisions of Article XIII hereof.

(b) The General Partner shall have the right and authority to require in all of the Partnership's contracts that he will not be personally liable thereon and that the person or entity contracting with the Partnership is to look solely to the Partnership and its assets for satisfaction of any claim, liability, expense, action, judgment or other matter arising thereunder or on account thereof.

XIII. Determination of Disputes

13.1. *General.* Any dispute or controversy arising under, out of, in connection with, or in relation to
   (a)   this Agreement, and any amendment thereof,
   (b)   the breach thereof, or
   (c)   the formation, operation or termination of the Partnership shall be determined and settled by arbitration by a panel of three members in accordance with the Rules of the American Arbitration Association. Any award rendered therein shall be final and binding upon the Partners and their legal representatives and judgment may be entered in any court having jurisdiction thereof. The expenses of such arbitration shall be paid by the party against whom the award shall be entered.

XIV. Miscellaneous Provisions

14.1. *Investment Representations.* Each partner acknowledges, warrants and represents as follows:
   (a)   That he is over twenty-one (21) years of age, is subject to no legal disability and has not relied and is not relying upon any information, statement or representation except those expressly set forth in this agreement.
   (b)   That he has consulted with and been advised by his own attorney and accountant with respect to his participation in the Partnership.
   (c)   That he and his advisors have reviewed this agreement and the exhibits annexed hereto.
   (d)   That nothing in this agreement or the exhibits annexed hereto or any other document or memorandum exhibited to him has been construed or relied upon by him as a representation by the General Partner or any other person of the income, expenses or value of the Property, the tax shelter or other tax consequences to the partners or of the future distributions, income and losses of the Partnership.

(e) That he is a sophisticated real estate investor.*

(f) That his capital contribution does not represent more than ten (10%) percent of his net worth.*

(g) That he has not had a professional, social and/or business relationship with the General Partners and their families prior to this transaction.*

(h) That this is a private placement exempt from registration under § 4(2) of the Securities Act of 1933, as amended, and not a public offering and that no registration statement, prospectus or offering circular is required by law or has been used in connection with this transaction.*

(i) That he is investing in the Partnership for his own account and for investment purposes only and not with a view to distribution or resale.*

(j) That he is prepared to hold this partnership interest indefinitely and will not sell, pledge, transfer or otherwise dispose of his interest in the Partnership or any portion thereof without the written legal opinion of counsel satisfactory to the General Partner that such transfer is not a violation of the Securities Act of 1933, as amended, or any other applicable securities law.

14.2. *Applicable Law.* This Agreement shall be governed by, and construed in accordance with, the laws and decisions of the State of [   ].

14.3. *Creditors.* A creditor who makes a non-recourse loan to the Partnership may not have or acquire at any time as a result of making such loan any direct or indirect interest in the profits, capital or property of the Partnership other than as a secured creditor. The Partnership shall not incur any non-recourse indebtedness unless the creditor agrees to the foregoing.

14.4. *Oral Modification.* This Agreement constitutes the entire understanding among the parties hereto. No waiver or modification of the provisions hereof shall be valid unless in writing and signed by the party to be charged and then only to the extent therein set forth.

14.5. *Notices.* All notices, demands, solicitations of consent or approval, and other communications hereunder shall be in writing and shall be deemed to have been given when the same are deposited in the United States Mail and sent by postage prepaid registered or certified mail, return receipt requested, addressed as follows: If intended for the Partnership, to its principal place of business, if intended for any Partner, at the address of such Partner set forth at the foot of this Agreement; or to such other address which any Partner shall have given to the Partnership for such purpose by notice delivered as aforesaid.

14.6. *Captions.* The captions used herein are intended for convenience of reference only, shall not constitute any part of this Agreement and shall not modify or affect in any manner the meaning or interpretation of any of the provisions of this Agreement.

14.7. *Amendments.* Any amendment of this Agreement may be made only by written consent of the General Partner and Limited Partners holding not less than 51% of the total Limited Partners' interests in the Partnership.

14.8. *Binding Effect.* Except as otherwise provided herein, this Agreement shall be binding upon and shall inure to the benefit of the respective heirs, executors, administrators, legal representatives, and permitted successors and assigns of the parties hereto.

---

*Note that these representations vary somewhat from the terms of Regulation D (see Appendix H). The requirements of Regulation D must be met independently if exemption from registration is to be obtained on that basis.

14.9. *Construction.* None of the provisions of this Agreement shall be for the benefit of or enforceable by any creditor of the Partnership.

14.10. *Separability.* In case any one or more of the provisions contained in this Agreement or any application thereof shall be invalid, illegal or unenforceable in any respect, the validity, legality and enforceability of the remaining provisions contained herein and other application thereof shall not in any way be effected or impaired thereby.

14.11. *Survival of Representations, Warranties and Agreements.* All representations, warranties and agreements shall survive until the final liquidation and termination of the Partnership, except to the extent that a representation, warranty or agreement expressly provides otherwise.

14.12. *Further Assurances.* The Partners will execute and deliver such further instruments and do such further acts and things as may be required to carry out the intent and purposes of this Agreement.

14.13. *Counterparts.* This Agreement may be executed in counterparts and all such counterparts taken together shall constitute one agreement.

IN WITNESS WHEREOF, the parties have executed this Agreement as of the date first written above.

GENERAL PARTNER

Name   Address

GP Associates

By: _____

CLASS B LIMITED PARTNERS

Name   Address

_____   _____

_____   _____

LIMITED PARTNERS

Name	Address	Capital Contribution	Percentage Interest

[Notarizations]

Appendix G

Rehab Associates Limited Partnership Pro Forma Accounting Projections with Accompanying Notes and Assumptions

(Projections as of September 23, 1983)

REHAB ASSOCIATES
STATEMENT OF PROJECTED

Year	1983 (3 months)	1984	1985	1986	1987	1988	1989	1990
Basic rental income (Note 3)			182500	980000	1855000	2230000	2230000	2811250
Additional rental income (Note 3)						200060	420000	590555
Interest income from capital contributions	423974	1639985	1376015	1005575	698922	418175	140849	
Total income	423974	1639985	1558515	1985575	2551922	2848235	2790849	3401805
Depreciation (Note 9)			1031073	2547293	2505793	2505793	2505793	1634293
Additional interest expense (Note 12)						200060	420000	493095
Interest on consolidated wraparound deed of trust (Note 15)			956134	3820638	3814689	3807260	3798567	3683151
Interest on supervisory services fee (Note 15)				270000	270000	270000	270000	270000
			67500					
Accrued interest on general partner deferred fee (Note 14)			12000	48000	48000	48000	48000	48000
Administrative fee (Note 10)			3750	15000	15000	15000	15000	16875
Monitoring fee (Note 11)			1075	7500	7500	7500	7500	8430
Other deductions (Note 5)	540780	962992	1062140	1442541	1166317	808437	401980	126073
Other administrative costs			6937	26775	25018	22958	20543	23307
Total deductions	540780	962992	3141410	8177746	7852216	7605016	7487383	6304031
Taxable income or (loss)	(116806)	676992	(1502895)	(6192172)	(5298294)	(4836781)	(4696454)	(2902226)

(Due to computer rounding, certain rows may not add.)

The notes and assumptions are an integral part of this projected statement.

LIMITED PARTNERSHIP
PARTNERSHIP TAXABLE INCOME (LOSS)

1991	1992	1993	1994	1995	1996	1997	1998	1999	2000 (9 months)
4555000	4555000	4635000	4875000	4887500	4925000	4925000	4932500	4955000	3716250
752080	923160	1104495	1296750	1500520	1716540	1945580	2188305	2445625	2038733
5307080	5478160	5739495	6171750	6388020	6641540	6870580	7120805	7400625	5754983
1634293	1634293	1634293	1634293	1634293	1634293	1634293	1634293	1634293	1225720
562320	635640	713355	795750	883080	975660	1073820	1177845	1288125	1018743
3356001	3344435	3329044	3312740	3292689	3269184	3241630	3209329	3171464	2349865
270000	270000	269918	267124	262762	257991	252772	247064	240821	176168
48000	48000	48000	48000	48000	48000	48000	48000	48000	36000
22500	22500	22500	22500	24175	30000	30000	30000	30000	22500
11250	11250	11250	11250	12100	15000	15000	15000	15000	11250
126073	126073	126073	107242	833	833	833	833	833	625
37742	35610	34621	33680	35570	55834	45894	42151	51920	30214
6069859	6128600	6190654	6232579	6193789	6286795	6342242	6404515	6480456	4871083
(762779)	(650440)	(451159)	(60829)	194231	354745	528338	716290	920169	883899

REHAB ASSOCIATES
STATEMENT OF PROJECTED

Year	1983 (3 months)	1984	1985	1986	1987	1988	1989
Taxable income or (loss)	(116806)	676992	(1582895)	(6192172)	(6290294)	(4836781)	(4696454)
Add:							
Depreciation			1031073	2547293	2505793	2505793	2505793
Accrued interest–consolidated wraparound deed of trust			371826	1485548	1483465	1480574	1477185
Accrued interest–supervisory services fee			67500	270000	270000	270000	270000
Accrued interest–general partner deferred fee			12000	48000	48000	48000	48000
Salvage	300000						
Pre-opening loan to lessee			46750	187000	187000	187000	187000
Other deductions	540545	962992	1062140	1442541	1166217	808437	401900
Class A limited partners' contribution	710500	853500	3268500	2543500	2256000	2132300	2235700
Class B limited partner's contribution	30000	34000	34000	34000	34000	34000	
Short-term loan	7400000						
Construction loan	1700000	6400000	5650000				
Subtract:							
Short-term loan–principal and interest payments	271241	1085463	1085463	2166703	2893782	2493755	2337812
Amortization–consolidated wraparound deed of trust			7380	32635	38250	44840	52575
Amortization–supervisory services fee							
Accrued interest paid–consolidated wraparound deed of trust							
Accrued interest paid–supervisory services fee							
General partner fees	800000						
Personal property	700000		700000				
Land	900000						
Building	1576000						
Construction costs	1030000	7600000	5995000	675000			
Developer costs	1001000	120000	379000	150000			
Architect costs	456000	111000	108000				
Financing fees	329000						
Real estate taxes	20000	40000	40000				
Closing costs	114000						
Preopening loan to lessee			185000	750000			
Legal fees	416000						
Accounting fees	70000						
Appraisal costs	17000						
Bank fees	74000						
Printing and filing costs	30000						
Miscellaneous	12765						
Selling commissions	840000						
Real estate advisory fee	280000						
Nonaccountable expense allowance	280000						
Note guarantee fee	930510						
Monitoring fee	40000	50000	50000	50000	50000	50000	
Reserve	376723	(263979)	846052	(708629)	(329860)	40720	38737
Cash available for partners' distribution	0	0	0	0	0	0	0
Limited partners' distributions – Class A							
Limited partners' distributions – Class B							
General Partner distribution							

(Due to computer rounding, certain rows may not add.)

The notes and assumptions are an integral part of this projected statement.

Appendix G

LIMITED PARTNERSHIP
PARTNERSHIP CASH FLOW

1990	1991	1992	1993	1994	1995	1996	1997	1998	1999	2000 (9 months)
(2902226)	(762779)	(650440)	(451159)	(60829)	194231	354745	528338	716290	920169	803899
1634293	1634293	1634293	1634293	1634293	1634293	1634293	1634293	1634293	1634293	1225720
1367996	1043025	1045136	1040576	1035231	1028965	1021620	1013009	1002915	991083	734333
270000	270000	270000	269918	267124	262762	257991	252772	247064	240821	176168
48000	48000	48000	48000	48000	48000	48000	48000	48000	48000	36000
140250										
126873	120873	126873	126073	107242	833	833	833	833	833	625
61632	77249	84696	99206	116391	136441	159946	187500	219801	257666	221982
			10988	46499	50861	55632	60850	66550	72802	59049
265394	1061405	1059648	1057588	1055173	1052343	1049025	1045136	1040576	1035231	771724
			67500	270000	270000	270000	270000	270000	270000	202500
357960	1231759	1329518	1433139	1542998	1659439	1782879	1913760	2052460	2199499	1801489
336661	1158460	1250413	1322128	1395185	1472618	1554705	1641741	1733977	1031758	156781
17719	60972	65811	69506	73431	77506	81827	86407	91262	96408	82478
3500	12510	13294	41425	74302	109315	146347	185612	227221	271333	153930

PROJECTED INVESTMENT SUMMARY FOR A $100,000
CLASS A LIMITED PARTNER INVESTOR IN A 50% TAX BRACKET

Year	(1) Capital Contribution	(2) Interest Expense	(3) Total Investment	(4) Investment Tax Credit	(5)(A) Taxable Income (Loss)	(6) Tax Savings (Cost)	Cash Distribution (7) Annual Amount	(8) Annual Percentage Return	After Tax Benefits (9)(B) Annual	(10)(C) Net	(11) Cumulative	(12)(D) Excess Investment Interest Expense
1983 (3 months)	5075	2990	8065	6171	(3808)	1904			8076	10	10	
1984	6096	11576	17672	14281	(6825)	3413			17694	21	31	
1985	23346	9722	33068	22665	(20830)	10415			33080	12	44	
1986	18168	7106	25274		(50562)	25281			25281	7	51	3916
1987	16114	4946	21060		(42129)	21065			21065	4	55	6448
1988	15231	2972	18203		(36416)	18208			18208	6	61	6448
1989	15970	1006	16976		(33965)	16983			16983	7	68	6448
1990					(20367)	10184	2405	2.40	12588	12588	12656	6448
1991					(5353)	2677	8275	8.27	10951	10951	23608	
1992					(4565)	2282	8932	8.93	11214	11214	34821	
1993					(3166)	1583	9444	9.44	11027	11027	45848	
1994					(427)	213	9966	9.97	10179	10179	56027	
1995					1231	(616)	10519	10.52	9903	9903	65930	
1996					2210	(1105)	11105	11.11	10000	10000	75931	
1997					3237	(1619)	11727	11.73	10108	10108	80639	
1998					4322	(2161)	12386	12.39	10224	10224	96263	
1999					5474	(2737)	13084	13.08	10347	10347	106610	
2000 (9 months)					5492	(2746)	11193	11.19	8447	8447	115058	
Total	100000	40318	140318	43118	(206448)	103224	109034					

(A) Column (5) includes interest on Capital Contributions (Column 2)

(B) Column (9) equals the sum of "Investment Tax Credit" (Column 4), "Tax Savings (Cost)" (Column 6) and "Cash Distributions - Annual Amount" (Column 7)

(C) Column (10) equals "Annual After Tax Benefits" (Column 9) minus "Total Investment" (Column 3)

(D) See Note (19)

(Due to computer rounding, certain rows may not add.)

The notes and assumptions contained in this report are an integral part of this projected statement.

PROJECTED INVESTMENT SUMMARY FOR A $50,000
CLASS A LIMITED PARTNER INVESTOR IN A 50% TAX BRACKET

Year	(1) Capital Contribution	(2) Interest Expense	(3) Total Investment	(4) Investment Tax Credit	(5)(A) Taxable Income (Loss)	(6) Tax Savings (Cost)	Cash Distribution		(9)(B) Annual	After Tax Benefits		(12)(D) Excess Investment Interest Expense
							(7) Annual Amount	(8) Annual Percentage Return		(10)(C) Net	(11) Cumulative	
1983 (3 months)	2538	1495	4033	3086	(1904)	952			4038	5	5	
1984	3048	5788	8836	7141	(3413)	1706			8847	11	16	
1985	11673	4861	16534	11333	(10415)	5208			16540	6	22	
1986	9084	3553	12637		(25281)	12640			12640	3	25	1958
1987	8057	2473	10530		(21065)	10532			10532	2	27	3224
1988	7615	1486	9101		(18208)	9104			9104	3	30	3224
1989	7985	503	8488		(16983)	8491			8491	4	34	3224
1990					(10184)	5092	1202	2.40	6294	6294	6328	3224
1991					(2677)	1338	4137	8.27	5476	5476	11804	
1992					(2282)	1141	4466	8.93	5607	5607	17411	
1993					(1583)	792	4722	9.44	5513	5513	22924	
1994					(213)	107	4983	9.97	5090	5090	28014	
1995					616	(308)	5259	10.52	4952	4952	32965	
1996					1105	(552)	5553	11.11	5000	5000	37965	
1997					1619	(809)	5863	11.73	5054	5054	43019	
1998					2161	(1081)	6193	12.39	5112	5112	48131	
1999					2737	(1368)	6542	13.08	5174	5174	53305	
2000 (9 months)					2746	(1373)	5597	11.19	4224	4224	57529	
	50000	20159	70159	21559	(103224)	51612	54517					

(A) Column (5) includes interest on Capital Contributions (Column 2)

(B) Column (9) equals the sum of "Investment Tax Credit" (Column 4), "Tax Savings (Cost)" (Column 6) and "Cash Distribution – Annual Amount" (Column 7)

(C) Column (10) equals "Annual After Tax Benefits" (Column 9) minus "Total Investment" (Column 3)

(D) See Note (19)

(Due to computer rounding, certain rows may not add.)

The notes and assumptions contained in this report are an integral part of this projected statement.

PROJECTED TAX AND ECONOMIC RESULTS OF THE ASSUMED SALE OF THE PARTNERSHIP PROPERTY ON SEPTEMBER 1, 2000 APPLICABLE TO A $100,000 CLASS A LIMITED PARTNERSHIP INTEREST (NOTE 18)
(000 OMITTED—EXCEPT FOR PER UNIT)

	Sale at 11% Capitalization Rate	Sale at $1 Above Existing Indebtedness	Sale at Cost
Net sales proceeds:			
Sales price	$ 80018	$32331	$33359
Less:			
Advisory fee to general partner	2401		1001
Existing indebtedness	32331	32331	32331
Net sales proceeds	$ 45286	$ -0-	$ 27
Distribution of net sales proceeds:			
Class A limited partners	$ 33244		$ 25
Class B limited partner	1750		1
General partner	10292		1
	$ 45286	$ -0-	$ 27
Gain on sale:			
Sales price (amount realized)	$ 80018	$32331	$33359
Less:			
Selling expenses	2401		1001
Adjusted basis	3165	3165	3165
Gain on sale	$ 74452	$29166	$29193
Class A limited partners' share of gain on sale:			
Ordinary	$ 3858	$ 3858	$ 3858
Capital	55593	23285	23310
Tax due (A)	$ 13119	$ 6586	$ 6590
Class A limited partners' share			
of net sales proceeds	$ 33244	$ -0-	$ 25
Less tax due	13119	6586	6590
Net after tax proceeds (cost)	$ 20125	($ 6586)	($ 6563)
Per unit (with 000)	$144000	($47000)	($47000)

(A) The projected tax does take into account any alternative minimum tax.

(Due to computer rounding, certain rows and columns may not add.)

The notes and assumptions are an integral part of this projected statement.

Accounting projections

The accounting projections have been prepared solely for purposes of illustration. They are based on estimates and assumptions which are inherently subject to uncertainty and variation depending upon evolving events. They are not represented to be, and should not be relied upon to indicate, results that will actually be obtained.

No representation or warranty of any kind is made respecting the accuracy, attainment or completeness of the accounting projections and no representation or warranty should be inferred from such projections. Prospective investors are urged to consult their own advisors with respect to the projections and the material assumptions underlying them.

Notes and assumptions

The attached statements analyzing the proposed Partnership transactions are based upon, among other things, the assumptions outlined herein. The more descriptive and informative Confidential Memorandum should be read in conjunction with the attached statements, especially materials set forth under "Fiduciary Responsibility of General Partner," "Conflicts of Interest," "Federal Tax Consequences and "Risk Factors."

The Internal Revenue Code (the Code), especially those sections enacted or amended by the Economic Recovery Tax Act of 1981 and the Tax Equity and Fiscal Responsibility Act of 1982 (TEFRA), may be affected by the adoption of further regulations. Accordingly, the reader should consult his own tax advisor with respect to the tax aspects as they may relate to his particular circumstances and tax situation.

As more fully discussed in the Confidential Memorandum, TEFRA enacted an alternative minimum tax (AMT). Limitations are imposed upon the amount of interest on the investors' notes that can be deducted in computing this AMT.

The reader is advised to consult with his tax advisor as to state and local taxes which may be payable in connection with tax preference items.

Projections are inherently subject to varying degrees of uncertainty and their achievability depends upon, among other things, the reliability of the underlying assumptions and the probability of the occurrence of a complex series of future events or transactions, many of which are not within the control of the General Partner.

THE ACCOMPANYING PROJECTIONS ARE AN ILLUSTRATION OF FINANCIAL RESULTS BASED UPON ASSUMPTIONS WHICH ARE NOT NECESSARILY THE MOST LIKELY. THE PROJECTIONS ARE PREPARED TO ILLUSTRATE WHAT WOULD HAPPEN IF THE ASSUMPTIONS CONTAINED HEREIN WOULD OCCUR.

(1) Principles of reporting: The projections are prepared in accordance with the tax accrual method of accounting and assume that all the limited partners will be admitted on October 1, 1983. It is assumed that all transactions will be completed on October 1, 1983. If an investor is admitted after October 1, 1983, the total amounts of income and deductions allocated or available to him will vary from those projected.

(2) Organization: The Partnership is a limited partnership organized under [state] law to acquire, substantially rehabilitate and refurnish, own and net-lease a 275-room hotel located in [   ] (the "Hotel"). The General Partner is GP Incorporated, a [   ] corporation.

(3) Total rental income: The Partnership will lease the property as described in the "Lease" section of the "Confidential Memorandum." The Lessee will be required to pay the Partnership an Annual Basic Rent as set forth in the Lease plus Percentage Rent in an amount equal to 14% of the Lessee's Gross Income in excess of $15,000,000 per year. The amount of the Lessee's Gross Income upon which the projected Percentage Rent is based is projected in the market study and financial projections prepared in June 1982 and supplemented in April 1983 (the "Study"). The Study projects Gross Income of the Lessee from Hotel operations of $11,568,000 for the calendar year 1986, $14,160,000 for 1987, $15,951,000 for 1988, $17,863,000 for 1989, $18,936,000 for 1990 and thereafter adjusted for inflation at an assumed rate of 6%. The projections contained herein estimate that the Lessee's Gross Income from Hotel operations will begin October 1, 1985 rather than January 1, 1986. The Study numbers were adjusted accordingly. The maximum impact on the Lessee's Gross Income from Hotel operations in any particular year as a result of the adjustment will be approximately $648,000.

(4) Syndication costs: The Partnership will incur approximately $1,542,765 of nondeductible costs in connection with the syndication of this offering. These expenditures consist of the following: $1,455,000 to [investment bank], $45,000 to Partnership counsel, $10,000 to [firm preparing market study] and $32,765 for printing, filing and other miscellaneous costs.

(5) Expenses:

It is assumed that the Partnership will deduct certain fees and expenses as ordinary and necessary business expenses. These fees and expenses are not being paid out of operating income:

REHAB ASSOCIATES LIMITED PARTNERSHIP

	1983 (3 months)	1984	1985	1986	1987	1988	1989	1990	1991	1992	1993	1994	1995-2015	Total
Partnership supervisory fee (A)			$ 15,625	$ 62,500	$ 62,500	$ 62,500	$ 46,875							$ 250,000
Loan guarantee fee (B)														50,000
Tax advice (C)	$202,000													202,000
Lease and consolidated wraparound deed of trust legal fee (D)			208	833	833	833	9,375							25,000
Transfer and mortgage taxes	92,065													92,065
Short-term loan costs (E)	3,800	$ 15,200	15,200	15,200	15,200	15,200	11,400	$ 833	$ 833	$ 833	$ 833	$ 833	$17,295	91,200
Note guarantee fee (F)	76,214	284,488	226,007	158,765	105,362	60,109	19,565							930,510
Construction loan costs (G)	6,344	25,375	19,031											50,750
Construction period costs (H)	16,505	62,020	67,146	126,040	126,040	126,040	126,040	126,040	126,040	126,040	126,040	106,409		1,260,398
Short-term loan interest (I)	143,852	575,909	703,297	1,016,703	793,782	493,755	187,812							3,915,111
Partnership monitoring fee (J)			12,500	50,000	50,000	37,500								150,000
Total	$540,780	$962,992	$1,062,140	$1,442,541	$1,166,217	$808,437	$401,900	$126,873	$126,873	$126,873	$126,873	$107,242	$17,295	

(Due to computer rounding, certain rows may not add.)

(A) Partnership supervisory fee: The General Partner will receive $250,000 in 1983 and $50,000 in 2000 (see Note 14) for supervising the Partnership affairs for the first four years of operations of the Hotel. This fee will be amortized over four years commencing with the date the property is placed in service.

(B) Loan guarantee fee: The General Partner will receive $50,000 in consideration of its obligation to make loans available to the Partnership during the rehabilitation period and for four years subsequent to the date the property is placed in service. This fee will be amortized over a four-year period commencing with the date the property is placed in service.

(C) Tax advice: It is assumed that $202,000 will be paid by the Partnership for tax advice in regard to the structuring of the transaction. This cost is comprised of a $125,000 Partnership counsel fee, $60,000 financial consulting fee and a $17,000 appraisal fee. This cost will be deducted in 1983.

(D) Lease and Consolidated Wraparound Deed of Trust legal fee: Legal fees of $25,000 pertaining to the Lease and Consolidated Wraparound Deed of Trust will be amortized over thirty years commencing with the date the property is placed in service.

(E) Short-Term Loan costs:

(i) A financing fee of $74,000 will be paid to the "Short-Term Lender" in connection with securing the loan. $66,200 of this fee will be amortized over a six-year period commencing in 1983 and the balance of $7,800 will be capitalized in accordance with Section 266 of the Code.

(ii) A legal fee of $15,000 will be paid to the counsel of the Short-Term Lender for the review of the loan documents. This fee will be amortized over a six-year period commencing in 1983.

(iii) A legal fee of $10,000 will be paid to the Partnership counsel for review of the loan documents. This fee will be amortized over a six-year period commencing in 1983.

(F) Note guarantee fee: A fee of $930,510 will be paid to a surety who will guarantee the payment of principal and interest on the Class Limited Partner notes. $184,207 of this fee will be amortized on a declining balance method over two years to reflect the amount of Class A Limited Partner notes assigned to the Lender and $746,303 will be amortized on a declining balance method over six years to reflect the amount of Class A Limited Partner notes assigned to the Short-Term Lender.

(G) Construction Loan costs: The Partnership will pay $50,750 to the counsel of the Lender for review of the construction loan documents. This fee will be amortized over the construction period.

(H) Construction period costs: The Partnership will capitalize, and thereafter amortize, $1,260,398 of interest and taxes incurred during the construction period in accordance with Section 189 of the Code.

(I) Short-Term Loan interest: The Partnership will deduct $3,915,111, which is the portion of interest attributable to loan proceeds which are not being used for acquisition or construction of the property. The balance of the interest will be capitalized and/or amortized.

(J) Partnership monitoring fee: Limited partners' monitoring agent will receive $150,000 for monitoring the affairs of the Partnership during the first three years of operations. This fee will be amortized over the three-year period.

(6) General Partner fees: The General Partner will receive a total of $1,465,000 from the Partnership in connection with the organization and operation of the Partnership and the rehabilitation and operation of the Hotel. The Partnership will amortize $300,000 (see Notes 5A and 5B) of these costs over a four-year period commencing when the property is placed in service. The Partnership will capitalize and depreciate as part of the cost of the Hotel $1,160,000, consisting of a $900,000 rehabilitation supervision (see Note 14) fee and a $260,000 construction financing fee. The Partnership will also capitalize $5,000 of reimbursed expenses which the General Partner incurred in connection with the acquisition of the property. These expenses will be allocated $2,000 to land and $3,000 to the cost of the Hotel.

(7) Source and application of initial funds:

Source of funds:

Class A Limited Partners' capital contributions	$14,000,000
Class B Limited Partner's capital contributions	200,000
Interest on Class A Limited Partners' capital contributions	5,644,589
Interest on Class B Limited Partner's capital contributions	58,905
Consolidated Wraparound Deed of Trust (A)	21,250,000
Salvage value of personal property	300,000
Services fee (A)	3,000,000
Short-Term Loan (A)	7,400,000
General Partner Deferred fee (B)	400,000
General Partner loan (C)	100,000
	$52,353,494

Application of funds:

Syndication costs (D)	$ 1,542,765
Land	1,622,274
Personal property	4,150,000
Real property	27,586,421
Transfer and mortgage taxes	92,065
General Partner fees (E)	300,000
Legal fees (F)	100,750
Tax advice (G)	202,000
Short-Term Loan fee	66,200
Note guarantee fee	930,510
Short-Term Loan interest	3,915,111
Short-Term Loan	7,400,000
Construction period costs	1,260,398
Preopening loan to Lessee	935,000
Monitoring fee	150,000
Portion of debt service short fall	2,000,000
Unallocated legal fees (C)	100,000
	$52,353,494

(A) See Note (15)
(B) See Note (14)
(C) See Note (8)
(D) See Note (4)
(E) See Note (6)
(F) See Note (5D, 5E, 5G)
(G) See Note (5C)

(8) Unallocated legal fees: The Partnership will pay additional counsel fees estimated to be $100,000. These fees will be funded by one of the following: (i) Partnership reserves, (ii) additional cash flow that may be available to the Partnership if the interest rate on the Short-Term Loan is less than the 14.7% average, or if (i) and (ii) are not available these fees will be paid through proceeds loaned by the General Partner to the Partnership.

(9) Cost recovery allowances: The cost of the property, excluding certain costs that will be expensed, is assumed to be $33,358,695. For purposes of the projections, this cost has been allocated and cost recovery allowances computed as follows:

	Estimated Cost
Personal property	$ 4,150,000
Real property	27,586,421
Land	1,622,274
	$33,358,695

The real property's cost will be recovered using the straight-line method over 15 years. A 25% investment tax credit will be taken on the real property expenditures which constitute "qualified rehabilitation expenditures." The basis of the real property will be reduced by one-half of the credit taken. It has been assumed that the building will be placed in service in October 1985.

The cost of the personal property will be recovered using an accelerated method over five years.

(10) Administrative fee: The General Partner will receive $3,750 in 1985, $15,000 each year in 1986 through 1989, $16,875 in 1990, $22,500 each year in 1991 through 1994, $24,375 in 1995, $30,000 each year in 1996 through 1999 and $22,500 in 2000 for services in the administration of the affairs of the Partnership.

(11) Monitoring fee: Limited Partners' monitoring agent will receive $1,875 in 1985, $7,500 each year in 1986 through 1989, $8,438 in 1990, $11,250 each year in 1991 through 1994, $12,188 in 1995, $15,000 each year in 1996 through 1999 and $11,250 in 2000 for monitoring the interest of the Limited Partners.

(12) Additional interest: Under the Consolidated Wraparound Deed of Trust, the Partnership will be obligated to pay additional interest to the Developer in an amount equal to 14% of the Lessee's Gross Income in excess of $15,000,000 but not in excess of $18,000,000 per year, and 6% of the Lessee's Gross Income in excess of $18,000,000 (see Note 3 in regard to Lessee's Gross Income).

(13) Class A Limited Partners' capital contributions: The purchase price for each Class unit is $100,000, of which $5,075 will be payable upon admission. The following schedule illustrates the principal and interest payments for a $100,000 unit. A rate of 12.6% per annum is assumed with principal payments payable on admission and on June 30 of each year. Interest payments will be payable in quarterly installments commencing December 31, 1983.

SCHEDULE OF PAYMENTS FOR A ONE UNIT CLASS A $100,000 INVESTMENT

Date of payment	Principal	Interest	Total payments
Upon admission	$ 5,075		$ 5,075
1983 payment		$ 2,990	2,990
1984 payment	6,096	11,576	17,672
1985 payment	23,346	9,722	33,068
1986 payment	18,168	7,106	25,274
1987 payment	16,114	4,946	21,060
1988 payment	15,231	2,972	18,203
1989 payment	15,970	1,006	16,976
	$100,000	$40,318	$140,318

(14) General Partner Deferred fee: The General Partner will defer $350,000 of the total $900,000 rehabilitation supervisory fee (see Note 6) and $50,000 of the total $250,000 Partnership supervisory fee (see Note 5A). Interest on the deferred fee will accrue at the rate of 12% per annum and will be payable along with the deferred fee subsequent to September 30, 2000. However, if the Partnership has available reserves not required to meet other obligations or if the interest rate on the Short-Term Loan is less than the 14.7% average, then available Partnership reserves and any cash flow available to Partners as a result of the interest savings on the Short-Term Loan will be applied first to reduce the accrued interest and then deferred.

(15) Financing: The following is only a summary of the financing for the property. For a full understanding, reference must be made to the "Acquisition Terms and Financing" section of the Confidential Memorandum.

GP Affiliates, an affiliate of the General Partner, has entered into an agreement to acquire the Hotel and six additional parcels of land from [   ], an unrelated limited partnership ("Developer"). GP Affiliates will assign its right to acquire the property to the Partnership. The purchase price for the property is $5,111,000. The Partnership has also agreed to bear certain additional costs that may be incurred in connection with the acquisition of the property in an amount not to exceed $50,000.

Purchase Money Note: To finance a portion of the purchase price of the property, the Partnership will issue a $1,935,000, 10-year, 16% nonrecourse Purchase Money Note to the Developer.

Construction Loan: The construction loan will be obtained from [   ] (the "Lender") in the amount of $13,750,000. This loan will mature 26 months from closing and will bear interest at a floating rate which will be 1.25% above the Lender's prime rate.

The Permanent Loan: The Partnership has obtained a permanent loan commitment from the Developer pursuant to which the Developer has agreed to:

    (A)   loan the Partnership $13,750,000 on the completion date or

(B) in the event that the Developer is unable to loan the $13,750,000 to the Partnership, the Developer will then assume the Partnership obligations under the construction loan at the completion date.

The Permanent Loan will be secured by the Consolidated Wraparound Deed of Trust.

The Interim Loan: The Developer has obtained a commitment from the Lender to loan the Developer $13,750,000 upon completion of the rehabilitation. The loan will be for 5 years and will bear interest at a floating rate which will be .5% over the Lender's prime rate plus 2% of Gross Room Income of the Hotel. To secure the obligation of the Developer, the Lender will have the first deed of trust on the property (subject to a $100,000 deed of trust).

Development Agreement Obligation: At the completion date $2,200,000 of the remaining obligations to the Developer will be consolidated into the Consolidated Wraparound Deed of Trust.

FF&E Agreement Obligation: At the completion date, a $2,750,000 obligation to the Developer will be consolidated into the Consolidated Wraparound Deed of Trust.

Turnkey Rehabilitation Agreement: By the completion date, it is estimated that $3,675,000 will be owed to [service company] under the Turnkey Rehabilitation Agreement. Of this amount, $675,000 together with interest at the rate of 12% per annum (accruing from the ninety-first day following the completion date) will be paid on June 30, 1986, and the balance of $3,000,000 together with interest at 9% per annum subject to certain deferrals and capitalizations, will be paid over a 30-year period.

The Consolidated Wraparound Deed of Trust: On the completion of the Hotel the Permanent Loan ($13,750,000), the Purchase Money Note ($2,550,000, including $615,000 of interest accrued), the Development Agreement Obligation ($2,200,000) and the FF&E Agreement Obligation ($2,750,000) will be consolidated and secured by a $21,250,000 Wraparound Deed of Trust on the property. This indebtedness will bear interest at 16% per annum and will be fully amortized over a 30-year period based on the constant monthly payments. During the first 15 years there will be a 5% interest deferral for 60 months. At the end of the fifteenth year, the portion of the interest during the prior 60-month period which has accrued but which has not yet been paid will be capitalized and, together with interest at 16%, will be amortized over a 10-year period commencing in the sixteenth year. In addition, during any year in which the Partnership is not required to pay and does not pay the 5% deferred interest (anticipated to be 9/1/85 through 8/31/90), additional interest on the outstanding indebtedness will accrue at the rate of 2% per annum. The additional interest will be payable at the end of the fifteenth year. The Consolidated Wraparound Deed of Trust will bear other interest as described in note 12.

Short-Term Loan: The Partnership will also be required to borrow $7,400,000. The Partnership has received a commitment from a lender for a loan at closing, bearing interest at the rate of 1.25% above the London Interbank Offered Rate ("LIBOR") on the date of the funding of the loan, and with a partial interest deferral of up to 1.25% if, and to the extent that, such interest rate exceeds an average of 14.7% per annum. Principal payments will be made in 1986 through 1989. The Partnership may arrange for such a loan under more favorable terms.

(16) Rehabilitation investment tax credit: It is assumed that the rehabilitation of the Hotel will qualify for a 25% rehabilitation investment tax credit.

This credit is available for qualified rehabilitation expenditures attributable to a certified historic structure incurred after 1981. It is assumed for these projections that the rehabilitation investment tax credit will be taken as qualified progress expenditures. As discussed in the "Federal Tax Consequences" section of the Confidential Memorandum, it is not clear that the Internal Revenue Service will agree that the credit can be taken prior to the building being placed in service.

(17) Allocation of Income and Losses from Operations and Cash Available for Distribution:

Income and losses: Income from Operations with respect to any year or portion thereof prior to the Anniversary Date (projected to be October 1, 1990) will be allocated 98.25% to the Class A Limited Partners, .75% to the Class B Limited Partner and 1% to the General Partner. Income from Operations with respect to any year or portion thereof on or after the Anniversary Date shall be allocated to the Partners as follows: First, to the extent of and in proportion to the distributions, if any, of cash flow with respect to that year or portion thereof; however, when income allocated to any Partner would result in the creation or continuation of a positive Capital Account for that Partner while any other Partner has a negative Capital Account, Income from Operations first will be allocated to Partners having negative Capital Accounts in proportion to such negative Capital Accounts until all such negative Capital Accounts have been eliminated; Second, to the Partners in proportion to any deficits in their respective Capital Accounts and to the extent necessary to eliminate such deficits; Third, 94.05% to the Class A Limited Partners, 4.95% to the Class B Limited Partner and 1% to the General Partner until the aggregate positive balances in the Class A Limited Partners' Capital Accounts equals $14,000,000 plus a return of $1,260,000 per annum commencing on the Anniversary Date, less an amount equal to all prior distributions of net proceeds and cash flow to the Class A Limited Partners. The balance, if any, 66.5% to the Class A Limited Partners, 3.5% to the Class B Limited Partner and 30% to the General Partner.

Losses from Operations will be allocated 98.25% to the Class A Limited Partner, .75% to the Class B Limited Partner and 1% to the General Partner; if, however, when losses allocated to any Limited Partner would result in the creation or continuation of a deficit Capital Account for that Limited Partner while any other Limited Partner has a positive Capital Account Losses from Operations first will be allocated to the Limited Partners having positive Capital Accounts in proportion to such positive Capital Accounts until all such positive Capital Accounts have been eliminated.

Cash available for distribution: Any cash flow that is available for distribution with respect to any year or portion thereof prior to the Anniversary Date will be distributed 98.25% to the Class A Limited Partners, .75% to the Class B Limited Partner and 1% to the General Partner.

Any cash flow that is available for distribution with respect to any year or portion thereof on or after the Anniversary Date shall be distributed 94.05% to the Class A Limited Partners, 4.95% to the Class B Limited Partner and 1% to the General Partner until an amount equal to $1,260,000 has been distributed to the Class A Limited Partners with respect to that year, on a noncumulative basis. This would represent a distribution to the Class A Limited Partners of 9% of their capital contributions. The balance, if any, will be distributed 66.5% to the Class A Limited Partners, 3.5% to the Class B Limited Partner and 30% to the General Partner.

(18) Sale of property: For the purpose of these projections, it is assumed that the property is sold on October 1, 2000. The schedule depicting the sale of property represents the projected tax consequences if the property were to be disposed under one of the following:

 (A) At a sale price of $80,018,000 which reflects a capitalization rate of 11% on the Annual Basic Rent plus the Projected Percentage Rent in year 2001 (see Note 3).

 (B) At a price equal to the outstanding Consolidated Wraparound Deed of Trust, Services fee, General Partner Deferred fee and accrued interest at that time plus one dollar.

 (C) At a sale price of $33,358,695 which reflects all capitalized property costs upon completion of the rehabilitation of the Hotel.

Upon the sale of the property the General Partner will receive a real estate advisory fee, which is projected to be 3% of the sale price. Ordinary income rate of 50% and a capital gain rate of 20% have been applied to the taxable gain. For full details as to the distribution of net proceeds see "Summary of The Limited Partnership Agreement" section of the Confidential Memorandum.

(19) Investment interest limitation: Investment interest expense is deductible by a partner only to the extent such expense attributable to the partner's interest in the Partnership plus any other investment interest expense attributable to sources other than the Partnership does not exceed the sum of (1) $10,000 ($5,000 for a married taxpayer filing a separate return), (2) the amount of a partner's total net investment income and (3) the amount by which certain expenses incurred with respect to property subject to a net lease exceed rent received under such lease.

In determining net investment income of the Partnership, a deduction must be claimed for depreciation based on the "useful life" of the Property. The Partnership based its estimate of useful life on 45 years. The IRS may claim that the calculation of depreciation for purposes of determining the Partnership's net investment income should be based on some shorter recovery period, in which case the amount of excess investment interest per unit might be substantially increased.

(20) Other assumptions: It has been assumed that federal income tax deductions for Partnership expenses will be allowable in accordance with their treatment in the accompanying projections. There can, however, be no assurance as to the deductibility of these items upon examination by the IRS. Certain areas of possible consideration are herein set forth and should be read in conjunction with the "Federal Tax Consequences" section of the Confidential Memorandum.

The projections are based upon the assumption that the tax effects of the relationships between the Partnership and all other parties to Partnership transactions will be accepted by the IRS as reflected herein. Should the IRS successfully challenge one or more of the aforementioned relationships, the projected tax benefits to the Limited Partners could be significantly reduced or possibly eliminated.

Particular note should be given to recently issued Revenue Ruling 83-84, pending amendment to Section 267 of the Code and pending proposed changes in the regulation 704(b) of the Code.

The foregoing is not an all inclusive itemization of areas of possible challenge. It is merely intended to set forth some of the areas which require the consideration of potential investors and their tax advisors. Reference is made to the "Federal Tax Consequences" section of the Confidential Memorandum for an expanded discussion of the federal tax aspects of investing in the Partnership.

It is anticipated that the tax treatment given in the projections to specific items of Partnership income and expense will be consistent with the treatment on the Partnership returns. However, this should not be considered by potential investors as an indication of the probability that such treatment would be sustained by the IRS upon examination. Should the tax treatment of one or more items of income or expense be denied, the tax benefits from an investment in the Partnership may be significantly reduced or possibly eliminated. Potential investors should seek the advice of their own tax advisors in order to satisfy themselves as to the tax consequences of investing in the Partnership.

Potential investors should also be aware of a new penalty provision enacted by TEFRA. Newly enacted Section 6661 provides for a 10% penalty on the underpayment of tax that is attributable to a substantial understatement of income tax. This refers to an understatement in excess of 10% of the correct tax. The penalty can be avoided under certain circumstances. Potential investors should seek the advice of their own tax advisors in order to satisfy themselves as to the possibility of tax and penalty consequences of investing in the Partnership in the event of an IRS tax examination.

The IRS presently is paying increased attention to "tax shelter" partnerships. Accordingly, there may be a substantial risk of audit. An audit by the IRS of the Partnership's information return could result in an audit of an investor's individual tax return and the adjustment of nonpartnership items. The Partnership will have no obligation to pay the costs of any such audit of an investor's individual return and the investors should assume that they will have to bear any such costs.

New rules are applicable to IRS audit procedures. Under provisions enacted by TEFRA relating to 1983 and subsequent tax returns, the limited partners may be bound by certain audit determinations reached by the "tax matters partner" with the IRS.

The projections and assumptions are contingent upon the following, without limitation: (a) that the Partnership will be treated as a partnership rather than as an association taxable as a corporation, (b) that no interpretation or amendments to the Internal Revenue Code will reduce or eliminate the tax benefits projected, and (c) that the treatment given in the projections to all tax items will be accepted by the IRS.

Appendix H

Securities and Exchange Commission, Regulation D-Rules Governing the Limited Offer and Sale of Securities Without Registration Under the Securities Act of 1933, 17 C.F.R. §§ 230.501–230.508

Preliminary Notes

1. The following rules relate to transactions exempted from the registration requirements of section 5 of the Securities Act of 1933 (the "Act") (15 U.S.C. 77a *et seq*, as amended). Such transactions are not exempt from the antifraud, civil liability, or other provisions of the federal securities laws. Issuers are reminded of their obligation to provide such further material information, if any, as may be necessary to make the information required under this regulation, in light of the circumstances under which it is furnished, not misleading.

2. Nothing in these rules obviates the need to comply with any applicable state law relating to the offer and sale of securities. Regulation D is intended to

be a basic element in a uniform system of federal-state limited offering exemptions consistent with the provisions of sections 18 and 19(c) of the Act. In those states that have adopted Regulation D, or any version of Regulation D, special attention should be directed to the applicable state laws and regulations, including those relating to registration of persons who receive remuneration in connection with the offer and sale of securities, to disqualification of issuers and other persons associated with offerings based on state administrative orders or judgments, and to requirements for filings of notices of sales.3. Attempted compliance with any rule in Regulation D does not act as an exclusive election; the issuer can also claim the availability of any other applicable exemption. For instance, an issuer's failure to satisfy all the terms and conditions of Rule 506 shall not raise any presumption that the exemption provided by section 4(2) of the Act is not available.

3. Attempted compliance with any rule in Regulation D does not act as an exclusive election; the issuer can also claim the availability of any other applicable exemption. For instance, an issuer's failure to satisfy all the terms and conditions of Rule 506 shall not raise any presumption that the exemption provided by section 4(2) of the Act is not available.

4. These rules are available only to the issuer of the securities and not to any affiliate of that issuer or to any other person for resales of the issue's securities. The rules provide an exemption only for the transactions in which the securities are offered or sold by the issuer, not for the securities themselves.

5. These rules may be used for business combinations that involve sales by virtue of Rule 145(a) (17 CFR 230.145(a)) or otherwise.6. In view of the objectives of these rules and the policies underlying the Act, Regulation D is not available to any issuer for any transaction or chain of transactions that, although in technical compliance with these rules, is part of a plan or scheme to evade the registration provisions of the Act. In such cases, registration under the Act is required.

6. In view of the objectives of these rules and the policies underlying the Act, Regulation D is not available to any issuer for any transaction or chain of transactions that, although in technical compliance with these rules, is part of a plan or scheme to evade the registration provisions of the Act. In such cases, registration under the Act is required.

7. Securities offered and sold outside the United States in accordance with Regulation S need not be registered under the Act. See Release No. 33-6863. Regulation S may be relied upon for such offers and sales even if coincident offers and sales are made in accordance with Regulation D inside the United States. Thus, for example, persons who are offered and sold securities in accordance with Regulation S would not be counted in the calculation of the number of purchasers under Regulation D. similarly, proceeds from such sales would not be included in the aggregate offering price. The provisions of this note, however, do not apply if the issuer elects to rely solely on Regulation D for offers or sales to persons made outside the United States.

§ 230.501 Definitions and terms used in Regulation D

As used in Regulation D (§§ 230.501-230.508), the following terms shall have the meaning indicated:

(a) *Accredited investor.* "Accredited investor" shall mean any person who comes within any of the following categories, or who the issuer reasonably believes comes within any of the following categories, at the time of the sale of the securities to that person:

(1) Any bank as defined in section 3(a)(2) of the Act, or any savings and loan association or other institution as defined in section 3(a)(5)(A) of the Act whether acting in its individual or fiduciary capacity; any broker or dealer registered pursuant to section 15 of the Securities Exchange Act of 1934; any insurance company as defined in section 2(13) of the Act; any investment company registered under the Investment Company Act of 1940 or a business development company as defined in section 2(a)(48) of that Act; any Small Business Investment Company licensed by the U.S. Small Business Administration under section 301(c) or (d) of the Small Business Investment Act of 1958; any plan established and maintained by a state, its political subdivisions, or any agency or instrumentality of a state or its political subdivisions, for the benefit of its employees, if such plan has total assets in excess of $5,000,000; any employee benefit plan within the meaning of the Employee Retirement Income Security Act of 1974 if the investment decision is made by a plan fiduciary, as defined in section 3(21) of such act, which is either a bank, savings and loan association, insurance company, or registered investment adviser, or if the employee benefit plan has total assets in excess of $5,000,000 or, if a self-directed plan, with investment decisions made solely by persons that are accredited investors;

(2) Any private business development company as defined in section 202(a)(22) of the Investment Advisers Act of 1940;

(3) Any organization described in section 501(c)(3) of the Internal Revenue Code, corporation, Massachusetts or similar business trust, or partnership, not formed for the specific purpose of acquiring the securities offered, with total assets in excess of $5,000,000;

(4) Any director, executive officer, or general partner of the issuer of the securities being offered or sold, or any director, executive officer, or general partner of a general partner of that issuer;

(5) Any natural person whose individual net worth, or joint net worth with that person's spouse, at the time of his purchase exceeds $1,000,000;

(6) Any natural person who had an individual income in excess of $200,000 in each of the two most recent years or joint income with that person's spouse in excess of $300,000 in each of those years and has a reasonable expectation of reaching the same income level in the current year;

(7) Any trust, with total assets in excess of $5,000,000, not formed for the specific purpose of acquiring the securities offered, whose purchase is directed by a sophisticated person as described in § 230.506(b)(2)(ii); and

(8) Any entity in which all of the equity owners are accredited investors.

(b) *Affiliate.* An "affiliate" of, or person "affiliated" with, a specified person shall mean a person that directly, or indirectly through one or more intermediaries, controls or is controlled by, or is under common control with, the person specified.

(c) *Aggregate offering price.* "Aggregate offering price" shall mean the sum of all cash, services, property, notes, cancellation of debt, or other consideration to be received by an issuer for issuance of its securities. Where securities are being offered for both cash and non-cash considerations, the aggregate offering price shall be based on the price at which the securities are offered for cash. Any portion of the aggregate offering price attributable to cash received in a foreign currency shall be translated into United States currency at the currency exchange rate in effect at a reasonable time prior to or on the date of the sale of the securities. If securities are not offered for cash, the aggregate offering price shall be based on the value of the consideration as established by bona fide sales of that consideration made within a reasonable time, or, in the absence of sales, on the fair value as determined by an accepted standard. Such valuations of non-cash consideration must be reasonable at the time made.

(d) *Business combination.* "Business combination" shall mean any transaction of the type specified in paragraph (a) of Rule 145 under the Act (17 CFR 230.145) and any transaction involving the acquisition by one issuer, in exchange for all or a part of its own or its parent's stock, of stock of another issuer if, immediately after the acquisition, the acquiring issuer has control of the other issuer (whether or not it had control before the acquisition).

(e) *Calculation of number of purchasers.* For purposes of calculating the number of purchasers under §§ 230.505(b) and 230.506(b) only, the following shall apply:

(1) The following purchasers shall be excluded:

(i) Any relative, spouse or relative of the spouse of a purchaser who has the same principal residence as the purchaser;

(ii) Any trust or estate in which a purchaser and any of the persons related to him as specified in paragraph (e)(1)(i) or (e)(1)(iii) of this section collectively have more than 50 percent of the beneficial interest (excluding contingent interests);

(iii) Any corporation or other organization of which a purchaser and any of the persons related to him as specified in paragraph (e)(1)(i) or (e)(1)(ii) of this section collectively are beneficial owners of more than 50 percent of the equity securities (excluding directors' qualifying shares) or equity interests; and

(iv) Any accredited investor.

(2) A corporation, partnership or other entity shall be counted as one purchaser. If, however, that entity is organized for the specific purpose of acquiring the securities offered and is not an accredited investor under paragraph (a)(8) of this section, then each beneficial owner of equity securities or equity interests in the entity shall count as a separate purchaser for all provisions of Regulation D (§§ 230.501-230.508), except to the extent provided in paragraph (e)(1) of this section.

(3) A non-contributory employee benefit plan within the meaning of Title I of the Employee Retirement Income Security Act of 1974 shall be counted as one purchaser where the trustee makes all investment decisions for the plan.

(f) *Executive officer.* "Executive officer" shall mean the president, any vice president in charge of a principal business unit, division or function (such as sales, administration or finance), any other officer who performs a policy making function, or any other person who performs similar policy making functions for the issuer. Executive officers of subsidiaries may be deemed executive officers of the issuer if they perform such policy making functions for the issuer.

(g) *Issuer.* The definition of the term "issuer" in section 2(4) of the Act shall apply, except that in the case of a proceeding under the Federal Bankruptcy Code (11 U.S.C. 101 *et seq.*), the trustee or debtor in possession shall be considered the issuer in an offering under a plan or reorganization, if the securities are to be issued under the plan.

(h) *Purchaser representative.* "Purchaser representative" shall mean any person who satisfies all of the following conditions or who the issuer reasonably believes satisfies all of the following conditions:

(1) Is not an affiliate, director, officer or other employee of the issuer, or beneficial owner of 10 percent or more of any class of the equity securities or 10 percent or more of the equity interest in the issuer, except where the purchaser is:

(i) A relative of the purchaser representative by blood, marriage or adoption and not more remote than a first cousin;

(ii) A trust or estate in which the purchaser representative and any persons related to him as specified in paragraph (h)(1)(i) or (h)(1)(iii) of this section collectively have more than 50 percent of the beneficial interest (excluding contingent interest) or of which the purchaser representative serves as trustee, executor, or in any similar capacity; or

(iii) A corporation or other organization of which the purchaser representative and any persons related to him as specified in paragraph (h)(1)(i) or (h)(1)(ii) of this section collectively are the beneficial owners of more than 50 percent of the equity securities (excluding directors' qualifying shares) or equity interests;

(2) Has such knowledge and experience in financial and business matters that he is capable of evaluating, alone, or together with other purchaser representatives of the purchaser, or together with the purchaser, the merits and risks of the prospective investment;

(3) Is acknowledged by the purchaser in writing, during the course of the transaction, to be his purchaser representative in connection with evaluating the merits and risks of the prospective investment; and

(4) Discloses to the purchaser in writing a reasonable time prior to the sale of securities to that purchaser any material relationship between himself or his affiliates and the issuer or its affiliates that then exists, that is mutually understood to be contemplated, or that has existed at any time during the previous two years, and any compensation received or to be received as a result of such relationship.

Note 1: A person acting as a purchaser representative should consider the applicability of the registration and antifraud provisions relating to brokers and dealers under the Securities Exchange Act of 1934 ("Exchange Act") (15 U.S.C. 78a et seq., as amended) and relating to investment advisers under the Investment Advisers Act of 1940.

Note 2: The acknowledgment required by paragraph (h)(3) and the disclosure required by paragraph (h)(4) of this section must be made with specific reference to each prospective investment. Advance blanket acknowledgment, such as for "all securities transactions" or "all private placement," is not sufficient.

Note 3: Disclosure of any material relationships between the purchaser representative or his affiliates and the issuer or its affiliates does not relieve the purchaser representative of his obligation to act in the interest of the purchaser.

§ 230.502 General conditions to be met.

The following conditions shall be applicable to offers and sales made under Regulation D (§§ 230.501-230.508):

(a) *Integration.* All sales that are part of the same Regulation D offering must meet all of the terms and conditions of Regulation D. Offers and sales that are made more than six months before the start of a Regulation D offering or are made more than six months after completion of a Regulation D offering will not be considered part of that Regulation D offering, so long as during those six month periods there are no offers or sales of securities by or for the issuer that are of the same or a similar class as those offered or sold under Regulation D, other than those offers or sales of securities under an employee benefit plan as defined in rule 405 under the Act (17 CFR 230.405).

Note: The term "offering" is not defined in the Act or in Regulation D. If the issuer offers or sells securities for which the safe harbor rule in paragraph (a) of this § 230.502 is unavailable, the determination as to whether separate sales of securities are part of the same offering (i.e. are considered "integrated") depends on the particular facts and circumstances. Generally, transactions otherwise meeting the requirements of an exemption will not be integrated with simultaneous offerings being made outside the United States in compliance with Regulation S. See Release No. 33-6863.

The following factors should be considered in determining whether offers and sales should be integrated for purposes of the exemptions under Regulation D:

(a) Whether the sales are part of a single plan of financing;
(b) Whether the sales involve issuance of the same class of securities;
(c) Whether the sales have been made at or about the same time;
(d) Whether the same type of consideration is being received; and
(e) Whether the sales are made for the same general purpose.

See Release 33-4552 (November 6, 1962) [27 FR 11316].

(b) *Information requirements (1) When information must be furnished.* If the issuer sells securities under § 230.505 or § 230.506 to any purchaser that is not an accredited investor, the issuer shall furnish the information specified in paragraph (b)(2) of this section to such purchaser a reasonable time prior to sale. The issuer is not required to furnish the specified information to purchasers when it sells securities under § 230.504, or to any accredited investor.

Note: When an issuer provides information to investors pursuant to paragraph (b)(1), it should consider providing such information to accredited investors as well, in view of the anti-fraud provisions of the federal securities laws. In addition, specific disclosure requirements regarding limitations on resale are contained in § 230.504(b)(2)(ii).

(2) *Type of information to be furnished.* (i) If the issuer is not subject to the reporting requirements of section 13 or 15(d) of the Exchange Act, at a reasonable time prior to the sale of securities the issuer shall furnish to the purchaser the following information, to the extent material to an understanding of the issuer, its business, and the securities being offered;

(A) *Offerings up to $2,000,000.* The same kind of information as would be required in Part II of Form 1-A (17 CFR 239.90), except that the issuer's balance sheet, which shall be dated within 120 days of the start of the offering, must be audited.

(B) *Offerings up to $7,500,000.* The same kind of information as would be required in Part I of Form S-18 (17 CFR 239.28), except that only the financial statements for the issuer's most recent fiscal year must be certified by an independent public or certified accountant. If Form S-18 is not available to an issuer, then the issuer shall furnish the same kind of information as would be required in Part I of a registration statement filed under the Act on the form that the issuer would be entitled to use, except that only the financial statements for the most recent two fiscal years prepared in accordance with generally accepted accounting principles shall be furnished and only the financial statements for the issuer's most recent fiscal year shall be certified by an independent public or certified accountant. If an issuer, other than a limited partnership, cannot obtain audited financial statements without unreasonable effort or expense, then only the issuer's balance sheet, which shall be dated within 120 days of the start of the offering, must be audited. If the issuer is a limited partnership and cannot obtain the required financial statements without unreasonable effort or expense, it may furnish financial statements that have been prepared on the basis of federal income tax requirements and examined and reported on in accordance with generally accepted auditing standards by an independent public or certified accountant.

(C) *Offerings over $7,500,000.* The same kind of information as would be required in Part I of a registration statement filed under the Act on the form that the issuer would be entitled to use. If an issuer, other than a limited partnership, cannot obtain audited financial statements without unreasonable effort or expense, then only the issuer's balance sheet, which shall be dated within 120 days of the start of the offering, must be audited. If the issuer is a limited partnership and cannot obtain the required financial statements without unreasonable effort or expense, it may furnish financial statements that have been prepared on the basis of federal income tax requirements and examined and reported on in accordance with generally accepted auditing standards by an independent public or certified accountant.

(D) If the issuer is a foreign private issuer, the issuer shall disclose the same kind of information required to be included in a registration statement filed under the Act on the form that the issuer would be entitled to use. The financial statements need be certified only to the extent required by paragraph (b)(2)(i)(B) or (C) of this section, as appropriate.

(ii) If the issuer is subject to the reporting requirements of section 13 or 15(d) of the Exchange Act, at a reasonable time prior to the sale of securities the issuer shall furnish to the purchaser the information specified in paragraph (b)(2)(ii)(A) or (B) of this section, and in either event the information specified in paragraph (b)(2)(ii)(C) of this section:

(A) The issuer's annual report to shareholders for the most recent fiscal year, if such annual report meets the requirements of § 240.14a-3 or 240.14c-3 under the Exchange Act, the definitive proxy statement filed in connection with that annual report, and, if requested by the purchaser in writing, a copy of the issuer's most recent Form 10-K (17 CFR 249.310) under the Exchange Act.

(B) The information contained in an annual report on Form 10-K under the Exchange Act or in a registration statement on Form S-1 (17 CFR 239.11), Form S-11 (17 CFR 239.18), or Form S-18 (17 CFR 239.28) under the Act or on Form 10 (17 CFR 249.210) under the Exchange Act, whichever filing is the most recent required to be filed.

(C) The information contained in any reports or documents required to be filed by the issuer under sections 13(a), 14(a), 14(c), and 15(d) of the Exchange Act since the distribution or filing of the report or registration statement specified in paragraphs (b)(2)(ii) (A) or (B), and a brief description of the securities being offered, the use of the proceeds from the offering, and any material changes in the issuer's affairs that are not disclosed in the documents furnished.

(D) If the issuer is foreign private issuer, the issuer may provide in lieu of the information specified in paragraphs (b)(2)(ii) (A) or (B) of this section, the information contained in its most recent filing on Form 20-F or Form F-1 (§ 239.31 of the chapter).

(iii) Exhibits required to be filed with the Commission as part of a registration statement or report, other than an annual report to shareholders or parts of that report incorporated by reference in a Form 10-K report, need not be furnished to each purchaser that is not an accredited investor if the contents of material exhibits are identified and such exhibits are made available to a purchaser, upon his written request, a reasonable time prior to his purchase.

(iv) At a reasonable time prior to the sale of securities to any purchaser that is not an accredited investor in a transaction under § 230.505 or § 230.506, the issuer shall furnish to the purchaser a brief description in writing of any material written information concerning the offering that has been provided by the issuer to any accredited investor but not previously delivered to such unaccredited purchaser. The issuer shall furnish any portion or all of this information to the purchaser, upon his written request a reasonable time prior to his purchase.

(v) The issuer shall also make available to each purchaser at a reasonable time prior to his purchase of securities in a transaction under § 230.505 or § 230.506 the opportunity to ask questions and receive answers concerning the terms and conditions of the offering and to obtain any additional information which the issuer possesses or can acquire without unreasonable effort or expense that is necessary to verify the accuracy of information furnished under paragraph (b)(2) (i) or (ii) of this section.

(vi) For business combinations or exchange offers, in addition to information required by Form S-4 (17 CFR 239.25), the issuer shall provide to each purchaser at the time the plan is submitted to security holders, or, with an exchange, during the course of the transaction and prior to sale, written information about any terms or arrangements of the proposed transactions that are materially different from those for all other security holders. For purposes of this subsection, an issuer which is not subject to the reporting requirements of section 13 or 15(d) of the Exchange Act may satisfy the requirements of Part I.B. or C. of Form S-4 by compliance with paragraph (b)(2)(i) of this § 230.502.

(vii) At a reasonable time prior to the sale of securities to any purchaser that is not an accredited investor in a transaction under § 230.505 or § 230.506, the issuer shall advise the purchaser of the limitations on resale in the manner contained in paragraph (d)(2) of this section. Such disclosure may be contained in other materials required to be provided by this paragraph.

(c) *Limitation on manner of offering.* Except as provided in § 230.504(b)(1), neither the issuer nor any person acting on its behalf shall offer or sell the securities by any form of general solicitation or general advertising, including, but not limited to, the following:

(1) Any advertisement, article, notice or other communication published in any newspaper, magazine, or similar media or broadcast over television or radio; and

(2) Any seminar or meeting whose attendees have been invited by any general solicitation or general advertising.

(d) *Limitations on resale.* Except as provided in § 230.504(b)(1), securities acquired in a transaction under Regulation D shall have the status of securities acquired in a transaction under section 4(2) of the Act and cannot be resold without registration under the Act or an exemption therefrom. The issuer shall exercise reasonable care to assure that the purchasers of the securities are not underwriters within the meaning of section 2(11) of the Act, which reasonable care may be demonstrated by the following:

(1) Reasonable inquiry to determine if the purchaser is acquiring the securities for himself or for other persons;

(2) Written disclosure to each purchaser prior to sale that the securities have not been registered under the Act and, therefore, cannot be resold unless they are registered under the Act or unless an exemption from registration is available; and

(3) Placement of a legend on the certificate or other document that evidences the securities stating that the securities have not been registered under the Act and setting forth or referring to the restrictions on transferability and sale of the securities. While taking these actions will establish the requisite reasonable care, it is not the exclusive method to demonstrate such care. Other actions by the issuer may satisfy this provision. In addition, §§ 230.502(b)(2)(vii) and 230.504(b)(2)(ii) require the delivery of written disclosure of the limitations on resale to investors in certain instances.

§ 230.503 Filing of notice of sales.

(a) An issuer offering or selling securities in reliance on § 230.504, § 230.505 or § 230.506 shall file with the Commission five copies of a notice on Form D (17 CFR 239.500) no later than 15 days after the first sale of securities.

(b) One copy of every notice on Form D shall be manually signed by a person duly authorized by the issuer.

(c) If sales are made under § 230.505, the notice shall contain an undertaking by the issuer to furnish to the Commission, upon the written request of its staff, the information furnished by the issuer under § 230.502(b)(2) to any purchaser that is not an accredited investor.

(d) Amendments to notices filed under paragraph (a) of this section need only report the issuer's name and the information required by Part C and any material change in the facts from those set forth in Parts A and B.

(e) A notice on Form D shall be considered filed with the Commission under paragraph (a) of this section.

(1) As of the date on which it is received at the Commission's principal office in Washington, DC; or

(2) As of the date on which the notice is mailed by means of United States registered or certified mail to the Commission's principal office in Washington, DC, if the notice is delivered to such office after the date on which it is required to be filed.

§ 230.504 Exemption for limited offerings and sales of securities not exceeding $1,000,000.

(a) *Exemption.* Offers and sales of securities that satisfy the conditions in paragraph (b) of this section by an issuer that is not subject to the reporting requirements of section 13 or 15(d) of the Exchange Act and that is not an investment company shall be exempt from the provisions of section 5 of the Act under section 3(b) of the Act.

(b) *Conditions to be met (1) General Conditions.* To qualify for exemption under this § 230.504, offers and sales must satisfy the terms and conditions of §§ 230.501 and 230.502, except that the provisions of § 230.502(c) and (d) shall not apply to offers and sales of securities under this § 230.504 that are made:

(i) Exclusively in one or more states each of which provides for the registration of the securities and requires the delivery of a disclosure document before sale and that are made in accordance with those state provisions; or

(ii) In one or more states which have no provision for the registration of the securities and the delivery of a disclosure document before sale, if the securities have been registered in at least one state which provides for such registration and delivery before sale, offers and sales are made in the state of registration in accordance with such state provisions, and such document is in fact delivered to all purchasers in the states which have no such procedure before the sale of securities.

(2) *Specific condition (i) Limitation on aggregate offering price.* The aggregate offering price for an offering of securities under this § 230.504, as defined in § 230.501(c), shall not exceed $1,000,000, less the aggregate offering price for all securities sold within the twelve months before the start of and during the offering of securities under this § 230.504 in reliance on any exemption under section 3(b) of the Act or in violation of section 5(a) of the Act, provided that no more than $500,000 of such aggregate offering price is attributable to offers and sales of securities without registration under a state's securities laws.

Note 1: The calculation of the aggregate offering price is illustrated as follows:

Example 1. If an issuer sells $500,000 worth of its securities pursuant to state registration on January 1, 1988 under this § 230.504, it would be able to sell an additional $500,000 worth of securities either pursuant to state registration or without state registration during the ensuing twelve-month period, pursuant to this § 230.504.

Example 2. If an issuer sold $900,000 pursuant to state registration on June 1, 1987 under this § 230.504 and an additional $4,100,000 on December 1, 1987 under § 230.505, the issuer could not sell any of its securities under this § 230.504 until December 1, 1988. Until then the issuer must count the December 1, 1987 sale towards the $1,000,000 limit within the preceding twelve months.

Note 2: If a transaction under this § 230.504 fails to meet the limitation on the aggregate offering price, it does not affect the availability of this § 230.504 for the other transactions considered in applying such limitations. For example, if an issuer sold $1,000,000 worth of its securities pursuant to state registration on January 1, 1988 under this § 230.504 and an additional $500,000 worth on July 1, 1988, this § 230.504 would not be available for the later sale, but would still be applicable to the January 1, 1988 sale.

Note 3: In addition to the aggregation principles, issuer's should be aware of the applicability of the integration principles set forth in § 230.502(a).

   (ii) *Advice about the limitations on resale.* Except where the provision does not apply by virtue of paragraph (b)(1) of this section, the issuer, at a reasonable time prior to the sale of securities, shall advise each purchaser of the limitations on resale in the manner contained in paragraph (d)(2) of § 230.502.

§ 230.505 Exemption for limited offers and sales of securities not exceeding $5,000,000.

 (a) *Exemption.* Offers and sales of securities that satisfy the conditions in paragraph (b) of this section by an issuer that is not an investment company shall be exempt from the provisions of section 5 of the Act under section 3(b) of the Act.

 (b) *Conditions to be met (1) General conditions.* To qualify for exemption under this section, offers and sales must satisfy the terms and conditions of §§ 230.501 and 230.502.

  (2) *Specific conditions (i) Limitation on aggregate offering price.* The aggregate offering price for an offering of securities under this § 230.505, as defined in § 203.501(c), shall not exceed $5,000,000, less the aggregate offering price for all securities sold within the twelve months before the start of and during the offering of securities under this section in reliance on any exemption under section 3(b) of the Act or in violation of section 5(a) of the Act.

Note: The calculation of the aggregate offering price is illustrated as follows:

Example 1. If an issuer sold $2,000,000 of its securities on June 1, 1982 under this § 230.505 and an additional $1,000,000 on September 1, 1982, the issuer would be permitted to sell only $2,000,000 more under this § 230.505 until June 1, 1983. Until that date the issuer must count both prior sales towards the $5,000,000 limit. However, if the issuer made its third sale on June 1, 1983, the issuer could then sell $4,000,000 of its securities because the June 1, 1982 sale would not be within the preceding twelve months.

Example 2. If an issuer sold $500,000 of its securities on June 1, 1982 under § 230.504 and an additional $4,500,000 on December 1, 1982 under this section, then the issuer could not sell any of its securities under this section until June 1, 1983. At that time it could sell an additional $500,000 of its securities.

   (ii) *Limitation on number of purchasers.* There are no more than or the issuer reasonably believes that there are no more than 35 purchasers of securities from the issuer in any offering under this section.

   (iii) Disqualifications. No exemption under this section shall be available for the securities of any issuer described in § 230.252(c), (d), (e), or (f) of Regulation A, except that for purposes of this section only:

    (A) The term "filing of the notification required by § 230.255" as used in § 230.252(c), (d), (e) and (f) shall mean the first sale of securities under this section;

    (B) The term "underwriter" as used in § 230.252(d) and (e) shall mean a person that has been or will be paid directly or indirectly remuneration for solicitation of purchasers in connection with sales of securities under this section; and

(C) Paragraph (b)(2)(iii) of this section shall not apply to any issuer if the Commission determines, upon a showing of good cause, that it is not necessary under the circumstances that the exemption be denied. Any such determination shall be without prejudice to any other action by the Commission in any other proceeding or matter with respect to the issuer or any other person.

§ 230.506 Exemption for limited offers and sales without regard to dollar amount of offering.

(a) *Exemption.* Offers and sales of securities by an issuer that satisfy the conditions in paragraph (b) of this section shall be deemed to be transactions not involving any public offering within the meaning of section 4(2) of the Act.

(b) *Conditions to be met (1) General conditions.* To qualify for an exemption under this section, offers and sales must satisfy all the terms and conditions of §§ 230.501 and 230.502.

(2) *Specific Conditions (i) Limitation on number of purchasers.* There are no more than or the issuer reasonably believes that there are no more than 35 purchasers of securities from the issuer in any offering under this section.

Note: See § 230.501(e) for the calculation of the number of purchasers and § 230.502(a) for what may or may not constitute an offering under this section.

(ii) *Nature of purchasers.* Each purchaser who is not an accredited investor either alone or with his purchaser representative(s) has such knowledge and experience in financial and business matters that he is capable of evaluating the merits and risks of the prospective investment, or the issuer reasonably believes immediately prior to making any sale that such purchaser comes within this description.

§ 230.507 Disqualifying provision relating to exemptions under §§ 230.504, 230.505 and 230.506.

(a) No exemption under § 230.504, § 230.505 or § 230.506 shall be available for an issuer if such issuer, any of its predecessors or affiliates have been subject to any order, judgment, or decree of any court of competent jurisdiction temporarily, preliminary [sic] or permanently enjoining such person for failure to comply with § 230.503.

(b) Paragraph (a) of this section shall not apply if the Commission determines, upon a showing of good cause, that it is not necessary under the circumstances that the exemption be denied.

§ 230.508 Insignificant deviations from a term, condition or requirement of Regulation D.

(a) A failure to comply with a term, condition or requirement of § 230.504, § 230.505 or § 230.506 will not result in the loss of the exemption from the requirements of section 5 of the Act for any offer or sale to a particular individual or entity, if the person relying on the exemption shows:

    (1) The failure to comply did not pertain to a term, condition or requirement directly intended to protect that particular individual or entity; and

    (2) The failure to comply was insignificant with respect to the offering as a whole, provided that any failure to comply with paragraph (c) of § 230.502, paragraph (b)(2)(i) of § 230.504, paragraphs (b)(2)(i) and (ii) of § 230.505 and paragraph (b)(2)(i) of § 230.506 shall be deemed to be significant to the offering as a whole; and

    (3) A good faith and reasonable attempt was made to comply with all applicable terms, conditions and requirements of § 230.504, § 230.505 or § 230.506.

  (b) A transaction made in reliance on § 230.504, § 230.505 or § 230.506 shall comply with all applicable terms, conditions and requirements of Regulation D. Where an exemption is established only through reliance upon paragraph (a) of this section, the failure to comply shall nonetheless be actionable by the Commission under section 20 of the Act.

Appendix I

National Park Service, "National Register of Historic Places"

(Final Rule, 36 C.F.R. Part 60)

§ 60.1 Authorization and expansion of the National Register.
§ 60.2 Effects of listing under Federal law.
§ 60.3 Definitions.
§ 60.4 Criteria for evaluation.
§ 60.5 Nomination forms and information collection.
§ 60.6 Nominations by the State historic preservation officer under approved State historic preservation programs.
§ 60.7-8 (Reserved)
§ 60.9 Nominations by Federal agencies.
§ 60.10 Concurrent State and Federal nominations.
§ 60.11 Requests for nominations.
§ 60.12 Nomination appeals.
§ 60.13 Publication in the Federal Register and other NPS notification.
§ 60.14 Changes and revisions to properties listed in the National Register.
§ 60.15 Removing properties from the National Register.

Authority: National Historic Preservation Act of 1966, as amended, 16 U.S.C. 470 *et seq.*, and EO 11593.
Source: 46 FR 56187, Nov. 16, 1981, unless otherwise noted.

§ 60.1. Authorization and expansion of the National Register.

(a) The National Historic Preservation Act of 1966, 80 Stat. 915, 16 U.S.C. 470 *et seq.*, as amended, authorizes the Secretary of the Interior to expand and maintain a National Register of districts, sites, buildings, structures, and objects significant in American history, architecture, archeology, engineering and culture. The regulations herein set forth the procedural requirements for listing properties on the National Register.

(b) Properties are added to the National Register through the following processes.

(1) Those Acts of Congress and Executive orders which create historic areas of the National Park System administered by the National Park Service, all or portions of which may be determined to be of historic significance consistent with the intent of Congress;

(2) Properties declared by the Secretary of the Interior to be of National significance and designated as National Historic Landmarks;

(3) Nominations prepared under approved State Historic Preservation Programs, submitted by the State Historic Preservation Officer and approved by the NPS;

(4) Nominations from any person or local government (only if such property is located in a State with no approved State Historic Preservation Program) approved by the NPS and;

(5) Nominations of Federal properties prepared by Federal agencies, submitted by the Federal Preservation Officer and approved by NPS.

§ 60.2. Effects of listing under Federal law.

The National Register is an authoritative guide to be used by Federal, State, and local governments, private groups and citizens to identify the Nation's cultural resources and to indicate what properties should be considered for protection from destruction or impairment. Listing of private property on the National Register does not prohibit under Federal law or regulation any actions which may otherwise be taken by the property owner with respect to the property.

(a) The National Register was designed to be and is administered as a planning tool. Federal agencies undertaking a project having an effect on a listed or eligible property must provide the Advisory Council on Historic Preservation a reasonable opportunity to comment pursuant to section 106 of the National Historic Preservation Act of 1966, as amended. The Council has adopted procedures concerning, *inter alia,* their commenting responsibility in 36 CFR Part 800. Having complied with this procedural requirement the Federal agency may adopt any course of action it believes is appropriate. While the Advisory Council comments must be taken into account and integrated into the decisionmaking process, program decisions rest with the agency implementing the undertaking.

(b) Listing in the National Register also makes property owners eligible to be considered for Federal grants-in-aid for historic preservation.

(c) If a property is listed in the National Register, certain provisions of the Tax Reform Act of 1976 as amended by the Revenue Act of 1978 and the Tax Treatment Extension Act of 1980 may apply. These provisions encourage the preservation of depreciable historic structures by allowing favorable tax treatments for rehabilitation, and discourage destruction of historic buildings by eliminating certain otherwise available Federal tax provisions both for demolition of historic structures and for new construction on the site of demolished historic buildings. Owners of historic buildings may benefit from the investment tax credit provisions of the Revenue Act of 1978. The Economic Recovery Tax Act of 1981 generally replaces the rehabilitation tax incentives under these laws beginning January 1, 1982 with a 25% investment tax credit for rehabilitations of historic commercial, industrial and residential buildings. This can be combined with a 15-year cost recovery period for the adjusted basis of the historic building. Historic buildings with certified rehabilitations receive additional tax savings by their exemption from any requirement to reduce the basis of the building by the amount of the credit. The denial of accelerated depreciation for a building built on the site of a demolished historic building is repealed effective January 1, 1982. The Tax Treatment Extension Act of 1980 includes provisions regarding charitable contributions for conservation purposes of partial interests in historically important land areas or structures.

(d) If a property contains surface coal resources and is listed in the National Register, certain provisions of the Surface Mining and Control Act of 1977 require consideration of a property's historic values in the determination on issuance of a surface coal mining permit.

§ 60.3. Definitions.

(a) *Building.* A building is a structure created to shelter any form of human activity, such as a house, barn, church, hotel, or similar structure. Building may refer to a historically related complex such as a courthouse and jail or a house and barn.

Examples

Molly Brown House (Denver, CO)
Meek Mansion and Carriage House (Hayward, CA)
Huron County Courthouse and Jail (Norwalk, OH)
Fairntosh Plantation (Durham vicinity, NC)

(b) *Chief elected local official.* Chief elected local official means the mayor, county judge, county executive or otherwise titled chief elected administrative official who is the elected head of the local political jurisdiction in which the property is located.

(c) *Determination of eligibility.* A determination of eligibility is a decision by the Department of the Interior that a district, site, building, structure or object meets the National Register criteria for evaluation although the property is not formally listed in the National Register. A determination of eligibility does not make the property eligible for such benefits as grants, loans, or tax incentives that have listing on the National Register as a prerequisite.

(d) *District.* A district is a geographically definable area, urban or rural, possessing a significant concentration, linkage, or continuity of sites, buildings, structures, or objects united by past events or aesthetically by plan or physical development. A district may also comprise individual elements separated geographically but linked by association or history.

Examples

Georgetown Historic District (Washington, DC)
Martin Luther King Historic District (Atlanta, GA)
Durango-Silverton Narrow-Gauge Railroad (right-of-way between Durango
  and Silverton, CO)

(e) *Federal Preservation Officer.* The Federal Preservation Officer is the official designated by the head of each Federal agency responsible for coordinating that agency's activities under the National Historic Preservation Act of 1966, as amended, and Executive Order 11593 including nominating properties under that agency's ownership or control to the National Register.

(f) *Keeper of the National Register of Historic Places.* The Keeper is the individual who has been delegated the authority by NPS to list properties and determine their eligibility for the National Register. The Keeper may further delegate this authority as he or she deems appropriate.

(g) *Multiple Resource Format submission.* A Multiple Resource Format submission for nominating properties to the National Register is one which includes all or a defined portion of the cultural resources identified in a specified geographical area.

(h) *National Park Service (NPS).* The National Park Service is the bureau of the Department of Interior to which the Secretary of Interior has delegated the authority and responsibility for administering the National Register program.

(i) *National Register Nomination Form.* National Register Nomination Form means (1) National Register Nomination Form NPS 10-900, with accompanying continuation sheets (where necessary) Form NPS 10-900a, maps and photographs or (2) for Federal nominations, Form No. 10-306, with continuation sheets (where necessary) Form No. 10-300A, maps and photographs. Such nomination forms must be "adequately documented" and "technically and professionally correct and sufficient." To meet these requirements the forms and accompanying maps and photographs must be completed in accord with requirements and guidance in the NPS publication, "How to Complete National Register Forms" and other NPS technical publications on this subject. Descriptions and statements of significance must be prepared in accord with standards generally accepted by academic historians, architectural historians and archeologists. The nomination form is a legal document and reference for historical, architectural, and archeological data upon which the protections for listed and eligible properties are founded. The nominating authority certifies that the nomination is adequately documented and technically and professionally correct and sufficient upon nomination.

(j) *Object.* An object is a material thing of functional, aesthetic, cultural, historical or scientific value that may be, by nature or design, movable yet related to a specific setting or environment.

Examples

Delta Queen Steamboat (Cincinnati, OH)
Adams Memorial (Rock Creek Cemetery, Washington, DC)
Sumpter Valley Gold Dredge (Sumpter, OR)

(k) *Owner or owners.* The term owner or owners means those individuals, partnerships, corporations or public agencies holding fee simple title to property. Owner or owners does not include individuals, partnerships, corporations or public agencies holding easements or less than fee interests (including leaseholds) of any nature.

(l) *Site.* A site is the location of a significant event, a prehistoric or historic occupation or activity, or a building or structure, whether standing, ruined, or vanished, where the location itself maintains historical or archeological value regardless of the value of any existing structure.

Examples

Cabin Creek Battlefield (Pensacola vicinity, OK)
Mound Cemetery Mound (Chester vicinity, OH)
Mud Springs Pony Express Station Site (Dalton vicinity, NE)

(m) *State Historic Preservation Officer.* The State Historic Preservation Officer is the person who has been designated by the Governor or chief executive or by State statute in each State to administer the State Historic Preservation Program, including identifying and nominating eligible properties to the National Register and otherwise administering applications for listing historic properties in the National Register.

(n) *State Historic Preservation Program.* The State Historic Preservation Program is the program established by each State and approved by the Secretary of Interior for the purpose of carrying out the provisions of the National Historic Preservation Act of 1966, as amended, and related laws and regulations. Such program shall be approved by the Secretary before the State may nominate properties to the National Register. Any State Historic Preservation Program in effect under prior authority of law before December 12, 1980, shall be treated as an approved program until the Secretary approves a program submitted by the State for purposes of the Amendments or December 12, 1983, unless the Secretary chooses to rescind such approval because of program deficiencies.

(o) *State Review Board.* The State Review Board is a body whose members represent the professional fields of American history, architectural history, historic architecture, prehistoric and historic archeology, and other professional disciplines and may include citizen members. In States with approved State historic preservation programs the State Review Board reviews and approves National Register nominations concerning whether or not they meet the criteria for evaluation prior to their submittal to the NPA.

(p) *Structure.* A structure is a work made up of interdependent and interrelated parts in a definite pattern of organization. Constructed by man, it is often an engineering project large in scale.

Examples

Swanton Covered Railroad Bridge (Swanton vicinity, VT)
Old Point Loma Lighthouse (San Diego, CA)
North Point Water Tower (Milwaukee, WI)
Reber Radio Telescope (Green Bay vicinity, WI)

(q) *Thematic Group Format Submission.* A Thematic Group Format submission for nominating properties to the National Register is one which includes a finite group of resources related to one another in a clearly distinguishable way. They may be related to a single historic person, event, or developmental force; of one building type or use, or designed by a single architect; of a single archeological site form, or related to a particular set of archeological research problems.

(r) *To nominate.* To nominate is to propose that a district, site, building, structure, or object be listed in the National Register of Historic Places by preparing a nomination form, with accompanying maps and photographs which adequately document the property and are technically and professionally correct and sufficient.

§ 60.4. Criteria for evaluation.

The criteria applied to evaluate properties (other than areas of National Park System and National Historic Landmarks) for the National Register are listed below. These criteria are worded in a manner to provide for a wide diversity of resources. The following criteria shall be used in evaluating properties for nomination to the National Register, by NPS in reviewing nominations, and for evaluating National Register eligibility of properties. Guidance in applying the criteria is further discussed in the "How To" publications. Standards & Guidelines sheets and Keeper's opinions of the National Register. Such materials are available upon request.

National Register criteria for evaluation. The quality of significance in American history, architecture, archeology, engineering, and culture is present in districts, sites, buildings, structures, and objects that possess integrity of location, design, setting, materials, workmanship, feeling, and association and

(a) that are associated with events that have made a significant contribution to the broad patterns of our history; or

(b) that are associated with the lives of persons significant in our past; or

(c) that embody the distinctive characteristics of a type, period, or method of construction, or that represent the work of a master, or that possess high artistic values, or that represent a significant and distinguishable entity whose components may lack individual distinction; or

(d) that have yielded, or may be likely to yield, information important in prehistory or history.

Criteria considerations. Ordinarily cemeteries, birthplaces, or graves of historical figures, properties owned by religious institutions or used for religious purposes, structures that have been moved from their original locations, reconstructed historic buildings, properties primarily commemorative in nature, and properties that have achieved significance within the past 50 years shall not be considered eligible for the National Register. However, such properties will qualify if they are integral parts of districts that do meet the criteria or if they fall within the following categories:

(a) A religious property deriving primary significance from architectural or artistic distinction or historical importance; or

(b) A building or structure removed from its original location but which is significant primarily for architectural value, or which is the surviving structure most importantly associated with a historic person or event; or

(c) A birthplace or grave of a historical figure of outstanding importance if there is no appropriate site or building directly associated with his productive life.

(d) A cemetery which derives its primary significance from graves of persons of transcendent importance, from age, from distinctive design features, or from association with historic events; or

(e) A reconstructed building when accurately executed in a suitable environment and presented in a dignified manner as part of a restoration master plan, and when no other building or structure with the same association has survived; or

(f) A property primarily commemorative in intent if design, age, tradition, or symbolic value has invested it with its own exceptional significance; or

(g) A property achieving significance within the past 50 years if it is of exceptional importance.

This exception is described further in NPS "How To", no. 2, entitled "How to Evaluate and Nominate Potential National Register Properties That Have Achieved Significance Within the Last 50 Years" which is available from the National Register of Historic Places Division, National Park Service, United States Department of the Interior, Washington, D.C. 20240.

§ 60.5. Nomination forms and information collection.

(a) All nominations to the National Register are to be made on standard National Register forms. These forms are provided upon request to the State Historic Preservation Officer, participating Federal agencies and others by the NPS. For archival reasons, no other forms, photocopied or otherwise, will be accepted.

(b) The information collection requirements contained in this part have been approved by the Office of Management and Budget under 44 U.S.C., 3507 and assigned clearance number *1024-0018*. The information is being collected as part of the nomination of properties to the National Register. This information will be used to evaluate the eligibility of properties for inclusion in the National Register under established criteria. The obligation to respond is required to obtain a benefit.

§ 60.6. Nominations by the State Historic Preservation Officer under approved State Historic Preservation programs.

(a) The State Historic Preservation Officer is responsible for identifying and nominating eligible properties to the National Register. Nomination forms are prepared under the supervision of the State Historic Preservation Officer. The State Historic Preservation Officer establishes statewide priorities for preparation and submittal of nominations for all properties meeting National Register criteria for evaluation within the State. All nominations from the State shall be submitted in accord with the State priorities, which shall be consistent with an approved State historic preservation plan.

(b) The State shall consult with local authorities in the nomination process. The State provides notice of the intent to nominate a property and solicits written comments especially on the significance of the property and whether or not it meets the National Register criteria for evaluation. The State notice also gives owners of private property an opportunity to concur in or object to listing. The notice is carried out as specified in the subsections below.

(c) As part of the nomination process, each State is required to notify in writing the property owner(s), except as specified in paragraph (d) of this section, of the State's intent to bring the nomination before the State Review Board. The list of owners shall be obtained from either official land recordation records or tax records, whichever is more appropriate, within 90 days prior to the notification in intent to nominate. If in any State the land recordation or tax records is not the most appropriate list from which to obtain owners that State shall notify the Keeper in writing and request approval that an alternative source of owners may be used.

The State is responsible for notifying only those owners whose names appear on the list consulted. Where there is more than one owner on the list, each separate owner shall be notified. The State shall send the written notification at least 30 but not more than 75 days before the State Review Board meeting. Required notices may vary in some details of wording as the States prefer, but the content of notices must be approved by the National Register. The notice shall give the owner(s) at least 30 but not more than 75 days to submit written comments and concur in or object in writing to the nomination of such property. At least 30 but not more than 75 days before the State Review Board meeting, the States are also required to notify by the above mentioned National Register approved notice the applicable chief elected official of the county (or equivalent governmental unit) and municipal political jurisdiction in which the property is located. The National Register nomination shall be on file with the State Historic Preservation Program during the comment period and a copy made available by mail when requested by the public, or made available at a location of reasonable access to all affected property owners, such as a local library, courthouse, or other public place, prior to the State Review Board meeting so that written comments regarding the nomination can be prepared.

(d) For a nomination with more than 50 property owners, each State is required to notify in writing at least 30 days but not more than 75 days in advance of the State Review Board meeting the chief elected local officials of the county (or equivalent governmental unit) and municipal political jurisdiction in which the property or district is located. The State shall provide general notice to property owners concerning the State's intent to nominate. The general notice shall be published at least 30 days but not more than 75 days before the State Review Board meeting and provide an opportunity for the submission of written comments and provide the owners of private property or a majority of such owners for districts an opportunity to concur in or object in writing to the nomination. Such general notice must be published in one or more local newspapers of general circulation in the area of the nomination. The content of the notices shall be approved by the National Register. If such general notice is used to notify the property owners for a nomination containing more than 50 owners, it is suggested that a public information meeting be held in the immediate area prior to the State Review Board meeting. If the State wishes to individually notify all property owners, it may do so, pursuant to procedures specified in Subsection 60.6(c), in which case, the State need not publish a general notice.

(e) For Multiple Resource and Thematic Group Format submission, each district, site, building, structure and object included in the submission is treated as a separate nomination for the purpose of notification and to provide owners of private property the opportunity to concur in or object in writing to the nomination in accord with this section.

(f) The commenting period following notifications can be waived only when all property owners and the chief elected local official have advised the State in writing that they agree to the waiver.

(g) Upon notification, any owner or owners of a private property who wish to object shall submit to the State Historic Preservation Officer a notarized statement certifying that the party is the sole or partial owner of the private property, as appropriate, and objects to the listing. In nominations with multiple ownership of a single private property or of districts, the property will not be listed if a majority of the owners object to listing. Upon receipt of notarized objections respecting a district or single private property with multiple owners, it is the responsibility of the State Historic Preservation Officer to ascertain whether a majority of owners of private property have objected. If an owner whose name did not appear on the list certifies in a written notarized statement that the party is the sole or partial owner of a nominated private property such owner shall be counted by the State Historic Preservation Officer in determining whether a majority of owners has objected. Each owner of private property in a district has one vote regardless of how many properties or what part of one property that party owns and regardless of whether the property contributes to the significance of the district.

(h) If a property has been submitted to and approved by the State Review Board for inclusion in the National Register prior to the effective date of this section, the State Historic Preservation Officer need not resubmit the property to the State Review Board; but before submitting the nomination to the NPS shall afford owners of private property the opportunity to concur in or object to the property's inclusion in the Register pursuant to applicable notification procedures described above.

(i) (Reserved)

(j) Completed nomination forms or the documentation proposed for submission on the nomination forms and comments concerning the significance of a property and its elibigility for the National Register are submitted to the State Review Board. The State Review Board shall review the nomination forms or documentation proposed for submission on the nomination forms and any comments concerning the property's significance and eligibility for the National Register. The State Review Board shall determine whether or not the property meets the National Register criteria for evaluation and make a recommendation to the State Historic Preservation Officer to approve or disapprove the nomination.

(k) Nominations approved by the State Review Board and comments received are then reviewed by the State Historic Preservation Officer and if he or she finds the nominations to be adequately documented and technically, professionally, and procedurally correct and sufficient and in conformance with National Register criteria for evaluation, the nominations are submitted to the Keeper of the National Register of Historic Places, National Park Service, United States Department of the Interior, Washington, D.C. 20240. All comments received by a State and notarized statements of objection to listing are submitted with a nomination.

(l) If the State Historic Preservation Officer and the State Review Board disagree on whether a property meets the National Register criteria for evaluation, the State Historic Preservation Officer, if he or she chooses, may submit the nomination with his or her opinion concerning whether or not the property meets the criteria for evaluation and the opinion of the State Review Board to the Keeper of the National Register for a final decision on the listing of the property. The opinion of the State Review Board may be the minutes of the Review Board meeting. The State Historic Preservation Officer shall submit such disputed nominations if so requested within 45 days of the State Review Board meeting by the State Review Board or the chief elected local official of the local, county or municipal political subdivision in which the property is located but need not otherwise do so. Such nominations will be substantively reviewed by the Keeper.

(m) The State Historic Preservation Officer shall also submit to the Keeper nominations if so requested under the appeals process in § 60.12.

(n) If the owner of a private property or the majority of such owners for a district or single property with multiple owners have objected to the nomination prior to the submittal of a nomination, the State Historic Preservation Officer shall submit the nomination to the Keeper only for a determination of eligibility pursuant to subsection (s) of this section.

(o) The State Historic Preservation Officer signs block 12 of the nomination form if in his or her opinion the property meets the National Register criteria for evaluation. The State Historic Preservation Officer's signature in block 12 certifies that:

(1) All procedural requirements have been met;
(2) The nomination form is adequately documented;
(3) The nomination form is technically and professional correct and sufficient;
(4) In the opinion of the State Historic Preservation Officer, the property meets the National Register criteria for evaluation.

(p) When a State Historic Preservation Officer submits a nomination form for a property that he or she does not believe meets the National Register criteria for evaluation, the State Historic Preservation Officer signs a continuation sheet Form NPS 10-900a explaining his/her opinions on the eligibility of the property and certifying that:

(1) All procedural requirements have been met;
(2) The nomination form is adequately documented;
(3) The nomination form is technically and professionally correct and sufficient.

(q) Notice will be provided in the Federal Reigster that the nominated property is being considered for listing in the National Register of Historic Places as specified in § 60.13.

(r) Nominations will be included in the National Register within 45 days of receipt by the Keeper or designee unless the Keeper disapproves a nomination, an appeal is filed, or the owner of private property (or the majority of such owners for a district or single property with multiple owners) objects by notarized statements received by the Keeper prior to listing. Nominations which are technically or professionally inadequate will be returned for correction and resubmission. When a property does not appear to meet the National Register criteria for evaluation, the nomination will be returned with an explanation as to why the property does not meet the National Register criteria for evaluation.

(s) If the owner of private property (or the majority of such owners for a district or single property with multiple owners) has objected to the nomination by notarized statement prior to listing, the Keeper shall review the nomination and make a determination of eligibility within 45 days of receipt, unless an appeal is filed. The Keeper shall list such properties determined eligible in the National

Register upon receipt of notarized statements from the owner(s) of private property that the owner(s) no longer object to listing.

(t)   Any person or organization which supports or opposes the nomination of a property by a State Historic Preservation Officer may petition the Keeper during the nomination process either to accept or reject a nomination. The petitioner must state the grounds of the petition and request in writing that the Keeper substantively review the nomination. Such petitions received by the Keeper prior to the listing of a property in the National Register or a determination of its eligibility where the private owners object to listing will be considered by the Keeper and the nomination will be substantively reviewed.

(u)   State Historic Preservation Officers are required to inform the property owners and the chief elected local official when properties are listed in the National Register. In the case of a nomination where there are more than 50 property owners, they may be notified of the entry in the National Register by the same general notice stated in § 60.6(d). States which notify all property owners individually of entries in the National Register need not publish a general notice.

(v)   In the case of nominations where the owner of private property (or the majority of such owners for a district or single property with multiple owners) has objected and the Keeper has determined the nomination eligible for the National Register, the State Historic Preservation Officer shall notify the appropriate chief elected local official and the owner(s) of such property of this determination. The general notice may be used for properties with more than 50 owners as described in § 60.6(d) or the State Historic Preservation Officer may notify the owners individually.

(w)   If subsequent to nomination a State makes major revisions to a nomination or renominates a property rejected by the Keeper, the State Historic Preservation Officer shall notify the affected property owner(s) and the chief elected local official of the revisions or renomination in the same manner as the original notification for the nomination, but need not resubmit the nomination to the State Review Board. Comments received and notarized statements of objection must be forwarded to the Keeper along with the revisions or renomination. The State Historic Preservation Officer also certifies by the resubmittal that the affected property owner(s) and the chief elected local official have been renotified. "Major revisions" as used herein means revisions of boundaries or important substantive revisions to the nomination which could be expected to change the ultimate outcome as to whether or not the property is listed in the National Register by the Keeper.

(x)   Notwithstanding any provision hereof to the contrary, the State Historic Preservation Officer in the nomination notification process or otherwise need not make available to any person or entity (except a Federal agency planning a project, the property owner, the chief elected local official of the political jurisdiction in which the property is located, and the local historic preservation commission for certified local governments) specific information relating to the location of properties proposed to be nominated to, or listed in, the National Register if he or she determines that the disclosure of specific information would create a risk of destruction or harm to such properties.

(y)   With regard to property under Federal ownership or control, completed nomination forms shall be submitted to the Federal Preservation Officer for review and comment. The Federal Preservation Officer, may approve the nomination and forward it to the Keeper of the National Register of Historic Places, National Park Service, United States Department of the Interior, Washington, D.C. 20240.

[46 FR 56187, Nov. 16, 1981, as amended at 48 FR 46308, October 12, 1983]

§§ 60.7–60.8 [Reserved]

§ 60.9. Nominations by Federal agencies.

(a) The National Historic Preservation Act of 1966, as amended, requires that, with the advice of the Secretary and in cooperation with the State Historic Preservation Officer of the State involved, each Federal agency shall establish a program to locate, inventory and nominate to the Secretary all properties under the agency's ownership or control that appear to qualify for inclusion on the National Register. Section 2(a) of Executive Order 11593 provides that Federal agencies shall locate, inventory, and nominate to the Secretary of the Interior all sites, buildings, districts, and objects under their jurisdiction or control that appear to qualify for listing on the National Register of Historic Places. Additional responsibilities of Federal agencies are detailed in the National Historic Preservation Act of 1966, as amended, Executive Order 11593, the National Environmental Policy Act of 1969, the Archeological and Historic Preservation Act of 1974, and procedures developed pursuant to these authorities, and other related legislation.

(b) Nomination forms are prepared under the supervision of the Federal Preservation Officer designated by the head of a Federal agency to fulfill agency responsibilities under the National Historic Preservation Act of 1966, as amended.

(c) Completed nominations are submitted to the appropriate State Historic Preservation Officer for review and comment regarding the adequacy of the nomination, the significance of the property and its eligibility for the National Register. The chief elected local officials of the county (or equivalent governmental unit) and municipal political jurisdiction in which the property is located are notified and given 45 days in which to comment. The State Historic Preservation Officer signs block 12 of the nomination form with his/her recommendation.

(d) After receiving the comments of the State Historic Preservation Officer, and chief elected local official, or if there has been no response within 45 days, the Federal Preservation Officer may approve the nomination and forward it to the Keeper of the National Register of Historic Places, National Park Service, United States Department of the Interior, Washington, D.C. 20240. The Federal Preservation Officer signs block 12 of the nomination form if in his or her opinion the property meets the National Register criteria for evaluation. The Federal Preservation Officer's signature in block 12 certifies that:

(1) All procedural requirements have been met;

(2) The nomination form is adequately documented;

(3) The nomination form is technically and professionally correct and sufficient;

(4) In the opinion of the Federal Preservation Officer, the property meets the National Register criteria for evaluation.

(e) When a Federal Preservation Officer submits a nomination form for a property that he or she does not believe meets the National Register criteria for evaluation, the Federal Preservation Officer signs a continuation sheet Form NPS 10-900a explaining his/her opinions on the eligibility of the property and certifying that:
    (1) All procedural requirements have been met;
    (2) The nomination form is adequately documented;
    (3) The nomination form is technically and professionally correct and sufficient.

(f) The comments of the State Historic Preservation Officer and chief local official are appended to the nomination, or, if there are no comments from the State Historic Preservation Officer an explanation is attached. Concurrent nominations (see § 60.10) cannot be submitted, however, until the nomination has been considered by the State in accord with Sec. 60.6 supra. Comments received by the State concerning concurrent nominations and notarized statements of objection must be submitted with the nomination.

(g) Notice will be provided in the Federal Register that the nominated property is being considered for listing in the National Register of Historic Places in accord with § 60.13.

(h) Nominations will be included in the National Register within 45 days of receipt by the Keeper or designee unless the Keeper disapproves such nomination or an appeal is filed. Nominations which are technically or professionally inadequate will be returned for correction and resubmission. When a property does not appear to meet the National Register criteria for evaluation, the nomination will be returned with an explanation as to why the property does not meet the National Register criteria for evaluation.

(l) Any person or organization which supports or opposes the nomination of a property by a Federal Preservation Officer may petition the Keeper during the nomination process either to accept or reject a nomination. The petitioner must state the grounds of the petition and request in writing that the Keeper substantively review the nomination. Such petition received by the Keeper prior to the listing of a property in the National Register or a determination of its eligibility where the private owner(s) object to listing will be considered by the Keeper and the nomination will be substantively reviewed.

§ 60.10. Concurrent State and Federal nominations.

(a) State Historic Preservation Officers and Federal Preservation Officers are encouraged to cooperate in locating, inventorying, evaluating, and nominating all properties possessing historical, architectural archeological, or cultural value, Federal agencies may nominate properties where a portion of the property is not under Federal ownership or control.

(b) When a portion of the area included in a Federal nomination is not located on land under the ownership or control of the Federal agency, but is an integral part of the cultural resource, the completed nomination form shall be sent to the State Historical Preservation Officer for notification to property owners, to give owners of private property an opportunity to concur in or object to the nomination, to solicit written comments and for submission to the State Review Board pursuant to the procedures in § 60.6.

(c) If the State Historic Preservation Officer and the State Review Board agree that the nomination meets the National Register criteria for evaluation, the nomination is signed by the State Historic Preservation Officer and returned to the Federal agency initiating the nomination. If the State Historic Preservation Officer and the State Review Board disagree, the nomination shall be returned to the Federal agency with the opinions of the State Historic Preservation Officer and the State Review Board concerning the adequacy of the nomination and whether or not the property meets the criteria for evaluation. The opinion of the State Review Board may be the minutes of the State Review Board meeting. The State Historic Preservation Officer's signed opinion and comments shall confirm to the Federal agency that the State nomination procedures have been fulfilled including notification requirements. Any comments received by the State shall be included with the letter as shall any notarized statements objecting to the listing of private property.

(d) If the owner of any privately owned property, (or a majority of the owners of such properties within a district or single property with multiple owners) objects to such inclusion by notarized statements) the Federal Historic Preservation Officer shall submit the nomination to the Keeper for review and a determination of eligibility. Comments, opinions, and notarized statements of objection shall be submitted with the nomination.

(e) The State Historic Preservation Officer shall notify the nonfederal owners when a concurrent nomination is listed or determined eligible for the National Register as required in § 60.6.

§ 60.11. Requests for nominations.

(a) The State Historic Preservation Officer or Federal Preservation Officer as appropriate shall respond in writing within 60 days to any person or organization submitting a completed National Register nomination form or requesting consideration for any previously prepared nomination form on record with the State or Federal agency. The response shall provide a technical opinion concerning whether or not the property is adequately documented and appears to meet the National Register criteria for evaluation in § 60.4. If the nomination form is determined to be inadequately documented, the nominating authority shall provide the applicant with an explanation of the reasons for that determination.

(b) If the nomination form does not appear to be adequately documented, upon receiving notification, it shall be the responsibility of the applicant to provide necessary additional documentation.

(c) If the nomination form appears to be adequately documented and if the property appears to meet the National Register criteria for evaluation, the State Historic Preservation Officer shall comply with the notification requirements in Section 60.6 and schedule the property for presentation at the earliest possible State Review Board meeting. Scheduling shall be consistent with the State's established priorities for processing nominations. If the nomination form is adequately documented, but the property does not appear to meet National Register criteria for evaluation, the State Historic Preservation Officer need not process the nomination, unless so requested by the Keeper pursuant to § 60.12.

(d) The State Historic Preservation Officer's response shall advise the applicant of the property's position in accord with the State's priorities for processing nominations and of the approximate date the applicant can expect its consideration by the State Review Board. The State Historic Preservation Officer shall also provide notice to the applicant of the time and place of the Review Board meeting at least 30 but not more than 75 days before the meeting, as well as complying with the notification requirements in § 60.6.

(e) Upon action on a nomination by the State Review Board, the State Historic Preservation Officer shall, within 90 days, submit the nomination to the National Park Service, or, if the State Historic Preservation Officer does not consider the property eligible for the National Register, so advise the applicant within 45 days.

(f) If the applicant substantially revises a nomination form as a result of comments by the State or Federal agency, it may be treated by the State Historic Preservation Officer or Federal Preservation Officer as a new submittal and processed in accord with the requirements in this section.

(g) The Federal Preservation Officer shall request the comments of the State Historic Preservation Officer and notify the applicant in writing within 90 days of receipt of an adequately documented nomination form as to whether the Federal agency will nominate the property. The Federal Preservation Officer shall submit an adequately documented nomination to the National Park Service unless in his or her opinion the property is not eligible for the National Register.

[48 FR 46308, Oct. 12, 1983]

§ 60.12. Nomination appeals.

(a) Any person or local government may appeal to the Keeper the failure or refusal of a nominating authority to nominate a property that the person or local government considers to meet the National Register criteria for evaluation upon decision of a nominating authority to not nominate a property for any reason when requested pursuant to § 60.11, or upon failure of a State Historic Preservation Officer to nominate a property recommended by the State Review Board. (This action differs from the procedure for appeals during the review of a nomination by the National Park Service where an individual or organization may "petition the Keeper during the nomination process," as specified in §§ 60.6(t) and 60.9(i). Upon receipt of such petition the normal 45-day review period will be extended for 30 days beyond the date of the petition to allow the petitioner to provide additional documentation for review.)

(b) Such appeal shall include a copy of the nomination form and documentation previously submitted to the State Historic Preservation Officer or Federal Preservation Officer, an explanation of why the applicant is submitting the appeal in accord with this section and shall include pertinent correspondence from the State Historic Preservation Officer or Federal Preservation Officer.

(c) The Keeper will respond to the appellant and the State Historic Preservation Officer or Federal Preservation Officer with a written explanation either denying or sustaining the appeal within 45 days of receipt. If the appeal is sustained, the Keeper will:

(1) request the State Historic Preservation Officer to submit the nomination to the Keeper within 15 days if the nomination has completed the proce-

dural requirements for nomination as described in Section 60.6 or 60.9 except that concurrence of the State Review Board, State Historic Preservation Officer or Federal Preservation Officer is not required; or

(2) if the nomination has not completed these procedural requirements, request the State Historic Preservation Officer or Federal Preservation Officer to promptly process the nomination pursuant to Section 60.6 or 60.9 and submit the nomination to the Keeper without delay.

(d) State Historic Preservation Officers and Federal Preservation Officers shall process and submit such nominations if so requested by the Keeper pursuant to this section. The Secretary reserves the right to list properties in the National Register or determine properties eligible for such listing on his own motion when necessary to assist in the preservation of historic resources and after notifying the owner and appropriate parties and allowing for a 30-day comment period.

(e) No person shall be considered to have exhausted administrative remedies with respect to failure to nominate a property to the National Register until he or she has complied with procedures set forth in this section. The decision of the Keeper is the final administrative action on such appeals.

[48 FR 46308, Oct. 12, 1983]

§ 60.13. Publication in the "Federal Register" and other NPS notification.

(a) When a nomination is received, NPS will publish notice in the Federal Register that the property is being considered for listing in the National Register. A 15-day commenting period from date of publication will be provided. When necessary to assist in the preservation of historic properties this 15-day period may be shortened or waived.

(b) NPS shall notify the appropriate State Historic Preservation Officer, Federal Preservation Officer, person or local government when there is no approved State program of the listing of the property in the National Register and will publish notice of the listing in the Federal Register.

(c) In nominations where the owner of any privately owned property (or a majority of the owners of such properties within a district or single property within a district or single property with multiple owners) has objected and the Keeper has determined the nomination eligible for the National Register, NPS shall notify the State Historic Preservation Officer, the Federal Preservation Officer (for Federal or concurrent nominations), the person or local government where there is no approved State Historic Preservation Program and the Advisory Council on Historic Preservation. NPS will publish notice of the determination of eligibility in the Federal Register.

§ 60.14. Changes and revisions to properties listed in the National Register.

(a) *Boundary changes.*

(1) A boundary alteration shall be considered as a new property nomination. All forms, criteria and procedures used in nominating a property to the National Register must be used. In the case of boundary enlargements only those owners in the newly nominated as yet unlisted area need be notified and will be

counted in determining whether a majority of private owners object to listing. In the case of a diminution of a boundary, owners shall be notified as specified in § 60.15 concerning removing properties from the National Register. A professionally justified recommendation by the State Historic Preservation Officer, Federal Preservation Officer, or person or local government where there is no approved State Historic Preservation Program shall be presented to NPS. During this process, the property is not taken off the National Register. If the Keeper or his or her designee finds the recommendation in accordance with the National Register criteria for evaluation, the change will be accepted. If the boundary change is not accepted, the old boundaries will remain. Boundary revisions may be appealed as provided for in §§ 60.12 and 60.15.

(2) Four justifications exist for altering a boundary: Professional error in the initial nomination, loss of historic integrity, recognition of additional significance, additional research documenting that a larger or smaller area should be listed. No enlargement of a boundary should be recommended unless the additional area possesses previously unrecognized significance in American history, architecture, archeology, engineering or culture. No diminution of a boundary should be recommended unless the properties being removed do not meet the National Register criteria for evaluation. Any proposal to alter a boundary has to be documented in detail including photographing the historic resources falling between the existing boundary and the other proposed boundary.

(b) *Relocating properties listed in the National Register.*

(1) Properties listed in the National Register should be moved only when there is no feasible alternative for preservation. When a property is moved, every effort should be made to reestablish its historic orientation, immediate setting, and general environment.

(2) (2) If it is proposed that a property listed in the National Register be moved and the State Historic Preservation Officer, Federal agency for a property under Federal ownership or control, or person or local government where there is no approved State Historic Preservation Program, wishes the property to remain in the National Register during and after the move, the State Historic Preservation Officer or Federal Preservation Officer having ownership or control or person or local government where there is no approved State Historic Preservation Program, shall submit documentation to NPS prior to the move. The documentation shall discuss:

    (i) The reasons for the move;
    (ii) the effect on the property's historical integrity;
    (iii) the new setting and general environment of the proposed site, including evidence that the proposed site does not possess historical or archeological significance that would be adversely affected by the intrusion of the property; and
    (iv) photographs showing the proposed location.

(3) Any such proposal with respect to the new location shall follow the required notification procedures, shall be approved by the State Review Board if it is a State nomination and shall continue to follow normal review procedures. The Keeper shall also follow the required notification procedures for nominations. The Keeper shall respond to a properly documented request within 45 days of receipt from the State Historic Preservation Officer or Federal Preservation Officer, or within 90 days of receipt from a person or local government where there is no

approved State Historic Preservation Program, concerning whether or not the move is approved. Once the property is moved, the State Historical Preservation Officer, Federal Preservation Officer, or person or local government where there is no approved State Historic Preservation Program shall submit to the Keeper for review

    (i)   a letter notifying him or her of the date the property was moved;

    (ii)   photographs of the property on its new site; and

    (iii)   revised maps, including a U.S.G.S. map;

    (iv)   acreage, and

    (v)   verbal boundary description.

The Keeper shall respond to a properly documented submittal within 45 days of receipt with the final decision on whether the property will remain in the National Register. If the Keeper approves the move, the property will remain in the National Register during and after the move unless the integrity of the property is in some unforeseen manner destroyed. If the Keeper does not approve the move, the property will be automatically deleted from the National Register when moved. In cases of properties removed from the National Register, if the State, Federal agency, or person or local government where there is no approved State Historic Preservation Program has neglected to obtain prior approval for the move or has evidence that previously unrecognized significance exists, or has accrued, the State, Federal agency, person or local government may resubmit a nomination for the property.

    (4)   In the event that a property is moved, deletion from the National Register will be automatic unless the above procedures are followed prior to the move. If the property has already been moved, it is the responsibility of the State, Federal agency or person or local government which nominated the property to notify the National Park Service. Assuming that the State, Federal agency or person or local government wishes to have the structure reentered in the National Register, it must be nominated again on new forms which should discuss:

    (i)   the reasons for the move;

    (ii)   the effect on the property's historical integrity, and

    (iii)   the new setting and general environment, including evidence that the new site does not possess historical or archeological significance that would be adversely affected by intrusion of the property.

In addition, new photography, acreage, verbal boundary description and a U.S.G.S. map showing the structure at its new location must be sent along with the revised nomination. Any such nomination submitted by a State must be approved by the State Review Board.

    (5)   Properties moved in a manner consistent with the comments of the Advisory Council on Historic Preservation, in accord with its procedures (36 CFR Part 800), are granted as exception to § 60.12(b). Moving of properties in accord with the Advisory Council's procedures should be dealt with individually in each memorandum of agreement. In such cases, the State Historic Preservation Officer or the Federal Preservation Officer, for properties under Federal ownership or control, shall notify the Keeper of the new location after the move including new documentation as dscribed above.

§ 60.15. Removing properties from the National Register

(a) Grounds for removing properties from the National Register are as follows:

(1) The property has ceased to meet the criteria for listing in the National Register because the qualities which caused it to be originally listed have been lost or destroyed, or such qualities were lost subsequent to nomination and prior to listing;

(2) additional information shows that the property does not meet the National Register criteria for evaluation;

(3) error in professional judgment as to whether property meets the criteria for evaluation; or

(4) prejudicial procedural error in the nomination or listing process. Properties removed from the National Register for procedural error shall be considered for listing by the Keeper after correction of the error or errors by the State Historic Preservation Officer, Federal Preservation Officer, person or local government which originally nominated the property, or by the Keeper, as appropriate. The procedures set forth for nominations shall be followed in such reconsiderations. Any property or district removed from the National Register for procedural deficiencies in the nomination and/or listing process shall automatically be considered eligible for inclusion in the National Register without further action and will be published as such in the Federal Register.

(b) Properties listed in the National Register prior to December 13, 1980, may only be removed from the National Register on the grounds established in paragraph (a)(1) of this section.

(c) Any person or organization may petition in writing for removal of a property from the National Register by setting forth the reasons the property should be removed on the grounds established in paragraph (a) of this section. With respect to nominations determined eligible for the National Register because the owners of private property object to listing, anyone may petition for reconsideration of whether or not the property meets the criteria for evaluation using these procedures. Petitions for removal are submitted to the Keeper by the State Historic Preservation Officer for State nominations, the Federal Preservation Officer for Federal nominations, and directly to the Keeper from persons or local governments where there is no approved State Historic Preservation Program.

(d) Petitions submitted by persons or local governments where there is no approved State Historic Preservation Program shall include a list of the owner(s). In such cases the Keeper shall notify the affected owner(s) and the chief elected local official and give them an opportunity to comment. For approved State programs, the State Historic Preservation Officer shall notify the affected owner(s) and chief elected local official and give them an opportunity to comment prior to submitting a petition for removal. The Federal Preservation Officer shall notify and obtain the comments of the appropriate State Historic Preservation Officer prior to forwarding an appeal to NPS. All comments and opinions shall be submitted with the petition.

(e) The State Historic Preservation Officer or Federal Preservation Officer shall shall respond in writing within 45 days of receipt to petitioners for removal of property from the National Register. The response shall advise the petitioner of the State Historic Preservation Officer's or Federal Preservation Officer's views on the petition.

(f) A petitioner desiring to pursue his removal request must notify the State Historic Preservation Officer or the Federal Preservation Officer in writing within 45 days of receipt of the written views on the petition.

(g) The State Historic Preservation Officer may elect to have a property considered for removal according to the State's nomination procedures unless the petition is on procedural grounds and shall schedule it for consideration by the State Review Board as quickly as all notification requirements can be completed following procedures outlined in § 60.6, or the State Historic Preservation Officer may elect to forward the petition for removal to the Keeper with his or her comments without State Review Board consideration.

(h) Within 15 days after receipt of the petitioner's notification of intent to pursue his removal request, the State Historic Preservation Officer shall notify the petitioner in writing either that the State Review Board will consider the petition on a specified date or that the petition will be forwarded to the Keeper after notification requirements have been completed. The State Historic Preservation Officer shall forward the petitions to the Keeper for review within 15 days after notification requirements or Review Board consideration, if applicable, have been completed.

(i) Within 15 days after receipt of the petitioner notification of intent to pursue his petition, the Federal Preservation Officer shall forward the petition with his or her comments and those of the State Historic Preservation Officer to the Keeper.

(j) The Keeper shall respond to a petition for removal within 45 days of receipt, except where the Keeper must notify the owners and the chief elected local official. In such cases the Keeper shall respond within 90 days of receipt. The Keeper shall notify the petitioner and the applicable State Historic Preservation Officer, Federal Preservation Officer, or person or local government where there is no approved State Historic Preservation Program, of his decision. The State Historic Preservation Officer or Federal Preservation Officer transmitting the petition shall notify the petitioner, the owner(s), and the chief elected local official in writing of the decision. The Keeper will provide such notice for petitions from persons or local governments where there is no approved State Historic Preservation Program. The general notice may be used for properties with more more than 50 owners. If the general notice is used it shall be published in one or more newspapers with general circulation in the area of the nomination.

(k) The Keeper may remove a property from the National Register on his own motion on the grounds established in paragraph (a) of this section, except for those properties listed in the National Register prior to December 13, 1980, which may only be removed from the National Register on the grounds established in paragraph (a)(1) of this section. In such cases, the Keeper will notify the nominating authority, the affected owner(s) and the applicable chief elected local official and provide them an opportunity to comment. Upon removal, the Keeper will notify the nominating authority of the basis for the removal. The state Historic Preservation Officer, Federal Preservation Officer, or person or local government which nominated the property shall notify the owner(s) and the chief elected local official of the removal.

(l) No person shall be considered to have exhausted administrative remedies with respect to removal of a property from the National Register until the Keeper has denied a petition for removal pursuant to this section.

Appendix J

Advisory Council on Historic Preservation, Regulations Implementing Section 106 of the National Historic Preservation Act, 36 C.F.R. Part 800

SUBPART A—BACKGROUND AND POLICY

§ 800.1 Authorities, purposes, and participants.

(a) *Authorities.* Section 106 of the National Historic Preservation Act requires a Federal agency head with jurisdiction over a federal, federally assisted, or federally licensed undertaking to take into account the effects of the agency's undertakings on properties included in or eligible for the National Register of Historic Places and, prior to approval of an undertaking, to afford the Advisory Council on Historic Preservation a reasonable opportunity to comment on the undertaking. Section 110(f) of the Act requires that federal agency heads, to the maximum extent possible, undertake such planning and actions as may be necessary to minimize harm to any National Historic

Landmark that may be directly and adversely affected by an undertaking and, prior to approval of such undertaking, afford the Council a reasonable opportunity to comment. These regulations define the process used by a federal agency to meet these responsibilities, commonly called the Section 106 process.

(b) *Purposes of the Section 106 Process.* The Council seeks through the Section 106 process to accommodate historic preservation concerns with the needs of federal undertakings. It is designed to identify potential conflicts between the two and to help resolve such conflicts in the public interest. The Council encourages this accommodation through consultation among the Agency Official, the State Historic Preservation Officer, and other interested persons during the early stages of planning. The Council regards the consultation process as an effective means for reconciling the interests of the consulting parties.

Integration of the Section 106 process into the normal administrative process used by agencies for project planning ensures early, systematic consideration of historic preservation issues. To this end, the Council encourages agencies to examine their administrative processes to see that they provide adequately for the efficient identification and consideration of historic properties, that they provide for participation by the State Historic Preservation Officer and others interested in historic preservation, that they provide for timely requests for Council comment, and that they promote cost-effective implementation of the Section 106 process. When impediments are found to exist in the agency's administrative process, the agency is encouraged to consult with the Council to develop special Section 106 procedures suited to the agency's needs.

(c) *Participants in the Section 106 Process*.

(1) *Consulting parties.* Consulting parties are the primary participants in the Section 106 process whose responsibilities are defined by these regulations. Consulting parties may include:

(i) *Agency Official.* The Agency Official with jurisdiction over an undertaking has legal responsibility for complying with Section 106. It is the responsibility of the Agency Official to identify and evaluate affected historic properties, assess an undertaking's effect upon them, and afford the Council its comment opportunity. The Agency Official may use the services of grantees, applicants, consultants, or designees to prepare the necessary information and analyses, but remains responsible for Section 106 compliance. The Agency Official should involve applicants for federal assistance or approval in the Section 106 process as appropriate in the manner set forth below.

(ii) *State Historic Preservation Officer.* The State Historic Preservation Officer coordinates State participation in the implementation of the National Historic Preservation Act and is a key participant in the Section 106 process. The role of the State Historic Preservation Officer is to consult with and assist the Agency Official when identifying historic properties, assessing effects upon them, and considering alternatives to avoid or reduce those effects. The State Historic Preservation Officer reflects the interests of the state and its citizens in the preservation of their cultural heritage and helps the Agency Official identify those persons interested in an undertaking and its effects upon historic properties. When the State Historic Preservation Officer declines to participate or does not respond within 30 days to a written request for participation, the Agency Official shall consult with the Council, without the State Historic Preservation Officer, to complete the Section 106 process. The State Historic Preservation Officer may assume primary responsibility for reviewing Federal undertakings in the State by agreement with the Council as prescribed in Section 800.7 of these regulations.

(iii) *Council.* The Council is responsible for commenting to the Agency Official on an undertaking that affects historic properties. The official authorized to carry out the Council's responsibilities under each provision of the regulations is set forth in a separate, internal delegation of authority.

(2) *Interested Persons.* Interested persons are those organizations and individuals that are concerned with the effects of an undertaking on historic properties. Certain provisions in these regulations require that particular interested persons be invited to become consulting parties under certain circumstances. In addition, whenever the Agency Official, the State Historic Preservation Officer, and the Council, if participating, agree that active participation of an interested person will advance the objectives of Section 106, they may invite that person to become a consulting party. Interested persons may include:

(i) *Local Governments.* Local governments are encouraged to take an active role in the Section 106 process when undertakings affect historic properties within their jurisdiction. When a local government has legal responsibility for Section 106 compliance under programs such as the Community Development Block Grant Program, participation as a consulting party is required. When no such legal responsibility exists, the extent of local government participation is at the discretion of local government officials. If the State Historic Preservation Officer, the appropriate local government, and the Council agree, a local government whose historic preservation program has been certified pursuant to Section 101(c)(1) of the Act may assume any of the duties that are given to the State Historic Preservation Officer by these regulations or that originate from agreements concluded under these regulations.

(ii) *Applicants for Federal Assistance, Permits, and Licenses.* When the undertaking subject to review under Section 106 is proposed by an applicant for Federal assistance or for a Federal permit or license, the applicant may choose to participate in the Section 106 process in the manner prescribed in these regulations.

(iii) *Indian Tribes.* The Agency Official, the State Historic Preservation Officer, and the Council should be sensitive to the special concerns of Indian tribes in historic preservation issues, which often extend beyond Indian lands to other historic properties. When an undertaking will affect Indian lands, the Agency Official shall invite the governing body of the responsible tribe to be a consulting party and to concur in any agreement. When an Indian tribe has established formal procedures relating to historic preservation, the Agency Official, State Historic Preservation Officer, and Council shall, to the extent feasible, carry out responsibilities under these regulations consistent with such procedures. An Indian tribe may participate in activities under these regulations in lieu of the State Historic Preservation Officer with respect to undertakings affecting its lands, provided the Indian tribe so requests, the State Historic Preservation Officer concurs, and the Council finds that the Indian tribe's procedures meet the purposes of these regulations. When an undertaking may affect properties of historic value to an Indian tribe on non-Indian lands, the consulting parties shall afford such tribe the opportunity to participate as interested persons. Traditional cultural leaders and other Native Americans are considered to be interested persons with respect to undertakings that may affect historic properties of significance to such persons.

(iv) *The Public.* The Council values the views of the public on historic preservation questions and encourages maximum public participation in the Section 106 process. The Agency Official, in the manner described below, and the State Historic Preservation Officer should seek and consider the views of the public when taking steps to identify historic properties, evaluate effects, and develop alternatives. Public participation in the Section 106 process may be fully coordinated with, and satisfied by, public participation programs carried out by Agency Officials under the authority of the National Environmental Policy Act and other pertinent statutes. Notice to the public under these statutes should adequately inform the public of preservation issues in order to elicit public views on such issues that can then be considered and resolved, when possible, in decision making. Members of the public with interests in an undertaking and its effects on historic properties should be given reasonable opportunity to have an active role in the Section 106 process.

§ 800.2 Definitions.

(a) "Act" means the National Historic Preservation Act of 1966, as amended, 16 U.S.C. §§ 470-470w-6.

(b) "Agency Official" means the federal agency head or a designee with authority over a specific undertaking, including any state or local government official who has been delegated legal responsibility for compliance with Section 106 and Section 110(f) in accordance with law.

(c) "Area of potential effects" means the geographic area or areas within which an undertaking may cause changes in the character or use of historic properties, if any such properties exist.

(d) "Council" means the Advisory Council on Historic Preservation or a Council member or employee designated to act for the Council.

(e) "Historic property" means any prehistoric or historic district, site, building, structure, or object included in, or eligible for inclusion in, the National Register. This term includes, for the purposes of these regulations, artifacts, records, and remains that are related to and located within such properties. The term "eligible for inclusion in the National Register" includes both properties formally determined as such by the Secretary of the Interior and all other properties that meet National Register listing criteria.

(f) "Indian lands" means all lands under the jurisdiction or control of an Indian tribe.

(g) "Indian tribe" means the governing body of any Indian tribe, band, nation, or other group that is recognized as an Indian tribe by the Secretary of the Interior and for which the United States holds land in trust or restricted status for that entity or its members. Such term also includes any Native village corporation, regional corporation, and Native Group established pursuant to the Alaska Native Claims Settlement Act, 43 U.S.C. § 1601, *et seq.*

(h) "Interested person" means those organizations and individuals that are concerned with the effects of an undertaking on historic properties.

(i) "Local government" means a city, county, parish, township, municipality, borough, or other general purpose political subdivision of a state.

(j) "National Historic Landmark" means a historic property that the Secretary of the Interior has designated a National Historic Landmark.

(k) "National Register" means the National Register of Historic Places maintained by the Secretary of the Interior.

(l) "National Register Criteria" means the criteria established by the Secretary of the Interior for use in evaluating the eligibility of properties for the National Register (36 C.F.R. Part 60).

(m) "Secretary" means the Secretary of the Interior.

(n) "State Historic Preservation Officer" means the official appointed or designated pursuant to Section 101(b)(1) of the Act to administer the State historic preservation program or a representative designated to act for the State Historic Preservation Officer.

(o) "Undertaking" means any project, activity, or program that can result in changes in the character or use of historic properties, if any such historic properties are located in the area of potential effects. The project, activity, or program must be under the direct or indirect jurisdiction of a federal agency or licensed or assisted by a federal agency. Undertakings include new and continuing projects, activities, or programs and any of their elements not previously considered under Section 106.

SUBPART B—THE SECTION 106 PROCESS

§ 800.3 General.

(a) *Scope.* The procedure in this subpart guides Agency Officials, State Historic Preservation Officers, and the Council in the conduct of the Section 106 process. Alternative methods of meeting Section 106 obligations are found in Section 800.7, governing review of undertakings in States that have entered into agreements with the Council for Section 106 purposes, and Section 800.13, governing Programmatic Agreements with federal agencies that pertain to specific programs or activities. Under each of these methods, the Council encourages federal agencies to reach agreement on developing alternatives or measures to avoid or reduce effects on historic properties that meet both the needs of the undertaking and preservation concerns.

(b) *Flexible Application.* The Council recognizes that the procedures for the Agency Official set forth in these regulations may be implemented by the Agency Official in a flexible manner reflecting differing program requirements, as long as the purposes of Section 106 of the Act and these regulations are met.

(c) *Timing.* Section 106 requires the Agency Official to complete the Section 106 process prior to the approval of the expenditure of any federal funds on the undertaking or prior to the issuance of any license or permit. The Council does not interpret this language to bar an Agency Official from expending funds on or authorizing nondestructive planning activities preparatory to an undertaking before complying with Section 106, or to prohibit phased compliance at different stages in planning. The Agency Official should ensure that the Section 106 process is initiated early in the planning stages of the undertaking, when the widest feasible range of alternatives is open for consideration. The Agency Official should establish a schedule for completing the Section 106 process that is consistent with the planning and approval schedule for the undertaking.

§ 800.4 Identifying historic properties.

(a) *Assessing Information Needs*.

(1) Following a determination by the Agency Official that a proposed project, activity, or program constitutes an undertaking and after establishing the undertaking's area of potential effects, the Agency Official shall:

(i) Review existing information on historic properties potentially affected by the undertaking, including any data concerning the likelihood that unidentified historic properties exist in the area of potential effects;

(ii) Request the views of the State Historic Preservation Officer on further actions to identify historic properties that may be affected; and

(iii) Seek information in accordance with agency planning processes from local governments, Indian tribes, public and private organizations, and other parties likely to have knowledge of or concerns with historic properties in the area.

(2) Based on this assessment, the Agency Official should determine any need for further actions, such as field surveys and predictive modeling, to identify historic properties.

(b) *Locating Historic Properties*. In consultation with the State Historic Preservation Officer, the Agency Official shall make a reasonable and good faith effort to identify historic properties that may be affected by the undertaking and gather sufficient information to evaluate the eligibility of these properties for the National Register. Efforts to identify historic properties should follow the Secretary's "Standards and Guidelines for Archeology and Historic Preservation" (48 FR 44716) and agency programs to meet the requirements of Section 110(a)(2) of the Act.

(c) *Evaluating Historical Significance*.

(1) In consultation with the State Historic Preservation Officer and following the Secretary's Standards and Guidelines for Evaluation, the Agency Official shall apply the National Register Criteria to properties that may be affected by the undertaking and that have not been previously evaluated for National Register eligibility. The passage of time or changing perceptions of significance may justify reevaluation of properties that were previously determined to be eligible or ineligible.

(2) If the Agency Official and the State Historic Preservation Officer agree that a property is eligible under the criteria, the property shall be considered eligible for the National Register for Section 106 purposes.

(3) If the Agency Official and the State Historic Preservation Officer agree that the criteria are not met, the property shall be considered not eligible for the National Register for Section 106 purposes.

(4) If the Agency Official and the State Historic Preservation Officer do not agree, or if the Council or the Secretary so request, the Agency Official shall obtain a determination from the Secretary of the Interior pursuant to applicable National Park Service regulations.

(5) If the State Historic Preservation Officer does not provide views, then the State Historic Preservation Officer is presumed to agree with the Agency Official's determination for the purpose of this subsection.

(d) *When No Historic Properties Are Found.* If the Agency Official determines in accordance with Sections 800.4(a)-(c) that there are no historic properties that may be affected by the undertaking, the Agency Official shall provide documentation of this finding to the State Historic Preservation Officer. The Agency Official should notify interested persons and parties known to be interested in the undertaking and its possible effects on historic properties and make the documentation available to the public. In these circumstances, the Agency Official is not required to take further steps in the Section 106 process.

(e) *When Historic Properties Are Found.* If there are historic properties that the undertaking may affect, the Agency Official shall assess the effects in accordance with Section 800.5.

§ 800.5 Assessing effects.

(a) *Applying the Criteria of Effect.* In consultation with the State Historic Preservation Officer, the Agency Official shall apply the Criteria of Effect (Section 800.9(a)) to historic properties that may be affected, giving consideration to the views, if any, of interested persons.

(b) *When No Effect Is Found.* If the Agency Official finds the undertaking will have no effect on historic properties, the Agency Official shall notify the State Historic Preservation Officer and interested persons who have made their concerns known to the Agency Official and document the finding, which shall be available for public inspection. Unless the State Historic Preservation Officer objects within 15 days of receiving such notice, the Agency Official is not required to take any further steps in the Section 106 process. If the State Historic Preservation Officer files a timely objection, then the procedures described in Section 800.5(c) are followed.

(c) *When An Effect Is Found.* If an effect on historic properties is found, the Agency Official, in consultation with the State Historic Preservation Officer, shall apply the Criteria of Adverse Effect (Section 800.9(b)) to determine whether the effect of the undertaking should be considered adverse.

(d) *When the Effect Is Not Considered Adverse.*

(1) If the Agency Official finds the effect is not adverse, the Agency Official shall:

(i) Obtain the State Historic Preservation Officer's concurrence with the finding and notify and submit to the Council summary documentation, which shall be available for public inspection; or

(ii) Submit the finding with necessary documentation (Section 800.8(a)) to the Council for a 30-day review period and notify the State Historic Preservation Officer.

(2) If the Council does not object to the finding of the Agency Official within 30 days of receipt of notice, or if the Council objects but proposes changes that the Agency Official accepts, the Agency Official is not required to take any further steps in the Section 106 process other than to comply with any agreement with the State Historic Preservation Officer or Council concerning the undertaking. If the Council objects and the Agency Official does not agree

with changes proposed by the Council, then the effect shall be considered as adverse.

(e) *When the Effect Is Adverse.* If an adverse effect on historic properties is found, the Agency Official shall notify the Council and shall consult with the State Historic Preservation Officer to seek ways to avoid or reduce the effects on historic properties. Either the Agency Official or the State Historic Preservation Officer may request the Council to participate. The Council may participate in the consultation without such a request.

(1) *Involving Interested Persons.* Interested persons shall be invited to participate as consulting parties as follows when they so request:

(i) The head of a local government when the undertaking may affect historic properties within the local government's jurisdiction;

(ii) The representative of an Indian tribe in accordance with Section 800.1(c)(2)(iii);

(iii) Applicants for or holders of grants, permits, or licenses, and owners of affected lands; and

(iv) Other interested persons when jointly determined appropriate by the Agency Official, the State Historic Preservation Officer, and the Council, if participating.

(2) *Documentation.* The Agency Official shall provide each of the consulting parties with the documentation set forth in Section 800.8(b) and such other documentation as may be developed in the course of consultation.

(3) *Informing the Public.* The Agency Official shall provide an adequate opportunity for members of the public to receive information and express their views. The Agency Official is encouraged to use existing agency public involvement procedures to provide this opportunity. The Agency Official, State Historic Preservation Officer, or the Council may meet with interested members of the public or conduct a public information meeting for this purpose.

(4) *Agreement.* If the Agency Official and the State Historic Preservation Officer agree upon how the effects will be taken into account, they shall execute a Memorandum of Agreement. When the Council participates in the consultation, it shall execute the Memorandum of Agreement along with the Agency Official and the State Historic Preservation Officer. When the Council has not participated in consultation, the Memorandum of Agreement shall be submitted to the Council for comment in accordance with Section 800.6(a). As appropriate, the Agency Official, the State Historic Preservation Officer, and the Council, if participating, may agree to invite other consulting parties to concur in the agreement.

(5) *Amendments.* The Agency Official, the State Historic Preservation Officer, and the Council, if it was a signatory to the original agreement, may subsequently agree to an amendment to the Memorandum of Agreement. When the Council is not a party to the Memorandum of Agreement, or the Agency Official and the State Historic Preservation Officer cannot agree on changes to the Memorandum of Agreement, the proposed changes shall be submitted to the Council for comment in accordance with Section 800.6.

(6) *Ending Consultation.* The Council encourages Agency Officials and State Historic Preservation Officers to utilize the consultation process to the fullest extent practicable. After initiating consultation to seek ways to reduce or avoid effects on historic properties, the State Historic Preservation Officer, the Agency Official, or the Council, at its discretion, may state that

further consultation will not be productive and thereby terminate the consultation process. The Agency Official shall then request the Council's comments in accordance with Section 800.6(b) and notify all other consulting parties of its requests.

§ 800.6 Affording the Council an opportunity to comment.

(a) *Review of a Memorandum of Agreement.*
    (1) When an Agency Official submits a Memorandum of Agreement accompanied by the documentation specified in Section 800.8(b) and (c), the Council shall have 30 days from receipt to review it. Before this review period ends, the Council shall:
        (i) Accept the Memorandum of Agreement, which concludes the Section 106 process, and inform all consulting parties; or
        (ii) Advise the Agency Official of changes to the Memorandum of Agreement that would make it acceptable; subsequent agreement by the Agency Official, the State Historic Preservation Officer, and the Council concludes the Section 106 process; or
        (iii) Decide to comment on the undertaking, in which case the Council shall provide its comments within 60 days of receiving the Agency Official's submission, unless the Agency Official agrees otherwise.
    (2) If the Agency Official, the State Historic Preservation Officer, and the Council do not reach agreement in accordance with Section 800.6(a)(1)(ii), the Agency Official shall notify the Council, which shall provide its comments within 30 days of receipt of notice.

(b) *Comment When There Is No Agreement.*
    (1) When no Memorandum of Agreement is submitted, the Agency Official shall request Council comment and provide the documentation specified in Section 800.8(d). When requested by the Agency Official, the Council shall provide its comments within 60 days of receipt of the Agency Official's request and the specified documentation.
    (2) The Agency Official shall make a good faith effort to provide reasonably available additional information concerning the undertaking and shall assist the Council in arranging an on site inspection and public meeting when requested by the Council.
    (3) The Council shall provide its comments to the head of the agency requesting comment. Copies shall be provided to the State Historic Preservation Officer, interested persons, and others as appropriate.

(c) *Response to Council Comment.*
    (1) When a Memorandum of Agreement becomes final in accordance with Section 800.6(a)(1)(i) or (ii), the Agency Official shall carry out the undertaking in accordance with the terms of the agreement. This evidences fulfillment of the agency's Section 106 responsibilities. Failure to carry out the terms of a Memorandum of Agreement requires the Agency Official to resubmit the undertaking to the Council for comment in accordance with Section 800.6.
    (2) When the Council has commented pursuant to Section 800.6(b), the Agency Official shall consider the Council's comments in reaching a final decision on the proposed undertaking. The Agency Official shall report the decision to the Council, and if possible, should do so prior to initiating the undertaking.

(d) *Foreclosure of the Council's Opportunity to Comment.*

(1) The Council may advise an Agency Official that it considers the agency has not provided the Council a reasonable opportunity to comment. The decision to so advise the Agency Official will be reached by a majority vote of the Council or by a majority vote of a panel consisting of three or more Council members with the concurrence of the Chairman.

(2) The Agency Official will be given notice and a reasonable opportunity to respond prior to a proposed Council determination that the agency has foreclosed the Council's opportunity to comment.

(e) *Public Requests to the Council.*

(1) When requested by any person, the Council shall consider an Agency Official's finding under Sections 800.4(b), 800.4(c), 800.4(d), or 800.5(b) and, within 30 days of receipt of the request, advise the Agency Official, the State Historic Preservation Officer, and the person making the request of its views of the Agency Official's finding.

(2) In light of the Council views, the Agency Official should reconsider the finding. However, an inquiry to the Council will not suspend action on an undertaking.

(3) When the finding concerns the eligibility of a property for the National Register, the Council shall refer the matter to the Secretary.

§ 800.7 Agreements with States for Section 106 reviews.

(a) *Establishment of State Agreements.*

(1) Any State Historic Preservation Officer may enter into an agreement with the Council to substitute a state review process for the procedures set forth in these regulations, provided that:

(i) The state historic preservation program has been approved by the Secretary pursuant to Section 101(b)(1) of the Act; and

(ii) The Council, after analysis of the state's review process and consideration of the views of federal and state agencies, local governments, Indian tribes, and the public, determines that the state review process is at least as effective as, and no more burdensome than, the procedures set forth in these regulations in meeting the requirements of Section 106.

(2) The Council, in analyzing a state's review process pursuant to Section 800.7(a)(1)(ii), shall:

(i) Review relevant state laws, Executive Orders, internal directives, standards, and guidelines;

(ii) Review the organization of the state's review process;

(iii) Solicit and consider the comments of federal and state agencies, local governments, Indian tribes, and the public;

(iv) Review the results of program reviews carried out by the Secretary; and

(v) Review the record of state participation in the Section 106 process.

(3) The Council will enter into an agreement with a state under this section only upon determining, at minimum, that the State has a demonstrated record of performance in the Section 106 process and the capability to administer a comparable process at the state level.

(4) A state agreement shall be developed through consultation between the State Historic Preservation Officer and the Council and concurred in by the Secretary before submission to the Council for approval. The Council may invite affected federal and state agencies, local governments, Indian tribes, and other interested persons to participate in this consultation. The agreement shall:

(i) Specify the historic preservation review process employed in the state, showing that this process is at least as effective as, and no more burdensome than, that set forth in these regulations;

(ii) Establish special provisions for participation of local governments or Indian tribes in the review of undertakings falling within their jurisdiction, when appropriate;

(iii) Establish procedures for public participation in the State review process;

(iv) Provide for Council review of actions taken under its terms, and for appeal of such actions to the Council; and

(v) Be certified by the Secretary as consistent with the Secretary's "Standards and Guidelines for Archeology and Historic Preservation."

(5) Upon concluding a state agreement, the Council shall publish notice of its execution in the Federal Register and make copies of the state agreement available to all federal agencies.

(b) *Review of Undertakings When a State Agreement Is in Effect*.

(1) When a state agreement under Section 800.7(a) is in effect, an Agency Official may elect to comply with the state review process in lieu of compliance with these regulations.

(2) At any time during review of an undertaking under a state agreement, an Agency Official may terminate such review and comply instead with Sections 800.4 through 800.6 of these regulations.

(3) At any time during review of an undertaking under a state agreement, the Council may participate. Participants are encouraged to draw upon the Council's expertise as appropriate.

(c) *Monitoring and Termination of State Agreements*.

(1) The Council shall monitor activities carried out under state agreements, in coordination with the Secretary of the Interior's approval of state programs under Section 101(b)(1) of the Act. The Council may request that the Secretary monitor such activities on its behalf.

(2) The Council may terminate a state agreement after consultation with the State Historic Preservation Officer and the Secretary.

(3) An agreement may be terminated by the State Historic Preservation Officer.

(4) When a state agreement is terminated pursuant to Section 800.7(c)(2) and (3), such termination shall have no effect on undertakings for which review under the agreement was complete or in progress at the time the termination occurred.

§ 800.8 Documentation requirements.

(a) *Finding of No Adverse Effect*. The purpose of this documentation is to provide sufficient information to explain how the Agency Official reached the finding of no adverse effect. The required documentation is as follows:

(1) A description of the undertaking, including photographs, maps, and drawings, as necessary;
(2) A description of historic properties that may be affected by the undertaking;
(3) A description of the efforts used to identify historic properties;
(4) A statement of how and why the Criteria of Adverse Effect were found inapplicable;
(5) The views of the State Historic Preservation Officer, affected local governments, Indian tribes, federal agencies, and the public, if any were provided, as well as a description of the means employed to solicit those views.

(b) *Finding of Adverse Effect*. The required documentation is as follows:
(1) A description of the undertaking, including photographs, maps, and drawings, as necessary;
(2) A description of the efforts to identify historic properties;
(3) A description of the affected historic properties, using materials already compiled during the evaluation of significance, as appropriate; and
(4) A description of the undertaking's effects on historic properties.

(c) *Memorandum of Agreement.* When a memorandum is submitted for review in accordance with Section 800.6(a)(1), the documentation, in addition to that specified in Section 800.8(b), shall also include a description and evaluation of any proposed mitigation measures or alternatives that were considered to deal with the undertaking's effects and a summary of the views of the State Historic Preservation Officer and any interested persons.

(d) *Requests for Comment When There Is No Agreement.* The purpose of this documentation is to provide the Council with sufficient information to make an independent review of the undertaking's effects on historic properties as the basis for informed and meaningful comments to the Agency Official. The required documentation is as follows:
(1) A description of the undertaking, with photographs, maps, and drawings, as necessary;
(2) A description of the efforts to identify historic properties;
(3) A description of the affected historic properties, with information on the significant characteristics of each property;
(4) A description of the effects of the undertaking on historic properties and the basis for the determinations;
(5) A description and evaluation of any alternatives or mitigation measures that the Agency Official proposes for dealing with the undertaking's effects;
(6) A description of any alternatives or mitigation measures that were considered but not chosen and the reasons for their rejection;
(7) Documentation of consultation with the State Historic Preservation Officer regarding the identification and evaluation of historic properties, assessment of effect, and any consideration of alternatives or mitigation measures;
(8) A description of the Agency Official's efforts to obtain and consider the views of affected local governments, Indian tribes, and other interested persons;
(9) The planning and approval schedule for the undertaking; and
(10) Copies or summaries of any written views submitted to the Agency Official concerning the effects of the undertaking on historic properties and alternatives to reduce or avoid those effects.

§ 800.9 Criteria of Effect and Adverse Effect.

(a) An undertaking has an effect on a historic property when the undertaking may alter characteristics of the property that may qualify the property for inclusion in the National Register. For the purpose of determining effect, alteration to features of the property's location, setting, or use may be relevant depending on a property's significant characteristics and should be considered.

(b) An undertaking is considered to have an adverse effect when the effect on a historic property may diminish the integrity of the property's location, design, setting, materials, workmanship, feeling, or association. Adverse effects on historic properties include, but are not limited to:

(1) Physical destruction, damage, or alteration of all or part of the property;

(2) Isolation of the property from or alteration of the character of the property's setting when that character contributes to the property's qualification for the National Register;

(3) Introduction of visual, audible, or atmospheric elements that are out of character with the property or alter its setting;

(4) Neglect of a property resulting in its deterioration or destruction; and

(5) Transfer, lease, or sale of the property.

(c) Effects of an undertaking that would otherwise be found to be adverse may be considered as being not adverse for the purpose of these regulations:

(1) When the historic property is of value only for its potential contribution to archeological, historical, or architectural research, and when such value can be substantially preserved through the conduct of appropriate research, and such research is conducted in accordance with applicable professional standards and guidelines;

(2) When the undertaking is limited to the rehabilitation of buildings and structures and is conducted in a manner that preserves the historical and architectural value of affected historic property through conformance with the Secretary's "Standards for Rehabilitation and Guidelines for Rehabilitating Historic Buildings"; or

(3) When the undertaking is limited to the transfer, lease, or sale of a historic property, and adequate restrictions or conditions are included to ensure preservation of the property's significant historic features.

SUBPART C—SPECIAL PROVISIONS

§ 800.10 Protecting National Historic Landmarks.

Section 110(f) of the Act requires that the Agency Official, to the maximum extent possible, undertake such planning and actions as may be necessary to minimize harm to any National Historic Landmark that may be directly and adversely affected by an undertaking. When commenting on such undertakings, the Council shall use the process set forth in Sections 800.4 through 800.6 and give special consideration to protecting National Historic Landmarks as follows:

(a) Any consultation conducted under Section 800.5(e) shall include the Council;

(b) The Council may request the Secretary under Section 213 of the Act to provide a report to the Council detailing the significance of the property, describing the effects of the undertaking on the property, and recommending measures to avoid, minimize, or mitigate adverse effects; and

(c) The Council shall report its comments, including Memoranda of Agreement, to the President, the Congress, the Secretary, and the head of the agency responsible for the undertaking.

§ 800.11 Properties discovered during implementation of an undertaking.

(a) *Planning for Discoveries.* When the Agency Official's identification efforts in accordance with Section 800.4 indicate that historic properties are likely to be discovered during implementation of an undertaking, the Agency Official is encouraged to develop a plan for the treatment of such properties if discovered and include this plan in any documentation prepared to comply with Section 800.5.

(b) *Federal Agency Responsibilities.*

(1) When an Agency Official has completed the Section 106 process and prepared a plan in accordance with Section 800.11(a), the Agency Official shall satisfy the requirements of Section 106 concerning properties discovered during implementation of an undertaking by following the plan.

(2) When an Agency Official has completed the Section 106 process without preparing a plan in accordance with Section 800.11(a) and finds after beginning to carry out the undertaking that the undertaking will affect a previously unidentified property that may be eligible for inclusion in the National Register, or affect a known historic property in an unanticipated manner, the Agency Official shall afford the Council an opportunity to comment by choosing one of the following courses of action:

    (i) Comply with Section 800.6;

    (ii) Develop and implement actions that take into account the effects of the undertaking on the property to the extent feasible and the comments from the State Historic Preservation Officer and the Council pursuant to Section 800.11(c); or

    (iii) If the property is principally of archeological value and subject to the requirements of the Archeological and Historic Preservation Act, 16 U.S.C. §§ 469 (a)-(c), comply with that Act and implementing regulations instead of these regulations.

(3) Section 106 and these regulations do not require the Agency Official to stop work on the undertaking. However, depending on the nature of the property and the undertaking's apparent effects on it, the Agency Official should make reasonable efforts to avoid or minimize harm to the property until the requirements of this section are met.

(c) *Council Comments.*

(1) When comments are requested pursuant to Section 800.11(b)(2)(i), the Council will provide its comments in a time consistent with the Agency Official's schedule, regardless of longer time periods allowed by these regulations for Council review.

(2) When an Agency Official elects to comply with Section 800.11(b)(2)(ii), the Agency Official shall notify the State Historic Preservation Officer and the Council at the earliest possible time, describe the actions proposed to take effects into account, and request the Council's comments. The Council shall provide interim comments to the Agency Official within 48 hours of the request and final comments to the Agency Official within 30 days of the request.

(3) When an Agency Official complies with Section 800.11(b)(2)(iii), the Agency Official shall provide the State Historic Preservation Officer an opportunity to comment on the work undertaken and provide the Council with a report on the work after it is undertaken.

(d) *Other Considerations*.

(1) When a newly discovered property has not previously been included in or determined eligible for the National Register, the Agency Official may assume the property to be eligible for purposes of Section 106.

(2) When a discovery occurs and compliance with this section is necessary on lands under the jurisdiction of an Indian tribe, the Agency Official shall consult with the Indian tribe during implementation of this section's requirements.

§ 800.12 Emergency undertakings.

(a) When a federal agency head proposes an emergency action and elects to waive historic preservation responsibilities in accordance with 36 C.F.R. § 78.3, the Agency Official may comply with the requirements of 36 C.F.R. Part 78 in lieu of these regulations. An Agency Official should develop plans for taking historic properties into account during emergency operations. At the request of the Agency Official, the Council will assist in the development of such plans.

(b) When an Agency Official proposes an emergency undertaking as an essential and immediate response to a disaster declared by the President or the appropriate governor, and Section 800.12(a) does not apply, the Agency Official may satisfy Section 106 by notifying the Council and the appropriate State Historic Preservation Officer of the emergency undertaking and affording them an opportunity to comment within seven days if the Agency Official considers that circumstances permit.

(c) For the purposes of activities assisted under Title I of the Housing and Community Development Act of 1974, as amended, Section 800.12(b) also applies to an imminent threat to public health or safety as a result of natural disaster or emergency declared by a local government's chief executive officer or legislative body, provided that if the Council or the State Historic Preservation Officer objects, the Agency Official shall comply with Sections 800.4 through 800.6.

(d) This section does not apply to undertakings that will not be implemented within 30 days after the disaster or emergency. Such undertakings shall be reviewed in accordance with Sections 800.4 through 800.6.

§ 800.13 Programmatic Agreements.

(a) *Application.* An Agency Official may elect to fulfill an agency's Section 106 responsibilities for a particular program, a large or complex project, or a class of undertakings that would otherwise require numerous individual requests for comments, through a Programmatic Agreement. Programmatic Agreements are appropriate for programs or projects:

    (1) When effects on historic properties are similar and repetitive or are multistate or national in scope;

    (2) When effects on historic properties cannot be fully determined prior to approval;

    (3) When nonfederal parties are delegated major decision making responsibilities;

    (4) That involve development of regional or land-management plans; or

    (5) That involve routine management activities at Federal installations.

    (b) *Consultation Process.* The Council and the Agency Official shall consult to develop a Programmatic Agreement. When a particular state is affected, the appropriate State Historic Preservation Officer shall be a consulting party. When the agreement involves issues national in scope, the president of the National Conference of State Historic Preservation Officers or a designated representative shall be invited to be a consulting party by the Council. The Council and the Agency Official may agree to invite other federal agencies or others to be consulting parties or to participate, as appropriate.

    (c) *Public Involvement.* The Council, with the assistance of the Agency Official, shall arrange for public notice and involvement appropriate to the subject matter and the scope of the program. Views from affected units of state and local government, Indian tribes, industries, and organizations will be invited.

    (d) *Execution of the Programmatic Agreement.* After consideration of any comments received and reaching final agreement, the Council and the Agency Official shall execute the agreement. Other consulting parties may sign the Programmatic Agreement as appropriate.

    (e) *Effect of the Programmatic Agreement.* An approved Programmatic Agreement satisfies the Agency's Section 106 responsibilities for all individual undertakings carried out in accordance with the agreement until it expires or is terminated.

    (f) *Notice.* The Council shall publish notice of an approved Programmatic Agreement in the Federal Register and make copies readily available to the public.

    (g) *Failure to Carry Out a Programmatic Agreement.* If the terms of a Programmatic Agreement are not carried out or if such an agreement is terminated, the Agency Official shall comply with Sections 800.4 through 800.6 with regard to individual undertakings covered by the agreement.

§ 800.14 Coordination with other authorities.

To the extent feasible, Agency Officials, State Historic Preservation Officers, and the Council should encourage coordination of implementation of these regulations with the steps taken to satisfy other historic preservation and environmental authorities by:

    (a) Integrating compliance with these regulations with the processes of environmental review carried out pursuant to the National Environmental Policy Act, and coordinating any studies needed to comply with these regulations with studies of related natural and social aspects;

(b) Designing determinations and agreements to satisfy the terms not only of Section 106 and these regulations, but also the requirements of such other historic preservation authorities as the Archeological and Historic Preservation Act, the Archeological Resources Protection Act, Section 110 of the National Historic Preservation Act, and Section 4(f) of the Department of Transportation Act, as applicable, so that a single document can be used for the purposes of all such authorities;

(c) Designing and executing studies, surveys, and other information-gathering activities for planning and undertaking so that the resulting information and data is adequate to meet the requirements of all applicable federal historic preservation authorities; and

(d) Using established agency public involvement processes to elicit the views of the concerned public with regard to an undertaking and its effects on historic properties.

§ 800.15 Counterpart regulations.

In consultation with the Council, agencies may develop counterpart regulations to carry out the Section 106 process. When concurred in by the Council, such counterpart regulations shall stand in place of these regulations for the purposes of the agency's compliance with Section 106.

Appendix K

New York City Administrative Code, Chapter 8-A, "Preservation of Landmarks and Historical Districts"

TITLE 25
CHAPTER 3
LANDMARKS PRESERVATION AND HISTORIC DISTRICTS

§ 25-301 Purpose and declaration of public policy.

(a) The council finds that many improvements, as herein defined, and landscape features, as herein defined, having a special character or a special historical or aesthetic interest or value and many improvements representing the finest architectural products of distinct periods in the history of the city, have been uprooted, notwithstanding the feasibility of preserving and continuing the use of such improvements and landscape features, and without adequate consideration of the irreplaceable loss to the people of the city of the aesthetic, cultural and historic values represented by such improvements and landscape features.

In addition, distinct areas may be similarly uprooted or may have their distinctiveness destroyed, although the preservation thereof may be both feasible and desirable. It is the sense of the council that the standing of this city as a world wide tourist center and world capital of business, culture and government cannot be maintained or enhanced by disregarding the historical and architectural heritage of the city and by countenancing the destruction of such cultural assets.

(b) It is hereby declared as a matter of public policy that the protection, enhancement, perpetuation and use of improvements and landscape features of special character or special historical or aesthetic interest or value is a public necessity and is required in the interest of the health, prosperity, safety and welfare of the people. The purpose of this chapter is to (a) effect and accomplish the protection, enhancement and perpetuation of such improvements and landscape features and of districts which represent or reflect elements of the city's cultural, social, economic, political and architectural history; (b) safeguard the city's historic, aesthetic and cultural heritage, as embodied and reflected in such improvements, landscape features and districts; (c) stabilize and improve property values in such districts; (d) foster civic pride in the beauty and noble accomplishments of the past; (e) protect and enhance the city's attractions to tourists and visitors and the support and stimulus to business and industry thereby provided; (f) strengthen the economy of the city; and (g) promote the use of historic districts, landmarks, interior landmarks and scenic landmarks for the education, pleasure and welfare of the people of the city.

§ 25-302 Definitions.

As used in this chapter, the following terms shall mean and include:

(a) "Alteration." Any of the acts defined as an alteration by the building code of the city.

(b) "Appropriate protective interest." Any right or interest in or title to an improvement parcel or any part thereof, including, but not limited to, fee title and scenic or other easements, the acquisition of which by the city is determined by the commission to be necessary and appropriate for the effectuation of the purpose of this chapter.

(c) "Capable of earning a reasonable return." Having the capacity, under reasonably efficient and prudent management, of earning a reasonable return. For the purposes of this chapter, the net annual return, as defined in subparagraph (a) of paragraph three of subdivision v of this section, yielded by an improvement parcel during the test year, as defined in subparagraph (b) of such paragraph, shall be presumed to be the earning capacity of such improvement parcel, in the absence of substantial grounds for a contrary determination by the commission.

(d) "City-aided project." Any physical betterment of real property, which:

(1) may not be constructed or effected without the approval of one or more officers or agencies of the city; and

(2) upon completion, will be owned in whole or in part by any person other than the city; and

(3) is planned to be constructed or effected, in whole or in part, with any form of aid furnished by the city (other than under this chapter), including, but not limited to, any loan, grant, subsidy or other mode of financial assistance, exercise of the city's powers of eminent domain, contribution of city property, or the granting of tax exemption or tax abatement; and

(4) will involve the construction, reconstruction, alteration or demolition of any improvement in a historic district or of a landmark.

(e) "Commission." The landmarks preservation commission.

(f) "Day." Any day other than a Saturday, Sunday or legal holiday; provided, however, that for the purposes of subdivision d of section 25-317 of this chapter, the term "day" shall mean every day in the week.

(g) "Exterior architectural feature." The architectural style, design, general arrangement and components of all of the outer surfaces of an improvement, as distinguished from the interior surfaces enclosed by said exterior surfaces, including, but not limited to, the kind, color and texture of the building material and the type and style of all windows, doors, lights, signs and other fixtures appurtenant to such improvement.

(h) "Historic district." Any area which:
    (1) contains improvements which:
        (a) have a special character or special historical or aesthetic interest or value; and
        (b) represent one or more periods or styles of architecture typical of one or more eras in the history of the city; and
        (c) cause such area, by reason of such factors, to constitute a distinct section of the city; and
    (2) has been designated as a historic district pursuant to the provisions of this chapter.

(i) "Improvement." Any building, structure, place, work of art or other object constituting a physical betterment of real property, or any part of such betterment.

(j) "Improvement parcel." The unit of real property which (1) includes a physical betterment constituting an improvement and the land embracing the site thereof, and (2) is treated as a single entity for the purpose of levying real estate taxes, provided however, that the term "improvement parcel" shall also include any unimproved area of land which is treated as a single entity for such tax purposes.

(k) "Interior." The visible surfaces of the interior of an improvement.

(l) "Interior architectural feature." The architectural style, design, general arrangement and components of an interior, including, but not limited to, the kind, color and texture of the building material and the type and style of all windows, doors, lights, signs and other fixtures appurtenant to such interior.

(m) "Interior landmark." An interior, or part thereof, any part of which is thirty years old or older, and which is customarily open or accessible to the public, or to which the public is customarily invited, and which has a special historical or aesthetic interest or value as part of the development, heritage or cultural characteristics of the city, state or nation, and which has been designated as an interior landmark pursuant to the provisions of this chapter.

(n) "Landmark." Any improvement, any part of which is thirty years old or older, which has a special character or special historical or aesthetic interest or value as part of the development, heritage or cultural characteristics of the city, state or nation, and which has been designated as a landmark pursuant to the provisions of this chapter.

(o) "Landmark site." An improvement parcel or part thereof on which is situated a landmark and any abutting improvement parcel or part thereof used as and constituting part of the premises on which the landmark is situated, and which has been designated as a landmark site pursuant to the provisions of this chapter.

(p) "Landscape feature." Any grade, body of water, stream, rock, plant, shrub, tree, path, walkway, road, plaza, fountain, sculpture or other form of natural or artificial landscaping.

(q) "Minor work." Any change in, addition to or removal from the parts, elements or materials comprising an improvement, including, but not limited to, the exterior architectural features or interior architectural features thereof and, subject to and as prescribed by regulations of the commission if and when promulgated pursuant to section 25-319 of this chapter, the surfacing, resurfacing, painting, renovating, restoring or rehabilitating of the exterior architectural features or interior architectural features or the treating of the same in any manner that materially alters their appearance, where such change, addition or removal does not constitute ordinary repairs and maintenance and is of such nature that it may be lawfully effected without a permit from the department of buildings.

(r) "Ordinary repairs and maintenance." Any:
    (1)   work done on any improvement; or
    (2)   replacement of any part of an improvement;
for which a permit issued by the department of buildings is not required by law, where the purpose and effect of such work or replacement is to correct any deterioration or decay of or damage to such improvement or any part thereof and to restore same, as nearly as may be practicable, to its condition prior to the occurrence of such deterioration, decay or damage.

(s) "Owner." Any person or persons having such right to, title to or interest in any improvement so as to be legally entitled, upon obtaining the required permits and approvals from the city agencies having jurisdiction over building construction, to perform with respect to such property any demolition, construction, reconstruction, alteration or other work as to which such person seeks the authorization or approval of the commission pursuant to section 25-309 of this chapter.

(t) "Person in charge." The person or persons possessed of the freehold of an improvement or improvement parcel or a lesser estate therein, a mortgagee or vendee in possession, assignee of rents, receiver, executor, trustee, lessee, agent or any other person directly or indirectly in control of an improvement or improvement parcel.

(u) "Protected architectural feature." Any exterior architectural feature of a landmark or any interior architectural feature of an interior landmark.

(v) "Reasonable return."
    (1)   A net annual return of six per centum of the valuation of an improvement parcel.
    (2)   Such valuation shall be the current assessed valuation established by the city, which is in effect at the time of the filing of the request for a certificate of appropriateness; provided that:

> (a) The commission may make a determination that the valuation of the improvement parcel is an amount different from such assessed valuation where there has been a reduction in the assessed valuation for the year next preceding the effective date of the current assessed valuation in effect at the time of the filing of such request; and

(b) The commission may make a determination that the value of the improvement parcel is an amount different from the assessed valuation where there has been a bona fide sale of such parcel within the period between March fifteenth, nineteen hundred fifty-eight, and the time of the filing of such request, as the result of a transaction at arm's length, on normal financing terms, at a readily ascertainable price, and unaffected by special circumstances such as, but not limited to, a forced sale, exchange of property, package deal, wash sale or sale to a cooperative. In determining whether a sale was on normal financing terms, the commission shall give due consideration to the following factors:

(1) The ratio of the cash payment received by the seller to (a) the sales price of the improvement parcel and (b) the annual gross income from such parcel;

(2) The total amount of the outstanding mortgages which are liens against the improvement parcel (including purchase money mortgages) as compared with the assessed valuation of such parcel;

(3) The ratio of the sales price to the annual gross income of the improvement parcel, with consideration given, where the improvement is subject to residential rent control, to the total amount of rent adjustments previously granted, exclusive of rent adjustments because of changes in dwelling space, services, furniture, furnishings, or equipment, major capital improvements, or substantial rehabilitation;

(4) The presence of deferred amortization in purchase money mortgages, or the assignment of such mortgages at a discount;

(5) Any other facts and circumstances surrounding such sale which, in the judgment of the commission, may have a bearing upon the question of financing.

(3) For the purposes of this subdivision v:

(a) Net annual return shall be the amount by which the earned income yielded by the improvement parcel during a test year exceeds the operating expenses of such parcel during such year, excluding mortgage interest and amortization, and excluding allowances for obsolescence and reserves, but including an allowance for depreciation of two per centum of the assessed value of the improvement, exclusive of the land, or the amount shown for depreciation of the improvement in the latest required federal income tax return, whichever is lower; provided, however, that no allowance for depreciation of the improvement shall be included where the improvement has been fully depreciated for federal income tax purposes or on the books of the owner; and

(b) Test year shall be (1) the most recent full calendar year, or (2) the owner's most recent fiscal year, or (3) any twelve consecutive months ending not more than ninety days prior to the filing (a) of the request for a certificate, or (b) of an application for a renewal of tax benefits pursuant to the provisions of section 25-309 of this chapter, as the case may be.

(w) "Scenic landmark." Any landscape feature or aggregate of landscape features, any part of which is thirty years old or older, which has or have a special character or special historical or aesthetic interest or value as part of the development, heritage or cultural characteristics of the city, state or nation and which has been designated a scenic landmark pursuant to the provisions of this chapter.

§ 25-303 Establishment of landmarks, landmark sites, interior landmarks, scenic landmarks and historic districts.

(a) For the purpose of effecting and furthering the protection, preservation, enhancement, perpetuation and use of landmarks, interior landmarks, scenic landmarks and historic districts, the commission shall have power, after a public hearing:

(1) to designate and, as herein provided in subdivision j, in order to effectuate the purposes of this chapter, to make supplemental designations as additions to, a list of landmarks which are identified by a description setting forth the general characteristics and location thereof;

(2) to designate and, in order to effectuate the purposes of this chapter, to make supplemental designations as additions to, a list of interior landmarks, not including interiors utilized as places of religious worship, which are identified by a description setting forth the general characteristics and location thereof;

(3) to designate and, in order to effectuate the purposes of this chapter, to make supplemental designations as additions to a list of scenic landmarks, located on property owned by the city, which are identified by a description setting forth the general characteristics and location thereof; and

(4) to designate historic districts and the location and boundaries thereof, and, in order to effectuate the purposes of this chapter, to designate changes in such locations and boundaries and designate additional historic districts and the location and boundaries thereof.

(b) It shall be the duty of the commission, after a public hearing, to designate a landmark site for each landmark and to designate the location and boundaries of such site.

(c) The commission shall have power, after a public hearing, to amend any designation made pursuant to the provisions of subdivisions a and b of this section.

(d) The commission may, after a public hearing, whether at the time it designates a scenic landmark or at any time thereafter, specify the nature of any construction, reconstruction, alteration or demolition of any landscape feature which may be performed on such scenic landmark without prior issuance of a report pursuant to subdivision c of section 25-318. The commission shall have the power, after a public hearing, to amend any specification made pursuant to the provisions of this subdivision.

(e) Subject to the provisions of subdivisions g and h of this section, any designation or amendment of a designation made by the commission pursuant to the provisions of subdivisions a, b and c of this section shall be in full force and effect from and after the date of the adoption thereof by the commission.

(f) Within five days after making any such designation or amendment thereof, the commission shall file a copy of same with the secretary of the board of estimate and with the department of buildings, the city planning commission, the board of standards and appeals, the fire department and the department of health.

(g) (1) The secretary of the board of estimate, within five days after the filing of such copy with such secretary, shall refer such designation or amendment thereof to the city planning commission, which, within thirty days after such referral, shall submit to the board of estimate a report with respect to the relation of such designation or amendment thereof to the zoning resolution, projected public improvements and any plans for the development, growth, improvement or renewal of the area involved.

(2) The board of estimate may modify or disapprove such designation or amendment thereof within ninety days after a copy thereof is filed with the secretary of the board provided that the planning commission has submitted the report required by this subdivision or that thirty days have elapsed since the referral of the designation or amendment to the commission by the secretary of the board. If the board shall disapprove such designation or amendment thereof, it shall cease to be in effect on the date of such action by the board. If the board shall modify such designation or amendment thereof, such modification shall be in effect on and after the date of the adoption thereof by the board.

(h) (1) The commission shall have power, after a public hearing, to adopt a resolution proposing rescission, in whole or in part, of any designation or amendment or modification thereof mentioned in the preceding subdivisions of this section. Within five days after adopting any such resolution, the commission shall file a copy thereof with the secretary of the board of estimate, who shall, within five days after such filing, refer such resolution to the city planning commission.

(2) Within thirty days after such referral, the city planning commission shall submit to the board of estimate a report with respect to the relation of such proposed rescission to the zoning resolution, projected public improvements and any plans for the development, growth, improvement, or renewal of the area involved.

(3) Such board may approve, disapprove or modify such proposed rescission within ninety days after a copy of the resolution proposing same is filed with the secretary of the board. If such proposed rescission is approved or modified by the board, such rescission or modification thereof shall take effect on the date of such action by the board. If such proposed rescission is disapproved by the board, or is not acted on by the board within such period of ninety days, it shall not take effect.

(i) The commission may at any time make recommendations to the city planning commission with respect to amendments of the provisions of the zoning resolution applicable to improvements in historic districts.

(j) All designations and supplemental designations of landmarks, landmark sites, interior landmarks, scenic landmarks and historic districts made pursuant to subdivision a shall be made pursuant to notices of public hearings given, as provided in section 25-313.

(k) Upon its designation of any improvement parcel as a landmark and of any landmark site, interior landmark, scenic landmark or historic district or any amendment of any such designation or rescission thereof, the commission shall cause to be recorded in the office of the register of the city of New York in the county in which such landmark, interior landmark, scenic landmark or district lies, or in the case of landmarks, interior landmarks, scenic landmarks and districts in the county of Richmond in the office of the clerk of said county of Richmond, a notice of such designation, amendment or rescission describing the party affected by, in the case of the county of Richmond, its land map block number or numbers, and its tax map, block and lot number or numbers, and in the case of all other counties, by its land map block and lot number or numbers.

§ 25-304 Scope of commission's powers.

(a) Nothing contained in this chapter shall be construed as authorizing the commission, in acting with respect to any historic district or improvement therein, or in adopting regulations in relation thereto, to regulate or limit the height and bulk of buildings, to regulate and determine the area of yards, courts and other open spaces, to regulate density of population or to regulate and restrict the locations of trades and industries or location of buildings designed for specific uses or to create districts for any such purpose.

(b) Except as provided in subdivision a of this section, the commission may, in exercising or performing its powers, duties or functions under this chapter with respect to any improvement in a historic district or on a landmark site or containing an interior landmark, or any landscape feature of a scenic landmark, apply or impose, with respect to the construction, reconstruction, alteration, demolition or use of such improvement or landscape feature or the performance of minor work thereon, regulations, limitations, determinations or conditions which are more restrictive than those prescribed or made by or pursuant to other provisions of law applicable to such activities, work or use.

§ 25-305 Regulation of construction, reconstruction, alterations and demolition.

(a) (1) Except as otherwise provided in paragraph two of this subdivision a, it shall be unlawful for any person in charge of a landmark site or an improvement parcel or portion thereof located in an historic district or any part of an improvement containing an interior landmark to alter, reconstruct or demolish any improvement constituting a part of such site or constituting a part of such parcel and located within such district or containing an interior landmark, or to construct any improvement upon land embraced within such site or such parcel and located within such district, or to cause or permit any such work to be performed on such improvement or land, unless the commission has previously issued a certificate of no effect on protected architectural features, a certificate of appropriateness or a notice to proceed authorizing such work, and it shall be unlawful for any other person to perform such work or cause same to be performed, unless such certificate or notice has been previously issued.

(2) The provisions of paragraph one of this subdivision a shall not apply to any improvement mentioned in subdivision a of section 25-318 of this

chapter, or to any city-aided project, or in cases subject to the provisions of section 25-312 of this chapter.

(3) It shall be unlawful for the person in charge of any improvement or land mentioned in paragraph one of this subdivision a to maintain same or cause or permit same to be maintained in the condition created by any work in violation of the provisions of such paragraph one.

(b) (1) Except in the case of any improvement mentioned in subdivision a of section 25-318 of this chapter and except in the case of a city-aided project, no application shall be approved and no permit or amended permit for the construction, reconstruction, alteration or demolition of any improvement located or to be located on a landmark site or in an historic district or containing an interior landmark shall be issued by the department of buildings, and no application shall be approved and no special permit or amended special permit for such construction, reconstruction or alteration, where required by article seven of the zoning resolution, shall be granted by the city planning commission or the board of standards and appeals, until the commission shall have issued either a certificate of no effect on protected architectural features, a certificate of appropriateness or a notice to proceed pursuant to the provisions of this chapter as an authorization for such work.

(c) (1) A copy of every application or amended application for a permit to construct, reconstruct, alter or demolish any improvement located or to be located on a landmark site or in an historic district or containing an interior landmark shall, at the time of the submission of the original thereof to the department of buildings, be filed by the applicant with the commission. A copy of every application, under article seven of the zoning resolution, for a special permit for any work which includes the construction, reconstruction or alteration of any such improvement shall, at the time of the submission of such application or amended application of the city planning commission or the board of standards and appeals, as the case may be, be filed with the commission.

(2) Every such copy of an application or amended application filed with the commission shall include plans and specifications for the work involved, or such other statement of the proposed work as would be acceptable by the department of buildings pursuant to the building code. The applicant shall furnish the commission with such other information relating to such application as the commission may from time to time require.

(3) Together with the copies of such application or amended application, every such applicant shall file with the commission a request for a certificate of no effect on protected architectural features or a certificate of appropriateness in relation to the proposed work specified in such application.

§ 25-306 Determination of request for certificate of no effect on protected architectural features.

(a) (1) In any case where an applicant for a permit from the department of buildings to construct, reconstruct, alter or demolish any improvement on a landmark site or in an historic district or containing an interior landmark, or an applicant for a special permit from the city planning commission or the board of standards and appeals authorizing any such work pursuant to article seven of the zoning resolution, or amendments thereof, files a copy of such application or amended application with the commission, together with a request for a certificate of no effect on protected architectural features, the commission shall determine:

> (a) whether the proposed work would change, destroy or affect any exterior architectural feature of the improvement on a landmark site or in an historic district or any interior architectural feature of the interior landmark upon which said work is to be done; and
>
> (b) in the case of construction of a new improvement, whether such construction would affect or not be in harmony with the external appearance of other, neighboring improvements on such site or in such district. If the commission determines such question in the negative, it shall grant such certificate; otherwise, it shall deny such request.

(2) Within thirty days after the filing of such application and request, the commission shall either grant such certificate, or give notice to the applicant of a proposed denial of such request. Upon written demand of the applicant filed with the commission after the giving of notice of a proposed denial, the commission shall confer with the applicant. The commission shall determine the request for a certificate within thirty days after the filing of such demand. If a demand is not filed within ten days after the giving of notice of the proposed denial, the commission shall determine such request within five days after the expiration of such ten-day period.

(3) In the event of a denial of such a certificate, the applicant may file with the commission a request for a certificate of appropriateness with respect to the proposed work specified in such application.

§ 25-307 Factors governing issuance of certificate of appropriateness.

(a) In any case where an applicant for a permit to construct, reconstruct, alter or demolish any improvement on a landmark site, or in an historic district or containing an interior landmark, files such application with the commission together with a request for a certificate of appropriateness, and in any case where a certificate of no effect on protected architectural features is denied and the applicant thereafter, pursuant to the provisions of section 25-306 of this chapter, files a request for a certificate of appropriateness, the commission shall determine whether the proposed work would be appropriate for and consistent with the effectuation of the purposes of this chapter. If the commission's determination is in the affirmative on such question, it shall grant a certificate of appropriateness, and if the commission's determination is in the negative, it shall deny the applicant's request, except as otherwise provided in section 25-309 of this chapter.

(b) (1) In making such determination with respect to any such application for a permit to construct, reconstruct, alter or demolish an improvement in an historic district, the commission shall consider (a) the effect of the proposed work in creating, changing, destroying or affecting the exterior architectural features of the improvement upon which such work is to be done, and (b) the relationship between the results of such work and the exterior architectural features of other, neighboring improvements in such district.

(2) In appraising such effects and relationship, the commission shall consider, in addition to any other pertinent matters, the factors of aesthetic, historical and architectural values and significance, architectural style, design, arrangement, texture, material and color.

(3) All determinations of the commission pursuant to this subdivision b shall be made subject to the provisions of section 25-304 of this chapter, and the commission, in making any such determination, shall not apply any regulation, limitation, determination or restriction as to the height and bulk of buildings, the area of yards, courts or other open spaces, density of population, the location of trades and industries, or location of buildings designed for specific uses, other than the regulations, limitations, determinations and restrictions as to such matters prescribed or made by or pursuant to applicable provisions of law, exclusive of this chapter; provided, however, that nothing contained in such section 25-304 or in this subdivision b shall be construed as limiting the power of the commission to deny a request for a certificate of appropriateness for demolition or alteration of an improvement in an historic district (whether or not such request also seeks approval, in such certificate, of construction or reconstruction of any improvement), on the ground that such demolition or alteration would be inappropriate for and inconsistent with the effectuation of the purposes of this chapter, with due consideration for the factors hereinabove set forth in this subdivision b.

(c) In making the determination referred to in subdivision a of this section with respect to any application for a permit to construct, reconstruct, alter or demolish any improvement on a landmark site, other than a landmark, the commission shall consider (1) the effects of the proposed work in creating, changing, destroying or affecting the exterior architectural features of the improvement upon which such work is to be done, (2) the relationship between such exterior architectural features, together with such effects, and the exterior architectural features of the landmark, and (3) the effects of the results of such work upon the protection, enhancement, perpetuation and use of the landmark on such site. In appraising such effects and relationship, the commission shall consider, in addition to any other pertinent matters, the factors mentioned in paragraph two of subdivision b of this section.

(d) In making the determination referred to in subdivision a of this section with respect to an application for a permit to alter, reconstruct or demolish a landmark, the commission shall consider the effects of the proposed work upon the protection, enhancement, perpetuation and use of the exterior architectural features of such landmark which cause it to possess a special character or special historical or aesthetic interest or value.

(e) In making the determination referred to in subdivision a of this section with respect to an application for a permit to alter, reconstruct or demolish an improvement containing an interior landmark, the commission shall consider the effects of the proposed work upon the protection, enhancement, perpetuation and use of the interior architectural features of such interior landmark which cause it to possess a special character or special historical or aesthetic interest or value.

§ 25-308 Procedure for determination of request for certificate of appropriateness.

The commission shall hold a public hearing on each request for a certificate of appropriateness. Except as otherwise provided in section 25-309 of this chapter, the commission shall make its determination as to such request within ninety days after filing thereof.

§ 25-309 Request for certificate of appropriateness authorizing demolition, alterations or reconstruction on ground of insufficient return.

(a) (1) Except as otherwise provided in paragraph two of this subdivision a, in any case where an application for a permit to demolish any improvement located on a landmark site or in an historic district or containing an interior landmark is filed with the commission, together with a request for a certificate of appropriateness authorizing such demolition, and in any case where an application for a permit to make alterations to or reconstruct any improvement on a landmark site or containing an interior landmark is filed with the commission, and the applicant requests a certificate of appropriateness for such work, and the applicant establishes to the satisfaction of the commission that:

    (a) the improvement parcel (or parcels) which includes such improvement, as existing at the time of the filing of such request, is not capable of earning a reasonable return; and

    (b) the owner of such improvement:

        (1) in the case of an application for a permit to demolish, seeks in good faith to demolish such improvement immediately (a) for the purpose of constructing on the site thereof with reasonable promptness a new building or other income-producing facility, or (b) for the purpose of terminating the operation of the improvement at a loss; or

        (2) in the case of an application for a permit to make alterations or reconstruct, seeks in good faith to alter or reconstruct such improvement, with reasonable promptness, for the purpose of increasing the return therefrom;

the commission, if it determines that the request for such certificate should be denied on the basis of the applicable standards set forth in section 25-307 of this chapter, shall, within ninety days after the filing of the request for such certificate of appropriateness, make a preliminary determination of insufficient return.

(2) In any case where any application and request for a certificate of appropriateness mentioned in paragraph one of this subdivision a is filed with the commission with respect to an improvement, the provisions of this section shall not apply to such request if the improvement parcel which includes such improvement has received, for three years next preceding the filing of such request, and at the time of such filing continues to receive, under any provision of law (other than this chapter or section four hundred fifty-eight, four hundred sixty or four hundred seventy-nine of the real

property tax law), exemption in whole or in part from real property taxation; provided, however, that the provisions of this section shall nevertheless apply to such request if such exemption is and has been received pursuant to section four hundred twenty-a, four hundred twenty-two, four hundred twenty-four, four hundred twenty-five, four hundred twenty-six, four hundred twenty-seven, four hundred twenty-eight, four hundred thirty, four hundred thirty-two, four hundred thirty-four, four hundred thirty-six, four hundred thirty-eight, four hundred forty, four hundred forty-two, four hundred forty-four, four hundred fifty, four hundred fifty-two, four hundred sixty-two, four hundred sixty-four, four hundred sixty-eight, four hundred seventy, four hundred seventy-two or four hundred seventy-four of the real property tax law and the applicant establishes to the satisfaction of the commission, in lieu of the requirements set forth in paragraph one of this subdivision a, that:

    (a) The owner of such improvement has entered into a bona fide agreement to sell an estate of freehold or to grant a term of at least twenty years in such improvement parcel, which agreement is subject to or contingent upon the issuance of the certificate of appropriateness or a notice to proceed;

    (b) The improvement parcel which includes such improvement, as existing at the time of the filing of such request, would not, if it were not exempt in whole or in part from real property taxation, be capable of earning a reasonable return;

    (c) Such improvement has ceased to be adequate, suitable or appropriate for use for carrying out both (1) the purposes of such owner to which it is devoted and (2) those purposes to which it had been devoted when acquired unless such owner is no longer engaged in pursuing such purposes; and

    (d) The prospective purchaser or tenant:

        (1) In the case of an application for a permit to demolish seeks and intends, in good faith either to demolish such improvement immediately for the purpose of constructing on the site thereof with reasonable promptness a new building or other facility; or

        (2) In the case of an application for a permit to make alterations or reconstruct, seeks and intends in good faith to alter or reconstruct such improvement, with reasonable promptness.

(b) In the case of an application made pursuant to paragraph one of subdivision a of this section by an applicant not required to establish the conditions specified in paragraph two of such subdivision, as promptly as is practicable after making a preliminary determination as provided in paragraph one of such subdivision a, the commission, with the aid of such experts as it deems necessary, shall endeavor to devise, in consultation with the applicant, a plan whereby the improvement may be (1) preserved or perpetuated in such manner or form as to effectuate the purposes of this chapter, and (2) also rendered capable of earning a reasonable return.

(c) Any such plan may include, but shall not be limited to, (1) granting of partial or complete tax exemption, (2) remission of taxes and (3) authorization for alterations, construction or reconstruction appropriate for and not inconsistent with the effectuation of the purposes of this chapter.

(d) In any case where the commission formulates any such plan, it shall mail a copy thereof to the applicant promptly and in any event within sixty days after giving notice of its preliminary determination of insufficient return. The commission shall hold a public hearing upon such plan.

(e) (1) If the commission, after holding a public hearing pursuant to subdivision d of this section, determines that a plan which it has formulated, consisting only of tax exemption and/or remission of taxes, meets the standards set forth in subdivision b of this section, as such plan was originally formulated, or with such modifications as the commission deems necessary or appropriate, the commission shall deny the request of the applicant for a certificate of appropriateness and shall approve such plan, as originally formulated, or with such modifications.

(2) Such plan, as so approved, shall set forth the extent of tax exemption and/or remission of taxes deemed necessary by the commission to meet such standards.

(3) The commission shall promptly mail a certified copy of such approved plan to the applicant and shall promptly transmit a certified copy thereof to the tax commission. Upon application made by the owner of such improvement pursuant to the provisions of paragraph five of this subdivision e, the tax commission shall grant, for the fiscal year next succeeding the date of approval of such plan, the tax exemption and/or remission of taxes provided for therein.

(4) In accordance with procedures prescribed by the regulations of the commission, it shall determine, upon application by the owner of such improvement made in advance of each succeeding fiscal year, the amount of tax exemption and/or remission of taxes, if any, which it deems necessary, as a renewal of such plan for the ensuing year, to meet the standards set forth in subdivision b of this section, and shall promptly mail a certified copy of any approved renewal of such plan to the applicant and shall promptly transmit a certified copy of such renewal to the tax commission. Upon application made by the owner of such improvement pursuant to the provisions of paragraph five of this subdivision e, the tax commission shall grant, for such fiscal year, the tax exemption and/or remission of taxes specified in such determination.

(5) Where any such plan or a renewal thereof is approved by the commission, pursuant to the provisions of the preceding paragraphs of this subdivision e, prior to January first next preceding the fiscal year to which the tax benefits of such plan or renewal thereof are applicable, the owner shall not be entitled to such benefits for such fiscal year unless he or she files an application therefor with the tax commission between February first and March fifteenth, both dates inclusive, next preceding such fiscal year. Where any such plan or a renewal thereof is approved by the commission between January first and June thirtieth, both dates inclusive, next preceding the fiscal year to which the tax benefits of such plan or renewal thereof are applicable, the owner shall not be entitled to such benefits for such fiscal year unless he or she files an application therefor with the tax commission on or before August first of such fiscal year.

(f) (1) In any case where the commission determines, after holding a public hearing pursuant to subdivision d of this section, that a plan which it has formulated, consisting in whole or in part of any proposal other than tax exemption and/or remission of taxes, meets the standards set forth in subdivision b of this section, as such plan was originally formulated, or with such modifications as the commission deems necessary or appropriate, the commission shall approve such plan, as originally formulated, or with such modifications, and shall promptly mail a copy of same to the applicant.

(2) The owner of the improvement proposed to be benefited by such plan mentioned in paragraph one of this subdivision f may accept or reject such plan by written acceptance or rejection filed with the commission. If such an acceptance is filed, the commission shall deny the request of such applicant for a certificate of appropriateness. If a new application for a permit from the department of buildings and a new request for a certificate of appropriateness are filed, which application and request conform with such proposed plan, the commission shall grant such certificate as promptly as is practicable and in any event within thirty days after such filing.

(3) If such accepted plan consists in part of tax exemption and/or remission of taxes, the provisions of paragraphs two, three, four and five of subdivision e of this section shall govern the granting of such tax exemption and/or remission of taxes.

(g) (1) Except in a case where the applicant is required to establish the conditions set forth in paragraph two of subdivision a of this section, if

(a) The commission does not formulate and mail a plan pursuant to the provisions of subdivisions b, c, and d of this section within the period of time prescribed by such subdivision d; or

(b) The commission does not approve a plan pursuant to the provisions of subdivision e or f of this section within sixty days after the mailing of such plan to the applicant; or

(c) A plan approved by the commission pursuant to the provisions of paragraph one of subdivision f of this section is rejected by the owner of such improvement pursuant to the provisions of paragraph two of such subdivision;

the commission may, within ten days after expiration of the applicable period referred to in subparagraphs (a) and (b) of this paragraph one, or within ten days after the filing of a rejection of a plan pursuant to paragraph two of subdivision f of this section, as the case may be, transmit to the mayor a written recommendation that the city acquire a specified appropriate protective interest in the improvement parcel which includes the improvement with respect to which the request for a certificate of appropriateness was filed, and shall promptly notify the applicant of such action.

(2) If, within ninety days after transmission of such recommendation, or, if no such recommendation is transmitted, within ninety days after the expiration of the period herein prescribed for such transmission, the city does not:

(a) Give notice, pursuant to section three hundred eighty-two of the charter, of an application to condemn such interest or any other appropriate protective interest agreed upon by the mayor and the commission; or

(b) Enter into a contract with the owner of such improvement parcel to acquire such interest, as so recommended or agreed upon;

the commission shall promptly grant, issue and forward to the owner, in lieu of the certificate of appropriateness requested by the applicant, a notice to proceed.

(h) No plan which consists in whole or in part of the granting of a partial or complete tax exemption or remission of taxes pursuant to the provisions of this chapter shall be deemed to have been approved by the commission unless it is also approved by the board of estimate within the period of time prescribed by this section for approval of such plan by the commission.

(i) (1) In any case where the applicant is required to establish the conditions set forth in paragraph two of subdivision a of this section, as promptly as is practicable after making a preliminary determination with respect to such conditions, as provided in paragraph one of subdivision a of this section, and within one hundred and eighty days after making such preliminary determination, the commission, alone or with the aid of such persons and agencies as it deems necessary and whose aid it is able to enlist, shall endeavor to obtain a purchaser or tenant (as the case may be) of the improvement parcel or parcels with respect to which the application has been made, which purchaser or tenant will agree, without condition or contingency relating to the issuance of a certificate of appropriateness or notice to proceed and subject to the provisions of paragraph three of this subdivision i, to purchase or acquire an interest identical with that proposed to be acquired by the prospective purchaser or tenant whose agreement is the basis of the application, on reasonably equivalent terms and conditions.

(2) The applicant shall, within a reasonable time after notice by the commission that it has obtained such a purchaser or tenant, which notice shall be served within the period of one hundred and eighty days provided by paragraph one of this subdivision i, enter into such agreement to sell or lease (as the case may be) with the purchaser or tenant so obtained. Such notice shall specify a date for the execution of such agreement, which may be postponed by the commission at the request of the applicant.

(3) The provisions of this section shall not, after the consummation of such agreement, apply to such purchaser or tenant or to the heirs, successors or assigns of such purchaser or tenant.

(4) (a) If, within the one hundred eighty day period following the commission's preliminary determination pursuant to paragraph one of subdivision a of this section, the commission shall not have succeeded in obtaining a purchaser or tenant of the improvement parcel, pursuant to paragraph one of this subdivision i, or if, having obtained such a purchaser or tenant, such purchaser or tenant fails within the time provided in paragraph two of this subdivision i, to enter into the agreement provided for by such paragraph two, the commission, within twenty days after the expiration of the one hundred eighty day period provided for in paragraph one of this subdivision i, or within twenty days after the date upon which a purchaser or tenant obtained by the commission pursuant to the provisions of such paragraph one fails to enter into the agreement provided for by said paragraph, whichever of said dates later occurs, may transmit to the mayor a written recommendation that the city acquire a specified appropriate protective interest in the improvement parcel or parcels which include the improvement or are part of the landmark site with respect to which the request for a certificate of appropriateness was filed, and shall promptly notify the applicant of such action.

(b) If, within ninety days after transmission of such recommendation, or, if no such recommendation is transmitted, within ninety days after the expiration of the period herein prescribed for such transmission, the city does not give notice, pursuant to section three hundred eighty-two of the charter, of an application to condemn such interest or any other appropriate protective interest agreed upon by the mayor and the commission, or does not enter into a contract with the owner of such improvement parcel to acquire such interest, as so recommended and agreed upon; the commission shall promptly grant, issue and forward to the owner, in lieu of the certificate of appropriateness requested by the applicant, a notice to proceed.

(5) Such notice to proceed shall authorize the work of demolition, alteration, and/or reconstruction sought with respect to the improvement parcel or parcels concerning which the application was made, only if such work (a) is undertaken and performed by the purchaser or tenant specified pursuant to the provisions of paragraph two of subdivision a of this section, in the application, or a bona fide assignee, successor, lessee or sub-lessee of such purchaser or tenant (other than the owner who made application therefor), and (b) is undertaken and performed with reasonable promptness after the issuance of such notice to proceed.

§ 25-310 Regulation of minor work.

(a) (1) Except as otherwise provided in section 25-312 of this chapter, it shall be unlawful for any person in charge of an improvement located on a landmark site or in an historic district or containing an interior landmark to perform any minor work thereon, or to cause or permit such work to be performed, and for any other person to perform any such work thereon or cause same to be performed, unless the commission has issued a permit, pursuant to this section, authorizing such work.

(2) It shall be unlawful for any person in charge of any such improvement to maintain same or cause or permit same to be maintained in the condition created by any work done in violation of the provisions of paragraph one of this subdivision a.

(b) The owner of an improvement desiring to obtain such a permit, or any person authorized by the owner to perform such work, may file with the commission an application for such permit, which shall include such description of the proposed work, as the commission may prescribe. The applicant shall submit such other information with respect to the proposed work as the commission may from time to time require. The commission shall promptly transmit such application to the department of buildings, which shall, as promptly as is practicable, certify to the commission whether a permit for such proposed work, issued by such department, is required by law. If such department certifies that such a permit is required, the commission shall deny such application, and shall promptly give notice of such determination to the applicant. If such department certifies that no such permit is required, the commission shall determine such application as hereinafter provided.

(c) (1) The commission shall determine:

(a) Whether the proposed work would change, destroy or affect any exterior architectural feature of an improvement located on a landmark site or in an historic district or interior architectural feature of an improvement containing an interior landmark; and

(b) If such work would have such effect, whether judged by the standards set forth in subdivisions b, c, d and e of section 25-307 of this chapter with respect to an improvement of similar classification hereunder, such work would be appropriate for and consistent with the effectuation of the purposes of this chapter.

(2) If the commission determines the question set forth in subparagraph (a) of paragraph one of this subdivision c in the negative, or determines the question set forth in subparagraph (b) of such paragraph in the affirmative, it shall grant such permit, and it shall deny such permit if it determines such question set forth in subparagraph (a) in the affirmative and determines such question set forth in subparagraph (b) in the negative.

(d) The procedure of the commission in making its determination with respect to any such application shall be as prescribed in subparagraph two of subdivision a of section 25-306 of this chapter, except that any period of thirty days referred to in such subparagraph shall, for the purposes of this subdivision d, be deemed to be twenty days.

(e) The provisions of this section shall be inapplicable to any improvement mentioned in subdivision a of section 25-318 of this chapter and to any city-aided project.

§ 25-311 Maintenance and repair of improvements.

(a) Every person in charge of an improvement on a landmark site or in an historic district shall keep in good repair (1) all of the exterior portions of such improvement and (2) all interior portions thereof which, if not so maintained, may cause or tend to cause the exterior portions of such improvement to deteriorate, decay or become damaged or otherwise to fall into a state of disrepair.

(b) Every person in charge of an improvement containing an interior landmark shall keep in good repair (1) all portions of such interior landmark and (2) all other portions of the improvement which, if not so maintained, may cause or tend to cause the interior landmark contained in such improvement to deteriorate, decay or become damaged or otherwise fall into a state of disrepair.

(c) Every person in charge of a scenic landmark shall keep in good repair all portions thereof.

(d) The provisions of this section shall be in addition to all other provisions of law requiring any such improvement to be kept in good repair.

§ 25-312 Remedying of dangerous conditions.

(a) In any case where the department of buildings, the fire department or the department of health, or any officer or agency thereof, or any court on application or at the instance of any such department, officer or agency, shall order or direct the construction, reconstruction, alteration or demolition of any improvement on a landmark site or in an historic district or containing an interior landmark, or the performance of any minor work upon such improvement, for the purpose of remedying conditions determined to be dangerous to life, health or property, nothing contained in this chapter shall be construed as making it unlawful for any person, without prior issuance of a certificate of no effect on protected architectural features or certificates of appropriateness or permit for minor work pursuant to this chapter, to comply with such order or direction.

(b) The department of buildings, fire department or department of health, as the case may be, shall give the commission as early notice as is practicable, of the proposed issuance or issuance of any such order or direction.

§ 25-313 Public hearings; conferences.

(a) The commission shall give notice of any public hearing which it is required or authorized to hold under the provisions of this chapter by publication in the City Record for at least ten days immediately prior thereto.

The owner of any improvement parcel on which a landmark or a proposed landmark is situated or which is a part of a landmark site or proposed landmark site or which contains an interior landmark or proposed interior landmark, or any property which includes a scenic landmark or proposed scenic landmark shall be given notice of any public hearing relating to the designation of such proposed landmark, landmark site, interior landmark or scenic landmark, the amendment to any designation thereof or the proposed rescission of any designation or amendment thereto. Such notice may be served by the commission by registered mail addressed to the owner or owners at his or her or their last known address or addresses, as the same appear in the records of the office of the commissioner of finance or if there is no name in such records, such notice may be served by ordinary mail addressed to "Owner" at the street address of the improvement parcel or property in question. Failure by the commission to give such notices shall not invalidate or affect any proceedings pursuant to this chapter relating to such improvement parcel or property.

(b) At any such public hearing, the commission shall afford a reasonable opportunity for the presentation of facts and the expression of views by those desiring to be heard, and may, in its discretion, take the testimony of witnesses and receive evidence; provided, however, that the commission, in determining any matter as to which any such hearing is held, shall not be confined to consideration of the facts, views, testimony or evidence submitted at such hearing.

(c) The commission may delegate to any member or members thereof the power to conduct any such public hearing and to hold any conference required to be held under the provisions of sections 25-306 and 25-310 of this chapter.

(d) The commission, may, in its discretion, direct that notice of any such public hearing on a request for a certificate of appropriateness, or on any plan formulated by the commission in relation thereto, be given by the applicant to such owners of property in the neighborhood of the improvement or improvement parcel to which such request relates, as the commission deems proper. When so directed, the applicant shall mail a notice of such hearing to such owners, at their last known addresses, as the same appear in the records of the office of the commissioner of finance, and shall likewise mail a notice of such hearing to persons who have filed written requests for such notice with the commission. A reasonable period of time, as prescribed by the regulations of the commission, shall be afforded the applicant for giving notice of such hearing to such owners and persons. Any failure to give or receive such notice shall not invalidate any such hearing or any determination made by the commission with respect to such request for a certificate or with respect to such plan.

§ 25-314 Extension of time for action by commission.

Whenever, under the provisions of this chapter, the commission is required or authorized, within a prescribed period of time, to make any determination or perform any act in relation to any request for a certificate of no effect on protected architectural features, a certificate of appropriateness or a permit for minor work, the applicant may extend such period of time by his or her written consent filed with the commission.

§ 25-315 Determinations of the commission; notice thereof.

(a) Any determination of the commission granting or denying a certificate of no effect on protected architectural features, a certificate of appropriateness or a permit for minor work shall set forth the reasons for such determination.

(b) The commission shall promptly give notice of any such determination, and of any preliminary determination of insufficient return made pursuant to paragraph one of subdivision a of section 25-309 of this chapter, to the applicant. Such notice shall include a copy of such determination.

(c) Subject to the provisions of section 25-304 of this chapter, any determination of the commission granting a certificate of no effect on protected architectural features, a certificate of appropriateness or a permit for minor work may prescribe conditions under which the proposed work shall be done, in order to effectuate the purposes of this chapter, and may include recommendations by the commission as to the performance of such work, provided that the provisions of this subdivision shall not apply to any notice to proceed granted pursuant to the provisions of subdivisions g and i of section 25-309 of this chapter.

§ 25-316 Transmission of certificates and applications to proper city agency.

In any case where a certificate of no effect on protected architectural features, certificate of appropriateness or notice to proceed is granted by the commission to an applicant who has filed with the commission a copy of an application for a permit from the department of buildings, the commission shall transmit such certificate or a copy of such notice to the department of buildings. In any case where any such certificate or notice is granted to an applicant who has filed an application for a special permit with the city planning commission or the board of standards and appeals pursuant to article seven of the zoning resolution, the commission shall transmit such certificate or a copy of such notice to the planning commission or the board of standards and appeals, as the case may be.

§ 25-317 Penalties for violations; enforcement.

(a) Any person who violates any provision of subdivision a of section 25-305 of this chapter shall be guilty of a misdemeanor and shall be punished by a fine of not more than one thousand dollars and not less than one hundred dollars, or by imprisonment for not more than one year, or by both such fine and imprisonment.

(b) Any person who violates any provision of subdivision a of section 25-310 of this chapter or any provision of section 25-311 shall be punished, for a first offense, by a fine of not more than two hundred and fifty dollars or less than twenty-five dollars or by imprisonment for not more than thirty days, or by both such fine and imprisonment, and shall be punished for a second, or any subsequent offense, by a fine of not more than five hundred dollars or less than one hundred dollars, or by imprisonment for not more than three months, or by both such fine and imprisonment.

(c) Any person who files with the commission any application or request for a certificate or permit and who refuses to furnish, upon demand by the commission, any information relating to such application or request, or who wilfully makes any false statement in such application or request, or who, upon such demand, wilfully furnishes false information to the commission, shall be punished by a fine of not more than five hundred dollars or by imprisonment for not more than ninety days, or by both such fine and imprisonment.

(d) For the purpose of this chapter, each day during which there exists any violation of the provisions of paragraph three of subdivision a of section 25-305 of this chapter or paragraph two of subdivision a of section 25-310 of this chapter or any violation of the provisions of section 25-311 of this chapter, shall constitute a separate violation of such provisions.

(e) Whenever any person has engaged or is about to engage in any act or practice which constitutes or will constitute a violation of any provision of this chapter mentioned in subdivisions a and b of this section, the commission may make application to the supreme court for an order enjoining such act or practice, or requiring such person to remove the violation or directing the restoration, as nearly as may be practicable, of any improvement or any exterior architectural feature thereof or improvement parcel affected by or involved in such violation, and upon a showing by the commission that such person has engaged or is about to engage in any such act or practice, a permanent or temporary injunction, restraining order or other appropriate order shall be granted without bond.

§ 25-318 Reports by commission on plans for proposed projects.

(a) Plans for the construction, reconstruction, alteration or demolition of any improvement or proposed improvement which:

(1) is owned by the city or is to be constructed upon property owned by the city; and

(2) is or is to be located on a landmark site or in an historic district or contains an interior landmark;

shall, prior to city action approving or otherwise authorizing the use of such plans with respect to securing the performance of such work, be referred by the agency of the city having responsibility for the preparation of such plans to the commission for a report. Such report shall be submitted to the mayor, the city council and to the agency having such responsibility and shall be published in the City Record within forty-five days after such referral.

(b) (1) No officer or agency of the city whose approval is required by law for the construction or effectuation of a city-aided project shall approve the plans or proposal for, or application for approval of, such project, unless, prior to such approval, such officer or agency has received from the commission a report on such plans, proposal or application for approval.

    (2) All such plans, proposals or applications for approval shall be referred to the commission for a report thereon before consideration of approval thereof is undertaken by any such officer or agency, and the commission shall submit its report to each such officer and agency and such report shall be published in the City Record within forty-five days after such referral.

    (c) Except as provided in subdivision d of section 25-303, where the commission so requests, plans for the construction, reconstruction, alteration or demolition of any landscape feature of a scenic landmark shall, prior to city action approving or otherwise authorizing the use of such plans with respect to securing the performance of such work, be referred by the agency of the city having responsibility for the preparation of such plans to the commission for a report. Such report shall be submitted to the mayor, the city council and to the agency having such responsibility and shall be published in the City Record within forty-five days after such referral. No such report shall recommend disapproval of any such plans where land contour work or earthwork is necessary in order to conform with applicable laws concerning regulation of lots, storm water disposal and water courses. The commissioner of parks and recreation may request an advisory report concerning work proposed to be performed on, or in the vicinity of, a scenic landmark, and such report shall be published in the City Record.

§ 25-319 Regulations.

The commission may from time to time promulgate, amend and rescind such regulations as it may deem necessary to effectuate the purposes of this chapter, including, but not limited to, regulations:

    (a) for the protection, preservation, enhancement, and perpetuation and use of landmarks, interior landmarks, scenic landmarks and historic districts, subject to the provisions of section 25-304 of this chapter. Such regulations may apply to one or more historic districts or to one or more portions of an historic district and may vary from area to area in their provisions;

    (b) relating to the determination of the earning capacity of improvement parcels by the commission pursuant to section 25-309 of this chapter;

    (c) relating to the procedures of the commission in carrying out its functions, powers and duties under this chapter, including procedures for the giving of notice by the commission by mail or otherwise, where notice is required by this chapter; and

    (d) relating to forms to be used in proceedings before the commission.

§ 25-320 Investigations and reports.

The commission may make such investigations and studies of matters relating to the protection, enhancement, perpetuation or use of landmarks, interior landmarks, scenic landmarks and historic districts, and to the restoration of landmarks, interior landmarks, scenic landmarks and buildings in historic districts as the commission may, from time to time, deem necessary or appropriate for the effectuation of the purposes of this chapter, and may submit reports and recommendations as to such matters to the mayor and other agencies of the city. In making such investigations and studies, the commission may hold such public hearings as it may deem necessary or appropriate.

§ 25-321 Applicability.

The provisions of this chapter shall be inapplicable to the construction, reconstruction, alteration or demolition of any improvement on a landmark site or in a historic district or containing an interior landmark, or of any landscape feature of a scenic landmark, where a permit for the performance of such work was issued by the department of buildings, or, in the case of a landscape feature of a scenic landmark, where plans for such work have been approved, prior to the effective date of the designation, or amended or modified designation, pursuant to the provisions of section 25-303 of this chapter, first making the provisions of this chapter applicable to such improvement or landscape feature or to the improvement parcel or property in which such improvement or landscape feature is or is to be located.

Appendix L

Current Text of S. 3196, a Bill to Amend the National Historic Preservation Act

The following bill was referred to the Public Lands Subcommittee of the Senate Committee on Energy and Natural Resources. Hearings on the bill are expected in 1992.

101ST CONGRESS

2d SESSION

S.3196

To amend the National Historic Preservation Act and the National Historic Preservation Act Amendments of 1980 to strengthen the preservation of our historic heritage and resources, and for other purposes.

IN THE SENATE OF THE UNITED STATES

October 12 (legislative day, October 2), 1990

Mr. FOWLER introduced the following bill; which was read twice and referred to the Committee on Energy and Natural Resources

A BILL

To amend the National Historic Preservation Act and the National Historic Preservation Act Amendments of 1980 to strengthen the preservation of our historic heritage and resources, and for other purposes.

Be it enacted by the Senate and House of Representatives of the United States of America in Congress assembled,

Section 1. Short title.

This Act may be cited as the "National Historic Preservation Amendments Act of 1990."

Section 2. Findings.

"(1)

"(A)

Section 1(b) of the National Historic Preservation Act (16 U.S.C. 470(b)) is amended—

(1) by redesignating paragraphs (2), (3), (4), (5), (6), and (7) as paragraphs (4), (5), (6), (7), (8) and (9); and

(2) by inserting after paragraph (1) the following new paragraphs:

"(2) historic properties, including prehistoric and historic sites, buildings, districts, structures, landscapes, and objects, prehistoric and historic archaeological resources, prehistoric and historic roads and trails, and places that have figured in the traditions and lifeways of our communities, of Native American and other ethnic groups, and of the Nation as a whole, are vital links to our past and contribute in major ways to the identity of our Nation and its communities;

"(3) a national preservation program is achieved by extending Federal Government concern to properties of significance to localities, Indian tribes, States and the Nation in private and public ownership;".

Section 3. Policy.

Section 2 of the National Historic Preservation Act (16 U.S.C. 470-1) is amended—

(1) in paragraph (2) by inserting "and in the administration of the national preservation program in partnership with States, Indian tribes, and local governments" after "community of nations"; and

(2) in paragraph (6) by inserting ", Indian tribes," after "local governments."

Section 4. Review of threats to properties.

Section 101(a) of the National Historic Preservation Act (16 U.S.C. 470a(a)) is amended—

(1) in paragraph (2)(F)—

(A) by striking "property, any" and inserting "property and any"; and

(B) by striking ", and the general public,"; and

(2) at the end thereof by adding the following new paragraph:

"(8) The Secretary shall, at least once every 3 years, in consultation with the Council, make a review of threats to properties included in or eligible for inclusion on the National Register, in order to—

"(A) determine what kinds of properties may be in particular danger;

"(B) ascertain the causes of the threats; and

"(C) develop and submit to the President and Congress recommendations for remedial action.".

Section 5. State historic preservation programs.

Section 101(b) of the National Historic Preservation Act (16 U.S.C. 470a(b)) is amended—

(1) by amending paragraph (2) to read as follows:

"(2) Periodically, but not less than every 4 years after the approval of any State program under this subsection, the Secretary, in consultation with the Council and the State Historic Preservation Officer, shall evaluate the program to determine whether it is consistent with the purposes and requirements of this Act. If at any time the Secretary determines that a State program is not consistent with the purposes and requirements of this Act, the Secretary shall disapprove the program and suspend, in whole or in part, assistance to the State under subsection (b)(1), unless there are adequate assurances that the program will be made consistent with the purposes and requirements of the Act within a reasonable period of time. At the discretion of the Secretary, a State system of fiscal audit and management may be substituted for comparable Federal requirements so long as the State system establishes and maintains substantially similar accountability standards. The Secretary may also conduct periodic fiscal audits of State programs approved under this section.";

(2) in paragraph (3)—

(A) by striking "and to" and inserting "and administer the State program of Federal assistance for historic preservation within the State, and to":

(B) in subparagraph (A), by striking "in cooperation with Federal and State agencies, local governments, and private organizations and individuals,";

(C) by amending subparagraph (B) to read as follows:

"(B) nominate eligible properties to the National Register of Historic Places;";

(D) by striking subparagraph (D) and redesignating subparagraphs (E), (F), (G), and (H) as subparagraphs (D), (E), (F) and (G);

(E) in subparagraph (F), as redesignated by subparagraph (D), by striking "relating to the Federal and State Historic Preservation Programs; and" and inserting "in historic preservation;";

(F) in subparagraph (G), as redesignated by subparagraph (D), by striking the period at the end thereof and inserting a semicolon; and

(G) by adding at the end thereof the following new subparagraphs:

"(H) consult with appropriate Federal agencies in accordance with this Act, on—

"(i) Federal undertakings that may affect historic properties; and

"(ii) the content and sufficiency of any plans developed to protect or to reduce or mitigate harm to such properties;

"(I) advise, assist, and evaluate proposals for rehabilitation projects that may qualify for Federal assistance (including grants, loans, and tax incentives); and

"(J) carry out such additional responsibilities as the State Historic Preservation Officer determines to be appropriate, consistent with the purposes of this Act.";

(3) in paragraph (5) by striking "1980" and inserting "1990"; and

(4) by adding at the end thereof the following new paragraphs:

"(6) (A) Subject to subparagraph (B), the Secretary or the Council may delegate to a State Historic Preservation Officer, through contracts and cooperative agreements, all or any part of their authorities within the State—

"(i) to identify and preserve historic properties;

"(ii) to determine the eligibility of properties for listing on the National Register;

"(iii) to expand the National Register;

"(iv) to maintain historical and archaeological data bases;

"(v) to certify eligibility for Federal preservation incentives;

"(vi) to comment on, approve, and enforce actions of Federal, State, or local governments, private individuals, and corporations pursuant to this Act, the Internal Revenue Code of 1986, and other Federal law; and

"(vii) to exercise such other authority as the Secretary or the Council may decide to delegate.

"(B) A delegation of authority under subparagraph (A) may be made if—

"(i) the State Historic Preservation Officer has requested the additional authority;

"(ii) the Secretary has approved the State historic preservation program pursuant to section 101(b) (1) and (2);

"(iii) the State Historic Preservation Officer agrees to carry out the additional authority in a timely and efficient manner acceptable to the Secretary or the Council, as the case may be;

"(iv) the Secretary or the Council agree to provide for a timely review of decisions when requested; and

"(v) the Secretary or the Council and the State Historic Preservation Officer agree on the terms of additional financial assistance to the State, if there is to be any, for the costs of carrying out the delegated authority.".

Section 6. Certification of local governments.

Section 101(c) of the National Historic Preservation Act (16 U.S.C. 470a(c)) is amended by adding at the end thereof the following new paragraph:

"(4) For the purposes of this section—

"(A) the term 'designation' means the identification and registration of properties for protection that meet criteria established by the State or the locality for significant historic and prehistoric resources within the jurisdiction of a local government; and

"(B) the term 'protection' means a local review process under State or local law for proposed demolition of, changes to, or other action that may affect historic properties designated pursuant to subsection (c).".

Section 7. Tribal historic preservation programs.

(a) REVISION OF EXISTING LAW.—Section 101 of the National Historic Preservation Act (16 U.S.C. 470a) is amended—

    (1) by redesignating subsections (d), (e), (f), (g) and (h) as subsections (e), (f), (g), (h), and (i); and

    (2) by inserting after subsection (c) the following new subsection:

"(d) (1) (A) The Secretary shall establish a program and develop regulations to assist Indian tribes in preserving their unique cultural heritage. The program shall have as its purpose the preservation, retention, and enhancement of the historic properties and cultural traditions of Indian tribes.

"(B) The program under subparagraph (A) shall be developed in such a manner as to ensure that tribal values are taken into account. The Secretary may waive or modify requirements of this section to conform to the cultural setting of tribal heritage preservation goals and objectives. The tribal programs implemented by specific tribes may vary in scope, as determined by each tribe's chief governing authority.

"(C) The Secretary shall consult with Indian tribes, other Federal agencies, State Historic Preservation Officers, and other interested parties and initiate the program under subparagraph (A) by not later than October 1, 1991.

"(2) Tribal historic preservation programs shall be administered by a tribal preservation official appointed by the tribe's chief governing authority or as a tribal ordinance may otherwise provide.

"(3) A tribal preservation official may assume all or any part of the functions of a State Historic Preservation Officer under subsection (b)(3) with respect to Indian lands of the tribe, if—

"(A) the tribe's chief governing authority so requests;

"(B) the tribal preservation official provides the Secretary with a plan describing how the functions the tribal preservation official proposes to assume will be carried out; and

"(C) the Secretary approves the plan, after consultation with the State Historic Preservation Officer, and with the Council if the tribe proposes to assume the functions of the State Historic Preservation Officer with respect to review of undertakings under section 106, and other Indian tribes, if any, whose tribal or aboriginal lands may be affected by conduct of the tribal historic preservation program.

"(4) At the request of a tribe whose preservation program has been approved to assume responsibilities pursuant to paragraph (3), the Secretary shall delegate to such tribe, through a contract or cooperative agreement, all or any part of the authorities described in subsection (b)(6) on Indian lands of the tribe, if—

"(A) the Secretary agrees to provide appropriate financial assistance to the tribe for the costs of carrying out the delegated authority;

"(B) the Secretary ensures that the tribal historic preservation program is sufficient to carry out the contract or cooperative agreement and this Act; and

"(C) the contract or cooperative agreement specifies any continuing responsibilities of the Secretary or of the appropriate State Historic Preservation Officers and provides for appropriate participation by—

"(i)   the tribe's traditional cultural authorities;
"(ii)   representatives of other Indian tribes whose traditional lands are under the jurisdiction of the tribe to which the Secretary's preservation responsibilities are delegated; and
"(iii)   the interested public.

"(5)   The Council may enter into an agreement with an Indian tribe to permit undertakings on Indian lands of the tribe to be reviewed under tribal historic preservation regulations in place of review under regulations promulgated by the Council to govern compliance with section 106, if the Council, after consultation with the tribe and appropriate State Historic Preservation Officers, determines that the tribal historic preservation regulations will afford historic properties protection at a level and of a kind equivalent to those afforded by the Council's regulations.

"(6)   At the request of a tribe whose preservation program has been approved to assume responsibilities pursuant to paragraph (3), and with the concurrence of the Council, the Bureau of Indian Affairs shall delegate such part of its preservation authorities as the tribe may request on Indian lands of a tribe to the tribal preservation official, or, when a tribe so requests, to the appropriate State Historic Preservation Officer.

"(7)   (A)   Properties of traditional religious and cultural importance to an Indian tribe or other Native American group shall be eligible for inclusion on the National Register.

"(B)   In planning an undertaking in compliance with section 106, a Federal agency shall consult with an Indian tribe that may attach religious and cultural values to properties described in subparagraph (A).".

(b)   CONFORMING AMENDMENTS.—(1) Section 102(a)(3) of the National Historic Preservation Act (16 U.S.C. 470b(a)(3)) is amended by striking "101(d) (1) and (2)" and inserting "101(e) (1) and (2)."

(2)   Section 110(c) of the National Historic Preservation Act (16 U.S.C. 470h-2(c)) is amended by striking "101(g)" and inserting "101(h)."

Section 8. Matching grants.

Section 101(e) of the National Historic Preservation Act, as redesignated by section 7(a)(1), is amended—

(1)   by amending paragraph (1) to read as follows:

"(1)   (A)   The Secretary shall administer a program of matching grants to the States for the purposes of carrying out this Act and for such other purposes as the Secretary may determine.

"(B)   The Secretary shall consult with the Council regarding the provision of grants related to the carrying out of authorities under subsection (b)(6)."; and

(2)   by adding at the end thereof the following new paragraphs:

"(4)   The Secretary shall administer a program of direct grants to Indian tribes for the purpose of carrying out this Act as it pertains to Indian tribes. Matching fund requirements may be waived or Federal funds available to a tribe may be used as tribal matching funds for the purposes of the tribe's conducting its responsibilities pursuant to this section.

"(5)   (A)   As part of the program of matching grant assistance to States, the Secretary shall administer a program of direct grants to the Federated States of Micronesia, the Republic of the Marshall Islands, and the

Republic of Palau (referred to as the 'Micronesian States') in furtherance of the Compact of Free Association between the United States and the Federated States of Micronesia and the Marshall Islands, approved by the Compact of Free Association Act of 1985 (48 U.S.C. 1681 note), and the Compact of Free Association between the United States and Palau, approved by the Joint Resolution entitled 'Joint Resolution to approve the "Compact of Free Association" between the United States and the Government of Palau, and for other purposes' (48 U.S.C. 1681 note). It shall be the goal of the program to ensure at the termination of the Compacts that each Micronesian State has established historic and cultural preservation programs that meet the unique cultural needs of those emerging nations, thus guaranteeing the continuation of the programs. The Secretary may waive or modify the requirements of this section to conform to the cultural setting of those nations in order to achieve that goal.

"(B) The amounts to be made available to the Micronesian States shall be determined by the Secretary on the basis of needs as determined by the Secretary. Matching funds shall not be required.".

Section 9. Education and training.

Section 101 of the National Historic Preservation Act (16 U.S.C. 470a), as amended by section 6, is amended by adding at the end thereof the following new subsection:

"(j) (1) The Secretary shall, in consultation and cooperation with—
"(A) the Department of Education;
"(B) the Council;
"(C) the Department of Labor;
"(D) the National Conference of State Historic Preservation Officers;
"(E) the National Trust for Historic Preservation;
"(F) the Smithsonian Institution;
"(G) the Society for American Archaeology;
"(H) the American Institute of Architects;
"(I) the Organization of American Historians; and
"(J) other Federal, tribal, and non-Federal organizations,
develop and implement a comprehensive preservation education and training program.

"(2) The education and training program described in paragraph (1) shall include—

"(A) new standards and increased preservation training opportunities for Federal workers involved in preservation-related functions;

"(B) increased preservation training opportunities for other Federal, State, tribal, and local government workers, students, and individuals with an avocational interest in preservation;

"(C) inclusion of provisions in federally-sponsored survey and excavation work to afford an opportunity for the participation of avocational archaeologists;

"(D) special assistance to historically black colleges and universities and to tribal colleges and colleges with a high enrollment of American Indians to establish preservation degree programs;

"(E) dissemination of information on preservation technologies;

"(F) implementation of a coordinated national informational and media program (such as public service announcements) on preservation topics;

"(G) distribution of model preservation curricula for elementary and high schools and adult education programs;

"(H) preservation internship programs for United States and foreign students;

"(I) provision of training and skill development in trades and crafts related to historic preservation in existing Federal training and development programs; and

"(J) support for research, analysis, curation, interpretation, and display related to preservation.

"(3) There are authorized to be appropriated to carry out this subsection $5,000,000 for each of fiscal years 1991, 1992, 1993, 1994, and 1995.".

Section 10. Requirements for awarding of grants.

Section 102 of the National Historic Preservation Act (16 U.S.C. 470b) is amended—

(1) by amending subsection (a)(3) to read as follows:

"(3) for more than 60 percent of the aggregate costs of carrying out projects and programs specified in section 101(b)(3) in any one fiscal year, except that the Secretary may provide up to 100 percent of the aggregate costs in any one fiscal year for the additional costs incurred by a State Historic Preservation Officer in carrying out activities pursuant to section 101(b)(6).";

(2) in subsection (b) by striking ", in which case a grant to the National Trust may include funds for the maintenance, repair, and administration of the property in a manner satisfactory to the Secretary"; and

(3) by adding at the end thereof the following new subsection:

"(e) The Secretary may make funding available to individual States and the National Trust for Historic Preservation as soon as possible after execution of a grant agreement. For purposes of administration, grants to individual States and the National Trust each shall be considered to be one grant and shall be administered by the National Park Service as such.".

Section 11. Apportionment of grant funds.

Section 103 of the National Historic Preservation Act (16 U.S.C. 470c) is amended—

(1) in subsection (a) by striking "for comprehensive statewide historic surveys and plans under this Act," and inserting "for the purposes of this Act"; and

(2) in subsection (b) by striking "The amounts appropriated and made available for grants to the States for purposes and programs under this Act for each fiscal year shall be apportioned among the States by the Secretary in accordance with needs as disclosed in approved statewide historic preservation plans.".

Section 12. Federal agency historic preservation programs.

Section 110 of the National Historic Preservation Act (16 U.S.C. 470h-2) is amended—

(1) in subsection (a)(1) by striking "101(f)" and inserting "101(g)";

(2) by amending subsection (a)(2) to read as follows:

"(2) In consultation with the Council and the Secretary and in cooperation with State Historic Preservation Officers, tribal preservation programs, and certified local governments, each Federal agency, unless exempted pursuant to section 214, shall establish and implement a preservation program for the identification, evaluation, nomination to the National Register of Historic Places, and protection of historic properties that ensures—

"(A) that historic properties under the jurisdiction or control of the agency, or subject to possible effect by actions assisted, licensed, permitted, or participated in by the agency or by programs subject to review and approval by the agency, are identified and evaluated to determine their eligibility for inclusion in the National Register;

"(B) that such properties under the jurisdiction or control of the agency as may be eligible for inclusion in the National Register—

"(i) are managed and maintained in a way that reasonably preserves their historic, archaeological, architectural, cultural, and other values; and

"(ii) are not inadvertently damaged, disposed of or allowed to deteriorate;

"(C) that the preservation, management, and maintenance of such properties not under the jurisdiction or control of the agency but subject to possible effect by actions assisted, licensed, permitted, or participated in by the agency or by programs subject to review and approval by such agency are given full consideration in planning;

"(D) that the agency's preservation-related activities are carried out in cooperation with other Federal, State, tribal, and local agencies and the private sector, and in coordination with Federal, State, tribal, and local historic preservation plans; and

"(E) that the agency's procedures for compliance with section 106—

"(i) are consistent with regulations issued by the Council pursuant to section 211; and

"(ii) provide for identification of historic properties and the development and implementation of agreements, in consultation with State Historic Preservation Officers, local governments, Indian tribes, and the interested public, regarding the means by which adverse effects on such properties will be resolved."; and

(3) by adding at the end thereof the following new subsections:

"(k) Each Federal agency shall ensure that the agency will not grant a loan, loan guarantee, permit, license, or other assistance to an applicant who, at any time prior to the making of the grant, has adversely affected a historic property to which the grant would relate, or being in a position to prevent it, allowed such adverse effect to occur, unless the agency, in consultation with the Council, determines that circumstances justify granting such assistance despite the adverse effect created or permitted by the applicant.

"(l) With respect to any undertaking subject to section 106 which adversely affects any property included in or eligible for inclusion in the National Register and for which the Federal agency has not entered into an agreement with the Council and the appropriate State Historic Preservation Officer, the head of the Federal agency shall approve the undertaking only if the head of the agency has determined that implementing the recommendations contained in the comments of the Council pursuant to section 106 is not feasible and prudent.

"(m) When the Council finds, after consultation with the Secretary, State Historic Preservation Officers, affected Indian tribes and local governments, and the interested public, that a Federal agency's procedures for compliance with the National Environmental Policy Act of 1969 (42 U.S.C. 4321 et seq.) provide adequately for consideration of cultural resources, including—

"(1) the identification of effects on cultural resources; and

"(2) the development and implementation of agreements with affected parties and others regarding the means by which adverse effects will be resolved, the agency may comply with those procedures in place of regulations promulgated by the Council in order to meet the requirements of sections 106, 110(a)(2), 110(b), and 111, as applicable. The Council shall review the procedures of such an agency from time to time to ensure that they continue to provide adequately for consideration of cultural resources.."

Section 13. Lease or exchange of federal historic properties.

Section 111 of the National Historic Preservation Act (16 U.S.C. 470h-3) is amended—

(1) in subsection (a) by striking "may, after consultation with the Advisory Council on Historic Preservation, lease" and inserting "shall, after consultation with the Council, establish and implement adaptive use alternatives for historic properties that are not needed for current or projected agency purposes, and may" and

(2) in subsection (b) by striking "may" and inserting "shall."

Section 14. Disposition of archaeological materials.

Title I of the National Historic Preservation Act (16 U.S.C. 470 et seq.) is amended by adding at the end thereof the following new section:

"SEC. 112. (a) Each Federal agency that is responsible for the protection of archaeological resources or that conducts, causes to be conducted, or permits archaeological surveys or excavations pursuant to this Act or any other law shall ensure that—

"(1) agency personnel and contractors supervising archaeological surveys and excavations meet professional standards under regulations developed by the Secretary in consultation with the Council and other affected agencies, taking into account, and, when appropriate, utilizing the pertinent standards and certification systems of, international, national, State, and local archaeological organizations;

"(2) programs for the protection of archaeological resources and for archaeological surveys and excavations are designed, when appropriate, to involve and inform the interested public, including volunteers, professional societies, avocational groups, Native American organizations and educational institutions;

"(3) archaeological surveys and excavations are designed, to the extent feasible, to address research topics of demonstrable significance to the sciences and humanities; and

"(4) data produced by archaeological surveys and excavations are maintained in perpetuity in appropriate data bases and disseminated to potential users.

"(b) (1) The analysis and disposition of materials and records produced by archaeological survey and recovery work conducted by or caused to be conducted or permitted by Federal agencies shall be determined pursuant to section 110(b) through consultation among concerned parties and need not require the permanent retention of all such materials if the responsible agency, in consultation with other parties, determines that disposition other than as prescribed under paragraph (2) is in the public interest.

"(2) Subject to a determination under paragraph (1), artifacts and other materials produced by archaeological surveys and excavations shall be—

"(A) analyzed as necessary to address significant research topics; and

"(B) (i) preserved in an appropriately equipped repository; or

"(ii) disposed of in a manner that reflects balanced consideration of their ownership, scientific and educational value, cultural or religious significance (where applicable), artistic and aesthetic qualities (where applicable), and any special conservation problems that the materials may present.

"(3) When artifacts or other materials are preserved in a repository, retained by their owner for study or exhibition, or donated, loaned, leased, or otherwise transferred to another party for study or exhibition, the Federal agency that gives up possession of the materials shall ensure that the materials are registered with an antiquities registration program in order to maintain a permanent record of such materials and their location.

"(c) Archaeological survey and recovery work conducted pursuant to an agreement executed under section 106 shall not require a separate permit under the Archaeological Resources Protection Act of 1979 (16 U.S.C. 470aa et seq.) if the work meets the requirements of section 4(a) of that Act (16 U.S.C. 470cc(a)).

"(d) The Secretary, in consultation with the Council and affected Federal agencies, State Historic Preservation Officers, tribal preservation officials, appropriate national and regional archaeological and anthropological organizations, and Native American organizations shall promulgate standards and guidelines to implement this section.

"(e) In order to promote the preservation of archaeological resources on private land that are eligible for listing on the National Register, the Secretary shall, in consultation with the Council, promulgate guidelines to ensure that Federal, State, and tribal historic preservation programs subject to this Act include plans to—

"(1) identify locations of archaeological resources on private land that have a demonstrated or likely research significance;

"(2) provide information to the owners of those resources concerning the significance of the archaeological resources, the need for protection of those resources, and the available means of protection;

"(3) encourage owners to preserve archaeological resources in place and offer the owners of those resources information on the tax and grant assistance available for the donation of the resources or of a preservation easement of the resources; and

"(4) encourage owners who are undertaking excavations to—

"(A) conduct excavations and analyses that meet the standards for federally-sponsored excavations established pursuant to this Act;

"(B) register artifacts found within the archaeological resource with an antiquities registration program;

"(C)   donate or lend artifacts of great significance in current or likely research to an appropriate research institution; and

"(D)   allow access to artifacts for research purposes.".

Section 15. Interstate and international traffic in antiquities.

Title I of the National Historic Preservation Act (16 U.S.C. 470 et seq.), as amended by section 13, is amended by adding at the end thereof the following new sections:

"SEC. 113. (a) In order to facilitate the control of illegal interstate and international traffic in antiquities, the Council shall study and report the suitability and feasibility of establishing a program for the registration of artifacts removed from archaeological sites in the United States and artifacts brought into the United States from abroad.

"(b) In conducting the study described in subsection (a) the Council shall consult with other Federal agencies that conduct, cause to be conducted, or permit archaeological surveys or excavations and with State Historic Preservation Officers, archaeological organizations, Indian tribes and Native American organizations, international organizations and other interested persons.

"(c) Not later than 18 months after the date of enactment of this section, the Council shall submit to Congress a report detailing its findings and recommendations from the study described in subsection (a).

"(d) There are authorized to be appropriated not more than $500,000 for the study described in subsection (a), such sums to remain available until expended.

"SEC. 114. (a) The Council shall, in consultation with the Cultural Property Advisory Committee established by section 306 of the Convention on Cultural Property Implementation Act (19 U.S.C. 2605), call for and organize United States leadership and participation in an international conference on the international antiquities trade.

"(b) The conference described in subsection (a) shall focus on—

"(1)   providing adequate controls, enforcement, and incentives to ensure that traded artifacts are the products of properly conducted excavations; and

"(2)   promoting an exchange between nations to enhance public knowledge of each nation's cultural heritage.

"(c) Invitations to the conference described in subsection (a) shall be extended to representatives of national governments, archaeological and anthropological organizations, Native American organizations, public and private museums, arts and antiquities dealers, private collectors, legislators, and law enforcement specialists.

"(d) The conference described in subsection (a) shall be held in 1992 as part of the commemoration of the 500th anniversary of the Columbus Discovery Voyage.

"(e) Funds for the conference described in subsection (a) shall be provided through appropriations of such sums as are necessary to the Council and other Federal agencies and by donations or transfer to the Council from other public and private sources.."

Section 16. Membership of advisory council on historic preservation.

Section 201(a) of the National Historic Preservation Act (16 U.S.C. 470i(a)) is amended—

(1) by striking "and" at the end of paragraph (9);
(2) by striking the period at the end of paragraph (10) and inserting ", and"; and
(3) by adding at the end thereof the following new paragraph:
"(11) one Native American appointed by the President.".

Section 17. Regulations of the advisory council on historic preservation.

Section 211 of the National Historic Preservation Act (16 U.S.C. 470s) is amended by striking the period at the end of the first sentence and inserting "in its entirety."

Section 18. Definitions.

(a) AMENDMENT AND ADDITION OF DEFINITIONS.—Section 301 of the National Historic Preservation Act (16 U.S.C. 470w) is amended—
(1) in paragraph (1) by striking "Code" and all that follows through the end of the paragraph;
(2) in paragraph (2) by striking "the Trust Territories of the Pacific Islands" and inserting "the Republic of the Marshall Islands, the Federated States of Micronesia, and the Republic of Palau";
(3) by amending paragraph (4) to read as follows:
"(4) 'Indian tribe' or 'tribe' means an Indian tribe, band, nation, or other organized group or community, including a Native village, Regional Corporation or Village Corporation, as those terms are defined in section 3 of the Alaska Native Claims Settlement Act (43 U.S.C. 1602), which is recognized as eligible for the special programs and services provided by the United States to Indians because of their status as Indians.";
(4) in paragraph (5) by—
(A) inserting "landscape," after "district,"; and
(B) striking "Register" and all that follows through the end of the paragraph and inserting "Register, including artifacts, records, and material remains related to such a property or resource.";
(5) by amending paragraph (7) to read as follows:
"(7) 'undertaking' means a project, activity, or program funded in whole or in part under the direct or indirect jurisdiction of a Federal agency, including—
"(A) those carried out by or on behalf of the agency;
"(B) those carried out with Federal financial assistance;
"(C) those requiring a Federal permit, license, or approval; and
"(D) those subject to State or local regulation administered pursuant to a delegation or approval by a Federal agency.";
(6) in paragraph (8) by—
(A) striking "maintenance and reconstruction," and inserting "maintenance, study, interpretation, reconstruction, and education and training regarding the foregoing activities,";
(7) in paragraph (9) by striking "urban area" and inserting "area";
(8) in paragraph (10) by striking "urban area of one or more neighborhoods and" and inserting "area";
(9) in paragraph (13)(A) by striking "archaeology" and inserting "pre-historic and historic archaeology, folklore and cultural anthropology,"; and
(10) by adding at the end thereof the following new paragraphs:

"(14) 'Indian land manager' means the official of an Indian tribe having primary management authority over lands under the tribe's jurisdiction.

"(15) 'Indian lands' means Indian country as that term is defined in section 1151 of title 18, United States Code, and to the extent not otherwise included in that definition, all lands conveyed or interim conveyed to Alaska Native villages and regional corporations pursuant to the Alaska Native Claims Settlement Act (43 U.S.C. 1601 et seq.).

"(16) 'Traditional cultural authority' means an individual in a Native American group or other social or ethnic group who is recognized by members of the group as an expert on the group's traditional history and cultural practices.

"(17) 'Certified local government' means a local government whose local historic preservation program has been certified pursuant to section 101(c).

"(18) 'Cultural resources' means the tangible and intangible elements of traditional culture, including—

"(A) historic resources;

"(B) American folklife, as that term is defined in section 3(1) of the American Folklife Preservation Act (20 U.S.C. 2102(1)); and

"(C) Native American cultural values protected by the American Indian Religious Freedom Act (42 U.S.C. 1996).

"(19) 'Council' means the Advisory Council on Historic Preservation established by section 201.".

(b) TECHNICAL AMENDMENT.—Section 201(a) of the National Historic Preservation Act (16 U.S.C. 470i(a)) is amended by striking "(hereafter referred to as the 'Council')."

Section 19. Cooperative agreements for the performance of functions of a federal agency.

Section 302 of the National Historic Preservation Act (16 U.S.C. 470w-1) is amended by inserting after "Act," the following: "and, in consultation with the Council, enter into an agreement with the Council, a State Historic Preservation Officer, or a tribal preservation official to perform functions of the Federal agency within a State or tribal territory, and may make funds available to the Council, State Historic Preservation Officer, or tribal preservation official for that purpose,".

Section 20. Access to information.

Section 304 of the National Historic Preservation Act (16 U.S.C. 4702-3) is amended to read as follows:

"(a) The head of a Federal agency or other public official receiving grant assistance pursuant to this Act, after consultation with the Secretary, shall withhold from disclosure to the public, information about the location, character, or ownership of a historic resource if the Secretary and the agency determine that disclosure may—

"(1) cause a significant invasion of privacy;

"(2) risk harm to the historic resource; or

"(3) impede the use of a traditional religious site by practitioners.

"(b) When the Secretary has determined that information should be withheld from the public pursuant to subsection (a), the Secretary, in consultation with the Federal agency, shall determine who may have access to the information for the purpose of carrying out this Act.

"(c) When the information in question has been developed in the course of an agency's compliance with section 106 or 110(f), the Secretary shall consult with the Council in reaching determinations under subsections (a) and (b).".

Section 21. International activities.

(a) TRANSFER OF TITLE. Title IV of the National Historic Preservation Act Amendments of 1980 (16 U.S.C. 470a-1 and 470a-2) is transferred to and added at the end of the National Historic Preservation Act.

(b) FEDERAL UNDERTAKINGS OUTSIDE THE UNITED STATES. Section 402 of the National Historic Preservation Act, as transferred by subsection (a), is amended to read as follows:

"SEC. 402. A Federal agency having direct or indirect jurisdiction over undertakings carried out outside the United States shall establish procedures, in consultation with the Advisory Council on Historic Preservation, the Department of Defense, and the Department of State, to ensure that

"(1) during the planning of each such undertaking the appropriate preservation authorities in the host country are consulted;

"(2) properties significant to the history or prehistory of the host country or included on or eligible for inclusion on the host country's equivalent of the National Register, which might be affected by a United States-sponsored undertaking, are identified and evaluated;

"(3) the undertaking's effects on such properties are taken into account; and

"(4) reasonable and effective steps are taken to avoid or mitigate adverse effects on such properties.".

Section 22. National center for preservation technology.

Title IV of the National Historic Preservation Act, as transferred by section 20(a), is amended by adding at the end thereof the following new sections:

"SEC. 403. The Congress finds and declares that the lack of adequate technology transfer for historic preservation demonstrates a clear need for a new national institution to coordinate research, disseminate information, and provide training about preservation technologies.

"SEC. 404. For the purposes of this title—

"(1) the term 'Board' means the National Preservation Technology Board established by section 406; and

"(2) the term 'Center' means the National Center for Preservation Technology established by section 405.

"SEC. 405. (a) There is established in the Department of the Interior a National Center for Preservation Technology.

"(b) It shall be the duty of the Center to—

"(1) develop and transfer preservation and conservation technologies for the identification, evaluation, conservation, and interpretation of prehistoric and historic resources (including archaeological sites, historic buildings and structures, cultural and designed landscapes, maritime sites, objects, and documents);

"(2) coordinate preservation technology transfer among Federal agencies, State and local governments, universities, international organizations and the private sector; and

"(3) conduct such other activities as are necessary to fulfill the purposes of this title.

"(c) The work of the Center shall be conducted through research, professional training, technical assistance, and programs for public awareness in conjunction with the National Park Service through consortia of regional centers and laboratories and service facilities designated or established under section 407.

"(d) The Center shall be headed by an Executive Director, appointed by the Secretary in consultation with the Board, who has demonstrated high level abilities and experience in the social or physical sciences and in organizational management and the use of technologies.

"(e) The Executive Director of the Center may appoint and fix the compensation of such officers and employees as are necessary to perform the functions of the Center.

"(f) The Director of the National Park Service shall provide the Center such additional personnel, equipment and facilities as may be needed for the Center to carry out its activities.

"SEC. 406. (a) There is established a Preservation Technology Board.

"(b) The Board shall—

"(1) provide leadership, policy direction, coordination and professional oversight to the Center;

"(2) advise on priorities and the allocation of funds among the activities of the Center; and

"(3) submit an annual report to the President and Congress.

"(c) The Board shall be comprised of—

"(1) The Director of the National Park Service (or the Director's designee);

"(2) 1 representative appointed by the head of each of—
"(A) the Department of the Interior;
"(B) the Smithsonian Institution;
"(C) the Department of Agriculture;
"(D) the Department of Commerce;
"(E) the Department of Defense;
"(F) the Department of Energy;
"(G) the Advisory Council on Historic Preservation;
"(H) the Department of State;
"(I) the Department of Transportation;
"(J) the General Services Administration;
"(K) the National Archives and Records Administration;
"(L) the National Science Foundation;
"(M) the Library of Congress;
"(N) the Office of Technology Assessment;
"(O) the National Trust for Historic Preservation;
"(P) the National Conference of State Historic Preservation Officers;
"(Q) the National Academy of Sciences; and
"(R) the Consortia of National Laboratories; and

"(3) 10 persons appointed by the President whose professional qualifications or experience include the disciplines included in the scope of the work of the Center.

"(d) The members of the Board shall serve one 5-year term each, except that the initial appointments shall be staggered so that 6 shall serve a 1-year term, 6 shall serve a 2-year term, 6 shall serve a 3-year term, 6 shall serve a 4-year term and 5 shall serve a 5-year term.

"SEC. 407. (a) The Center shall select regional preservation technology centers from among applicants with a demonstrated institutional commitment to continuing preservation.

"(b) A regional preservation technology center shall develop, coordinate, and implement preservation technology transfer functions in an area of the United States designated by the Board.

"(c) Eligible applicants from areas of the United States designated by the Center may include—

"(1) Federal and non-Federal laboratories;
"(2) museums;
"(3) universities;
"(4) non-profit or for-profit corporations;
"(5) Cooperative Park Study Units of the National Park Service;
"(6) State Historic Preservation Offices; and
"(7) tribal preservation officers.

"(d) The Center may establish or designate analytical or technical research laboratories and service facilities to further the purposes of the Center.

"SEC. 408. The Center may accept—

"(1) grants and donations from private individuals, groups, organizations, corporations and foundations; and
"(2) transfers of funds from other Federal agencies.

"SEC. 409. The Center may enter into contracts and cooperative agreements with Federal, State, tribal, and local governments, nonprofit organizations, for-profit corporations and educational institutions to carry out the Center's responsibilities under this Act and to provide grants and loans to the regional centers and laboratories or service facilities pursuant to section 407.

"SEC. 410. There are authorized to be appropriated for the purposes of the Center $500,000 in fiscal year 1991 and $5,000,000 in each of fiscal years 1992, 1993 and 1994, such sums to remain available until expended.".

Section 23. Report.

Not later than the end of fiscal year 1992, the Secretary, in consultation with the Council, State Historic Preservation Officers, and others, as appropriate, shall undertake a study and report to Congress on the status of the inclusion of artifacts, records, and material remains and on the advisability of including traditional cultural practices and lifeways on, the National Register of Historic Places.

Index

Abatement, real property tax, 5.1.3, 5.1.4, 9.1.3, 9.2.4
Accelerated cost recovery system:
  anti-churning, and, 1.2.4, 1.3.2
  component depreciation, 1.3.2
  generally, 1.1, 1.3.2, 1.4
  175% declining balance method, 1.3.2
  recapture of depreciation, 1.3.3
  straight line depreciation, 1.3.2, 1.4.1
  tax-exempt organization, depreciation of property used by, 1.6, 1.7.2
  Tax Reform Act of 1984, 1.3.2
  200% declining balance method, 1.3.2
Acquisition costs, 1.2.2
Administrative Procedures Act, 6.1.7, 6.1.9, 6.2
Advisory Council on Historic Preservation:
  environmental impact statement, duty to comment, 6.3.4
  generally, 6.1
  Section 106 role, 6.1.3, 6.1.4, 6.1.5, 6.1.6, 6.1.9
Aggregate losses, 3.2.5
Alterations, building:
  generally, 7.4.1
  landmark property, to, 7.4.1, 7.4.2
  maintenance and repairs, 7.4.7
  notice to proceed, 7.4.7
  standards, 7.4.2
  unlawful, penalties for, 7.4.10
Alternative minimum tax, 3.2.4
Amortization, 60-month, 1.1, 1.3
Amtrak Improvement Act of 1974, 4.1.10
Anti-churning, 1.2.4, 1.3.2

Appraisal, easement, 1.4.4, 1.5.4
Appropriateness, certificate of, 7.4.1, 7.4.3, 7.4.5, 7.4.7, 9.1.2
Archeological and Historic Preservation Act, 6.1.6
Architect, role in preservation project, 9.1.2, 9.1.3
Architectural review, boards of, 7.1.4
Asbestos Hazard Emergency Response Act, 1986, 8.1.3
Asbestos, 8
  audits, 8.3.3
  avoiding liability., 8.3.1
  Hazard Emergency Response Act, 8.1.3
  rehabilitation projects, 8.3
  state regulation, 8.1.6
  testing for, 8.1.1
Assessment, real property tax:
  current use, 5.1.5
  frozen, 5.1.7, 9.2.2
  highest and best use, 5.1.5
  restricted use, 5.1.6
At risk rule, real estate partnership:
  applicability to, 3.1.2, 3.2.2
  non-recourse debt financing, 3.2.2
  qualified non-recourse financing, 3.2.2
Attorney, role in preservation project, 9.1.2

Basis:
  adjustments, 1.3.1, 1.4.1
    for Certified Historic Structure, 1.3.1
    for Investment Tax Credit, 1.2.2
    under TEFRA, 1.3.1
  cost of rehabilitation to exceed, 1.2.4

Index

Basis *(Continued)*
  easement donation, effect upon, 1.4.5, 1.5.5
  land cost, 1.2.4
  qualification for Investment Tax Credit, 1.2.4
  reduction, methods, 1.2.4
  time for determination, 1.2.4
Beach and Dune Regulation Law, 7.4.5
Blue sky laws, *see* Securities law, state
Boards of architectural review, 7.1.4
BOCA, *see* Building Officials & Code Administrators International
Building alterations, *see* Alterations, building
Building code requirements, 5.2, 5.2.1, 5.2.2, 9.1.2
Building enlargement, 1.2.2
Building Officials & Code Administrators International, 5.2.1

California Environmental Quality Act, 6.5.2
California State Historical Building Code, 5.2.2
California State Historical Resources Commission, 6.5.1
Cambridge, Massachusetts Half Crown Neighborhood Conservation District, 7.2
Capital view corridor, 7.4.1
Carryback and carryforward, rehabilitation tax credit, 1.2.7
Category of hazardous substances, 8.2.2
CERCLA, 8.1.4, 8.2.2
Certificate of no effect, 7.4.7
Certification:
  historic district, 2.2, 7.5, 7.5.2
  local preservation statutes, 2.2, 7.5, 7.5.1
Certification of appropriateness, 7.4.1, 7.4.3, 7.4.5, 7.4.7, 9.1.2
Certification of Historic Significance:
  appeals, 2.2.4
  application procedure and requirements, 2.2.2–2.2.4, 2.2.3
  generally, 2.2
  standards for evaluation, 2.2.1
Certification of nonsignificance, 2.2, 2.2.3, 9.1.2, 9.2.3
Certification of rehabilitation:
  appeal of denial, 2.2.4, 2.3.3
  application procedure, 2.3.3
  generally, 2.3
  standards for rehabilitation, 2.3.1

Certified historic structure:
  differences in tax treatment from non-historic structures, 1.5, 1.6
  easement donations, 1.4.3, 1.5.3
  rehabilitation expenditures, 1.2.2
  rehabilitation percentage, 1.2.1
  standards for rehabilitation of, 2.3
Charitable institution, hardship application, 7.4.5
Civil penalties, 8.2.3
Coastal Zone Management Act, 4.1.10
Commercial building, as qualified rehabilitation, 1.2.3
Community development block grant, 4.1.4, 4.3.3, 9.1.3
Community Reinvestment Act, 4.1.8
Component depreciation, 1.3.2
Comprehensive public development projects, 9.2.4
Condemnation, 9.2.4
Condominium conversion, investment tax credit passthrough to owner, 1.2.6
Connecticut State Housing Authority, 9.2.2
Conservation purposes, defined, 1.4.3, 1.5.3
Contractor, role in preservation project, 9.1.3
Council on Environmental Quality, regulations, 6.3.1, 6.3.7
Cranston-Gonzales Act, 4.1.6
Critical Issues Fund, 4.3.7
Current-use valuation, 5.1.5

Demolition:
  disincentives, historic buildings, 1.1
  economic hardship grounds, 7.4.5
  generally, 1.1, 7.4.4, 7.4.5
  unlawful, penalties for, 7.4.10
Department of Energy, 4.1.10
Department of the Interior:
  certification, role in, 2.1, 2.1.3
  environmental impact statement, duty to comment, 6.3.4
Department of Transportation Act of 1966, 6.2
Depreciation:
  accelerated 1.3, 1.3.2, 1.4
  accelerated cost recovery system, 1.3.2, 1.4.1
  component, 1.3.2
  disincentive to demolition as, 1.1
  generally, 1.1, 3.2.2, 9.1.3
  and passive loss, 3.2.5
  150%, 200% balance rate, 1.1, 1.3

125% declining balance rate, 1.1, 1.3.1
recapture, 1.3.3
  upon donation of easement, 1.4.5, 1.5.5
  upon installment sale, 1.3.3
straight line, 1.1, 1.2.2, 1.3, 1.3.2, 1.4, 1.4.1
tax exempt participation, 1.6.2
transition rules, 1.4.2
Designation:
  historic district, 2.1.1, 2.2, 7.3.4
  landmarks, see Landmark designation
District of Columbia Commission of Fine Arts, 7.1.6
District of Columbia Historic Preservation Review Board, 7.1.6, 7.4.4

Easements, preservation:
  effect of donation:
    on basis, 1.2.4
    upon rehabilitation tax credit, 1.2.8, 1.4.5, 1.5.5
  eligibility of building for, 1.4.3, 1.5.3
  enforcement, 1.4.2, 1.5.3
  facade, 9.1.3, 9.2.1, 9.2.3
  maintenance, 1.4.2, 1.5.2
  public access, 1.4.1, 1.5.1
  purposes for which granted, 1.4.3, 1.5.3
  sales and disposition of property, effect of, 1.4.1, 1.5.1
  tax treatment, 1.4, 1.5
  Tax Treatment Extension Act of 1980, 1.4, 1.5
  transfer restrictions, 1.4.1, 1.5.1
  valuation, 1.4.4, 1.5.4
Economic Development Administration, 4.1.9
Economic hardship application, see Hardship application
Economic Recovery Tax Act of 1981:
  accelerated cost recovery system, 1.3.2
  generally, 1.1
  rehabilitation incentives, 1.1
Energy, Department of, 4.1.10
Energy credit, 1.2.1
Environmental assessment, 6.3.3, 6.5.2
Environmental audits, 8.3.3
Environmental impact statement:
  content, 6.3.6
  duty to supplement, 6.3.6
  judicial review, 6.3.7
  lead agency, 6.3.4
  New York State Environmental Quality Review Act, under, 6.5.2
  preparation:
    responsibility for under NEPA, 6.3.4
    time for, 6.3.5
  public participation, 6.3.4
  requirement for, 6.3, 6.3.2, 6.3.3
  when required, 6.3.1, 6.3.3
Executive order 11593, 6.1, 6.1.7
Exemption, real property tax, 5.1.1, 9.1.3, 9.2.4

Facade easement, 9.1.3, 9.2.1, 9.2.3
Farmers Home Administration Programs, 4.1.7
Federal and state laws re hazardous substances, 8.2.2
Federal Housing Administration Insurance Program, 4.1.5, 9.1.3, 9.2.2
Federal Register, 2.1, 2.1.3
Financing, access to, for preservation projects, 4, 4.1.8
Financing sources:
  federal:
    Coastal Zone Management Act, 4.1.10
    Commerce, Department of, 4.1.9
    community development block grant, 4.1.3, 4.1.4, 4.3.3
    Economic Development Administration, 4.1.9
    Energy, Department of, 4.1.10
    Farmers Home Administration, 4.1.7
    Federal Housing Administration, 4.1.5
    guaranteed and insured loans, 4.1, 4.1.5, 4.1.6, 4.1.9, 9.1.3
    Historic Preservation Loan Program, 4.1.5
    home improvement loan insurance (Title I), 4.1.5
    Housing Development Grant (HODAG), 4.1.6
    Housing and Urban Development, Department of, 4.1.2
    National Endowment for the Arts, 4.1.10
    National Endowment for the Humanities, 4.1.10
    National Historic Preservation Fund grants, 4.1.1
    rehabilitation mortgage insurance, 4.1.5
    rental rehabilitation program, 4.1.6
    rent subsidies, 4.1.6
    section 8 housing assistance payments program, 4.1.6, 9.2.2
    Small Business Administration loans, 4.1.9

Index

Financing sources *(Continued)*
  special economic development and adjustment assistance grants (Title IX), 4.1.9, 4.3.3
  Transportation, Department of, 4.1.10
  Urban Development Action Grant (UDAG), 4.1.3, 4.3.3
  urban homesteading program, 4.1.6
  National Trust Programs:
    critical issues funds, 4.3.7
    Historic Properties Preservation Fund, 4.3.7
    Inner City Ventures Fund, 4.3.7
    National Main Street Center, 4.3.7
    National Preservation Loan Fund, 4.3.7
    Preservation Services Fund, 4.3.7
  private:
    charitable donations, 4.3.8
    corporate donations, 4.3.6
    foundations, 4.3.5, 9.1.3
    nonprofit organizations, 4.3.7
    revolving funds, 4.2, 4.3.1–4.3.4, 9.1.3
  state and local:
    generally, 4.2, 4.2.1, 4.2.2, 9.1.3
    industrial development bonds, 4.2.1, 9.2.3
    industrial revenue bonds, 4.2.1
    mortgage credit certificates, 4.2.1
    municipal bonds, 4.2.1
    private activity bond, 4.2.1
    qualified mortgage subsidy bonds, 4.2.1
    qualified redevelopment bonds, 4.2.1
    single family mortgage revenue bonds, 4.2.1
    tax revenue, 4.2.1
Foreign investors, entities, 1.6.1, 1.7.1
Forty-Second Street Development Project, New York, New York, 4.2.2, 9.2.4
Foundation Center, The, 4.3.5
Foundation Directory, The, 4.3.5, 4.3.6
Foundation grants, 4.3.5
Foundation Grants Index, 4.3.5
Foundation News, 4.3.5
Frozen tax assessment, 5.1.7, 9.2.2

General partner:
  corporation as, 3.2.1
  fiduciary duty, 3.1.2
  liability, 3.1.2, 3.2.1
  rights and powers, 3.1.2
  role, 3.1.2
General partnership, 3.1

Hardship application:
  charitable institution, 7.4.5
  religious institution, 7.4.5
Hazardous Materials Transportation Act, 8.1.5
Hazardous substances, 8
  other, 8.2
  PCB regulation, 8.2.1
  state regulation, 8.2.2
Historic district:
  boundary designation, 7.3.4
  certification, 2.2, 2.2.2, 7.3.5, 7.5, 7.5.2
  designation, 7.3.4
  examples, 9.2.1, 9.2.2
  generally, 7.3.4
  preliminary certification, 2.2
  standards for evaluation, 2.2.1
Historic preservation certification application, 2.2.2
Historic Preservation Fund, 4.1.1
Historic preservation loan program, 4.1.5
Historic properties preservation fund, 4.3.7
Historic resources inventory, 7.2
Historic Sites, Buildings, and Antiquities Act of 1935, 6.1
Home Improvement Loan Insurance (Title I), 4.1.5
Home programs, 4.1.6
Homestead property, 5.1.4
Housing Act, Low Income, 4.1.6
Housing Development Grants (HODAG), 4.1.6
Housing and Community Development Act of 1987, 4.1.3, 4.1.4, 4.1.6
Housing and Urban/Rural Recovery Act, 4.1.6

Industrial development bonds, 4.2.1, 9.2.3
Industrial revenue bonds, 4.2.1, 9.2.3
Inner City Ventures Fund, 4.3.7
Inspection of maintenance and repairs, 7.4.8
Installment sale, recapture of depreciation, 1.3.3
Internal Revenue Code 52(a), 1.3.2
Internal Revenue Code 52(b), 1.3.2
Internal Revenue Code 170, 1.4, 1.5
Internal Revenue Code 216, 4.2.1
Internal Revenue Code 267(b), 1.3.2
Internal Revenue Code 707(b)(1), 1.3.2
Internal Revenue Code 611, 3.2.3
Internal Revenue Procedure, 3.1.2
Inventory, historic resources, 7.2

Investment tax credit:
  age and use of building, 1.1
  building qualifications, 1.2.3, 2.2
  condominium conversion, 1.2.6
  depreciation, qualifying methods, 1.3
  disallowance of rehabilitation expenses, 1.2.1
  factors dictating availability, 1.2
  generally, 1.1, 9.1.3
  lessee as recipient, 1.2.6
  owner as recipient, 1.2.6
  partial rehabilitation, availability for, 1.2.4
  pass-through to lessee, 1.2.6
  recapture, 1.2.6, 1.2.8
  residential property, availability for, 1.2.3, 1.5, 1.6
  transferee, pass-through to, 1.2.6
  transferee as recipient, 1.2.6
  see also Rehabilitation tax credit

John Jay Estate, 9.2.6, 9.2.7

Land costs, as affecting basis, 1.2.4
Landmark designation:
  appeals, 7.3.10
  hearing requirements 7.3.8
  initial, 9.2.7
  nomination process, 7.3.1
  notice requirements, 7.3.6, 7.3.9
  publication requirements, 7.3.6, 7.3.9
  record of decision, 7.3.9
  standards, 7.3.2–7.3.4
  upholding, 9.2.7
Landmark Preservation Law, 7.4.5
Leases, to tax-exempt organization, 1.6.1, 1.7.1
Lessee:
  investment tax credit, received by, 1.2.6
  qualified rehabilitation expenditures made by, 1.2.2
Liabilities of PRP, 8.2.2
Limited partner:
  assignment of partnership interest, 3.1.3, 3.2.1
  liability of, 3.1.3
  role in limited partnership, 3.1.3
Limited partnership:
  advantages, 3.1
  defined, 3.1
  formation, 3.1.1
  general partner, role of, 3.1.2
  limitation of liability, 3.1
  limited partner role, 3.1.3
  management, 3.1, 3.2.1

recognition by Internal Revenue Service, 3.2.1
  securities law, as affecting, 3.3
  special allocation, 3.2.2
  tax advantages, 3.1, 3.2.2
  tax treatment, 3.2
  termination, 3.1.2, 3.2.1
Limited partnership agreement, 3.1.1, 3.2.1, 3.2.2
Limited partnership certificate, 3.1.1, 3.2.1
Local preservation commissions, 7.1.4
  appointments to, 7.1.4
  composition, 7.1.4
  enforcement powers, 7.4.10
  establishment, 7.1.3, 7.1.4
  generally, 7.1.3
  members, 7.1.4
  procedural standards, 7.3.5
  scope of authority, 7.1.5, 7.1.6
Local preservation ordinances:
  alteration provisions, 7.4.1, 7.4.2
  authority for, 7.1.5
  certification of, 7.5, 7.5.1
  commission, creation of, 7.1.3, 7.1.4, 7.1.6
  definitions, 7.1.2
  demolition provisions, 7.4.4, 7.4.5
  designation procedures, 7.3
  designation standards, 7.3.4
  economic hardship provisions, 7.4.5
  enabling legislation, 7.1.5
  enforcement provisions, 7.4.10
  historic districts, 7.3.4
  procedural standards, 7.3.5, 7.3.6
  publicly owned property, 7.4.9
  purpose, statement of, 7.1.1
  standards for designation, 7.3.4
  violations provisions, 7.4.11
Low-Income Housing Act of 1990, 4.1.6
Low-Income Housing Credit, 4.1.6
  amount of credit, 1.3.1
  income guidelines, 1.3.3
  qualification of project, 1.3.3
  qualified basis, 1.3.2
  Tax Reform Act of 1986, 1.2.7, 1.3
Lowell Historic Preservation Community, 9.2.3
Lucas Case discussion, 7.4.5

Maintenance and repair of landmarks:
  compliance inspection, 7.4.8
  generally, 7.4.6
  owner responsibility, 7.4.6
  routine, 7.4.7
Memorandum of Agreement, 6.1.5

Index

Minnesota Environmental Rights Act, 6.5.2
Mobile homes regulation, 7.4.5
Mortgage credit certificate, 4.2.1
Municipal bonds, 4.2.1

National Conference of Commissioners on Uniform State Laws, 1.4.1, 1.5.1
National Emission Standards for Hazardous Air Pollution (NESHAP), 8.1.1
National Endowment for the Arts, 4.1.10
National Endowment for the Humanities, 4.1.10
National Environmental Policy Act (NEPA):
 applicability, 6.3.1
 challenges under, 6.3.7
 environment, as including historic resources, 6.3.1
 environmental assessment, 6.3.3
 environmental impact statement, 6.2, 6.3, 6.3.2, 6.3.3, 6.3.6, 6.3.7
 federal action, as defined under, 6.3.1
 finding of no significant impact, 6.3.3
 generally, 6.3
 judicial review, 6.3.1, 6.3.7
 lead agency, 9.2.4
 National Historic Preservation Act, coordination with, 6.4
 purpose and effect, 6.3
National Historic Landmarks, 6.1.11, 6.2
National Historic Preservation Act (NHPA):
 consultation process under, 6.1.4
 coordination with, 6.4
 enforcement, section 106, 6.1.7–6.1.9
 exempted federal activities, 6.1.6
 federal officials, responsibility under, 6.1.1
 generally, 2.1, 6.1
 memorandum of agreement, 6.1.5, 6.1.7, 6.1.8
 National Environmental Policy Act, coordination with, 6.4
 protection afforded under, 6.1
 purpose and effect, 6.1, 6.3
 section 106 review procedures, 6.1, 6.1.1, 6.1.2, 6.1.3, 6.1.4, 6.1.6, 6.1.7–6.1.9
National Historic Preservation Fund Grants, 4.1.1
National Main Street Center Program, 4.3.7
National Park Service:
 National Register, 2.1
 role in certification, 2.2, 7.5.1

National Preservation Loan Fund, 4.3.7
National Priorities List, 8.2.2
National Register of Historic Places:
 eligibility for listing, 2.1.1, 2.1.2
 generally, 6.1
 nomination by federal agency, 2.1.3
 nomination procedure, 2.1.3, 2.1.4
 objection to listing, 2.1.3, 2.1.4
 owner consent to listing, 2.1.4, 6.1
 purpose, 2.1
 removal or delisting, 2.1.5
National Trust for Historic Preservation programs, see Financing sources, National Trust programs
Negative declaration, 6.5.2
New York City Board of Estimate, 7.1.6, 9.2.4
New York City Landmarks Commission, 5.1.1, 7.1.6, 9.2.4
New York City Planning Commission, 5.3.4
New York City Public Development Corporation, 4.1.3
New York City Special Theatre Subdistrict, 5.3.1, 5.3.2, 5.3.4, 9.2.4
New York City Theatre Advisory Council, 5.3.4
New York City Uniform Land Use Review Procedure (ULURP), 9.2.4
New York City Zoning Resolution, 5.3.1, 5.3.4, 9.2.4
New York State Eminent Domain Procedure Law, 9.2.4
New York State Environmental Conservation Law, 6.5.2
New York State Environmental Quality Bond Act of 1986, 4.2.1
New York State Environmental Quality Review (SEQRA), Act, 6.5.2
New York State General Business Law; 352-e(b), 3.4.1
New York State Historic Preservation Act of 1980, 6.5.1, 9.2.4
New York State Register of Sites and Structures, 6.5.1
New York State Uniform Fire Prevention and Building Code, 5.2.1
New York State Urban Development Corporation, 4.2.2, 9.2.4
New York State Urban Development Corporation Act, 9.2.4
Nonrecourse debt financing, 3.1.2, 3.2.2

Occupational Health and Safety Act (OSHA), 8.1.2

Old Georgetown Historic District, 7.1.6
Omnibus Budget Reconciliation Act (OBRA), 1.3
Ordinances, local preservation, *see* Local preservation ordinances

Palo Alto Historical Association, 7.1.4
Palo Alto Historic Resources Committee, 7.1.4
Partial rehabilitation:
  certification of, 2.3
  investment tax credit, availability for, 1.2.4
Partners and partnership:
  investment tax credit, eligibility for 3.2.2
  investment tax credit pass-through, 1.2.6
  property transferred to partnership, 1.2.4
  special allocation, 3.2.2
  tax-exempt entity, as partner, 1.6.2, 1.7.2
  see also General partner; General partnership; Limited partner; Limited partnership
Passive loss amendments, 3.2.5
Passive loss rules:
  rehabilitation credit, effect on, 3.2.4
  tax benefits, effect on, 3.2.4, 3, 3.2.2
  Tax Reform Act of 1986, 3.2.4
  PCB regulations, 8.2.1
  Penn Central ruling, 7.4.5
Philadelphia preservation commission, 7.4.4
Potential liability, 8.3.2
Preservation Services Fund, 4.3.7
Private Activity Bond, 4.2.1
Private placement memorandum, 9.1.3
Property selection, 9.1.1
Public hearings, 7.3.8, 9.2.4
Publicly owned property, applicability of local preservation ordinances, 7.4.9
"Public support" test, 1.4.2, 1.5.2
Public Works and Development Facilities Programs Department of Commerce, 4.1.9

Qualified conservation contribution, 1.4, 1.5, 9.1.3
Qualified mortgage subsidy bonds, 4.2.1
Qualified non-recourse financing, 3.2.2
Qualified organization:
  defined, 1.4.1, 1.4.2
  "public support" test, 6.2
Qualified real property interest, 1.4.1
Qualified redevelopment bond, 4.2.1
Qualified rehabilitated buildings, 1.2.3
Qualified rehabilitation expenditures:
  accelerated cost recovery and, 1.2.2
  acquisition costs, 1.2.2
  certified historic structure, 1.2.2
  defined, 1.2.2
  depreciation, 1.3, 1.4.1
  enlargement of building, 1.2.2
  excluded expenditures, 1.2.2
  by lessee, 1.2.2
  methods for increasing, 1.2.4
  soft costs, 1.2.2

RCRA, 8.2.2
Real Estate Syndicate Act (New York), 3.4.1
Real Property taxes:
  abatement, 5.1.3, 5.1.4, 9.1.3, 9.2.4
  credits and deduction, 5.1.2
  exemptions, 3.2.5, 5.1.1, 9.1.3, 9.2.4
  frozen assessment, 5.1.7, 9.2.2
  reductions in assessment, 5.1.3–5.1.6
Reasonable return, 7.4.5
Redlining, bank, 4.1.8
Registered historic district, 7.5
Regulation D exemption, 3.3
  accredited investor, 3.3.2, 3.3.3
  integration, 3.3.2, 3.3.3
Regulation of asbestos, 8.1.2
Rehabilitation, partial, *see* Partial rehabilitation
Rehabilitation mortgage insurance, 4.1.5
Rehabilitation percentage, 1.2.1, 1.5, 1.6
Rehabilitation tax credit:
  amount usable, 1.2.7
  carryback and carryforward, 1.2.7
  eligibility of building within historic district, 2.2
  eligibility criteria, 9.1.1
  generally, 1.2, 1.2.7, 1.3.4, 9.1.3
  preservation easement, effect of donation, 1.4.5
  qualified rehabilitated building, 1.2.3
  qualified rehabilitation expenditures, 1.2.2
  recapture, 1.2.8
  recipients, 1.2.8
  rehabilitation percentage, 1.2.1
  substantial rehabilitation, 1.2.4
  tax-exempt organization, availability to, 1.6, 1.7
  tax-exempt participation, effect upon, 1.6.2, 1.7.2
  transition rules, 1.4.2
  walls, retention, to qualify, 1.2.5
  see also Investment tax credit

Index

Religious institution, hardship application by, 7.4.5, 7.4.10
  ownership of historic property by, 7.4.10
Rental rehabilitation program, 4.1.6
Rent subsidies, 4.1.6
Residential property:
  as qualified rehabilitation, 1.2.3, 1.5, 1.6
  easement deduction, 1.4.3, 1.5.3
Resource Conservation and Recovery Act (RCRA), 8.2.2
Requirement for testing for asbestos, 8.1.1
Restricted use valuation, 5.1.6
Revenue Act of 1978:
  "at risk" rule, 3.2.2
  rehabilitation incentives, 1.1
Revolving fund, 4.2, 4.3.1–4.3.4
Rural rehabilitation program, 4.1.6
Rural rental housing and loan program, 4.1.7

Sale and disposition of property:
  changes in use, 1.2.8
  preservation easement, effect upon, 1.4.1, 1.5.1
  recapture of depreciation, 1.3.3
  recapture of tax credit, 1.2.8
Sale and leaseback, tax-exempt organizations, by, 1.6, 1.7
San Antonio Preservation Commission, 7.4.4
Secretary of the Interior:
  National Register role, 2.1.3, 6.1
  Standards for Rehabilitation, 1.4.1, 1.5.1
Section 8 Housing Assistance Payments Program, 4.1.6, 9.2.2
Section 38 property:
  disposition, effect on tax, 1.2.8
  easement, timing of donation, 1.4.5, 1.5.5
  generally, 1.2.1
  investment tax credit, 1.2
Section 106, see National Historic Preservation Act (NHPA)
Securities, definition of, 3.3
Securities Act of 1933, 3.3
Securities Exchange Act of 1934, 3.3
Securities and Exchange Commission, Rules 501–506, 3.3.1–3.3.3
Securities law:
  federal, 3.3
    anti-fraud provision, 3.3
    exemption from registration, 3.3
    generally, 3.3
    intrastate offering exemption, 3.3.4
    "no action" letter, 3.4.1

private placement exemption, 3.3.4
registration, 3.3
Rule 10b-5, 3.3, 3.3.5
small offering exemption, 3.3.4
state:
  California, 3.4.2
  New York, 3.4.1
SEQRA, 9.2.8
Single family mortgage revenue bond, 4.2.1
Small business administration, 4.1.9
Soft costs:
  generally, 1.2.2, 3.2.2
  tax treatment, 1.2.2
Solarz Bill of 1991, 7.4.10
Standards for rehabilitation:
  air-conditioning, heating, ventilation, 2.3.2
  generally, 2.3.1, 9.2.3
  incompatible uses and additions, 2.3.2
  masonry and plaster, 2.3.2
  storefront alteration, 2.3.2
  window replacement, 2.3.2
State constitution, 7.1.1
State Historic Preservation Officer:
  generally, 2.1.3
  National Historic Preservation Act, role under, 6.1, 6.1.1, 6.1.3, 6.1.4, 6.1.5
  taxation, role in, 5.1.7
State historic preservation statutes, 6.5, 6.5.1, 6.5.2
State review board, National Register nomination, 2.1.3
Statutes, state and local preservation, see Local preservation ordinances
Straight line depreciation, 1.1, 1.2.2, 1.3, 1.4
Subdivision and SEQRA, 9.2.8
Substantial improvement:
  defined, 1.3.2
  depreciation, 1.3.2
Substantial rehabilitation, 1.2.4, 9.1.1
Substantial rehabilitation test:
  basis, relationship to, 1.2.4
  criticism of, 1.2.4
Surface Transportation Act of 1978, 4.1.10
Syndication, 3.1 et seq., 9.1.3, 9.2.1
Syndication agreement, 9.1.3
Syndicator, role in preservation project, 9.1.3

Taking of property, 7.4.5, 9.2.4
Tax abatement, real property, 5.1.3, 5.1.4, 9.1.3
Tax assessment, real property, 5.1.5, 5.1.6, 5.1.7

Tax exemption, real property, 5.1.1
Tax-exempt organizations:
  foreign investors and entities, 1.6.1, 1.7.1
  leases to, 1.6.1, 1.7.1
  participation in rehabilitation project, 1.6.2, 1.7.2
  preservation organizations as, 4.3.2, 4.3.8
  sale-leaseback by, 1.6.1, 1.7.1
  taxation of foreign property leased to, 1.6, 1.6.1, 1.7, 1.7.1
Tax-exempt use property, 1.6.1, 1.7.1
Tax Reform Act of 1976:
  "at-risk" rule, 3.2.2
  conservation easements, 1.1
  generally, 1.1
  rehabilitation incentives, 1.1
Tax Reform Act of 1984:
  accelerated cost recovery system, 1.3.2
  depreciation, recapture, 1.3.3
  depreciation under, 1.3
  easement valuation, 1.4.4, 1.5.4
  investment tax credit, availability to tax-exempt organizations, 1.6, 1.7
  tax shelter, registration of, 3.2.3
  wall retention requirements, 1.2.5, 1.2.6
Tax Reform Act of 1986:
  at-risk rule, 3.2.2
  generally, 3.2.4
  historic preservation certifications, 2, 2.1.5, 2.2, 2.2.2
  low income housing credit, 1.3
  passive loss rule under, 3.2.4
  rehabilitation tax credit under, 3.2.4
  syndication 3, 3.1
Tax shelters:
  abusive, 3.2.3
  registration requirement for, 3.2.3

Tax Treatment Extension Act of 1980, 1.4, 1.5
Technical and Miscellaneous Revenue Act of 1988, 1.2.7
Toxic Substance Control Act (TSCA), 8.2.1
Transferable development rights:
  amount transferable, 5.3.3
  conditions of transfer, 5.3.4
  generally, 5.3, 9.1.2, 9.2.4
  property eligible, 5.3.1
  transfer zone, 5.3.2
Transferee, passthrough of investment tax credit, 1.2.6

Underground storage tanks, 8.2.3
Uniform Conservation Easement Act, 1.4.1, 1.5.1
Uniform Limited Partnership Act, 3.1, 3.1.1, 3.1.3
United Artists ruling, 7.4.5
Urban development action grant, 4.1.3, 4.3.3, 9.1.3
Urban Homesteading Program, 4.1.6

Valuation:
  current use, 5.1.5
  easement, 1.4.4, 1.5.4
  highest and best use, 5.1.5
  historic property, 5.1.5
  restricted use, 5.1.6

Walls, retention, 1.2.5
Washington State Environmental Protection Act, 6.5.2
Westchester Reform Temple ruling, 7.4.10

Zoning laws for religious institutions, 7.4.10